Revised and Enlarged Fifth Edition

THIS BUSINESS OF MUSIC

by Sidney Shemel and
M. William Krasilovsky

Billboard Publications, Inc.
New York

To our wives, Shirley and Phyllis,
for their constant encouragement

Copyright © 1964, 1971, 1977, 1979,1985
by Sidney Shemel and M. William Krasilovsky

Revised and enlarged 5th edition
first published 1985 in New York by Billboard Publications, Inc.
1515 Broadway, New York, New York 10036

Library of Congress Cataloging in Publication Data
Shemel, Sidney.
   This business of music.
   Bibliography: p.
   Includes index.
   1. Music trade—United States. 2. Music—Economic
aspects. 3. Copyright—Music. 4. Music, Popular
(Songs, etc.)—Writing and publishing. I. Krasilovsky,
M. William. II. Title.
ML3790.S5   1985   338.4'778'0973   85–1293
ISBN 0–8230–7754–3

Manufactured in U.S.A.

Revised, enlarged, 5th edition
1 2 3 4 5 6 7 8 9/88 87 86 85

PREFACE

In this fifth edition, an attempt has been made to discuss and clarify some of the modifications in business, economics, and legal facts and concepts that have transpired since the previous edition. Outstanding new developments have been the fields of music videos and Compact Discs. The music industry has been learning to live with the extensive changes wrought by the Copyright Act of 1976 regarding such matters as duration and divisibility of copyrights, jukeboxes, cable television, public broadcasting, compulsory licenses, fair use and the Copyright Royalty Tribunal.

The authors wish to acknowledge their special indebtedness for this revision to the following persons: Paul S. Adler, Nicholas Arcomanno, Lewis M. Bachman, Albert Berman, Noel Berman, Lisa Castano, Ralph F. Colin, Robert Crothers, Steven D'Onofrio, Peter M. Eichler, Ron Eyre, Leonard Feist, Herman Hernandez, Jules Kurz, Thomas R. Levy, Milton Posner, Milton Schnapf, Eileen L. Selsky, Edward S. Slattery, Norman N. Stollman, and Theodora Zavin. Susan D. Susman was especially helpful with the chapter on "Work Permits for Foreign Artists," and Robert S. Meloni rendered valuable aid in research for and the drafting of the chapter on "Music Videos."

Over the years in connection with the preparation of prior editions, the authors have received the gracious and unstinting help of many other persons in the music industry. The inspiring assistance of the Billboard staff with respect to all the editions is gratefully acknowledged.

CONTENTS

PART FOUR   **Appendixes and Music Industry Forms**

INTRODUCTION

The business of music is an ever-changing and dynamic field. Its consumers include listeners as well as amateur and professional performers. According to the American Music Conference, 38 percent of the U.S.A. households contain musicians. About one-half of amateur musicians play more than one instrument, with the piano alone being played by more than 18 million amateurs. The category of "listener" encompasses practically the entire population. Many listeners are involuntary, such as those who hear background music in restaurants, hotel lobbies, elevators and factories, but the average American listens to over 23½ hours of radio programs per week. Much of the listening to music is done while in transit, in cars, airplanes, or even through "Walkman" headphones while jogging.

There is a very large stake in the United States music industry. Broadcasters operate about 9,000 commercial radio and television stations in the U.S.A. The American public has invested in over 450 million radio sets and more than 140 million television sets. Ninety-eight percent of all United States households have at least one television set and these homes watch television on the average of 6.8 hours a day. There are radios in 99 percent of all United States homes, and an average of more than five radio sets in each home. Presently there are over 9 million video-cassette recorders in consumers' homes, and 1983's sales of prerecorded home video programming were double those in 1982. About 4 million video-cassette recorders were sold in the U.S.A. in 1983, roughly twice the 1982 number.

Industry Volume

There are over 75 million phonographs in use in the United States. Sales of separate audio components exceed a billion dollars a year. For 25 years, starting from the mid-1950s, the record business grew an average of 20 percent a year. In 1977 and 1978 sales peaked, in a period when the "Saturday Night Fever" soundtrack album and the "Rumours" LP by Fleetwood Mac had sales in excess of 20 million copies apiece. Then sales fell sharply. By 1983, as compared to 1978, unit sales had declined 20 percent (578 million versus 726.2 million) and, despite rising list prices, dollar volume of net shipments of records and prerecorded tapes, at suggested retail list prices, had dropped 8 percent, i.e. from $4.13 billion to $3.8 billion. However, classical record sales increased from 3 percent of the market to 6 percent between 1979 and 1982 ($111 million in 1979 to $216 million in 1982).

In 1983 the record industry had a 5 percent rise over 1982 in dollar value at suggested retail list price of net shipments of records and tapes.

But overall unit shipments remained flat. Cassette sales in 1983, as compared to 1982, increased 30 percent in unit figures and 31 percent in dollar volume. For the same years LP/EP unit shipments dropped 14 percent and there was an 11 percent decline in dollar volume. Unit sales of cassettes finally reached virtual parity with 12-inch discs in 1983. Singles decreased 9 percent in unit figures and 5 percent in dollar volume. Eight-tracks declined 57 percent in units and 42 percent in dollar volume.

However, in considering the lackluster market statistics of the 1980s it should be recognized that the record industry has shown substantial long-term growth as indicated by retail sales of $200 million in 1950, $600 million in 1960, $1.7 billion in 1970 and $3.8 billion in 1983.

Aggregate annual sales of printed editions reached $241 million in 1983, a slight increase over the corresponding figure of $239 million in 1982. The aggregate figure has changed comparatively little since 1977 when it totalled $228 million. On a long-term basis comparison may be made to sales of only $72 million in 1967.

The total annual sales of musical instruments, accessories and printed music passed the $1 billion mark in 1970, reached $2.09 billion in 1977, and were $2.3 billion in 1983, as against $2.2 billion in 1982. As to traditional instruments, dollar volume is up but unit sales are falling. The increase in dollar volume in 1983 over 1982 has been achieved largely through the unusual growth of electronic keyboard sales.

New Phonograph Records

According to the Record Industry Association of America, there were about 2,300 new LPs in 1983, which is 13 percent fewer than the 2,630 in 1982 and 45 percent less than the high of 4,170 in 1978. New cassettes in 1983 aggregated approximately 2,500 which is 8 percent less than the 2,710 in 1982. There were 2,105 new 7-inch singles in 1983, down 7 percent from the 2,285 in 1982. The number of new 12-inch singles increased 33 percent, from 460 in 1982 to 610 in 1983. Cassette EPs were up 300 percent, from 50 in 1982 to 150 in 1983.

Purchasing Trends

According to the Record Industry Association of America, the following shows the trends in purchases by music type, in terms of percentage of dollars spent for the years 1982 and 1983.

	Retail Sector		Direct Marketing Sector	
	1982	1983	1982	1983
Rock	34%	35%	27%	30%
Country	15	13	24	20
Pop/Easy Listening	14	14	17	19
Black/Dance	7	11	2	4
Gospel	6	5	6	4

Classical	6	5	7	8
Shows/Soundtracks	4	3	3	3
Jazz	3	2	4	2
Children's	3	3	2	2
Other	8	9	8	8

At the retail level the Rock share of 1983 total music expenditures showed a small increase over 1982, while Pop/Easy Listening remained stable. Country, Jazz, Classical and Gospel decreased their market share of retail sales in 1983. Black/Dance displayed a strong upward surge.

In 1983 as compared to 1982, Rock's share of the Direct Marketing Sector went up 3 percent, Pop/Easy Listening and Black/Dance each rose 2 percent and Classical showed a 1 percent rise. Country, Gospel and Jazz had considerable declines. The percentages allocable to Shows/Soundtracks and to Children remained unchanged.

During the same period in the Retail Sector, as to percentage of dollars spent, LPs decreased from 62 to 55 percent, eight-tracks dropped from 5 to 2 percent, singles grew from 5 to 6 percent, and cassettes surged from 28 to 37 percent. In the direct marketing field LPs fell to 48 percent from 53 percent in 1982, eight-tracks diminished from 15 percent to 9 percent, and cassettes moved ahead smartly from 32 percent to 43 percent.

Performing-Right Organizations

Collections by performing-right organizations have climbed notably. In 1983, the American Society of Composers, Authors and Publishers (ASCAP) received $198 million on behalf of a membership which at year end included over 26,500 writers and nearly 11,000 publishers. This compares with 1970 collections of some $73.5 million and $94 million in 1976. Broadcast Music Inc. (BMI) had for the fiscal year ending June 30, 1984 collections of $124.6 million, about 63 percent of the ASCAP collections, and represented some 45,000 writers and over 26,500 publishers; in 1970 BMI collections were about $34 million and in 1976 $60 million. BMI states that its goal is to reach equality with ASCAP as to income. BMI asserts that this will be accomplished eventually through the renegotiations of agreements with television and radio broadcasters. The third U.S.A. performing-right organization, SESAC, Inc. acknowledges a 1983 income of about $5 million and affiliates numbering some 1,070 publishers and over 1,600 writers. Its earnings for 1976 were stated to be some $3 million.

Factors Relating to Growth

In part, past industry growth has been due to new technology, such as the introduction of the LP in 1948 and the dominance of stereo toward the close of the sixties. Added to this was the mid-sixties introduction of prerecorded cartridges and cassettes, which opened an entirely new market for record manufacturers. Another sales area, that of video cassettes, is relatively recent. Sales of video cassette recorders passed the $1 billion annual mark by 1981 and continue to increase rapidly, broadening the market for video cassettes. Whether the video cassettes feature full-length films, with background or incidental music, or musical motion pictures or concerts, the music industry would appear to be the ultimate gainer.

Another recent new sales area is that of Compact Discs ("CD"), also called digital audio discs, which were introduced into the United States market in 1983 after their success in Europe and Japan. CDs rely on computer and laser technology to produce near-perfect sound reproduction. Imperfections that produce surface noise in conventional disc records are eliminated in CDs. Under present techniques a CD contains about one hour of music and can remain in good condition indefinitely. Many observers predict that CD records will replace LP records within the next ten years.

Some of the more conventional earlier music industry growth is accounted for by new marketing methods such as rack jobbing, mail-order, record clubs, and discount record stores. Rack jobbing, introduced into drug and grocery stores in the mid-1950s, services supermarkets, variety stores, department and discount stores, drug stores and other retail outlets with records and tapes.

CBS Records entered the record club field in 1955 and RCA in 1958. Clubs sell both records and prerecorded tapes. Since 1955, when the volume was approximately $6 million, annual sales for clubs and mail orders have increased to where such sales reached $439 million in 1983.

Inhibition of Growth

A potent factor to inhibit growth has been counterfeiting, piracy, and bootlegging in the record field. It has been estimated that in 1982 the total dollar value of pirate, counterfeit, and bootleg products in North America was $400 million, which is indicative of the amount of lost legitimate sales. Another inhibitor is the widespread practice of home taping of records, tapes, and video cassettes. According to a study authorized by the Recording Industry Association of America, home taping results in lost sales of records and prerecorded tapes equal to 325 million albums annually, and at least 84 percent of blank tapes are used to record music. Rentals of video cassettes, which are widespread, act as a severe limitation on video cassette sales. Recent statistics have shown a ratio of nine-to-one of rental transactions as against retail sales. The record industry is seeking federal legislative relief from what is known as the First Sales Doctrine, which is the legal basis for allowing retailers to rent out video cassettes without compensating copyright owners. Under that doctrine, the first sale of a product in effect is the last one over which the manufacturer has control. In 1984 the First Sale Doctrine by federal legislation became inapplicable to the commercial rental of audio recordings and such rentals now require the consent of copyright owners; this legislation does not affect audiovisual works such as videocassettes.

Growth in the record field has been adversely impacted from time to time by conditions of general economic recession.

Distribution

The record industry in the past has been characterized by chaotic distribution and intense competition, which in many instances result in minimal or no profits.

Five charts at the end of this introduction show the phases of development of record and sheet music distribution. Chart 1 presents the normal record distribution pattern existing in the 1930s and into the 1940s. Chart 2 shows a change in the pattern caused by the introduction of one-stops. Chart 3 shows the distribution niche attained by record clubs. Chart 4 demonstrates the place in the distribution pattern accorded to rack jobbers, television packagers, importers, and chain-store buying services. Chart 5 shows the basic methods of distributing popular music in sheet music and folio form. A sixth chart at the close of this introduction portrays the usual pattern of music video distribution in 1984.

With the rise in business costs in recent years, combined with the business slump, it became more difficult for smaller record companies to continue on their own. Many independent record companies, which do not have their own manufacturing and distribution facilities, have made arrangements for manufacturing and distribution by major record companies. Chrysalis is linked up with CBS, Motown is distributed by MCA, and A&M and Arista Records are handled by RCA. Although the big record companies have become larger, the independent record distributors, who relied for hits on the larger independent record companies to subsidize smaller record labels, have lost considerable ground.

Leisure and Purchaser Ages

Of great long-range importance to the music industry is the benefit flowing from the expansion of leisure time in the nation as a whole. Older persons retire earlier and on higher retirement incomes, and those in the current work force have shorter hours and larger entertainment budgets. Presently, persons 25 and over account for about 57 percent of the total dollars spent on all records and tapes purchased, while persons 10–19 buy approximately 19 percent and those 20–24, 24 percent. Studies indicate that more adults than in past generations have continued a habit of buying records, frequently well into their 20s and beyond. Demographic studies predict a substantial increase in the 25–44 age groups, a smaller decrease in the 10–19 age group and a slight rise in the 20–24 segment. With the decrease in the teen group of record buyers, previously considered the key segment of the record-buying public, it is anticipated that the record industry will develop new programs and campaigns to increase the interest of the after-teen market.

Television and Direct Mail Packages

For many years there has been a substantial secondary market for record albums in the field of direct sales to consumers, through television or mail offers.

The contents of the albums are often new compilations of popular hits of erstwhile record stars such as Connie Francis or of former featured record groups such as The Five Platters. The albums consist of from 14 to 18 songs per LP or cassette. Sometimes the offer relates to sets of LPs covering as many as 50 songs.

In the field of direct marketing through television some of the significant companies are Candelight Music, a division of K-Tel International of Minneapolis, Minnesota and Winnepeg, Canada; Suffolk Marketing of New York; Sessions Records of Chicago; and Heartland Advertising and V&R Advertising of New York. A number of the leading companies that market to consumers by direct mail include Franklin Mint of Philadelphia, Pennsylvania; Readers Digest of Pleasantville, New York; Silver Eagle Records of Palm Springs, California; and Time Life Records of Alexandria, Virginia.

Many of these companies utilize the services of larger record companies, such as the Special Services Division of CBS Records, to assemble and license packages for their mail order sales. Usually, major campaigns by the marketing companies, whether through television or direct mail offers, are undertaken only after scientific testing in a trial area.

Proposed Legislative Changes

An important pending legislative proposal by the record companies, strongly opposed by record merchants, is the abolition of the First Sale doctrine which bars the collection of fees by record companies for the rental of video cassettes.

Another significant legislative proposal is for a royalty from blank tape or recording equipment manufacturers to compensate copyright owners for the home dubbing of music. Such a royalty is now in effect in Austria, West Germany, Sweden, Hungary, and Congo, and is under consideration in other foreign countries.

A legislative proposal, with a possible strong impact on potential income of record companies and artists, relates to the granting of a performance right for recordings. This right does not now exist under the 1976 Copyright Act. Broadcasters at present may play records and tapes without paying license fees to the record companies or artists. In many foreign countries such as England, Canada, and France, fees are required. Pursuant to the 1976 Copyright Act, the Register of Copyrights rendered a report which recommended that the Act be amended to provide a performance right for recordings, subject to a compulsory license.

Under another pending proposal the 1976 Copyright Act would be amended to eliminate compulsory licenses for cable television.

The above description of proposals is incomplete and should not be taken as indicating that any of the proposals will be enacted.

Songwriters and Entertainers

Songwriters offered an innumerable number of songs for publication in 1983 with over 125,000 actually reaching the point of copyright registration in the 12 months ended June 30, 1983. Hundreds of thousands of persons considered themselves entertainers, with the membership in 1983 of the American Federation of Musicians alone totalling over 270,000. Millions were on the sidelines as amateurs.

International Music Tastes

Music has long been identified as an international language and as a common unifying cultural denominator. With advances in methods of communication, transportation, and trade, music tastes have advanced the One World concept. Artists such as Julio Iglesias, Stevie Wonder, Michael Jackson, the Rolling Stones, Frank Sinatra, and Nana Mouskouri are some of those who have achieved global popularity. Certain records attain hit status in their original language versions and others when adapted into local language lyrics. Examples of foreign records which have been adapted for the American public are "It's Impossible" (from the Spanish), "Strangers In The Night" (from the German), and "El Condor Paso" and "The Girl from Ipanema" (from Brazilian Portuguese).

Music and Advertising

Music has become an essential part of the advertising industry. Interwoven with commercial jingles, which no longer merely introduce but also contain the commercial message, the music contributes immeasurably to the success of the advertising. Who can deny the importance of the jingles for the products of McDonald's and Pepsi-Cola and the commercials for various airlines? License fees of as much as $100,000 and possibly more may be commanded for a license to use a standard song in a commercial jingle. Advertising agencies have also learned the value of employing music for trade and industrial shows, and many recognized composers have been commissioned to fashion musical settings for the display of a line of automobiles and other products.

New Ventures

The expansion of the music industry has not barred the door to new entrants. The industry still remains one where fortunes can be rapidly built and lost. There are many annual dropouts from the ranks of publishers, record companies, and managers, but also many replacements who are attracted by the possibility of large financial rewards.

CHART I

RECORD DISTRIBUTION IN THE 1930s AND EARLY 1940s

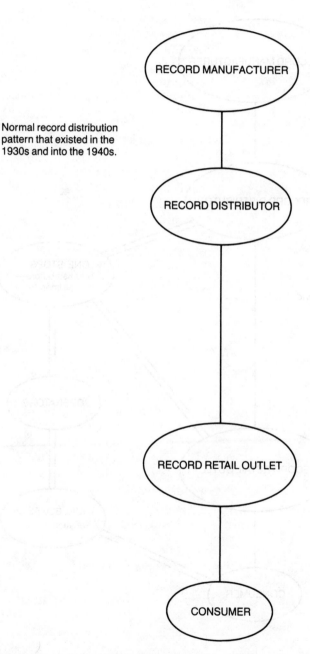

Normal record distribution
pattern that existed in the
1930s and into the 1940s.

RECORD MANUFACTURER

RECORD DISTRIBUTOR

RECORD RETAIL OUTLET

CONSUMER

Produced by RECORD MARKET RESEARCH, a division of *Billboard*

CHART II

RECORD DISTRIBUTION FROM THE LATE 1940s TO 1955

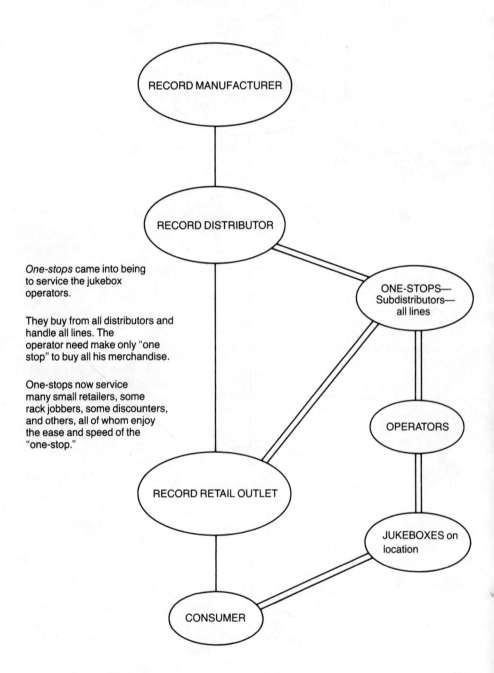

One-stops came into being to service the jukebox operators.

They buy from all distributors and handle all lines. The operator need make only "one stop" to buy all his merchandise.

One-stops now service many small retailers, some rack jobbers, some discounters, and others, all of whom enjoy the ease and speed of the "one-stop."

RECORD MANUFACTURER

RECORD DISTRIBUTOR

ONE-STOPS—Subdistributors—all lines

OPERATORS

RECORD RETAIL OUTLET

JUKEBOXES on location

CONSUMER

Produced by RECORD MARKET RESEARCH, a division of Billboard

CHART III

RECORD DISTRIBUTION FROM 1955 TO 1957

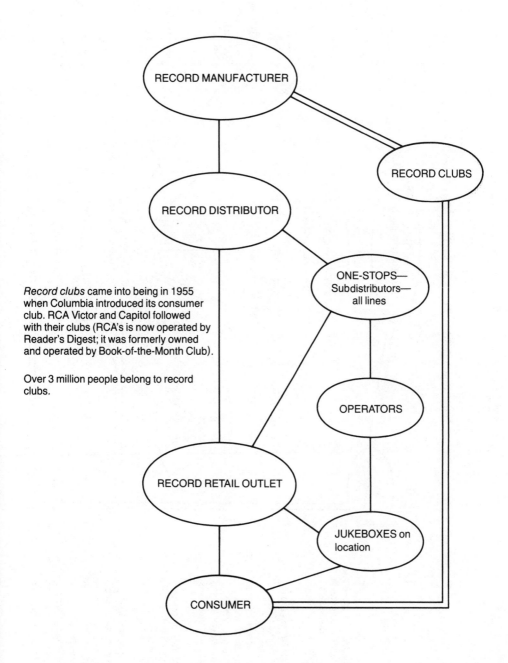

Record clubs came into being in 1955 when Columbia introduced its consumer club. RCA Victor and Capitol followed with their clubs (RCA's is now operated by Reader's Digest; it was formerly owned and operated by Book-of-the-Month Club).

Over 3 million people belong to record clubs.

Produced by RECORD MARKET RESEARCH, a division of *Billboard*

CHART IV

RECORD DISTRIBUTION AFTER 1957 THROUGH 1984

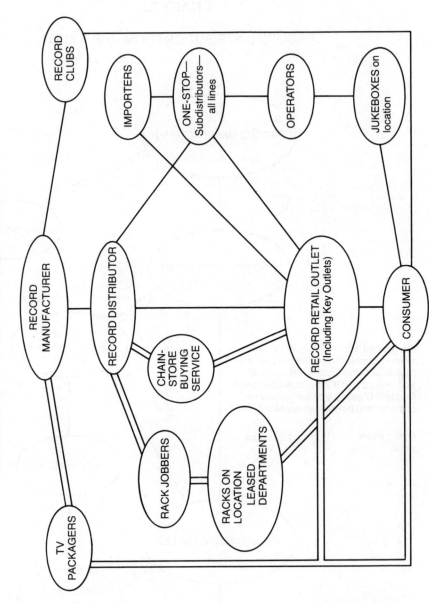

Rack Jobbers came into the record business in 1957 and their sales quickly increased.

TV Packagers are a later aspect of the business. They receive licenses from record manufacturers and they sell to key outlets and directly to consumers.

Importers of foreign records handled major quantities in the 1980s.

Chain-Store Buying Services, for chains such as Tower Records and Sam Goody, with consolidated warehousing, handle increasing volume since 1970s to service their own stores.

CHART V

POPULAR SHEET MUSIC AND FOLIO DISTRIBUTION

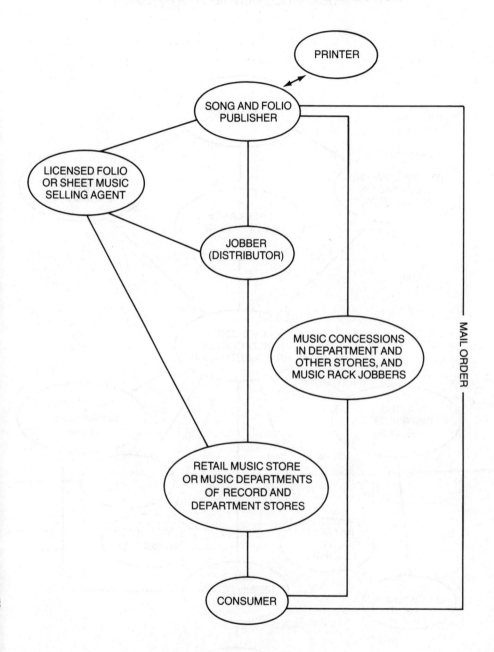

Produced by RECORD MARKET RESEARCH, a division of *Billboard*

CHART VI

MUSIC VIDEO DISTRIBUTION—1984

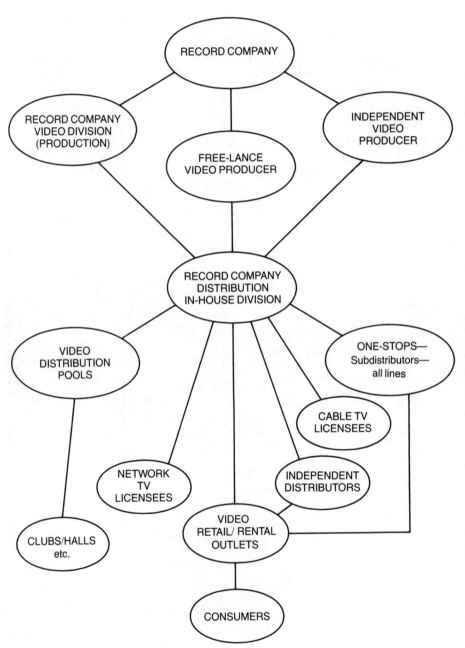

Part 1

RECORDING COMPANIES AND ARTISTS

Recording Artist Contracts

Becoming a recording star is the aim of many attractive youngsters. They desire the fame and fortune of a Michael Jackson, Elton John, Stevie Wonder, or Boy George.

How to attract the attention of record companies and an artist contract is an intricate subject beyond the scope of this book. In brief, it is a matter of arranging for necessary exposure to artists and repertoire men or record producers. Recommendations may come from friends, agents, other artists, music publishers, etc. Results may sometimes be obtained by making a demonstration record and haunting the offices of the publishers and record companies.

Assuming that a successful contact has been made, and a record company contract is offered, the budding artist must then negotiate a fair and reasonable agreement either by himself or with the aid of knowledgeable representatives, such as managers or attorneys. For such negotiations, it is wise for the artist to have an understanding of the basic elements in a form recording contract.

Under the usual agreement, a sample of which is included in Part 4 as Form 12, it is stated that the artist is employed to render his personal services as a recording performer on an exclusive basis for the purpose of manufacturing phonograph records. He will be required to appear at such reasonable times and places as are designated by the record company to perform for recordings. The musical selections to be recorded will be chosen by the record company, although, in practice, the company will give the artist a substantial voice in choosing the selections. For his services he will be paid no less than union scale established in agreements with the applicable union, which is for vocalists the American Federation of Television and Radio Artists (AFTRA) and for instrumentalists the American Federation of Musicians (AF of M); commonly the artist receives monies in excess of union scale.

The record company will agree to pay all of the recording costs of the record session, including payments to the artist, the arranger, the copyist, and the musicians. These costs shall be deemed to be advances against and recoupable out of royalties which might otherwise become due to the artist. Companies usually include studio rentals and editing costs in the recording costs which are recoupable out of artist royalties.

Royalties

A typical artist contract will provide that the artist be paid a royalty which may be a percentage of the suggested retail list price, less excise taxes and duties, of records sold or a percentage (usually double that applied to the suggested retail list price) of the wholesale price of records sold. For a new artist, the royalty may be about 7 to 9 percent of the suggested retail list price for United States sales and a lesser percentage, frequently one-half the United States sales percentage, for sales outside the United States. As the artist increases in stature the royalty rate for United States sales may increase to 10 to 12 percent and the corresponding rate on foreign sales will also go up; in the case of "superstars," the royalty may start at 13 percent or even higher for United States sales, with commensurate increases for foreign sales.

Where high royalty rates are requested, record companies frequently insist on a sliding scale escalation of royalty rates based on the quantity of sales. For example, there might be a higher rate for all sales of albums over 200,000 up to 400,000 and an additional escalation in rates for sales over 400,000. This type of escalation may be compared with a common practice in contracts to increase royalty rates upon the exercise of options to extend contract years. Extension escalations usually apply to all sales of product recorded in the extension period, whereas sales escalations are ordinarily limited to sales over certain plateaus.

For singles records sold, the companies will require a lower rate than that for albums. For example, a 13 percent album artist may be paid only 10 percent on singles sold. This may be justified on the ground that with respect to distributing and marketing costs a record company's profit margin for singles is less than its profit margin for albums.

Frequently royalties are based on 90 percent of the records sold. The 10 percent allowance seems to have originated years ago to cover returns of records to the record company for breakages and other reasons. Companies today do not pay royalties on records returned, on the ground that they are not sold, and thereby the 10 percent allowance has tended to become merely a standard reduction in the rate of royalties. In bargaining as to royalty terms, an increasing number of artists are insisting upon being paid royalties on 100 percent of records sold and not returned; whether they will prevail depends on their bargaining position.

For singles records marketed in the United States, the suggested retail list price is presently $1.95. Assuming a royalty of 6 percent on 90 percent sold, this would aggregate 10.53 cents per record sold in the United States.

LPs (long play albums) and cassettes contain an average of about ten selections. Whereas singles records in the United States are practically 100 percent monaural, LPs are marketed in stereo only. There is a present industry trend to list prices of $8.98 for popular music LPs, motion picture soundtrack albums, and show albums. The list price for tapes is generally the same as for vinyl discs; the list price for Compact

Discs is discussed hereinafter in this chapter in the section entitled "Compact Discs."

In computing royalties on albums, the retail list price is subject to reduction for the portion of the price allocated to the packaging of the album. The deduction for packaging is on the theory that the artist is paid on the sales price of the actual disc, rather than on the artwork, wrapping, and sales appeal added by the packaging ingenuity and expense of the record company. In this regard the record company may point out that the artwork and cover origination charges paid by the record company are substantial in relation to the recording costs of the record itself and there is no reason to pay the artist on income from covers. On the other hand, the artist may assert that the essence of sales is his performance, and that he is entitled to compensation based on all income from the recording. Most artists do accept reductions for the price of packaging. For the purpose of computing the price base for royalty computations, record companies may deduct up to about 10 percent to 15 percent of the retail price for packaging of singlefold (and about 12½ to 17 percent for doublefold) disc albums and a generally higher percentage, such as 15 percent to 25 percent, for albums in tape form.

Assuming that an LP retails for $8.98, a typical computation of royalties would reduce the price to $8.08 by allocating 90 cents to the deduction for packaging. A royalty of 9 percent on 90 percent of those sold would result in a figure of 65.4 cents per album. As indicated before, royalties are usually applied by the record company to recoup recording costs before any moneys become due to the artist.

Lest it be believed that the lower royalty payable to new artists generally indicates high profits to record companies, it should be borne in mind that most albums fail to recoup their recording costs and represent a loss. Furthermore, many LPs are recorded by artists whose royalty rate is higher than 9 percent.

Royalty percentages payable on sales of records outside the United States are ordinarily lower than those on United States sales. Frequently, the foreign rate is 50 percent of the United States rate, but where the United States company owns and operates foreign subsidiaries the rate may be higher, for example, 75 percent. Sometimes, especially when the United States company owns the Canadian distributor, Canadian rates are the same as those for United States sales. With rare exceptions American record companies do not derive substantial business from exporting records abroad. They license their masters to foreign record companies, which manufacture from the masters. Under agreements with foreign record companies the American company will be paid a royalty percentage on the suggested retail list price (less taxes and the cost or price of packaging) of records manufactured and sold in foreign countries. The royalty may range from about 8 to as high as about 17 percent and may be based on 90 to 100 percent of records sold. The limited return to the United States companies causes them to insist on the reduced royalty payable to artists for foreign sales. The ultimate percentage that goes to the artist will depend on his bargaining position if he opposes the percentage offered by the record company.

As to tape sales in the United States, it was at one time common for record companies to offer reduced royalty rates, such as half the regular artist royalty. Originally these reductions were justified by the fact that distribution was effected through licensees. In recent years, distribution of most tapes has tended to be handled in the same way as discs. The market for tapes has grown to the point that on an overall basis 52 percent of the combined LP/tape market in 1983 was attributed to tape sales. Presently, the larger record companies are likely to pay the same royalty rate on tape sales as on disc sales. Smaller record companies which distribute tape through third parties may still attempt to obtain reduced tape royalties but many artist negotiations result in raising the royalty rates for United States tape sales to two-thirds, three-quarters, or even 100 percent of the rates applicable to disc sales.

In the United States, two large record companies, CBS Records and RCA, have their own record clubs. It is common for record clubs to distribute the product of diverse record companies. For example, the Columbia Record Club of CBS distributes, nonexclusively, records manufactured by Capitol, A&M, Atlantic, and MCA.

A common provision in artists' contracts is that the royalty payable to the artist for record club sales will be 50 percent of the royalty rate for retail sales. The clause may further state that no royalty will be payable for "bonus" or "free" records given away to members or subscribers to the club for joining or subscribing to the club and/or as a result of purchasing a requisite number of records.

The Columbia and RCA record clubs, in their arrangements to distribute products of other companies, normally obtain a license for the masters and pay a royalty which is in essence a percentage of the club's regular price to members. This price is substantially equal to the suggested retail list price less a packaging deduction. The current royalty of the Columbia Record Club is approximately 9½ percent on 85 percent of records manufactured and sold; the royalty for soundtrack, original cast and classical albums is commonly higher. It is typical of clubs that they usually pay no royalty on bonus or free records. There is a large membership turnover in record clubs and a continual need to encourage both new and old members by a bonus or free record offer. It is apparent that in artists' contracts, record companies have negotiated bonus or free record clauses similar to those found in agreements between clubs and the record companies.

Popular artists may fear that a record club will unconscionably flood club members with free or bonus records of their performances, for which royalties will not be payable. To meet this objection, the artist contract can provide that the number of records of the artist given away by a club cannot exceed those sold. The record company can achieve similar protection in its agreement with a club.

It has been contended by the Columbia Record Club that many record club sales, at least in the United States, represent sales which would not be made by retailers in the absence of a club, and that the artist benefits by the additional exposure and sales. The Columbia Record Club has also argued that its availability to record companies other than CBS Records enables these companies to compete with the major record companies in distribution channels and makes them more effective in retaining their artists and in bidding for new artists.

Record clubs also exist in Europe and Australia.

Compact Discs

Compact Discs ("CDs"), also called digital audio discs, were first introduced into the United States in 1983, following their successful acceptance in Europe and Japan. A CD is a small disc, about 4.7 inches in diameter, which contains digitized music that is incorporated as microscopic pits in the aluminum base. The music is read by a laser beam in a CD player. Each disc is coated with a layer of plastic which prevents scratches and other deterioration. At present, a CD contains about one hour of music.

A CD produces near-perfect sound reproduction. The recording technique results in the preservation of the full dynamic range of sound, including complete loudness and softness of music passages. The imperfections that cause surface noise in conventional discs are eliminated. A CD can remain in good condition indefinitely. It has been called the most significant advance in home audio quality since the introduction of the 12-inch LP in 1948. Many industry sources anticipate that CDs will replace LP records in the next decade.

High suggested retail list prices set at the launching of CDs are gradually dropping. Prices still represent a premium over the suggested retail list prices of conventional LPs.

In a manner akin to the practices at the introduction of tapes, record companies are requiring concessions from artists in order to encourage the production and distribution of CDs by lowering the costs associated with CDs. A common contract clause provides that royalties on CDs will be computed on a suggested retail list price base equivalent to that of conventional 12-inch vinyl LPs. Another usual contract provision is that the container charges deductible for CDs are equal to as much as 25 percent, a percentage higher than typically applied to conventional LPs.

For their protection artists may limit the concessions to a stipulated period, such as two years. Or they may obtain a clause stating that if the record company's future policy for newly signed artists calls for a CD royalty computation formula more favorable than that in the present artist contract, then the record company will, prospectively, compute royalties on the more favorable basis.

Length of Contract

The standard artist contract runs for a term of one year, during which the artist will record exclusively for the company. Under the contract, the company will be granted options to renew the agreement for one or more successive years. Up to four option periods may be observed in many artist agreements.

New York and California are the states in which most recording contracts are entered into. New York has not legislated the maximum period for which an adult may bind himself under an artist contract. It would be up to a court to decide whether a long period might be against public policy. It is noteworthy that New York has provided a statutory procedure whereby artist contracts with minors under 18 years of age may be approved by a court and whereby the recording company is thus assured that the contract will not be voidable by the minor because of his age, as was the case under common law. Under the statute, the contract will not be approved if the term is longer than three years. Thus a period of one year and up to two one-year options would satisfy the statute; more options would prevent court approval. Since record companies may wish to have the benefit of court approval for young artists who become successful, the effect of the statute in New York is to make record companies, which desire court approval, limit the term of agreements with minors to one year plus two one-year options. For further discussion, reference should be made to Chapter 37, "Contracts with Minors."

The New York statute with respect to minor contracts acts as a declaration of public policy as to the reasonableness of a particular term and in the long run may affect the enforceable term in contracts with adults. However, in the case of adults, the courts would investigate all facets of the employment, including the guaranteed compensation, before reaching a determination as to an allowable term. For example, if an older artist were guaranteed $150,000 a year for ten years, it is difficult to believe that a New York court would find the term unreasonable.

Some contracts with artists permit a suspension and corresponding extension of the exclusive term of rights to their services for their failure to perform. Theoretically this could bind the artist forever if he continues to fail to perform. In a case involving the artist Larry Coryell, a New York court refused to grant an injunction against him, holding that whether the restraints were "unreasonable and harsh" was a proper subject for a trial. The court noted that in this type of personal service contract, courts will "look critically on provisions which restrict the employee in his right to earn a livelihood by imposing unreasonable restrictions on his activities."

Under a California statute the term of any personal service contract is limited to a maximum of seven years. The chapter on "Contracts with Minors" contains a discussion of the rights of minors to disaffirm contracts in California in the absence of court approval. A California court will carefully review all aspects of the agreement before approving it.

There has been a California court case in which MCA Records attempted to enjoin Olivia Newton-John, the recording artist, from recording for another record company, after an alleged breach by the artist in the delivery of recordings. A California Court of Appeals in 1979 stated that the artist could not be enjoined for more than the period in which her commitments could have been fully performed. This was considered to be the five-year overall contract term, consisting of a two-year initial period and three one-year options. MCA had unsuccessfully contended that the contract term could be suspended and extended for up to seven years by reason of contractual language permitting suspension and extension of the contract term until delivery of recordings was completed. As a consequence, some record companies, in their contracts, eliminate references to a term shorter than seven years. They define contract periods by the date albums are delivered, instead of by the expiration of a certain number of months.

By virtue of agreements between recording companies and the American Federation of Musicians, recording contracts with instrumentalists must be approved by the International Executive Board of the union. A contract submitted for union approval will be deemed approved if not rejected within thirty days. A standard form of such a recording contract has been promulgated by the union, which has indicated that it favors agreements which do not extend beyond five years.

Selection of Material

A new artist will often be required to permit the record company to choose the compositions to be recorded. For this purpose the record company employs artists and repertoire men (A & R men) or independent producers who search for material suitable to the artist. It is obviously in the best interest of both artist and company that there be a selection of the musical works most appropriate to the artist.

More mature artists will seek the right to choose or at least approve material to be recorded. In the past, record companies were content to take a less active role and might readily permit the artist to exercise creative control. The companies recognize that experienced artists can be very helpful in finding worthwhile material. In fact, some artists have been notably successful in composing their own hits, and it is not unusual for artists to write their own material. Rock music groups often compose the songs they record. Many contemporary artists such as Stevie Wonder, Billy Joel and Carly Simon rely heavily on their own original material for audience appeal. Often their original songs are then recorded again by other artists.

With the onset of economic difficulties in the record business in the late 1970s, the attitude of the record companies has changed to the position where they insist on being seriously involved in creative aspects of recordings. There may be exceptions in the case of some superstars with a strong negotiating stance. Where an artist is given the right to select or to approve the material to be recorded, an impasse may occur as between the artist and the record company; this may destroy the essence of the agreement unless provision is made to resolve the impasse.

Certain artists, such as Paul McCartney, Johnny Cash, Lawrence Welk, and others, have formed their own music publishing companies. It is known that artists with their own publishing firms may favor recording material in which their firms have an interest. Some publishers, in order to be assured of a recording by a top artist, will offer to assign to the artist's publishing company an interest in the copyright. These publishers may feel that the artist may make the composition into a hit and therefore deserves an ownership participation in the copyright.

Independent producers such as Gamble-Huff of Philadelphia have a vital role in song selections and they may also be the writer or publisher of the songs.

Exclusivity

Most artist recording contracts require the artist to record exclusively for the record company. Otherwise, different companies could be issuing competing versions of the artist's recordings, and confusion and chaos might result. Furthermore, the record company would very likely be unwilling to spend time and money in developing and promoting the artist if he were also recording for other labels.

Exceptions exist, especially in the field of classical and jazz albums. In these fields it is common to find the same artist featured on albums issued by various companies. The very multiplicity of albums by the same artist will encourage nonexclusive recording arrangements in the future.

With respect to instrumentalists, many performers make a livelihood by playing as so-called "sidemen" in different bands on recording dates. They are not the featured performers on such dates, and the resultant albums will not stress their participation. If a contract specifically provides that the artist cannot perform as a sideman, this can be enforced; on the other hand, the artists and their union will claim their right to perform as sidemen in the event the contract language does not expressly forbid such performance. It is customary to give a credit on the LP jacket to the sideman's recording company in a form such as "By the courtesy of the XYZ Record Company" after the sideman's name. The sideman's recording company will usually insist, when granting permission for their artists to record as sidemen, that they not be prominently featured on the covers of, and advertising with respect to, the LP for which they have acted as sidemen.

Prominent vocalists who hope to perform in Broadway shows and motion pictures may require the right to have their performance in such media issued as a part of a show album or a soundtrack album on the label of another company. Whether this right will be granted depends on the bargaining position of the parties, including the other concessions made by the record company. The company may feel that the exception is worthwhile since it promotes the exposure of the artist.

Since an artist's performance is unique, the courts will enjoin the artist from recording for another company in violation of the exclusivity clause.

In addition to prohibiting recordings for others during the term of the agreement, the recording contract will usually forbid recording the same selection for another company for a period of years. This period is ordinarily stated as five years but it may aggregate more by virtue of the starting date of the restrictive period set forth in the agreement. In some agreements the five-year period does not commence at the date of the recording; it may begin instead at the date of release of the recording or at the expiration of the term of the contract.

An artist who specializes in recordings of standard, folk, or jazz material may argue against the recording restriction period on the ground that he may be barred from effective repertoire in recordings for other record companies. On the other hand, in view of the extensive material available in these fields of music, record companies will oppose the artist's contention.

Recording Costs

Agreements with most artists provide that the recording costs for the artist's records are recoupable by the record company from the royalties otherwise payable to the artist. Until the royalty equals the recording costs no royalty is payable to the artist, and he will be paid only on royalties earned thereafter.

It is clear that new artists with lower percentage royalties will have to wait longer for royalty payments than artists with higher royalty percentages, assuming that all other things are equal. Obviously, it will take longer to recoup recording costs out of a lower royalty fund than out of a higher one. An established artist with a high royalty percentage benefits both from the speed of recoupment and from the increased subsequent payments.

In determining when they will receive royalties, artists must also consider the fact that the record company will recover its costs, for all recordings made by the artist prior to the end of an accounting period, out of the royalties earned for the period on all such records. Thus, if five single records of an artist are released, and only the last one is successful, no royalties will be payable to the artist until the recording costs for all five records have been recouped from the royalties earned on the successful record.

Record companies may liken the system of recoupment of recording costs from royalties to a joint enterprise or venture for the manufacture of a product, where the cost of production and the overhead must be repaid before the joint venturers divide any profits. With respect to records, the artist is paid union scale or more for his services, and he must wait until the costs of the enterprise are earned before he shares in additional income. The record companies may contend that while the system may be inexact, considering their large financial risk and the fact that the artist invests only his time, substantial justice results. An artist is rarely dependent in the main on his record royalties; most performers derive their major income from personal appearances in concert halls and nightclubs and on television, and the record company will not share in such earnings, although recordings may have been essential in building the popularity required for personal appearances.

Recording costs vary with the type of recording. A two-sided singles record, containing one popular composition on each side, may be recorded for as little as $3,000 to $4,000 although the costs may aggregate $6,000 to $7,000 or more for an involved singles recording. Albums or LPs may range in cost from as low as $5,000 for a few musicians who use stock or informal "head" arrangements, to as much as $100,000 or more for large band recordings; well-known rock groups with a search for perfection have been known to run up costs in excess of $300,000 for an album. Recording costs for relatively new artists can range from $80,000 to $130,000 or more for one album. Original cast albums of Broadway shows may cost as much as $80,000 to $90,000 or more. Some LPs entail little or no additional recording costs since they are assembled from existing singles recordings.

Ownership and Use of Masters

A recording agreement is usually an employment contract, and the results and proceeds of the artist's services, unless otherwise provided, will belong to the record company, including the copyright in sound recordings recorded on or after February 15, 1972.[1] The artist retains no interest in the physical tapes or masters or the copyright in the sound recordings and is restricted to a claim for contractual compensation and royalties. Exclusive rights under the copyright in sound recordings are limited to reproduction, the preparation of derivative works, and distribution; the right of public performance is not included.

A record company will jealously guard its ownership rights in

[1]Prior to January 1, 1978, the effective date of the Copyright Act of 1976, copyright extended to sound recordings both recorded and distributed on or after February 15, 1972.

masters and copyrights. However, in the case of certain successful artists, record companies, in order to secure their services, have agreed in relatively rare instances that the ownership of the masters and copyrights will revert to the artists after a period of years. Artists who desire to transfer to another record company find that the reversion of their recordings is a valuable right which enhances their worth to a new company. Where a reversion right is not granted, artists and their new company have been known to bid substantial sums to acquire ownership of the old masters and copyrights. To protect itself, a record company may agree to a reversion right provided that reversion will be delayed until all recording costs and advances to the artist have been recouped.

A record company can usually use a recording as it sees fit. It may issue the recording on any label it desires, and it may couple the recording with the recordings of other artists.

Lower Price Labels

Some record companies have several labels; one may be the top label and the others may denote secondary or specialty labels or a cheaper line of records. For example, RCA uses the name RCA for its prime label and Camden for lower priced albums. In certain instances a record will be issued originally on the top label and after a period of time will be reissued on a secondary label. This practice may be found in the Camden line referred to above and on the Okeh label of CBS Records.

An artist may request that the recording contract provide for issuance solely on the top label of a company, at least in the United States. The company may grant the request for the United States, where it controls the pressing of the records, and may refuse the restriction for other countries where licensees are used and where flexibility in release is necessary. Alternatively, the company may insist on reserving the right to reissue the recording in the United States on a secondary label after a period of years, since thereby new sales may be stimulated at lower list prices.

Coupling

It is common for record companies to issue recordings which couple the performances of various artists. It has been found that the public is interested in such multiple performances, and increased sales result. Such sales will enhance royalties payable to the artists whose performances are included in the composite albums. Nevertheless, there is the danger that an artist may be cheapened and damaged by poor association in an album with other artists, and to protect themselves artists will at times attempt to obtain the right to approve the coupling of their recordings with other recordings. The company will want the protection of a provision that approval will not be unreasonably withheld.

Packaging

A potent sales factor is the packaging of an album. Eye appeal is very important in attracting buyer interest. Included in eye appeal will be pictures of scenes or artists, designs, and various types of printing of the album title and the names of the artists. The company will claim to be the best judge of packaging that will appeal to buyers and promote the career of the artist. However, as in the case of coupling, an important artist may achieve the right to approve the packaging of the albums or even to prepare and furnish it subject to the company's approval. The contract may provide that the approval of the artist may not be unreasonably withheld, in order to obviate the development of an impasse which would bar the release of an LP. Since the foreign market is different from the domestic, the company may limit the right of approval of packaging to the domestic area; the company may claim that it cannot supervise packaging by its foreign licensees.

Recording and Release Requirements

A contract with an artist will set forth the minimum number of record sides to be recorded during each contract year. A side customarily consists of a single composition, with about a three-minute duration. For a singles vocal artist the minimum number of sides is usually four, six, or eight; for a singles instrumentalist the minimum number of sides required by the AF of M is eight. For an album artist the minimum is usually 10 to 12 sides, the equivalent of an LP. The agreement may also provide that the artist will make additional recordings at the company's election. Sometimes the parties agree that an excess over a certain maximum number of recordings must be mutually approved.

Renewal periods may be marked by an increase in the minimum number of sides to be recorded. The agreement may contain a provision favorable to the company, namely, that the company may at its option be credited with the excess over the minimum recorded in any one year toward meeting the minumum recording requirements in the succeeding year.

A recording agreement with an artist signifies that the company's intention is to produce recordings by him. After the initial recordings are made, the record company may become disillusioned and try to avoid further recording obligations to the artist. For such purpose, agreements with artists sometimes provide that the extent of the company's liability for failure to record shall be the payment to the artist of union scale for the deficient number of recordings.

Artists can sense quickly when companies have cooled toward them, and they may request a release from their contract, which the companies may be pleased to grant. But where the parties are unable to agree on a release their unhappy relationship may drag on until the expiration of the recording agreement.

Often the first single or album recorded by an artist is a dismal failure, and the record company will not make a move to schedule a new recording session. The artist faces the prospect of requesting a release or sitting out the balance of the contract year. Visualizing this situation, the artist may have inserted a provision in the recording agreement whereunder he is released in the event the company allows six months or a comparable period to lapse between recording sessions.

From the artist's point of view, recordings are meaningless unless released commercially. A company will naturally oppose being forced to release recordings. Its position is that it will have made a sizeable investment in the recordings which it would be pleased to release if of commercial quality. To be compelled to release recordings may amount to throwing good money after bad. The artist who does not want to be at the mercy of an arbitrary judgment on the part of the company will seek to have a release requirement inserted in the contract or will request at least a right of termination as to future commitments if a certain release schedule is not met. For example, a contract may call for the company to release a minimum of two albums per 18-month period, and if the company fails to comply the artist may end the agreement. But agreements with many artists leave the matter of record releases to the discretion of the company. To force a release does not mean that the company can be compelled to promote and exploit it, and the record can still die in its infancy. However, the investment of a company in a released recording and its pride in its product may cause a favorable sales program despite its initial opposition to a release.

It is rare that release requirements apply to countries other than the United States, where the company has complete control over manufacturing and distribution.

Promotional and Tour Support

Artists in their negotiations with record companies may seek promotional and tour support. For example, they may ask that there be a minimum amount of advertising of their releases and concerts in trade papers, on radio, or other media. An artist may request that if he goes on performance tours at stadiums, festivals, music halls, or theaters, the record company either will contribute a fixed amount towards the expense of the tour or will, up to a certain sum, make up any deficiency in recoupment by the artist of his tour expenses. Typical expenses are for transportation, hotels, food, and equipment rentals. An artist may urge that the tours are necessary to expose the artist and to build up his popularity as a record seller.

Another form of promotional tour includes traveling to certain major cities to meet the press and local disc jockeys.

Before 1979, when record company economic straits ensued, a company might occasionally accept an artist's request and make provision for a certain budget for promotional and tour support. It might refuse such support to established artists and concentrate on artists who require a public buildup. But the trend today is for record companies to seldom agree by contract to promotional and tour support. At this writing, negotiations between record companies and artists place their emphasis regarding promotional support on video productions, which are discussed later in this chapter and in Chapter 7, "Music Videos."

Where such financing is to be provided, a subject for negotiation is how much, if any, of the funds will be recoupable from the artist's royalties. The company's position is that all such moneys should be regarded as advances recoupable from artist royalties. The artist naturally will be opposed and will claim that the funds constitute normal company promotional expenses.

Assignments

A situation may develop which leads a record company to assign its rights in masters to another entity. This may arise by virtue of sales, mergers, etc. In most instances the agreement with the artist will not prohibit assignment of masters, and assignment would therefore be permitted; the artist can readily understand the freedom in this regard that the recording company desires. On the other hand, an assignment to an irresponsible assignee can cause great harm to the artist.

The company may also desire to assign its interest in the entire recording contract. In essence, what would be assigned is the right to future recording services of the artist. Since personal services are involved, doubt would exist as to assignability of a contract if it did not grant express authority for that purpose. Most agreements convey such authority.

Artists are concerned with the stature and personnel of their recording company. A small company may be financially unsound and unable to invest sufficiently in good personnel and quality recordings. A new artist may not be in a position to quibble about assignability of his contract, although a successful performer will seek to limit such assignability.

One form of restriction on assignments of masters or contracts is to require the artist's approval. The company, for its protection, may provide that the approval may not be unreasonably withheld. Or the artist may grant his consent in advance to an assignment to companies having an equal or better standing in the industry in terms of gross receipts and credit rating. Or an artist may be willing to authorize an assignment provided that the original record company continues to be liable for the fulfillment of all obligations.

Artists may wish to authorize assignments of all of the recording company's artists and masters, as in the case of sale of the entire business, or in the event of a merger. In such instances, there is a good likelihood of a stronger company emerging, with resulting benefits to the artist.

Duet or Group Recordings

One record contract may cover several artists who perform together as duets or groups. So long as the duet or group functions as a unit special problems may not arise. But the time may come when for various reasons the artists become estranged, or their paths diverge. A performer may leave the field of entertainment altogether. Or one member of the group may become a solo star and no longer wish to record with the others; or he may alternate solo and group recordings.

If a group has a special name, such as The Constellations or The Echoes, the record company will contract for the exclusive right to the use of the name on records during the term of the agreement. As to artists who have recorded previously on another record label, it will be appropriate to provide that their group name will continue to be available to the prior record companies for earlier recordings.

When a member of a duet or group drops out, a satisfactory replacement must be arranged. The record company will wish to choose or at least approve the replacement so as to ensure the continuation of the group's special sound or quality. The group may prefer, and fight for, autonomy in the selection of a replacement.

The record company will contend it is entitled to continue to record the dropout artist, as a solo performer, if the record company so desires. This is especially understandable if the artist is a standout performer in the duet or group. The terms of an agreement covering a potential solo artist will entail separate negotiations when the duet or group is first signed. The provisions will ordinarily run the gamut of those commonly contained in a solo artist agreement, including the initial period, renewal options, royalties, advances, and recording and release commitments.

Royalties for a duet or group recording will be apportioned among the members, after the recoupment of recording costs. It is likely that the suggested retail price of a duet or group recording will be the same as the price for a recording by a solo artist. Since the total sales of a duet or group recording may not exceed the aggregate sales for a solo disc, the royalties for each member may be low in comparison with royalties to solo artists. To avoid discontent, a record company may be persuaded to increase its royalty rate for a group recording, although companies can readily argue that the higher rate is unjustified by sales.

An A & R man may conclude that two artists under separate agreements should jointly perform on one or more records. For example, artists of the caliber of Julio Iglesias and Willie Nelson may be requested to make a combined recording, which may achieve greater sales than records featuring each artist alone. Record contracts will anticipate the royalty problems created thereby by providing that the royalty of each artist shall be reduced proportionately by the total number of royalty artists, and that joint recording costs charged against each artist's royalties shall also be reduced proportionately. An established artist will be granted the right to approve a proposed joint recording with another royalty artist.

Publishing

Many record companies are affiliated with music publishing firms, and some record companies and publishing firms are under common management. Often artists are also successful composers. As a part of negotiations with an artist, a record company may require the artist to assign to its affiliated publishing company all compositions owned or controlled by the artist and recorded during the term of the agreement. A publishing interest in a composition reduces the risk of the recording company in investing in and exploiting a record of the composition.

Record companies may claim that activities financed by the record company accrue to the benefit of publishers who may be riding on the coat-tails of the record manufacturer. A record company may contend that, in fact, except for a publisher's distribution of printed copies and his attempting to secure multiple records of the same composition, it is difficult to differentiate between what a record company and a publishing firm will do to exploit a musical composition. A record firm sends promotional copies of records to radio and television stations and has promotional men call upon disc jockeys to encourage the playing of records. Companies may buy radio time to plug their records. They advertise in trade publications. All of these activities will result in publishing income, since there will be broadcasting performances for which the performing-right organization will pay royalties, sales of records for which the record company will remit mechanical-license fees, and sales of sheet music if the composition becomes popular.

Under the circumstances, the record company can argue strongly for a publishing interest in compositions controlled by the artist and recorded under the recording agreement. The artist may believe that the additional interest of the record company, through its affiliated publishing firm, is worthwhile because it may cause greater exploitation efforts on the part of the record company. On the other hand, the artist may conclude that the record company does not need the additional incentive and that it is not entitled to any publishing income. Or the artist may be willing to compromise by granting an interest in publishing income only for the life of the particular record issued by the record firm.

If the artist has his own publishing firm, he is particularly likely to oppose an assignment of an interest in the copyright or publishing income. An argument used by some artists in contesting a publishing clause may be that the record company's publishing enterprise is a mere shell and does not offer usual publishing services other than the activities of the record company. According to them, a recognized publisher has the staff and budget to supplement that of the record company and exploitation will be effected. However, in employing an established publisher, the artist may be defeating himself if the publisher obtains a so-called cover version of the same composition by a competing recording artist; this is less probable where the publisher is an affiliate of the artist's record company.

The record company may settle for a provision whereby the record company pays at a bargain rate for a mechanical license for compositions controlled by the artist. Thus the fee for United States sales may be 75 percent instead of 100 percent of the compulsory mechanical-license rate, under the 1976 Copyright Act, per record side. While 100 percent of such rate in the latter half of 1984 would be typically 4.5 cents per composition, the bargain rate would amount to only 3.375 cents. The matter of a reduced mechanical-license rate is discussed further under "Controlled Compositions" below.

Controlled Compositions

A common paragraph in record contracts relates to "controlled compositions." This covers the terms of the mechanical license issued to a record company by a copyright proprietor or its agent for the right to record and distribute any composition written or owned, in whole or in part, by the artist. The paragraph will set forth the royalty rate negotiated by the company and the artist, which rate is customarily three-quarters of the compulsory license rate under the 1976 Copyright Act.

Despite the fact that albums may contain more than ten compositions, record companies have generally decided that they would pay a maximum overall rate per album equal to that on ten compositions. This is in order to limit their increasing costs for mechanical licenses, the rates having risen from $2\frac{3}{4}$ cents per composition in 1978 to $4\frac{1}{2}$ cents in the last half of 1984. Further, the contracts with the artists may provide that to the extent mechanical license fees in the aggregate on controlled and *noncontrolled* compositions exceed the maximum overall compulsory license rate for ten compositions, the excess is deductible from moneys otherwise payable to the recording artist for royalties or advances. In effect, this places a responsibility on the artist to negotiate favorable mechanical-license rates with outside publishers for compositions that the artist proposes to record.

Another point for negotiation of the controlled composition paragraph relates to "free goods." In essence, these are records considered to be given free of charge by a record company to its retail distributor in order to encourage the retailer to buy the records of a certain artist. While the record company does not pay artist royalties usually on such records, the retailers actually sell these "free" records at retail. The controlled composition paragraph may provide that no mechanical-license fees for controlled compositions are payable for "free goods" despite their sale at retail. The artist may contend that such fees should be paid because free goods are merely a form of discount that the record company should absorb. Often the company and the artist may compromise by the payment of mechanical-license fees on 50 percent of the albums distributed by the company as free goods.

Under a controlled composition clause, the record company will fix the reduced mechanical-license fee as of a particular date. The artist will attempt to provide for the latest possible date, such as the date of record release, in order to have the advantage of any increases in the compulsory license rate. The company will insist on an earlier date such as the recording or delivery date of the master recording. Typically the applicable rate on this date remains in effect forever and does not change with increases in the compulsory license rate.

Video Rights

Key issues in contract negotiations between artists and record companies concern music video rights. These videos are usually three-to-five minute visualizations of pop songs performed by the artist. They are recognized as significant promotional aids that encourage record and tape sales. Music videos have had an important influence on record companies' resurgence in economic well-being. They are also part of a growing commercial market aimed at pay, cable, and free television, video-cassette sales, nightclub exhibitions, and video jukebox plays.

In most contracts the definition of "records" or "phonograph records" includes audiovisual devices such as video cassettes. Negotiations will deal with the extent of a record company's right to control the use of recordings in audiovisual form and to restrict the artist from performing in such media, such as in feature films, for other companies.

A common issue is whether there must be consent of the record company and the artist for commercial exploitation of music videos.

Another issue is the allocation of profits from the marketing of videos. This in turn raises the question of how the costs of producing the videos are to be advanced and recouped. Shall recoupment be from the artist's record royalties or from the artist's share of video receipts or a combination of both?

Under copyright law, a video producer must obtain from a copyright proprietor or its agent a synchronization license in order to record protected music in synchronization with or timed relation to the pictures in a video. Permission is also necessary to publicly perform, make copies of, and distribute the music as a part of the music videos. Where there are compositions written, owned, or controlled by an artist, record companies will demand that the artist contract provide for free licenses. While artists may agree to this in the case of promotional usages, they may balk in respect of commercial exploitation. If fees are to be paid, what is to be the form of payment? Will there be a flat one-time fee, or a per-copy royalty or a combination of both? There are presently no fixed standards.

The foregoing and other facets of music videos are discussed in further detail in Chapter 7, "Music Videos."

Accountings and Defaults

Artist recording agreement will usually provide that the recording company will account to the artist semiannually. The parties may covenant that the artist waives any protests against accountings if he fails to complain within a certain period, such as one year. This provision should not be overlooked by the artist since the courts will uphold a provision which appears reasonable. The clause is designed to safeguard the company from disputes arising long after the facts are made known to the artist.

In the absence of a contractual right to audit the record company's books, an artist will have to sue in the courts in order to obtain the right to audit. The record company will not otherwise be obliged to open its books for inspection.

Artists may be confronted with a company's failure to account for or pay royalties when due. For such failure the artist may commence legal proceedings against the company to require an accounting and for moneys owed. In addition, the artist may desire to treat the breach as justification for termination of the agreement, so that he is no longer obliged to render services to the company. However, unless the agreement specifically authorizes such termination, if the company opposes the artist, a court will have to determine whether or not the breach is a material one which justifies the cancellation. This will depend on the facts. It may be anticipated that a slight delay in rendering accountings and payments would not be regarded as material, whereas long delays after many demands for accountings might be considered material.

Other events of default also may arise. The company may refuse to allow an inspection of books and records although the contractual right is granted to the artist. The company may fail to release recordings, or to record the artist at given periods as provided by the agreement. Here again the artist will be running a risk of court reversal if he acts to terminate an agreement which does not specifically authorize cancellation.

Risks of court reversal can be eliminated by the insertion of an appropriate default clause in the artist's contract. Under the clause it will be stated that under certain specified conditions the artist may terminate the agreement. The agreement may also provide, in order to avoid expensive court actions, that all disputes must be submitted to arbitration.

The company may strongly oppose a default clause which does not adequately protect it by requiring a written notice of defaults and a sufficient opportunity to remedy them. Or the company may completely refuse to accept a unilateral right of termination by the artist, although it is willing to agree to an arbitration clause.

Bankruptcy

In a normal recording contract, there may be a potential term of five years, consisting of an initial period of one year and four one-year options. If there are sales of the artist's records beyond the five years, the relationship of the record company and the artist will continue as long as royalties are earned and payable. Relations between an artist and his record company may, however, be interrupted or revised by proceedings under bankruptcy laws involving either party.

In the 1980s there have been the bankruptcies of record labels such as Stax, General Recorded Tapes (Chess), All Platinum, and Springboard. In each instance the debtor's master recordings were sold and the funds collected by the bankruptcy creditor for distribution among the creditors. Delinquent artist royalties are ordinarily general debts with no priority in bankruptcy. Future artist royalties constitute a continuing obligation to be met at the prebankruptcy contractual rates. This obligation is commonly assumed by the purchaser of the master recordings. Under some record contracts, it is provided that the agreement will terminate and record masters are subject to recapture by the artist or producer in case of bankruptcy. This would remove record masters from the assets of a bankrupt and make them unavailable to creditors.

At times recording artists have resorted to the bankruptcy courts to free them from onerous exclusive recording contracts. Willie Nile (professionally known as Noonan), an Arista Records recording artist, had accumulated a deficit royalty recoupment account which required the sale of a large number of records before it would become positive. He also had significant financial obligations for prebankruptcy legal expenses and his manager's $60,000 arbitration award. He had a limited cash flow and insubstantial assets. Arista Records, despite low sales, exercised its options to extend the agreement for 18 months, during which Nile would have to record two albums, in addition to two already made. Arista refused further advances to Nile that he had requested in order to help pay his financial obligations. In a Chapter 7 "straight bankruptcy" proceeding Nile became entitled to reject, and he did reject, his recording contract with Arista as an executory agreement; this is in contrast to the need for bankruptcy court approval to reject an executory contract in a proceeding for reorganization under Chapter 11 of the Bankruptcy Code.

Record companies may raise a good faith argument in opposition to an artist who files for bankruptcy for the sole purpose of breaking his recording contract or to place pressure on the record company to renegotiate his agreement. This contention is of dubious merit when a performing artist is in actual financial distress and is evidencing a need for the protection of the Bankruptcy Code. Arista Records did not raise the question of good faith in the Nile bankruptcy proceeding, although in view of Nile's financial distress it is unlikely that the bankruptcy court would have found in favor of Arista.

In a case involving the artist George Jones, then under contract to CBS Records, a bankruptcy court held that the trustee in bankruptcy was vested with the artist's right to receive record royalties on pre-bankruptcy recordings. The court also decided that CBS could continue to recoup its advances in respect of such recordings from royalties on sales generated by the recordings. It is of interest that Jones' discharge in bankruptcy was ultimately denied for his failure to produce records of his financial status and business transactions for the year preceding the filing of his petition.

Foreign Record Deals

Record companies in the United States use various methods of foreign distribution. Large companies such as CBS, RCA, and Warner Communications have their own independent companies in certain countries, and in others they distribute through licensees. Smaller companies, in most instances, use only licensees for foreign distribution. There is also a hybrid arrangement in which substantial companies may organize their own foreign branches which will use the facilities of local record companies in these countries for pressing and distributing and also will perform various independent functions.

A number of record companies exist in each of the major foreign countries, and an American company seeking overseas representation must face the problems of making a wise choice of a company to represent it.

CBS, RCA, and Warner are large American companies which offer to represent American catalogs in various foreign countries.

A substantial worldwide record company based in England is E.M.I. Records Ltd. Its affiliate in the United States is Capitol Records, and it has record affiliates in all other principal countries. E.M.I. Records Ltd. has been known to seek representation of American catalogs outside of England, as well as for England.

Another large international record combine is the Polygram Record group with headquarters in the Netherlands and West Germany. Polygram includes and coordinates the interests of the Phonogram and Polydor subgroups of record companies throughout the world. The Polygram Record group has actively sought the representation of American record catalogs for foreign territories.

There is a proposal pending for the merger of the worldwide record, music video, and music publishing businesses of RCA Corporation and the West German conglomerate Bertelsmann AG. It is contemplated that each company would continue to exercise autonomous control in the creative area but would combine in the fields of manufacture, distribution, and administration. Arista Records, a U.S.A. company, is now jointly owned by RCA and Bertelsmann. The Bertelsmann record label is Ariola and Bertelsmann has wholly owned subsidiaries in the United Kingdom, France, Benelux, Spain, Austria, and Switzerland. As noted above, RCA offers to represent American catalogs in foreign countries.

An American record company may decide to facilitate its contractual and servicing problems by dealing with a large international company such as E.M.I. for many areas. On the other hand, other American companies prefer to make separate representation agreements for each important country. They fear being swallowed up by a large international company with a plethora of its own product and with varying needs for American record repertoire in different countries. A copy of a foreign record licensing agreement is included in Part 4 as Form 15.

Royalty Terms

Foreign licensees of American recordings tend to pay similar royalty rates to the licensors. The range has been from approximately 8 to 17 percent of the retail list price in the country of manufacture or sale (less excise and purchase taxes and the price of packaging), based on 90 to 100 percent of records sold. Ordinarily the country of sale is the price situs.

However, in recent years the prevailing tendency has been to compute royalties upon other than the retail price. Where this takes place it is likely that the alternate royalty sought will be the approximate equivalent of the 8 to 17 percent referred to above. In the United States the equivalent royalty computed on the wholesale price is roughly double the royalty based on the retail price. In Europe the price fixed by the mechanical-right societies for the computation of copyright royalties on sales of records is generally used as the base, with appropriate adjustments, for the calculation of record royalties. In such computations, the rate of royalty would be adjusted in order to achieve the equivalence referred to above.

A further predominating recent trend in respect of new contracts has been to depart from the base of 90 percent of records sold, and to use instead the criterion of 100 percent of net sales remaining after the deduction from gross sales of disc jockey and other promotional records, record returns, and other credits.

For special categories of records, higher royalty rates may be negotiated. These recordings entail high royalty rates payable by the American licensor, so that little or no profit would be derived by the licensor from customary sublicensing royalties. Well-known classical artists may command royalties from 10 percent to as high as 16 percent of the retail list price worldwide. Similar royalties may be payable for original Broadway musical cast albums. Royalties on some motion picture soundtrack albums may rival the royalties payable for Broadway cast albums, especially if the motion picture is one based on a popular Broadway musical. For records of this type, sublicensing royalties may rise to 15 percent or more of the retail list price, or its equivalent, or be governed by a formula such as a figure which is 5 percent higher than the royalties payable by the American licensor.

With the growing importance of lower priced or budget record lines in foreign markets, foreign licensees are insisting more and more on the right to market records in such categories and to pay a reduced royalty on such sales. The rate is subject to bargaining and is usually one-half the rate applicable to regular sales.

To limit the deduction from the retail list price for packaging, some contracts provide that the deduction may not exceed a percentage of the retail list price (less excise and purchase taxes). The figure sometimes used here is 6½ percent. Other agreements set forth specific amounts, such as 45 cents for LPs, representing the packaging allowance.

The foreign licensee will also normally pay an additional royalty, based on sales of records, to two funds established by the American Federation of Musicians, or to the licensor for payment to the funds. One fund is known as the Music Performance Trust Fund and the other is sometimes referred to as the Special Fund. The rate of the additional royalty ranges from about 1 percent overall of the suggested retail list price of recordings produced before December 1, 1983, to approximately 0.85 percent in the aggregate as to later recordings. Payments by the licensee of the additional royalty to the two funds would be in fulfillment of the licensor's obligations under its union agreements covering AF of M members. In some instances, the foreign licensee's royalty payments to the American licensor include compensation for the two funds, and the American licensor makes the payments to the funds. For a further discussion of the two funds, see Chapter 6, "Labor Agreements."

Guarantees

In negotiations with licensees, the American licensor will strive to obtain money advances or guarantees. Apart from the objective of immediate financial gain, it will be contended that the advances or guarantees ensure vigorous action by licensees in promoting and exploiting the licensor's record catalog.

The American record company will seek also to have the contract require the licensee to release a minimum number of LPs or singles during the life of the agreement. A clause which has found some acceptance by licensees provides that the licensor's singles in the top 50 hit charts of *Billboard* or *Cash Box* magazines will be released in the local territory. Record companies which are subsidiaries of motion picture companies may insist on the release of all soundtrack or other motion picture music recordings in conjunction with the exhibition of the films. American record companies with original Broadway cast albums may demand the release of such albums in at least English-speaking countries, as soon as the copyright owners of the music permit such release outside the United States; the licensee may provide that release may not be required if there is a local cast album of the same show made in the licensee's territory.

In record contracts with top artists, an American company may at times be forced to agree to release recordings not only in the United

States but also in other territories. For this reason, a licensee may be requested to agree to release recordings by artists who are entitled contractually to territorial releases.

Sales of American recordings can be promoted by the territorial tours of American artists. They appear on local radio and television and in concert halls, auditoriums, and nightclubs, thereby becoming known to the local populace. Release of their recordings to coincide with their appearances in a territory is important to the careers of artists and to sales of their recordings. Agreements may contractually commit a licensee to make such releases, and to cooperate in promoting an artist on tour.

Another form of exploitation is the use of video clips of the artists on television. Contracts may require the licensee to order copies of the video clips and to arrange for appropriate exposure in the territory.

Rights granted to licensees will extend for different periods, although a common minimum term is three years from the date of the agreement. Most licensees will insist on a one-year minimum period of exploitation, including the right of manufacture, of any master recording delivered in the latter part of the term.

To protect itself against large losses if a licensee has made substantial guarantees of royalties or releases and the licensor's catalog has failed to meet expectations, a licensee may reserve the right to cancel the agreement at an anniversary date prior to the end of the agreement.

On the other hand, as a defense against the licensee's incompetence or lack of effort, the licensor may reserve the right to cancel the agreement if the licensee fails to achieve a minimum of royalty earnings within a certain period during the term of the agreement.

As a bargaining point and an incentive to greater efforts by the licensee, licensors may condition an extension of the original term upon royalty earnings having exceeded the guarantee in the original term. The licensors may also require an increase in the guarantee of royalties applicable to the extended year or years.

Centralized Manufacture—Exclusivity

A common complaint by licensees is that the anticipated sale of an American recording does not warrant the expense in manufacturing the recording locally. The licensee will further point out that customs and duties on the importation of finished recordings, at their regular export prices, are prohibitively high. At the regular export price, the customs and duties would be imposed on the cost of manufacture plus the profit markup. To reduce the customs and duties to manageable proportions, it is sometimes arranged that the licensor will export records at its cost and will rely on the payment of royalties on sales for its profits. In effect, the American licensor then acts as the manufacturing plant for the licensee. This procedure has the advantage of promoting the exposure of the licensor's records in a territory until they become popular enough to merit local manufacture. In some instances, a licensee, working under this arrangement, may agree to purchase a minimum number of records from a selected group in the licensor's catalog.

In recent years, import duties have been abolished among the European Economic Community, popularly known as the Common Market, which includes, England, France, West Germany, Italy, Holland, Belgium, Luxembourg, Ireland, Greece, and Denmark. It is now possible for records and jackets manufactured in one country to be shipped to another with no additional expense except for freight charges. To reduce manufacturing charges, in Common Market countries licensees of the same American licensor may make contractual arrangements to purchase the licensor's product from each other. The diminished costs of manufacturing through centralized fabrication can result in the release of more items in the licensor's catalog than might otherwise prevail. Centralized manufacture tends to be facilitated where the licensees are affiliated with each other as subsidiaries of a large international record company. In fact, the Common Market's abolition of tariff barriers has accelerated in recent years the tendency to enter into licensing arrangements with a single licensee covering more than one territory, instead of on a territory-by-territory basis with different licensees. Centralized manufacture has been encouraged by increasing acceptance of original language covers, including artwork. The benefits of centralized manufacture are obviously restricted by local taste in recordings.

Licensees will desire exclusivity for their particular territory. This will be especially true where there are substantial guarantees of royalties and releases.

In the Common Market countries exclusivity may be prohibited by articles in the Treaty of Rome which governs the relations among the member countries. Therein the accent is upon free competition, the unrestricted crossing of goods across borders, nondiscrimination and market unity. Territorial sales restrictions in license agreements among the Common Market countries would appear to be barred, so that records first sold anywhere in the Common Market under authority of the copyright holder or its licensee may be imported into or exported out of any member State. Thus if an American record company licenses its Dutch subsidiary to manufacture and sell certain records, a British company may buy them in bulk and export them to England, in contravention of the so-called exclusive rights granted by the American company to another British company.

While exclusive selling rights and territorial sales restrictions in license agreements are generally invalid by reason of the Treaty of Rome in Common Market countries, the effect of the Treaty on exclusivity and territorial restrictions in other areas such as manufacturing and sublicensing is not as clear. For such matters American and other companies would be well-advised to consult with local counsel.

Performance Fees

In contrast to United States practice, the principal European broadcasting systems, whether owned by the state or privately, pay fees to the representatives of record companies for the right to broadcast recordings. These fees are apart from those payable to owners of copyrighted compositions for the right to perform the music. Fees are also collected from jukebox proprietors and other users of recordings, such as dance halls and nightclubs.

If American recordings are released abroad, a portion of the foregoing fees will be attributable to the American records. In agreements with licensees, licensors are frequently granted an interest in the fees; a 50 percent participation is common. But the trend is for major licensees to insist upon retaining broadcast performance fees until such time as the United States passes legislation under which United States broadcasters would pay similar performance fees. Where fees paid to the licensee are not allocated in direct relation to the broadcasts of particular records, the agreement with the licensee may provide for an allocation to the licensor in the ratio of the licensee's sales of the licensor's records to the total sales of records by the licensee. For the average American record company the fees will not prove to be substantial. Nevertheless, the licensor appears to be entitled to a share of the fees which, over the long run, may increase through bargaining among the licensee record companies and the commercial users of recordings.

In 1961, delegates from more than 40 countries, including the United States, met in Rome, Italy, and drafted an international convention for the protection of performers, manufacturers of records, and broadcasting organizations. At the conclusion of the conference, 35 countries voted for the newly drafted instrument, three abstained, and none voted against it. Eighteen countries signed the convention at the end of the conference, including Argentina, Austria, Belgium, Brazil, Cambodia, Chile, Denmark, France, Germany (Federal Republic), the Holy See, Iceland, India, Italy, Mexico, Spain, Sweden, United Kingdom, and Yugoslavia; subsequent signatories are Israel, Finland, Monaco, Ecuador, Lebanon, Ireland, Colombia, and Paraguay. The United States did not sign the convention. Under the convention, the states which signed may thereafter ratify or accept it. For states which did not affix their signature to the convention, the convention is open for "accession." The convention became effective on May 18, 1964, as a result of six countries having deposited ratifications. These countries are the United Kingdom, Mexico, Sweden, Ecuador, Niger, and Congo (Brazzaville); subsequently Austria, Brazil, Chile, Costa Rica, Czechoslovakia, Denmark, El Salvador, Fiji, the German Federal Republic, Guatemala, Ireland, Italy, Luxembourg, Norway and Uruguay ratified the convention.

Under the convention, provision is made for equitable remuneration by the user of a record for broadcasting or any communication to the public, to the performers, or to the producers of the record, or to both, depending on local law.

Copyright Clearances

The licensee will customarily assume the obligation to obtain clearances from the owners of copyrighted musical material in connection with the manufacture or sale of records which embody such material. This will involve the payment of a mechanical-license fee, which in Europe is based on the number of copies of a recording that are sold. The fees in Europe range from about 6 to 8 percent of the retail price of the records.

Labels

A number of substantial record companies in America have arranged with licensees for the issuance of the licensor's records in a local territory on the licensor's label. Among such companies are RCA and MCA.

Companies which are not substantial and whose labels are not well known experience difficulties in securing release on their own labels in foreign areas. As a compromise, a licensor may propose the use of a split label, composed of the licensor's and the licensee's label.

American companies seek the use of their own label for various reasons, including of course the matter of prestige. A primary aim is to achieve identification and acceptance by local dealers and the public apart from and independent of the particular licensee. This will permit an easier transition to a new licensee and will facilitate the licensor's establishing its own local enterprise. Further, with an identifiable label it is simpler for the licensor to take appropriate steps to promote its product through advertising and other methods. Finally, it is more feasible to sign foreign artists to an American company which has a foreign release on its own label.

Foreign licensees may resist a request for a label if they fear the buildup of a potential competitor thereby. The licensee may claim the loss of valuable sales on the ground that the public will not purchase records on new, unknown labels; the answer may be the establishment of a transitional period during which a split label is used.

To protect their labels American companies should give serious consideration to registering their labels promptly as trademarks in foreign countries. Companies which delay may find that their labels have been pre-empted by local registrants in certain countries.

First Refusal

If an American company licenses its recordings to a foreign licensee, the latter is likely to pick and choose among the available recordings for the purpose of a territorial release. Many recordings may never be released by the licensee, either because of unsuitability to the locality or because of other commitments of the licensee or its incapacity to handle additional recordings. Needless to say, the failure to release recordings does not necessarily mean that the recordings are unsalable in the area.

Under the circumstances, a licensor may be unwilling to commit its entire catalog exclusively to a licensee. Provision may be made that the licensee have a priority right to select recordings from the catalog for local release, but also that recordings unselected within a stated period can be placed with other licensees by the licensor. This priority arrangement is often referred to as a right of first refusal.

A licensee committed to substantial guarantees of release or money royalties may balk at receiving merely a right of first refusal. It will claim an exclusive right to all of the licensor's recordings whether or not released locally. The licensee may point out that with the passage of time recordings which were unreleased may become timely and the licensee is entitled to release them at the later date. It will be claimed that confusion may result from the possible release of recordings by the same artist on different record labels.

The licensor with substantial release guarantees may conclude that such releases will skim the cream off its catalog so that there is little reason for striving for a right of first refusal arrangement.

As a prerequisite to a right of first refusal, it may be expected that the regular licensee will require that releases by other licensees will not give prominent credit to the original licensor. Otherwise there may be confusion in the local market concerning the local source of the licensor's recordings.

Record Clubs

There are now record clubs in England, France, West Germany, Netherlands, Belgium, Switzerland, Austria, Denmark, Finland, Sweden, Australia, and Canada. Foreign licensees with club arrangements will seek the right to release through clubs. Some licensors may refuse to permit sales through clubs unless they approve the particular club and its methods of operations. Licensees frequently request the right to pay reduced royalty rates on club sales. They may contend that they themselves receive merely a limited licensing royalty from clubs owned and operated by third parties. Or if they own their own record clubs they may assert that sales are at discounted prices and there are high advertising costs and large amounts of uncollectable moneys. The rates will be the subject of bargaining and are usually one-half of the rates applicable to regular retail sales.

Coupling

In certain areas the licensee, in order to promote sales, may wish to combine the recordings of different artists from the same or unrelated labels. Or the licensee may be interested in coupling on one record selections drawn from separate records by the same artist. In some countries such as Israel where the singles market is insignificant, coupling is essential if singles hits are to reach the consumer. The licensor may fear the downgrading of its image or its artists by this procedure and may therefore prohibit any coupling without its consent. As a compromise the licensor may permit coupling from among its recordings but not with the recordings of other labels. Where the licensor's recordings are released locally on the licensor's label, it is unusual for a licensee to propose the coupling of such recordings with those of other labels.

Reciprocal Arrangements

Many foreign recordings are released in the United States and some reach the top of the popularity charts. Prominent examples include the recordings of British groups such as the Rolling Stones; their recordings have consistently sold in large quantities.

In negotiating for the foreign release of their record catalogs, American licensors should and do give weight to the possibility of reciprocal record-licensing agreements, so that the flow of product is westward as well as to Europe and other areas. In the past, American recordings were sought more avidly for foreign territories than were foreign recordings for the United States. However, foreign countries have become more nationalistic in their record tastes and Americans have become more receptive to foreign artists. It is natural to expect that, as foreign recordings achieve success in the United States, American record companies will be eager to acquire the exclusive rights to foreign record catalogs.

As consideration for granting an exclusive license for its American recordings, the American licensor may negotiate for either an exclusive right to the recordings of the foreign licensee or a right of first refusal to accept or reject the records of the licensee for distribution in the United States and possibly other areas, such as Canada. The terms for the distribution will tend to be similar to those observed in the arrangement for distribution by the licensee of the American recordings.

The possibilities of reciprocal arrangements may be limited where the licensee is a member of one of the large international record combines. As may be expected, the foreign recordings of the CBS, RCA, Warner Bros., E.M.I., Polydor, and Phonogram groups will be channeled to their respective affiliates in the United States. It is unusual when foreign recordings not absorbed by the American affiliates are placed with unaffiliated American record companies.

Cover Records

The phrase "cover record" denotes a competing record of the same tune made after the original record of the song has been issued. Cover records may be a great source of friction between a licensor and a licensee. It is not uncommon for a licensee to release a locally made cover record of tunes contained in a prior recording made by the licensor and licensed to the licensee. Obviously, a licensor will be hostile to a cover record, and the licensor, as a condition of a licensing agreement, may insist on a clause prohibiting cover records made by the licensee. Some artists record in various foreign languages and thereby tend to head off cover records.

If the licensed recording is suitable for the local market, a licensee may be willing to exclude a cover version. This is especially true for instrumental rather than vocal versions. However, where the licensed recording includes an English lyric, its release in a foreign language area may be ineffectual, and the licensee may be unwilling to preclude a local language cover record. The licensee will point out that otherwise its competitors will obtain a great advantage.

A possible compromise is to provide that the licensed recording will be released before a local cover version, and that a minimum period—one month, for example—must elapse before the release of the local record.

The large international record companies with affiliates in many countries, as a matter of good relations with their licensors, generally avoid cover versions.

Publishing Rights

Most of the important record companies outside the United States are affiliated with music publishing enterprises. For example, the Polydor and E.M.I. companies have sister publishing companies in many areas.

The important record companies in the United States are in general linked with music publishing firms. Record companies in foreign areas state that for similar reasons they tend to be affiliated with publishing enterprises. In the smaller record markets, such as Scandinavia, it is argued that the economics of the record business require the possibility of additional income from music publishing in order to support full exploitation of a record catalog.

The American licensor with publishing interests may be faced with a request that the licensee's publishing affiliate be appointed as the exclusive subpublisher for the American publisher in the particular area. This is clearly a bargaining point, and the American firm will have to evaluate many aspects in reaching a decision on the matter. The strength of the local publisher, other commitments of the licensor, the increased guarantees to the record licensor, and other items will have to be considered. An unfavorable aspect may be the tendency of the subpublisher to restrict record releases on a copyright to its affiliated record firm so as to avoid any record competition for the firm. On the other hand, it may be found that in practice this is only a theoretical and not a practical disadvantage.

Samples and Materials

In the servicing of licensees, samples of old and new recordings will be sent to them so that the licensee may determine the recordings to be released in the local territory. In the case of old recordings where there is no time urgency, samples may be dispatched by boat at a lower cost than by mail. Airmail will probably be used for samples of new recordings, since the licensee may wish to review them quickly. It may be sufficient to send new singles by airmail and to rely on boat transportation for new LPs.

Agreements with licensees will provide for samples to be forwarded to the licensees. Although there may be no charge for the samples, it is common to require the licensee to pay for packing and for freight and other transportation costs.

Import duties in the major foreign countries encourage local pressing rather than the importation of finished records from the United States. For the purpose of manufacture, the licensee will order master tapes from which lacquers or metal parts can be made locally as a preliminary to pressing, or the licensee may order lacquers or metal parts. For the production of album covers, the licensee may request negatives of cover pictures or may order copies of printed front covers or printed back liners. The licensee will usually pay at the licensor's cost price for orders of tapes, lacquers, metal parts, negatives, and printed covers or liners, as well as the costs of packing and shipping.

For mutual convenience, the parties may agree that all materials will be shipped to the licensee via a freight forwarder whose charges will be paid by the licensee. The forwarder will be experienced in the required documentation, packaging, and routing necessary for expeditious shipment to, and entry through the customs of, the different foreign countries.

Handling of Materials on Termination

At the end of a licensing agreement, the licensee will have on hand tapes, lacquers or metal parts, and possibly an inventory of finished records. The licensor, to protect its interests and those of a successor licensee, will want to control the licensee's disposition of such items.

As to the inventory of finished records, it is common to provide for a six-month sell-off period after the final date of the agreement. It must be recognized that in the absense of a sell-off period, the licensee, in order to reduce its risk, would have to desist from releasing any new product for months before the final date of the agreement term. This would operate to the detriment of both parties, especially since they may be negotiating for, and may eventually enter into, a new agreement during the final months of the original term. To protect itself, the licensor may provide that all sales in the sell-off period shall be in the normal course of business and at regular prices since otherwise the product may be down-graded by severe discounting and other practices;

in the Common Market countries referred to above under "Exclusivity," care must be taken that this clause does not fall foul of the restrictions under the Treaty of Rome.

The licensor may condition the right to sell-off on there being a written list of the inventory, supplied to the licensor within a short period after the expiration of the licensing agreement. The list will provide information useful to the licensor and any new licensee regarding the prospects of competition between the old and new licensees during the sell-off period, and may also serve as the basis for evaluating a further right, which the licensor may require, that the licensor shall have the opportunity at any time after the expiration of the licensing agreement to purchase from the licensee at the licensee's cost (and perhaps a small additional percentage) all or part of the inventory not theretofore sold by the licensee. The new licensee may be interested in purchasing such inventory through the licensor. Where the old licensee is distrusted, the licensor may wish to encourage the acquisition of the inventory so as to avoid the risk of new pressings continuing to be sold under the guise of inventory.

As to materials in the hands of the licensee, other than finished records, it is often provided that the licensee, at the option of the licensor and upon its instructions, will (1) deliver the same to the licensor in the United States or the licensed territory, or (2) transfer the same to a new licensee, or (3) destroy the same under the licensor's supervision or, at the licensor's request, destroy the same and supply an appropriate affidavit to that effect. The licensee and the licensor may also provide as to whether the costs of delivery are borne by the licensee or the licensor, and whether the licensee will be entitled to reimbursement for the costs of the materials that are to be transferred.

Accountings and Auditing

In any dealings with foreign licensees it is important to appoint licensees which are reputable and financially responsible. Otherwise, with or without proper protective provisions, the licensor may be faced with a plethora of disputes over many items, including accountings and royalty payments.

The agreement between the licensee and licensor may require quarterly or semiannual accountings. From the point of view of the licensor it is preferable to receive quarterly accountings; licensees prefer semiannual accountings. The accountings should set forth in detail the computation of the amounts included therein, and should show the number of records sold from each master recording during the accounting period, as well as all charges, royalties, and deductions.

The American licensor should obtain the right to inspect and audit the books of account of the licensee; licensees usually require that such an inspection and audit be done at the expense of the licensor and be conducted by a certified public accountant. In the event of an inspection and audit it may be insisted that the licensee show its accountings to the mechanical-rights society with respect to the number of copies of the record that have been sold. This should afford a simple check on the accuracy of the reports to the licensor.

Default Clauses

It is advisable that the licensing agreement between the American licensor and the foreign licensee contain a complete, detailed clause setting forth the rights and obligations of the parties in the event of a default.

A default would be material and important to an American licensor if the licensee failed to (1) pay guarantees and royalties when due, (2) make complete accountings when due, or (3) comply with contractual requirements as to minimum releases of the licensor's records. The licensor will also provide that the bankruptcy or insolvency of the licensee will constitute a material default.

The licensee will strive for a provision under which it is entitled to a notice of default and a period in which to remedy it.

Ordinarily, where there is a material default, the American licensor will have the right to cancel the agreement. It may also be provided that where there is such a cancellation the licensee will not have the right, usually granted at the end of an agreement, to sell off any inventory of finished goods.

The default clause should reserve to the licensor all rights to seek damages, accountings, or other relief, despite cancellation of the agreement.

Variations in Currency Values

Licensors to foreign licensees should be aware of frequent currency variations relative to U.S.A. dollars. Extreme cases such as Brazil and Israel can make the time of measurement of royalty computation and payments of vital importance. Contractual negotiations should specify whether the time for computing royalty conversions to U.S.A. dollars is at the date of (a) sale of records, (b) receipt of payment by the licensee for records sold, (c) the close of the accounting period, or (d) contractually required payment to the licensor. Within the space of 3 to 12 months, major changes can occur. If advances to the licensor from the licensee are obtained in U.S.A dollars, at which of these four possible dates is the recoupment by the licensee to be measured?

Frozen Funds

For the few areas in the world where governmental regulations impede the free flow of local funds to the United States for the payment of record royalties and guarantees, the licensing agreement may stipulate that the licensor may direct the licensee to deposit locally the requisite funds to the credit of the licensor in a depository designated by the licensor. The money then becomes available for local use by the licensor.

Jurisdiction over Disputes

Disputes may occur between the licensor and the licensee regarding the interpretation of the licensing agreement or regarding royalty statements and other compliance with the agreement. The American licensor will seek to have American courts or American arbitration bodies appointed as the exclusive forum for the consideration and determination of the controversies. This will avoid the great expense of litigation in a foreign tribunal. The foreign licensee will assert that the forum should be local because the facts are local. Negotiations will be necessary to determine who will prevail.

Branch Operations

As noted previously, a hybrid type of foreign arrangement, which is used rarely, has arisen in recent years. This entails the establishment of foreign subsidiaries or branches by American record companies, combined with pressing and distribution agreements with foreign record companies.

Typically a branch organization handles local recordings, the scheduling of releases of American and local product, the ordering of records from pressing plants, the promotion of product, and accountings to publishers and the American company. The foreign record company presses at a stipulated amount per record and buys the finished product from the branch organization at a price which represents a distributor's discount from the price to retail dealers. In effect, the discount represents the compensation to the foreign record company for its distribution services.

The amount of the discount will be determined to some extent by whether or not unsold products can be returned to the branch organization. If they can be, there is a lesser discount than if they cannot.

Usually, the branch organizations can contract for additional services to be performed by the record company for a stipulated charge. For example, the foreign record company may supply accounting services and obtain mechanical reproduction licenses from publishers.

One advantage of this type of arrangement to the American record company is better control over the release and promotion of its own catalog. It can also engage in the making of local recordings with local artists under contract to the branch organization. If the activities are successful, the profits derived can be considerably greater than the limited return under a licensing agreement. Eventually a profitable operation can lead to the initiation of pressing and distribution facilities owned by the branch organization itself.

On the other hand, the American company is likely to have to forgo the advances or guarantees of moneys which might otherwise be obtained in a licensing situation. There may be losses due to overhead, unsold product, and other factors in a branch setup, in contrast to the more certain profits from a licensing deal. In some instances, American companies have liquidated their unprofitable branch organizations and reverted to licensing agreements.

While the foreign record company may not profit as much under the branch arrangement, its risk is probably less. It will be relieved of advances, guarantees, and the expense of onerous release obligations. In many cases, it will not assume the hazard of unsold merchandise. It is assured of pressing business and can rely on a given amount of product for its distribution facilities.

Copyright in Sound Recordings

Federal protection for "sound recordings" has been in effect since February 15, 1972 by an amendment to the Copyright Act of 1909. Protection applies to such recordings fixed and published on or after February 15, 1972. Until the 1976 Copyright Act, generally effective on January 1, 1978, statutory copyright did not exist in respect of unpublished sound recordings. However, provision was made in that Act for their copyright protection.

What Is a Sound Recording?

The Senate Committee on the Judiciary, in connection with an antecedent draft of the 1976 Copyright Act, has stated as follows:

> copyrightable "sound recordings" are original works of authorship comprising an aggregate of musical, spoken, or other sounds that have been fixed in tangible form. The copyrightable work comprises the aggregation of sounds and not the tangible medium of fixation. Thus, "sound recordings" as copyrightable subject matter are distinguished from "phonorecords," the latter being physical objects in which sounds are fixed. They are also distinguished from any copyrighted literary, dramatic, or musical works that may be reproduced on a "phonorecord."

As discussed hereinafter, a "sound recording" by definition in the copyright statutes does not include the sounds accompanying a motion picture or other visual work.

Local Protection

Sound recordings fixed and published before February 15, 1972 are not eligible for federal copyright protection.

But such recordings may be protected under common law or under the state antipiracy statutes prevalent in most states in the United States; this is discussed further in Chapter 12, "Counterfeiting, Piracy and Bootlegging." The 1976 Copyright Act, however, limits the duration of their protection under state law. Such protection will no longer be effective on or after February 15, 2047. As a consequence, on February 15, 2047, 75 years from the effective date (February 15, 1972) of the federal statute that initiated federal protection of sound recordings, the recordings fixed before February 15, 1972 will fall into the public domain.

Authorship

Under the 1976 Copyright Act, copyright in a sound recording vests initially in the "author" or "authors." With respect to sound recordings it may be difficult to decide who is the author, inasmuch as the final result reflects the contributions of various persons who perform in different areas. It is usual for the copyrightable elements in a sound recording to involve authorship both by the performers on the recording and by the record producer in charge of planning the recording session, recording and electronically processing the sounds, and assembling and editing them into the final sound recording. In some cases the record producer contributes very little and the performance must be relied on for the only copyrightable element. In other cases, such as recordings of birdcalls and airplane motors, the record producer's contribution is the sole copyrightable aspect.

The 1976 Copyright Act was not designed to fix the authorship or the resulting ownership of the recordings. These were left to employment relations and to bargaining by the parties involved. If the work is prepared by an employee in the course of his employment, it is a work for hire and the employer is the author. If there is no employment relationship or agreement by performers to assign the copyright to the record producer, the copyright in the sound recording will be owned by the performing artists, or, if there are creative contributions by the record producer, jointly by the producer and the artists.

Where a notice of copyright on a sound recording fails to set forth the copyright owner, the name of the producer will be deemed part of the notice if his name appears on the record label or container.

Publication

The 1976 Copyright Act defines publication to mean the distribution "to the public by sale or other transfer of ownership, or by rental, lease or lending." It also includes the offering to distribute "phonorecords to a group of persons for purposes of further distribution."

A recording will thus be deemed published if it is sold to the public or offered to wholesalers or retailers for ultimate sale to the public.

Rights of Copyright Owner

The copyright owner of a sound recording has the exclusive rights to reproduce it, to distribute the records to the public, and to make derivative works based thereon. The rights do not extend to the making or duplication of another sound recording that is an independent fixation of other sounds, although such sounds imitate or simulate the copyrighted sound recording. Thus, the copyright owner cannot prevent cover records or sound-alike records which imitate the original recording.

Performance rights in sound recordings are not granted by the 1976 Copyright Act or any prior federal statute. Therefore the copyright owner is not entitled to license or receive royalties for the public performance and broadcasting of the recordings.

Congress considered at length whether a performance right should be given to copyright owners of sound recordings. The conclusion was that the matter required further study. It provided in the 1976 Copyright Act that the Register of Copyrights must submit to the Congress a report making recommendations on whether performance rights should be made available to performers on, and copyright owners of, sound recordings. The report was to "describe the status of such rights in foreign countries, the views of major interested parties, and specific legislative or other recommendations, if any."

A report has been submitted in which the Register of Copyrights recommends that the Copyright Act be amended to provide performance rights, subject to compulsory licensing, in sound recordings and that the benefits, in the form of royalties, be extended to performers and record producers. The report suggests that Congress legislate the initial schedule or royalty rates, which the Copyright Royalty Tribunal (established under the Act) would review at stated intervals. Specific legislative recommendations, including suggested royalties, are embodied in the report. At this writing the report has not been implemented by statute.

Under the Copyright Act of 1909, as amended, the term of copyright protection in sound recordings is limited to 28 years from the date of publication plus a renewal period of 28 years. Sound recordings which qualify for registration under that Act are entitled to the basic protection period of 56 years, plus the added 19 years provided under the 1976 Copyright Act.

For sound recordings which are protected initially under the 1976 Copyright Act, the term of protection under that Act applies. If the author is an individual the term would be 50 years from the death of the author. In the event there are two or more authors who did not work for hire, the term endures for 50 years from the death of the last surviving author. In the case of a recording made for hire or where the author is not a human being, the term would be 75 years from the year of first publication of the recording or a period of 100 years from the year of its creation, whichever expires first.

Under the 1976 Copyright Act, provision is made that all terms of copyright will extend to the end of the calendar year in which they would otherwise expire. The statute also permits the termination of grants of rights of licenses after certain periods. For a further discussion, see Chapter 16, "Duration of Copyright and Limitation of Grants."

Notice of Copyright

If a sound recording protected by the 1976 Copyright Act is published in the United States or elsewhere by authority of the copyright owner it is required to contain a copyright notice.[1]

Under the copyright statutes the copyright notice on a sound recording should appear on the surface of the copies or on the label or container in such manner and location as to give reasonable notice of the claim of copyright. The notice is to comprise the symbol ℗ (i.e., the letter P in a circle), the year date of the first public distribution of the sound recording, and the name of the copyright owner of the sound recording. A typical notice of copyright might be: ℗ 1985 Arch Records Corporation.

The copyright statutes permit the substitution, in the place of the name of the copyright owner, of an abbreviation by which the owner's name can be recognized or a generally known alternative designation of the name of the owner. Thus a notice might read: ℗ 1985 Arch Rec. Corp., since the name can be recognized as an abbreviation of Arch Records Corporation. An example of a known alternative designation of the name of the owner might be the use of the owner's trademark (e.g., the trademark "ARCH").

If the producer of the sound recording is named on the record labels or containers, and if no other name appears in conjunction with the notice, his name is considered to be part of the notice.

Protection of Underlying Works

Generally speaking a sound recording is not deemed to be a "copy" of the musical composition or other material contained in the recording. As a consequence it is unnecessary to place a copyright notice such as "© 1985 M.B.Y. Music Publishing Co. Inc." on a sound recording in order to protect the underlying musical work.

Public Broadcasting

Under the 1976 Copyright Act, effective for the most part on January 1, 1978, exclusive rights in sound recordings do not apply insofar as they are included in educational television and radio programs distributed by or through public broadcasting entities. This is on condition that copies or records of the program are not commercially distributed by or through the public broadcasters to the general public.

Deposit for Library of Congress

The 1976 Copyright Act, generally effective January 1, 1978, requires that within three months from the date of publication of a phonorecord,

---

[1]The phrase "or elsewhere" does not appear in the Copyright Act of 1909 as amended; otherwise the requirement is similar.

the copyright owner or the owner of the exclusive right of publication shall deposit in the Copyright Office, for the use or disposition of the Library of Congress, two complete phonorecords of the best edition, together with any printed or visually perceptible material published with such phonorecords. The deposit includes the entire container or package as well as the disc or tape inserted therein.

The best edition of a work is that published in the United States before the date of deposit that the Library of Congress determines most suitable for its purpose. The Register of Copyrights may by regulation exempt such deposit or require deposit of only one copy. The deposit is not a condition of copyright protection.

Copyright Registration

There is no requirement for copyright registration under the 1976 Copyright Act and registration is not a condition of copyright protection. Registration of any published or unpublished work is permissive at any time during the existence of copyright in the work.

For registration the applicant must file an application on a form prescribed by the Register of Copyrights, together with a $10 fee and the following deposits:

(1) for an unpublished sound recording, one phonorecord
(2) for a published sound recording, two complete phonorecords of the best edition
(3) for a sound recording first published outside the United States, one complete phonorecord as so published

A deposit of phonorecords for the Library of Congress referred to above will satisfy the deposit provisions for registration if the phonorecords deposited are accompanied by the application and fee described in this section and by any additional identifying material that the Register of Copyrights may require by regulation.

The Register is authorized by regulation to require or permit the deposit of one phonorecord where two would normally be required or the deposit of identifying material instead of phonorecords.

While registration is not a condition of copyright protection, no action for infringement can be brought until registration has been made. It is further provided that no award of statutory damages or of attorneys' fees shall be made for (1) infringements of an unpublished work commenced before its registration and (2) infringement of a published work begun after first publication and before registration unless registration is made within three months of such publication.

In a court proceeding a certificate for a registration made before or within five years after first publication of the work is prima facie evidence of the validity of the copyright and of the facts stated in the certificate. For a later registration the evidentiary weight for the certificate is in the Court's discretion. For a further discussion of copyright deposits and registration see Chapter 15, "The Nature of Copyright in the United States."

Albums

Notices of copyright may appear complicated in relation to an album consisting of, say, ten separate recordings. Where there is a single copyright owner, a single notice will suffice, for example, ℗ 1985 Arch Records, Inc., and the album may be registered for copyright as a collective work in one application. In that event, only the overall title of the collective work will be indexed and cataloged in the records of the Copyright Office. For the separate indexing and cataloging of individual selections, the copyright owner may file a different application for registration together with a separate fee for each selection. If the album has been the subject of a registration, the application for registration of an individual title should indicate that the single is from the album.

Derivative Works

Sound recordings are treated under the copyright law like other works with respect to the copyrightability of derivative works. If there is a new version of a public domain work, or a new version of a copyrighted work produced with the consent of the copyright proprietor, the new version is regarded as a "derivative work" which is copyrightable as such.

Insofar as a sound recording comprises recordings reissued with substantial new recorded material, or recordings republished with materially edited abridgements or revisions of the basic recording, the sound recording is deemed a copyrightable derivative work. The copyright in the derivative work applies only to the new material or the changes or revisions in the underlying work. Where there are only minor additions to or variations from the original recording, there is not an original work of authorship that is required for a registerable derivative work. Mechanical changes merely to rechannel a monaural recording into a stereophonic or quadraphonic mode, using the same sequence of sounds, would not ordinarily justify registration as a derivative work. Similarly the issuance of a tape of a sound recording previously released only in disc form would not qualify for a new registration.

In the notice of copyright for derivative works incorporating previously published material, the year date of first publication of the derivative work suffices without the need to show the year date of the earlier published material.

Compilations

Under the 1976 Copyright Act a compilation is defined so as to include collective works. According to the Act, a compilation "is a work formed by the collection and assembling of pre-existing materials." As an alternative it consists "of data that are selected, coordinated or arranged." The resulting work must be such that as a whole it "constitutes an original work of authorship."

It is common for sound recordings to appear in compiled albums which are very saleable. "Greatest Hits" series are released by many record companies. Thus there may be an album entitled "The Greatest Hits of Ferrante and Teicher." It may consist solely of recordings produced before February 15, 1972, when federal statutory copyright in sound recordings became effective, or may include only recordings made after that date, or may be a combination of recordings created before and after February 15, 1972.

Each compilation is afforded statutory protection as such, without adding to or diminishing from the protection under the copyright law for individual selections. If the compilation contains selections which have had a substantial remixing or alteration or addition of sounds, these selections, in respect of the new matter or changes, are entitled to protection as new works.

The notice of copyright for a compilation need contain only the year date of the first publication of the compilation, without setting forth the earlier year dates of publication of the component selections or the names of the different owners of the individual selections. Unless there is an express transfer of the entire copyright in a contribution in a compiled work or of any rights under the copyright, the copyright owner in the compiled work is presumed to have acquired only the privilege to reproduce and distribute the separate contribution.

The 1976 Copyright Act provides that an innocent infringer of a separate contribution has a complete defense if he proves he was misled by the notice of copyright on a compilation and acted under a purported transfer or license from the named copyright proprietor. However, he is not exonerated if a search of the Copyright Office records would have revealed a registration by the true owner or a document showing the true ownership executed by the person named in the compilation notice of copyright. To avoid this defense, owners of the individual selections may require the proprietor of the compilation to set forth a separate copyright notice for each contribution.

Audiovisual Recordings

Under the 1976 Copyright Act and the 1909 Act, as amended, sound recordings are defined so as to exclude "sounds accompanying a motion picture or other audiovisual work." Such excluded recordings are protected under the copyright of the motion picture or other audiovisual work and are ineligible for the copyright notice (℗etc.) applicable to sound recordings.

Where in fact a soundtrack album is released before the motion picture in which the soundtrack is contained, the recording is generally deemed eligible for the ℗ copyright notice and to copyright protection as a separate sound recording. The earlier release removes the recording from the category of "accompanying" the film.

Despite the fact that a soundtrack album is distributed initially after the release of the motion picture, it is common for record companies to use the ℗ copyright notice and to file an application for copyright registration of the album as a sound recording. This is justified on the ground that the soundtrack album usually contains edited, assembled, or rearranged versions of the basic soundtrack music or dialogue, and may be construed as a compilation or derivative work.

Foreign Sound Recordings

Many sound recordings originate outside the United States. While they are unpublished they are subject to copyright protection in the United States without regard to the nationality or domicile of the authors.

Foreign recordings that are published with the special notice of copyright applicable to domestic recordings may also be entitled to United States copyright protection. This is on condition that (1) the author is a national or domiciliary of a foreign country with which the United States has copyright relations pursuant to a treaty, or (2) the work is first published in the United States or a foreign nation that is a party to the Universal Copyright Convention, or (3) the work is within the scope of a Presidential proclamation extending protection to works of nationals or domiciliaries of a foreign nation that protects works of United States citizens or domiciliaries or works first published in the United States on substantially the same basis as the foreign country protects works of its citizens or works first published there.

The United States is a party to the Convention for the Protection of Phonograms against Unauthorized Duplication of Their Phonograms, Geneva, 1971. The effective date for the United States was March 10, 1974. As of July 31, 1983, there were 37 nations that were parties to the Convention.

For a further discussion relating to international aspects of sound recordings, see Chapter 32 entitled "International Copyright Protection," and Chapter 12, "Counterfeiting, Piracy and Bootlegging."

Independent Record Producers

In the past, particularly in the 1950s and 1960s, Artist and Repertoire (A&R) men reigned supreme at record companies. They selected the artists, taught, encouraged and supervised them, and were credited with nurturing the hits. Their high salaries were sometimes augmented by special bonuses, or by small royalties which were rarely at the expense of the artist royalty accounts.

The importance of the independent producer surged in the late 1970s and early 1980s. Previously a record company may have dealt with an independent producer who made a speculative "hot single" and sold it at a profit with an override royalty to himself. However, the new trend has been to look to the independent producer to assume more and more of the A & R function. Thus, entire recording budgets or specific recording funds are delivered into the hands of a "track record" producer, with carte blanche as to supervision of sessions and post-production editing of tapes.

Some noteworthy pairings of artists and producers are:

Producer	Artist
Arif Mardin	Meat Loaf, Aretha Franklin, Melissa Manchester, Chic, Leo Sayer, Chaka Khan
Richard Perry	Barbra Streisand, Ringo Starr, The Pointer Sisters
Quincy Jones	Michael Jackson, Aretha Franklin
Barry Manilow	Dionne Warwick
Burt Bacharach	Dionne Warwick, Neil Diamond
Barry Gibb	Barbra Streisand
Peter Asher	Linda Ronstadt

Artists have often been coproducers or sole producers of their own recording sessions. They thus achieve a track record as producers in their own right and can carry on the parallel career of producer and artist. Thus a great superstar such as Stevie Wonder, Todd Rundgren, or certain members of Chic or of Earth, Wind, and Fire have built careers as producers. For example, Luther Vandross has produced Aretha Franklin and Cheryl Lyn, Todd Rundgren has produced Meat Loaf and Patti Smith, and Nile Rodgers and Bernard Smith of Chic have produced recordings of Blondie, Sister Sledge, and David Bowie.

The Album Market

The growth of the role of the independent producer has largely paralleled the emphasis of the record industry on LP products rather than singles. Since the latter part of the '70s most singles records in and of themselves have failed to achieve sufficient sales to recoup required production and marketing costs. Singles have been looked to as promotional aids for the sales of LPs and are essential in that role. But the record market is largely an album market and the potential for recurring hit albums of a successful artist justifies the substantial investments by a record company. In respect of albums, entrusting large recording budgets to a proven successful producer by record companies is considered good business.

In the field of disco or dance, there are enlarged "singles" which sell at higher prices than 45 rpm singles and are packaged like albums. They are often purchased from independent production companies or are authorized for production with little regard to the artist or to a long term artist commitment, and with more attention to the song, the arrangement, and the producer.

Record Producer Functions

The independent record producer assumes important functions. He sometimes performs as a talent scout in the discovery of new artists. He usually participates significantly in choosing appropriate musical material and in selecting and supervising arrangers, accompanists, studios, and engineers. He is deeply involved in controlling recording costs within the limits of budgets or recording funds. At times another individual is appointed as an executive producer, to assist the independent producer or to perform some of his functions, particularly with regard to business affairs. Overall, the independent producer is engaged as an expert to deliver marketable potential hit product within specified financial budgets or appropriations. If excess costs are incurred, the producer is held responsible unless the excess is approved by the record company.

Label Deals

An independent producer, with particularly desirable artists under contract to him, may be able to negotiate a "label deal" with a record company. Such deals, which are rare, provide that the manufactured records and tapes will bear the trade name and label of the producer. A producer may claim that the deal enhances his prestige and aids in attracting artists to his fold. It may also be advantageous to a producer who wishes to establish the name of his firm, with an eye towards the future development of his own recording and manufacturing operation. In the case of label agreements, producers will seek both fixed and royalty compensation from record companies. The fixed compensation may be in the form of a weekly overhead payment, and other periodic payments, or so much per recorded master, or a variation thereof. The royalty compensation will be a percentage of the wholesale or retail list price, computed usually on 90–100 percent of the records manufactured and sold. The percentage will depend on the results of the bargaining between the producer and the record company. It is common for the producer to be responsible for paying royalties due to recording artists. Where the producer is so committed the producer royalty must be sufficiently high to cover both the artist royalty and an override royalty to the producer.

Pressing and Distribution Deal

An alternate form of a label deal is a "pressing and distribution" arrangement. Therein the production company relies upon a profit participation instead of a royalty. In such deals, the record company deducts from receipts the pressing charges, mechanical license fees, and other specified expenses, including a negotiated distribution fee. The distribution fee which is akin to a royalty is taken by the record company as payment for its services. Distribution charges of 15 to 17 percent of gross dealer prices on LPs and cassettes are common, with slightly higher rates for singles and extended play records (i.e. EPs).

A major problem of a label deal involving more than one artist is whether the royalties or profits from the hits of one artist can be used by the record company to recoup the losses on other artists. This can create financial difficulties for a production company in paying its artist royalties when the company's hit royalties or profits are appropriated by the record company to cover losses on other artists. Through negotiations an independent producer may cause the record company to agree that the amount payable by the producer to an artist is excluded from such crossrecoupment.

Royalties

If a producer is engaged to supervise artists already under contract to a record company, the producer's royalty may range from 3 to 5 percent of the retail list price, with a reduced royalty for record club, foreign and other special sales. The royalty will not ordinarily be payable until recording costs have been recouped out of the artist royalty. Sometimes the recoupment provision is more favorable to the artist and the producer in that recoupment will be from the aggregate of the artist and producer royalties. Where recoupment is solely out of the artist royalty, it may be provided that the producer will, upon such recoupment, be paid royalties retroactively to the first record sold.

Where a producer supplies a new artist, the total royalties for the package may range from about 10 to 14 percent of the retail list price. From the record company viewpoint, it may be attributing from 7 to 10 percent to the artist and from 3 to 4 percent to the producer. For sales outside the United States, the traditional royalty has been not more than one-half the domestic royalty. But there has been an upward trend as foreign licensees have increased their royalties to United States licensors, and especially when the foreign licensee is owned by the domestic record company. A common provision is that all moneys paid for obtaining a master recording, whether as payments to the producer or as expenditures for recording costs, will be deemed an advance against and recoupable from the total royalties for the package otherwise payable to the production firm.

There may be an alternative package deal for an important artist and his producer where a major royalty and a major recording fund are involved. The major recording fund may be several hundred thousand dollars per album, or even more. The package may provide for a total royalty of up to 18 percent or higher, with royalties as much as 22 percent having been observed.

For deals with lesser artists, the ultimate share of the production firm will vary, depending on the contract between the artist and the producer. Participation by the producer may range from 50 percent down to a third, and may go higher than 50 percent when the producer has a favorable agreement with the artist. In a simple arrangement, the producer and the artist may agree to share all receipts on a fixed ratio basis such as 50–50, resulting in clearly delineated participations which the parties can anticipate. A producer may benefit particularly if a fixed, negotiated royalty is payable by the producer to the artist. For example, the contract may provide that the artist will be paid a royalty of 7 percent, based on 90 percent of sales, with half royalties for foreign sales and with no royalty payable until the artist royalty equals the amount of the recording costs. On the other hand, the record company may have agreed to pay on 100 percent of sales, with a three-quarters royalty for foreign sales and with recoupment against the total package royalty.

Artist/Producer Joint Ventures

Often an independent producer may establish a working relationship with a new artist, without either having a commitment from a record company. They may enter into a special joint venture contractual relationship which portrays their rights and obligations, including the sharing of advances and royalties if a record company contract is obtained.

The contract may provide for the making of a demonstration recording in advance of a record company contract. For that purpose, the producer may be obligated to furnish or procure studio facilities and musicians, with the cooperation of the artist. To cause the studio to defer or reduce its charges, the producer may be authorized to offer the studio a small royalty participation in a resultant recording. The producer and the artist may seek to have musicians defer or reduce their charges. Payment to a studio or musicians may be provided for as off-the-top deductions from advances or royalties that are received. The contract may call for certain minimum payments to the artist and the producer as the next off-the-top deductions, before an ultimate sharing between the artist and the producer on a basis such as 50–50.

Under the contract the parties may agree to cooperate in obtaining and accepting a recording contract that contains specified minimum terms. Over and above an understanding that the record company will be a major one, the parties may stipulate that the contract must contain an LP recording commitment by the record company and that the net artist royalty, after the producer's share, must not be less than a certain percentage, such as 5 percent of the retail list price.

While the producer may be delegated the responsibility to negotiate with the record company, the artist may retain a right of full consultation. Also the artist may insist on the right to replace the producer, if the resultant recordings do not achieve best-selling chart action; the producer may require the right to approve the new producer, with such approval not to be unreasonably withheld. Or in such instance the artist may be entitled to call for the appointment of a coproducer. Under the contract the costs of the new producer or coproducer would be deductible from the share otherwise due to the first producer.

Not all record company renewal contract options are exercised. To protect the producer's interest in the artist, it may be provided in the contract between them that the producer shall have a three to six month period in which to obtain a new record contract to replace the old one.

A recurring issue in the contract between the producer and the artist is whether the recording costs will be recoupable solely out of the artist royalties or out of the combined artist and producer royalties. Usually recording costs are chargeable as an advance against the artist royalties, but often they are shared by the artist and producer in the proportion of their royalty participations. Where the recording costs are recouped only from the artist royalties, the producer commonly receives royalties initially after the record company has fully recouped from the combined artist and producer royalties; thus the producer will be paid royalties prior to the artist becoming entitled to receive any royalties.

A form of an artist/producer development agreement is included in Part 4 as Form 13.

Producer Advances

Producers will rarely produce recordings of an artist under contract to a record company without requiring the payment of cash fees. Usually these constitute advances recoupable from the producer royalties, although on few occasions they are deemed to be nonrecoupable bonuses. Advance payments to producers with respect to artists on minor labels may be as low as $1,000 a single record side, and producer advances of from $20,000 to $50,000 per album incorporating 8 to 10 sides are not unusual.

Where a recording fund is available, the balance remaining after the deduction of the recording costs is retained by the producer, or in some cases shared between the producer and the artist. The said balance is deemed to be a recoupable advance chargeable against the person or persons entitled to retain it.

While an advance to a producer will be chargeable against the producer's royalty, it will also be regarded as an additional recording cost recoupable from the artist royalty. If negotiations with the record company result in recoupment of the producer advance out of the aggregate of the producer and artist royalties, this will prove beneficial to both royalty participants as compared to having 100 percent recoupment from each of their respective shares. Each royalty participant will then bear a proportional share of the producer advance in the ratio that his respective royalty rate is to the combined royalty rates.

Producer advances and royalties are separately accounted for and are distinct from royalties payable to songwriters or publishers for mechanical-license fees. Where there are mechanical-license fees which become payable to the artist or producer in their capacity as songwriter or publisher, they should scrutinize with care a proposed clause in a contract with the record company which makes all advances chargeable against payments *of any kind* that may become due to them.

Music Publishing

Producers often derive additional compensation through their control of the music publishing rights in original material that is recorded. They thereby receive performance fees when their record is played and mechanical-license fees when their record is manufactured and sold. On the other hand, the record company may bargain for the entire music publishing rights controlled by a producer, for half the rights, or at least for an interest in the publishing income. Sometimes the record company may be willing to settle for a reduced mechanical-license rate.

Artist Follow-Up Rights

If a producer is engaged to work with an artist under contract to a record company, the producer may seek the right to continue as the producer of future recording sessions. He may request a contractual clause stating that if a certain level of sales in the United States are achieved within a specified time period, he will be given the right to produce future sessions on the basis of the same or higher advance payment and royalty provisions. Under the clause, only if he refuses may the company proceed to use other producers for the artist. The time period should be short enough to be within the normal production period for a follow-up record and yet long enough for the sales plateau to be achieved. For purposes of the sales plateau computation, there may be a provision that "free" records and records in the reserve for returns must be counted. Often the time period utilized is eight to nine months.

When acquiring master recordings of a new artist from a producer, a record company will usually insist on obtaining rights to subsequent recordings by the artist. It will be the company's position that, having expended time and money in establishing an artist, the company is entitled to continue with an artist who thus becomes successful.

There are various avenues which the company may take for follow-up rights. In the first place, the company may be content with an agreement with the producer to produce and supply further recordings by the artist.

On the other hand the company may prefer a direct recording contract with the artist, with a separate agreement with the producer covering his right, if any, to supervise the future recordings and to receive fixed and royalty compensation.

Or the company may take an option to enter into a recording contract with the artist within a given period of time. For example, the period may be four months after the acquisition of the initial master. Assuming that the record is issued within 30 days after its purchase, the company will then have 90 days in which to evaluate the market acceptance of the record before having to act to pick up the option. For convenience the company may execute a record agreement with the artist at the same time as the company makes a master purchase agreement with the producer; however, it will be provided that the agreement with the artist will not become effective unless and until the option is exercised.

Contractual Safeguards

If the producer refuses to consent to a recording agreement between the artist and the company because the producer wishes to retain his contractual relations with the artist, the company may still safeguard itself against a breach by the producer of his contract with the artist. This can be done through the device of an agreement between the company and the artist stating that (1) the artist is familiar with the agreement between the producer and the company, including any right of first refusal as to subsequent recordings by the artist, (2) the artist will abide by the master purchase agreement insofar as it covenants for his personal performance, (3) the artist will look solely to the producer for royalty statements and the payment of royalties, and (4) a breach of the agreement between the producer and the artist will not excuse performance by the artist in accordance with the master purchase agreement.

The company may wish to secure protection against the possibility that the producer may become unavailable, for any reason, to produce further recordings by the artist. For such protection it may be necessary to insist that such unavailability will give rise to a right to an assignment of the recording contract between the producer and the artist, and that for such purpose, if the producer fails to make the assignment when the company is entitled thereto, the company is deemed to be the attorney-in-fact of the producer.

In respect of new artists to be discovered by and pacted to the producer, the company may demand that the agreement between the artist and producer be in a form satisfactory to the company. Thereby the company may include provisions that the recording agreement shall be deemed for the benefit of the company, that it may be enforced by the company, that the company shall receive notice of any defaults by the producer and an opportunity to cure the defaults, and that, should the defaults be incurable, the company has the right to take over the recording agreement with the artist with no responsibility for past defaults of the producer. Such provisions are enforceable by the company against the artist.

For master recordings of artists under contract to the producer the company will rely on the producer for appropriate warranties of the originality of the material and of the fact that the recordings, including the performance of the artist, will not interfere with the rights of third parties. The company will also look to the producer for warranties that all recording costs for the master have been paid, so that no claims will be made against the company for unpaid bills. Under its agreements with the American Federation of Musicians and the American Federation of Television and Radio Artists the company must procure a warranty from the producer that the musicians and vocalists who made the master were paid union scale for their services; this warranty must therefore appear in the master purchase agreement and, in accordance with the union agreements, be stated to be for the benefit of the unions. Unless the producer is a signatory to the agreement with the AF of M, the company, under its agreement with the AF of M, guarantees the accuracy of the representation as to instrumentalists. Similarly the record company, under its AFTRA agreement, guarantees the accuracy of the producer's warranty as to vocalists if the producer was not a signatory to the AFTRA code when the recording was made or acquired by the company. Finally, the company will require the producer to agree not to permit the artist to rerecord the same material within a period of, usually, five years, so that for that period the company will not be faced with competition by the same artist performing the same material.

To guard against manufacture and sales directly by the producer, the contract will prohibit such activities.

As indicated heretofore, because the producer is an intermediary between the artist and the company, the company must obtain from the producer the contractual safeguards that the company would include in agreements with the artist. The company will also seek from the producer additional provisos to protect the company from the effects of a default or misunderstanding in the relations between the producer and the artist.

The producer, on the other hand, must realize that he stands to some extent in the position of the artist and that he must attempt to secure the contractual clauses which would be required by artists. Thus, he should watch for appropriate provisions relating to accountings, audits, renewal of the agreement, prohibitions against re-recordings, guarantees of release of records pressed from the master recordings, etc. Furthermore, the producer must bulwark his special position as a producer by clauses ensuring his control of the artist and material; the company may try to limit such control so as to give the company a voice in future productions involving the artist.

Record Clubs and Premiums

Between five and six million Americans belong to record clubs. Total club and mail order sales in 1983 were $439 million. Over 60 percent of this figure is attributable to purchases made under traditional club membership plans. The remaining portion of the total consists largely of so-called package sales of sets of several records designed to appeal generally to the over-35 market of record buyers. Often, the recordings are not of a current vintage.

Record club sales are made mostly on an installment or credit basis. The RCA Music Service (the RCA club name) and the Columbia Record Club are among the most active in the field.

The major record clubs handle the catalogs of various record companies. In addition to the records released by CBS Records, the Columbia Club also currently distributes all the major labels except RCA, such as Capitol, MCA and Polygram, and many of the other labels. The RCA Club distributes its own line and currently licenses the product of certain other companies such as A&M, Arista, Capitol, Mercury, and London.

The Columbia Record Club is part of Columbia House, a division of CBS, Inc. RCA Music Service is part of RCA Records.

Federal Trade Commission Proceedings

In 1962, the Federal Trade Commission charged Columbia and its parent firm, the then Columbia Broadcasting System, with monopoly practices and the illegal suppression of competition. The complaint was based, among other things, on the practice of the club of making exclusive arrangements with labels other than those handled by CBS Records. It was alleged that this was unfair to retail dealers and the competing record clubs.

Under the terms of a Federal Trade Commission consent order issued in 1971, Columbia is prohibited from acting as the exclusive record club for the labels of other record manufacturers. It is now the common practice of all major record clubs to obtain their product from manufacturers on a nonexclusive basis.

Membership Plans

Record clubs offer various purchasing plans to prospective members. Under one arrangement, a new member can buy 11 albums or tapes for $1.00 if he makes a commitment to purchase an additional eight albums or tapes at regular club prices over a three-year period. Other plans make individual albums available to members at reduced prices. Still other plans are illustrated by such offers as "3 for free spectacular," "one free with every one you buy," and "disc dividends."

Outside Label Agreements

In their contractual agreements with outside labels, Columbia and the other clubs normally provide that the licensed product will bear the original label and jacket when sold through the club.

Royalties payable by the Columbia club to the outside labels are about 9 ½ percent of the club's regular price (less a charge allocated to the record container), based on 85 percent of the records sold and not returned; the royalty for soundtrack, original cast, and classical albums is typically about 12 percent. Other clubs may pay a similar royalty. It is common that no royalty is payable by clubs on "bonus" or "free" records distributed to members either as a part of an enrollment offer or as the result of the purchase of a required number of records. However, the clubs will sometimes accept a limitation on the number of bonus or free records, in terms of such records not exceeding a percentage of the records on which royalties are payable; and the clubs will pay royalties on the excess as if sold, although in some contracts such royalties will be at a lower rate than that applicable to regular club sales.

Ordinarily the Columbia club and certain other labels take master tapes from the outside labels and then press records based on the tapes. The operation in that regard is similar to that of a foreign licensee of an outside label. The club pays, as in the case of foreign licensees, mechanical copyright license fees and payments on sales which become due to the Music Performance Trust Fund and the Special Fund established through the American Federation of Musicians.

Artist Royalties

A fairly standard provision in agreements with American artists is that they receive one-half their usual royalty rate on sales through clubs and that no royalties are payable on bonus or free records distributed by clubs. The bonus and free record clauses tend to match the provisions in agreements between record companies and the record clubs, and the lower royalties have been negotiated in the light of the royalties from the clubs.

A further impetus toward reduced artist royalties has been added by the operations of record clubs outside the United States. Club operations exist in England, France, West Germany, Netherlands, Belgium, Switzerland, Austria, Denmark, Finland, Sweden, Australia, and Canada. It is common for foreign licensees of American records to place such records in clubs on the basis of lower royalties payable to the United States licensors, as compared to the royalty rates on regular sales.

Mechanical-License Fees

A problem faced by the clubs in the United States has been the amount of payments due for mechanical copyright license fees to music publishers whose selections are included in records released by clubs. While publishers have been willing to accept reductions in the customary mechanical-license rate, and a rate of 75 percent of the rate payable by the original record company is often obtained, The Harry Fox Agency, which represents many publishers, has balked at waiving royalties on free or bonus records and such royalties are normally paid by the clubs. The Harry Fox Agency will accept the 75 percent rate provided that it does not reduce the royalty below 75 percent of the statutory compulsory mechanical-license rate.

Premiums

A premium offer may arise when a company such as a supermarket or a tire company, in order to encourage patronage for its regular products, sells records at an unusually low price, such as $1 per LP. This is a promotional plan which frequently involves a guarantee to the record company of a substantial number of sales.

Since the price paid to the record company is low, it must keep its costs at a reduced level. The margin of profit on each record will be small, but a premium transaction will entail large volume and low distribution expenses. In connection with a premium offer, the record company will seek low mechanical-license rates from the music publishers and the record company will have to evaluate the royalty rates which must be paid to the performing artists. Some agreements with artists provide for no royalties in the case of premium sales; others may establish reduced royalty rates. Where the artist agreement does not provide for low royalty rates the record company may have to negotiate with the artist, stressing the promotional exposure and publicity values, and the volume of sales which may result in sizable royalty payments even at lower royalty rates.

Labor Agreements

The unions for performers in the phonograph record industry are the American Federation of Musicians (AF of M) and the American Federation of Television and Radio Artists (AFTRA). Musicians, including leaders, contractors, copyists, orchestrators, and arrangers of instrumental music, are covered by the AF of M. Vocalists, actors, announcers, narrators, and sound effects artists are represented by AFTRA.

Required Membership

It is a condition of employment, under the employers' agreements with both unions, that the employees be members of the union or become members by the thirtieth day following the beginning of their employment.

Agreements

The present agreement with AFTRA is entitled the "National Code of Fair Practice for Phonograph Recordings," and is in effect from April 1, 1983 to March 31, 1986.

There are two direct agreements with the AF of M, effective for the period from December 1, 1983 through November 30, 1986: the "Phonograph Record Labor Agreement (December, 1983)," and the "Phonograph Record Manufacturers' Special Payments Fund Agreement (December, 1983)."

In addition, record companies which sign the agreements with the AF of M are parties to a "Phonograph Record Trust Agreement (December, 1983)," for which the Trustee is Martin A. Paulson.

Arbitration

Under the AFTRA agreement, any dispute or controversy of any kind and nature whatsoever between a record company and AFTRA is to be submitted to arbitration. Also subject to arbitration is any dispute or controversy between a record company and a member of AFTRA arising out of the AFTRA agreement or out of any contract made on or after April 1, 1983.

However, if there is an exclusive recording agreement with an artist, and "the Company has reason to believe that the artist has recorded or contemplates recording in violation of the contract," the company may apply to a court for an injunction and other relief arising out of the particular act.

There is a specified procedure for requesting an arbitration. AF-TRA or the record company or the artist (with the written consent of AFTRA) appoints an arbitrator designated by the initiating party. The other party must then name its arbitrator within three days, or an arbitrator will be named by the American Arbitration Association. The two arbitrators have five days to name a third from a panel submitted by the American Arbitration Association, or a third arbitrator will be named by the Association.

The award of a majority of the arbitrators is final and binding upon the parties, and judgment upon the award may be entered by any party in the highest court of the forum, state or federal, having jurisdiction.

While the AF of M agreements do not specifically provide for arbitration, the agreements incorporate the current provisions of the union's Constitution and By-Laws. The Constitution provides that every "claim, dispute, controversy or difference . . . arising out of, dealing with, relating to, or affecting the interpretation of (the) contract or the violation or breach or threatened violation or breach thereof . . ." is to be adjudicated by binding arbitration. The arbiter for any dispute involving recording, radio, or television activities is the International Executive Board of the American Federation of Musicians. According to the Constitution, the award of the Board shall be final and binding and is enforceable by the courts.

Contractors

Under the AFTRA Code a contractor is required on all engagements of group singers consisting of three or more. If the sex of the group does not preclude the use of the contractor's singing services, the contractor must be a performing member of the singing group.

Contractors for group singers are defined in the Code as "those artists who perform any additional services, such as contacting singers, pre-rehearsing, coaching, or conducting singers, arranging for sessions or rehearsals, or any other similar or supervisory duties, including assisting and preparation of production memorandum." The contractor is to be present at all times during the recording session.

For his services the contractor for group singers receives, in addition to his fee as a singer, certain additional fees.

Under the AFTRA Code, a contractor is also required for all original cast show albums employing a singing group of three or more. He need not be a member of the singing group. His duties include (1) liaison between the cast and producer, (2) responsibility for completion of appropriate forms and filing same with AFTRA within 48 hours, and (3) responsibility for enforcement of AFTRA provisions. The contractor for original cast albums receives, in addition to his fees as a performer, certain additional fees.

It is the duty of the contractor, in respect of each recording session, to fill out the pertinent information on the AFTRA Member Contractor

Standard Report Form, and to deliver a copy to the record company representatives. After the record company initials it to indicate that a recording session has been held, the contractor must file the report with AFTRA. This report is over and above Schedule A, a production memorandum, which the record company must furnish to AFTRA within 21 calendar days after the recording session. The production memorandum is to provide sufficient information to permit a computation of the appropriate performing fee, and also sets forth the gross fee paid.

Under the Phonograph Record Labor Agreement with the AF of M, the functions of a contractor are not generally defined. In practice, however, the contractor engages the necessary musicians for the recording session; he often hires the AFTRA contractor, who in turn engages the required singers. An AF of M contractor must be used if 12 or more sidemen are employed for any session. The contractor must attend throughout the session and may be one of the sidemen who play at the session. The contractor's pay must be not less than double the applicable sideman's scale, with no extra payment for his services as sideman. It is the duty of the contractor to supply to the record company, for each record session, a completed Form B and completed W–4 forms. The forms are the basis for payment of union scale by the record company, within 15 days (excluding Saturdays, Sundays, and holidays) after the date of receipt of the completed forms.

New Rights for Performing Artists

The agreement with AFTRA contains a provision relating to new laws which create new rights for performing artists, with regard to their performances on phonograph records used directly for broadcasting or any other communication to the public.

These laws may be in the form of new domestic legislation or, if adopted, the International Convention for the Protection of Performers, Producers of Phonograms, and Broadcasting Organizations, dated October 26, 1961. The Convention contemplates the payment of remuneration for such performances. The AFTRA agreement provides that if the remuneration is in fact received by the record company, upon 30 days written request by either party, the record company and the union will bargain in good faith as to what portion shall be paid to the performers. The provision is not applicable if the legislation or Convention provides for separate payments to the performers.

The principal countries of Europe have adopted the Convention.

Dubbing

One meaning of "dubbing" is the addition of vocal or instrumental performances to music already recorded. This is also called "overdubbing."

Under the AF of M agreement, there is a general prohibition

against dubbing except as specifically permitted by other provisions of the agreement. Dubbing is allowed if the record company gives prior notice to the union and, in the event of the dubbing, pays union scale and fringe benefits for the new use. Also, during a session the record company may add live performances to a recording made at the same session, without additional compensation to the musicians; and, after the completion of a session, the record company may add vocal performances or additional instrumental performances, without further payment to the musicians at the original recording session.

The AFTRA agreement does not prohibit overdubbing. It provides that if the "artist participates in multiple tracking (i.e., sings again to the original track at the same session), he shall be paid for the session as if each overtracking were an additional [record] side."

Under the AFTRA agreement, the word "dubbing" is also applied to characterize converting or transferring the performance of artists in a medium other than phonograph records, e.g., radio, television, or motion pictures, for use as phonograph recordings. This is sanctioned by AFTRA provided that certain conditions are met by the record company. These include notice to AFTRA, payment of AFTRA scale to the performers, obtaining the consent of the "star or featured or overscale artist," if any, and acquiring the consent of the artist who has performed the vocal soundtrack if any for the "star or featured or overscale artist." The provisions for payment are comparable to AF of M required re-use fees.

Royalty Performers

Under the AF of M agreement, a distinction is made between a musician who is a phonograph record "royalty artist" and one who is not. A "royalty artist" is defined as one "(a) who records pursuant to a phonograph record contract which provides for a royalty payable to such musician at a basic rate of at least 3% of the suggested retail list price of records sold (less deductions usual and customary in the trade) or a substantially equivalent royalty, or (b) who plays as a member of (and not as a sideman with) a recognized self-contained group. . . ."

The agreement also defines a "recognized self-contained group." It consists of "two or more persons who perform together in fields other than phonograph records under a group name. . . ." In addition, the group must be recording under a phonograph record contract providing for a royalty "at a basic rate of at least 3% of the suggested retail list price of records sold (less deductions usual and customary in the trade) or a substantially equivalent royalty." Furthermore, all musicians in the group must be members of the AF of M.

Provision is made that at the first session for a single record side the royalty artist receives only the basic session rate and related overtime rate irrespective of whether he plays multiple parts, doubles, overdubs, or "sweetens."

The AFTRA agreement provides that, for recordings of the same side, a royalty artist shall receive minimum union scale, with a maximum payment of three times scale irrespective of the length and number of sessions. The production memorandum to be filed by a record company after a recording session must indicate whether or not the performer is a royalty artist.

Special protection for the AFTRA royalty artist is afforded by a provision that the record company must furnish the artist "at least semiannually and to AFTRA upon request, . . . so long as there shall be sales, a full and proper accounting in order to correctly ascertain the amount of royalty . . . due artist." The AF of M agreement goes even further by its insistence that recording contracts contain a covenant that the contract "shall become effective unless it is disapproved by the International Executive Board of the American Federation of Musicians of the United States and Canada, or a duly authorized agent thereof, within 30 working days after it is submitted to the International Executive Board. The parties acknowledge that this provision is not intended to provide a device for the parties hereto to avoid their obligations."

With respect to AFTRA Pension and Welfare Funds, the record company is required to pay to the funds an amount equal to 9 percent of the gross compensation paid to the performer by the company. Included in the "gross compensation" are all forms of payment, of any kind or nature, whether they be "salaries, earnings, *royalties,* fees, advances, guarantees, deferred compensation, proceeds, bonuses, profit-participation, shares of stock, bonds, options and property of any kind or nature whatsoever paid to the artist directly or indirectly . . ." (italics ours). The 9 percent payment is limited, however, to the first $100,000 of gross compensation paid to the artist in any calendar year.

Foreign Recordings

The AFTRA agreement states that it applies to the making of phonograph recordings in the United States of America, its territories and possessions, all of which is referred to as the "Recording Territory." No clause attempts to regulate recordings made outside the Recording Territory.

On the other hand, the AF of M agreement is not so restricted. In the first place, it covers recordings made in Canada as well as in the United States, or in a present territory or possession of either country, all of which is called the "Domestic Area." The agreement also encompasses any residents of the Domestic Area engaged within or without that area to perform as instrumental musicians or as leaders, contractors, copyists, orchestrators, or arrangers of instrumental music in the recording of phonograph records outside the Domestic Area. However, the 10 percent of earnings payment to the AF of M Pension Welfare Fund applies only to services performed in the Domestic Area.

The constitution of the AF of M is incorporated by reference in contracts for engagements with AF of M members. Thereunder the AF of M prohibits its members from rendering services outside the Domestic Area unless the member is expressly so authorized in writing by the union. Penalties for a violation include a fine not exceeding $5,000, or the loss of membership rights up to and including expulsion, or both.

Acquired Masters

Purchases or leases of master recordings by record companies are an accepted part of the music business. There are well-established and well-financed independent producers of master recordings who sell or lease them to record companies. There are also young musicians who make master recordings on speculation, inspired by faith in their own talents. Without the capital to operate under union standards, these young entrepreneurs may record in makeshift studios with nonunion musicians or with union musicians who are willing to accept less than scale.

AFTRA and the AF of M are fully aware of the illicit practices in the field. The unions recognize the threats inherent therein to the employment of union members and to the maintenance of minimum union pay rates. Certain provisions in the AFTRA and AF of M agreements may be regarded as having been included in the light thereof. They appear designed to make the record companies assist in policing the field. Thus Paragraph 17 of the AF of M agreement addresses itself to the use by a record company of acquired recordings which were recorded in the Domestic Area or by a resident of the Domestic Area. The use is prohibited unless the instrumentalists, leaders, contractors, copyists, orchestrators, and arrangers have been paid not less than union scale and fringe benefits.

To satisfy its obligations, the record company in its agreement to acquire the master recordings, may include certain stipulated clauses. These are: (1) a representation and warranty by the seller or licensor that the recorded music does not come within the terms of Paragraph 17 of the union agreement or that the requirements of Paragraph 17 are satisfied, and (2) a statement that the representation and warranty were included for the benefit of the union and may be enforced by the union or by the person it may designate. The record company guarantees the representation and warranty if the seller or licensor was not a party to a Phonograph Record Labor Agreement with the union when the recording was made.

The AFTRA agreement specifically covers master recordings made in the United States of America, its territories and possessions. In the acquisition of such master recordings, the record company must obtain from the seller or lessor the following warranty and representation for the direct benefit of AFTRA and the performing artists:

That all artists whose performances embodied thereon were recorded in the recording territory, have been paid the minimum rates specified in the 1983–1986 AFTRA Code of Fair Practice for Phonograph Recordings or the applicable Code then in effect at the time the recording was made, and that all payments due to the AFTRA Pension and Welfare Funds have been made.

It is the record company's obligation to furnish to AFTRA, on the form known as Schedule D, the said warranty and representation when masters are acquired from third parties. In the alternative, the record company may file a Schedule A which lists performers and payments by the company. Schedule A is the form used for reporting usual recording engagements.

If the AFTRA representation and warranty quoted above are false and the seller or lessor was not a signatory to an AFTRA Phonograph Recording Code when the recording was made or when acquired by the record company, then the company must make the minimum scale payments plus any applicable contributions to the AFTRA Pension and Welfare Funds.

Transferee Royalty Obligations

From time to time attorneys in the music field may be asked to advise the transferee of master recordings as to his royalty obligations to the artists on the recordings. Unless a third-party transferee specifically agrees to pay royalties to the artist, there may be a question under law as to the privity of obligations between the artist and the third party.

The AFTRA agreement clearly attempts to solve this problem. It refers to any transfer of title to or rights in a master recording by "sale, assignment, pledge, hypothecation, or other transfer, or by attachment, levy, lien, garnishment, voluntary bankruptcy, involuntary bankruptcy, arrangement, reorganization, assignment for benefit of creditors, probate, or any other legal proceeding. . . ." Under the AFTRA Code the transferee is responsible to the artist for royalties due under the artist contract for sales of phonograph records made by the transferee or its licensees. Such responsibility accrues after default by the producer of the records in the payment of artist royalties and receipt by the transferee of written notice by the artist specifying the default, together with due proof of the artist's royalty arrangements. The transferee's responsibility is only in respect of sales after receipt of such notice.

The AFTRA agreement also requires that any transferee of title or rights in a master recording, who is not a signatory to the AFTRA Code, shall sign an agreement with AFTRA assuming the obligations referred to in the previous paragraph. The transferee continues to have the same responsibility to the artist for all sales by the transferee's successor in interest, unless the successor is a Code signatory.

In agreements transferring an interest in a master recording, every record producer must include provisions incorporating the aforementioned royalty responsibility to the artist on the part of the transferee, as will as a covenant requiring the same undertaking in all subsequent transfers.

Union Scale Payments

As is normal in union agreements, the AFTRA Code makes provision for minimum compensation rates in various classifications. Among these are "Soloists and Duos," "Group Singers," "Actors and Comedians, Narrators and Announcers," and "Sound Effects Artists." There are special rates payable to performers in original cast show albums and to the vocalists "stepping out" of groups in recording sessions. The AFTRA rates applicable, effective April 1, 1985, appear in Appendix S.

Exhibit A to the AF of M agreement covers minimum wages and other working conditions for instrumentalists, leaders, contractors, arrangers, orchestrators, and copyists. The provisions are detailed and extensive, and reference should be made to the union agreement for specific terms.

Effective December 1, 1983, a musician for nonclassical recordings became entitled to $178.15 as a basic session rate for a three-hour session. There are premium rates for recording sessions held on Saturdays after 1:00 p.m., Sundays, listed holidays, and during certain late night hours. Rates increased by 5 percent on December 1, 1984 to $187.06 and will increase another 5 percent to $196.41 on December 1, 1985.

Leaders and contractors receive not less than double the applicable sideman musician's scale.

A musician who doubles in certain instruments is paid an additional 20 percent of the base rate and the overtime related thereto.

AFTRA Contingent Scale Payments

Under the AFTRA Code there are additional union scale payments to be made by record companies to AFTRA members, contingent upon the sales success in the United States of phonograph records recorded on or after December 15, 1974. The payments are due from record companies only to those AFTRA members who participated in the recording and who are not entitled to receive royalty payments. A recording ceases to be considered as a basis for additional payments at the expiration of ten years after the date of its first release to the public as a single or as a part of an album.

In determining contingent scale payments, only sales in normal retail channels, less (1) an allowance for a reasonable reserve for returns and (2) records distributed as free goods or promotional goods, are counted. Sales through record clubs or by mail order and premium sales are excluded.

A recorded side which has been previously released in album form does not earn contingent scale payments for further release in any other album and if released as a single it does not accrue contingent scale moneys for release in any other single. However, a recording initially released as a single will qualify for additional contingent scale payments in connection with the first album in which it appears, and a recording first sold in an album will be eligible for such payments with respect to the initial single in which it is contained.

As for albums, other than cast albums, there are incremental fees of 50 percent of minimum scale per plateau to be paid if sales reach levels of (a) 157,500, (b) 250,000, (c) 375,000, (d) 500,000, (e) 650,000, (f) 825,000, and (g) 1,000,000.

As for single sales, there are contingent scale payments of $33\frac{1}{3}$ percent per plateau to be paid when sales of (a) 500,000, (b) 600,000, (c) 750,000, (d) 850,000, (e) 1,000,000 and (f) 1,500,000 are arrived at.

Contingent scale payments may not ordinarily be recouped or charged against royalties or other payments due to AFTRA royalty artists. However, the record company may, subject to the consent of the covered artist, credit overscale payments in excess of $2\frac{1}{2}$ times the minimum scale against contingent payments. All contingent scale payments are subject to contributions to the AFTRA Pension and Welfare Funds.

Special Payments Fund and Trust Fund

Each record manufacturer is required to enter into the Phonograph Record Manufacturers' Special Payment Fund Agreement with the AF of M. The manufacturer also becomes a signatory to a Phonograph Record Trust Agreement.

Pursuant to the Special Payments Fund Agreement, the record company must make certain payments, based on record sales, to the Administrator under the Agreement, the United States Trust Company of New York, 45 Wall Street, New York, N.Y. 10005. Provision is made in the Phonograph Record Trust Agreement for the record manufacturer to pay lesser amounts, calculated similarly on record sales, to the Trustee, Martin A. Paulson, of 1501 Broadway, New York, N.Y. 10036.

Each agreement applies only to records containing music "which was performed or conducted by musicians covered by, or required to be paid pursuant to, (the) Phonograph Record Labor Agreement." If the services of union members in respect of a particular record consist solely of arrangements, orchestrations or copying, then that record is not subject to either agreement.

Moneys collected by the Administrator under the Special Payments Trust Agreement, after deduction of expenses, are ultimately disbursed to members of the AF of M who participated in the recordings.

The Trustee under the Phonograph Record Trust Agreement has the obligation to expend the money in the Trust Fund, less expenses, for the purpose "of arranging and organizing the presentation of personal performances by instrumental musicians in the area throughout the United States, and its territories, possessions and dependencies, and the Dominion of Canada . . . on such occasions and at such times and places as in the judgment of the Trustee will contribute to the public knowledge and appreciation of music." The performances are to be organized for live audiences, which may be broadcast when no admissions fees are charged, "in connection with activities of patriotic, charitable, educational, civic, and general public natures." The activities must be without profit to the Trust Fund.

Payments to the Administrator

The schedule for payments to the Administrator of the Special Payments Fund calls for 0.6 percent of the manufacturer's suggested retail price for each record and tape sold where the suggested retail price is $3.79 or less. For records having a higher manufacturer's suggested retail price, up to a maximum of $8.98, the sum to be paid is 0.58 percent of the suggested retail list price. For tapes the amount is 0.5 percent of the manufacturer's suggested retail price up to a maximum of $8.98.

In computing payments, the record company must report 100 percent of net sales. There are certain allowances in connection with the computation of payments. First, there is a packaging deduction from the suggested retail list price in the country of manufacture or sale, of 20 percent of the suggested retail list price for phonograph records and 30 percent of the suggested retail list price for tapes and cartridges. There is an exemption for singles of the first 100,000 sold of each title. Excepting record clubs, an exemption of up to 25 percent of the total records, tapes, and cartridges distributed is granted for "free" records, tapes, and cartridges actually distributed. As to record clubs, the exemption for "free" and "bonus" records, tapes, and cartridges actually distributed may be up to 50 percent of total distribution, with the record manufacturer to pay the full rate on one-half of the excess of the "free" and "bonus" records, tapes, and cartridges over the 50 percent, in addition to full rate payments for all records actually sold by clubs.

Suggested retail list prices shall be computed exclusive of any sales or excise taxes on sales of records, tapes, and cartridges. If a record company discontinues using manufacturers' suggested retail prices, it agrees to negotiate a new basis for computing payments which shall be equivalent to that required when there are such suggested retail prices.

Payments to the Trustee

Payments to the Trustee of the Phonograph Record Trust Agreement are calculated on the basis of 0.35 percent of the manufacturer's suggested retail list price, up to a maximum of $8.98, for each record and tape sold, whether singles, albums, or extended play records. The allowances and exemptions in the computation of payments are generally similar to those in the calculations of payments to the Administrator of the Special Payments Fund. However, the exemption for singles is the first 150,000 sold of each title, instead of the 100,000 provided for the Special Payments Fund.

Periods of Payments

As to each record which is subject to the Special Payments Fund Agreement, there is a ten-year limitation, from the date of release, on the sales for which payments thereunder must be made. For example, if a record is released for sale initially in February, 1977, payments will be due for all sales made only during the calendar years 1977–1986, inclusive. There is a corresponding five-year limitation for payments to the Trustee of the Phonograph Record Trust Agreement.

Transfers or Licenses

No sales, assignments, leases or licenses of master recordings to a firm or person doing business in the United States, Canada, or Puerto Rico may be made unless the transferee or licensee is, or becomes, a signatory to the Special Payments Fund Agreement and the Phonograph Record Trust Agreement.

Grants or licenses of rights to firms or persons in other areas are prohibited unless the transferee or licensee agrees to pay the record company the amount, based on sales, called for under both agreements. The record company is obligated in turn to pay the Administrator or Trustee the sums received from the transferee or licensee.

Payment by Administrator

A complicated weighting formula is employed by the Administrator in arriving at the amount payable to a particular musician. The total union scale paid to the musician over the five years preceding the payment by the Administrator is related to the aggregate union scale paid over the same period in respect of all recordings subject to the Special Payments Fund Agreement, with the more recent scale payments being accorded a greater weighting than the older payments. The amount available for distribution by the Administrator is then multiplied by the resulting proportion to determine the payment to the single musician.

The following illustration of the computation is taken from the Special Payments Fund Agreement:

> If the scale wages payable to a musician participating in the 1975 distribution have been $50.00 in 1974, $100.00 in 1973, $70.00 in 1972, none in 1971, and $30.00 in 1970, and if the total scale wages payable to all musicians during the same five years

have been $10,000 in 1974, $9,000 in 1973, $7,000 in 1972, $5,000 in 1971, and $5,000 in 1970, the fraction of the distribution payable to that musician would be determined as follows:

Year	Musician's Scale Wages	Total Scale Wages Payable to All Musicians
1974	$ 50 × 5 = $250	$10M × 5 = $50,000
1973	100 × 4 = 400	9M × 4 = 36,000
1972	70 × 3 = 210	7M × 3 = 21,000
1971	0 × 2 = 0	5M × 2 = 10,000
1970	30 × 1 = 30	5M × 1 = 5,000
	$890	$122,000

The musician's 1975 special payment would be 890/122,000 [of the 1975 distribution].

Video Promotional Tapes

Master recordings are used in video promotional tapes which are employed to promote the sale of phonograph records and tapes. This involves negotiations with unions as to the permissibility of the usage and, if permissible, the terms and conditions applicable to the compensation of the union members engaged therein.

There is an AF of M Video Promo Supplement in effect for the period July 1, 1983 to November 30, 1986. Thereunder the AF of M allows the practice, provided that certain payments are made by the record company. As to video promo selections produced on or after July 1, 1984 through November 29, 1985, each non-royalty musician who performs "on camera" is to be paid $125 per day for each such selection; for selections produced thereafter the payment is increased to $140 per day. Pension and welfare payments are to be made at the rates set forth in the Phonograph Record Labor Agreement with the AF of M.

If a video promotional tape is marketed to consumers as a video cassette or video disc, then, as when the record company receives $5,000 in worldwide revenues from the sale or licensing thereof, the company is obligated to pay to the AF of M the sum of $500 for distribution to the musicians whose services were employed in the production of the underlying master recording. When the record company receives worldwide revenues from the sale or licensing of a particular video tape in excess of $60,000 for a tape produced on or after July 1, 1984 through November 29, 1985 (or $70,000 for a tape produced thereafter), it is required to pay to the AF of M 1 percent of any excess, less the $500 referred to above, for distribution to the same musicians. If a royalty artist's contract provides for his participation in the said revenues and if the contract so allows, then the foregoing payments to the AF of M based upon revenues may be reduced to the extent the payments would otherwise be due to the royalty artist.

The above payments constitute the only ones owed to the AF of M and the musicians arising out of the production and exploitation of video promotional tapes.

At this writing AFTRA had not negotiated an agreement specifically covering video promotional tapes. The AFTRA Code of Fair Practice for Phonograph Recordings provides that the "Company agrees not to make master tapes or portions of master tapes . . . available for use of any kind or nature whatsoever in any other medium . . ."

The production of a video tape or film goes beyond the general scope of this publication insofar as it concerns film production unions such as the Screen Actors Guild, the Writers Guild of America, the Directors Guild of America, the Producers Guild of America, and the International Association of Theatrical and Stage Employees. The appropriate unions must be considered in planning any video production.

Music Videos

A highly significant factor in the music scene has been the development of electronic audiovisual devices which record and/or play back prerecorded programs through a conventional television receiver. These videoplayer systems may use programming in the form of cassettes, cartridges, or discs.

Equipment makers are known as hardware manufacturers, whereas firms which specialize in creating and marketing programming for the videoplayer systems are referred to as software manufacturers or producers. There are two major incompatible, competitive videoplayer systems, the Beta-format originated by Sony and the VHS-format sponsored by Matsushita, with the latter now predominating. In early 1984 there were over 9 million video cassette recorders in American households and sales were proceeding at an annual rate estimated at 7 million. Cassettes are preferred by purchasers over cartridges and discs; in 1984 RCA discontinued the manufacture of videodisc players and CBS ceased its production of videodiscs.

A further important factor in the music business has been the creation and marketing of music videos. These are primarily 3-5 minute visualizations of pop songs, usually featuring the visual and audio performances of the artist who recorded the songs. The release of most major new records is accompanied by a music video. The videos are significant promotional aids that foster record and tape sales and are credited with much of the record companies' recent rebound in economic health. Showings on the MTV 24-hour cable music channel, which in the latter part of 1984 reached 24 million households, and on other cable music channels clearly produce increased record and tape sales. Music videos, with their surging popularity, are also part of a growing commercial market. The emphasis of music videos has been on their television exhibition as a promotional tool, rather than on their status as commercial entertainment. Free licenses by record companies to programs such as MTV have been prevalent in the past but this practice has changed. MTV has agreed with a number of major record companies to make multimillion dollar payments for exclusive rights to selected video clips for periods ranging from one week to 30 days. It is anticipated that the exploitation of music videos will result in revenues derived from the sale of video cassettes and videodiscs, exhibition on network, cable and local television, viewings in commercial clubs, and plays on video jukeboxes.

Music videos directly involve contractual rights and obligations among record companies, artists, producers, music publishers and others. Possibly to a lesser extent, other software programming may be concerned with all or some of the same entities, persons or factors. Insofar as music videos and other software programming are audivisual motion picture productions, the legal and contractual principles and standards are related to those discussed in Chapter 28, "Music and the Movies," and in Chapter 10, "Licensing of Recordings for Motion Pictures."

Record manufacturers engaged in video programming, whether in the form of music videos or other software, have enlarged the scope of their operations to include film making and its attendant problems. The increasing length of record company/artist contracts bears witness to this phenomenon, as record companies, artists, and producers attempt to cover contractually the multiplying complexities of the record and film business.

In the following discussion, aspects of music videos will be a primary focus. Music videos directly impact the record and music publishing business and are also subject to many of the problems inherent in the creation and production of other software.

Contractual Standards

The music video scene is characterized by much uncertainty as it relates to contractual rights and obligations among record companies, artists, producers and others engaged in the production and marketing of the videos. Industry-wide contractual standards for music videos are likely to remain in a state of flux until their market potential is more clearly defined. Some very general criteria have emerged in recording artist and video production agreements. But specifics vary from record company to record company and even these specifics are prone to later modification.

Negotiations for Video Rights

The potential of the music video promotional and commercial markets has impelled record companies to strive vigorously to obtain video rights from artists. The rights have become key issues in contractual negotiations. In support of their claims to video rights, record companies contend that audiovisual products can offer and will offer strong competition to phonograph records and tapes for the consumer home market. They state it is a natural development for record companies, based on their artist associations and their recording experience, to produce audiovisual programming. Some record companies are engaged alone or with coproducers in the development of both promotional and longer videos of their artists.

Definition of Records

There is some uniformity among record companies in that for years they have included in their artist contracts language permitting the record company to use recordings in audiovisual form and restricting the artists from appearing in audiovisual media for other companies. One form provides that the artist's rendition may be used exclusively

> . . . in any medium and by any means whatsoever, including but not limited to audio-visual records, motion pictures, television or any medium or devices now or hereafter known, and to utilize photographs, drawings, and pictorial animation in connection therewith.

In another form the definition of "record" or "phonograph record" embraces a

> . . . film, video tape or similar device which embodies the artist's audio performance with a visual rendition of the artist's performance, i.e., a sight and sound device.

Length and Use of Videos

While music videos are primarily three to five minute "clips," like those used by MTV, the cable music channel, the typical definition of "records" or "phonograph records" contains no time or length limitations. As defined, an artist would be disqualified from performing for third persons in films or video tapes of live concerts, full-length feature films or documentaries, or film television programs in which an artist visually performs only a single song. For example, a record company could require consent for an artist's participation in the Woodstock Concert film or in a featurelength film such as "Rock 'n Roll High School." The record company could refuse consent or, theoretically, might even condition approval on its being granted the right to distribute the film theatrically, on television, and in video cassettes for home use. This can be intolerable to an artist who treasures and seeks film appearances.

Artists may therefore try to limit the definition of a record to audiovisual productions of a short duration, or to audiovisual productions of one or two songs, or to copies to be marketed to the public for home use only. A common issue is whether there can be any commercial exploitation of audiovisual products without the express consent of the artist. While artists may agree to promotional uses of music videos, they may refuse to allow commercial exploitation without their prior written approval. Some companies may accept this restriction but others will resist it strongly. A new artist may find it very difficult to obtain the right to approve commercial uses of music videos.

Certain record companies have acquiesced in limiting their rights to audiovisual performances of sound recordings produced under the recording artist agreement. Even in such cases the record company would probably retain exclusive control over the video exploitation rights for promotional purposes and for home video sales.

Product Commitment

Although it is common for a record company to have the exclusive right to make videos of an artist, more often than not, the record company will not be obligated to finance and produce such videos. This is similar to the typical lack of specific obligations of a record company to carry out and finance promotional activities in support of phonograph records. But established artists, in contrast to new artists, do obtain commitments from record companies to produce music videos such as on a per-record basis. Because of the substantial costs to produce a music video, a record company will generally agree to creating one only after a record appears to be a commercial success.

An artist will ordinarily have no rights to produce and finance independently a music video in the absence of his record company's consent. This is despite the record company's lack of any obligation to grant such approval or to produce a music video itself. In the light of such circumstances an artist may attempt to protect himself by reserving video rights subject to granting the record company a right of first refusal, for a limited period of time, to produce and exploit the music video. Under the right of first refusal, the record company would have the prerogative to match offers of third parties. The record company might also be the beneficiary of a right of first negotiation, which would entitle it to be approached first and negotiated with before any third parties.

It is not uncommon for the artist and record company to agree that neither shall have the exclusive right to produce and exploit a music video and that both parties are proscribed from making a music video without mutual approval. This serves to delay their negotiations for control of music video rights until a future time when it may be easier to determine the value of the rights in the background of the developed industry-wide status.

Record Company Ownership Interest

The record company will ordinarily acquire the entire ownership interest in the physical video tapes and other physical materials, and also the copyright in the audiovisual work itself, including the visual images and the accompanying sounds.

The copyright is that accorded to a motion picture or other audiovisual work and the music video is generally deemed eligible for the © copyright notice. It is not qualified for the copyright notice ℗ applicable to sound recordings.

In the case of most artists the agreement between a record company and the artists constitutes an employment contract. The copyright in the audiovisual work, at least to the extent of an artist's contributions, would belong to the record company as a "work made for hire" under the 1976 Copyright Act. The Act also grants a work for hire status to one "specially ordered or commissioned for use . . . as a part of a motion picture or other audiovisual work . . ." where the parties have expressly agreed in writing "that the work shall be considered a work made for hire ." Thus a music video may be characterized as a work for hire either because of an employee-employer relationship or by reason of being deemed ordered or commissioned under the record contract. As a work for hire the record company is the "author" for copyright purposes, as well as being the owner of the video. The Copyright Act provides that for works made for hire the copyright will endure for a term of 75 years from the year of its first publication, or a term of 100 years from the year of its creation, whichever first expires. As "author" the record company could not have its rights terminated by others under the termination provisions of the Copyright Act. In any event there would be the protection against termination under such provisions accorded to a music video as a derivative work. For further discussion of termination rights, see Chapter 16, "Duration of Copyright and Limitation of Grants."

Exploitation Rights

Whether or not a record company owns the audiovisual work, as one made for hire or otherwise, a record company will demand that the artist grant it all exploitation rights in a music video. This will include not only promotional usages and home video sales but also licensing to third parties for broadcast or exhibition over free, pay or cable television and in nightclubs.

Increasingly, the major record labels are requesting fees for the broadcast of music videos on television and for showings in nightclubs. For television use, fees may range from $1,000 for a one-time exposure, such as on NBC's "Friday Night Videos," to sums in excess of $250,000 for the exclusive and first right to exhibit for a specific period of time, such as MTV's rights to the lengthy Michael Jackson "Thriller" documentary video and the 14 minute promotional video made therefrom. Some major record labels have entered into license agreements with video library agencies, for example, Rockamerica. These agencies license music videos to nightclubs on a semiannual or annual subscription basis at present rates of about $5 per video per month, or on a nonsubscription basis at rates of approximately $75 per video per month.

Production Costs and Their Recoupment

Under most artist agreements a record company will advance production costs of music videos produced under the contracts. These costs may range from $15,000 to over $500,000, with the amounts usually below $100,000. Whether or not the music video is considered a promotional or a commercial vehicle will largely influence the method for recoupment of production costs by the record company. Unlike most other record promotion expenses, which are borne entirely by the record companies, the companies will commonly insist on a form of recoupment that involves the artist.

Under most record artist contracts, the record company becomes entitled to recoup a certain percentage of the video production costs out of the artist's record royalties or the artist's share of the video income or a combination of both. Income derived by record companies from the exploitation of music videos is nominal in today's market. Accordingly, record companies will look to the artist's record royalties for the recoupment of from 50 to 75 percent, and sometimes more, of the video production costs. At times the percentages will be reduced if the underlying album achieves a high plateau of sales, for example 300,000.

Typically video production costs are also recoupable from the artist's share of net video receipts from the commercial exploitation of the music video. The usual artist participation is 50 percent of such net video receipts. These net receipts are defined as the gross receipts from commercial exploitation, less video production costs, distribution fees and expenses, and payments to third parties. In lieu of payment to the artist of a portion of the net video receipts, a less common approach is to pay a royalty to the artist on units of video cassettes and videodiscs sold. This royalty will be from 10 to 25 percent of the wholesale selling price.

Under recoupment from the combination of record royalties and the artist's share of net video receipts or his video royalties, the artist may well bear at least 75 percent and as much as 100 percent of the video costs. However, an established artist may be successful in breaking the recoupment mold described above. He may cause the creation of separate royalty accounts for videos and for phonograph records, with no earnings from one source being used to recoup the production costs attendant on the other source. At least one major record company has been amenable to providing for such separate royalty accounts for most of its artists, whether new or established.

Musical Composition Licenses

Ownership interests in musical compositions embodied in a music video are generally held by the music publisher of the compositions. In many cases the music publisher is the publishing affiliate of the record company. Among the essential rights for a music video controlled by the publisher or other copyright proprietor are the right to couple the music in timed relation to the visual images (often called the synchronization right), the right to publicly perform the compositions as a part of the video, the right to make copies of the compositions as included in the video, and the right to distribute to the public copies of the compositions as integrated into the music video.

There are compositions written, owned, or controlled by the recording artist and embodied in music videos ("controlled compositions"). As to controlled compositions, record companies will demand the issuance of a free synchronization license and also free licenses with respect to the other essential rights referred to above. Publishers and artists will ordinarily acquiesce in respect of promotional uses of the music videos. As to commercial exploitation, provisions for remuneration will vary. In justification of free licenses, the record company may contend that the artist does not lose a fee entirely since license fees are deductible in calculating the artist's share of net video receipts, and the artist's share is thereby increased if there is no deduction of license fees. Some record companies will provide for a fee, royalty or other remuneration in case of commercial exploitation of a controlled composition. This may be immediately particularized or the fixing of the fee may be delayed until industry standards have further evolved. At issue is the form of payment. Should there be a flat one-time fee, or a per-copy remuneration, or perhaps a combination of a flat fee plus per-copy compensations?

Where compositions are not controlled, there are differing approaches to their licensing by the copyright proprietors or their representatives. Independent publishers may be willing to give free synchronization and other licenses for strictly promotional usages, although there is no uniformity. But for commercial exploitation, the requirement that there be compensation is probable. While record companies will favor a complete flat-fee buyout of rights, many publishers will demand a flat fee plus per-copy remuneration. The fixing of the fee may be immediate or it may be delayed until the evolution of further industry standards.

A copy of a video synchronization and performance rights license from a publisher is included in Part 4 as Form 9B. A copy of sample video rights contract clauses is contained in Part 4 as Form 12B.

8

Record Covers and Liner Notes

Album covers are comprised of several elements. They are the title, the photographs or artwork, and the back liner notes.

Titles
There are various categories of titles. In Broadway cast albums the name of the show is the title and the phrase "original cast album" is featured. Motion picture soundtrack albums name the film in the title and prominently display the phrase "original soundtrack album," or, in the case of a re-recorded score, "original motion picture score."

Other albums have diverse types of titles. Some albums will simply set forth the name of the performer, for example, Gordon Lightfoot. Other titles will describe the musical contents, thus, "Songs of the West" or "Love Songs" or "Golden Hits."

The noncopyrightability of titles is discussed in Chapter 35, "Protection of Ideas and Titles."

Photographs or Artwork
Photographs of the performing artists grace the covers of many record albums. Original or unoriginal artwork appears on other covers.

Under the 1976 Copyright Act, "pictorial, graphic, and sculptural works" are copyrightable. These are defined to include "fine, graphic, and applied art, photographs, prints and art reproductions." For copyright protection there must be a notice of copyright affixed to each copy publicly distributed in the United States or elsewhere. The form of the notice must include the word "Copyright," or the abbreviation "Copr.," or the symbol ©, accompanied by the name of the copyright proprietor or an abbreviation by which the name can be recognized, or a generally known alternative designation of the proprietor. For photographs, works of art, and reproductions of works of art depicted in or on useful articles, the United States law does not require the year date in the notice; protection under the Universal Copyright Convention is conditioned upon the year of first publication appearing in the notice.

Album Backs
The descriptive material on the back of an album is known as the "liner notes." It may consist of biographical material relating to the performers or comments on the contents of the record, or a combination of both.

Liner notes are protected by copyright under United States Copyright law, provided a proper copyright notice appears with the word "Copyright," "Copr.," or ©, the name of the proprietor, or an abbreviation by which the name can be recognized, or a generally known alternative designation of the copyright proprietor, and the year of first publication. Although such a notice on the back cover of an album may also serve to protect the artwork on the front cover, several authorities on the subject suggest the cautious approach of placing two notices: one on the front and one on the back.

Placement of the copyright notice on the spine of an album cover is not recommended.

Record Company Practices

An examination of record album covers of different record companies reveals dissimilar practices in respect of copyright notices for artwork and liner notes. Some covers contain no copyright notice, possibly on the assumption that the record company anticipates no copying or invites copying. Certain covers contain full copyright notices, including the year date in Arabic numerals. On other covers the year date is in Roman numerals which the average consumer may be unable to decipher.

In respect of the artwork, a record company may decide to omit the year date of the album's initial release, as it may discourage sales of the album after it is no longer new. As noted previously, the omission of the year date with regard to art or photographs does not impair copyright protection in the United States. However, the benefits of the Universal Copyright Convention will not be available outside the United States.

On the other hand, to safeguard the sound recording itself, the copyright notice for sound recordings must contain the year date of its first publication and it is unlikely that a record company will wish to omit a copyright notice for the sound recording; the notice can appear on the back cover or the label or the record itself where it will not be as obvious as on the front cover.

Copyright Registration

The separate elements of a record album may qualify for different forms of copyright registration in the Copyright Office. In the past, prior to the 1976 Copyright Act, a record cover as a composite could be registered on Form KK, which related to a print or label, or, for longer pieces, placed in Class A, which was comprised of "Books."

The new forms for registration under the 1976 Copyright Act supersede the old forms. Form VA replaces the prior Form KK, and new form TX is to be used instead of Form A. For a further discussion of the new forms see Chapter 15, "The Nature of Copyright in the United States," and for copies of the forms see Appendix F in Part 4.

Name and Address of Record Company

Under the statutes of about 34 states, including New York, California, Ohio, Pennsylvania, Florida, Tennessee, and Illinois, the name of the record company and its address must appear on each record distributed in the state.

One purpose of such statutes is to protect the public by revealing the party to whom a consumer may address a request for redress for defective or mislabeled merchandise. The statutes facilitate state regulation designed to prevent deceptive practices such as mislabeling records to suggest they are soundtrack or Broadway cast albums or that they contain entirely performances by well-known artists.

By virtue of the statutes, record companies or artists aggrieved by misleading practices of other companies are better able to institute appropriate action to protect their rights by suits for injunction or damages or by complaints to federal, state, and local authorities.

Country of Manufacture

Under the 1976 Copyright Act, until July 1, 1986, with certain exceptions, books consisting of predominantly nondramatic literary material by domestic authors in the English language must be manufactured in the United States or Canada. This requirement is not a condition to the copyright owner's exclusive rights to reproduce and distribute copies, make derivative works, and perform the work.

However, failure to comply with the manufacturing requirement is generally a complete defense in any civil or criminal action for infringement of the exclusive rights of reproduction or distribution of copies. The copyright owner can restore his exclusive rights by manufacturing and registering an edition in the United States.

Since album covers, including liner notes, may be treated as books for copyright purposes, it is customary to affix to album covers a legend indicating the place of manufacture, for example, "Printed in the U.S.A."

In practice, the legend becomes significant for exporting covers to Canada. Under the Canadian Copyright Act, any person may apply to the Minister of Trade and Commerce for a license to print and publish in Canada an edition of any copyrighted book which the author has failed to have printed in Canada. The Canadian customs authorities, in connection with imports of books, including record covers, require a statement thereon as to the place of manufacture.

Simulated Stereo

Prior to the advent of stereophonic reproduction, recordings were made solely for monaural record players. Many of the old recordings are of interest to the present generation of record buyers who have only stereophonic record players. To bridge the gap, record companies have altered the monaural masters so that they can be played on stereophonic equipment.

Complaints were registered with the Federal Trade Commission to the effect that such altered recordings were being sold by record companies as if originally recorded for multichannel stereophonic reproduction. Acting on these complaints, the Federal Trade Commission promulgated a standard legend which must be printed prominently on such recordings. The legend states: "This Recording Altered To Simulate Stereophonic Reproduction." It must be printed over the title of the recording.

Trademarks

In Chapter 34, there is a full discussion of the protection of trademarks.

In relation to album covers, trademarks registered under the Federal Lanham Act should have printed, in proximity to the mark, the words, "Registered in U.S. Patent and Trademark Office," or "Reg. U.S. Pat. and TM Off.," or the letter R enclosed in a circle, thus ®.

On occasion, a cover will include a trademark not as yet registered. Prior to issuance of a registration certificate by the Patent Office, it is improper to use the notices referred to in the preceding paragraph. However, it is common to utilize the word "trademark" or the abbreviation "TM" in conjunction with a mark and this usage is considered acceptable for the purpose of giving actual notice to the public of a claim to the mark.

Soundtrack Albums

The album covers on motion picture soundtrack albums present certain special problems. The sounds will be taken from the soundtrack of the film. Artwork may be that used to advertise the film.

In respect of the recordings, the record company will probably use a ℗ notice of copyright in its own name on the album cover. For a further discussion see Chapter 3, "Copyright in Sound Recordings."

Assuming that the artwork and the photographs are derived from material used in connection with the film, the copyright notice on the album cover should be consistent with the copyright notices employed by the motion picture company for the protection of the artwork and the photographs. Thus, if the name of the motion picture company and a particular year and date appear in its notice, caution prescribes that the same name and date be contained in the album copyright notice placed in proximity to the artwork or photos. The copyright notice in the name of the motion picture company will also have the function of protecting the recording insofar as it is derived from the soundtrack of the film.

Album Packaging

Each year the National Academy of Recording Arts and Sciences, familiarly known as NARAS, makes awards for best album packaging to art directors. Awards by NARAS for album packaging have been made yearly since 1958.

At the same time, NARAS confers honors for other aspects of recordings, including best vocalist, best instrumentalist, etc.

Model Releases

Photographers who supply pictures for album covers are trained to require their models to sign releases granting the right to use the photographs for commercial purposes. In the absence of releases, the models may claim an invasion of their rights to privacy and of publicity, and in particular a violation of specific statutes which forbid the use of photographs for commercial endeavors unless the model consents in writing.

Anticounterfeit Products

To combat the counterfeiting of records, Polaroid and 3M offer special custom made labels for record jackets. They resist photo offset duplication in that they present a three dimensional effect utilizing the logo, signature or seal of the manufacturer.

Bar Coding

The system known as bar coding, which uses imprinted variant lines and numbers, is utilized as an aid to inventory and sales control of LPs. The bar codes are usually printed on the jackets but are sometimes included in affixed stickers. Through computer readers, the retailer, wholesaler and manufacturer can keep track of sales and inventory by categories such as record label, artist, title, and release number.

9

Agents and Managers

The role of the agent and manager in the music business is essentially one of representing artists rather than nonperforming composers and lyricists. Songwriters who are not involved in writing music for the stage, motion pictures, or television often feel no need for a manager or an agent. If they have a music publisher, the publisher administers copyrights so as to promote and exploit them through performances, recordings, printed editions, and foreign subpublishing. However, when a recording artist is also a songwriter, as is often true, especially in the fields of country, black, and rock and roll music, or when publishing rights are linked with dramatic rights, as in the fields of show and film music, a manager is sometimes used.

Definitions of Personal Representatives

The phrase "personal representative" is a generic term encompassing professional and business representatives of talent. Some agents or managers prefer to be known under this appellation, which has no distinctive definition of its own. In actuality, the representation field is divided between agents and managers. The agent is a business finder and negotiator. An agent will have a much larger stable of talent than a manager can cope with; this is because of their differing functions. The agent finds or receives offers of employment for the talent and negotiates the contract. He leaves to the manager the day-to-day career development, personal advice, and guidance, and the planning of the long-range direction of the artist's career in cooperation with the agent. An agent is compensated by a commission, which is normally 10 or 15 percent, the rate depending on the particular talent union involved and the duration of the engagement negotiated; the commission usually applies for the life of the contract and any renewals.

Leading the field for general agency services are the William Morris Agency, Inc. and International Creative Management, each with thousands of clients and with extensive staffs of agents, lawyers and accountants in offices throughout the entertainment cities of the United States and in major foreign countries.

Examples of prominent booking agents and their special fields are: Premier Talent Associates, Inc. (rock and roll); Norby Walter Associates (black, dance); Associated Booking Corp. (jazz, big band); Jim Halsey Co. Inc., and Top Billing Inc. (country). Regency Artists Ltd. specializes in live performances.

Areas where advice and counsel to artists are given by personal managers are:

(1) The selection of literary, artistic, and musical materials.
(2) Any and all matters relating to publicity, public relations and advertising.
(3) The adoption of the proper format for the best presentation of the artists' talents.
(4) The selection of booking agents to procure maximum employment for the artists.
(5) The types of employment which the artists should accept and which would prove most beneficial to their careers.
(6) The selection and supervision of accountants and attorneys other than those used by the manager.

Personal managers rarely travel with their artists. More often they engage, at the artists' expense, and supervise road managers to handle the numerous business matters "on the road," such as transportation, hotels, collections, and stage, sound, and lighting needs. Personal managers may serve as buffers to insulate the artist from unattractive offers and from requests for charitable gifts, free appearances, and the like. Many managers play important roles in the relationships with record companies as well as in the selection of songs and accompanists. They supervise relations with the talent agency to obtain the maximum benefits for the artist. They sometimes administer, or select and supervise publishers who administer, publishing firms which handle copyrights of songs which have been written by the artist or in which the artist has acquired an interest. The reliance of some artists on managers for repertoire and creative guidance, as well as for business decisions, is such that there is sometimes as much truth as humor in the statement that the artist is a mere figment of his manager's imagination. Certain managers assume such control over the artist's career, business, and even personal relationships that the manager functions as the alter ego of the artist.

A tribute to the role of a manager may be found in a favorable review of Linda Ronstadt which stated that one of the obvious reasons for her becoming one of the most popular woman singers in the world is " . . . the symbiosis between her evolving artistic gifts and her manager and record producer, Peter Asher, who has guided her career for four years." A previous tribute to the role of a manager appears in an exchange of compliments between the English-born Peter Frampton and his then manager, Dee Anthony. Frampton said: "I've never been a wheeler-dealer businessman, so my success has been because of the experienced people around me." His manager commented: "Acts just don't happen in this business. There are usually some extremely bad times before they make it . . . Peter Frampton took 3½ years to get to the top and part of it had to do with the belief in him by us, Frank [agent] and Jerry Moss [of A&M Records] and various promoters." Some time after this exchange Frampton and his manager severed their relationship and resorted to litigation to resolve their problems. In so doing they joined an increasing number of artists and managers who have dissolved their arrangements and have become opponents in court litigations.

Managers receive commissions of between 10 and 25 percent of the artist's gross receipts and reimbursement of travel and other special expenses. In a few instances in the popular recording business there are managers who receive payment on a net receipts computation rather than gross receipts. Such arrangements will often be at a higher percentage rate while sometimes resulting in a lesser cash expense to the artist. The simple reason is that a net receipts computation base is after deduction of the considerable expenses of agency commissions and the costs of instruments, sound equipment, travel, hotels, road manager and crew, backup musicians, publicity, and costumes.

Commissions payable to the manager are usually in addition to the commission that goes to the agent; in some instances the manager is entitled to a large commission, reducible to the extent agency commissions are charged to the artist. Many management agreements, especially those with new artists, provide for the escalation of commissions, from 10 percent to 25 percent in stipulated increments, depending upon the amount of the weekly or monthly gross earnings of the artist. In such instances, there may be a separate commission rate for record royalties or other earnings received semiannually so as to avoid having to fit these special earnings into a weekly or monthly commission escalation format. A common commission rate for such periodic earnings is 20 percent.

Business Manager

Although many personal managers undertake financial guidance and investment advice as a part of their functions, the usual practice of recognized, successful artists is to engage a business manager. He will often be an accountant or a tax attorney who will hold the purse strings, manage investments, and keep a close watch over the tax consequences of the artist's affairs. Fees for these services range from 2 to 6 percent of the gross receipts handled, unless a flat monthly or annual fee is arranged.

Fields of Exclusive Representation

Agents and managers generally obtain exclusive rights for representation in all fields in which the talent operates so that they can plan for or obtain engagements in one field without fear of conflict in another field. If they have exclusive rights, they are entitled to commissions even on earnings which do not result from the direct efforts of the agent or manager; this is justified by the fact that their efforts in other areas serve to generate the prominence of the artist. In some instances such exclusivity is a necessary assurance to the personal representatives that they will be adequately compensated for building the artist's career.

However, some agents or managers have no interest or ability in certain fields, such as music publishing, and the artist may limit their commissions to the areas in which they can be active and helpful. A recording artist would normally be represented for personal appearances, television shows, films, stage, and recording contracts by the same manager or agent, but it is conceivable that one or more of these fields would be excluded, especially by a more successful artist who desires to retain control and to avoid commissions. Some artists negotiate the exclusion of particular high-pay territories such as Atlantic City and Las Vegas/Reno. They thereby exclude agency services and commissions, working through their managers or in-house staff. The writers of a stage musical should be aware that the sale of their motion picture rights may be negotiated in conjunction with and approved by the official Dramatists Guild negotiator. Pursuant to the Dramatists Guild agreement, an agent is limited to a 10 percent commission on the sale of motion picture rights, and up to $1\frac{1}{2}$ percent is deducted from the commission to pay for the services of the negotiator when he is so used.

In the field of serious music, concert artists are frequently represented by personal managers who also serve as booking agents for combined fees. Firms active in this area include ICM Artists, Ltd., Shaw Concerts, Inc. and (largest of all) Columbia Artists Management, Inc. Some concert agents sometimes act as the employer, as for a community concert touring series, in which event commissions are waived.

Duration of Manager's Contract and Commissions

A typical manager's contract with a performing artist provides for an original term of one or two years plus enough one-year consecutive options (available to the manager) to extend the term to an aggregate of five years. Whether or not the manager ever exercises an option, the contractual term eventually comes to an end and the manager's obligation to give advice and counsel terminates, as, one might assume, does the artist's financial obligation to his manager. However, almost every manager's contract provides that commissions continue after the end of the term on "substitutions, modifications and extensions by options or otherwise" of the contracts or engagements entered into during the term of the contract. Thus, for example, a recording artist with a vague memory of a manager participating in an early career decision to select a record company may be obliged to pay commissions as long as royalties still flow from that record contract. In addition, if there is no hiatus (for example, a contract with another label) before resuming relations with the first record company, there may be a claim that recordings made after the end of the manager's term are under an extension of or substitution for the original contract. Another example of a continuing commission might be one for a concert or nightclub engagement, negotiated during the manager's term, but which occurred after the term's expiration. In this case the question may be compounded by a return engagement at the same hall.

The dilemma of how to achieve an amicable termination of a manager's role may be solved by an arms-length negotiation of the original management contract, which becomes a sort of prenuptial agreement. Terms to be covered could include the following:

(1) Early termination of a management contract if an achievement plateau is not quickly reached, in either earnings or some other accomplishment such as landing a major record contract or booking a significant promotional tour. This might be labeled a "kick-out" clause.

(2) No exercise of an option unless a minimum of earnings has been achieved. For example, a 50 percent increase in the level of gross receipts during a basic two-year contract might be a condition to the exercise of an option by the manager.

(3) A fixed period of time following the "end" of a term after which the manager may make no further claim to a commission, regardless of whether the contract or other relationship commenced during the basic term of the manager's contract. A six-month secondary term for such purposes may not be offensive to either party. An alternative would be to have a longer secondary term, for example one year, but with descending rates of regular commissions during the period, such as half rates for the first three months and quarter rates for the balance of the year. The diminishing rates would reflect reduced costs to the manager in the avoidance of overhead or other responsibilities.

(4) In the event of the manager's death, some provision for reduced commissions on previously obtained engagements or contracts; possibly a continuing payment of 50 to 75 percent of regular commissions might be fair if death occurred after some substantial measure of success had been accomplished, akin to the "plateau" referred to in (1) above.

The close and often trying relationship between artists and managers during years of active management makes it desirable that there be a full exploration of compatibility before entering into binding contracts. An alternative to a brief "handshake" period would be the negotiation, referred to above, of a complete contract with the assistance of attorneys experienced in the field. Perhaps an artist's negotiation with the would-be manager would reveal failings which the artist would prefer to reject at the outset. An extremely weak or phlegmatic manager might, in early discussions, demonstrate that he should not be trusted to negotiate for the artist.

Regulation of Managers and Agents

While all states regulate employment agencies by statute, agents and managers will not admit that they merely find jobs for their clients. California statutes specifically govern talent and literary agents and control the fees of and duration of the contracts with such agents. The Labor Code of California requires administrative review by the Labor Commissioner in the first instance of all controversies between artists and managers of that State. New York State regulates theatrical employment agencies by statute under its General Business Law.

Of more significance is the regulation of agents by unions, such as the American Federation of Musicians, the American Federation of Television and Radio Artists, and the American Guild of Variety Artists. Only the AF of M attempts to regulate managers, whereas all three unions strongly supervise agents through the granting of franchise certificates without which union members are barred from dealing with the agents. Subjects of regulation include such matters as maximum commission rates, duration, and conflicts of interest. Copies of standard AFTRA and AF of M approved forms of agreements between artist and representatives are included in Part 4 as Forms 17A and 17B, respectively.

Agreements between the agencies and unions provide that only approved forms of contracts will be used. Under the contracts an artist is afforded an opportunity to terminate if the agency has not offered a designated number of engagements.

AGVA Regulation of Agents

The American Guild of Variety Artists governs the area of musical performance in nightclubs, cabarets, theaters, and other areas of live entertainment. It limits its members' contracts with agents through an agreement entered into with those agents who are franchised by AGVA. The representative of the authorized agents is Artists' Representatives Association (ARA).

The agreement between AGVA and ARA was last negotiated in April of 1967 and it expired in March of 1969. Further negotiations and attempts to reach a new agreement have bogged down largely in the area of "packaging" of complete shows by agents and the status of AGVA members as independent contractors or employees for such purposes. The continued absence of a basic contract has resulted in treating the 1967 agreement as "Interim Regulations" for pending matters.

The AGVA Interim Regulations governing agents provide that their maximum commission is 10 percent, but no commission can reduce a member's compensation to a net of less than union scale. For exclusive representation, the maximum term allowed is an original period of three years plus an option for an additional three years. However, after an official advance written notice of extension by an agent, the artist can send a counter-notice refusing to consent thereto, and if the agent persists in his desire to continue the matter is referred to arbitration to determine if "the agent has contributed assiduously and definitely to the artist's career." Arbitration is also provided for other disputes, claims, controversies, and disciplinary proceedings as between artists and agents or between their respective associations, AGVA or ARA, or between members of AGVA and ARA. Initial proceedings are before a three-man panel made up of one AGVA representative, one ARA representative, and one impartial representative chosen by the other two representatives, and appeal thereafter to the American Arbitration Association is permitted.

Despite the uncertainty of AGVA/agency contractual relations, one may refer to the AGVA Interim Regulations for areas of potential concern as to undesirable agent activities in any field. They include:

(1) Wrongful withholding by the agent of any moneys belonging to an artist.

(2) Unlawfully entering into any arrangement with an operator whereby compensation is paid directly by the operator to the agent, under terms not disclosed to the artist, with intent to exact more than a 10 percent commission.

(3) Theft, embezzlement, misappropriation of funds, forgery, fraud or dishonest conduct.

(4) Putting any artist on a "black list" for any reason, or circulating an artist's name among other agents, booking offices, owners, employers, producers, operators and similar persons for any malicious purpose, or participating therein.

(5) Unlawfully and improperly holding himself out in any manner as the representative of an artist when he has no corresponding authorization from the artist.

(6) Misuse of his franchise for purposes not directly connected with his business as an agent; such purposes being in particular the advertisement of the fact that he is a franchised agent in order to attract business for a theatrical school, coaching school, dancing or singing academy, recording studio, sale of special music, arrangements, material or routines to performers, or misuse of his franchise unfairly and unethically to exploit amateur or nonprofessional persons hopeful of entering the theatrical profession. . . .

(7) Collecting moneys belonging to an artist without having written authority from the artist to do so. All moneys belonging to the artist received by the agent shall be faithfully accounted for by the agent and promptly paid over to the artist or as directed by the artist in writing;

provided, however, that the agent may deduct from such moneys any commission. . . . The moneys belonging to the artist shall not be co-mingled with moneys belonging to the agent but shall be segregated and kept in a separate account which may be known as a "client's account" or "trust account," or an account similar in nature. . . .

Conference of Personal Managers

There is a professional organization called The Conference of Personal Managers to which many leading managers belong. The organization operates in two sections, namely, The Conference of Personal Managers East and The Conference of Personal Managers West. Slightly more members are in the West than in the East. The organization has regional and national officers. While many managers are not members, the numerous leading managers who belong set certain standards which are also respected by nonmembers. One important contribution is a standard form of personal manager agreement promulgated by The Conference of Personal Managers.

Professionals Competing With Managers

For years managers have viewed with alarm the invasion of attorneys, accountants, business managers, and even public relations representatives into the ranks of managers. It has been recognized that the complexities of record company/artist negotiations often require the intercession of skilled attorneys to represent artists. At times an experienced music attorney may be regarded as more significant in making a recording deal for an artist than a lesser-skilled but highly paid manager.

Where an attorney is engaged and paid by the manager, few disputes may arise therefrom. But if the attorney is an important negotiator and expects substantial fees, often on a contingent basis, from the artist, the more sophisticated artist may question the role and rights of the manager. Similar problems are presented where the intercession of skilled accountants, business managers, or publicity representatives tends to supersede the functions of a manager.

The Conference of Personal Managers East has undertaken a campaign against the professionals who are competing with managers. One member of the committee reviewing such complaints contends that artists are entitled to full-time managers, that the attorney/accountant has a built-in conflict of interest, and that managers, faced with growing competition, must "do something to protect themselves." A prominent music attorney, who has acted as a personal manager for important artists, has said he prefers to work with an artist who has a separate personal manager. He has stated that it is difficult, if not impossible, to stay up all night reviewing personal and career problems in the capacity of manager and then to appear in his office at regular attorney's hours to conduct legal business.

Conflicts of Interest

The federal government has intervened actively in the role of talent agents who have interests adverse to those of their clients. In 1962, MCA, then a leading talent agency, was forced to divest itself of its talent agency function as the price for continuing to produce television and other films. It was deemed incompatible for MCA to represent talent while also acting as a user of talent in its production of films. Similarly, in the early 1940s, the Columbia Artist Bureau in the concert field was forced to dissociate itself from the then Columbia Broadcasting System network, and the agency affiliated with the National Broadcasting System was required to take like action.

Questions continue as to whether an artist is properly represented by agents with other competitive clients. Most artists appreciate being included by their agent in deals in which they are presented in a single package with other talent. For example, an agent may sell to the same television show not only the services of a leading writer but also the director, conductor, and artists. In such an instance—where the agent represents the producer of the package—the agent does not charge double fees. Instead, he collects his commission from the packager and usually foregoes any commission from the individual talent. If the agent is the packager, he also relinquishes his commission.

By its very nature, personal representation, be it by manager or agent, involves artistic decisions rather than pure mathematical or scientific ones. Thus, a manager or agent who is actively promoting and planning the career of one artist may actually benefit the artist by actions which in other situations might appear to involve a conflict of interest. Thus, Jerry Weintraub of Management Three has probably enhanced the careers of clients Frank Sinatra and John Denver by having them share television and nightclub audiences for an unusual mixture of diverse talents. The result of such joint billing is a benefit to both artists as well as the manager. In other situations, however, a popular artist may question why his manager or agent allows a relatively unknown opening act to tour or appear with him. If the motivation is to obtain new sources of commissions for a weak or unscrupulous manager or agent, at the expense of the main act which does not participate in the commissions, then a conflict of interest might be present. Obviously, a qualitative judgment is required that should not be based merely upon a single or isolated instance.

Special precaution should be taken when an attorney is a stockholder or officer or employee of a management firm. In that instance the artist, in dealing with the management firm, should be encouraged to seek separate counsel because of the possibility of conflict of interest if the artist relies on the attorney connected with the management firm.

Personal Relationships

The press reports from time to time that a famous agency has merged with a smaller agency, or that a well-known agent, who has handled this and that motion picture and recording star, has moved from one agency to another or has established his own agency. Or a recognized personal manager has undertaken to represent several artists in addition to those now represented by him, or has joined a talent organization.

The artist who appreciates the greater services and facilities that may accompany a merger may be happy to be associated with the merged agency. He may conclude that the larger agency will have more to offer in packaging or deals, and that he may benefit thereby. Another artist who loves being the stellar attraction of a small agency may be dissatisfied to find himself unwillingly a small fish in a big pond. Artists who have developed close personal relations with an individual agent who has moved on to another agency or his own business may be disgruntled unless they can follow the agent to his new connection.

Personal objections may be even more intensified if managers change their mode of operations. This is understandable because the manager-artist relationship is by nature extremely close.

Courts appreciate the significance of a personal relationship and they may stretch in favor of the artist who is objecting to a material change in the basic relations with his manager and wants to terminate the management agreement. Nevertheless they must respect the intentions of the parties as revealed by their agreement. Thus, in the case of the contract with a large talent agency, where the relationship is not necessarily very personal, the court may be unwilling, if no specific provision has been made in the agreement, to free the artist from the agency when the artist objects to a merger or wishes to follow an individual agent who has left the agency. It is up to the artist to have provided in the agreement for such contingencies. Some union agreements protect the personal relationship by requiring the talent agency to name several "key" individuals who will actually service the artist. Some artists designate their own particular "key man" with whom they anticipate a close working relationship. Certain union agreements permit termination of the agency agreement in the event of a merger of the agency with another agency.

The termination of obligations to an agency is deemed to apply only to new contracts not previously handled by the agency. There is a continuing right to commissions provided for in past contracts, such as recording contracts entered into under the aegis of the old agency.

Notices and Payments

Agreements negotiated by agents with record companies will provide that all notices and payments shall be made through the office of the agency. This protects both the artist and the agency, in that the agency can calendar and spot check the artist's receipts to determine that the accounting is generally proper, and it enables the agency to deduct its appropriate commission. Insofar as the record company is concerned, it may be better and easier to send notices of future record sessions to the agency and work through it on the selection of recording material than to attempt to contact the artist, who is often on tour.

In the case of ASCAP's and BMI's payments of performance moneys, commissions are not normally charged by the agencies on such receipts, which are usually paid directly to the client.

Music Contractors

Musicians for recording dates are often selected and assembled by a music contractor. Instead of charging the musicians an agent's commission in connection with the engagement, pursuant to union agreements with the American Federation of Musicians, the contractor looks to the record company or record producer for his fee. The fee is generally fixed at twice the minimum-scale payments to a musician. When one of the playing musicians arranges to assemble the others and thus assumes the duties of a contractor he will be paid twice the union scale of a musician for acting in the dual capacity of musician and contractor. For a further discussion of music contractors, see Chapter 6, "Labor Agreements."

10

Licensing of Recordings for Motion Pictures

Record companies with sizable catalogs or with current hits will from time to time receive requests for permission to use their recordings in films. There are usually four categories of films to which requests relate:

(1) A full-length theatrical film, such as *Saturday Night Fever* which includes recordings by The Bee Gees and other groups.
(2) Nonprofit, educational or religious films, such as a film on race relations which might contain recorded recitals by black poets.
(3) Television commercials, such as a Diamond Crystal Salt commercial which incorporated a recording of the song "Chitty, Chitty, Bang, Bang."
(4) Television features or series.

Film producers may favor certain recordings because they present in tangible form the exact flavor desired for particular scenes. A rendition by Aretha Franklin issued by Atlantic Records or a performance by Herb Alpert on an A&M release may present a background that a studio orchestra would be hardpressed to duplicate. The actual recordings dispel the need to guess at how a future rendition, made especially for the film, will sound.

Film producers may also consider the right to use recordings in films as an inexpensive, simple method for obtaining soundtrack music. This belief may be without merit. Multiple hurdles may have to be cleared before a recording becomes available for a motion picture. Appropriate consents or permissions may have to be acquired from artists, record companies, unions, and music publishers. A copy of an agreement for licensing a record for a film is included in Part 4 as Form 10.

Protection of Recordings
Legitimate film producers will always seek approvals before utilizing recordings in motion pictures. They recognize the property rights of the record companies, the music publishers, the recording artists, and the affected unions. It is rare that recordings are used for publicly exhibited films without proper authorization.

The legal bases for the protection of property interests in recordings are multiple and complicated. The rights of the copyright proprietors in sound recordings fixed and published on or after February 15, 1972, and before January 1, 1978 are protected under the Copyright Act of 1909, as amended. Effective January 1, 1978, sound recordings fixed on or after that date, irrespective of whether published or unpublished, are given copyright protection under the 1976 Copyright Act. The rights of the owners of the underlying compositions are protected under copyright statutes and also safeguarded under the motion picture copyright, irrespective of the date the recordings are made or released. Pre-February 15, 1972 recordings are safeguarded locally under judge-made common law and under the statutes in most states against record piracy, but pursuant to the 1976 Copyright Act the recordings will enter the public domain on February 15, 2047. For a further discussion, see Chapter 3, "Copyright in Sound Recordings."

As to pre-February 15, 1972 recordings, performers and record producers have depended largely upon two legal theories to secure recognition of their rights in recordings, namely, unfair competition and common law copyright. The two concepts are frequently confused in the decisions. To a lesser degree, plaintiffs have resorted to the performer's right of privacy in respect of his name and likeness, and to the artist's right to control and profit from publicity values which he has achieved.

Unfair Competition

Traditionally, the courts have held that for a case of unfair competition there must be the elements of (1) competition between the plaintiff and defendant, (2) the misappropriation of a business asset, and (3) the defendant's fraudulent passing off of the appropriated asset as the plaintiff's. However, courts in later decisions have tended to discard the elements of direct competition or passing off, relying instead on the "misappropriation" or "free ride" theory.

Common Law Copyright

There has been a maze of conflicting opinions on the question of common law copyright in sound recordings. It has been settled that the performances of recording artists in a pre-February 15, 1972 sound recording constitute an original artistic or intellectual creation which is eligible for common law copyright protection against unauthorized use. However, there has been a split of authority on whether sales or public distribution of records comprises a general publication of the work that throws it into the public domain. The present tendency is for the courts to oppose the forfeiture of common law copyright protection by the sales of records. In contrast, the concept of unfair competition is not affected by publication through sales of records.

Statutes

While statutes in many states bar the unauthorized dubbing and sale of phonograph records, it appears that these laws are addressed to sales of dubbed records and do not relate to the unauthorized integration of records into films.

Under United States copyright laws, a motion picture film, including its soundtrack, is the subject of statutory copyright. Copyright in sound recordings is considered fully in Chapter 3, with a separate treatment of the status of audiovisual works which include motion picture soundtrack recordings. Audiovisual works as such do not qualify for a copyright in sound recordings, but they are protected by the copyright in audiovisual works.

The exclusive right of a copyright owner of sound recordings fixed on or after February 15, 1972 to "reproduce the copyrighted works in copies or phonorecords" covers reproduction in visual media. There is therefore a statutory basis for requiring the consents of record companies for the use of their copyrighted recordings in motion pictures.

Consent of the Publisher

Chapter 28, "Music and the Movies," discusses film synchronization and performance licenses to be sought from music publishers. These relate ordinarily to music in existence before the production of the particular picture and proposed to be recorded in the soundtrack of the film. The same types of licenses must be acquired for music embodied in existing recordings proposed to be integrated in a film.

Union Re-Use Fees

Under the union agreements with the American Federation of Musicians and those with the American Federation of Television and Radio Artists, there are re-use fees to be paid by the record company if domestic phonograph recordings are utilized in different media, such as theatrical films, television films, or film commercials. The record company would be liable to the vocalists, musicians, conductors, arrangers, orchestrators, and copyists for re-use fees in an amount equal to present union scale for the services previously performed. The re-use fees may be substantial, depending upon the number of union members involved in the original recording and the extent of their services. The chief counsel for Capitol Records stated in 1968, at a time of much lower union scale than today, relative to requests for the re-use of existing records: "When a record company says 'yes,' the record company would be obligated to pay all the musicians, all the AFTRA performers, the arranger, the copyist, everybody, a new additional scale payment. If you want to do that for a symphony, the cost to the record company may well be $50,000." Standard licensing agreements provide that the cost of union re-use fees will be assumed by the licensee.

In certain instances, the unions upon application may grant waivers of re-use fees if the film is of a nonprofit public service nature. Since the record company may be charging little or nothing for its consent, it may require the film producer to apply for the waiver. Otherwise, unremunerative staff time may have to be devoted to the application.

Artist Contract Restrictions

If the film producer is not discouraged by re-use fees and by the need for music publisher licenses, the record company must still examine its own files to determine whether permission may be granted and on what terms. The record company will turn first to the recording contract under which the recording was originally made. In most cases, the contract will not limit the type of usage of a recording. This is especially true as to recordings by newer artists. For the established artist, another situation may prevail. The artist may have negotiated a restriction of his recording to the field of home phonograph records or tapes, or the contract may require the artist's consent for the synchronization of his recordings in films.

In the case of contract restrictions, the record company will have to advise the film producer thereof and arrange for either itself or the film producer to obtain the appropriate consent of the artist. If a license fee is to be paid to the record company, the artist may request a portion of the fee as the price of his consent.

Soundtrack Albums

The record manufacturer may be informed that the film producer proposes to issue a soundtrack album which includes the recording. This poses additional problems. In the first place, the record company may have granted exclusive foreign phonograph record rights in the recording to foreign record companies. Therefore, worldwide record rights may not be licensed to the film company unless the foreign record companies consent.

Assuming other problems have been solved, the record company may request a royalty based on sales of the proposed soundtrack album. This may be necessary in order to meet commitments to the artist who is entitled to a royalty on all sales of the recording. The royalty will vary with what the traffic will bear. If, for example, the artist must be paid a royalty of 7 percent of sales, pro rata in relation to the number of selections in the album, the record company will seek a higher royalty to afford the company a profit after deduction of the artist royalty.

In many instances, the record company will reserve all singles rights to the recording. If the film becomes popular and the soundtrack album emerges as a good seller, the record manufacturer may benefit by a resurgence in singles sales. Thus, RCA, which licensed its recording by Nilsson of "Everybody's Talking" for the motion picture *Midnight Cowboy,* reissued the recording as a single after the release of the film and derived additional sales on the reissue of the record.

11

Work Permits for Foreign Artists

American artists such as the Duke Ellington Orchestra conduct successful tours of Europe or Africa. The Rolling Stones, Paul McCartney, and other European artists have achieved tremendous acceptance in the United States. Underlying the exchanges of artists and their performing in foreign countries may be a world of red tape and procedures involving international policy questions of safeguarding native artists from job insecurity and protecting local balances of trade.

For a foreign artist who desires to perform or record in the United States, there is a complicated process which sometimes involves alien employment certification preliminary to the issuance of a temporary work visa. An understanding of the procedures and rules of the United States Department of Labor and of the Immigration and Naturalization Service of the Department of Justice is essential to any concert producer, booking agent, record company, and television or film producer that desires to import musical talent from other countries.

Types of Work Visas

There are two categories of temporary work visas available to alien artists. The preferred H-1 status is available to those artists who can support a claim of "distinguished merit and ability" by evidence of the nature discussed below. To qualify an entertainer for H-2 status, the Secretary of Labor or his designated representative is required to certify that there are no qualified persons in the United States available for the employment, and that the pay and other facets of such employment satisfy prevailing standards.

The Proper Petitioner and Petitions

Although vitally interested, the alien musician or musical group is only the beneficiary of the alien employment certification and the immigration petition and is not the proper party to act as the official petitioner. The petitioner should be in the category of the "importing employer" or his agent, and he need not be a United States resident or citizen. Petitions are commonly filed by booking agencies, concert promoters, and the like, who are deemed to have the proper status for such filings. Caution should be exercised to assure that the petitioner's status and relationship to the beneficiaries should be continued throughout the

United States engagement for which application is made. If there is a switch in persons holding the particular petitioner status, an application by the new party will be necessary. Thus, a Boston concert promoter may be an appropriate petitioner for a single appearance in that city. But if a six-city tour is planned, the booking agency handling the entire tour should be the over-all petitioner rather than having six individual petitions, with one for each city. If a tour is part of a record promotion, as well as for other purposes, the record company as employer, even though only indirectly involved in specific concert appearances, can be the petitioner for the entire tour, including employment at a record studio. More normally, a general agency (e.g., William Morris Agency, Inc., Associated Booking Corporation) serves as petitioner representing an interested party in all facets of United States employment.

Services of entertainers are restricted to the activity, area, and employer specified in the petition. A new petition is required for further engagements or if there is a change of employer or a change in the area of performance. An exception, where the performer is already in the United States, is an appearance without compensation on a charity show, for which no musician or other performer receives any compensation or reimbursement of expenses. When there are changes in the itinerary of an H-1 or H-2 entertainer beneficiary within the time period of the original itinerary, it is common to just notify the Immigration and Naturalization Service office which handled the original petitions by submitting a letter of notification, preferably either in person or by certified mail, return receipt requested. Any new or separate engagement on other media such as television or radio requires a new petition.

An H-1 status petitioner may petition directly to the Immigration and Naturalization Service, without the necessity for a prior Department of Labor application. Some cautious petitioners who seek the H-1 status also apply at the same time (without advising the other agency) to the Department of Labor. The latter's certification may be used for obtaining an H-2 or other status in the event of rejection of the claim of distinguished merit and ability by the adjudicating officer of the Immigration and Naturalization Service.

If the artist is not as well established as a Sheena Easton, Paul Mauriat, or Vienna Philharmonic, it may be especially valuable to buttress the claim of distinguished merit and ability, as the basis for an H-1 petition, with all the supporting proof available. The following extract from the applicable regulations governing the Immigration and Naturalization Service indicates the criteria involved in the determination of distinguished merit and ability:

> . . . whether the alien has performed and will perform as a star or featured entertainer, as evidenced by playbills, critical reviews, advertisements, publicity releases, averments by the petitioner, and contracts; the acclaim which the entertainer has achieved, as evidenced by reviews in newspapers, trade

journals, and magazines; the reputation of theaters, concert halls, night clubs, and other establishments in which the entertainer has appeared and will appear; the reputation of repertory companies, ballet groups, orchestras and other productions in which he has performed; the extent and number of commercial successes of his performances, as evidenced by contracts; whether the alien has been the recipient of national, international or other significant awards for his performances; the opinions of unions, other organizations and recognized critics and other experts in the field in which the alien is engaged; whether previous petitions filed in behalf of the alien seeking his services in a similar capacity have been properly approved by the Service, and, if so, whether there have been any changes in circumstances. . . .

The foregoing standards are designed to show whether the alien entertainer is clearly preeminent in his or her specialty.

Forms of Petition to File

Most visiting alien musicians and singers will not choose to apply as regular immigrants from their native lands. They will, rather, seek to qualify as nonimmigrants for temporary work visas. As such, and as the basis for an H-2 petition, they will require a certification of the Secretary of Labor or his designated representative, on a form ETA, Part A, that their employment will not take jobs from American artists. This is a preliminary to a petition to the Immigration and Naturalization Service on form I-129B. The only exception from this dual petition procedure is in the case of persons who can documentarily establish that they are of "distinguished merit and ability" coming to perform services "of an exceptional nature" (H-1 status) in which case the petitioner may skip the initial petition to the Department of Labor and apply directly to the Immigration and Naturalization Service of the Department of Justice.

When an entire orchestra, band, or other group with a single itinerary requests a temporary work visa, it is desirable to file petitions in group form rather than individually. One reason is that the $35 filing fee covers all members of the group. A more important reason is that it avoids duplicative adjudications and the risk that one group member may hold up others whose petitions were approved earlier. If there is a change in group personnel and group qualification before the commencement of a tour, the original petition may be amended. However, a change in personnel after initial entry into the United States will usually require a new petition and new filing fee. The new petition should be sent to the same district office as the previous petition with a copy of the original or the file number and should make reference to the file number and the date of the earlier approval. It is to be assumed that a group known and regularly appearing under a group name is an entity and that the qualifications are of the group rather than the individuals. In fact, the petition should use the group name in the space for "name of beneficiary," and individual member names can be attached on an accompanying schedule showing names, citizenships, birth dates, places of birth, and current addresses.

Accompanying Documents

Whether for an H-1 or H-2 petition, it is appropriate to accompany the petition with documentary proof of professional standing. This may be in the form of record or concert reviews, or hit charts. It is also advisable to have letters from recognized experts in the applicant's field of music, such as critics, concert promoters, recognized artists, publishers, or record company personnel (when the record company is not acting as petitioner), or a certificate of membership in a select professional society. Such endorsements should be in the English language or accompanied by an English translation made by a translator who submits a certificate of competency to translate and a notarized statement of the accuracy of the translation.

All documents must be submitted in duplicate. If the return of documents is desired, this must be explicitly requested, and two photocopies must accompany the originals when submitted.

Where to File Petitions

There are three United States departments normally concerned with alien entry into the United States for employment purposes. They are the Department of Labor, the Immigration and Naturalization Service of the Department of Justice, and the Department of State. The Departments of Labor and of Justice are the primary agencies concerned with alien employment petitions in the United States.

Department of Labor filings for certification (required only in an H-2 case) are handled initially by the applicable state employment service local office where the employment is to take place. The state office then forwards the papers to the regional office of the Manpower Administration of the United States Department of Labor, without the further intervention of the petitioner. In some areas of greater alien employment (e.g., Los Angeles, Chicago, and New York), the applicable state office may set up a special division to handle requests for certification. For example, in New York City, all entertainment field petitions should be sent to the Central Immigration Office, New York State Department of Labor, Room 7157, Two World Trade Center, New York, N.Y. 10047 (telephone 212-488-5772).

The Immigration and Naturalization Service of the Department of Justice maintains 37 District Offices spread throughout the United States, plus four District Offices in foreign countries (Italy, Mexico, Philippines, and Germany). They are further identified on the map and list of addresses included in Appendix R. Any district office can handle all territorial employment included in the itinerary of an artist, so long as the petition at least partially involves employment in the territory of the district office. It is not necessary or desirable to send multiple petitions to a number of district offices. In fact, it is sometimes advisable to select one district office in preference to another. Factors to consider include the convenience of the petitioner or its attorney or simply the possibility of faster service and more personal attention in one district office as against another. One district office may be reputed to be more difficult to deal with than another, and this may be significant since each office has a high degree of discretion, although decisions are subject to review. Of course, a particular office's familiarity with entertainment industry problems may sometimes compensate for logjams and longer waiting periods.

A matter of convenience to all parties concerned is the use of the long distance telephone by distant district offices to confirm to petitioners located in other cities entry approval for an alien. This may also be available in special cases to notify U.S. consular offices abroad of the petition approval so that they may process the visa applications of the artist beneficiaries. Such long distance telephone notification is afforded when the petitioner or his attorney or agent writes a letter to the district office authorizing that telephone costs be charged to the authorizing party's account. Often, when time is of the essence and any delay may be costly, a telephone authorization can be of great value.

Personal appearance by the petitioner with all necessary immigration and naturalization forms and supporting documents is an accepted procedure for expediting processing. In many offices, however, the busy schedule of adjudicating officers may still cause a long wait. Expedited determinations are available in certain districts but only under limited and urgent circumstances. Planning ahead is therefore crucial. Attorneys may not appear on behalf of a petitioner unless a special authorization form is signed by the petitioner.

The Department of State is primarily involved with handling requests for information, forms, the processing of papers in foreign countries through the various United States Consular Offices, and the issuance of visas where requested.

Artist's or Group's Accompanying Personnel

Performing artists attract ticket buyers and high fees on the basis of their individual reputations and talent. However, hardly any major artist is truly a solo entity. He depends upon back-up musicians, accompanists, road managers, publicity agents, sound technicians, and, in some instances, even on special hairdressers, valets, or maids. When applying for work visas in the United States, the unique and special talent of the major artist often cannot envelop all of his or her entourage. The hairdresser who is so essential in London might be replaced in New York by an equally qualified American. A bass player or pianist who accompanies the artist in Rome may be regarded by an American musicians' union representative as merely a competitor of an equally competent American musician.

In one petition application for the Canadian orchestra named Lighthouse, which used electronic instruments and equipment, a sound technician was recognized as a uniquely qualified member of the orchestra despite having talents no greater than those of available American technicians. His special status arose from the fact that the orchestra itself was using special sound equipment designed by this foreign sound technician. The equipment was subject to constant repair and rearrangement to fit different concert halls, for which functions the equipment designer had special training and experience that was not interchangeable with that of other technicians who did not have such familiarity with the orchestra or equipment. The road manager familiar with the personal whims and needs of the orchestra personnel as to dining, accommodations, and travel was held not so exceptional that his duties could not be similarly performed by an American citizen without special and extensive training. In summary, necessary accompanists and staff for an H-1 artist cannot be approved—on the same or a separate petition—without proving unique qualifications.

Of course, many such decisions are highly subjective and supporting affidavits and explanations should clearly delineate the unique qualities of accompanying personnel. A frequent factor is foreign language ability, where the artists require a staff familiar with a foreign language.

Immigrant Status

The prior discussion in this chapter has been based on the nonimmigrant status of the alien artist. The alternative, however, of immigrant status is not to be disregarded. Immigrant status, sometimes referred to as permanent resident status, is reflected by issuance of a "green card" which is actually now issued in blue. Because of the unlimited duration of the right under such card to work in the United States, it is in many instances more desirable to the foreign artist than an H-1 or H-2 nonimmigrant status. It is to be noted that an immigrant does not automatically lose foreign citizenship or commit himself to accepting U.S. citizenship, which may be available upon application after five years of permanent residence, or three years if living with one's United States citizen spouse.

In the past there were immigrant "quotas" for each national group, beyond which no more applicants could be accepted. Since 1968 national origin quotas have been abolished. In their place there is a worldwide quota of 270,000 immigrants annually, with a maximum of 20,000 from any one country. Spouses and parents of over-21 age children who are U.S.A. citizens are exempt from this quota, and if the alien fits into this group, known as "immediate relatives," he should consider applying for permanent resident status by this route, rather than through his profession.

All green cards, except for immediate relatives, are reserved for people in different categories known as preferences. For those without family ties here, there is a category known as "third preference" for members of the professions and persons "of exceptional ability in the arts and sciences." Ten per cent, or 27,000 visas, are allotted annually to these aliens and their families. Persons who qualify for the H-1 status can sometimes avail themselves of this preference although the "exceptional ability" required for a third preference status is deemed to be a much more stringent standard than the "distinguished merit and ability" which qualifies for H-1 status. To obtain the preference a petition by a sponsor offering full-time employment must be filed with and approved by the Attorney General. Aliens in this preference category must obtain a certification from the Secretary of Labor that their coming to the United States will not adversely affect American labor. However, where the Secretary determines that the alien is of exceptional ability the certification routinely issues. Once the third preference is approved, the alien must apply for an immigrant visa, either at the U.S.A. consulate in his home country or in the U.S.A. if he is in the United States and has never been employed there without government permission. There are waiting lists for immigrant visas, however, and the process can be a lengthy one, lasting a year or more. After the process has begun to procure an immigrant visa, it is inadvisable for the performer to travel in and out of the U.S.A. on any temporary visa, such as a tourist or visitor visa. This is because the intent to reside in the U.S.A. permanently is inconsistent with the intent to return abroad which is required for a temporary visa. To use a temporary visa while taking steps to obtain a "green card" may therefore be regarded as possible visa fraud.

Rejection and Right of Appeal

In the fast-moving world of musical entertainment, the frequent concern in alien employment is undue delay in clearing the artist for an engagement. Delay may force a prospective employer to find substitute artists to fill a concert hall or other place of engagement. Rarely will the employer be able to wait for the extended time involved in new applications or appeals. However, the beneficiary will be interested in the reasons for a refusal to admit and in the possibility of curing the refusal through appeal or a subsequent application.

As to H-1 and H-2 petitions, the regulations of the Immigration and Naturalization Service require that, if a petition is denied, the petitioner must be notified of the reasons therefor and of his right to appeal.

As to H-1 petitions, the regulations further require that if an adverse decision is proposed, based upon any evidence not submitted by the petitioner, then the petitioner must be so notified and invited to rebut such third party evidence. The third party evidence may have been submitted by parties such as unions, other organizations, critics, or experts in the related entertainment field who are frequently consulted by the adjudicating officer of the Immigration and Naturalization Service in order to obtain an advisory opinion regarding the qualifications of the alien and the nature of the services to be performed by him. The advisory opinions are sometimes given orally in the interest of expeditious handling of applications. For purposes of appeal from a rejected petition, even an oral opinion is subject to review by a petitioner because the opinion must be confirmed in writing within 15 days from the date when it was requested.

With respect to H-2 petitions, the Secretary of Labor must certify that (1) qualified persons are not available in the United States and (2) the employment will not adversely affect the wages and working conditions of workers in the United States similarly employed. If a notice is attached to the petition by such official that such certification cannot be made, the petitioner can produce countervailing evidence.

Under statutory standards H-1 and H-2 petitions will be denied for such items as insanity, chronic alcoholism, narcotics addiction, conviction of trafficking in narcotics, and the alien's evasion of the United States military draft, unless waived by the Government.

Union Comity

Although not required by law or regulation, it is advisable for alien artists on a United States tour to consult the applicable American union as to its requirements. For example, Canadian musicians, being members of the AF of M for the United States and Canada jointly, must pay a "work dues equivalent" to certain AF of M locals which charge United States members the same. These dues, which run as high as 4 percent of gross receipts in some instances, are not charged at all by other locals. The dues are not charged foreign musicians who are not from Canada.

Another example of continuing union review of alien employment is in the case of members of the British Musicians Union. They are expected to abide by the category and hours of employment of American musicians for whom reciprocal employment in the British territory was obtained. Although such a "trade" of work is sometimes arranged through a booking agency, the international unions themselves may at times informally facilitate such an exchange and thereby clear the way for the American union to advise the applicable government office of no objection to the permit. International union arrangements with the union in the alien artist's home country often cover membership status in the United States. Nonunion members can be required to join the United States union after 30 days from the commencement of employment in a "union shop."

Multiple Entry into United States and Extensions

Performing artists may interrupt a United States tour to perform in other countries before returning to the United States. This interruption does not require duplicate work clearances inasmuch as multiple entry permission is available. In such cases the alien should ask the Consul for a multiple entry visa. On the alien's arrival in the United States, the Immigration and Naturalization Service will determine the length of that particular stay. People with H-1 visas may be granted up to two years initially, with the possibility of extending the visit for a total of three years. Persons with H-2 visas may be given up to one year, with a possible extension of 45 days.

Applications for extensions of the permits are made to the Immigration Service for a continuation of the previous engagement on form I–539. In addition the petitioner must request an extension of the validity of the petition on form I–129B. The two are considered separately. A denial of extension of a stay is not appealable; a denial of extension of the petition is. If the petition is extended but the stay is not, the alien could go to another country, such as Canada, and ask the U.S. Consul there for a new visa based on the extended petition. If new engagements are involved, a new I–129B petition must also be filed with the Immigration Service. An extension of an H-2 permit also requires submission of a new labor certification to cover the continued or additional employment.

International Tax Treatment

Compensation for professional appearances in the United States is subject to the income taxes of either the United States, the country of origin of the artist, or both countries. Artists from countries such as the United Kingdom, France, West Germany, Canada, Sweden, and many other countries can avoid the payment of the United States federal income tax on United States earnings. This is due to the existence of treaties between the United States and such nations called "Conventions for the Avoidance of Double Taxation." Artists from nontreaty countries, such as East Germany, India, Brazil, and Czechoslovakia, are subject to a United States tax on their earnings from appearances in the United States. Tax clearance before departure from the United States is required from the Bureau of Internal Revenue District Director.

Eligibility under double taxation treaties requires the filing of proof with the Bureau of Internal Revenue District Director that the artist qualifies as a taxpayer in the artist's country of origin. For example, English taxpayers obtain such certificate from HM Inspector of Foreign Dividends, Malden House, 1 Blandon Road, New Malden, Surrey, England.

Resident (immigrant) status artists are considered the same as United States citizens for income tax status regardless of where the income originates. In recent years the United States, as well as Canada, has initiated a fixed percentage of withholding tax on foreign artists present on a temporary basis unless qualification under a tax treaty is first established. Where not so established applications for refunds are later required.

12

Counterfeiting, Piracy and Bootlegging

Counterfeiting in the record business consists of the unauthorized manufacture and distribution of copies of records under the guise of products of the authorized manufacturer. A typical example of counterfeiting might be the following hypothetical case: A guitarist on the roster of MCA Records recorded the theme of a television show, and it was a significant commercial success. If the Brigand Record Company, without the consent of MCA Records, were to manufacture and sell copies of the record to which there was affixed the label of MCA Records, this would constitute counterfeiting.

Piracy in the record business applies to the unauthorized duplication of tapes or records sold openly as manufactured without permission of the record company. The pirates may sell under their own label or with no label identification at all. Tape pirates, prior to federal copyright protection of sound recordings and prior to state laws against record piracy, had become bold enough to advertise their products through mail solicitation. In a typical advertisement, they offered to sell duplicates of bestselling albums at bargain prices, including recordings by the Beatles, Glen Campbell, Elvis Presley, the Rolling Stones, and Bob Dylan. It was common for pirates to purchase a tape or record for a few dollars, and then transfer the music from the authorized record or tape to the pirated tape, which tape could be sold at a reduced price in competition with the legitimate product.

Bootlegging is akin to piracy except that it involves products incorporating an unauthorized recording of a live or broadcast performance rather than the duplication of existing products.

Counterfeiting of discs is facilitated by the ease of making metal parts for the pressing of records from taped recordings of released records. Illegal duplication of tapes is even easier since it is unnecessary to acquire the metal presses or any of the other expensive equipment it takes to make records. Tape duplication requires a tape recorder, a tape playback machine, and some machines that will produce many copied tapes at one time. Years ago an industry source stated that the "cost of going into business as a tape pirate is less than $10,000."

Clearly the counterfeiter and the pirate are brothers in their nefarious endeavors. Both are obviously misappropriating the services of the artist and a product owned and paid for by a legitimate manufacturer. Both benefit at the expense and detriment of record companies, performing artists, music publishers, unions, and the federal and local government. The counterfeiter and the pirate fail to pay the recording costs incurred by the record company, and they steal the profits which might otherwise accrue to the record company. Detriment to the artist results from inferior-quality recordings manufactured by the counterfeiter or pirate and from the nonpayment of artist royalties. Mechanical-license fees are not paid to music publishers. Payments computed as a percentage of the retail price of records sold are not made to the American Federation of Musicians Trust Fund and musicians. Income tax payments are avoided.

The only significant costs of the counterfeiter and pirate would appear to be pressing and duplication charges, the costs of covers and labels, and distribution expenses. Obviously, they can afford to charge substantially less than the legitimate manufacturer and still make a profit.

The seriousness of the problem is illustrated in this excerpt from a 1970 memorandum from the record industry to a United States Senate subcommittee:

> Atlantic Recording Corporation paid approximately $80,000 to record an album by Crosby, Stills and Nash, and then another $20,000 to advertise and promote the album. Atlantic's costs for manufacturing discs and prerecorded tapes of the album exceeded $600,000.
>
> It is just at this point—after the record company has invested enormous sums on a high-quality album, produced a hit and achieved wide market popularity—that the pirate swoops in to reap the benefits at little or no expense.

The statements above regarding the deleterious practices of counterfeiting and piracy also apply in the main to bootlegging, with the obvious exception that there is a misappropriation of a live or broadcast performance rather than an existing product.

Information supplied by the International Federation of Phonogram and Videogram Producers (IFPI) is that in 1982 the total dollar value of pirate, counterfeit and bootleg product sold in North America was $400 million. Of such sales in the United States, IFPI estimates that pirate material represents 25 percent, counterfeit 55 percent and bootleg 20 percent. IFPI also estimates that the total of such products amounts to 10 to 20 percent of all retail sales. Thus from one-tenth to one-fifth of all sales is of material having an unauthorized origin.

Federal Counterfeit Label Law

Until 1962 there were no federal laws directly applicable to the prosecution of persons who transported or sold phonorecords on which counterfeit labels were affixed, and state laws were either nonexistent or ineffectual. Finally, in 1962, Congress passed an anti-counterfeiting label law which was signed by the President. The 1962 law, however, was plagued with difficulties such as the requirement that the prosecution had to prove both knowledge and fraudulent intent on the offender's part in transporting, receiving, selling, or offering for sale records to which the counterfeit labels were stamped, pasted or affixed. Moreover, the 1962 law imposed relatively modest penalties.

In 1982, the law was substantially amended, and now has the heading "Trafficking in counterfeit labels for phonorecords, and copies of motion pictures or other audiovisual works." Under the present law, any person who knowingly traffics in a counterfeit label affixed or designed to be affixed to a copyrighted phonorecord or a copy of a copyrighted motion picture or other audiovisual work, can be fined up to $250,000 and/or imprisoned for up to five years. Thus, the fraudulent intent requirement has been eliminated. It is now sufficient for the prosecution to prove that the offense of trafficking in counterfeit labels was knowingly committed. In addition, all counterfeit labels which have been affixed or which were intended to have been affixed are to be forfeited and destroyed or otherwise disposed of by the court upon conviction under this statute.

Federal Legislation

A federal copyright in sound recordings was established effective February 15, 1972, relating to sound recordings fixed and published on and after that date. Effective January 1, 1978, sound recordings fixed on or after that date, irrespective of whether published or unpublished, are granted copyright protection under the 1976 Copyright Act.

A violation of the exclusive rights of the copyright owner of a sound recording is a copyright infringement and subject to a civil action for infringement. Among the court remedies for civil infringement are injunctions, the impounding and the destruction or other reasonable disposition of the infringing articles, and the award under the 1976 Copyright Act, effective January 1, 1978, of either (1) the copyright owner's actual damages and any additional profits of the infringer, or (2) statutory damages for any one work of generally from $250 to $10,000, or in the case of willful infringement from $250 to $50,000, in the court's discretion. The court may also award court costs and reasonable attorney's fees to the prevailing party.

The court may order destruction of not only all records and tapes made or used in violation of the copyright owner's rights but also matrices, masters, tapes, film negatives, or other articles by which the records and tapes may be reproduced.

Until 1982 a first time copyright infringer was only subject to a misdemeanor charge under the Copyright Act. As indicated by industry sources, federal prosecutors were unlikely to pursue criminal copyright infringers, and offenders were subject to relatively small penalties in light of the enormous profits to be made. Finally, in 1982, Congress amended the federal criminal code which now provides that criminal infringement of the copyright in a sound recording, involving willful action for purposes of commercial advantage or private financial gain is punishable as a felony. As a result, federal prosecutors are more willing to pursue these crimes and possible offenders are more effectively deterred.

Under this new penalty system as set forth in the "Piracy and Counterfeiting Amendments Act of 1981" and depending on the number of phonorecords reproduced or distributed within a 180 day period, an individual may be fined up to $250,000 and/or imprisoned up to five years. For a further discussion of criminal penalties, see Chapter 26, "Infringement of Copyrights."

Prior to federal copyright protection, the record industry was forced to rely largely on suits in state courts under theories of unfair competition, in order to prohibit the piracy of recordings. The industry and its performers contended that effective relief could not be obtained from the state courts. Apart from the different interpretations of law in the 50 separate states, it appeared that an injunction in one state did not bar a pirate from renewing his operations in another state. Further, a pirate enjoined by one record company from duplicating its product could simply switch to copying records and tapes manufactured by another record company.

As noted above, federal copyright protection has been provided for sound recordings fixed and published on or after February 15, 1972. This has supplied the legislative relief needed to halt the widespread illegal duplication and sale of more recent sound recordings. An injunction obtained against a pirate for infringement of the federal copyright is enforceable nationwide. Moreover, there are criminal penalties to dissuade willful infringers from committing additional infringements by pirating the records of another record company.

However, federal copyright protection does not extend to a vast number of recordings which predate February 15, 1972. Under the 1976 Copyright Act, state law is not preempted in respect of such recordings until February 15, 2047. Consequently, there is still available the remedy of civil lawsuits in state courts under theories of unfair competition. The large profits attendant upon record piracy have tended to cause pirates to defy the risks of such civil suits.

The recording industry, aware of the need for criminal sanctions, has been successful in convincing practically all the states in the United States to pass penal legislation specifically prohibiting the unauthorized reproduction and sale of recordings. These laws have proved very effective in limiting record piracy. For example, the antipiracy law of California provides that first offenses are punishable by a fine of up to $25,000 or imprisonment of up to a year and one day, or both; subsequent offenses could draw a fine of up to $50,000 or a jail term, or both.

Under the antipiracy law of New York, the unauthorized manufacture or duplication of sound recordings is punishable by imprisonment from 1 to 3 years or a fine up to $5,000, or both.

Compulsory License

Under the 1976 Copyright Act a compulsory license for musical compositions is not available to those reproducing sound recordings without the consent of their owners. This represents a statutory enactment of the decisions of the federal courts interpreting the provisions of the prior Copyright Act. These decisions were the outcome of protracted litigation brought in the main by publishers affiliated with The Harry Fox Agency, Inc., the mechanical licensing agency for most United States publishers; the Agency has been active in these lawsuits.

The pirating of recordings without the consent of the copyright owner of the music in the recordings constitutes a willful infringement of the music copyright. The pirate is subject to civil actions for such infringement under the 1976 Copyright Act; the remedies include injunctions, the impounding and destruction of infringing materials, money awards for damages, the infringer's profits, court costs and attorney's fees. For willful infringements of the music copyright there are also criminal penalties of a fine of up to $25,000 and imprisonment of up to one year, or both. It is the announced decision of the United States Department of Justice to prosecute those who pirate pre-February 15, 1972 sound recordings on the grounds of infringement of the copyrights in the musical compositions contained in the recordings.

Many record companies are associated with music publishers who publish original music. The music publishers are therefore strongly motivated to pursue civil and criminal actions against pirates of the recordings issued by their affiliated record companies.

International Treaty

In 1971, representatives from approximately 50 nations including the United States met in Paris and drafted an international treaty to protect sound recordings against piracy. The treaty is known as the "Geneva Convention of October 29, 1971, for the Protection of Producers of Phonograms Against Unauthorized Duplication," and became effective in 1973. On March 10, 1974, the United States became a member of the Convention. Other members are: Argentina, Australia, Austria, Brazil, Chile, Costa Rica, Denmark, Ecuador, Egypt, El Salvador, Fiji, Finland, France, the Federal Republic of Germany, Guatemala, Holy See, Hungary, India, Israel, Italy, Japan, Kenya, Luxembourg, Mexico, Monaco, New Zealand, Norway, Panama, Paraguay, Spain, Sweden, United Kingdom, Uruguay, Venezuela, and Zaire.

The treaty provides that contracting states will protect the nationals of other states against the making or importation of duplicate recordings without the consent of the legal producer, if the intent is to distribute them to the public. Each national legislature would decide the method by which this result would be brought about.

The law providing for United States federal copyright protection for sound recordings serves to implement the agreement of the United States, as a signer of the treaty, to protect the producers of sound recordings who are nationals of other contracting countries against piracy of sound recordings.

For a further discussion of the treaty see Chapter 3, "Copyright in Sound Recordings," and Chapter 32, "International Copyright Protection."

13

Payola

Since 1960, payola has been a federal criminal offense for which the sentence may be a fine of up to $10,000 or imprisonment for up to one year, or both.

As commonly used in the music industry, payola is a term describing secret payment to and acceptance by broadcasting station personnel (usually disc jockeys, record librarians, or program directors) of money, service, or other valuable consideration in return for their broadcast use of a particular record or song. It is not an offense if the payment is disclosed to the station and to the independent or other program producer or person for whom the program is produced or supplied.

Where the station licensee has knowledge of the payment, it must inform the public by means of an announcement on the program involved. The station cannot willingly remain in ignorance while its employees supplement their income by payola. The Communications Act provides that "reasonable diligence" must be exercised.

Incentive to Payola

The obvious incentive for engaging in payola is to create a public illusion of spontaneous and genuine popularity of a record or song and thereby to promote the sale of records and the performance and other use of a song. Payola is a crutch upon which a promotion man with a second-rate product or insufficient contacts or ability may be tempted to lean. Unfortunately, even meritorious material can fall prey to payola when, in the absence of payola, a record may be bottled up and kept from the public ear by a bribe-taking disc jockey, record librarian, or other station employee.

Contacts and promotion are recognized as essential and legitimate factors in the popular music industry. An excellent song or record is worthless on a record company or music publisher's shelf, without public exposure. One witness in the 1960 congressional hearings on payola said: "Until the public actually hears your product, you can't tell whether you have a hit or not." The editorial work of a music publisher, therefore, must be supplemented by the vital work of joining with the record company in convincing disc jockeys to play the particular record and song. This is a function of music publishers' promotional employees.

A good disc jockey or record librarian considers that he has music selection problems equal to those of any record company or music publisher. It is normal for personnel in the broadcasting and music industries to have mutual interests and rapport. Some music and record company promotion men achieve a "friend of the family" status with each other and with broadcasting personnel that may be expressed by tips on employment opportunities and other favors. Some disc jockeys help music men by calling attention to new songs and master recordings from their local area or an up-and-coming "regional breakout" of records or songs. It becomes a matter of degree as to when gifts and entertainment at theaters, restaurants, and nightclubs leave the realm of socializing and enter the area of payola through implication of a promise of air play.

Commercial Bribery

Relationships of music publishers and songwriters to record company personnel are not subject to the federal payola statute but may constitute another type of payola. Such relations, as well as those in broadcasting station payola, are subject to state commercial bribery laws, in effect in over one-third of the states, when they involve the payment of money or other valuable consideration to an employee behind the back of his employer.

Payola, in the sense of pay-for-pay or plugging, has been with the music industry for a long time. In 1916, the Music Publishers Protective Association noted that as much as $400,000 a year was being paid to artists to plug their songs. The publishers agreed to levy a fine of $5,000 upon any member who continued the practice, but the agreement was unenforced and ineffective. In the late 1930s a group of publishers retained the late Joseph V. McKee, attorney and onetime acting mayor of New York City, to work with the Federal Trade Commission and obtain a Code outlawing payola. This move collapsed.

Publishing Interests

It has been reported that an important recording star who is often his own composer and publisher saw fit to pay $250,000 for the United States and Canadian rights to publish about 100 songs written and recorded by himself in years prior to the formation of his own publishing firm. While he was creating a greater incentive to record his own songs, this does not comprise payola. Nor is there payola when a recording star who is not a writer acquires a financial publishing interest in a song which may be suitable for his recording. This is similar to the ownership of music publishing firms by record companies which may be motivated to record songs in their publishing catalog. In fact, some record firms make special incentive payments to artist and repertoire men who obtain publishing rights to material recorded.

Trade Paper Payola

Temptations of payola have also been evidenced with respect to trade paper hit charts. A prominent trade paper research director reported that he personally turned down a bribe of $3,000 to put a song on the charts, and that he had to discharge two employees of his department who received valuable gifts from record manufacturers. Erstwhile *Billboard* publisher Hal B. Cook has advocated an independent audit of industry rating systems, stating: "If charts are unduly influenced by economic considerations, a false market condition is created."

Practices of Payola

The 1960 report of the congressional subcommittee investigating payola reported:

> The subcommittee held 19 days of hearings on "payola" and related unfair and deceptive practices. . . . Fifty-seven witnesses were heard; they included disc jockeys and other programming personnel, network and licensee executive personnel, phonograph record manufacturers and distributors, independent data processors, trade paper representatives, songwriters and publishers, and members of the subcommittee staff. Testimony appears to indicate that the selection of much of the music heard on the air may have been influenced by payments of money, gifts, etc., to programming personnel. In some instances, these payments were rationalized as licensing fees and consultation fees.

The practices of payola revealed by the testimony were varied. Automobiles were purchased for disc jockeys. Television sets were given as gifts. Weekly or monthly checks were remitted. Stipulated payments based on the number of records sold in an area were made. "Cut-ins" on publishing rights were arranged. The ways were many but the motivation was the same.

After its extensive study of payola in the broadcasting of music, the congressional committee successfully introduced amendments to the law in 1960, making payola a federal criminal offense. In recommending the amendments, the committee offered numerous examples of situations that would be affected by the amendments now in force. These examples, as they involve the music industry, are helpful guides. Committee examples 1, 2, 3, 4, 10, and 20 follow:

> Example 1: A record distributor furnishes copies of records to a broadcast station or disc jockey for broadcast purposes. No announcement is required unless the supplier furnished more copies of a particular recording than are needed for broadcast purposes. Thus, should the record supplier furnish 50 or 100 copies of the same release, with an agreement by the station, express or implied, that the record will be used on a broadcast, an announcement would be required because consideration beyond the matter used on the broadcast was received.

Example 2: An announcement would be required for the same reason if the payment to the station or disc jockey were in the form of cash or other property, including stock.

Example 3: Several distributors supply a new station, or a station which has changed its program format (e.g., from "rock and roll" to "popular" music), with a substantial number of different releases. No announcement is required under Section 317 where the records are furnished for broadcast purposes only; nor should the public interest require an announcement in these circumstances. The station would have received the same material over a period of time had it previously been on the air or followed this program format.

Example 4: Records are furnished to a station or disc jockey in consideration for the special plugging of the record supplier or performing talent beyond an identification reasonably related to the use of the record on the program. If the disc jockey were to state, "This is my favorite new record, and sure to become a hit; so don't overlook it," and it is understood that some such statement will be made in return for the record and this is not the type of statement which would have been made absent such an understanding and the supplying of the record free of charge, an announcement would be required, since it does not appear that in those circumstances the identification is reasonably related to the use of the record on that program. On the other hand, if a disc jockey, in playing a record, states: "Listen to this latest release of performer 'X,' a new singing sensation," and such matter is customarily interpolated into a disc jockey's program format and would be included whether or not the particular record had been purchased by the station or furnished to it free of charge, it would appear that the identification by the disc jockey is reasonably related to the use of the record on that particular program and there would be no announcement required.

Example 10: Free books or theater tickets are furnished to a book or drama critic of a station. The books or plays are reviewed on the air. No announcement is required. On the other hand, if 40 tickets are given to the station with the understanding, express or implied, that the play would be reviewed on the air, an announcement would be required because there has been a payment beyond the furnishing of a property or service for use on or in connection with a broadcast.

Example 20: A well-known performer appears as a guest artist on a program at union scale because the performer likes the show, although the performer normally commands a much higher fee. No announcement is required.

Federal Trade Commission

Payola also concerns the Federal Trade Commission, which is charged with regulation of competition in supplying of goods in interstate commerce, under Section 5 of the Federal Trade Commission Act. Under that section, unfair or deceptive acts or practices as well as unfair competition are declared unlawful. The Commission construed payola as a violation of this section and investigated numerous record manufacturers and distributors. As a result many such companies entered into consent decrees under which they agree to cease and desist from payola practices. Violations of the decree will usually subject the companies to penalties, in contrast to the warnings likely to be meted out to companies not parties to a decree.

Bureau of Internal Revenue

Another blow to the practice of payola was given by the Bureau of Internal Revenue, which, having been apprised of facts indicating possible understatement of taxable income of disc jockeys and other persons, initiated its own investigation. Firms making payola payments were not allowed to deduct such bribery expenses from their income, and they also became subject to audit by the tax authorities.

14

Trade Practice Regulation

The Federal Trade Commission administers statutes designed to foster and promote the maintenance of fair competitive conditions in interstate commerce in the interest of protecting industry, trade, and the public. Pursuant to the jurisdiction granted it, the Commission has intervened to bar the practice of giving "payola" to broadcasting station personnel in order to achieve a preferred position in the exposure of records and musical compositions over the air to the public. This abuse is considered at greater length in the preceding chapter, "Payola."

But the problem of "payola" is only one of the many abuses that have been called to the attention of the Commission. A substantial number of complaints relate to discrimination among purchasers with respect to prices, services, and facilities. Other complaints deal with misrepresentation and deception by various members of the industry engaged in the manufacture, distribution, and sale of recordings.

The Commission has adopted a procedure developed for the purpose of clarifying and defining practices deemed violative of the statutes administered by the Commission and for the purpose of voluntary compliance by the industry members with the laws. This procedure comprises trade practice hearings at which all members of the industry and other interested parties are afforded an opportunity to present views, information, and suggestions regarding the establishment of rules to furnish guidance in the requirements of the applicable laws. Following consideration of comments and suggestions, the Commission promulgates trade practice rules for the industry.

In 1964, the Commission scheduled a trade practice hearing for the phonograph record industry in Washington, D.C., and all of the important segments of the industry were represented and participated. In connection with the hearing, a set of proposed rules, consisting of industry proposals which the Commission staff felt should be considered, were made available, and written comment was invited to be submitted prior to the hearing. The proposed rules were also the subject of the hearing.

On October 9, 1964, the Commission promulgated Trade Practice Rules for the phonograph record industry. The rules became operative on November 9, 1964, but were rescinded on December 3, 1979. However, the rules, as promulgated, are still helpful in indicating practices that violate the statutes administered by the Federal Trade Commission. Reference will now be made to certain of the rules.

Discriminatory Price Differential Practices

Rule 1, which was declaratory of the statutes, prohibited discriminatory price differential practices where the effect may be substantially to lessen competition or to tend to create a monopoly or to injure, destroy or prevent competition with a competitor or its customers. The rule bars both secret and open direct and indirect rebates, refunds, discounts, credits, or other forms of price differential to purchasers of goods of like grade and quality.

Various examples are presented under the rule. It would be a violation if freight were paid on shipments to one customer and not to others, if a higher price were charged one customer than another, if some customers and not others were permitted to take discounts above the usual discounts, if one customer and not others were allowed a discount based on a percentage of total purchases in a given period, and if "free" records were supplied to some and not to all customers. It was stated that the rule was not intended to prohibit differentials which make only due allowance for differences in the cost of manufacture, sale, or delivery resulting from differing methods or quantities in which products are sold or delivered. It was further indicated the rule should not be construed to bar the granting of different prices to customers in different functional categories. For example, a seller could grant a lower price to wholesalers than to retailers, to the extent that such wholesalers resell to retailers. On the other hand, if the wholesalers also sell at retail in competition with their customers, the prices charged to the wholesalers should not be lower, on that portion of the goods they sell at retail, than the prices charged to competing retailers.

While there appears to be no contention about the right to fix different prices for customers in varying functional categories, there can be factual disputes regarding whether a purchaser qualifies for the classification of "distributor," "rack jobber," "one-stop" or "retailer." Although there is little argument about the functions of a distributor, which is the first link in the chain of distribution headed by manufacturers, some distributors simultaneously operate as rack jobbers on the side and service locations that undersell their regular dealer customers. There are distributors who own one-stops. The rack jobber, as commonly understood, services supermarkets, variety stores, drug stores, and other busy retail outlets, whereas the one-stop stocks the records of many manufacturers so that jukebox operators and small dealers can purchase their requirements at one location instead of having to contact a number of distributors.

A number of retailers who are affected adversely by the rack jobbers have contended that a rack jobber should be classified as a retailer and therefore not entitled to a lower price than that charged to retailers. The rack jobber argues that he operates as a subdistributor in furnishing racks and record stocks to retailers who actually own the operation; some rack jobbers have even claimed the status and privileges of a distributor. Retailers in competition with the rack locations assert that in reality the entire risk and control are vested in the rack jobber and that he should therefore be regarded as a retailer. These contentions appear to present a factual problem underlying proper functional classification upon which differing prices depend.

Advertising, Promotional Allowances, or Facilities

The rules required proportional equality of treatment of competing customers with respect to the supplying of advertising or promotional allowances, marketing services, or facilities. Where the allowance, service, or facility offered to certain customers is not suitable to others, an equivalent, alternative allowance, service, or facility should be afforded the latter.

It was stated that there would be a violation if racks, browsers, bins, displays, special packaging, and other similar services and facilities were supplied to certain customers but not made known and available on proportionally equal terms to all competing customers. A similar conclusion would apply to preferential treatment in cooperative advertising allowances, to the furnishing of free merchandise with the proviso that it be used for advertising or that the proceeds of its sale be used for advertising purposes, or to the granting of allowances for advertising based on a fixed percentage of a customer's purchases.

Price Fixing and Other Practices

Under the rules, a planned common course of action to fix or maintain prices was forbidden. Also prohibited were tie-in sales which involved the coerced purchase of one product through its being made a prerequisite to the purchase of other products. Under another rule, members of the industry could not sell products or fix prices on condition that the purchaser not deal in the products of competitors.

Deceptive Practices

A number of rules were addressed to misleading and deceptive practices. The misuse of "stereo" and "stereophonic" was attacked by a prohibition against referring thereby to a record which does not have two distinctly separate modulations derived from an original live recording in which a minimum of two separate channels was employed; however, the words may be used with a monaural recording having two separate modulations provided there is clear disclosure that the recording was originally monaural and was altered to simulate stereophonic reproduction.

The rules also represented a thrust against deception regarding performing artists, misrepresentation of the contents of recordings, and deception involving reissues, new titles, and date or origination.

Use of the terms, "close-outs," "discontinued lines," "special bargains," and similar phrases was barred by a rule which applied when the terms are false or lead the public to believe wrongly that products are being offered at bargain prices.

Deceptive pricing was the subject of another rule.

It should be cautioned that the rules were rescinded in late 1979 and that they have been referred to solely for the purpose of discussing practices that violate the statutes administered by the Federal Trade Commission.

Sound-Alike Recordings

With the crackdown on record piracy referred to in Chapter 12, there seems to have been a concomitant growth in what have been called sound-alike recordings. These are recordings of hit songs by artists other than the original artist.

For example, suppose there is a recording entitled "The Sounds of Elton John" with a picture of the artist on the cover. However, the contents may be simply the hit songs made famous by Elton John, but performed by another artist. This practice has proved misleading to the public, which would expect the recording to contain the voice of the original artist.

In a case involving one distributor of sound-alike recordings, Magnetic Video Corp., the Federal Trade Commission accused the company of false and misleading practices. The Commission asserted that the company's use of the names and likenesses of the original performers deceived record purchasers who were persuaded that the recordings were made by the original artists.

Under the Federal Trade Commission order, signed by the company, it consented to not employing any likeness of the original performer or any artwork similar to that on the original cover or tape label, in the packaging or advertising of the company's records. Furthermore, the company was required to use in bold letters the following disclaimer: "This is not an original artist recording" on the package, label, and advertising of the sound-alike recordings. Under the order the name of the actual artist on the recording must be disclosed.

Part 2
MUSIC PUBLISHERS AND WRITERS

15

The Nature of Copyright in the United States

The Copyright Office offers the following description of the meaning of copyright:

> "Copyright" literally means the right to copy. The term has come to mean that body of exclusive rights granted by statute to authors for protection of their writings. It includes the exclusive right to make and publish copies of the copyrighted work, to make other versions of the work, and, with certain limitations, to make recordings of the work and to perform the work in public.

The concept of copyright as an intangible property right is best understood by distinguishing it from the physical property. If a purchaser of a set of letters written by a famous person were to claim that he thereby acquired the right to make copies of the letters in printed form, he could be restrained under copyright infringement principles. In the words of the 1976 copyright statute:

> Ownership of a copyright, or of any of the exclusive rights under a copyright, is distinct from ownership of any material object in which the work is embodied. Transfer of ownership of any material object, including the copy or phonorecord in which the work is first fixed, does not of itself convey any rights in the copyrighted work embodied in the object. . . .

The right to copyright is founded on authorship and exists separate and apart from the physical expression.

Copyright protects the expression of ideas, not the ideas themselves. The films *Jaws* and *Shark's Treasure* are based on the idea of shark terror; the films *Rosemary's Baby* and *The Exorcist* are both based upon the idea of satanism. Similarly, the musical compositions "The Twist," "Twist and Shout," and "Let's Twist," all relate to the dance craze of the 1960s. Similar examples in the 1970s occur with the Hustle and Reggae. None is a copyright infringement of another since each constitutes an original expression of the idea.

The United States Copyright Act of 1790 followed Constitutional authorization: "To promote the Progress of Science and useful Arts, by securing for limited Times to Authors and Inventors, the exclusive

Right to their respective Writings and Discoveries." The Act of 1790 was restricted to protection against copying of certain printed material. The now valuable performance right was granted statutory sanction in 1889. The right of mechanical reproduction presently applicable to phonograph records was added in 1909, when piano rolls were prominent. It was not until 1972 that the copyright statute was extended to cover the duplication of phonograph renditions. As discussed hereinafter, retransmission on cable TV and performances on jukeboxes and public broadcasting were made subject to copyright licensing by the 1976 Copyright Act. The establishment of a Copyright Royalty Tribunal was first enacted in that statute.

The 1976 Copyright Act, with a generally effective date of January 1, 1978, appears in Part 4 as Appendix A. A list of current regulations of the Copyright Office promulgated under the 1976 Copyright Act is contained in Part 4 as Appendix B. Selected extracts from such current regulations of the Copyright Office are included in Part 4 as Appendix C.

History of Copyright Law Revision
Until the 1976 Copyright Act, in which the 1909 copyright statute was generally revised and brought up to date, the music business, along with other copyright owners, adjusted to, and sometimes suffered under, the earlier statute. A Supreme Court opinion of then Justice Fortas (later quoted with approval by Chief Justice Burger) described this antiquated law as one calling "not for the judgment of Solomon but for the dexterity of Houdini." In just such dextrous fashion did the law through court innovation try to cope with technological changes not dreamed of by the 1909 legislators, such as television, cable television, transcriptions, synchronization with film, offset printing, Xerox reprography, and long-playing records.

It was in 1955 that the Copyright Office, with congressional authorization, initiated studies preparatory to a general revision of the 1909 Copyright Act. Under the program, 34 definitive and valuable studies were completed and printed for general circulation to the public at large as well as to a panel of consultants. The studies covered the multitude of problems to be reviewed in the drafting of a new statute; they included the essence of comments from the panel and from interested persons. These comments were considered by the Copyright Office in preparing and circulating for review drafts preliminary to, and the 1964 initial congressional bills for, the general revision of the copyright statute. There followed numerous bills and many years of controversial hearings and industry compromises before the final enactment of a revision statute in 1976. Progress was slowed by the opposition of interested groups to particular provisions, including those relating to cable television and jukebox performance fees, and performers' rights in sound recordings. Cable television and performers' rights were especially controversial.

During the long period of legislative review, it was decided to give interim protection to some works which would otherwise have gone irretrievably into the public domain and have now been preserved for further extended protection. By a series of joint resolutions passed by Congress, emergency interim extensions were provided for those copyrights that would otherwise have fallen into the public domain on or after September 20, 1962. Among the well-known songs so reprieved are "St. Louis Blues," "By the Beautiful Sea," "Missouri Waltz," and "There's a Long Long Trail."

As noted previously, with certain exceptions, the effective date of the copyright revision statute enacted in 1976 is January 1, 1978. In substance, all copyright matters then existing or thereafter arising are subject to and governed by the revised law. For further discussion, see the section on "Transitional Provisions" at the close of this chapter.

Single Federal System

Under the system prior to the 1976 Act, works were subject to a dual system of protection before they were published. They could have been either registered for unpublished copyright under the Copyright Act of 1909, as amended (assuming their eligibility under the standards of the act), or, if not registered, they were subject to perpetual protection under state common law. After publication, only the 1909 Copyright Act, as amended, applied.

The 1976 copyright revision statute has replaced the dual system for unpublished works by a single system of federal statutory protection for all works covered by the bill, published or unpublished. The single system governs whether the work was created before or after the effective date of the copyright revision act. An exception until February 15, 2047, applies as to sound recordings first issued prior to February 15, 1972, which is discussed in Chapter 3, "Copyright in Sound Recordings."

Thus, under the 1976 statute, the large body of unpublished musical works, which is "fixed" by recordings or writings, comes automatically under the federal system. Special provisions as to duration of previously fixed but unpublished and unregistered works are discussed hereinafter.

Common Law Copyright

Protection of copyright under the provisions of the copyright statute is provided for any song or recording once fixed in any tangible medium of expression. However, there is a parallel system of copyright called common law copyright which protects works that are not so fixed and therefore do not qualify for statutory copyright, such as a musical composition improvised or developed from memory without being recorded or written down. Common law protection is available not under federal law but under individual state law.[1]

Protection under common law springs into being without any formality, registration, or notice. It offers an author, composer, or artist complete protection against the unauthorized commercialization of his work as long as it is not fixed in a tangible form sufficiently permanent or stable to permit it to be perceived, heard, or otherwise communicated for a period of more than transitory duration. Even a widely viewed "live" television or radio presentation of a song can be protected under common law if it is not recorded simultaneously with its transmission.

Common law protection is generally perpetual. It is not limited to any number of years, and is thus dissimilar to statutory protection.

Prior to the January 1, 1978, effective date of the 1976 copyright revision law, common law protection would cover works not "published." Except as to sound recordings first fixed before February 15, 1972 (for which preemption is delayed until February 15, 2047), the revision law has preempted any state common law or statutory protection for any of such works fixed in tangible form. It has legislated, with exceptions noted below, the same duration of protection for previously existing common law works as is granted for new works created on or after January 1, 1978. The period of protection is generally the life of the author plus 50 years, with anonymous works, pseudonymous works, and works made for hire being protected for 75 years from the year of first publication or 100 years from the year of creation, whichever expires first. But in no event is the period of protection to be less than 25 years, regardless of when the work originated. Thus there would be a minimum of 25 years of protection even if the author died 100 years ago. The statute provides an incentive toward publication in granting a further 25 years of minimum protection if the work is published before the end of the first 25 year period, that is, on or before December 21, 2002; in that event the copyright will expire on December 31, 2027.

Statutory Copyright

As discussed above, under the 1976 Copyright Act there is copyright in musical compositions, which have been "fixed" in some visible or recorded form, only under the federal copyright law, except with regard to sound recordings first fixed before February 15, 1972. The federal statutory copyright applies to both unpublished and published works.

The statute defines "Publication" as "the distribution of copies of phonorecords of a work to the public by sale or other transfer or ownership, or by rental, lease or lending." It goes on to provide that the

[1]Protection under any applicable state common law or statute is specifically preserved until February 15, 2047, for sound recordings first fixed before February 15, 1972.

offer "to distribute copies or phonorecords to a group of persons for purposes of further distribution, public performance, or public display, constitutes publication." Public performance is not a publication, regardless of the size of audience. The 1976 Copyright Act requires in respect of published compositions that all publicly distributed copies bear a notice of copyright which is discussed hereinafter.

Under the 1909 Copyright Act the sale of recordings was not considered a "publication" of a composition, which would have classified it as a published work for purpose of copyright registration. This has been changed under the 1976 Act. While the 1976 law requires that a notice of copyright be placed on "publicly distributed copies" of the work, a phonorecord is not deemed such a copy. Accordingly, notice of copyright in the underlying music, as distinct from notice of copyright in the recording itself, is not necessary on a record.

Registration for copyright is discussed hereinafter.

Copyright Formalities—Introduction

Registration in the Copyright Office of the United States of a claim to copyright is a relatively simple procedure. It is not a condition of copyright protection in a published or unpublished work. It rather makes a public record of statutory copyright already existing. It does not bar someone from contesting the registrants' claim.

There is no specific timetable under the 1976 Act for when a registration must be made. Registration may be obtained at any time during the copyright protection period by the owner of copyright or of any exclusive right in a published or unpublished work. It is the view of the Copyright Office that under the 1976 Act the basic registration by the owner of an exclusive right in a work secures the statutory benefits of registration to all authors and other owners of rights in the work.[2] However, except for a minor instance, under the 1976 Copyright Act no action or proceeding may be maintained for infringement until there has been registration and the deposit of copies of the work required in connection with the registration.[3] The action for infringement can proceed promptly thereafter, even in respect of past infringement, except that the remedies of statutory damages or of attorney's fees are not available for (1) infringements of copyrights in unpublished works prior to registration or (2) infringements between first publication and the effective date of registration unless registration is made within three months after first publication.[4]

The 1976 Copyright Act provides that in a judicial proceeding a registration certificate for a "registration made before or within five years after first publication of the work shall constitute prima facie

---

[2] Under the 1909 Act only the copyright owner could register a work for copyright protection.
[3] This was also true under the 1909 Act.
[4] The 1909 Act did not restrict the remedies available after registration and the deposit of copies.

evidence of the validity of the copyright and of the facts stated in the certificate." For subsequent registrations, the evidentiary weight of a registration certificate is within the court's discretion. Therefore the statutory presumption is not available to late registrants who wait more than five years from the initial publication of their song. The five year registration deadline for the statutory presumption is not applicable to unpublished songs.

It appears prudent under the 1976 statute for a copyright owner to register and deposit promptly both published and unpublished works and thereby place the public on notice of his claims to copyright. As indicated above, the absence of registration impedes the right to sue promptly for infringement, the remedies of statutory damages and attorney's fees, and the evidentiary presumption as to copyright validity and the facts in the certificate. There is a further benefit in registration in that a claimant who desires to replace lost or mislaid certificates or deposits can apply for copies. Unpublished manuscripts or facsimile reproductions are kept for the entire period of copyright protection. Published manuscripts are retained for the longest period deemed practicable and desirable by the Register of Copyrights and the Library of Congress. Under their most recent determination published deposits will not be retained for more than five years from the date of deposit except that works of the visual arts (pictorial, graphic or sculptural works) will be kept for ten or more years. However, the depositor or the copyright owner may request retention of deposited material for a period of 75 years, pursuant to regulations, including fees, to be prescribed by the Register of Copyrights. In a 1983 Interim Regulation the fee for such retention of each copyright deposit has been fixed at $135.

There is a practice of certain songwriters to attempt to avoid registration of unpublished songs by mailing a copy of their manuscripts to themselves by registered mail, and then leaving the sealed envelopes unopened. They believe that the date on the envelope and the contents of the envelope, when shown in a court proceeding, will conclusively demonstrate the priority of their authorship in suits against third parties for infringement. While there may be some merit to their position, the procedure is obviously inferior to the protection and advantages, including an evidentiary presumption, to be achieved by a copyright registration. The copyright registration is likely to be immeasurably better than a self-addressed sealed envelope in proving that the work deposited with the registration was in existence on the date of the application and was not fraudulently concocted or modified, just prior to the initiation of an infringement action, so as to be similar to the defendant's song.

Very few rejections by the Copyright Office of applications for registration occur. According to the Copyright Office, it has a policy of liberal acceptance of claims to copyright. It has stated: "We will register material which we feel a court *might* reasonably hold to be copyright-able, even though personally we feel that it is not subject to copyright." Thus an attempt to register an original version of a public domain item such as Scott Joplin's "Entertainer," which a claimant may have unearthed in an attic, might be rejected summarily if recognized as a public domain composition. But a brief melodic variation of a segment of the same work might be registered as an arrangement of a public domain work even if some doubt existed as to the substantiality of the new material.

Copyright Formalities—Items Involved

For many years the United States was in a unique position in insisting upon copyright formalities as a condition to the preservation or asser-tion of legal rights in copyrights. Such formalities are:

(1) Copyright notice
(2) Copyright registration
(3) Deposit of copyrighted works with the appropriate govern-ment agency.

Other countries, such as those which were members of the Berne Convention, the then-leading international treaty concerning copyright, refused to conform to such copyright formalities for protection under their appropriate copyright laws, and the United States refused to waive such formalities as to foreign works. However, under the Universal Copyright Convention which became effective in 1955 and to which the United States and many other countries adhere, the American concept of copyright notice as a requisite formality was accepted. This is more generally discussed under Chapter 32, "International Copyright Protec-tion." The specific formalities as they exist under the United States Copyright Act are separately discussed hereinafter under the following headings: "Registration of Published Works," "Registration of Unpub-lished Works," "Copyright Notice," and "Deposit of Copyrighted Works."

Registration of Published Works

Copyright registration of an unpublished work is not a prerequisite to registering the work when published, although frequently an unpub-lished copyright registration will have been obtained. If a work has been registered in unpublished form it is unnecessary to make another registration when published, although the copyright owner may register the published edition, if desired.

Although the 1976 Copyright Act requires that copies be deposited in the Copyright Office within three months of publication, there is no loss of copyright merely for failure to file an application for the copy-right registration of a published work.

To register under the 1976 Act the copyright claim in a published work, the following should be sent to the Copyright Office:

(1) Two copies of the best edition of the work, except one copy (as first published) for a work first published outside the United States. If published only in phonorecords, send two complete phonorecords of the best edition. In the case of a contribution to a collective work, send one complete copy of the best edition of the collective work.

(2) A completed application on the form supplied by the Copyright Office.[5]

(3) A registration fee of $10.00 by check, money order, or bank draft made payable to the Register of Copyrights.[6] Currency is sent at the remitter's risk.

For a definition of "best edition" see the section on "Deposit of Copyrighted Works" in this chapter.

The Copyright Office makes available, under the 1976 Act, without charge, the following copyright application forms which are used in the music business:

(1) Form PA (for *works in the performing arts*): This encompasses published or unpublished musical works, including any accompanying works; dramatic works, including any accompanying music; and motion pictures and other audio-visual works. It supersedes 1909 Act Forms D, E, E-Foreign, and L-M. It does not cover sound recordings.

(2) Form SR (for *sound recordings*): This includes published or unpublished sound recordings and supersedes 1909 Act Form N. Only Form SR need be filed if the copyright claimant for both the musical or dramatic work and the sound recording are the same and the claimant is seeking a single registration to cover both of these works.

(3) Form TX (for *nondramatic literary works*): Except for dramatic works and certain kinds of audiovisual works the Form includes all types of published and unpublished works written in words (or other verbal or numerical symbols). It supplants the 1909 Act Form A, which includes books manufactured in the United States. The form comprehends lyric books as well as poems that may be used as lyrics.

(4) Form VA (for *works of the visual arts*): This embraces published and unpublished "pictorial, graphic, or sculptural works," including: two-dimensional and three-dimen-

---

[5]Under the 1909 Act the form for musical composition was known as Form E and the form for sound recordings as Form N.

[6]The fee under the 1909 Act was $6.

sional works of fine, graphic, and applied art; photographs, prints and art reproductions; and maps, globes, charts, technical drawings, diagrams, and models. It covers pictorial or graphic labels and advertisements, as well as works of "artistic craftsmanship."

(5) Form RE (for *renewal registrations*): It supersedes the 1909 Act Form R.

In addition to the above basic application forms under the 1976 Act, there is an additional form which is used in the music business. This is:

(6) Form CA (for *supplementary registration*): It is utilized to apply for a supplementary registration under Section 408(d) of the 1976 Act, in order to correct an error in a copyright registration or to amplify the information given in a registration.

Each form contains simple instructions for its completion and filing. Copies of Copyright Office Forms PA, SR, TX, VA, RE and CA are included in Part 4 as Appendix F. No form has been promulgated for the recording of assignments and transfers of copyrights in the Copyright Office. The parties to such assignments or transfers merely file the written instruments.

Applications for registration under the 1976 Act generally require information similar to that which was called for in applications for registration under the 1909 Act. There is, however, new information to be supplied pursuant to Section 409 of the 1976 Act. This includes the date of any author's death, a statement of whether the work was made for hire, a statement of how the claimant obtained ownership of the copyright if the claimant is not the author, previous or alternative titles under which the work can be identified, and the year in which creation of the work was completed. There is also a requirement that pre-existing works, on which a compilation or derivative work is based, or which are incorporated in the work, shall be identified in an application to register a compilation or derivative work. This information must go along with a description of the new additional material which was also requested under the 1909 Act forms.

Forms of applications, prescribed by the Register of Copyrights, may further require any other information regarded by the Register as having a bearing on the preparation, identification, existence, ownership, or duration of the copyright. While the statute does not call for information on an author's date of birth, this is an item to be supplied in the application forms; the Register of Copyrights states that an answer is optional but it is useful as a form of identification.

Most applications for copyright registration of musical compositions will be made on Form PA, which is designated as an "Application for Copyright Registration for a Work of the Performing Arts." The Copyright Office has stated that a:

Work of the Performing Arts includes works prepared for the purpose of being "performed" directly before an audience or indirectly "by means of any device or process." Examples of works of the performing arts are: (1) musical works, including any accompanying words; (2) dramatic works, including any accompanying music; (3) pantomines and choreographic works; and (4) motion pictures and other audiovisual works.

Following registration under the 1909 Act the Copyright Office issued a certificate with an EP copyright number. There is a new numbering system for 1976 Act registrations. For example, when registration is on Form PA, the certificate for a published work has a PA copyright number.

Registration of Unpublished Works

To register a claim for copyright registration of an unpublished work, the following should be sent to the Copyright Office:

(1) One complete copy or phonorecord of the work, whichever best represents the work. Since manuscripts or phonorecords are not returned the applicant should retain a duplicate.
(2) An application properly completed on the form supplied by the Copyright Office. Reference should be made to the preceding discussion under "Registration of Published Works" for the appropriate form to be used.[7]
(3) A registration fee of $10.00 by check, money order, or bank draft made payable to the Register of Copyrights.[8] Currency is sent at the remitter's risk.

Following registration under the 1909 Act the Copyright Office issued a certificate with an Eu copyright number. There is a new numbering system for 1976 Act registrations. Thus when registration is on Form PA the certificate for an unpublished work has a PAU copyright number. Upon registration of an unpublished or published work, the Copyright Office prepares a copyright card for its files to add to the millions of similar cards recording registration since 1870. Applicable information will also be published in the Catalog of Copyright Entries which is issued in microfiche form by the Copyright Office.

Copyright Notice

A record company about to sponsor the recording of a song, or a motion picture producer planning to use a song in a film, will easily find whom

---

[7]Under the 1909 Act the form for musical compositions was known as Form E. There was no form for unpublished sound recordings under the 1909 Act since recordings were registrable only if published.

[8]Under the 1909 Act, the fee was $6.

to deal with for the requisite permission or license in the copyright notice on published copies of the song. This notice shows the year date of original publication and the name of the proprietor of the copyright.

A composer or publisher whose claim to copyright has been rejected may find that the problem is caused by the failure to use or to present properly or locate properly the copyright notice in a prior publication. The copyright notice requirements are relatively simple to follow and yet can have most dire consequences for the unwary. One argument for retaining provisions for copyright notice in the 1976 revised law, in a form largely similar to the requirement which has existed since 1802, is that the burden should be on the copyright claimant to notify the public at large of his claim in the most clear and unambiguous fashion.

Publication of a work must be accompanied by a notice of copyright on each copy published in the United States or elsewhere.[9] Otherwise, unless the omission is excused under the 1976 Copyright Act, the work will be deemed dedicated to the public and all claims to copyright will have been permanently abandoned.[10]

There are statutory requirements as to the notice of copyright. According to paragraph 401 of the 1976 Copyright Act, the notice shall consist either of the word "Copyright," the abbreviation, "Copr.," or the symbol ©, accompanied by the name of the copyright owner or an abbreviation by which the name can be recognized, or a generally known alternative designation of the owner. In the case of printed, literary, musical, or dramatic works, the notice must also include the year of initial publication. A copyright notice usually looks like this: "© 1985 John Doe" or "Copyright 1985 by John Doe."[11] The copyright notice for phonorecords utilizes a ℗ instead of the © and is discussed separately under Chapter 3, "Copyright in Sound Recordings."

For certain categories of works, the 1909 copyright statute prescribed where the notice should appear. As to musical works, the notice had to be placed either upon the title page or the first page of music.

Under the 1976 Copyright Act, the notice is to be placed on "copies in such manner and location as to give reasonable notice of the claim of copyright." It is also provided that the Register of Copyrights may prescribe by regulation, as examples, specific notice positions to satisfy this requirement, although these specifications are not "exhaustive" of what may be otherwise "reasonable" notices. See Appendix C3 in Part 4 for a regulation of the Copyright Office on methods of affixation and positioning of copyright notices.

---

[9]Under the 1909 Act there was the requirement of a notice on each copy published or offered for sale in the United States.

[10]The 1909 Act, as amended, in Section 21 made provision that omissions under certain circumstances would not invalidate the copyright.

[11]Notices in this form also satisfied the requirements of the 1909 Act.

To achieve international protection under the Universal Copyright Convention, which is adhered to by many of the leading countries of the world, including the United States, each copy of a published work should bear the symbol © accompanied by the name of the copyright proprietor and the year of first publication, placed in such manner and location as to give reasonable notice of claim of copyright. Other formalities, such as registration and deposit of copies, are waived, except that each country can require formalities pertaining to its own nationals and to works first published there. Since the 1976 copyright law revision, the United States standard for the placement of notice is the same as under the Universal Copyright Convention.

Deposit of Copyright Works

Under the 1976 Copyright Act, within three months from publication in the United States with notice of copyright, the copyright owner or the owner of the exclusive right of publication must deposit in the Copyright Office, for the use or disposition of the Library of Congress, two copies of the best edition of the work. This is irrespective of whether there is an application for copyright registration. If the work is a sound recording there must be deposited two complete phonorecords of the best edition, together with any printed or visually perceptible material published with said phonorecords; the deposit includes the entire container or package as well as the disc or tape inserted therein.

The best edition of a work is that published in the United States before the date of deposit that the Library of Congress deems most suitable for its purpose. The Register of Copyrights may by regulation exempt such deposit or require deposit of only one copy. Literary, dramatic and musical compositions published only in the form of phonorecords are exempt from deposit. For a regulation of the Copyright Office on deposits for the Library of Congress and for copyright registration, see Part 4, Appendix C4. For a statement by the Library of Congress on what it considers to be the best edition of published copyrighted works, see Appendix C5 in Part 4.

At any time after publication the Register of Copyrights may in writing demand the required deposit. For failure to comply within three months there is a liability (a) to a fine of not more than $250 for each work, (b) to pay the Library of Congress the total retail price of the copies or phonorecords demanded and (c) for an additional fine of $2,500 for willful or repeated failure or refusal to comply.

The deposit is not a condition of copyright protection.

The deposit of copies of copyrighted works serves two purposes: to identify the copyrighted work in connection with copyright registration, and to provide copies for the use of the Library of Congress. The deposit of copies for the first purpose has been an integral part of the United States copyright system from its beginning in 1790. Since the administration of the registry system was placed in the Library of Congress in 1870, a single deposit has served both purposes.

Deposit as record evidence of the copyrighted work must be viewed with some caution. While unpublished manuscripts or facsimile reproductions are kept on file for the life of the copyright, the Register of Copyrights and the Librarian of Congress may determine in their discretion to dispose of published works after their retention for the longest period deemed practicable and desirable. At this point such period for most works has been fixed at five years from the date of deposit. As noted previously a procedure has been established under the 1976 Copyright Act for a request to be made for retention of deposited material for the full term of copyright.

In 1939, music deposits received prior to 1928 and to the extent then retained were transferred to the Library's Music Division, where they are preserved and are available for consultation. Since then, additional musical compositions deemed appropriate for such preservation have regularly been so transferred.

Assignments or Mortgages of Copyright

Under the 1976 Copyright Act, there may be a "transfer of copyright ownership" in a copyright or any of the exclusive rights comprised in a copyright. The transfer may be by means of a conveyance or by operation of law. The copyright or exclusive rights may also be transferred by will or by intestate succession. A transfer of ownership includes an assignment, mortgage, exclusive license, or any other conveyance or hypothecation, whether or not limited in time or place. It does not include a nonexclusive license.

A transfer of ownership, other than by operation of law, must be in writing and signed by the owner of the rights conveyed or his authorized agent. If the transfer is acknowledged before a notary public or other person authorized to administer oaths in the United States, the certificate or acknowledgment becomes prima facie evidence of the execution of the transfer.

Transfer of copyright ownership may be recorded in the Copyright Office. For a document of six pages or less, covering only one title, the fee is $10. For each page over six and for each additional title there is a further fee of 50 cents. Upon recordation the Register of Copyrights returns the document together with a certificate of recordation.

Following recordation under the 1976 Act, all persons are on constructive notice of the facts in the document recorded. This is on condition that the work has been registered for copyright and that the material recorded specifically identifies the work involved so that a reasonable search under the title or registration number of the work would reveal the document. Recordation is encouraged by a provision that the transferee cannot commence an infringement action until recordation. After recordation the suit may cover past infringements.

In the event of conflicting transfers, the prior one will prevail if it is recorded so as to give constructive notice within (1) one month after execution in the United States, or (2) within two months after execution abroad,[12] or (3) at any time before recordation of the later transfer. Absent such recordation the later transfer prevails if recorded first in the manner required to give constructive notice, provided that the later transfer is made in good faith for a valuable consideration, or on the basis of an agreement to pay royalties, without notice of the prior transfer.

Nonexclusive licenses in writing signed by the owner of the rights licensed or his agent will be valid against later transfers. Such licenses will also prevail against a prior unrecorded transfer if taken in good faith and without notice of the transfer.

A transfer will always be valid as between the transferee and the transferor, with or without recordation, since both parties are on notice of their own acts.

Regardless of the transfer, the copyright notice may continue to contain the name of the prior owner. The new owner may substitute his name in the copyright notice. This change of name in the notice of copyright need not be preceded by recording the transfer in the Copyright Office.[13] However, as noted previously, the new owner will be unable to initiate an infringement action prior to such recordation.

If the real owner's name is not substituted in the notice of copyright, an innocent infringer who has been misled by the notice and has taken a transfer from or license by the person named in the notice has a complete defense to an infringement action. But the defense is unavailable in the event the work has been registered in the name of the real owner of copyright or a recorded document executed by the person named in the notice shows the true ownership of the copyright.

A copy of a short form assignment of copyright is included in Part 4 as Form 7.

Copyright Notice Omissions or Errors

Under the 1909 Copyright Law the omission of a copyright notice would generally invalidate the copyright.

The 1976 Act, on the other hand, does not treat the omission of a notice as automatically forfeiting copyright protection and throwing the work into the public domain. If notice is omitted from "no more than a relatively small number of copies" or phonorecords distributed publicly the copyright is not invalidated. Even the omission from more than a relatively small number of copies does not affect the copyright's validity

---

[12]Under the 1909 Act comparable periods were three months after execution in the United States or within six months after execution abroad.

[13]Under the 1909 Act, failure to record an assignment before substituting the assignee's name in the copyright notice might invalidate the copyright.

where registration of the work has already been made or is made within five years after the publication without notice, and there are reasonable efforts exerted to add the notice to copies or records publicly distributed in the United States after discovery of the omission. Similarly, there is continued copyright protection if the omission violated a written requirement by the copyright owner that authorized copies or records were to bear a prescribed notice.

Before the 1976 Act, a postdated copyright notice or a notice without a name or without a date would ordinarily constitute a fatal defect in the copyright. Under the 1976 Act, the omission of a name or a date in the notice or postdating a notice more than one year from the date of first publication is treated as if the work had been published without any notice.

Although copyright may be preserved despite an error which is considered as amounting to publication without notice, an innocent infringer who proves he was misled by the error incurs no liability for actual or statutory damages for infringing acts committed prior to actual notice of registration of the work. A Court in its discretion may permit or disallow recovery of the infringer's profits. Thus in the case of relatively minor infringements by teachers, librarians, journalists and the like, completed before actual notice of registration, the liability, if any, would be restricted to the innocent infringer's profits. Should the infringement continue, the copyright owner may seek an injunction against any new acts of infringement, and the Court may grant the injunction or may permit future uses on condition that the copyright owner be paid a reasonable license fee in a sum and on terms fixed by the Court.

Persons who plan a long-range business which proposes to use works published without a notice of copyright should follow the cautious approach of having the Copyright Office registration records checked before beginning. Under the 1976 Copyright Act the omission of a notice does not necessarily mean that the copyright is no longer protected.

While under prior law an error in the name of the copyright owner in the copyright notice might be a fatal defect, the 1976 Act states that such an error does not affect the validity or ownership of the copyright. In such a case an innocent infringer who relies on a license or transfer from the person erroneously named in the copyright notice has a complete defense to an action for infringement unless a Copyright Office search would show a registration in the name of another person or a document executed by the person named in the notice indicating ownership by another person.

Correction of Errors

Under the 1976 statute the Register of Copyrights may establish by regulations procedures whereby an earlier copyright registration may be corrected or amplified by a supplementary registration, but not superseded. Thus, if a registration has been made with an incorrect name of the owner or an inaccurate date of publication, the error can be indicated in an application for a supplementary registration which identifies the earlier registration and is accompanied by a $10 registration fee, the same amount required for the prior registration. The Copyright Office has promulgated Form CA for such supplementary registrations.[14]

Titles of works are not subjects of copyright but merely a means of identification of a work. A change of title does not require a new copyright registration. It is the practice of the Copyright Office, upon receiving a request in writing, to prepare without charge a cross-reference card under the new title, to appear in the general card indexes. If a permanent official record is desired, a formal signed statement, outlining the pertinent facts, can be submitted for recordation in the same manner as an assignment of copyright, with the same fee as for recording an assignment.

Fair Use

It is surprising to note how frequently songwriters and others in the music business think that as a general rule and regardless of circumstances copying four bars or less of music is permissible despite copyright protection. This error may stem from a misinterpretation of the doctrine of "fair use" which recognizes the right of the public to make a reasonable use of copyrighted material in special instances without the copyright owner's consent. A clear example of fair use is the practice of a book reviewer to quote lines from the book reviewed to illustrate his critical appraisal. Similarly, musicologists and other researchers may use reasonable extracts of copyrighted works in preparing a new scholarly text or commentary.

Fair use has been applied for many years as a judicial exception to the exclusive rights of a copyright owner to print, publish, copy, and vend a copyrighted work. Under the 1976 Act, the doctrine of fair use has been included in the copyright statute itself. The provisions of the fair use section of the statute are generally consistent with what had been the treatment under judge-made law prior to the statute.

It may be difficult to determine in advance what will be held to be a fair use. The language of the statute is illustrative rather than absolute. It recognizes that fair use of a copyrighted work may be utilized "for purposes such as criticism, comment, news reporting, teaching (includ-

---

[14]See Part 4, Appendix F, for Form CA. Under Copyright Office regulations promulgated prior to the 1976 Act, a statement could be submitted indicating an omission or other error and supplying the correct facts and it was within the discretion of the Register of Copyrights to determine whether an annotation should be placed on the original registration to indicate that there exists elsewhere in the Copyright Office information referring to the corrected facts. In exceptional cases corrections might be made by filing a new application for copyright registration.

ing multiple copies for classroom use), scholarship, or research. . . ." It states that the factors to be considered in determining whether a use is fair use include "(1) the purpose and character of the use including whether such use is of a commercial nature or is for nonprofit educational purposes; (2) the nature of the copyrighted work; (3) the amount and substantiality of the portion used in relation to the copyrighted work as a whole; and (4) the effect of the use upon the potential market for or value of the copyrighted work."

To help clarify fair use of music for educational purposes, a text of guidelines was prepared by representatives of the Music Publishers' Association of the United States, Inc., the National Music Publishers' Association Inc., the Music Teachers National Association, the Music Educators National Conference, the National Association of Schools of Music, and the Ad Hoc Committee on Copyright Law Revision. These guidelines were invited by the House Committee of the Judiciary, were included in the 1976 report of the Committee on the proposed bill for the general revision of the copyright law, and were accepted by House and Senate conferees on the 1976 Copyright Act as part of their understanding of fair use for educational uses of music. The guidelines set forth the extent of permissible copying of music for educational purposes, with a caveat that the conditions might change in the future so that the guidelines may have to be restricted or enlarged. Also the guidelines are not intended to limit the types of copying which are permissible under fair use as defined in the 1976 Act.

In substance, the guidelines permit emergency copying for a performance, making a single copy of a sound recording of copyrighted music for aural exercises or examinations, editing or simplification of printed copies, and making multiple copies (not more than one per pupil) of partial excerpts not comprising a performable unit and not exceeding 10 percent of a whole work. There is a general prohibition, except as specifically exempted, against copying for performances, copying of workbooks, exercises, and tests, and copying to substitute for the purchase of music. A copy of the text of the guidelines is included in Part 4 as Appendix A1.

In a 1972 decision of a Court faced with the defense of fair use by Catholic priests who had presented their revised version of "Jesus Christ, Superstar," the Court made a ruling consistent with the 1976 statutory statement of fair use. It held that the defendants' production could not qualify as "literary and religious criticism of the plaintiffs' work." It stated that the defendants' presentation: "(1) is obviously a substitute for plaintiffs' work; (2) copies almost all of the plaintiffs' lyrics, score, and sequence of songs; (3) undoubtedly has and will injure plaintiffs financially; (4) is definitely in competition with plaintiffs' performances; and (5) does not serve or advance the greater public interest in the development of news, art, science or industry."

There is an application of fair use where song lyrics have been employed as background for the historical setting of a nonfiction magazine article.

A Court has held that the reproduction of "some more or less disconnected 'snatches' or quotations from the words of . . . [a] song" was fair use. On the other hand, another Court decided that the use in a commercial of a short extract of the basic melody of a work was not fair use. All factors in respect of fair use must be considered, and the *quality* of the use—not only the *quantity* used—is important.

Parody and burlesque of a copyrighted work are dependent on fair use and require caution. *Mad Magazine* was upheld by a Federal Circuit Court of Appeals in its defense of parodies, such as "The Last Time I Saw Maris" based on "The Last Time I Saw Paris," on the ground of fair use for humorous critical purposes. The court's decision pointed out that the copying did not exceed the amount required to recall reasonably and evoke in the reader the original version being parodied; public policy was stressed in favor of parody.

But Jack Benny was stopped from a parody of "Gaslight." The Court found that his extensive use in burlesque form would diminish the commercial value of the original version. The same Court permitted Sid Caesar to make a parody use without authorization of "From Here To Eternity" where the parody made more limited use of the original.

A controversial area of copyright law is the audio or video taping of a copyrighted work as broadcast by radio or television. In general, it constitutes copyright infringement to tape a copyrighted work off the air for commercial purposes. However, off-the-air video taping in the home for private use has been held by the U.S. Supreme Court, in the so-called Sony Betamax case, to be permissible as fair use.[15] The practice involved was largely time-shifting—the taping of a program for delayed viewing at home.

Litigation has not as yet settled the propriety of home audio recording of a broadcast or phonorecord for private use. However, in connection with the passage of the act in 1971 creating a limited copyright in sound recordings, the then House Judiciary Committee commented that "it is not the intention of the Committee to restrain the home recording, from broadcasts or from tapes or records, of recorded performances where the home recording is for private use and with no purpose of reproducing or otherwise capitalizing commercially on it."

The music industry has for many years contained "answer songs," which have been common in the country and western, and rhythm and blues fields—areas that are now part of the pop music business. An original song might have been entitled, for example, "We Always Walk in the Rain." If this should achieve success, another writer might shortly thereafter pen a song called "We Never Walk in the Rain," as a humorous reply to an aftermath of the former song. The facts must be

---

[15]Sony Corporation of America v Universal City Studios, Inc. (1984).

weighed carefully to decide whether the answer song has gone beyond the bounds of fair use. Should the answer song be written by the writer or writers of the original song, as is often the case, it would ordinarily be with the consent of the original publisher and a problem of fair use would not arise.

In cases involving fair use, where there is doubt regarding its applicability, it appears prudent to apply for a license from a copyright proprietor. The existence of the fair use exception tends to strengthen the bargaining position of the applicant for the license.

Titles

Copyright protection does not extend to titles of songs or other copyrighted materials insofar as they are titles. Indirectly, copyright may become involved if the words in the title are an important segment of the song lyric. However, while court decisions have tended to cloud the matter, titles which achieve a secondary meaning in the minds of the public by becoming associated with a particular work have traditionally been safeguarded by the doctrine of unfair competition. This doctrine will be invoked by the courts to prevent deception or defrauding of the public by the passing off of a product as if it were the product of the plaintiff.

Phonograph albums frequently use an individual song title as the major featured title for the album itself. Use of the titles of popular songs helps to set the mood of the album, identifies the type of music contained, and attracts album buyers. No extra payment to the music publisher over usual mechanical royalties is customary. It is common for the publisher to insist upon the full statutory mechanical rates when the title of his song is so used, even though the songs in the remainder of the album are licensed at lower rates customary for budget line albums.

Property rights in titles can be extremely valuable. Motion picture producers regularly pay large sums for the use of titles such as "Ode to Billy Joe," or "Alexander's Ragtime Band."

Not all titles are sufficiently unique for the assertion of legal rights against a motion picture use of the title. For example, Walt Disney issued a movie using the title "The Love Bug" without a license from the publisher of the musical composition, "The Love Bug Will Bite You (If You Don't Watch Out)." Disney was able to show that the film involved a "Volkswagen automobile with human attributes," and was not based upon or related to the musical composition of the plaintiff. The Court found that the "Love Bug" phrase was "oft used" and that the plaintiff had failed to establish the requisite secondary meaning and likelihood of confusion to support relief.

Compulsory License for Phonorecords

Under the 1976 Copyright Act, when phonorecords of a nondramatic musical composition have been distributed to the public with the authorization of the copyright owner, any other person may record and distribute phonorecords of the work upon giving certain notice and paying a royalty. Commencing on July 1, 1984 the royalty is 4½ cents for each record made and distributed or 0.85 cent per minute or fraction thereof, whichever is larger. On January 1, 1986 the rates are scheduled to increase to 5 cents and 0.95 cent, respectively. A record is deemed to be distributed if possession has been "voluntarily and permanently parted with." These provisions are commonly referred to as the "compulsory license" or "compulsory mechanical license," and, although provisions have varied in the past, there has been a statutory compulsory license since 1909.[16]

The Register of Copyrights has characterized the compulsory license provisions as being severe on the copyright owner:

> Once he exploits his right to record his music he is deprived of control over further recordings. He cannot control their quality nor can he select the persons who will make them. There have been many complaints of inferior recordings and of recordings by financially irresponsible persons.

The Register indicated that a further disadvantage, which may be even more important, is that the "statute places a ceiling . . . per record on the royalty he can obtain." While author and publisher groups have argued vehemently against the continuation of the compulsory license, record industry representatives have contended strongly and successfully for the retention of the compulsory license.

The compulsory license for phonorecords, under the 1976 Copyright Act, allows the making of an "arrangement of the work to the extent necessary to conform it to the style or manner of interpretation of the performance." Even a "sound-alike" recording, with an arrangement similar to that in a prior recording, is permitted. However, a compulsory licensee must avoid changing the basic melody or fundamental character of the work.[17] There can be no claim made to an arrangement as a derivative copyright, unless consented to by the copyright owner.

Compulsory mechanical licenses under the 1976 Copyright Act apply solely to phonorecords primarily intended to be distributed to the public for private use. They are unavailable for purposes of background music services, broadcast transcriptions or commercial motion picture synchronization. A compulsory license may not be obtained as to a musical work to be used in the duplication of a sound recording made by another, unless consent is acquired from the owner of the original sound recording,[18] which itself was fixed lawfully. This acts as a restriction on the pirating of recordings.

---

[16]The royalty under the 1909 Act was 2 cents for each record manufactured.
[17]These provisions as to arrangements do not differ from prior applicable law.
[18]This is in accord with prior judicial holdings.

Anyone who proposes to invoke the benefit of compulsory mechanical-licensing provisions must serve a "notice of intention" to obtain a compulsory license. This is similar to the "notice of intention to use" under the prior law. Pursuant to Section 115 of the 1976 Act the notice must be sent to the copyright owner before any records are distributed, with service to take place before or within 30 days of making the record. If the records of the Copyright Office fail to identify the copyright owner and his address, then the notice requirements can be met by sending the notice to the Copyright Office together with a $6 fee.

Notice of Use by Copyright Owner

Under the 1909 Act a copyright owner was required to file a "notice of use" in the Copyright Office if he used the composition himself for a mechanical reproduction or licensed others to do so. His failure to file such a notice was a complete defense to any suit, action, or proceeding for any infringement of the recording or mechanical reproduction rights, prior to the filing of a notice, although infringements subsequent to the filing were not subject to the defense.

The 1976 Copyright Act eliminates any formal "notice of use" requirements to be fulfilled by the copyright proprietor. It provides that "To be entitled to receive royalties under a compulsory license, the copyright owner must be identified in the registration or other public records of the Copyright Office." The copyright owner cannot recover for records made and distributed before he is so identified, although he can recover for records made and distributed after such identification.

To protect the right to recover mechanical-license fees under the 1976 Act, it is prudent for a copyright owner to register his copyright before records are made and distributed.

It is customary for reliance to be placed on negotiating a mechanical license from the copyright owner instead of following the procedure for a compulsory license. A negotiated license will ordinarily permit quarterly accountings and payments, instead of the monthly ones under oath called for by the 1909 and 1976 statutes, and will probably dispense with the requirement under the 1976 Act for cumulative annual statements certified by a Certified Public Accountant.

For a further discussion of compulsory mechanical-license provisions see Chapter 20, "Mechanical Rights."

The compulsory mechanical-license fee is subject to review by the Copyright Royalty Tribunal established under the 1976 Copyright Act. Reviews are scheduled for 1987, and in each subsequent tenth year. At the reviews the Tribunal may adjust the fee.

Record Rentals

Under a recent federal statute, effective as to copies of sound recordings acquired on or after October 4, 1984, there can be no commercial rental, lease or lending by the owners of the copies unless authorized by the copyright proprietors of the recordings and of the underlying musical works. A record company desiring to sanction such activities can negotiate a license from the music copyright proprietor or may obtain a compulsory license of the musical works in accordance with the established system applicable to the making and distribution of recordings. However for rentals, leasing and lending, a compulsory license requires the payment of a royalty to the music copyright owner over and above that payable for the sale of records. The compulsory licensee must share its rental, lease or lending revenues with the music copyright owner in the proportion that revenues from the sale of recordings are allocated between the copyright proprietors of the sound recording and the underlying music. For a further discussion, see Chapter 20, "Mechanical Rights."

The Jukebox Public Performance Fee

Under the Copyright Act of 1909, owners of jukeboxes were generally exempted from the payment of public performance fees to copyright proprietors of music. The only direct benefits to copyright owners from jukebox use were mechanical-license fees paid by record manufacturers who sold records to the jukebox industry. The exemption was termed a "historical anomaly" by the Register of Copyrights during studies preliminary to copyright revision. Finally, after heated conflicts during legislative hearings, a compromise resulted whereby the 1976 Copyright Act repealed the exemption of jukeboxes from public performance fees.

Under the current Act, a jukebox owner may obtain a compulsory public performance license as to nondramatic musical works by filing an application in the Copyright Office and by paying to the Register of Copyrights a yearly fee per box. The jukebox license fee which was originally set in the 1976 Copyright Act at $8 per box is subject to periodic reviews by the Copyright Royalty Tribunal, of which the first review under the statute was carried out in 1980; later reviews are to be held in each subsequent tenth year. At these reviews the Tribunal may change the fee. Pursuant to the Tribunals' review the license fee was increased to $25 in 1982 and later to $50 on January 1, 1984. Provision has been made by the Copyright Royalty Tribunal for a cost of living adjustment in the $50 fee commencing August 1, 1986 if so indicated by the Consumer Price Index.

Of the sums collected, the Register, after deducting reasonable administrative costs, deposits the balance in the United States Treasury for later distribution by the Copyright Royalty Tribunal to copyright owners, or to their designated agents. In January of each year persons claiming a share in the payments for the previous year by jukebox owners are required to file a claim with the Copyright Royalty Tribunal in accordance with regulations prescribed by the Tribunal. Distribution is made by the Tribunal after the first of October of each year unless there is a controversy among the claimants. Controversies are determined by the Copyright Royalty Tribunal. Under the statute, the act of filing a claim constitutes an agreement by the claimants to be bound by decisions of the Copyright Royalty Tribunal. While a controversy is being considered, the Tribunal has the discretion to distribute amounts not being disputed.

The formula for the distribution of royalty fees to claimants calls for the payment of a pro-rata share of the fees to copyright owners not affiliated with a performing right society, and the balance to the performing right societies in their pro-rata shares as determined by their mutual agreement; or, in the absence of such agreement, their pro-rata shares as shown by their claims.

Jukeboxes are not to be confused with background music or disco establishment equipment, which does not qualify for the jukebox compulsory license. To be a jukebox, or in the words of the statute "a coin-operated phonorecord player," the following criteria must be met under the statute: it performs nondramatic musical works and is activated by insertion of a coin; it is located in an establishment making no direct or indirect admission charge; and it affords a choice of works by patrons from a readily available list of titles.

Cable Television

The technical nature of television broadcasting limits the geographic area covered by the initial transmission. Unless there is a network extension of a broadcast area or syndicated usage of videotaped programs by many stations, the normal audience of an originating television broadcast is necessarily confined. Nevertheless by use of sophisticated "Community Antenna Television" facilities (CATV), signals from distant metropolitan stations are brought to more rural environs. The audience of originating television broadcasters is thereby extended beyond the area anticipated by copyright owners that licensed the broadcaster.

Cable television systems may be described as commercial subscription services which pick up television broadcasts of programs initiated by others and cause them to be retransmitted to paying subscribers. In a typical system there is a central antenna for the receipt and amplification of television signals plus a network of cables by which the signals are transmitted to the receivers of subscribers. In some cases CATV systems initiate their own programming.

In ruling upon claims by copyright owners against CATV facilities, commencing in 1968, the Supreme Court of the United States held that cable television systems were not liable to copyright owners for the retransmission of copyrighted material. According to the court, the cable systems were not active "performers" but merely retransmitters of already licensed material. They were only extensions of the passive viewers whom they serviced.

The 1976 Copyright Act, in substance, changed preexisting law and requires that cable television systems obtain a license from copyright owners for the retransmission of distant nonnetwork programming. Provision is made whereby a cable television system can receive a compulsory license upon compliance with various formalities, including the recording of certain information with the Copyright Office. Accountings must be rendered semiannually to the Register of Copyrights, showing the number of channels used, the stations carried, the total number of subscribers, and the gross receipts from providing secondary transmission of primary broadcast transmitters.

Royalty rates to be paid by the cable systems semiannually are set forth in Section 111 of the 1976 Act, and are computed on the basis of specified percentages of the gross receipts from providing secondary transmissions of primary nonnetwork broadcasts. For such purpose there are not included receipts from subscribers for other services such as pay-cable or installation charges. Separate lower fee schedules are provided for smaller cable systems.

After deducting administrative costs, the Register will deposit the balance in the Treasury of the United States. Subsequently there is a distribution by the Copyright Royalty Tribunal, after deduction of its reasonable administrative costs, among the copyright owners entitled, or to their designated agents, once a year. Controversies among claimants are determined by the Tribunal.

Cable television royalties are subject to periodic review by the Copyright Royalty Tribunal on the basis of standards and conditions set forth in the 1976 Act. The first basic review was made in 1980 and there may be further reviews in each subsequent fifth calendar year. The Tribunal has the authority to revise the royalty rates.

Noncommercial Broadcasting

The 1976 Act grants to noncommercial public broadcasting a compulsory license with respect to the use of published nondramatic literary and musical works and also published pictorial, graphic, and sculptural works. The grant is subject to the payment of reasonable royalty fees to be established by the Copyright Royalty Tribunal. In effect, as to music, public broadcasters are thereby enabled to synchronize nondramatic musical works with their programs and to perform the programs. The rights do not include the unauthorized dramatization of a nondramatic musical work or the unauthorized use of any portion of an audiovisual work.

The Act seeks to encourage voluntary private agreements between copyright owners and public broadcasters. Voluntary agreements between such parties, negotiated before, during, or after determination of terms and rates by the Tribunal, supersede, as between the parties, such terms and rates. Additional proceedings for review by the Tribunal of rates and terms may occur in 1987 and in each ensuing fifth year.

Copyright Royalty Tribunal

The 1976 Copyright Act created a new concept in United States law. It established a special review board called a Copyright Royalty Tribunal, with powers to set and distribute royalties in certain compulsory rate situations. The concept has some similarity to the Performing Right Tribunal which has existed in the United Kingdom for similar purposes since 1956.

It was a function of the Copyright Royalty Tribunal to establish initially reasonable terms and rates as to compulsory license fees to be paid for performances by public noncommercial broadcasters. In accordance with statutory scheduling the Tribunal will make adjustments in those terms and rates and in the specific fees enunciated in the 1976 Copyright Act for compulsory licenses for jukeboxes, cable television, and the mechanical reproduction of records. The Tribunal distributes compulsory license fees to be deposited with the Register of Copyrights with respect to jukeboxes and cable television, and determines, in cases of controversy, the division of such fees. As to jukebox license fees, the 1976 Act provides that making a claim constitutes an agreement by the claimant to abide by the Tribunal's decision in a controversy regarding the distribution of jukebox fees.

Members of the five-person Tribunal are appointed by the President of the United States with Senate confirmation, for staggered terms of seven years each. The Tribunal chairperson is chosen by the members. Any rate changes by the Tribunal of mechanical royalties or jukebox, public broadcasting, or cable television fees would be subject to a judicial review in the United States Court of Appeals.

Under the 1976 Copyright Act the Tribunal was scheduled to review rates for mechanical reproduction in 1980, 1987 and thereafter at ten-year intervals. Fees to be paid for performance by jukeboxes were to be reappraised in 1980 and in each subsequent tenth year. Cable television compulsory license rates were required to be reviewed in 1980 and in each ensuing fifth year. As to rates and terms with regard to compulsory licenses for public noncommercial broadcasters, the reviews were scheduled for 1982 and in each subsequent fifth year.

Transitional Provisions

The effective date of the 1976 Copyright Act, with certain exceptions, is January 1, 1978. How does that date affect relationships which began under the 1909 Act?

The new Act does not restore to copyright status works which went into the public domain before January 1, 1978.

If before that date a person was manufacturing records or tapes under the compulsory mechanical-license provisions of Section 1(e) of the 1909 Act, he can continue under that license without obtaining a new compulsory license under the 1976 Act. However, he must comply with the provisions of the 1976 Act relating to royalties and accountings.

In the event a cause of action or a legal breach arose under the 1909 Act before January 1, 1978, the same continue to be governed by the 1909 Act rather than the new Act.

In the case of works published before January 1, 1978, notices of copyright need not be changed, because of the enactment of the new Act, on copies publicly distributed on or after that date.

16

Duration of Copyright and Limitation of Grants

In authorizing exclusive rights under copyright law, the United States Constitution provides that such exclusive rights are to be of limited duration. After the limited period of copyright expires, the works become a part of the public domain and "free as the air," as more generally discussed in Chapter 23, "Uses and New Versions of Public Domain Music."

The extent and duration of the limited period of protection is a matter of statutory definition, which has varied throughout the history of copyright in the United States.

In the Copyright Act of 1909 there was the concept of an original term of copyright of 28 years, and a renewal term whereunder the copyright was renewable by certain persons for another 28 years. The technicalities surrounding the renewal term have produced a difficult maze which has been the subject of confusion and numerous lawsuits. The United States Supreme Court, speaking through Justice Frankfurter, stated that the basic purpose of the renewal period was to enable "the author to sell his 'copyright' without losing his renewal interest," and that "if the author's copyright extended over a single, longer term, his sale of the 'copyright' would terminate his entire interest."

The 1976 Act retains the copyright renewal concept as to certain existing works in their original term of copyright, while providing for a 19-year extended term beyond the aggregate 56-year period of protection under the prior copyright statute. As to the extended period, however, a right of termination is provided in favor of the author or his heirs. This is more fully discussed under "Limitations of Old Transfers and Licenses" hereinafter in this chapter.

For post-1977 works, the 1976 Act institutes a period of protection which is usually the life of the author plus 50 years. There is no longer a renewal period of copyright applicable to such works, although provision is made in essence for the right to terminate copyright transfers and licenses after their 35th year. This right of termination is considered at greater length under "Limitation of New Transfers and Licenses" later in this chapter.

Duration of Term Computations

There are different categories under the 1976 Act with respect to the duration of copyright protection. These are essentially the following:

(1) New works created after 1977.
(2) Pre-1978 works in their original term of copyright.
(3) Pre-1978 works in their renewal term of copyright.
(4) Pre-1978 works not previously published or copyrighted.

New Works

For works created on or after January 1, 1978, the duration of copyright protection is the life of the author plus 50 years. Where there is a joint work the 50 years are measured from the death of the last surviving co-author.

However, as to anonymous or pseudonymous works where the identity of the author remains unrevealed, or in the case of works made by an employee-for-hire, the duration is 75 years from the year of first publication, or 100 years from creation, whichever expires first. If the author of an anonymous or pseudonymous work is later officially identified in the records of the Copyright Office, the copyright endures for the life of the identified author plus 50 years.

If records maintained by the Copyright Office as to dates of death of authors do not disclose a date of death of an identifiable author, then after a period of 75 years from first publication or 100 years from creation, whichever is earlier, it is presumed that the author has been dead at least 50 years. Reliance on this presumption in good faith is a complete defense to an infringement action.

Existing Works in Original Term of Copyright

For works in their original term of copyright on January 1, 1978, the 1976 Act makes provision for the term to continue for 28 years as under the prior copyright statute. It also preserves a renewal term of copyright but extends the same by 19 years, from the 28-year period under the previous act to a renewal and extension term of 47 years. As under the 1909 Act, there is an obligation to file an application for renewal and extension within one year prior to the expiration of the original term of copyright, failing which the copyright expires at the end of the initial 28-year term. As more fully discussed under "Terminal Date" hereinafter in this chapter, the initial 28-year term, under the 1976 Act, will end at the close of the calendar year in which it would otherwise terminate. The one-year period, prior to the expiration of the 28-year term, in which to file an application for renewal and extension, will therefore begin at the commencement of the calendar year in which the 28-year term ends.[1]

---

[1]Under the 1909 Act the 28-year term would terminate on the anniversary date on which the copyright was originally secured, and the one-year period for a renewal application would commence 12 months before the anniversary date.

Existing Works in Their Renewal Term

As to copyrights in their renewal term before 1978, or for which a renewal registration is made before 1978, the renewal period is extended so that the copyrights will be protected for 75 years from the date copyright was originally secured. This represents a 19-year extension of the 28-year renewal term under the 1909 Copyright Act. Here, too, it should be noted that under the 1976 Act the 75th year will end at the close of the calendar year in which it would otherwise terminate.

Interim copyright extension statutes had previously extended until December 31, 1976, the renewal term of copyrights such as "Alexander's Ragtime Band" which would otherwise have expired between September 19, 1962 and December 31, 1976. This was in anticipation of general copyright revision legislation being enacted which would further extend their terms. The 1976 Act specifically makes provision for such copyrights to endure for a period of 75 years from the date copyright was originally secured; the expiration date would be December 31, of the 75th year. Thus a work in its sixtieth year on December 31, 1976 would receive extended protection for 15 years, in contrast to the 19 years afforded works not subject to the interim copyright statutes. While the effective date of the 1976 Act is January 1, 1978 for most purposes, the effective date is in reality December 31, 1976 for the extension of the copyright terms of works that benefited by the interim copyright extension acts.

Many copyrighted works which were advantaged by the interim 19-year copyright extension statutes have existed for more than 75 years and have entered the public domain in the United States. Among these are "Anchors Aweigh," "Take Me Out to the Ball Game," "By the Light of the Silvery Moon," and "On the Road to Mandalay."

Pre-1978 Works Not Published or Copyrighted

Prior to the 1976 Act, a work not under statutory copyright or in the public domain was covered by common law copyright under applicable state law. The 1976 Act provides that such works are protected by federal copyright for the same period as new works, in other words, for the life of the author plus 50 years. If the works are anonymous, pseudonymous, or works made for hire, the copyright endures for 75 years from first publication or 100 years from creation, whichever first expires. In all cases, however, such works have a minimum 25-year duration until December 31, 2002, and if published before then the period of minimum duration is 50 years until December 31, 2027.

Terminal Date

All terms of copyright, pursuant to the 1976 Act, are extended to run to the end of the calendar year in which they would otherwise terminate. This may result in a slight prolongation of terms that might otherwise expire in another part of the year. It facilitates the computation of dates such as when renewal applications must be filed or when 100-year and 75-year periods terminate.

For example, for a copyright secured on July 1, 1960, the first 28-year term of copyright would, under the 1909 Act, have ended on June 30, 1988, as contrasted with December 31, 1988, by reason of the 1976 Act. A renewal and extension application would have had to be filed between July 1, 1987 and June 30, 1988 under the 1909 Act, as compared with between January 1, 1988 and December 31, 1988 pursuant to the 1976 Act. The 28-year renewal period would have expired on June 30, 2016 under the earlier act, but the 47-year renewal period by reason of the 1976 Act would continue until December 31, 2035.

For new works under the 1976 Act, such as one fixed on July 1, 1978, the term of copyright protection will ordinarily be the life of the author plus 50 years. If the author dies on February 15, 1980, the 50-year period will expire on December 31, 2030, and not on February 14, 2030.

With respect to 1950 copyrights and later copyrights now in their first term of copyright, it is worthy of special note that the principle of year-end termination of copyright terms has affected the computation of the one-year period in which to file a renewal and extension application. Under the 1909 Act the one-year period would have run from one anniversary date to another, for example, April 30 to April 30. But by reason of the year-end termination of the term of copyrights, the one-year period is a calendar year, that is, January 1 to December 31. In the case of 1950 copyrights the one-year period was prolonged from the anniversary date in 1977 until the end of 1978. For example, if a song were copyrighted on April 30, 1950, its first term under the 1909 Act would expire on April 29, 1978, and the one-year period to file a renewal application would run from April 30, 1977 to April 30, 1978. By reason of the 1976 Act the 28-year first term ended on December 31, 1978, and therefore the period for a renewal application to be filed was between April 30, 1977 and December 31, 1978.

Joint Works

A joint work is defined in the 1976 Copyright Act as one "prepared by two or more authors with the intention that their contributions be merged into inseparable or interdependent parts of a unitary whole."

A song can qualify as a joint work in the case of authors who write words and music together or where one or more authors write words and other authors separately write the music.

For joint works fixed on or after January 1, 1978, the statutory term of protection is 50 years from the death of the last surviving author. This is beneficial to the heirs of the earlier-deceased co-authors.

Copyright Office Records

The computations of copyright terms under the 1976 Act present practical problems with respect to ascertaining the dates of death of obscure or unknown authors. The Register of Copyrights is obligated to maintain current records of author deaths. Any person having a copyright interest may record in the Copyright Office statements of the death or living status of an author, in form and content complying with regulations of the Register of Copyrights.

After a period of 75 years from publication of a work or 100 years from its creation, whichever expires first, any person may obtain a certification from the Copyright Office that its records disclose nothing to indicate the author is living or has been dead less than 50 years. In that case, as indicated heretofore, the person may rely upon a presumption that the author has been dead for over 50 years. Such reliance in good faith is a complete defense to an infringement action.

Copyright Renewal Registrations

As noted previously, the concept of copyright renewal applies to pre-1978 works in their original term of copyright as of January 1, 1978. The procedures for applications for copyright renewal are similar to those prevalent under the Act of 1909. For the regulation promulgated by the Copyright Office on renewal of copyright, pursuant to Section 304(a) of the 1978 Copyright Act, see Appendix C2 in Part 4.

The timing and manner of an application to renew a copyright constitute very technical requirements under copyright law. Even a sophisticate such as the late Howard Hughes may make a fatal error, as happened in the filing of a late claim to copyright renewal of his film "The Outlaw," starring Jane Russell. Many musical compositions fall into the public domain for failure to file an application for renewal in the final year of protection under the original 28-year term; this filing requirement is continued under the 1976 Act.

Separate and additional renewal applications should be filed where a work has both an unpublished and a published copyright registration. Similarly, where there are copyrights on different versions or arrangements, each registration should be renewed at the appropriate time if the new material or arrangement is to continue under copyright. It should be emphasized that the 1909 and 1976 Copyright Acts leave no doubt that, with respect to copyrights originating before January 1, 1978, in default of application for renewal and extension, a copyright terminates after its initial 28 years.

For a renewal application, it is unnecessary to file a copy of the manuscript or printed edition. The following should be sent to the Copyright Office:

(1) A completed renewal application in a form supplied by the Copyright Office, signed by, or on behalf of, the appropriate renewal claimant. The form promulgated by the Copyright Office under the 1976 Act is designated Form RE.[2]

---

[2]For a copy of Form RE, see Part 4, Appendix F. With respect to renewal applications under the 1909 Act, the form supplied by the Copyright Office was known as Form R.

(2) A fee of $6.00 by check, money order, or bank draft made payable to the Register of Copyrights. Currency is forwarded at the remitter's risk.

The 1909 and 1976 Copyright Act specify the same persons who may claim the renewal copyright. The right to renew is ordinarily the author's if he lives until the 28th year of the copyright. If he does not survive, the right is given to designated beneficiaries in a particular order of preference. For certain works, the copyright proprietor is accorded the right of renewal.

If the renewal right was originally the author's, the appropriate renewal claimants are:

(1) The author, if still living.
(2) If the author is dead, the widow, widower, or children of the author.
(3) If there is no surviving widow, widower, or child, the executor named in the author's will.
(4) If there is no surviving widow, widower, or child, and the author left no will, the next of kin of the deceased author.

The application for renewal may be submitted in the name of the appropriate claimant by a person having either an express or implied power of attorney by virtue of a written assignment of the renewal right. Thus, a publisher who has been assigned the renewal right will file the application for renewal in the name of the author if the author is not available.

In the case of certain works which were originally copyrighted by a proprietor, the right to renew is in the proprietor. This includes posthumous works and periodical, cyclopedic or other composite works, or works copyrighted by an employer or corporation that hired someone to create the work.

Where there is a collaborator on a song, the timely filing for renewal by one author will be deemed sufficient to protect the entire copyright for all interested persons. Similarly, when there is a class of appropriate claimants, such as the widow, widower, or children, the filing by a child or the widow or widower will safeguard the copyright for all persons in the class. Caution dictates that reliance should not be placed on the application of one interested person if other applications can also be filed.

The Songwriters Guild, formerly known as The American Guild of Authors and Composers, provides a service for its members under which it watches over copyrights and at the appropriate time files renewal applications.

A renewal copyright is a new and independent right and grant, and not merely a prolongation of the first term. While the courts uphold assignments of the renewal right, the fulfillment of the assignment depends upon the survival of the author into the renewal year. In the event the author does not survive, the assignee's rights are defeated by the beneficiaries designated in the Copyright Act, such as the widow, widower, children, executor, or next of kin.

Limitations of Old Transfers and Licenses

The following is with respect to existing copyrights in their first or renewal terms as of the end of 1977. Exclusive or nonexclusive transfers or licenses of the renewal copyright or of any right under it made prior to 1978, covering the extended renewal period under the 1976 Act, can be terminated at any time during the period of five years beginning at the end of 56 years from the date the copyright was originally secured or from January 1, 1978, whichever is later. Such termination, which applies only to the 19-year extension period under the 1976 Act, can be effected by a written notice served at least two years and not more than ten years in advance of the termination date within the five-year period.

For the purpose of termination of grants, the principle of year-end expiration of terms of copyright, enacted under the 1976 Act, is inapplicable. The measurement of 56 years from the date a copyright was first secured is from the actual date and there is no prolongation to December 31. The five-year period and the two- to ten-year notice periods are also measured without reference to year-end expiration of copyright terms.

For an example of typical computations involved in the termination of a grant, it may be assumed that a copyright in a musical work was secured on April 30, 1944. Its 56th year would be completed on April 29, 2000. Its termination might be made effective in the five-year period from April 30, 2000 to April 30, 2005. Assuming that the author is alive and decides to terminate on April 30, 2000 (the earliest possible date), the advance notice must be served between April 30, 1990 and April 30, 1998.

As noted previously, there are copyrights whose 28-year renewal terms were extended by interim copyright extension statutes in contemplation of the enactment of a copyright revision act. These copyrights are older than 56 years from the date they were first secured and would have otherwise expired after September 19, 1962, and before January 1, 1978. Pursuant to the 1976 Act they were extended for a period no longer than the end of the 75th year from the initiation of their copyright protection, rather than 19 years. Some copyrights have exhausted much of the 19-year period. The five-year period during which a termination could become effective was measured from January 1, 1978, the effective date of the 1976 Act, and ended on December 31, 1982. There was a minimum two-year notice of termination that would have had to be served within the five-year period.

In the case of an author who made the transfer or license, termination notice has to be authorized by the author, if alive, or if dead by his widow and children (or the children of a deceased child) who under the

1976 Copyright Act own more than half of the owner's "termination interest." A widow who survives without any children owns the entire termination interest, as would a child without parents. If a widow has children, her share is 50 percent and her children as a group possess the other 50 percent. Rights of children are exercised by majority rule, on a per stirpes basis; in other words, the children of a dead child succeed to the interest of their parent, which interest is computed as if the parent were alive. Children of a dead child are bound by majority action among themselves in voting the share of their parent. If a widow survives and opposes termination, no action by her children can effect a termination.

Where there are joint authors, there can be a termination of a particular author's share by that author, or if dead by his widow and children who own more than 50 percent of the author's termination interest. There need not be a termination as to the whole work nor does a majority of all the authors have to consent to the termination of a partial interest. It is thus possible to recapture the lyrics of a song alone, or the music alone, or an undivided interest in the whole song.

There sometimes are grants of rights in renewal copyrights made by persons other than an author. A widow or children or others entitled to renewal copyright such as the next of kin may have assigned their interests in renewal copyrights. Under the 1976 Act, a pre-1978 grant by a person or persons other than an author covering the extended renewal period is subject to termination by the surviving person or persons who executed the grant, at any time during the five years after the 56th year from the date the copyright was originally secured.

A termination is effective regardless of any prior agreement to the contrary by any person, whether an author or an heir. The form of such prior agreement is immaterial, including an agreement to make a will or to make a future grant. The termination does not affect derivative works, such as motion pictures, made before termination under authority of a transfer or license. Works made for hire, or bequeathed by will by statutory renewal beneficiaries, are also excluded from any right of termination.

Notices of termination are to comply in form, content and manner of service as prescribed by the Register of Copyrights. A copy must be recorded in the Copyright Office before the effective date of termination, as a condition to its effectiveness. The Register, by regulation, has set forth the requisite contents of a notice of termination, although not prescribing a form. See Appendix C1 in Part 4.

Limitation of New Transfers and Licenses

The right of termination of past grants discussed above involves only pre-1978 works and those persons who would benefit from the 19-year extension of the prior overall 56-year copyright period applicable to pre-1978 works. A right of termination, as described below, also applies to new exclusive or nonexclusive grants of a transfer or license of copyright or of any right under a copyright made by the author, other than by will, on or after January 1, 1978. There is no right of termination as to grants made by the author's successors in interest, for example, members of his family, or as to the author's own bequests. It is immaterial whether the new grant is in respect of old or new works.

The right of termination represents a resolution of the basic question whether there should be any limitation on the term of a new assignment or license of rights by authors in order to protect them against transfers of their rights for an inadequate remuneration. The Copyright Act of 1909, as amended, sought to accomplish this by providing for the renewal copyright to vest in the author or his heirs. It was the conclusion of the Register of Copyrights that this concept should be eliminated "because it has largely failed to accomplish the purpose of protecting authors and their heirs against improvident transfers, and has been the source of much confusion and litigation." The Register recommended that some other provision be made to protect the authors and their successors.

Under the 1976 Act, new grants of a transfer or license executed by the author may be terminated at any time during a period of five years beginning at the end of 35 years from the date of execution of the grant. However, if the grant covers the right of publication of the work (as do most songwriter agreements) the termination may become effective during a period of five years beginning at the end of 35 years from the date of publication or 40 years from the date of execution of the grant, whichever is earlier. Termination is effected by written notice served not less than two or more than ten years before the desired date of termination within the stated five-year period.

Publication under the 1976 Act includes the distribution of copies or phonorecords to the public. (See Chapter 15, "The Nature of Copyright in the United States.") It is likely that an initial song publication in the form of printed editions or recordings will occur close to the date of execution of a songwriter contract. Consequently 35 years from the publication date will ordinarily mark the commencement of the five-year period of termination, rather than 40 years from the date of execution of the agreement. The significance of the publication date makes it imperative that publishers and writers keep careful records of that date.

An example of time computations might be as follows. Assuming the date of execution of the songwriter agreement is April 10, 1980 and the date of publication June 10, 1980, the five-year period of termination would begin on June 10, 2015 (35 years from publication) rather than April 10, 2020 (40 years from execution). For a termination date of, say, June 10, 2015, the notice of termination must be served between June 10, 2005 and June 10, 2013.

For another example, it may be assumed that a songwriter contract with a music publisher, granting the publisher all rights in a song including the right of publication, is executed on April 10, 1980; the song is published on August 23, 1987. Inasmuch as the contract covers the right of publication, the five-year period of termination would commence on April 10, 2020 (40 years from execution) rather than August 23, 2022 (35 years from publication). If the author wishes to effectuate the termination on January 1, 2023, he will have to serve the advance notice of termination between January 1, 2013 and January 1, 2021.

The notice of termination of new grants must be authorized by the surviving author who executed the grant, or, if he had collaborators, by the majority of all collaborators who signed the grant. If the author is dead, or any collaborator is dead, at the time of notice of termination, the rights of such deceased author may be exercised by his widow and children (or the children of a deceased child), who under the 1976 Act would own more than one-half of the deceased author's termination interest.

Thus as to new grants of a transfer or license, as distinguished from old grants of interests in renewal copyrights, the failure or refusal of any coauthor of a joint work who executed the grant to join in a notice of termination may defeat the notice and benefit the then publisher if a majority of the collaborators who signed the grant do not join in the notice.

As with old grants of renewal interests, the right of termination does not apply to works made for hire and to grants made under the author's will, and derivative works, such as motion pictures, prepared before termination under authority of the transfer may continue to be used under the terms of the transfer. The right to terminate a new grant exists regardless of any agreement or contract to the contrary.

A surviving author who has contracted away all his rights in a new grant is in a better position under the 1976 Act than under the 1909 Act. The grant of a renewal copyright interest was enforceable against an author under the 1909 Act if he survived. However, under the 1976 Act a living author can terminate a new grant after the 35th year, irrespective of any agreement to the contrary.

It is true that an author who did not grant away renewal rights under the 1909 Act could recapture at the end of 28 years, instead of at the close of 35 years under the 1976 Act. Also, in the case of a deceased author who predeceased the copyright renewal period, under the 1909 Act rights reverted to his heirs at the end of the initial 28 years regardless of the assignment of renewal rights by the author.

The 1976 Act requires that a notice of termination as to new grants comply in form, content, and manner of notice with regulations of the Register of Copyrights. For a copy of the applicable regulation, see Appendix C1 in Part 4. To be effective, a copy of a notice must be recorded in the Copyright Office before the effective date of termination.

Terminated Old Author Grants—Further Grants

Pre-1978 grants of a transfer or license covering the extended renewal term may consist of those by authors and those by other persons who may be his widow, children, executor, or next of kin.

When old grants by authors are terminated, the rights revert at the effective date of termination to all persons who own the termination interest on the date of service of the notice of termination. This includes owners who did not join in the notice of termination. The reversion is in the same proportions as the ownership of the termination interest.

If, for example, a dead author has left a widow and two living children, the widow will own 50 percent of the reverted interest and each child 25 percent. Where there were also two grandchildren by a deceased third child, the share would be: widow 50 percent, each live child 16²/₃ percent and each grandchild 8¹/₃ percent.

In case rights under a grant by the author have reverted to his widow, children, or both, further grants of a transfer or license are to be made only by the action of those persons who own more than one-half the author's termination interest; their grant binds the owners of the reverted interest. For the purpose of further grants, the deceased holder of a reverted interest is represented by his legal representatives, legatees, or heirs at law.

Terminated Old Nonauthor Grants—Further Grants

As noted previously, old grants of a transfer or license may have been made by persons other than an author. These would be among statutory beneficiaries entitled to claim renewal rights under the 1909 Act on the death of an author before the renewal term of copyright. Such beneficiaries are his or her widow or widower, children, executors, or next of kin. Termination may be made only by the unanimous action of the survivors of those persons who executed the grant. Upon termination, there is reversion to all such survivors, with each co-owner having the independent rights of a tenant in common to dispose of his share or to use or license the musical composition subject to an obligation to account to co-owners.

Terminated New Grants—Further Grants

There is a right to terminate new exclusive or nonexclusive grants of a transfer or license of copyright or any right under copyright made by the author, other than by will, on or after January 1, 1978. New grants made by others are not terminable.

On termination, rights revert, as in the case of old grants by authors, at the effective date to the persons owning the termination interest at the date of service of the notice of termination. Those owners who did not join in the notice of termination are also included. The reversion is in the proportion of the owners' share of the termination interest. An earlier example is also apropos here. If a dead author has as survivors a widow and two living children, the widow will own 50 percent of the reverted rights and each child 25 percent. Should there also be two grandchildren by a deceased third child, the participations would be: widow 50 percent, each living child 16⅔ percent, and each grandchild 8⅓ percent.

Further grants of rights terminated under new grants may be made by the same proportion of owners of a termination interest, that is, more than one-half, that are required to join in a termination notice.

Period for Further Grants

Further grants, or agreements to make a further grant, of rights terminated in old or new grants are valid only if made after the effective date of termination. There is an exception in favor of the grantees, or their successors, whose rights were terminated. An agreement made with them in the interim between service of the notice of termination and the date of termination will be valid. This is of course beneficial to publishers who after receipt of a termination notice may enter into new agreements with the owners of the termination interest, before any other publishers may so do.

Publisher Rights After Termination

Notwithstanding termination, a derivative work made under authority of a grant before termination can continue to be used. In a case involving termination of the song "Who's Sorry Now," the former publisher contended that under the "derivative works exception" it had the right to collect and share in mechanical royalties from the sale of old recordings. The Supreme Court of the United States in a 5 to 4 decision, has upheld this contention on appeal.[1]

Aspects of Termination

In respect of termination, publishers and writers should keep in mind the following aspects of *old grants* of renewal rights made before 1978:

(1) There can be a statutory termination under the 1976 Act of the publisher's rights in respect of only the extended 19-year term. The rights as to the original and renewal terms, a 56-year period in the aggregate under the 1909 Act, remain unchanged.

(2) Since the publisher's rights as to the new 19-year extension can be terminated, its domestic licensing agreements should be expressly subject to such termination.

(3) Termination of old grants by the author of renewal rights can be effected in respect of the 19-year extension by the

[1]Mills Music, Inc. v. Snyder, decided January 8, 1985.

author, if living, or, if deceased, his widow and children (or the children of a deceased child). An old grant made by the executor or next of kin if they owned the renewal right can also be terminated with regard to the 19-year extension.

(4) Termination by widows and children (or the children of a dead child) of old grants of renewal rights by the author, in respect of the 19-year extension, is ineffective unless a majority in the termination interest concur. A widow cannot act without the approval of one or more of the children and vice-versa. If persons other than the author make a grant, for example, widows, children, or other statutory beneficiaries of renewal rights, the termination must be made unanimously by the survivors who executed the grant. If there are several writers, each writer's share is treated separately for termination purposes.

(5) Only the old publisher can enter into a valid new agreement for continuing rights between the date of the termination notice and the effective date of termination; valid agreements with other publishers as to reverting rights can be made only after the effective date of termination.

(6) If there is no termination notice, rights of the old publisher extend for the period in the old grant to the publisher, including the extended 19-year term.

Publishers and writers should be reminded of the following in respect of *new grants* made after 1977:

(1) The publisher's rights can generally be terminated after 35 years from publication or 40 years from execution of the grant, whichever is earlier, and therefore its domestic licensing agreements should be expressly subject to such termination. This is akin to licensing subject to termination under The Songwriters Guild songwriter agreements, which are discussed in Chapter 17, "Songwriter Contracts and Statements."

(2) Termination of new grants can be made only by the widow and children (or the children of a dead child) of a deceased author. If there are no such blood relatives, a termination will be ineffective.

(3) There can be no termination of new grants unless those entitled to a majority of the termination interest are in favor. Thus a widow cannot act without her children and vice-versa. If there are several writers a majority of the collaborators must concur; dead writers are represented by their widows and children (or the children of a dead child).

(4) Only the old publisher can make a new agreement for

> continued rights between the notice of termination and the effective date of termination; agreements with other publishers as to reverting rights can be made only after the effective date of termination.
>
> (5) In the absence of a termination notice, the new grant continues to be effective and the old publisher will keep its rights.

As noted previously, a termination does not affect the right to use derivative works, such as motion pictures, made before termination under authority of a new or old grant of a transfer or license.

Foreign Duration

The United States law as to the duration of copyright does not govern the period of protection in foreign countries. Although copyright in works may have expired in the United States, the works may still be protected in other countries. The term of protection in most foreign countries is the same as that in the 1976 Copyright Act, life of the author plus 50 years. This standard has existed for many years in the foreign countries which have adopted it. Some countries have a shorter term of copyright and others a longer term but the international norm is life plus 50 years. The term of protection for the works of an American author in a foreign country will not exceed that afforded under the domestic copyright law of that country.

Reference should be made to the law of a particular foreign country as to the protection given to American works. As more fully discussed in Chapter 32, "International Copyright Protection," American publishers and authors may rely for international protection on the Berne Convention or the Universal Copyright Convention or on special laws and treaties. The United States is not a member of the Berne Convention but it has been an adherent to the Universal Copyright Convention (UCC) since September 16, 1955. The Universal Copyright Convention does not protect works of an American author published in the United States before that date.

The UCC provides for a so-called *elective* rule of the shorter term. Thereunder a work first published in the United States or an unpublished work of an American national will be protected in a foreign country for the shorter of (a) a period equal to the U.S.A. copyright term or (b) the copyright term in the foreign country. While this rule has considerable following, with the notable exception of the United Kingdom, it is unlikely to have a significant effect on recent works. This is because the standard of life plus 50 years in the 1976 Copyright Act is also the international norm. As to older works, the extension of the U.S.A. copyright renewal period by the 1976 Act from 28 years to 47 years, making a total 75-year period of copyright protection, narrows the difference between that period and the life plus 50-year criterion.

Moreover, many older American works have qualified for protection in Berne Union countries under the so-called "back-door" approach by first or simultaneous publication in Canada, England, or another Berne county. Berne members apply the minimum life plus 50-year Berne standard.

The net result is that most American works qualify for protection abroad through the UCC, the Berne Convention, or both. Even those works not technically entitled to benefits of either Convention may be advantaged by administrative inertia abroad and be treated as if so protected.

17

Songwriter Contracts and Statements

An article in *Billboard* once remarked that the music business was similar to the meat-packing business in that it used everything on the animal but the squeal. (Some music critics might even include the squeal in today's market.) Yet there are songwriters who sign royalty agreements which make specific provision for writer participation in printed piano copies, mechanical royalties, and film synchronization receipts but fail to provide for writer participation in many other commercial uses, such as commercial jingles, lyric folios, future jukebox collections, and income from important foreign rights. Many writers have found a solution to this problem by providing that they must share equally in all receipts from unspecified sources. Other writers, notably show writers, put the burden on the publisher to specify sources of income in which the publisher shall have any participation.

Unfortunately, many a novice writer fears he will be jeopardizing the publisher's willingness to exploit the writer's song, and for this reason he signs whatever agreement is placed before him. Unlike the typical book publisher's contract, or the show music contract, all copyright rights covering popular music are customarily assigned to the publishers, and if the writer is not protected within the confines of the contract he has little chance to be safeguarded by custom in the industry.

It is essential that both parties to a songwriter contract be fully aware that the relations thereby undertaken between a writer and a publisher are likely to last a long time. Prior to passage of the 1976 Copyright Act, most songwriter contracts granted rights to the publisher for the then original term of United States copyright, 28 years, and in many instances for the 28-year renewal period of United States copyright; for foreign areas the grant would often be for the full duration of copyright protection in such territories. The 1976 statute, as to compositions first fixed after January 1, 1978, eliminates the concept of an original term and a renewal period, as such. Under the 1976 Act, copyright protection is generally for the life of the author plus 50 years, but an author who assigns his rights can nevertheless generally terminate the assignment at the end of 35 years. For a further discussion see Chapter 16, "Duration of Copyright and Limitation of Grants." This tends to establish a 35-year period as the minimum duration of the term of a publisher's rights, as compared to the 28-year term under the 1909

Act. In any event, whether 28 years or 35 years, or longer, the extensive length of the relationship between a composer and publisher emphasizes the importance of a carefully drawn publishing agreement.

The Songwriters Guild-AGAC

There is an organization of songwriters whose name was recently changed from the American Guild of Authors and Composers (AGAC) to The Songwriters Guild. The organization was formed as the Songwriter's Protective Association in 1931 and has a present membership of close to 4,000 writers. For convenience the organization will be referred to by the initials of its predecessor name, AGAC. The organization recommends to its members that they use a standard form of writer contract promulgated by AGAC. The contract was originally issued in 1948, revised slightly in 1969, and amended substantially in 1978 in the light of the 1976 Copyright Act. Under the 1969 AGAC form of contract, the grant of worldwide rights to the publisher was for the original period of United States copyright under the 1909 Act, that is, 28 years or for 28 years from publication, whichever was shorter. However, under that form, the right to recapture foreign copyrights, other than in Canada, would be forfeited, if the writer did not give to the original publisher written notice, at least six months in advance, of the writer's intention to sell or assign to a third party his rights in the United States renewal copyright or any of his rights in the United States or elsewhere for the period beyond the original grant. The 1978 AGAC form of contract increases the 28-year period to a worldwide maximum of 40 years from the date of the agreement or 35 years from the first release of a commercial sound recording of a composition, whichever is earlier; however, the parties can specify a lesser period. At the expiration, worldwide rights would be returned to the writer despite the fact that in most countries the term of copyright extends until 50 years from the death of the last surviving collaborator on a song.

Many publishers argue that a recapture right on the part of the writer is wrong in principle because it fails to recognize the importance of the publisher's efforts and expenditures in establishing the popular acceptance of compositions. They continue to attempt to obtain, in the songwriter agreement, an assignment of copyright and full administration and publishing rights for the maximum possible duration for any and all countries of the world. In negotiations between publishers and songwriters, a full understanding of the applicable statutory provisions as to duration and right of termination is essential. Such provisions are further discussed in this chapter under the subheading "Duration" and in Chapter 16, "Duration of Copyright and Limitation of Grants."

While recognizing the merit of certain provisions in the AGAC form of contract, such as the right granted to the writer to participate in all possible revenue from a song, publishers contend that some clauses are outdated and tend to impede the proper administration of a publisher's functions. Publishers assert, for instance, that a writer's consent should not be required for issuance of television or motion picture synchronization licenses.

References to other provisions of the AGAC 1978 form of contract appear in later portions of this chapter. That contract form and a publisher's popular song contract appear in Part 4 as Forms 1 and 2 respectively.

Duration

How long a publisher may continue to publish, exploit, and administer rights in a song is determined both by the songwriter contract and by statute. As noted above, some contracts, such as the 1948 and 1969 AGAC contract forms, expressly limit the publisher's worldwide rights to 28 years, subject to certain notices applicable to foreign rights. With respect to songs originating (first fixed) before 1978, the 1909 United States copyright statute included the concept of an original 28-year term of copyright and a 28-year renewal period; generally speaking, rights reverted to the author or his successors at the end of the first term of copyright unless they granted rights for the renewal term to the publisher. The 1976 Copyright Act has added a 19-year extension to the renewal term, subject to a right of termination in favor of the author or his specified statutory heirs.

As to compositions first fixed on or after January 1, 1978, the 1976 Copyright Act created a right of termination as to grants or licenses of United States rights by the author. The termination becomes effective within a period of five years from the end of the 35th year from the date of the grant or license provided that certain notice is given by the terminating writer or his designated successors; if the grant or license covers publication,[1] the five-year period begins at the end of 35 years from the date of publication or 40 years from the execution of the grant, whichever is earlier. This right of termination takes precedence over contrary contractual provisions. However, the parties are free to contract for a term of rights which is less than 35 years.

As noted previously, the AGAC contract forms were revised in 1978 so as to reflect the impact of the 1976 Copyright Act. The prior contract forms limited the grant of rights to the publisher to 28 years, after which worldwide rights would revert to the author or his successors. The new AGAC form has increased the maximum to 40 years from the date of the agreement or 35 years from the release of a phonorecord, whichever is sooner. The parties are nevertheless able to contract for a lesser period. Because of the contractual limitation on duration there is no need for designated statutory notices to effectuate the right of termination under the 1976 Act. Termination will be automatic and will

[1]Publication includes the distribution of copies or phonorecords to the public.

apply to worldwide rights, whereas the statutory right of termination covers only United States rights.

Divisibility

Except in rare instances, the music industry customarily treats all aspects of music copyright as a single "bundle of rights" exclusively owned and administered by the music publisher. As owner and administrator the publisher handles the separate rights of mechanical reproduction, preparation of derivative works, reproduction in printed editions, and other publication.

Before the 1976 Copyright Act, copyright was generally considered indivisible. There could be only an inseparable ownership of the rights under copyright, although such rights might be the subject of exclusive or nonexclusive licenses. Under the 1976 statute there is for the first time an express statutory recognition that copyright is divisible. There can be a separate transfer and ownership of any of the exclusive rights that comprise a copyright.

It is therefore possible under the 1976 statute for a writer to assign to a publisher the ownership of certain exclusive rights under copyright while reserving the ownership of one or more other such rights. The writer might assign the ownership of some rights to one publisher and of other rights to another publisher. On the other hand, for administrative convenience it seems likely that the practice of a single publisher owning and handling all rights will continue in the main.

With respect to "small" (i.e., nondramatic as compared to "grand" or dramatic) public performance rights, it is customary to allow ASCAP and BMI to handle the licensing thereof, irrespective of who owns the rights. For a further discussion of "small" and "grand" performance rights, reference should be made to Chapter 18, entitled "Performing-Right Organizations." The performing-right organizations make direct payments separately to writers and publishers. Songwriter contracts with publishers usually specify that publishers are not responsible to writers for the payment of public performance fees where the performing-right organizations make direct payments to writers.

Royalty Statements

Obtaining a satisfactory contract is only part of the basic obligation of an intelligent writer. He should also know how to read the royalty statement which accompanies royalty payments. Many an old-time songwriter boasted of ignorance in this respect by saying he filed royalty checks in the bank and royalty statements in the wastepaper basket. This ignorance can seem even more justifiable in an era of computerized royalty statements with code letters or numerals instead of clearly understandable designation of the nature of payments. A machine-prepared royalty statement can obviously be erroneous, since the machine has a human operator and each operator works from a publisher's royalty summary card. Reading the royalty statement not only informs the writer as to the source of his livelihood but it can also keep the writer alert as to possible exploitation angles for a particular song or songs which may be dormant in his catalog.

Some questions that an alert writer should have in mind when reading royalty statements are: Is an advance given for a certain song being charged against other songs of the writer handled by the same publisher? Is the division of 50 percent of mechanical royalties being properly allocated among collaborators, as in the case of a song with two lyricists and only one composer? Are foreign royalties being paid immediately in respect of an advance obtained by the publisher, or are they being withheld pending the often delayed receipt of foreign royalty statements? Are The Harry Fox Agency fees of 4½ percent being deducted in full by the publisher from mechanical receipts? Are the performance license fees for United States theater performances collected from a motion picture producer being distributed at the same time as the synchronization license fees? These and other questions can be raised only if the contract contains appropriate terms.

Publication or Recordings

One problem that faces writers is to ensure that a composition does not lie unnoticed on a publisher's shelf for an extended period of time. Under the 1978 AGAC form of contract, the writer will automatically recapture rights from the publisher after one year from the date of the agreement, or such shorter period as may be specified, if during the applicable period the publisher has not caused the making and distribution of a commercial recording. However, if prior to the end of the initial period, the publisher pays the writer a non-recoupable bonus of $250, the initial period to obtain a released commercial recording is extended for up to an additional 6 months or such lesser period as may be specified by the parties.

Under the AGAC contract, the publisher is required, at the writer's option, to either (1) print and offer for sale regular piano copies within 30 days after the initial release of a sound recording, or (2) make a piano arrangement or lead sheet within 30 days after execution of the agreement and furnish six copies to the writer. Failure of the writer to designate option (1) above shall automatically invoke option (2). The publisher may contend that the printing requirement is unfair to publishers who cause a composition to be recorded by a record company since a recording shows proper effort on the part of the publisher and usually implies that lead sheets were prepared and submitted to the record company.

Some non-AGAC publishing agreements make no provision for recapture of rights by the writer for a publisher's failure to obtain recordings. Other agreements may forestall recapture by one or more of the following acts on the part of the publisher: (1) printing sheet music copies, (2) obtaining a commercial recording of the composition, (3) licensing the music for inclusion in a television or motion picture or dramatic production, or (4) paying a certain sum, such as $100. The publisher may protect himself by a clause which requires the writer to give a 30-day (or longer) notice of intention to recapture, during which period the publisher may cure any default by arranging for any one of the four items set forth above.

Printed Editions

Sales of single copies of sheet music of most songs have in recent years slowed to a mere trickle in the United States, although sheet music sales in foreign countries retain greater importance. Some hit songs can still sell in large quantities in their first year of United States sales. A customary provision in a songwriter's contract is for the payment to the writer of 6 to 8 cents per copy of sheet music sold in the United States and Canada, plus 50 percent of the sheet music royalties received by the publisher for sales in other countries. (The publisher usually contracts to be paid 10 to 12½ percent of the retail selling price of sheet music sold outside the United States and Canada.) Under the 1978 AGAC form of contract, the minimum payment for copies of sheet music sold and paid for in the United States and Canada is based on a sliding scale percentage of the wholesale selling price. The minimum royalty is 10 percent for the first 200,000 copies, 12 percent for the next 300,000 copies and 15 percent for any excess.

For compositions included in printed song folios or albums, the AGAC form provides for the writer to be paid a royalty of 10 percent of the wholesale selling price (less trade discounts, if any) prorated downward by the ratio between the number of compositions written by the writer and the number of other copyrighted compositions in the folio or album. If the publication contains more than 25 compositions, the 10 percent royalty rate is increased by an additional ½ percent for each additional composition. It is becoming increasingly frequent for publishers to issue deluxe higher-priced folios containing as many as 45 to 50 songs, and usually writers will gladly consent to such editions and waive extra royalties.

Many publisher agreements, with respect to folios or albums, provide for the payment of a one-time fixed sum to a writer, ranging anywhere from $1 up to about $25, to cover all uses of a composition in each folio or album irrespective of the number sold. In many instances no substantial harm ensues from a reasonable fixed fee, rather than a royalty based on copies sold, since the sales of folios or albums are often very small. There have been exceptional folios which sold in excess of 100,000 copies, such as those comprised of Paul Simon, Bacharach-David, or Lennon-McCartney songs.

In his exploitation of music the publisher will be called upon to hand out promotional or professional copies of printed editions. These may be given to artist and repertoire men (frequently designated as A & R men) employed by record companies, since it is their function to acquire material which will be recorded by artists under contract to their companies. Other copies may be delivered to orchestras or vocalists in order to encourage their performance of the composition. Additional copies may be sent to managers and agents for artists. The AGAC form and most songwriter agreements provide that the publisher is not obligated to pay royalties for promotional or professional copies.

Mechanical Rights

Among the rights under copyright granted by a songwriter to a publisher is that of licensing the reproduction of the music by mechanical means, including tapes and records. The publisher is said to give a mechanical license to a record company.

For a singles record, that is, a 45 r.p.m. record with one composition on each side, the customary license fee in the United States prior to January 1, 1978, was 2 cents per composition for each record sold. The statutory compulsory mechanical-license fee pursuant to the Copyright Act of 1976 has tended to become the prevailing rate after the generally effective date of the Act, January 1, 1978. Commencing on July 1, 1984 the royalty is 4½ cents per composition for each phonorecord made and distributed or 0.85 cent per minute or fraction thereof, whichever is larger. On January 1, 1986 the rates are scheduled to increase to 5 cents and 0.95 cent, respectively.

In most instances, the license fee for a composition included in an album is the same as the singles rate, although sometimes the publisher will allow a reduced rate to the record company. A great majority of the active publishers in the United States use the services of a licensing agent named The Harry Fox Agency, Inc., whose office was established by an association of leading publishers known as the National Music Publishers Association. The functions and charges of The Harry Fox Agency are considered in Chapter 20, "Mechanical Rights."

In the agreement between a songwriter and a publisher, provision is made for the writer to share in mechanical-license fees received by the publisher. The customary share is 50 percent of the publisher's receipts in the United States. This means 50 percent of 100 percent of license fee payments from United States record companies, after deducting from the 100 percent the 4½ percent collection charge made by The Harry Fox Agency.[2] For mechanical-license earnings outside the United States, the writer is usually entitled to 50 percent of the net sums received in the United States by the American publisher.

---

[2]Under pre-1978 AGAC contract forms the amount deductible for The Harry Fox Agency mechanical-license fee was limited to 2½ percent. The new AGAC contract raises the percentage to 5 percent.

A similar provision prevails with regard to a publisher's receipts from licensing the synchronization or reproduction of music on television and motion picture soundtracks. Such licenses are referred to as synchronization licenses. Many publishers also utilize The Harry Fox Agency for the issuance of synchronization licenses. In the AGAC form of agreement, the licensing fee of The Harry Fox Agency which is deductible by the publisher is limited to $150 or 10 percent of the gross license fee, whichever is the lesser amount.

In promoting a new recording, a publisher may expend money in trade paper advertising and in the purchase and distribution of promotional records. These expenses are not normally chargeable either in whole or in part to the writer. However, a device has often been employed by publishers as a means of charging the writer's royalty account for one-half of these expenses. This device consists in the authorization by the publisher to the record company to undertake the entire expense of the advertisements or promotional records and to deduct from mechanical record royalties otherwise payable to the publisher the portion of the expense that the publisher would usually bear. This deduction "off the top" by the record company in its remittances to the publisher diminishes the proceeds received by the publisher, and the publisher then pays the writer only one-half of the reduced receipts. This practice is a violation of the AGAC standard songwriter agreement and most other songwriter agreements. It is difficult to ascertain the extent of the use of this device by a publisher without a detailed audit of the firm's books.

Accountings and Audits

The AGAC agreement stipulates that the publisher will account to writers either quarterly or semiannually, depending on what period is customary for the publisher, within 45 days after the end of the applicable period. Other agreements usually provide for semiannual accountings. Quarterly accountings are obviously more desirable for a writer than semiannual accountings. Naturally, a publisher will seek fewer accountings, which will lessen administrative costs and overhead.

Songwriters should be alert to provisions by which a songwriter waives any protests against accountings unless complaints are lodged within given periods, such as six months. These provisions are generally enforceable. A publisher is of course entitled to some protection against complaints received long after events transpire.

Frequently, a basis for a complaint regarding an accounting can be found only upon an audit of the books of the publisher. Many reputable publishers will cooperate with a request for an audit in the absence of a contractual provision permitting the songwriter to audit. Other publishers require such contractual sanctions on behalf of a writer before they are willing to allow an audit. A contractual provision has the advantage of fixing rights and obligations without requiring court construction, although courts may permit audits in the absence of contractual provisions.

Under the AGAC contract, any writer may demand a detailed breakdown of royalties on 60 days' written notice, showing the receipts attributable to each record label for each song as well as the details of other uses and the number of copies sold in each royalty category. If the writer undertakes an audit, the publisher must pay the cost of the examination, provided that the audit reveals the writer is owed 5 percent or more of the amount shown on the royalty statement; the payment by the publisher is not to exceed 50 percent of the amount found to be due to the writer. In case a record company and a publishing company are under common ownership and the publishing company does its own licensing of sound recordings, the writer may examine the books of the record company if royalty payments are questioned.

The AGAC Collection Plan is a compulsory system of collection and auditing required of all members of AGAC. It is designed to obviate the expense and delay involved for a songwriter in the auditing of publisher books. The charge is 5.75 percent of the writer royalties collected from publishers, with a maximum charge of $1,750 a year. Under the system, the writer directs publishers to send his checks and statements to the AGAC office. Not all publisher accounts are audited since the time and expense would be inordinate. AGAC accountants make a random selection of publishers for the purpose of auditing the accounts for several years at the same time. Many responsible publishers welcome the opportunity to be audited so as to reassure their writers of their accounting integrity. Furthermore, by dealing with an accountant who represents many writers, the publisher avoids the loss of time required to make individual explanations to the writers.

Many songwriters have requested that AGAC charge only for collections and audits with respect to particular publishers designated by the writers, rather than all publishers dealt with by the writers. This is not permitted on the ground that the 5.75 percent fee in respect of publishers that pay regularly and honestly is required to subsidize the expense of auditing and collecting with regard to the less scrupulous publishers. However, if a publisher is owned in whole or in part, to the extent of at least 25 percent, by an AGAC writer, he can exclude the royalties from that publisher in the collection plan and still avail himself of the collection service for other publishers.

Default

Occasionally a songwriter complains that royalties are not paid when due and that statements are insufficient in detail. What recourse has a writer under such circumstances if the agreement does not specifically cover the matter?

In the face of continued refusals to account, a claim can be made of a breach in the contract between the writer and the publisher. The writer can sue in the courts for an accounting, and under usual court procedure the writer will be able to examine the books and records of the publisher in support of the writer's action.

The writer may also take the position that the breach justifies his termination of the contract and that upon such a termination all rights in the copyright revert to him. It may be expected that the publisher will strongly oppose the writer in this regard. A court will have to decide whether the breach is material or immaterial—that is, whether or not it goes to the essence of the agreement and therefore permits the aggrieved party to cancel it. A refusal to account for one period may well be deemed immaterial, whereas failure to account for several periods, during which repeated requests for accountings were made by the writer, may be judged material.

The prospect of court litigation will discourage many songwriters from moving to obtain accountings or to nullify their agreements with publishers. There are at least two practical approaches to avoiding litigation financed by the writer. Using one approach, the writer may assign all publication rights to another publisher, and the writer and publisher may join in notifying the performing-right organization that the original publisher's rights have been canceled and that the publication rights have been vested in a new publisher. Upon such notice BMI may hold up payments of the publisher's share of performance royalties to the original publisher with a doubtful credit standing; ASCAP, by its rules, will hold back payments of the publisher's share of performance moneys but will resume payments within six months if a suit is not filed or within one year if a filed suit is not adjudicated, provided the original publisher files an agreement to indemnify ASCAP against claims by the other publisher and in addition, in disputes over renewal rights, files documentary support of its position. The performing-right organization's action may by itself be sufficient to make the original publisher willing to negotiate an agreeable settlement of the controversy.

Using a second approach, the writer, as a condition of the assignment to the new publisher, may require it to finance all litigation to establish the new publisher's rights to the material.

Obviously, it is to the writer's advantage to insert a clear and appropriate default clause in the songwriter's agreement. It should be provided that certain specified events constitute grounds for requesting arbitration or for the termination of the agreement. Among these events would be the failure to supply royalty statements and remittances and the publisher's refusal to allow an inspection of his books and records.

The publisher may strongly oppose the default clause and claim, with some merit, that the writer is protected by law in case of a material breach. While this is true, it entails the potentiality and expense of litigation to establish the materiality of a breach and does not meet the objective of the writer to avoid litigation. The writer can counter with an offer to give adequate notice to the publisher of a default and a sufficient opportunity to cure it. Another counter-offer may be one calling for arbitration rather than termination if the publisher and writer disagree as to whether statements and remittances are complete.

Performance Fees

Performance fees are collected by a performing-right organization, such as ASCAP or BMI, from radio and television stations, and from other commercial users of music such as nightclubs and hotels, for the right to perform copyrighted music. Under the 1909 Copyright Act the performance would ordinarily have to be for profit; the 1976 Copyright Act deletes the "for profit" requirements, but it substitutes certain specific and limited exemptions set forth in Section 110, such as noncommercial performances during religious services in places of worship or in face-to-face classroom instruction. ASCAP or BMI, as the case may be, remits separately to the writers and the publisher of a musical composition. Neither organization will pay the writer's share to the publisher. As a consequence, songwriter agreements with publishers do not provide for the payment of performance fees by the publisher to the writer. To clarify the matter, agreements will often state that the publisher is not obligated to pay any performance fees to the writer.

The AGAC contract specifically denies the right of the writer or publisher to share in the revenues distributed to the other by the performing-right organization with which both are affiliated. The now outdated 1947 AGAC form of agreement and the old 1939 Songwriter Protective Association form, which is the forerunner of the AGAC form, did not unqualifiedly state that the writer is not entitled to share in performance fees distributed to the publisher. They only negated the right of the writer to participate in the publisher's performance fees if the particular performing-right organization made writer distributions which were at least equal to publisher distributions.

Assignments

Many songwriter agreements permit a publisher to assign his rights. Thus a songwriter who enters into an agreement relying on the personnel and integrity of a particular publisher may find that by virtue of an assignment he is dealing with a different entity. The AGAC form meets this problem by requiring the writer's consent to an assignment by the publisher, except if the song is included in a bona fide sale of the publisher's business or entire catalog, or in a merger, or as part of an assignment to a subsidiary or affiliate. However, in all cases there must be delivered to the writer a written assumption of obligations by the new assignee-publisher.

It is clear that over the relatively long life of a copyright many situations may arise which can be handled more flexibly and expeditiously if a publisher can assign his rights. Publishers die and estates may be forced to sell interests in a copyright. Publishers retire and are desirous of disposing of their copyrights. Publishers become interested in other ventures. There can be little cause for complaint when the assignment is made to an established, reputable publisher; the tendency is for smaller firms and their copyrights to become acquired by larger, reputable publishers.

Lyrics versus Music

A commercial song may be written for instruments alone, without lyrics, but more frequently it consists of both music and lyrics. While there are writers who write both music and lyrics, it is more common for an individual to be either a composer or a lyricist. The wedding of lyrics and music is an integral part of the business of a music publisher. A good publisher must know the commercial potential of various types of lyrics as well as be acquainted with lyricists who can produce them.

Through the grant of all rights under copyright, the publisher obtains the right to set words to the music and to modify and adapt the music. These powers are usually necessary for the proper exploitation of a composition. A publisher must be careful to ascertain whether the writer has the right to approve changes in the music, including any lyrics, and whether the writer has agreed to share his royalties with the lyricist or other writer engaged by the publisher. Where the AGAC form of agreement has been used, it is prudent to draw a new agreement which includes all of the writers of the final version of the song and thus avoid any later problem of consent or sharing of royalties.

Earlier sections of this chapter are concerned with royalties payable to writers for printed editions and mechanical licenses. Normally these royalties cover the writers as a collective unit, rather than composer and lyricist separately. The aggregate writer royalties will ordinarily be shared equally between the composer and lyricist. Specifically, a royalty of 6 cents per copy of sheet music sold would be remitted as follows: 3 cents to the composer and 3 cents to the lyricist. Similarly, mechanical-license royalties, which are usually 50 percent of the publisher's collections, will be paid half to the composer and the other half to the lyricist. If there are three or more collaborators on a song, they will usually determine among themselves their respective shares of the aggregate writer royalties. It should also be recognized that some songs never reach the public eye and that the writers may wish to attempt to salvage their individual contributions of title, words, or music for future use. A copy of an agreement canceling collaboration in an unpublished composition not registered for copyright is included as Form 5 in Part 4.

Trust Funds

A potent weapon to ensure that a songwriter receives the moneys due to him is to provide that moneys collected by the publisher which are due to the writer are held in trust by the publisher. Thereby, a fiduciary relationship between the publisher and the writer is created in place of a debtor-creditor relationship. Under the debtor-creditor status, the failure to account to the writer might entail only a simple claim against the publisher. This claim would have the same standing as that for any other debt owed by the publisher. The bankruptcy of the publisher would erase the debt to the writer in the same way that other debts would be canceled.

However, under the trust concept the writer becomes the legal owner of the funds, and the publisher is the custodian on behalf of the writer. The claim of the writer is not then dischargeable in the bankruptcy of the publisher, and the writer achieves a preferred status in relation to other creditors. Furthermore, there is a basis for criminal prosecution of the publisher if he becomes insolvent and does not pay writer royalties, since there will have been a misappropriation of funds which belong to another, namely, the writer. A similar charge may be brought in case the publisher refuses to pay.

Under the AGAC form the trust concept is clearly established. Publishers using other songwriter forms will oppose the insertion of trust clauses because of the drastic consequences which may ensue. They point out, and with merit, that they may be unjustly prosecuted criminally if an honest dispute develops, for example, as to whether moneys are actually owed to the writer. They contend further that innocent officers in a publishing enterprise may become tarred with a criminal brush because of acts or defaults of other officers. They argue that, for full protection of personnel, there will have to be established separate and burdensome trust accounts and other administrative procedures which the average publisher cannot afford in terms either of time or expense.

Arbitration

As may be expected, disputes arise between publishers and writers concerning their respective rights and obligations under their agreements. If they cannot compromise, the AGAC form relegates both parties to arbitration, before a sole arbiter, under the prevailing rules of the American Arbitration Association. A decision by the arbitrator is enforceable by the courts. Some songwriter agreement forms follow the example of the AGAC form in providing for arbitration. Many do not.

From the writer's point of view, arbitration appears to be a desirable procedure, since it affords a relatively inexpensive and expeditious method for resolving conflicts which must be settled by third-party intervention. Many publishers favor arbitration for the same reason. Other publishers, because of the technical aspects of copyright law and the tendency of arbitration tribunals to compromise differences rather than decide disputes on principle, prefer to have recourse to the courts; moreover, publishers can often bear the expense of litigation more readily than writers, and the expense may well force writers to settle for less than they might be entitled to under a court decision.

Exclusive Writer Agreements

Publishers who are interested in a continuous supply of good material may attempt to negotiate an exclusive agreement with a desirable composer or lyricist. Under the agreement and for its term, the writer must submit all compositions solely to the publisher and the publisher can claim all rights under copyright in music written by the writer during the term. Royalties payable to the writer for his compositions are usually the same as those on compositions which are accepted for publication in the absence of an exclusive writer's agreement. A copy of an exclusive songwriter term contract and a supplemental letter regarding individual songs are included as Forms 3A and 3B, respectively, in Part 4.

A writer is not likely to sign an exclusive writer's contract unless he is to be paid a cash consideration either in the form of a lump sum or in the form of weekly payments, or unless he receives other special consideration such as a recording artist contract. Under the exclusive writer's contract the payments are commonly deemed to be an advance against and recoupable out of royalties which otherwise become payable to the writer.

It is a customary provision in exclusive writer agreements that the publisher has one or more options to extend the term of the agreement, either on the same terms or on modified terms. Sometimes the publisher cannot exercise the option unless he has passed certain performance tests which indicate that the publisher is actually working in the interest of the writer. One test may be that the writer's compositions have been recorded commercially a required number of times. Another test may be that the cash advances paid to the writer have been earned in the form of royalties. Some agreements provide for an increase in the cash consideration to be paid in the extended period.

Since many minors become songwriters and are requested to sign exclusive writer contracts, questions arise as to whether the minors can be legally bound and, if so, in what manner. A discussion of these questions appears in Chapter 37, "Contracts with Minors."

18

Performing-Right Organizations

The greatest source of revenue in the music industry comes from public performance payments collected and distributed by ASCAP and BMI. Yet, the basis of operation of each of these organizations was nonexistent until 1897 because Congress had failed to include public performance rights within the copyright statute prior to that date. Even after inclusion in the statute, there was no practical way to collect substantial moneys, since only less important sources such as concerts, dance halls, and cabarets were available before the development of broadcasting, and the numerous copyright owners were not sufficiently organized to license and collect.

In 1983, ASCAP alone collected some $198 million in performance fees from broadcasters and other sources. BMI's collection from such sources for the fiscal year ending June 30, 1984 was almost $125 million, and SESAC, a third licensing organization, for 1983 collected about $5 million. The three organizations thus received an aggregate of some $328 million. This may be compared with 1976 collections of approximately $94 million for ASCAP, about $60 million for BMI, and over $3 million for SESAC, or a total of some $157 million.[1] Total collections thus more than doubled in the interval. In considering this growth it should be remembered that additional sources of income, discussed below, were provided under the 1976 Copyright Act, such as public broadcasting, jukebox licensing, and retransmission cable licensing.

The 1983 ASCAP figures indicate that television licensing produces approximately 46 percent of the United States performance collections, with radio about 35 percent and other sources of relatively minor significance. Television contributed about 41 percent, radio approximately 38 percent, and other sources around 21 percent of BMI U.S.A. performance fees. SESAC reports that, in its licensing operations, radio share of income was 66 percent, television 18 percent, and other sources 16 percent.

The many years of lobbying by the performing-right organizations and their author and publisher members or affiliates for repeal of the statutory exemption of jukeboxes reached success in the 1976 Copyright Act. Under the statute, commencing in 1978, jukebox owners were

---

[1]BMI states that its goal is to reach equality with ASCAP as to income and it anticipates that this will be ultimately accomplished through renegotiations of broadcaster licenses.

required to pay license fees of $8 per box. Following review by the Copyright Royalty Tribunal, pursuant to the act, the license fee was increased to $25 in 1982 and to $50 in 1984. There is to be a cost of living adjustment commencing August 1, 1986, if so indicated by the Consumer Price Index.

The performing-right organizations also benefit from their right, provided under the 1976 Copyright Act, to license cable television. This vast field, although still in its infancy, grosses in the billions and is growing rapidly. Cable retransmissions are covered by a compulsory statutory license fee, whereas cable originated programs such as in the case of HBO or Showtime are licensed through negotiations with the copyright licensors. At the present time revenues to music licensors are relatively small. The statutory license fees are collected by the Register of Copyrights and distributed by the Copyright Royalty Tribunal to both music and nonmusic claimants, with the aggregate share of the performing-right organizations totalling only between 4 and 5 percent of the Tribunal's distributions. For the year 1982, the aggregate compulsory statutory license fees collected from some 7,000 cable systems were almost $40 million, of which about 90 percent was paid by the largest 2,000 cable systems. Due to the continued growth of the cable television industry and potential rate increases, it is anticipated that the statutory license fees for 1983 and thereafter will be larger than in 1982.

Another new source of income under the 1976 Copyright Act is represented by license fees from public and educational broadcasters. In the absence of voluntary agreements between copyright owners and public broadcasters, actual fees are determined by the Copyright Royalty Tribunal pursuant to the Act. It is noteworthy that ASCAP has negotiated a license fee of $11.5 million to be paid by National Public Radio and the Public Broadcasting System for the five-year period 1983–87.

The burgeoning area of college concert dates is a further possible source of increasing performance revenues. It was formerly assumed that college concerts were to be specially treated as low-budget nonprofit events largely in the field of serious music. However, rock and roll and other popular artists regularly appear at stadiums and halls before major audiences on a highly profitable tour basis having little or no relationship to nonprofit educational ventures. Higher performing-right music fees have been required for college concerts in recent years.

Organization of ASCAP, BMI, and SESAC

ASCAP is a membership organization of some 26,500 composers and authors and nearly 11,000 publishers. Founded in 1914, ASCAP shares revenue equally between writers and publishers. It collects on the basis of a general license to stations for its entire catalog, with the fee founded not on extent of use of music but on gross receipts of the station less some adjustments, such as agency commissions and wire charges. Its basic rate amounts to somewhat under 2 percent of adjusted gross receipts of stations. In distributing revenues to members, ASCAP pays an equal amount to publishers as a group and to writers as a group after an actual overhead deduction. The overhead expense of about 18½ percent of total ASCAP receipts was $37.7 million in 1983. Formerly, ASCAP absorbed the costs of distributing royalties received from foreign societies, but, in 1976, a service charge was initiated equal to actual costs and averaging between 3 and 4 percent in recent years.

BMI is a competitor of ASCAP owned by some 470 broadcasters and successors to the station owners who established BMI in 1940 as a move towards increasing broadcasting industry bargaining power with ASCAP. As of April, 1984, it represented about 45,000 writers and over 26,500 publishers. BMI, like ASCAP, charges broadcasters a fee based on formulas applied to adjusted gross receipts. The rate is also somewhat under 2 percent, but the adjustments are such that the same licensees who utilize music of both societies pay less to BMI than to ASCAP. The original prospectus used for selling BMI to broadcasters set forth that no dividends were to be expected from the company, and no dividends have been paid. Except for operating expenses and reserves, BMI pays all of the money it collects to its affiliated composers and publishers.

For many years BMI encouraged Canadian publishers and writers to join a wholly owned subsidiary, BMI/Canada. In 1976, all ownership was transferred to a Canadian trust so as to constitute PRO/Canada, a fully Canadian operation in the same sense as CAPAC, the ASCAP affiliate.

It is generally accepted that SESAC is by far the smallest of the three major performing-right organizations in the United States.

SESAC is a private licensing company which has been owned by the Heinecke family for over 50 years. It represents publishers who own approximately 1,070 catalogs, as of 1984. It also represents some 1,680 writers who became affiliated with SESAC since 1972. SESAC differs from BMI and ASCAP in that it allocates to its publisher and writer affiliates 50 percent of the profits of its operations after first deducting specified overhead expenses, with SESAC retaining the balance of the profits.

SESAC further differs from the other societies in that its formula for allocation of payments to affiliates places less emphasis upon actual surveys of performances on the air. Rather than paying strictly on the basis of a work's appearance on a performance survey, SESAC has decided that chart position is a dominant factor in airplay rotation and, therefore, a fair measure of performances. SESAC's formula also takes into consideration: the number of copyrights made available, the diverse kinds of music, and the growth of the catalog due to new works added during each quarter.

Under an incentive program, SESAC grants points to its writers and publishers in the performance category for single record releases (in 1984, a minimum of $240 per side each to the publisher and writer), for album releases (in 1984, $100 per selection each to the publisher and writer), for trade press picks, for cover records, and for the chart activity of each SESAC composition that appears in the trade press: *Billboard* and *Cash Box*. Additional bonus payments to both writers and publishers with respect to a song are awarded for crossovers (appearing on more than one type of chart), longevity (being on the charts for a minimum of 11 weeks), and for carryover (for any work that has achieved top-ten status). These bonus payments are computed as follows:

Crossover Bonus: If a record crosses over from, say, pop to country, the writer and the publisher will each receive full pop position money plus 50 percent of the country chart position money. Chart status is determined by averaging the positions of the record in *Billboard* and *Cash Box*.

Longevity Bonus: If a record appears on the charts of those publications for a minimum of 15 weeks, a bonus of 25 percent of total chart money will be paid to both the writer and the publisher; for a minimum of 13 weeks, a bonus of 20 percent of total chart money will be paid; and for a minimum of 11 weeks the bonus payment is 10 percent of total chart money.

Carryover Bonus: If a record appears in the top-ten position on the charts or if a record is on the charts for 15 or more weeks, there will be a bonus payment made to both the writer and the publisher of 10 percent of chart money on a quarterly basis for two years. An additional 5 percent will be paid on a quarterly basis for the third year.

SESAC reviews and analyzes all national network logs, pay-TV logs, and PBS/NPR cue sheets. It spotchecks the programming of local radio and television stations. SESAC utilizes the *Billboard Information Network* (BIN) and can directly derive the playlists from over 600 stations reporting to *Billboard* and to *Radio and Records* on a daily basis. Each quarter, SESAC considers the results of such reviews and analyses as part of its formula for making allocation payments to its affiliates.

Although SESAC does receive logs from all three major networks, and also does a small amount of spotchecking through monitors, it does not have the resources to duplicate the type of in-depth surveys conducted by the other two performing-right organizations.

Fees charged by SESAC to licensees differ from those charged by ASCAP and BMI inasmuch as they are based on fixed determinants rather than a percentage of gross receipts. SESAC uses a national rate card applicable to all its broadcast licensees which gives consideration to the factor of market classification (population). Fees for a full-time

AM radio station range from $330 to $7,200 per year. For example, a typical AM station with an average market population of 300,000 and a maximum one-minute advertising spot rate of $30, will pay an annual fee of $1,020. SESAC, like ASCAP and BMI, licenses virtually the entire broadcasting industry.

SESAC services all its affiliates by licensing and collecting fees for domestic mechanical and synchronization rights. It is also available to arrange for licensing and collecting in foreign countries. For such functions SESAC charges a fee of 5 percent of domestic mechanical license collections, 10 percent of domestic synchronization license collections, and 10 percent of the receipts from foreign licensees.

In 1966, SESAC published a two-volume catalog of compositions contained in the SESAC repertory; annual supplements to the basic two-volume catalog are published each year. In the same year, SESAC also published a Record-A-Ref which lists SESAC-represented musical compositions that have been recorded by commercial record companies. Annual supplements are also published.

Logging Procedures

ASCAP and BMI employ extensive systems of logging and statistical sampling of actual broadcasts to determine amounts to be paid to writers and publishers. Each television network performance is logged and credited for payment purposes by both organizations on the basis of a universal count without resort to sampling. This is possible because there are only three networks and these networks and the program producers supply program logs and music cue sheets to the performing-right organizations. ASCAP also makes audio and video tapes of network television performances to verify the accuracy of the information furnished by the networks and program producers.

On the other hand, most local radio station performances are sampled to the extent of only a small percentage of the total. This small sample is then multiplied by formulas established separately for each organization by leading statisticians selected by the organization. The formulas are used in order to have the sample represent most fairly total national performances, without undertaking the inordinate expense of a universal count. The sampling approach is also applied to local television performances.

For local television performances both ASCAP and BMI supplement their sampling techniques by resorting to cue sheets and to TV GUIDE program listings. TV GUIDE has some 95 regional editions. ASCAP uses the printed issues of the magazine, whereas BMI relies on the computerized electronic materials of the publication.

Where samples are used for logging purposes, the two organizations resort to different approaches. ASCAP utilizes tape and video recording teams throughout the United States to bring back actual recordings of the programs performed, which are then analyzed and identified regardless of whether or not the songs are in the ASCAP repertory. In a recent report ASCAP advised that as to some 800 local television stations in the United States, its television sample consisted of 30,000 hours of local programming. ASCAP states that, under its recording system, the stations and the ASCAP management have no prior knowledge as to which stations are being taped.

BMI does no actual taping other than some network shows to check the accuracy of the information furnished by the networks. It requires its broadcast licensees to supply, approximately once every 18 months, a station-prepared log of music used in a particular period. BMI uses a private accounting firm to select the stations so utilized and takes pains to keep the list of logging stations secret from its publishers and writers. As a further precaution BMI uses only a portion of the logs so obtained.

The ASCAP system of logging is definitely more costly than the BMI procedure and results in fewer stations being actually logged. But ASCAP claims that the secrecy factor involved in taping avoids any possibility of fictional entries or favoritism. BMI points out that the payment per station, even when multiplied by the applicable factor, is relatively low and the influence of any manipulation would be very small. BMI contends that, especially in the fields of country, black, latin and jazz music, its access to more logs from small cooperating station licensees offers a broader basis for judging nationwide performance of songs less likely to be programmed as frequently on big city stations.

In utilizing samples, both organizations statistically weight the samples received, in accordance with the size and importance of the logged station and the time of day of the program. ASCAP's procedure is generally on the basis of "follow the dollar"; weight is given relative to the percentage of dollar receipts from the station involved. BMI also adjusts in a less exact manner for the economic importance of the station-licensee by paying more for a network station television performance than for a local television station performance, and by compensating more for a "Radio 1" and a radio network station performance than for a "Radio 2" radio performance. A Radio 1 station is one which has paid BMI $4,000 or more for a recent calendar year period, whereas a Radio 2 station for the same period has paid BMI less than $4,000.

SESAC, having no accurate local station logging procedure, relies, among other factors as noted above, upon review of network logs, limited spot-checking of local stations, and increased emphasis upon commercial record releases and results shown in trade paper charts for the purpose of allocation of performance moneys.

ASCAP Songs versus BMI Songs

ASCAP is under a United States Court-administered consent decree, entered into with the approval of ASCAP and the United States Department of Justice, with respect to the antitrust laws; the decree guides nearly every aspect of its operations. BMI also is subject to a consent decree which not only relates to relations with users of music but also covers relations with affiliated publishers and writers.

The ASCAP decree requires ASCAP to accept any applicant for membership who, as a writer, has at least one song regularly published or commercially recorded, or as a publisher, actively engages in the business and whose musical publications have been "used or distributed on a commercial scale for at least one year." ASCAP actively solicits membership of writers and publishers through full-time staff members located in New York, California, and Tennessee, as well as by regularly placed trade paper advertisements inviting membership. In fact, ASCAP acts promptly to accept publisher applications by active publishers, without any prerequisite period of operations. The ASCAP decree also requires ASCAP to permit members to resign and compels the establishment of procedures available for resignation. A member of ASCAP may resign at the end of any calendar year by giving three months' advance notice in writing. Forms of ASCAP writer and publisher applications are included as Appendixes G and H, respectively. The form of ASCAP membership agreement, which is equally applicable to both writers and publishers, is included as Appendix I.

The 1966 BMI decree is similar to the ASCAP decree in respect of the acceptance of writers or publishers as affiliates. Under the decree BMI must accept as a writer affiliate any writer who has had at least one composition commercially published or recorded, and any publisher actively engaged in the business and whose compositions "have been commercially published or recorded and publicly promoted and distributed for at least one year." The decree prohibits contracts with writer or publisher affiliates from having a duration in excess of five years, except that BMI may continue to license compositions in existence at the date of termination until advances to the particular writer or publisher have been earned or repaid. In practice, the term of the publisher agreeement is five years, and the term of the writer agreement is two years, except for extensions as to existing copyrights at date of termination until advances have been earned or repaid. Throughout its history, BMI has been aggressive in the solicitation and attraction of new affiliates. Forms of BMI writer and publisher applications are included as Appendixes K and L, respectively. The forms of BMI writer and publisher agreements are included as Appendixes M and N, respectively.

ASCAP charges a $50 yearly membership fee for publishers and $10 yearly for writer members. BMI has a $25 application fee for new publisher affiliates, with no comparable fee for writers; there are no annual charges for either publishers or writers.

SESAC is not bound by a consent decree in any of its operations. However, it actively solicits new publisher and writer members. The basic term of its publisher agreement is five or ten years and the term of its writer agreement is three years. Such terms are automatically extended for similar periods unless canceled on three months prior notice.

No writer or publisher can collect from more than one performing-right organization for the same songs, as dual membership or affiliation is not permitted. However, a writer or publisher can resign from one of the organizations as to future songs, retaining collection rights as to songs previously registered with the organization and which continue to be licensed by it. Although ASCAP and BMI speak of release at the end of the license period of all rights to past songs of members or affiliates who resign, it is rarely accomplished. The difficulty arises from the fact that the song is originally placed with one or the other performing-right organization by the writer as well as by the publisher. This split origin of rights is rarely matched by joint resignations, and it has been judicially held that either the writer or the publisher can insist on maintaining the status quo with the first organization to which the performing right was jointly entrusted. This principle was established in a case involving the resignation, in 1940, of Edward B. Marks Music Corp. from ASCAP in order to join BMI. This occurred at the inception of BMI.

BMI acts to discourage writer resignations by terminating any bonus status of such writers. If a song remains in BMI after a resignation, because of continued affiliation of the publisher or another writer, the resigning writer will be thenceforth paid at only basic BMI writer rates.

With respect to writer resignations from ASCAP, a writer on a four-fund basis, after resignation, will receive payments only on a current performance basis if the song is still licensed by ASCAP by virtue of the membership of an ASCAP publisher or another ASCAP writer. A writer on a current-performance basis will remain on that basis.

Where an ASCAP writer collaborates with a BMI writer and the song is licensed by both societies, both will pay their own publishers and writers.

In case of collaboration between an ASCAP writer and a writer not affiliated with a performing-right organization, ASCAP will pay both writers if the unaffiliated writer's contribution is published by an ASCAP publisher and the unaffiliated writer does not give licensing rights to another performing-right organization. When a BMI writer collaborates with a writer not affiliated with another performing-right organization, BMI will not pay the unaffiliated writer.

Clearing Functions

Despite frequent grumbling by broadcasters at the necessity for paying sums akin to a gross receipts tax to performing-right organizations for the right to perform music, it is generally conceded that without such organizations inordinate expense and chaos would result. There would be endless searches and bargaining for performing rights, involving the owners of both established and obscure songs. Each station would require copyright clearance experts and would undergo programming delays while contacting the owners for each performance. The concept of a general clearance agency for a large group of music rights, undertaking a uniform system of collection and payment, is necessary for the orderly supply of music to stations. If it were not so, the government might close all performing-right organizations on the ground of violation of antitrust laws.

A Solicitor General's brief, submitted to the United States Supreme Court in 1967, supported a lower court finding; the brief stated "... that a central licensing agency such as ASCAP is the only practical way that copyright proprietors may enjoy their rights under the federal copyright laws and that broadcasters and others may conveniently obtain licenses for the performance of copyrighted music. It (the lower court) found that single copyright owners cannot deal individually with all users or individually police the use of their songs; and that a single radio station may broadcast as many as 60,000 performances of musical compositions involving as many as 6,000 separate compositions."

In a late 1970s lawsuit in a Federal court, CBS sought to require the U.S.A. performing-right organizations to offer for network television programming a per-use license price list which would be available in case of no direct licensing by copyright owners. A Federal Court of Appeals held in favor of ASCAP and BMI, stressed that CBS had sufficient economic bargaining power and strength to avoid antitrust factors alleged by CBS. The United States Supreme Court refused to review the decision. In the Buffalo Broadcasting case, an appellate Federal court has held that antitrust laws do not prohibit ASCAP and BMI from requiring blanket licenses from non-network local television broadcasters. The broadcasters have announced that they intend to seek an appeal to the United States Supreme Court.

ASCAP Credit System

One result of government review under the ASCAP consent decree has been the requirement that any ASCAP writer be free to choose payment on the basis solely of current performances of his works instead of the more complicated "spreading of payments" four-fund system preferred by older members.

The new ASCAP writer was formerly given this choice immediately upon joining. However, any new writer was better off with the current performance basis inasmuch as he had neither length of membership nor any recognized works. Accordingly, the possibility of error was removed by a 1976 amendment to the Writers Distribution Formula which provides that all new writer members are to be on a current performance basis. It is only in the third or fourth full survey years of a new writer's membership in ASCAP that he may elect, by written notice not later than March 31st, to switch to the four-fund basis. An election made on either the four-fund or the current performance basis is binding for not less than ten calendar quarters (2½ years). Except for such restriction the basis can be changed by a notice prior to April 1st electing to switch to the four-fund basis effective for the September distribution and by a notice before October 1st to switch to the current performance basis effective for the succeeding March distribution.

The manner in which ASCAP determines current performance payment to writers may be described as follows: the writer's current performance credit point value is calculated by dividing the total number of dollars available for distribution each quarter by the total number of ASCAP performance credits in the four most recent quarters then serving as a basis for distribution to writer members of ASCAP. Each individual member's credits are then multiplied by that point value to determine his actual share of the distribution. The point value will fluctuate with ASCAP receipts and the total number of ASCAP credits. For the most recent complete survey years the current performance point value has been $1.95.

In the "follow the dollar" policy of valuation of surveyed performances, ASCAP, with respect to network TV loggings, recognizes that a sponsor pays more on weekends and during prime hours. Performances on Monday through Friday receive 50 percent, 75 percent, and 100 percent of full credits, depending on the time of day whether morning, midday, or after 7 p.m. For weekends, the midday credits are eliminated in place of a full payment prime time commencing at 1 p.m.

The four-fund basis is designed to give steadier income to a writer as compared to the income based on a current performance computation. After the allocation of the amounts to be distributed on a current performance basis is made, the remainder left for distribution to writers on a four-fund basis is allocated as follows: 20 percent goes into the Current Performance Fund where credits are based on the most recent four quarters of performances, and the balance is distributed to three other funds in accordance with long-range factors: the Average Performance Fund (40 percent) for five-year averaged current performances; the Membership Continuity Fund (20 percent) for length of ASCAP membership (with a maximum of 42 years) multiplied by a factor based on a ten-year average of performances; and the Recognized Works Fund (20 percent) for five-year averaged performance of the writer's "recognized works," which are generally works of more than a year's age from their first logged performance.

It should be noted that the goal of greater stability over the years through the four-fund system is enhanced even beyond the stated factors, such as five- and ten-year averages of performances. This stability factor is increased by avoiding strict arithmetic computation of performance credits in arriving at the averages to be utilized. Performance credits are equated to "points" earned in certain plateaus, with credits in a lower range of performances being worth more than credits in a higher range.

No money is actually put aside for distribution in subsequent years under the four-fund system. Rather, a member receiving distributions on that system is opting to share in current income in later years on the basis of performances averaged over an extended period of years instead of being limited to each current period. The dollar value of future credits is determined anew each year.

It would appear that a new writer is wise to continue to avoid the four-fund basis; he has neither length of membership nor many active songs over a year old. On the other hand, an established writer will probably adhere to the four-fund basis, since the three long-range funds give an element of steady earnings and security and remove some of the gambling elements of the music business. Illustrative of the further benefits of regularizing earnings through the four funds are ASCAP's rules governing the 40 percent Average Performance Fund distribution, which provide in part as follows:

> ASCAP may . . . limit the rise in such payments for one year by not more than one-half of any increase for any writer member; ASCAP may limit any fall in such payments by assigning one third of the fall in the first year, another third in the second year and the remaining third in the third year.

ASCAP publishers receive distributions solely on a current performance basis.

Qualified Works

One of the most novel concepts in the ASCAP system of credits is the "qualified work" designation. Under this part of the system, a song with a history of over 20,000 feature performances, of which the most recent five years contributed an average of 500 feature performances a year, is given special higher credits when used in nonfeature roles such as background, cue, bridge, or theme. There is also a partial qualification for higher credits if a work which passes the five-year test has accumulated 15,000 or 10,000 feature performance credits. The justification for higher credits lies in the fact that when a background strain or a theme is based on a well-known old standard, such as "Moon over Miami," the user is getting more value from the use, and the user, accordingly, recognizes that ASCAP's bargaining power for general license fees is greater than if the tune were a new song previously unknown to the public and commissioned by the user especially for that purpose. Background uses of well-known songs are also deemed to advance the plot by public identification with special moods or images associated with the song. This simplified explanation leaves aside the more difficult factor of describing or justifying the different rates of payment. A "qualified work" employed as a theme is accorded half a feature credit, while an unqualified work in the same form would receive one-tenth of a feature credit. A background use of even five seconds of a qualified work gets half a feature credit, but an unqualified work requires a three-minute aggregate use for 36 percent of a feature credit, with reduction for lesser use, so that a use of between 16 and 30 seconds would earn only 6 percent of a feature credit and any such aggregate use of less than 16 seconds involving works written by the same writer(s) and published by the same publisher(s) would earn only 1 percent of a credit. However, nonqualifying works with at least five local radio feature credits in the most recent five years receive special credit for background, bridge or cue use in a single program. They are allotted not less than 20 percent of a use credit for the first performance and 2 percent additional for each subsequent use, with a maximum of 40 percent for all uses of an individual work in a single program.

A summary by the authors of the ASCAP Weighting Formula for purposes of credit as well as a full copy of the ASCAP Weighting Formula upon which the summary is based are included as Appendixes J1 and J2, respectively.

BMI Payments

The BMI standard form of writer contract and the BMI standard publisher contract do not mention payment rates. Each states in effect that payments will be made in accordance with the current practices and rates of BMI. The regular rates of payment to writers are the same as those for publishers. Actual payments to writers or publishers by BMI distinguish between radio and television performances and between network and local performances. In the case of a network performance, the rate allotted is multiplied by the number of interconnected stations carrying the broadcast. The rate allocated a local station performance is multiplied by a statistical multiplier based on the ratio of stations logged to stations licensed in each station classification.

BMI has a payment schedule, effective January 1, 1984, which is distributed to all its affiliates. Each payment rate covers combined writer and publisher compensation and should ordinarily be divided in half to arrive at the separate payments to a writer and a publisher. In the absence of a publisher the rate stipulated in the payment schedule is payable entirely to the writer. Also the publisher and writer can agree that the writer may receive more than 50 percent of the total payments, but the publisher's share can never equal more than one-half. BMI states that the new system is "similar to that of other performing rights organizations throughout the world." Under the new approach the need for a writer to form a publishing firm in order to collect more than 50 percent of the total performance fees paid is eliminated, and the number of prospective BMI music publishing firms is reduced.

On the assumption that there is a publisher and that the writer and publisher share equally in the payment rate, the following indicates their respective shares under the BMI payment schedule. Six cents are payable for a feature radio performance of a popular song on each radio network station and on each "Radio 1" station, which is a station that pays BMI $4,000 or more per year. Three cents are specified for feature radio performances on "Radio 2" stations, which are stations that pay less to BMI. A local television feature performance is allocated a rate of 75 cents. Network television feature performances in prime time, between 7 p.m. and 1 a.m., earn $4.50 per station, and in other than prime time, $2.50. There is no distinction made between AM and FM feature performances on radio. Concert works on radio receive substantially higher payments than performances of a popular song.

Commencing in 1977, every BMI song became eligible for a bonus. Under this system an individual song receives the base rate in the BMI payment schedule until a certain plateau of United States feature broadcast performances of the song is reached, at which point a higher payment rate ensues. Later, when stipulated higher levels of cumulative performances are attained, greater bonus rates become effective. Works receive credit for all feature broadcast performances from January 1, 1960, and after.

The BMI payment schedule as revised in 1984 provides for the following bonus plateaus:

Plateau A: 25,000 to 49,999 performances: 1½ times the base payment rate

Plateau B: 50,000 to 299,999 performances: 2 times the base payment rate

Plateau C: 300,000 to 999,999 performances: 2½ times the base payment rate

Plateau D: 1 million performances and over: 4 times the base payment rate

The achievement of Plateau D status is heralded by a special BMI awards ceremony. Some of the songs in this category are: "Amapola," "Bye Bye Love," "Don't Be Cruel," "Killing Me Softly With His Song," "Never On Sunday," "Sounds of Silence," "Sunrise, Sunset," and "Up, Up and Away." There are over 350 songs in this category.

Provision is made by BMI for special Plateau D status for songs identified originally as "show music." These songs originate in (1) a Broadway show, or (2) an off-Broadway show that opened after October 1, 1966 and had an original-cast LP released. Special credit is also stipulated for a "movie work." This is a complete musical work originating in, and performed for not less than 40 seconds as a feature work or theme in, a full-length theatrical or television motion picture released in the United States after October 1, 1966. A movie work cleared prior to January 1, 1980 is entitled to start at Plateau B or, if cleared after January 1, 1980, at Plateau C.

While United States television network, cable, and public broadcasting station feature performances are counted in computing the plateau of a musical work, such performances themselves do not qualify for bonuses.

A copy of the current BMI payment schedule for television and radio performances is included as Appendix O.

Advances to Writers and Publishers

From its inception in 1940, BMI followed a policy of granting advances of moneys to publishers and writers that negotiated for them. As of 1966 ASCAP followed suit. In each case the advances were recoupable and payable only out of earnings which would otherwise be payable to the recipient of the advance. Soon after the 1983 Federal court antitrust decision against ASCAP and BMI in the Buffalo Broadcasting case, both ASCAP and BMI ceased the making of advances. The decision limited the right of performing-right societies to require blanket licenses from non-network local television broadcasters. At this writing the case has been reversed on appeal to a Federal appellate court; the broadcasters have stated that they intend to seek an appeal to the United States Supreme Court. The outcome may affect the attitude of the societies toward making advances in the future.

ASCAP, however, for such contingencies as disability and death may make emergency payments to its members out of funds created by membership dues. These payments are chargeable against the member's future earnings.

SESAC continues to make advances and claims the distinction of being the only performing-right organization to do so. Its practice of making payments based upon the release of records and top hit chart activity makes advances a matter of its normal business operation.

Writer and Publisher Loans

With the cessation of advances by ASCAP and BMI there has arisen a greater need on the part of some writers and publishers for bank loans or loans from other third parties.

As to bank loans, both ASCAP and BMI cooperate by recognizing an irrevocable assignment of publisher or writer royalties for repayment of the loans. In fact, BMI will ordinarily honor an irrevocable assignment to any third party, whether a member of the borrower's family or otherwise, that lends money to a BMI writer or publisher. ASCAP too will accept an irrevocable assignment in connection with a nonbank loan, but only if the lender is another ASCAP writer or publisher.

ASCAP Writer Awards

ASCAP has a system of "awards to writers whose works have a unique prestige value for which adequate compensation would not otherwise be received by such writers, and to writers whose works are performed substantially in media not surveyed by the Society."

There is a Special Awards Panel, composed of people of standing who are not ASCAP members, and divided into a Popular-Production Panel and a Standard Awards Panel. The Popular-Production Panel makes special monetary awards to popular music composers and the Standard Awards Panel allocates such awards to composers of symphonic and concert music.

For popular music awards, applications must be filed by December 1 and May 1 of each year for writer members receiving $15,000 or less a year from regular ASCAP distributions. For a further discussion, reference may be made to *More About This Business of Music,* by Shemel and Krasilovsky, 3rd edition (Billboard Books, 1982), page 46.

Foreign Collections

Both ASCAP and BMI fulfill a valuable international role for publishers, writers, and users of music. They collect from abroad for their members or affiliates and collect from users in the United States on behalf of foreign societies. Foreign collections are made through affiliated societies in each country and remitted through the domestic organization. It would be a most difficult task for each writer or publisher to supervise the licensing of rights in every country of the world where American music is used. ASCAP has more than 40 foreign affiliates, and BMI has substantially the same; most often the same foreign society represents both of them, since the United States is unusual in having more than one performing-right organization.

BMI charges 5 percent of foreign collections as a service fee, which is deducted from remittances to its affiliated writers and publishers. Revenues received by ASCAP from foreign sources are distributed to writer and publisher members on a current performance basis. ASCAP makes an overhead charge of about $3\frac{1}{2}$ percent for its foreign collection services. ASCAP distributes foreign revenues to members on the basis of performances reported by the foreign society if the revenue from the society exceeds $200,000 a year and the reports furnished ASCAP allocate credit in reasonably identifiable form separately by compositions performed and indicate the members in interest. ASCAP seeks to distribute foreign income to its members based on reports received from local societies, even when the fees remitted are under $200,000, as long as the reports identify the works performed and the ASCAP members in interest. ASCAP receives more than $200,000 per year from Austria, Australia, Belgium, Canada, Denmark, England, France, Holland, Italy, Japan, Spain, Sweden, Switzerland, and West Germany. Except for Canada, a member's credits in these countries are used as the basis of distribution of all other foreign income which is not distributed in accordance with logging reports.[2] A similar procedure is used for the

---

[2]ASCAP deems Canadian performances to be more like United States performances than European performances, so that they are not considered a good guide for the distribution of unallocated monies.

distribution of foreign film and television income which is also not distributed in accordance with logging reports.

A great majority of American publishers, despite the convenience of collecting through ASCAP or BMI, have their share of foreign collections in important countries paid to foreign subpublishers or agents. They explain that a local subpublisher will expedite collections and will be more vigilant in claiming rights; some desire to have foreign revenue collected abroad and retained there for capital acquisitions or other local expenditures.

A major cause of alarm to American publishers and writers is the large sum of foreign performance collections not accounted to Americans because of claimed difficulties in identifying American songs under translated or new local titles. Such so-called unclaimed moneys go into general funds which are distributed by the foreign performing-right society among its membership, without participation by American writers or publishers. This "black box" distribution can be increased by the failure of the American publisher to appoint a local representative to identify and claim a song in its varied forms. On the other hand, the advantage of having a local subpublisher or agent will tend to be offset by the participation of the local representative in the publisher receipts. The terms of foreign subpublishing are discussed more fully in Chapter 19, "Foreign Publishing."

ASCAP and BMI Grievance Procedures

It is prudent for writers and publishers to recognize that the logging and tabulation techniques of ASCAP and BMI are subject to interpretation, and that the reports by the organizations should be carefully reviewed. The late Billy Rose, for example, once observed that ASCAP's performance reports on certain of his songs showed in the column "Share" a lesser percentage for his participation vis-à-vis his collaborators than appeared on royalty statements rendered by his publishers. Where there were two other writers involved, he had been credited with one-third of the writers' share of performance fees. He pointed out in an informal ASCAP Committee proceeding that he had written the words alone and that therefore his share was 50 percent and the other two collaborators should receive 25 percent apiece, instead of one-third each. Rose prevailed in his contentions, but ASCAP was careful to stress, in informing other members of the decision, that the writer has the burden of proving unusual divisions of performance fees.

Pursuant to the ASCAP consent decree entered in 1960, the Court appointed the late Judge John E. McGeehan, formerly a Justice of the Supreme Court of the State of New York, to examine periodically the design and conduct of the ASCAP survey of performances which establishes the basis of its distribution of revenues to members. He reported to the Court and to ASCAP and the United States government, making recommendations as to modifications of the ASCAP procedures and practices.

Similar services as Special Distribution Advisors have been recently performed by Seth M. Hufstedler, and Leo Kaplan, Esq., operating from their respective West and East Coast offices. Recognized functions of these Special Distribution Advisors include making themselves available in person or by correspondence to consult with members of ASCAP who have questions concerning or problems with the ASCAP distribution system.

Distribution Advisor inquiries have been made into such matters as the credits for music performed at football games, the reduction of credits for qualifying works utilized as feature songs in films, and the basis for distribution of money received from unsurveyed background wired music licensees.

Grievance procedure for publisher and writer members of ASCAP was formalized in the Article of Association of the Society pursuant to the 1960 consent decree. A Board of Review, elected in the same manner as the ASCAP Board of Directors, was established to have jurisdiction in the first instance over every complaint by a member relating to the distribution of ASCAP's revenues or to any rule or regulation of ASCAP directly affecting the distribution of revenues to the member. Each complaint must be filed within nine months from the receipt of the annual statement or of the rule or regulations on which the complaint is founded. The relief which may be granted by the Board of Review in terms of monetary payment may not extend back beyond the time covered by the annual statement, except that if the alleged injustice is such that the aggrieved party would not reasonably be put on notice of it by his annual statement, the relief given may reach back as far as, in the opinion of the Board, is required to do justice. The Board of Review is obligated to set forth in detail the facts and grounds underlying its decision. There is a right of appeal from any decision of the Board of Review to an impartial panel of the American Arbitration Association.

The BMI grievance procedure is set out in the 1966 consent decree as requiring reference of "all disputes of any kind, nature or description" between BMI and any writer, publisher, or music user to arbitration in the City of New York under the prevailing rules of the American Arbitration Association. SESAC is not subject to a court consent decree and has no established grievance procedure covering its relations with its affiliates.

Dramatic Performance Rights

Dramatic performance rights (frequently called "grand rights") are to be distinguished from nondramatic performance rights ("small rights"). They differ in the type of use involved and in the practical manner of who administers the rights.

The 1976 Copyright Act, as did the 1909 Act, grants the exclusive right to perform or represent a copyrighted work publicly if it be a dramatic work. A dramatic work includes material dramatic in character such as plays, dramatic scripts designed for radio or television broadcast, pantomimes, ballets, musical comedies, and operas. In contrast to a nondramatic work such as a musical composition, compulsory licenses under the 1976 Act for phonograph recordings, for jukebox performances, and for performances on public broadcasting systems do not apply to dramatic works. Thus the copyright owner of the dramatic work *My Fair Lady* has the absolute exclusive right to authorize or to withhold authorization of the recording or performance in public of the musical play.

It should be understood that a dramatic performance does not cause material to constitute a dramatic work. An example of a dramatic performance might be the portrayal of the story-line of the song "Moonlight Cocktail" in a dramatic fashion, such as for a television show using background scenery, props, and character action to depict the plot of the composition.

In practice, however, it is not simple to define a dramatic performance, and a leading negotiator on behalf of broadcasters, the late Joseph A. McDonald, has said in connection with ASCAP negotiations:

> What constitutes a dramatic rendition is a very difficult thing to define . . . even though we undertook to be as specific as possible in defining what would constitute a dramatic performance, it still leaves room—wide room—for interpretation.

The ASCAP television license represents the best efforts of music industry and broadcasting industry representatives toward reaching a definition of dramatic performance rights. The effort is necessary because ASCAP obtains from members only nondramatic public performance rights and not dramatic performance rights. Concerning the dramatization on television of a single musical composition that does not necessarily stem from a musical play or other dramatic production, the latest television license states:

> Any performance of a separate musical composition which is not a dramatic performance, as defined herein, shall be deemed to be a nondramatic performance. For the purposes of this agreement, a dramatic performance shall mean a performance of a musical composition on a television program in which there is a definite plot depicted by action and where the performance of the musical composition is woven into and carries forward the plot and its accompanying action. The use of dialogue to establish a mere program format or the use of any nondramatic device merely to introduce a performance of a composition shall not be deemed to make such performance dramatic.

With respect to the dramatic performance of dramatic musical works such as musical plays, the television license provides:

This license does not extend to or include the public performance by television broadcasting or otherwise of any rendition
or performance of (a) any opera, operetta, musical comedy,
play or like production, as such, in whole or in part, or (b) any
composition from any opera, operetta, musical comedy, play
or like production (whether or not such opera, operetta, musical comedy, play or like production was presented on the stage
or in motion picture form) in a manner which recreates the
performance of such composition with substantially such distinctive scenery or costumes as was used in a presentation of
such opera, operetta, musical comedy, play or like production
(whether or not such opera, operetta, musical comedy, play or
like production was presented on the stage or in motion picture
form).

Radio stations must also take care not to make dramatic uses of music
without specific authorization over and above their regular ASCAP or
BMI license. Most radio station problems in this field relate to playing
original cast albums in the same sequence as the dramatic presentation.
Under industry practice, no objection is ordinarily made by the copyright owners to the unlimited playing in sequence of instrumentals from
cast albums or to the playing in sequence of up to two vocals and an
instrumental. Some record companies and publishers obtain clearances
for the unrestricted playing of tunes from cast albums and so notify the
broadcasting stations.

The standard BMI contract with affiliated writers and publishers
gives BMI the right to license dramatic performances but these rights
are restricted. Thus, BMI is not authorized to license the performances
of more than one song or aria from an opera, operetta, or musical
comedy, or more than five minutes from a ballet, if such performance is
accompanied by the dramatic action, costumes, or scenery of that
opera, operetta, musical comedy, or ballet. The writers and publishers
of a work may jointly, by written notice to BMI, exclude from the grant
of rights to BMI any performances of more than 30 minutes duration of
a work that is an opera, operetta, or musical comedy; exceptions are
(1) the score of a theatrical film when performed with the film and (2)
the score written for a radio or television program when performed with
the program.

The standard SESAC license excludes "grand rights," which it
states include "dramatic renditions in whole or in part, with or without
costume . . . e.g., dramas, plays, operas, operettas, revues, musical
comedies, sketches and like productions. . . ." These rights are licensed
separately by SESAC.

Where a performance is found to be dramatic, who administers the
right to license it? The presentation of the whole or part of a musical
play will usually be administered by the writers, pursuant to rights
reserved to them by Dramatists Guild contracts. In the case of most

music publishers who publish show music, copyright is maintained in the name of the writer, and, accordingly, publishers do not acquire dramatic rights. In many instances, shows previously produced on the Broadway stage are licensed by agents for writers, such as Tams-Witmark Music Library, Inc. and Rodgers & Hammerstein Repertory, to amateur and stock groups, and to television for dramatic performances.

For music not originating in plays or operas and the like, the copyright is normally vested in the music publisher, who thereby obtains the dramatization rights, although some writer contracts, such as those of the AGAC, require consent of the writer for the dramatization of a composition. There are also some contracts, especially older ones, wherein the writer specifically reserved all dramatic rights.

19

Foreign Publishing

In the past, American publishers derived the great preponderance of their income on a composition from its exploitation in the United States and Canada. Only a rare song, such as one from a motion picture or musical play, could pierce the barrier of foreign language and taste. It is thus understandable that many foreign subpublishing deals were negotiated by American publishers with an emphasis on obtaining a locally originated foreign recording (in trade parlance a "cover record") or an immediate advance of moneys and with minimum bargaining as to the amount of royalty, the extent of the territory licensed, the duration of the license, and the minimum exploitation to be guaranteed by the subpublisher.

Today the international aspect of the music industry is firmly established and foreign earnings have become a major factor in the profit and loss figures of American publishers. It is possible for sales of a United States hit in a country such as West Germany to rival and even surpass sales in the United States. Even the language barriers of yesterday have tended to disappear and many a German and Japanese youth have learned some English from popular records originating in the United States, England, Australia, Holland and indeed in almost every country. English has become the most important language for lyrics on a world-wide basis. Some countries such as Canada, France, Italy, Australia, and Spain have gone so far as to issue government edicts as defensive measures, requiring minimum broadcasts of nationally originated music.

Factors contributing to the internationalization of popular music include playings on local stations, the influence of Armed Forces radio stations, international bookings of recording and concert stars, promotional videos, cheaper airfreight charges for finished records, the marketing of motion pictures and syndicated television shows in the world market, and the growth of leisure time and the broadening of the middle class in numerous countries.

In the past, American popular, show, film, and jazz music were of particular strength in the international sphere. More recently, American rhythm and blues and rock music have also shown popular acceptance. Competition among foreign subpublishers for the rights to successful United States songs is very marked.

Sales in World Market

Based on statistics compiled by the International Federation of Phonogram and Videogram Producers (IFPI), the worldwide record market in

1982 had total retail sales of 11.2 billion dollars. These sales had approximately the following percentage breakdown at retail selling prices: United States 35.3 percent; remainder of the world 64.7 percent. The latter figure is comprised roughly as follows: Europe exclusive of Iron Curtain countries, 29.47 percent; Japan, 11.3 percent; U.S.S.R., Czechoslovakia, Poland, Hungary and Yugoslavia, 7.3 percent; Canada, 3.2 percent; Australia and New Zealand, 2.1 percent; remainder of world, 11.33 percent.

Representation by Subpublishers

The United States publisher is confronted with alternative methods of achieving proper representation by foreign publishers. If he chooses to deal with large international publishers such as Chappell & Co., Ltd., or the EMI or CBS music publishing groups, he enjoys the convenience of a single point of contact in placing any material for world exploitation. On the other hand, by wise and studied selection of separate publishers in each foreign country, he may arrive at a better overall representation, including separate advances for and recoupable from only the earnings from particular countries. The latter approach necessarily assumes a much greater investment in the time and expense required to investigate and become familiar with the music business and publishers in each area and to correspond and enter into contractual relations with them.

Foreign publishers who handle United States musical material are called subpublishers, while the United States publisher is referred to as the original publisher. Agreements with subpublishers are commonly designated as subpublication agreements or contracts.

Apart from differences in the extent of territory covered, subpublication agreements vary according to the number of compositions included. If all of the compositions of a United States publisher are the subject of a subpublication agreement, the agreement may be considered as a catalog subpublication contract, and in this case all compositions for the term of the agreement are usually certified to the particular subpublisher.

Whether the arrangement with a publisher includes a single composition or an entire catalog, there are certain basic royalty provisions and, in addition, other fundamental points to be considered. A copy of a foreign subpublication agreement is included in Part 4 as Form 11.

Over 30 performing-right societies in the principal countries of the world have been organized specifically to collect performing-right license fees. The better known societies outside the United States and Canada are in Europe, Australia, and Japan. The functions of these foreign societies are discussed in Chapter 18, "Performing-Right Organizations." In considering the area of foreign publishing and subpublishing contracts, one should note that some societies, such as the United Kingdom's Performing Right Society (P.R.S.) and France's SACEM, also operate in numerous foreign territories no longer politically related to the home territories. Examples are SACEM collections in Southeast Asia and African countries formerly administered by the French government, and the P.R.S. collections in India, and in African, Caribbean, and other areas formerly within the British Empire.

American publishers are accustomed to the collection services of The Harry Fox Agency for mechanical royalties. In Europe, the usual method of collection of such fees is by the respective national mechanical-rights societies affiliated on a multinational basis in a confederation known as BIEM (Bureau International des Sociétés Gérant les Droits d'Enregistrement et de Reproduction Mécanique). Licenses for mechanical reproduction by record companies are negotiated on an industry-wide basis with the trade association of the record industry, IFPI (International Federation of the Phonographic Industry). These negotiations are on two levels. BIEM on an international basis negotiates with IFPI the general licensing system, the mechanics of licensing, the rate, and the principle of minimum royalty. The national societies settle such things as the amount of deductions from the standard rate and the minimum royalty.

The BIEM structure has undergone some changes in recent years. In 1960, GEMA, the West German authors' society which was handling both public performance and mechanical reproduction licensing, withdrew from BIEM, but rejoined in 1967. In 1970, Italy's public performance society, SIAE, took over SEDRIM, the Italian mechanical collection society. GEMA and SIAE are now affiliated with BIEM, and those two societies, together with the French society SACEM are permanently on the negotiating committee of BIEM. Other societies are elected to limited term seats on the negotiating committee.

The Harry Fox Agency, Inc., is agent in the United States for most of the foreign mechanical-right societies. The Fox Agency is available through these affiliations to represent European publishers for the collection of their mechanical earnings in the United States.

Many of these foreign societies will accept direct representation from United States publishers and act as their agent to collect foreign mechanical-license fees without the intercession of a local publisher. Through the foreign societies abroad, the Fox Agency can act as an agent for those United States publishers who have not entered into direct affiliation with the foreign societies and who have not authorized a local foreign subpublisher to subpublish their copyrights. For a further discussion of foreign mechanical-right societies and their respective territories, see Chapter 20, "Mechanical Rights."

As noted previously, mechanical-license fees relate in the main to a license to use copyrighted compositions on records. Fees are normally paid in accordance with the number of copies of a recording that are sold. In Europe, mechanical-license fees range from about 6 to 8 percent of the suggested retail list price of the records; European mechanical-license fees are divided proportionately among the copyright owners of the music used on the particular record.

When subpublishers are granted subpublication rights in a composition, they customarily receive the power to collect mechanical-license fees and, less frequently, the publisher's share of performance fees; the U.S.A. writer's share of performance collections, usually 50 percent of total performance fees, is reserved for the writers by the performing-right organization, and it is only the balance which is remitted to the subpublisher when it has the right to collect performance fees. The historically standard fee payable to the United States publisher is 50 percent of the moneys collected by the subpublisher, but forces of competition have tended to increase the percentage; payment of 75 percent is often required.

If a composition has been released on a United States commercial record and the same recording is likely to be released in the foreign territory, the United States publisher may insist on receiving more than the usual original publisher's share of performances fees and mechanical fees. His argument is likely to be that the local publisher is only a collecting agent and therefore only a collection charge, from 10 to 25 percent, should be deducted and the balance remitted to the United States publisher. Some subpublishers will accede to such arguments.

Other subpublishers will oppose any reduction in their fee. They contend that they may be the moving force in causing the release of the original United States recording in the locality. They argue that they must expend time and money in promoting the United States recording to make it successful. They point out that performance fees are earned by live as well as record performances, and that a reduced fee would unfairly compensate them for their efforts in printing, arranging, and distributing the composition so that it will be performed by orchestras and vocalists. Their position is reinforced in the event they obtain locally-originated recordings. They argue that the performing-right society's records do not adequately separate performance earnings from the imported recordings and other performance earnings. In one activity, namely, the collection of motion-picture and television-film performance fees, the subpublisher will readily agree to a collection fee of 10 to 25 percent, because only a collection arrangement is involved. Music cue sheets which list the music in United States films are received from the United States and are filed with the performing-right society. The society makes clear and separate accountings for each film, and the subpublisher can do little to affect the amounts accounted for. Principally in Europe, motion-picture performance fees for theatrical films are collected from theaters and are a small percentage of box office receipts. Television-film performance fees are received from the television stations.

Under some contractual arrangements a subpublisher will retain from 10 to 25 percent of receipts in its territory in respect of compositions for which there is no locally originated recording and a higher percentage after a local recording is obtained. The increased rate may be 30 to 50 percent of all receipts from the compositions or the higher rate may be limited to mechanical and synchronization income from the local version only. If the local version has a new title, as compared to the original song, the differentiation in titles makes it possible to distinguish the performance earnings of the original and local versions and to have a lower rate for nonlocal recordings and a higher rate applicable to all income from the local version.

Synchronization Fees

A synchronization license fee is payable for a publisher's consent to the recording of a composition as a part of the soundtrack of a motion picture or television film.

When a composition is subpublished, it is standard for the subpublisher to acquire the right to grant worldwide nonexclusive synchronization licenses for motion picture or television films originating in the local territory. Fifty percent or more of the fees will be payable to the United States publisher. However, for films originating outside the subpublisher's territory the United States publisher will usually reserve the right to issue worldwide synchronization licenses for fees in which the local publisher does not share even though the film may be shown in the local territory; however, the subpublisher will commonly participate in the collection of local film performance fees for the film. The United States publisher may also reserve the power to grant exclusive synchronization licenses which will have the effect, on issuance, of barring the local publisher from the exercise of any synchronization rights. Under the AGAC form of songwriter agreement, the writer must approve vocal renditions or dramatic representations or exclusive uses of a composition in films. As a consequence, American publishers may reserve all synchronization rights or may insist upon the right to be notified and to approve synchronization licenses proposed for issuance by a subpublisher. Irrespective of the AGAC form, American publishers may desire this notice and right of approval in order to pass upon the proposed price to be charged for the synchronization license.

In connection with the production of video cassettes or videodiscs, film companies request worldwide licenses for synchronization and marketing rights. To facilitate such licenses, original publishers may decide to exclude subpublishers from the right to license and collect fees on such productions originating outside the subpublisher's territory, although distribution will be made in the subpublisher's country.

Printed Editions

The common royalty payable by the subpublisher to the United States publisher for printed editions is 10 to 12½ percent of the suggested retail price of the editions. If folios or albums are printed, and the United States publisher's composition is included with other compositions, he will receive a pro-rata share of 10 to 12½ percent computed in the ratio that his composition bears to the total number of compositions in the edition. Many agreements provide that public-domain compositions in the editions will be excluded in calculating the United States publisher's pro-rata share.

Provision should be made for sample copies of printed editions to be supplied gratis to the original publisher. A reasonable number of copies—four, for example—may be required.

Local Lyrics and Versions

A subpublisher will usually acquire the right to make translations, adaptations, and arrangements of the composition, so that it may be exploited commercially in the territory. This will include the right to provide new lyrics and a new title.

It is obvious that for compositions other than instrumentals the subpublisher will be hampered in his efforts to market the composition if he cannot adapt it to the people in the territory via local language lyrics, a new title, and apt arrangements. The popular song known as "Never on Sunday" in English-speaking countries is called "Les Enfants du Piré" (Children of Piraeus) in France and "Ein Schiff Wird Kommen" (A Ship Will Come) in Germany, and there are different lyrics in each language. It would not have achieved its local popularity without adaptations to the areas concerned. In fact, a criterion in selecting a subpublisher is his ability to make appropriate and profitable adaptations of a United States composition.

Local Writer Royalties

Royalties payable to the local version lyric writer are frequently 12½ percent of the subpublisher's gross receipts for mechanical and synchronization uses, 25 percent of the total writers' share payable in the territory in respect of territorial public performance fees and one-half of usual lyric writer royalties for territorial printed edition sales. It is customary for the subpublisher to bear, out of its share, the royalty payable to the local lyric writer for mechanical and synchronization uses and for the sale of printed editions. The subpublisher can more easily afford such sharing where provision is made for its retained royalties to increase when there are local cover records. The local lyric writer's share of public performance fees is usually deducted by the local public performance society from the share of the original lyric writer. If the music and lyrics of the original song were written jointly by two original writers, the public performance fees payable to the local lyric writer would be deducted equally from the shares of the original writers.

Some public performance societies provide for local arrangers to receive a portion of the original music writer's share of public performance fees.

Copyright and Term of Rights

Subpublishers formerly would seek to have rights conveyed to them for the term of copyright in their territory. In most European countries, copyright subsists for the life of the writer plus 50 years. In Germany, the term is the life of the writer plus 70 years. However, in recent years the trend has been toward much shorter terms, with three-year retention of rights being common except for a possible further two years where cover records are obtained.

It is in the interest of the United States publisher to limit the term of rights, but not to the point of discouraging activity by the subpublisher. Some subpublishers have been willing to accept a period equal to the original term of the United States copyright under the Copyright Act of 1909, namely, 28 years. The author's right under the 1976 Copyright Act to terminate new grants to publishers after 35 years (where publication is involved the period is 35 years from publication or 40 years from execution of the grant, whichever is earlier) will influence United States publishers to make that period the maximum for a subpublication license.

Many subpublishers will acquiesce to a shorter term; in fact, one large United States publisher historically followed a policy of making subpublishing arrangements which were terminable by the United States publisher in its sole discretion by a brief written notice. It must be remembered that, where reciprocal relations are involved and the United States publisher expects to acquire rights in foreign compositions for the United States, the United States publisher must expect similar treatment to be required by the foreign subpublisher. Some foreign societies, such as those of West Germany and Italy, may not recognize a subpublication agreement with a local subpublisher unless there is a minimum period of duration, ordinarily three years, although they may accept a reversionary clause which is activated sooner by the subpublisher's failure to achieve certain performance tests.

While all rights under copyright may be granted to a subpublisher, the original publisher will normally reserve the ownership of the copyright. This is a necessity if the agreement with the writer is an AGAC form. The subpublisher will agree that each copy of the composition published by the subpublisher will bear a notice of copyright in the name of the original publisher.

A problem may arise in respect of local arrangements, translations, and adaptations of the composition and local lyrics and titles. The subpublisher may attempt to retain the copyright for such local modifications and versions insofar as the new material is concerned. This will be opposed by an experienced United States publisher since, unless the United States publisher acquires the copyright in new material, he may be unable to exploit the composition fully in the local territory after the subpublisher's rights expire; also, the subpublisher who owns the copyright in new material would have to be asked to consent to its use by another subpublisher in a different territory and would presumably require a royalty payment as the price for the consent. The United States publisher will seek to possess all rights in new material outside of the particular local territory so that the material may be made available to other subpublishers who represent the United States publisher.

In catalog deals, it is common to provide that compositions will revert to the original publisher at the end of the term of the catalog arrangement. Exceptions are sometimes made for compositions which have been printed locally or released on a locally originated record, or both printed and so released on records. The subpublisher may contend that the local release of the original United States recording should justify continuing rights in a composition, since the subpublisher may cause such release. The duration of the continuing rights would be a matter of negotiation between the original publisher and the subpublisher. Sometimes provision is made for some extension of rights in compositions which are made available to the subpublisher only towards the end of the catalog deal and for which there has been printing or release on a local record, or both, before the close of the term; otherwise the subpublisher would have little or no incentive to promote such songs.

Fees from All Usages

Subpublication contracts specify the royalties payable for various uses of a composition. In order to avoid penalizing itself because of failure to set forth all conceivable uses, the American publisher must be careful to provide that it is entitled to a stipulated percentage of all moneys collected by the subpublisher for any use other than those particularized in the agreement. There should be no objection by the subpublisher to the inclusion of this provision.

Accountings and Audits

Unless a subpublisher is a reputable firm, many problems may develop regarding accountings and royalty payments due to the American publisher. The subpublication contract should clearly define the obligation to account and make payment.

A common provision requires the subpublisher to forward to the original publisher an itemized and detailed statement within 90 days after the end of each calendar half-year, for that half-year, together with a remittance of all amounts shown to be due. It is advisable to delineate the items to be set forth in the itemized statement, so that disputes about the completeness of the accounting may be avoided. For mechanical fees, these items may consist of a list of the individual records released in the territory, the names of the artists and record companies on the records, the number of records sold, and the total fees received; in brief, one may request a copy of the entries in accountings by the mechanical-right society. For performance fees, the subpublisher may be required to supply all entries made by the performing-right society in its accountings to the subpublisher. Accountings for printed editions should separately show the different editions, the retail price, and the number of copies sold.

In certain instances, the subpublisher may agree to furnish a photocopy of all statements received from the mechanical-right society and the performing-right society. It is more likely that this will apply to a single song than to a catalog since the societies account alphabetically, with many compositions on a page, and hundreds of pages may be involved in the latter instance. On the other hand the subpublisher may so strongly desire the rights to a catalog that it will agree to the extra work entailed in making many photocopies.

United States publishers, in order to verify and facilitate the collection of fees due them, may wish to arrange for accountings of foreign performance fees to be made to them by way of ASCAP or BMI. For this purpose, the subpublisher may be asked to agree to inform his performing-right society to pay the original publisher's share of performance fees to ASCAP or BMI for the account of the American publisher. Where the United States publisher has entered into an agreement with a local mechanical-right society, the society may be advised to pay the original publisher's share of mechanical-right collections directly to the United States publisher. Or, if the original publisher is represented through The Harry Fox Agency for mechanical-right collections in a foreign country, the local mechanical-right society can be instructed to arrange for payment of the original publisher's share to The Harry Fox Agency for remittance to the American publisher. Inherent, however, in payments through the societies may be years of delays in receiving remittances as well as service charges in the United States by BMI, ASCAP, and The Fox Agency when they are involved. (For discussion of the BMI and ASCAP charges see Chapter 18, "Performing-Right Organizations" and as to The Fox Agency charges see Chapter 20, "Mechanical Rights.") There are also risks of a possible loss due to commingling with the accounts and moneys of many other publishers, through failure to identify foreign version titles. The charges and risks may prove to be worthwhile if they result in greater overall receipts of royalties, some of which might otherwise fail to be accounted for.

A prudent United States publisher will obtain the right to inspect and audit the account books of the subpublisher. It may be impracticable for the United States publisher to exercise the right through its own employees because of the distance between the publishers and the expense that may be entailed. But an American publisher may retain a local accountant on a reasonable basis and make effective use of the right of audit.

Subpublication for Diverse Territories

An American publisher may contract with a subpublisher for several countries under one agreement. The contract may state that the subpublisher is granted rights for all European countries, or all English-speaking countries, etc. To the American publisher, it will appear advantageous to provide for such coverage by one agreement. Otherwise a series of contracts, one for each country, may be required. There are certain subpublishing territories that frequently are licensed alone or together with other territories as a matter of custom or convenience. They are indicated below, with the italicized names representing countries that may also be licensed alone.

(1) *Germany,* Austria, and Switzerland

(2) Scandinavia, including Sweden, Norway, Denmark, Finland, and Iceland

(3) *Spain* and Portugal

(4) *United Kingdom,* Northern Ireland, Republic of Eire, Australia, New Zealand, Israel, Rhodesia, and miscellaneous territories of the British Commonwealth of Nations other than Canada

(5) *France,* and territories under the jurisdiction of SACEM, the French performing-right society

(6) *Japan*

(7) *Belgium, Holland,* and Luxembourg (sometimes Belgium is included with France, and Luxembourg is split between West Germany and France on a language basis)

(8) *Italy,* Vatican City, and San Marino

(9) *Australia* and New Zealand (see United Kingdom above)

(10) *Union of South Africa*

(11) *Mexico,* Venezuela, Colombia, Ecuador, and Peru

(12) Central America

(13) *Argentina,* Uruguay, Chile, Paraguay, and Bolivia

(14) *Brazil*

(15) *Greece*

(16) *East Germany,* Poland, Czechoslovakia, Romania, and Hungary

Since different performing- and mechanical-right societies commonly exist in each country, it is to be anticipated that the original subpublisher will have to use the services of other subpublishers for full territorial coverage. These subpublishers may be affiliated with the original subpublisher through common ownership, or they may operate with the original subpublisher solely through contractual relationships.

Customarily, the United States publisher receives a percentage, which is likely to be at least 50 percent, of the performance and mechanical royalties collected by the original subpublisher. Through such a provision, the United States publisher may be expecting to be paid at least half of all earnings in each country in the licensed territory. Where the original subpublisher employs the services of a subpublisher in another country, the latter will deduct a fee before remitting collections to the former. This fee may be 50 percent of the collections. As a consequence, the original subpublisher may be paid only 50 percent of the funds earned at the source. Applying the subpublication contract with the American publisher literally, the United States publisher, assuming its royalty percentage is 50 percent, would then be entitled to be paid one-half of the original subpublisher's collections or only 25 percent of the earnings at the source.

It is conceivable that the 25 percent figure may be decreased even further if the earnings which flow to the original subpublisher are screened through a series of separate publishers, despite the fact that they may be owned by the same principals.

Where various subpublishers are unaffiliated except through contractual arrangements, the original subpublisher may contend that the fee deductions in each country are legitimate and represent only a service fee in which the American publisher must participate. Otherwise, runs the argument of the original subpublisher, he would have to remit to the American publisher 100 percent of what is received from the other subpublishers (assuming that they have deducted 50 percent as their fee), and would earn no compensation for having arranged for the other subpublications. The American publisher may believe that there is merit in this argument. The extra fee may be warranted for the run-of-the-mill copyright with limited earnings by the convenience of dealing with one subpublisher who will handle the details of exploitation in additional territories. However, for a valuable copyright and for overall catalog subpublishing, the American publisher will seek to be protected from the duplication of fees. The obvious solution is to deal directly with a subpublisher in each country.

A simpler approach, which preserves the advantages of having a single subpublisher handle several territories and thereby avoids multiple communications and contracts, is to safeguard the United States publisher through contractual provisions. Under these clauses the subpublisher will agree to account for the earnings from each country in the licensed area as if he were the original subpublisher in the country; a provision may state that there will be accountings of royalties "computed at the source." Or, better still, it may be agreed that there will be direct accountings from the subpublisher designated by the original subpublisher, in each country on the basis of the terms in the contract with the original subpublisher. There undoubtedly are subpublishers who will accede to such terms; some may have their own affiliated firms in the other countries; others will have contracted with the other subpublishers for a finder's fee or some other minor compensation. The foregoing may be combined with provisos that the performing-right and mechanical-right society in each country will be instructed to make deductions at the source for transmission of performance fees to the American publisher's performing-right organization for performance fees, and, where the United States publisher has made appropriate arrangements with the local mechanical-right society or The Harry Fox Agency, for remittance of mechanical fees to the United States publisher or The Harry Fox Agency.

Common Market Territories

There are ten European countries in the Common Market: England, France, West Germany, Italy, Holland, Belgium, Luxembourg, Greece, Ireland, and Denmark. Their relations are governed by the Treaty of Rome, which provides for the abolition of tariff barriers and the free and unrestricted movement of goods across state borders. Territorial sales restrictions in license agreements among the Common Market countries are invalid.

Questions arise as to the legality of exclusive subpublishing agreements with publishers in different Common Market states. For example, there may be one agreement with a subpublisher in England covering exclusive rights there, and another with a subpublisher in France providing for exclusive rights in that country. Must each of these subpublishers respect and recognize the exclusive rights of the other? In practice, if a subpublishing agreement is for a limited term such as three years, it may be anticipated that fear of no renewal of the agreement by the original American publisher may tend to keep each subpublisher within the bounds of its own territory. But third parties such as companies which buy phonograph records lawfully licensed for manufacture in France are free, under the Treaty of Rome, to export the records into England and other Common Market countries. The same would also seem to apply to printed editions manufactured in one Common Market state and bought for export to another.

But the Treaty of Rome has been said to not affect the exclusive rights of copyright proprietors in respect of such matters as rented sheet music or the licensing of the public performance of copyrighted works. To what extent the Treaty of Rome will restrict exclusivity and territorial restraints in subpublishing agreements is not entirely clear and the advice of local counsel should be obtained. Infringements of the Treaty may not only involve the negation of business deals but also in certain cases prosecution and fines by the European Economic Community Commission.

Frozen Funds

In a few areas of the world, because of governmental regulations, funds may not be readily transmittable to the United States in payment of royalties due to the United States publisher. For such areas, a clause in the subpublication contract may provide that in the event remittances are prohibited or delayed by governmental authority, the United States publisher may direct the subpublisher to deposit the funds to the account of the United States publisher in a depository designated by the American publisher. It is possible that the United States publisher may be able to utilize the moneys on deposit for local purchases, transportation, and living expenses; some American publishers affiliated with motion picture companies have been able to use portions of frozen funds for the production of motion pictures in the frozen-funds country. In addition, the money may earn interest and be invested locally. It is also removed from the perils of insolvency or defalcations on the part of the subpublisher.

Default Clauses

In a subpublication agreement, the subpublisher assumes diverse obligations. It is difficult and often well-nigh impossible to define the legal effect, especially in a distant territory, of a default by a subpublisher in the performance of an obligation, in the absence of a clear statement in the agreement of the effect intended by the parties. For example, if an accounting statement or a royalty payment is delayed, is this to be a ground for canceling the agreement?

It is advisable to include in the agreement a clause which defines the rights and obligations of the parties in case of a default. From the American publisher's point of view it can be provided that there will be a material default if the subpublisher fails to: (1) make periodic accountings, (2) pay royalties when due, or (3) cause the release of locally originated recordings which have been promised. It can be provided that for such a failure the United States publisher can terminate the agreement and cause a reversion of all rights in the composition. The subpublisher can in turn guard himself against cancellation by a clause under which the subpublisher is to receive a written notice of the default and an opportunity for a certain period, perhaps 30 days, to cure the default. The default clause may further state that the American publisher can cancel the subpublication agreement in the event an insolvency or bankruptcy proceeding is commenced by or against the subpublisher and is not dismissed within a given period, such as 30 to 60 days. This clause will protect the American publisher against administration of his copyright by a trustee or an assignee by reason of an insolvency or bankruptcy action. Should the subpublisher continue in control of the copyright the clause will place the American publisher in a position to reassess the financial and other capability of the subpublisher and to terminate the agreement in case the United States publisher becomes dissatisfied.

Jurisdiction over Disputes

Despite careful draftsmanship, subpublication contracts may still give rise to disputes regarding their interpretation. Recognizing this fact, and the expense entailed in litigating a matter in a foreign country, American publishers may strive to provide that the exclusive forum for the determination of controversies will be American courts, or an American arbitration tribunal, in a given state. Subpublishers may contend that all the facts are indigenous to their locality and therefore it is reasonable for the local courts or a local arbitration body to have exclusive jurisdiction; the matter is one to be resolved through negotiations.

Catalog Agreements

It has been previously stated that, if all the compositions of a United States publisher are the subject of a publication agreement, the agreement may be considered as a catalog subpublication contract under which all compositions are subpublished by the subpublisher for the term of the agreement. A catalog subpublication agreement has the advantage of relieving the United States publisher of the burden of negotiating separately for representation in the territory of each composition in the catalog. It entails the disadvantage of prohibiting the United States publisher from shopping for the largest cash advance among the various foreign subpublishers who may be interested in a musical work. On the other hand, a United States publisher can require an overall cash advance for his catalog as the price for committing his catalog to a subpublisher, and it is possible, although unlikely, that the overall advance will exceed the separate advances that might be negotiated for individual compositions. In negotiating a catalog deal, a United States publisher may be able to obtain other concessions, such as increased royalty rates and a shorter term for the subpublisher's interest in copyrights, which would not be granted if single compositions were involved.

Local Firms

Larger United States publishers may eventually try to establish their own firms in a local territory. The attempt may prove to be unfeasible economically unless their catalog is suitable for and potentially strong in the locality. Otherwise the investment for office space, personnel, and overhead may be unwarranted.

Certain foreign performing-right societies abroad, such as that in France, tend to discourage foreign-controlled firms. Thus in France not only is investment by a foreign company subject to authorization by the French government but also SACEM, the French society, requires a minimum number of French copyrights in the firm's catalog as a condition to becoming a publisher member.

On the other hand, performing-right societies abroad generally will permit any publisher to become an associate member with the right to be represented by the society and to receive publisher distributions. Becoming a full member with additional voting and other rights can be more difficult. P.R.S., the British Society, for example, has required that an associate publisher earn a minimum amount of about £10,000 a year before being promoted to full membership. GEMA, the German society, has insisted on at least five years of membership at a lower level and on a minimum total income level of 100,000 DM for five consecutive years, with minimums of 6,000 DM in each of four consecutive such years, before a publisher can be considered for full membership; despite such qualifications GEMA has been denying such membership to companies owned by United States firms. At times, the problem of attaining full membership may be solved by the purchase of local publishing firms which have already qualified for such membership. On the other hand, a United States publisher may be satisfied with an associate membership provided that, as is commonly observed by societies, associate members receive distributions on an equal basis with full members. The practices of each society should be investigated prior to the establishment of a local firm by a United States publisher.

Joint Firms

Recognizing the perils and problems represented by a wholly owned local firm, many United States publishers have in the past embarked on joint publishing ventures with an established local publisher. A firm is organized which is owned jointly by both parties. In this way, the United States publisher acquires local management and "know-how" at a minimum of cost, since advantageous arrangements can be made whereby the local partner manages the joint company and supplies necessary office and other facilities for a fee which is commonly a percentage of gross revenues of the joint company. The fee may approximate 10 to 15 percent, and is generally exclusive of direct expenses billed to the joint company for costs of demonstration records, trade paper advertising, salaries of personnel who work solely for the joint company, and special legal and accounting services. In some instances the local partner may absorb all expenses in return for a negotiated fee.

Where a new joint firm is organized, the local partner will arrange for its formation through territorial counsel. Expenses of organization may be advanced by the local partner as a charge against future net income of the joint company. It is advisable for the United States publisher to be fully cognizant of the impact of territorial laws and practices, and for this purpose the United States publisher should give serious consideration to being represented by his own local counsel, who, for adequate representation, should be familiar with the music business in the area, including the practices of the performing-right society.

In the event the local performing-right society will not qualify a new firm for membership unless it controls locally originated material, arrangements must be made with the territorial partner to supply this material. Otherwise the joint firm may never achieve membership in the society and may continue to be dependent on firms with membership for relations with the society.

It may be that the local performing-right society will not qualify a new firm for full membership unless certain standards are met, and the United States publisher desires full membership for the proposed joint firm. The contract with the territorial partner may provide for the acquisition of a local publishing company which is a full member.

A problem in the operation of joint firms is that they may be administered by the local partner as if they were catalog deals. In other words, only the material from the United States publisher goes into the joint firm, and nothing is done by the local partner to develop the firm into the status of a local publisher that vigorously seeks to acquire and exploit territorial copyrights. This is easily understood, since as to any new material unearthed by the local partner he must decide whether to place it with his own 100 percent owned publishing enterprise or with the joint firm in which he has merely a 50 percent interest. In effect, the local partner tends to treat a joint firm as a catalog deal in which the United States partner's 50 percent interest is equivalent to an increased royalty; in return for the increased royalty the territorial partner is assured of a flow of desirable product for a number of years.

Overcoming the inertia of the territorial partner is not simple. One approach may be to employ a professional manager who will work solely for the joint firm. This may result in a large financial burden for the firm, which the United States partner and the territorial partner may be unwilling to risk. A professional manager will ordinarily be chosen by the local partner, who may be able to influence the professional manager to permit choice copyrights to continue to vest in the local partner's publishing firm. The territorial partner may consciously choose an ineffective professional manager so that the joint firm may not be built up as a strong competitor in local publishing.

Perhaps the answer lies in a formula, undoubtedly difficult to administer, whereby a certain proportion of local copyrights acquired by the territorial partner must vest in the joint firm. Of course, even with a formula, the United States partner cannot be sure of receiving an interest in quality copyrights.

What are the advantages of joint firms as compared with catalog arrangements? In the first place, were the joint firm to be a member of the local performing-right and mechanical-right societies, the accountings for copyrights controlled by the firm would be completely segregated, and losses due to improper accountings by the local partner would be avoided. Where the subpublisher's honesty and dependability are entirely clear, this advantage may not be significant.

A joint company may be formed because the United States publisher anticipates a greater overall return than would be derived from a catalog deal. However, the American publisher may fail to assess adequately all of the factors which will affect the ultimate earnings which redound to his benefit.

Let us take a practical example. It may be assumed that the joint firm will gross $50,000 during a given year, of which by contract $25,000

(50 percent) is paid to the American partner as customary subpublication royalties. A balance of $25,000 remains. From the $25,000 the local partner will deduct his management fee of 10 percent of the gross ($5,000) leaving $20,000. Direct expenses, such as demonstration records and advertising, are also deductible. Assuming direct expenses of $5,000 or about 10 percent of the gross, the balance is $15,000, which constitutes net profits. Taxes on profits in European countries vary, but a range of about 30 to 55 percent has been observed. Assuming in this instance a 50 percent tax rate, the taxes on net profits would be $7,500. The remaining profits, $7,500, would be split equally between the partners so that each would receive $3,750.

In terms of the gross of $50,000 the profit share of each partner in the example given is about 7½ percent. For comparison with a catalog deal, it would thus appear that the United States publisher, instead of a 50 percent of gross royalty, is apparently receiving the equivalent of a 57½ percent royalty. This figure is fallacious in that the 7½ percent increase should in reality be doubled to 15 percent or a total of 65 percent. The doubling occurs because under international tax conventions the 50 percent (or other percentage) tax paid in the principal foreign countries can be offset against domestic taxes in the United States. Under catalog arrangements, on the other hand, royalties received are subjected to domestic U.S.A. taxes, whereas the profit collected would in a real sense be exempt from domestic taxes.

Even the figure of 65 percent will not offer an absolutely true comparison with a catalog arrangement, since in the case of catalog royalties 50 percent of moneys received in the United States on account of foreign mechanical fees and foreign printed editions would be payable to the writers. Thus, an extra 15 percent for mechanical fees and a printed editions royalty, under a catalog deal, would in effect be halved insofar as the United States publisher is concerned, although it is doubtful that writers would share in any part of an equivalent 15 percent received in the form of profits. Of course, the writers would not participate in any performance fees collected under a catalog deal, and such fees can be expected to total at least a significant percentage of additional earnings from increased royalty rates.

It can be argued that an American publisher with a joint firm is better able to acquire from other American publishers foreign territorial rights in American copyrights. With a joint firm an American publisher may effectively represent that he is actually in business in a territory. He may actively engage in pursuing territorial rights in attractive United States copyrights. He may have the authority to execute subpublication agreements with and make cash advances to United States publishers on behalf of the joint firm. His representatives outside the United States may also seek to obtain rights in local copyrights for areas where there are joint firms.

In the absence of a joint firm, arrangements can be made with subpublishers for an American publisher to receive a commission or finder's fee for copyrights acquired for subpublication by the sub-publishers, and these commissions or fees may equal the compensation accruing through an interest in a joint firm. But such arrangements are unlikely to operate as flexibly and as well as those with a joint firm. In the one instance the American publisher will be merely an agent for the subpublisher with limited powers and authority; in the other he is a partner striving to increase the profits and minimize the risks and losses for a jointly owned business.

Finally, it must be recognized that while a catalog deal is designed to exploit a catalog and result in a profit to the American publisher, the joint firm not only accomplishes the same purpose but can also act as a necessary prelude to a wholly owned local publishing enterprise. It has been pointed out that many American publishers cannot afford the expense and overhead of a completely owned firm. This may be true only for the period of years during which the United States publisher's catalog is becoming established in an area. At the end of the period, the American publisher may have both the earnings and the vehicle, namely the joint company, for his own publishing business. To convert the joint firm into one owned entirely by the American publisher means that he must acquire the interest of the local partner.

Termination of Joint Ownership

Inherent in the formation of a joint company is the agreement on the part of the American partner to make a catalog deal with the company for a period of years. The number of years is subject to negotiations and may range from three upwards. An average of five years would appear to be common.

It is usual to provide for the manner in which the joint firm will continue after the period of years expires. The American partner will wish to have an option to buy out the local partner so that the United States publisher may have a wholly owned firm in the territory. This option may be exercised in many ways.

It may be covenanted that the purchase price for the half interest of the local partner will be computed as a certain number times the average net income or the last year's net income of the company. Assuming that it is reasonable to value a publishing company's net income in a range of six times such income, then the parties might fix the purchase price for a half interest at three times the net income. To this might be added half the costs of organizing the company, which may come to only a few hundred dollars. For example, if the company's net income is $10,000 the purchase price for the half interest may be stipulated as $30,000.

Another method is to provide for negotiations on the price and, if the parties are unable to agree, to have the price settled by designated arbitrators.

A further method is to have a local partner divide the copyrights into two lists of equal quality and give to the American partner the right to elect to take either list plus the stock interest of the territorial partner. Again the parties may agree to have half of the costs of organizing the company reimbursed to the local partner.

A different approach may be for the parties to offer successive bids, each a stipulated amount higher than the previous bid until the highest bidder prevails. For example, bids might start at $500 and each counter-bid must be $500 greater. The problem here is that the local partner may prevail and the American partner will be defeated in his attempt to have a wholly owned firm.

The parties may agree on a buy or sell clause, which means that either party may make an initial bid to buy the other's interest, on the understanding that the other party may instead buy out the bidder at the same price. Here once more the local partner may be the final buyer and thus frustrate the purpose of the American partner.

To avoid the necessity for a complicated procedure for either party to acquire the other's interest, the American partner may trade a long-term catalog deal—for example, ten years with the joint company—in return for an assignment to him gratis of the local partner's interest at the end of the ten-year period. Or an alternative approach, with practically the same economic results to the local partner, might be for the American partner to retain 100 percent ownership at all times but have the firm managed by the local publisher on a basis which would give the same net return to the local publisher that he would receive if he were a partner; this may not be practicable where the joint firm must have some local ownership in order to qualify for membership in local societies.

The parties may not only provide a procedure by which one partner may acquire the interest of the other but may also set forth their rights and obligations in the event an acquisition is not made. The partners would own a company which is no longer receiving new copyrights from the American partner. It will be at that time largely a repository of the copyrights previously certified to it. It will require accounting, administrative, and legal services but to a limited extent. In such circumstances the United States partner will want to limit the management fee of the local partner, who may have been receiving 10 to 15 percent of the gross receipts of the joint firm for providing physical facilities and services. It may be provided that the management fee will drop to a lower percentage, such as 5 percent, when the catalog deal with the American partner expires. It may be further agreed that the direct expenses of the company will not exceed specific amounts for any one item, perhaps $100, without the consent of both partners.

In determining whether the American partner will wish to buy out the local partner or to have complete ownership from inception, consideration should be given to the effect of American tax laws. Especially where the local firm will be largely a repository of copyrights without substantial operating activities, sole ownership by the American partner may be a factor in a potential decision by United States tax authorities that the American partner is a foreign personal holding company, subject to specified high taxes in America. If the local firm is to be run from the United States, as though a branch operation, the local government may possibly declare that the American owner has a permanent establishment in the foreign territory and that the usual tax exemption on original publisher royalties, under international tax conventions, is inapplicable. This may be somewhat offset by the ability in certain cases to reduce United States domestic taxes by the additional foreign taxes that would be payable. For a further discussion of tax aspects, see Chapter 38, "Taxation in the Music Business."

20

Mechanical Rights

The rights to reproduce a copyrighted composition in copies or phonorecords and to distribute them to the public are exclusive to owners of copyright. They are important and lucrative aspects of copyright.

Phonograph records and tapes, electrical transcriptions, and audio tapes for broadcast and background music purposes are included under the right of reproduction. Also encompassed is the use of a composition for synchronization with motion pictures, television films, and video tapes. Based on language in the 1909 Copyright Act and industry usage, the right of reproduction for phonograph records and tapes, electrical transcriptions, and audio tapes for broadcast and background music purposes is commonly referred to as a "mechanical right" and licenses thereof as "mechanical licenses" or "mechanical-right licenses." The right of reproduction, for the purposes of synchronization with films or video tapes, is under industry parlance ordinarily referred to as a "synchronization right" and licenses thereof as "synchronization licenses." For a further discussion of synchronization with films and video tapes reference should be made to Chapter 28, "Music and the Movies." and to Chapter 7, "Music Videos."

History

Until 1909, there was no copyright protection for the right to record a composition on phonograph records or other mechanical devices. Anyone might with perfect freedom and without any compensation to the copyright owner reproduce copyrighted music by mechanical means. Under the United States Copyright Act of 1909, recording and mechanical reproduction rights, with regard solely to compositions "published and copyrighted" subsequent to July 1, 1909, were for the first time recognized as exclusively vested in the copyright owner, except as such rights were restricted by compulsory license provisions. Although the statute referred to "published and copyrighted" compositions, the courts held that it also applied to unpublished copyrighted songs. Under Section 1(e) of the Act, it was provided that the copyright owner had the right "to make . . . any form of record in which the thought of an author may be recorded and from which it may be read or reproduced."

Congress was concerned not only with protecting the composer as to mechanical reproduction rights but also with preventing a music monopoly which might result from such protection. The Aeolian Co., a leading mechanical reproduction company which manufactured piano rolls, had made exclusive contracts with the major publishers whereby there would be a pre-emption of the mechanical reproduction rights to the catalogs of the publishers upon recognition of mechanical rights by court decision or by statute. Under the contracts, exclusive mechanical rights would be acquired for a period of at least 35 years, with the possibility of almost indefinite extension.

To avoid the potential monopoly, Congress provided in Section 1(e) of the 1909 Act that if the copyright owner used or permitted the use of a copyrighted composition for mechanical reproduction, then all others might reproduce the music on payment by the manufacturer to the copyright proprietor of a royalty of 2 cents "on each such part manufactured." This is often referred to as the compulsory license or the compulsory mechanical license.

Although the compulsory license provision called for "2 cents on each such part manufactured," the music industry interpreted the clause as meaning 2 cents per composition contained in a recording. Referring to the word "part," which might be construed to mean the entire disc or other mechanical contrivance for the production of sound, it had been sometimes argued that the compulsory license would cover the rerecording of a copyrighted composition in a motion picture or television soundtrack. The motion picture and television industries have, however, been unanimous in seeking synchronization licenses from copyright owners on negotiated terms and no reliance has been placed on the compulsory license clause.

Compulsory License under 1976 Act

Under the 1976 Copyright Act, which became generally effective January 1, 1978, when phonorecords of a nondramatic composition have been distributed to the public with the authorization of the copyright owner, any other person may record and distribute phonorecords of the work upon giving certain notice and paying a statutory royalty. Commencing on July 1, 1984 the royalty became 4½ cents for each record of a composition made and distributed or .85 cent per minute or fraction thereof, whichever is larger. On January 1, 1986 the rates are scheduled to increase to 5 cents and .95 cent, respectively. The alternate rate of .85 cent per minute or fraction thereof, as compared to the 4½ cent rate, will require an extra payment on songs 5:01 minutes or longer. For a 5:01 minute song the royalty thus will be 5:10 cents. A record is deemed to be distributed if possession has been "voluntarily and permanently parted with."

The compulsory license, under the 1976 Copyright Act, allows the making of an "arrangement of the work to the extent necessary to conform it to the style or manner of interpretation of the performance." Even a "sound alike" recording, with an arrangement similar to that in a prior recording, is permitted. However, a compulsory license must avoid changing the basic melody or fundamental character of the work.[1] There can be no claim made to an arrangement as a derivative copyright, unless consented to by the copyright owner.

Compulsory mechanical licenses under the 1976 Copyright Act apply solely to audio recordings primarily intended to be distributed to the public for private use. They are not available for purposes of background music services, broadcast transcriptions or commercial motion picture synchronization. A compulsory license applies only to musical works reproduced in new recordings. There can be no compulsory license as to compositions to be used in the duplication of a prior sound recording, unless consent has been obtained from the owner of the prior recording which itself was fixed lawfully.[2] This acts as a significant restriction on the pirating of recordings.

Parting with Possession-Returns

As noted previously, under the 1976 Act a record is not deemed to be distributed and no compulsory mechanical license fee is due unless possession of the record has been "voluntarily and permanently parted with." The House of Representatives Committee on the Judiciary has said that

> the concept of "distribution" comprises any act by which the person exercising the compulsory license voluntarily relinquishes possession of a phonorecord (considered as a fungible unit), regardless of whether the distribution is to the public, passes title, constitutes a gift, or is sold, rented, leased, or loaned, unless it is actually returned and the transaction canceled.

In the legislative history preceeding the 1976 Act there is recognition of a record industry practice to distribute records with return privileges. The House Committee on the Judiciary has stated:

> phonorecords are distributed to wholesalers and retailers with the privilege of returning unsold copies for credit or exchange. As a result, the number of recordings that have been "permanently" distributed will not usually be known until some time—six or seven months on the average—after the initial distribution. In recognition of this problem, it has become a well-established industry practice, under negotiated licenses, for record companies to maintain reasonable reserves of the mechanical royalties due the copyright owners, against which royalties on the returns can be offset. The Committee recognizes that this practice may be consistent with the statutory

---

[1]This is similar to the practice under the 1909 Act.
[2]This principle was followed by the courts under the 1909 Act.

requirements for monthly compulsory license accounting reports, but recognizes the possibility that, without proper safeguards, the maintenance of such reserves could be manipulated to avoid making payments of the full amounts owing to copyright owners.

The Committee recommended that the regulations to be promulgated by the Register of Copyrights

should contain detailed provisions ensuring that the ultimate disposition of every phonorecord made under a compulsory license is accounted for, and that payment is made for every phonorecord "voluntarily and permanently" distributed. In particular the Register should prescribe a point in time when . . . a phonorecord will be considered "permanently distributed," and should prescribe the situation in which a compulsory licensee is barred from maintaining reserves (e.g., situations in which the compulsory licensee has frequently failed to make payments in the past).

The Register of Copyrights has prescribed a regulation which in effect gives a compulsory licensee nine months at the most, from the month in which the records were relinquished from possession, to hold mechanical royalties in a reserve fund. However, the regulation denies such reserve to a habitual nonpayer of mechanical royalties. Such a licensee is one who, within three years from when a phonorecord was parted from possession, has had final judgment rendered against it for failing to pay mechanical royalties on phonorecords, or within such period has been found in any proceeding involving bankruptcy, insolvency, receivership, assignment for the benefit of creditors, or similar action, to have failed to pay such royalties.

The Register of Copyright did not establish any criteria for what a reasonable reserve would be and this is governed by general accounting procedures.

Notice of Intention

Anyone who proposes to invoke the benefit of compulsory licensing provisions under the 1976 Act must serve a "notice of intention" in a form and manner of service prescribed by the Register of Copyrights. The notice is similar to the "notice of intention to use" under the prior 1909 law. Pursuant to Section 115 of the 1976 Act the notice must be sent to the copyright owner before any records are distributed, with service to take place before or within 30 days after making the record.[3] If the records of the Copyright Office fail to identify the copyright owner

[3]Under the 1909 Act the notice of intention to use had to be served by registered mail on the copyright owner at his last address on record at the Copyright Office, with a duplicate to that office.

and his address, then the notice requirements can be met by sending the notice to the Copyright Office together with a $6 fee.

For failure to serve a compulsory license notice, the 1976 Act, in its words, "forecloses the possibility of a compulsory license." Absent a negotiated license, the making and distribution of phonorecords are thereby rendered actionable as acts of copyright infringement.

Compulsory License Accountings

A compulsory licensee under the 1976 Act must make monthly royalty payments on or before the twentieth of each month, for records made and distributed during the preceding month. With each payment there must be accompanied a detailed accounting statement made under oath.[4] The copyright owner is also entitled to cumulative annual statements that are certified by a Certified Public Accountant.

There is an automatic termination under the 1976 Act of a compulsory license for failure to render monthly payments and the monthly and annual accounts when due, if the default is not cured within 30 days after written notice by the copyright owner.[5]

Copyright Owner Identification

There is no obligation under the 1976 Act to pay royalties to a copyright owner pursuant to a compulsory license unless he is identified in the registration or other records of the Copyright Office. This provides an incentive for early copyright registration by an owner.

A copyright owner is entitled to compulsory license royalties for phonorecords made and distributed after he makes such identification, but he cannot recover for phonorecords made and distributed before the identification.

Negotiated License

The procedure for monthly accountings and payments under the 1976 Act is a considerable deterrent to resorting to compulsory licensees.[6] In the music industry it is standard for a record manufacturer to account for and pay royalties quarterly and not monthly, and statements are not usually required to be made under oath. The possibility of obtaining a royalty rate of less than the statutory rate also militates in favor of a negotiated license. By reason of the 1976 Act compulsory license clause, 4½ cents per composition or .85 cent per minute or fraction thereof, whichever is larger, is likely to serve as a ceiling on royalties in United States negotiated licenses for a previously recorded and pub-

---

[4]Under the 1909 Act monthly accountings under oath could be required by the Copyright proprietor.

[5]The 1909 Act made no provision for termination of the license in such circumstances, although a suit for money was provided.

[6]The same deterrent operated under the 1909 Act.

lished copyrighted composition until higher statutory rates go into effect on January 1, 1986 and then such higher rates will serve as a ceiling.[7] In addition, it is unnecessary to serve a notice of intention to obtain a compulsory license if the publisher issues a negotiated license. A copy of a mechanical-license form is included in Part 4 as Form 8.

The compulsory license provision is inapplicable to the first recording of a copyrighted composition. The copyright owner has complete discretion with respect to consenting to the first recording and imposing terms and conditions for such consent. Thus, the copyright proprietor may insist on such terms as higher mechanical royalties (for example, 5½ cents per composition), or that the record couple two compositions controlled by the copyright owner, or that the next recording by the same artist include a copyrighted composition from the catalog of the copyright proprietor. In practice, however, publishers usually grant initial licenses at the prevailing statutory rate and without additional restriction.

The Harry Fox Agency

In the United States, the predecessor of an association of leading publishers, now known as the National Music Publishers Association, Inc. (NMPA), established The Harry Fox Agency, Inc. (formerly known as The Harry Fox Office) of 205 East 42nd Street, New York, N.Y. 10017. It was created to act as agent-trustee to administer in the United States and Canada mechanical licenses on behalf of publishers who wish to avail themselves of its services on a fee basis. In 1976, the Canadian functions of The Fox Agency were taken over by the Canadian Musical Reproduction Rights Agency Limited, known as CMRRA.

The Harry Fox Agency represents over 3,500 publishers, many of whom are unaffiliated with the NMPA. The Agency's annual gross receipts exceed $81 million. Its services include the issuance of mechanical and synchronization licenses and the supervision of collections from record companies. The agency employs an auditing firm to check periodically the books of record companies so as to ensure proper accountings of mechanical-license fees. Litigation has been instituted at the instigation of publishers represented by The Harry Fox Agency to pursue delinquent record firms and record pirates, as well as to settle disputes regarding interpretations of the Copyright Act. For its mechanical license services, the agency charges 4½ percent of the collections made for publishers.

There is one basic type of mechanical license issued by The Harry Fox Agency on behalf of the publishers it represents. Thereunder the manufacturer must account and pay for all records manufactured and distributed.

---

[7]The ceiling under the 1909 Act was 2 cents per composition; under that act it was required that the composition need only be recorded with the permission or acquiescence of the copyright owner as a prerequisite to the invocation of a compulsory license.

The license calls for quarterly accountings and payments. The license provides that failure to make accountings and payments constitutes grounds for revocation of the license. It also states that service of a notice of intention to obtain a compulsory license is waived.

The license sets forth that the proposed users wish to use the copyrighted work under the compulsory license provision of the copyright statute. The license provides that the licensees have all the rights granted to, and all the obligations imposed upon, users of copyrighted works under the said compulsory license provision, with certain exceptions. These exceptions relate to quarterly instead of monthly or annual accountings, and a waiver of the notice of intention to obtain a compulsory license.

In respect of The Harry Fox license form used under the 1909 Act, the courts have held that the form is merely an agreement modifying a compulsory license and does not comprise a private contract as such. The courts have treated the matter as involving a compulsory license. The Harry Fox license form utilized since the 1976 Act is also designed to be only an agreement modifying a compulsory license.

An important provision of the 1976 statute specifically states that, if a default continues after a 30-day written notice of overdue royalties, there is an automatic termination of the compulsory license.[8] Furthermore, the termination results in the making and distribution of phonorecords for which royalties are unpaid, being actionable as acts of copyright infringement.

Other United States Mechanical-Rights Organizations

The American Mechanical Rights Association (AMRA), which is located at 2112 Broadway, New York, N.Y. 10023, was organized in 1961. AMRA licenses mechanical and synchronization rights for music publishers and writers. It charges a fee of 5 percent of the gross collections. AMRA also represents a number of foreign mechanical-rights societies, of which the largest is GEMA, the performing-right and mechanical-right society of West Germany.

Another firm offering services to publishers and writers is Mietus Copyright Management of 2351 Laurance Road, Union, New Jersey 07083. Mietus handles administration, licensing and collections worldwide. It invokes a one-time setup fee and charges 10 percent of worldwide collections received in the United States. It does not offer publisher accounting services, such as writer royalty statements.

The Copyright Service Bureau Ltd, which is located at 221 West 57th Street, New York, N.Y. 10019, performs the same licensing functions as Mietus Copyright Management. In addition to licensing, registering copyrights and other administrative functions, the Copyright Service Bureau acts as the publisher's accounting office for the render-

---

[8]It is rephrased in the Harry Fox license.

ing of statements to writers and to other publishers. Its fee is 15 percent for international and 10 percent for domestic collections.

The respective annual receipts of AMRA, the Copyright Service Bureau Ltd and Mietus Copyright Management are very small by comparison with those of The Harry Fox Agency, Inc.

The Songwriters Guild, formerly known as the American Guild of Authors and Composers, of 276 Fifth Avenue, New York, N.Y. 10001, has a catalog administration plan for its songwriter members who retain publishing rights. For a further discussion, see Chapter 24, "The Writer as His Own Publisher."

The Canadian Mechanical-Rights Organization

As indicated previously, the Canadian Musical Reproduction Rights Agency Limited (CMRRA) of 198 Davenport Road, Toronto, Ontario M5R1J2, in 1976 assumed the functions previously carried out by The Fox Agency in Canada. For its services CMRRA charges a fee of 5 percent of the collections made for any publishers. United States publishers can deal only with CMRRA for Canada since The Fox Agency will not undertake representation for that country.

International Mechanical-Right Societies

The Harry Fox Agency through affiliations with various territorial mechanical-right societies can make arrangements for them to act as agents to collect local mechanical-license fees on behalf of United States publishers in countries other than Canada. The fees charged by the local societies tend to approximate 15 percent, to which is added the 4½ percent charge which The Fox Agency applies to receipts handled by it. The Société Pour l'Administration du Droit de Reproduction Mécanique (SDRM) based in France will make collections for The Fox Agency in France, the former French colonies, Italy, Belgium, Holland and Luxembourg. The German society, known as GEMA, collects on behalf of The Fox Agency in Germany, Austria, Bulgaria, Rumania, Turkey, Israel, and the Philippines. The Mechanical Copyright Protection Society of Great Britain (MCPS) acts for the agency in the British Commonwealth, including Great Britain, Scotland, Ireland, and South Africa. Nordisk Copyright Bureau (NCB) handles collections for Scandinavia. The Agency is represented by the Spanish society (SGAE) in Spain and Portugal, the Russian society (VAAP) in the Soviet Union, the Swiss society (SUISA) in Switzerland, and the ANZ Musical Copyright Agency in Australia and New Zealand. JASRAC, the Japanese society, makes collections in Japan. Some of the societies handle performing-rights licensing and collections as well as mechanical-rights licensing and collections. In respect of certain mechanical-right societies, American publishers can make direct arrangements for the collection of mechanical-right fees in foreign areas; among these are MCPS, SDRM, GEMA, and NCB. JASRAC and the Italian society (SIAE) do not permit such arrangements. Through direct dealings with mechanical-right societies American publishers can eliminate The Harry Fox Agency charge of $4^1/2$ percent, but they forgo the convenience of having different territories serviced through the one agency.

Writer Share of Mechanical Fees

In contracts between publishers and songwriters it is standard for the writer to receive 50 percent of the mechanical-license fees collected by the contracting ("original") publisher. Thus, of every four cents paid to the original publisher the writer will be entitled to two cents. Where foreign subpublishers are entitled to retain 50 percent of the mechanical fees collected by them and they remit the balance to the original publisher, the writer will in effect receive one-quarter of the collections by the foreign subpublisher. In computing royalties due to the original publisher (and which the original publisher shares with the writer), it is common to disregard charges made by the local mechanical-right society which collected mechanical-license fees from local record companies and remitted the balance, after its charges, to the subpublisher, since it is this balance on which the royalty to the original publisher is customarily computed.

Record Clubs

Mechanical licenses are not issued separately by The Harry Fox Agency to record clubs which reissue original products, and the clubs do not obtain compulsory licenses at the statutory rate for such reissues. The clubs claim to be an extension of the original record manufacturer, and they have been relying on industry custom in most instances in respect of paying 75 percent of the compulsory license rate in respect of a composition re-released through a club. In the past, problems have arisen because a club has assumed that it need pay only 75 percent of reduced rates granted in some licenses. The Harry Fox Agency has taken the position that clubs must remit the higher of 75 percent of the original rate or 75 percent of the compulsory license rate. The Agency will abide by lower club rates negotiated by the publisher it represents.

Title Use Restriction

Pursuant to instructions from certain publishers, a Fox Agency license may contain a restriction against the use of a licensed song as the title of a record album. Such uses may be the special concern of publishers affiliated with motion picture companies or with record companies which release soundtrack albums or original cast albums. Where the title song of a film is named after the film, for example, "Never on Sunday," an album with the same title as the song may be confused by the public with the soundtrack album from the motion picture. The same would apply to a song from a show which has a title identical to that of the show, for example, "Promises, Promises." The publishers who impose the restriction seek to avoid this confusion and to regulate this type of usage.

Record Rentals

Effective as to copies of sound recordings acquired on or after October 4, 1984, there can be no commercial rental, lease or lending by the owner of the copies unless authorized by the copyright proprietors of the recordings and of the underlying musical works. The applicable legislation,[9] to that extent, is a modification of the First Sale Doctrine of copyright law, pursuant to which a purchaser of a phonorecord or an audiovisual recording, whether disc, tape, Compact Disc or other configuration, has been permitted to rent, lease or lend it without the consent of such copyright proprietors. The First Sale principle continues to apply to audiovisual recordings such as videocassettes.

An unauthorized commercial rental, lease or lending constitutes a copyright infringement subject to civil but not criminal infringement penalties under existing copyright laws.

A record company may place itself in a position to authorize unilaterally the commercial rental, lease or lending of records. This may be accomplished by the record company by either negotiating a voluntary license from the music copyright owner or resorting to the established system of obtaining a compulsory mechanical license for the making and distribution of records. However, for the compulsory licensing of rentals, leasing or lending the statute requires the payment of a royalty over and above that applicable to sales of records. The compulsory licensee must share its rental, lease or lending revenues with the music copyright proprietor in the same proportion as revenues from the sales of recordings are allocated between the copyright owners of the sound recording and the underlying music. At this writing the royalty formula remains to be implemented by regulations to be issued by the Copyright Office.

Congressional hearings leading up to the passage of the act regulating record rentals, leasing and lending indicated a direct link between those activities and the making of copies of records without the permission of or compensation to the copyright owners, the recording artists, the musicians and the composers. There was the threat of potentially substantial lost sales for manufacturers, distributors, and retail record stores. These factors were involved in the economic and policy concern behind the legislation.

The Act of October 4, 1984 enacting the above regulation of record rental, leasing and lending provides that its provisions will become ineffective after five years from that date.

[9]Act of October 4, 1984 (Pub. Law 98-450)

21

Arrangements and Abridgements of Music

The public does not hear songs or see them in written form until arrangements of the songs have been made. Nor are foreign songs presented, except in rare cases, to the American public with foreign lyrics. Songs usually require some development by arrangers, whose efforts may vary from mere transposition of keys and elaboration of chord structures to important creative work. Foreign lyrics must be substantially revised and not just translated, in view of the necessary adaptation of rhyme and accents.

Arrangers have sometimes been lauded as being more important to the success of a popular record than the original writers. In a statement submitted to Congress, it was contended that the creativity embodied in popular records played on a jukebox is often less attributable to composers than to persons without copyright status.

Jazz performers commonly make such substantial revisions of the basic song that it would take an expert musicologist to identify the source of the melodic material.

Many rock and roll singers make their own impromptu arrangements while performing because of inability to read music as well as their desire for spontaneity.

The vital impact of rock music upon the role of the arranger is well described in Milt Okun's "Great Songs of the Sixties." He there sets out the musical characteristics of rock music as differentiated from previous standards of popular music. "What basically happened was that the rhythm section, consisting of bass, guitar, drums and piano, which formerly gave the underpinning to a band, stepped to the front and became the whole band. . . ." He says further: "Rhythm like this must be worked out in rehearsal. It is much more complex and demanding than the reading of standard rhythm charts. Since most of the excitement comes from rhythmic development, plus improvisation, the trained arranger is not needed. Now there is arranging by group. One by-product of rock thus has been the unemployment of arrangers."

Control by Copyright Proprietor
Both the 1976 Copyright Act and the previous act permit arrangements to be copyrighted only if made by the copyright owner of the original

work or with his consent. Arrangements used on popular records rarely qualify for copyrighting under either of these conditions. The copyright owner, whether publisher or writer, ordinarily does not prepare the record arrangement and makes no claim for copyright in the arrangement. Nor is the consent of the music publisher obtained for the arrangement to be copyrighted by another person. The copyright owner issues a more or less standard mechanical license to record, which in practice is deemed to indicate that no objection will be made to the arrangements required for purposes of recording. The license in this instance amounts to an agreement not to object rather than a consent or grant of rights.

There can be no question that in popular music the English version of a foreign song is truly a new version that requires creative effort over and beyond mechanical translation. English versions are nearly always undertaken on assignment from the music publisher controlling the basic copyright and, unlike arrangements for purposes of record company sessions, the publisher will claim a further copyright in the new lyric version and the author of the new version will be given credit and royalties.

Arrangers for record company sessions rarely have any relationship to the music publisher and achieve no copyright status; they receive compensation solely from the record company or artists.

Some arrangers work directly for or with music publishers and printed music licensees, and copyrights are obtained on their arrangements. These arrangers are the musically knowledgeable and trained persons who prepare songs for printing in sheet music, orchestration, or folio form. Frequently the songs have already been recorded. Separate arrangements may be required for single instruments and voice and for the diverse parts for different instruments in bands and orchestras. These arrangers are customarily employed on a weekly salary or assignment basis, with no right to royalties, and, although their names may sometimes appear on the printed edition, as employees for hire they have no copyright or renewal status. A copy of an arranger's acknowledgment of his status as an employee for hire is included in Part 4 as Form 4.

Statutory Treatment of Arrangements

Most arrangements by their very nature may be categorized as supplemental works. As stated above they are usually prepared by employees for hire who acquire no rights in the copyright or in renewal copyrights, and with the employer being considered as the author of the work and the initial copyright owner.

The 1976 Copyright Act clarifies the status of works prepared on special order or commission for use "as a supplementary work." In the past there were disputes as to whether such works were prepared by an employee within the scope of employment or whether the person was acting as an independent contractor. Under the 1976 Act, if the parties expressly agree in writing that a supplementary work shall be deemed to be "a work made for hire," the agreement is binding and the employer is regarded as the author and initial owner of the copyright. The Act specifically defines "musical arrangements" as supplementary works as to which such an agreement can be made.

The 1976 Copyright Act sets forth certain standards for permissible arrangements in sound recordings in connection with provisions for compulsory licenses. Under Section 115 of the Act there can be a compulsory license for making and distributing phonorecords of a work once phonorecords of the work have been distributed to the public in the United States under authority of the copyright owner. A compulsory license, under the Act, permits the "making of a musical arrangement of the work to the extent necessary to conform it to the style or manner of interpretation of the performance." But the compulsory licensee cannot "change the basic melody or fundamental character of the work." The arrangement is not "subject to protection as a derivative work . . . except with the express consent of the copyright owner." For a further discussion of compulsory licenses, see Chapter 20, "Mechanical Rights."

Effect on Duration of Basic Work

The nature of musical arrangements or English-lyric versions assumes the prior existence of the basic work. A question arises as to whether the "derivative work," founded as it is on an earlier composition, has the effect of prolonging the term of copyright in the basic work. The Copyright Office has stated simply that "protection for a copyrighted work cannot be lengthened by republishing the work with new matter." The 1976 Act provides that the copyright in the derivative work "is independent of, and does not affect or enlarge the scope, duration, ownership, or subsistence of, any copyright protection in the pre-existing material."

In practical effect, however, copyrighted new versions may be used during the copyright term of the basic version to cause the public to accept the new version in place of the earlier version, and the publisher may thereby obtain the benefit of the longer copyright term of the new version; the lengthier term may arise from the 75th year from publication or 100th year from creation, whichever is earlier, period of protection under the 1976 Act of the work of an arranger who is an employee for hire or the life-plus-50-year term in the case of an arranger who is an independent contractor.[1] For example, under the 1909 Act, the publisher of Debussy's "Claire de Lune" benefited from a new English version of the song recorded some years before the basic copyright

---

[1] Under the 1909 Act the new matter would be protected for two 28 year terms.

expired and before any other publisher could issue a new version. The English version represents an application of two rights regarding new versions granted to copyright owners by copyright statutes: the exclusive right to prepare derivative works by the arrangement or adaptation of musical works and the right to copyright derivative works.

Standards of Originality

Not all arrangements are capable of copyright protection even if prepared with the consent of the copyright owner or, without such consent, during the public domain status of the arranged work. An element of creative authorship must be involved. How much is a matter of qualitative judgment which may eventually require judicial determination in case of conflict. The Copyright Office does not purport to compare the new version with the earlier work, but it requires the copyright claimant to state what new material has been added. The Copyright Office has said:

> When only a few slight variations or minor additions of no substance have been made, or when the revisions or added material consist solely of uncopyrightable elements, registration is not possible.

There are no maximum boundaries on the extent of originality and creativity that can be contributed by arrangements. The melodic basis of Brahms' "Academic Festival Overture" is found in the student songs of his day. Beethoven's "Country Dances" were, similarly, developed from contemporary folk dances, and already existing hymns were utilized by Bach in most of his chorales. The great originality and creativity of each of these masterpieces lie in the development of the material.

The minimum requirements of originality and creativity for copyrightable arrangements are indefinite. Courts analogize to the rejection of patents for improvements "which a good mechanic could make." In music situations, they have said:

> . . . anything which a fairly good musician can make, the same old tune being preserved, could not be the subject of copyright. . . . The musical composition contemplated by the statute must, doubtless, be substantially a new and original work, and not a copy of a piece already produced, with additions and variations, which a writer of music with experience and skill might readily make.

Applying such requirements, a Court rejected a claim of copyright infringement on an arrangement of public domain music even in the face of clear proof of copying. The new material in the arrangement, as copied by the defendant, involved adding an alto part and some few notes and rhythmical beats to smooth the transposition from Russian to

English lyrics; the English words were not copied. Another Court held that a student's piano collection of public domain songs could be protected as having "at least a modicum of creative work." This included editorial ingenuity in "fingering, dynamic marks, tempo indications, slurs and phrasing." The Court also recognized some value in an original editorial grouping of a series of public domain works, together with original titles.

The determination of the "modicum of creative work" may be difficult. In one case, a Sicilian sailor was fortunate to have a bad memory and insufficient musical training since his necessary improvisations of folk songs were deemed to warrant a copyright. In another instance, a respected teacher of music theory who was a choir master was found to have followed an original melody too faithfully to qualify for an arrangement copyright.

The rationale of denying copyright to changes that could be developed by any experienced writer is better understood by reference to a decision by a California leading copyright jurist, the late Judge Yankwich. He said that too broad a basis of copyright in arrangements would lead to restricting the use of many works. It would result in permitting a Charles Laughton to forbid other actors from portraying Henry VIII in the same creative manner as that which he employed; or in a Sir Laurence Olivier monopolizing the innovations in his portrayal of Hamlet. Judge Yankwich felt that a basic copyrighted work should not be subject to division into segments to the detriment of the original author or, in the case of public domain works, to the detriment of the public.

An important practical consideration in determining the extent of originality or creativity to be required by a court is the reluctance of members of the judiciary to qualify themselves as art or music experts.

The prevalent judicial position, which is equally applicable to music and art, has been stated by Justice Holmes as follows:

> It would be a dangerous undertaking for persons trained only to the law to constitute themselves final judges of the worth of pictorial illustrations, outside of the narrowest and most obvious limits. At the one extreme some works of genius would be sure to miss appreciation. Their very novelty would make them repulsive until the public had learned the new language in which their author spoke. It may be more than doubted, for instance, whether the etchings of Goya or the paintings of Manet would have been sure of protection when seen for the first time. At the other end, copyright would be denied to pictures which appealed to a public less educated than the judge.

This refusal to become a critic of art and music is not just an expression of judicial modesty; it is essential for orderly and efficient operation of the courts. The judge who passes upon the minimum standards of originality or creativity of an arrangement (which standards are equally applicable to a completely new composition) does not have to put a stamp of cultural approval on the piece. In the words of the late Judge Ryan of the Federal District Court for the Southern District of New York, he must merely find sufficient "fingerprints of the composition" in the arrangement or succession of musical notes which can "establish its identity."

Derivative Work Problems

In engaging or commissioning a lyricist or an arranger to improve upon a pre-existing work, the publisher and writer of the earlier version should be aware of the work thereby created. The 1976 Copyright Act categorizes a derivative work as one that involves the recasting, transformation, or adaptation of a prior work. Among the examples given are musical arrangements. Lyric versions of formerly instrumental works are also in that category.

The sharing of writer royalties and performance society credits is an immediate practical effect of adding lyrics to former instrumental works. This hardly ever occurs for musical arrangements since major changes are not generally made. If the previous work is relatively dormant and can only achieve commercial value through the suggested change, the original writer is unlikely to object to the sharing of his income. But the original writer of an established and popular work, such as an instrumental to which a lyric is being added, may resent the new writer who "horns in" on the original material, except where it is used in conjunction with the lyric, the new title of the lyric version, or other new arrangement.

The original writer and the publisher will be concerned with the selection of the new writer, his authorship credit, the publishing rights to be acquired from him, whether he will be credited with future earnings on the instrumental version as well as the new lyric version, and whether there will be a contractual limitation on obtaining still another lyric version.

Since the publisher usually selects and engages the lyricist or arranger, the publisher may protect itself and the original writer contractually from some of the problems arising in derivative work situations. As to arrangements, the 1976 Copyright Act makes special provisions for an arranger, by express agreement in writing, to be treated as an employee for hire, with all rights under copyright in the publisher as author. In the absence of such agreement, the arranger or the new lyricist may still be an employee for hire acting in the course of his employment, as was also permissible under the 1909 Act. Where there is an employment for hire, all rights under copyright in the new versions will reside in the publisher subject only to agreed-on accounting and credit obligations. No right to terminate the grant of rights to the publisher at any time will vest in the new writer or his statutory heirs or successors. For the protection of the original writer, the agreement with the lyricist or arranger can provide that the first writer will continue to receive all writer royalties for the use of the earlier material in its original form.

As to works originating on or after January 1, 1978, the 1976 Act states that the owner of a lawful derivative work can continue to use and license uses despite the exercise by an author of his right of termination. In the case of relatively simple musical arrangements of pre-existing works, questions arise as to whether the resultant works are the kind of derivative works contemplated by the statute. It may be assumed that only arrangements with sufficient originality to be copyrightable will result in derivative works envisaged by the act. As an example of such works, the legislative history refers to motion pictures which may continue to be used despite termination by authors. The ownership of substantial new lyrics in an otherwise terminated song may well qualify the owner-publisher to continue to exercise rights in the entire song.

Sound Recordings—Sound-alikes

A Court case concerns the song "Who's Sorry Now," as to which the heirs of a co-author had terminated the composer's grant to the publisher of all rights in respect of the extended 19-year term under the 1976 Copyright Act. The parties recognized that a sound recording is a derivative work. The publisher asserted that the "derivative works exception" under Section 304(c) of the Act preserved the publisher's right to participate in mechanical royalties from the sale of recordings licensed by it and produced by record companies prior to termination by the heirs. On appeal to the United States Supreme Court, in a 5 to 4 decision, it held in favor of the music publisher.[1]

Under the Copyright Act, the copyright owner of a sound recording cannot prevent the making or duplication of another sound recording that is an independent fixation of other sounds, despite the fact that the later recording imitates or simulates the earlier copyrighted recording. In effect, the copyright owner cannot prohibit cover records or sound-alike records that imitate the earlier recording. In this sense there is no protection of arrangements made for record company sessions.

Joint Works

In engaging a lyricist or arranger for pre-existing works, the publisher should bear in mind that thereby a new joint work may be created. Aspects of a joint work are discussed in Chapter 22, "Co-ownership and Joint Administration of Copyrights."

[1]Mills Music, Inc. v. Snyder, decided January 8, 1985.

While the 1909 Act did not define a joint work, leaving such definition to the courts, the 1976 Copyright Act defines a joint work as one "prepared by two or more authors with the intention that their contributions be merged into inseparable or interdependent parts of a unitary whole." It has been stated by the House of Representatives Committee on the Judiciary, in its 1976 report on the proposed 1976 Copyright Act, that a work is joint ". . . if the authors collaborate with each other, or if each of the authors prepared his or her contribution with the knowledge and intention that it would be merged with the contributions of other authors as 'inseparable or interdependent parts of a unitary whole.' The touchstone here is the intention, at the time the writing is done, that the parts be absorbed or combined into an integrated unit."

The status of a joint work is significant in that the owners possess undivided interests in the whole work and are not relegated to ownership of only their contributions. Under the 1909 Copyright Act the new writer would obtain copyright renewal rights in the entire composition. As to joint works under the 1909 Act, if the author of the new version has not contracted his renewal rights to the publisher, he may grant rights in the copyright renewal period to another publisher. That publisher will co-own the work and may use and license the use of the entire joint work subject to the obligation to account to the other co-owner for a fair share of the proceeds. Even if the new writer has assigned renewal rights to the original publisher, the assignment may prove to be ineffective should the writer die before the 28th year of the first copyright period and his statutory beneficiaries or successors refuse to recognize the assignment for the renewal copyright period. The foregoing rights as to joint works originally subject to the 1909 Act are continued under the later 1976 copyright statute.

Under the 1976 Act, for works fixed on or after January 1, 1978, there are no copyright renewal rights, although there are statutory rights of termination of grants of rights, generally after 35 years, where the works were not composed or written for hire. Under that act as to a pre-1978 grant, the statutory right of termination of grants in respect to the 19-year extension period after the 56th year can be effected separately as to each contributor. But termination of post-1977 grants as to later or earlier works, usually after 35 years, requires the action of a majority of the collaborators who joined in the grant of rights. This presumes a single grant of rights. Often where there are several writers it may be expected that there will be separate grants, and the original publisher, without an employment for hire relationship, may have to face the spectre of one author terminating and granting co-ownership rights to another publisher.

A subject of considerable discussion in the music industry has been the "12th-Street Rag" case brought under the 1909 Act with respect to the creation of joint works. In the "12th-Street Rag" proceedings, the facts were that the original composition was an instrumental and the composer did not contemplate the addition of lyrics. Years later the publisher caused lyrics to be written. Yet, the Court found that a joint work had been created.

Whereas a joint work usually depends upon a preconcerted common design and intent in its creation, the case seems to depart from this standard. The 1976 Copyright Act would appear to overrule the "12th-Street Rag" case, at least as to works created on or after the effective date of the Act, January 1, 1978, by defining a joint work as one requiring actual collaboration or one where each author had the knowledge and intention that his contribution would be merged with those of other authors.

Renewals

When must the renewal right be exercised for a copyrighted arrangement or abridgement or other new version under the 1909 Act? Based on a case such as "12th-Street Rag," it has been contended that the new version as a joint work under that Act must be renewed in the 28th year of the original work. While this contention has been criticized as being in contradiction of the fundamental nature of new versions as separately copyrightable works, prudent advisors have advocated the filing of renewal applications in both the 28th year of the original work and the 28th year of the new version.

Arrangement of Public Domain Works

In the printed form contracts of many record companies, it is provided that the recording artist grants to the company a free mechanical-right license for copyrighted arrangements of public domain songs which are recorded and controlled by the artist. This result in greater profits to the record company, inasmuch as there is no adjustment in the price at which the record may be sold. Where special provision is not made, normal mechanical-license fees are charged for the use of copyrighted arrangements of public domain compositions.

ASCAP and BMI pay substantial performance moneys to writers and publishers of copyrighted arrangements of public domain works. In the practice of ASCAP, there are various categories calling for payment of from 2 percent to 100 percent of the credit available for an original song. The minimum of 2 percent applies where the works are copyrighted only in a printed folio. A 10 percent figure is used where the song is separately copyrighted and published, or, lacking publication, where the song is primarily an instrumental work and is available on a rental basis. A special classification committee can award additional credit under certain circumstances. Thus it may grant up to 35 percent additional credit for new lyrics, up to 50 percent for new lyrics plus a new title, from 10 percent to 50 percent for changes in the music, or, if the work is primarily instrumental, (1) up to 35 percent for a transference from one medium to another, and (2) from 35 percent to 100 percent should there be creative originality and the work is identifiable as a set piece apart from the source material.

BMI pays performance moneys for copyrighted arrangements of public domain works at a rate based on administrative valuation of the new material and ranging upwards to as high as 100 percent of the rate applicable to original songs. Standards of evaluation appear to be comparable to those followed by ASCAP.

Some important folk artists refuse to join the ranks of those who would "rather be rich than ethnic." They eschew claiming copyright in folk-music versions that they popularize. Their failure to qualify for ASCAP or BMI performance royalties does not benefit the listener or the broadcasting station. Most stations pay general license fees based on their gross receipts and unrelated to the number of copyrighted songs used. But lack of participation in public performance royalties is salutary in that it increases the fund from which true original writers are paid. On the other hand, many folk artists and folk-music publishers are not so moral. They change titles without modifying lyrics or melody. They may claim full originality when they are really only "finders" of public domain songs. They register copyright claims to such songs as "original" works and fail to set forth accurately the limited amount of any new material. They thereby falsely and unfairly obtain the benefit of the Copyright Act provision which places on an unauthorized user the burden to prove the invalidity of a certificate of copyright registration. This burden may be extremely difficult to sustain because the copyright claimant as the true finder of public domain songs may be the only witness who can describe the source of the particular song, and he may be unwilling to admit the public domain origin. The finder of such a song who wishes to legally protect his discovery may embellish it with new copyrightable material.

An additional category of new copyrightable versions of public domain songs is based on the compilation of parts of different compositions. While copyright cannot be obtained on a segment of a public domain work, the linking of various segments may require such editorial creative endeavor, aside from original bridge music, that copyright will subsist in the collection as such. The "folk process" of developing folk songs by endless passage from person to person tends to add compilation material. The end product, a song in the hands of a finder, may still be a public domain work. However, the fashioning of a compilation composition by combining, say, a prison folk song with a riverboat work song, and perhaps adding another bit or piece from other sources, may result in a copyrightable work.

Foreign Treatment

It is of interest to note that England, France, and some other major nations differ with the United States in their treatment of writers of arrangements, abridgements, translations, and other new versions.

They do not require consent for the second copyright to arise, but they insist on consent of *both* the original version proprietor and the second version owner before use. This results in a parallel set of protective rights which, without prejudice to the original owner, safeguards the creator of the second version.

In France and other countries in the European continent, the local performing-right societies recognize the rights of arrangers of copyrighted published vocal works and generally allocate to them $2/12$ths of the total performance royalties payable to writers and publishers. This is deductible from the total writer royalties, which, for works of European origin, usually equal $8/12$ths of the entire performance royalties payable to writers and publishers. If in the case of a subpublished work there is both a local lyric writer and an arranger, the continental society will ordinarily allocate the $2/12$ths between them.

As to noncopyrighted works, foreign continental societies normally have plans for grading arrangements in accordance with the amount of original work done by the arranger, and the arranger's share of performance royalties is determined by such grading.

22

Co-ownership and Joint Administration of Copyrights

Even a cursory review of current trade press hit charts reveals a practice of the sharing by two publishers of the ownership of popular songs. Sharing often occurs when the record artist who introduces the new song owns a publishing firm. It also appears when a record company's publishing affiliate is granted a stake in the copyright as an inducement to the release of the record by the record company. There are further instances if an established song is in the renewal term of copyright and each of the two writers has granted his renewal rights to a separate music publisher.

The concept of "joint ownership," or "co-ownership," of copyright is recognized by the music industry, which frequently identifies the concept under the phrase "split copyright." Technically, this phrase has been a misnomer because in theory, prior to the 1976 Copyright Act, the courts have regarded a copyright as "indivisible." In practice, however, while there was only one legal overall ownership of a copyright, this was not regarded as barring a joint ownership of undivided interests or shares in the bundle of rights that constitute a copyright. As of January 1, 1978, under the 1976 Copyright Act, there is statutory recognition of the divisibility of copyright so that any of the exclusive rights under copyright, and any subdivision of them, may be transferred and owned separately. Most agreements between joint owners relate to the entire copyright and to undivided interests or shares therein, although under the 1976 Act there is no bar to joint ownership of a particular exclusive right such as the right to reproduce printed copies of a musical work. A copy of a form of agreement between joint owners is included in Part 4 as Form 6A.

Limited problems arise in the administration of a jointly owned copyright for purposes of licensing and collection. The operation of ASCAP, BMI, and SESAC in the field of performing rights is adapted to eliminating difficulties in administering joint rights in that area, provided that each of the co-owners is an affiliate or member of the same organization as the other co-owner. Each of these organizations will honor directions to divide publisher credits as directed by the co-owners. A copy of a form of publisher instruction for division of performance credits is included in Part 4 as Form 6B. While some dissatisfied publishers claim that they are forced to share copyrights with recording stars and record company publishing affiliates and that this is akin to payola, the practice appears uncoerced from a legal point of view. None of the performing-right organizations in the United States questions the practice as such, although they balk at dividing the credits between publishers in different performing-right organizations.

The operation of The Harry Fox Agency as agent and trustee for music publishers is also suited to the purposes of joint copyright proprietors. The Fox Agency will abide by instructions for the division of mechanical royalties and synchronization fees. A copy of a form of publisher instructions to The Harry Fox Agency is included in Part 4 as Form 6C. For a further discussion of The Harry Fox Agency, reference may be made to Chapter 20, "Mechanical Rights." SESAC's mechanical-licensing department similarly will follow instructions of joint owners as to the division of net receipts which remain after the deductions of SESAC's fees.

Even the field of printing and distribution of printed sheet music and folios is adapted to co-ownership. Firms such as Warner Bros. Music and Hal Leonard Publishing Corporation serve as licensees to handle printing and distribution and to remit to the joint owners their respective shares of the net receipts.

General Rights of Co-owners

A joint owner of a copyright is free to use or license the use of the work without the knowledge or consent of the other owner, provided that the use does not amount to a destruction of the work. Judges analogize to joint ownership of real estate. If two or more persons own a cabin on a wooded plot of land, any of the owners may make use of the property or may authorize third parties to use it, but no joint owner may chop down the trees or authorize third parties to destroy the joint property without consent of the other owners.

The courts have uniformly held that when any one of the co-owners of a copyright licenses the use of the work, he must account to the other co-owners for their share of the profits derived therefrom. While in an early case decided in 1873 a co-owner was not required to account for the profits derived from his own use of the property, under modern decisions there has been developed the principle that there must be an accounting. In practice, there remains a split of opinion among music publishers regarding the need to account to co-owners for profits from printed editions handled directly and not licensed for exploitation through third parties, although the better view would seem to favor the requirement to account.

Conflicts of Interest

At times, the co-owners will suffer from a conflict of interests. A record company co-owner may wish to grant itself a favorable, reduced mechanical-licensing rate, despite the decrease in publisher receipts which will result. Record company and artist co-owners may desire to discourage obtaining and exploiting cover records of the same song by other artists and record companies.

In making a deal with a record company to share in the copyright, the publisher should contractually provide for the mechanical licensing rate which the record company must pay. Otherwise, the record company may be in a position to grant itself a decreased rate, despite the objections of the co-owner, subject to a possible claim for breach of trust.

As to cover records, neither joint owner can bar the other, except contractually, from seeking and exploiting such records. On the other hand, no joint owner can insist, in the absence of a contractual right, on joint expenditures for advertising and exploitation of any nature, whether they be for a cover record or otherwise.

Synchronization Rights

Although it is simple to instruct The Harry Fox Agency to divide synchronization fees in the same manner as mechanical-right royalties received from record companies, it must be recognized that synchronization rights may require different treatment. Since synchronization rights apply worldwide, the joint-administration agreement must provide for an allocation of the synchronization fee between the United States and elsewhere when the co-ownership involves only United States rights, as may occur in the case of joint ownership during the renewal term of the United States copyright of pre-1978 works.

Many publishers agree that 50 percent of the synchronization fee should be considered as attributable to the United States and the balance to the rest of the world. Some knowledgeable industry accountants, however, state that the percentages should be: United States 45 percent and Canada 5 percent, with 50 percent for the remainder of the world.

A motion picture producer or other user of music who seeks a synchronization license must also acquire an additional license. In the United States, ASCAP and its members are barred by a Court decree based on antimonopoly laws from licensing theaters for the performance therein of music contained in film soundtracks; in the case of music not composed for the specific motion picture, licenses for such performance are customarily issued to the producer by the publisher. For both ASCAP and BMI music, it is usual for the publisher to issue, either directly or through The Harry Fox Agency, the requisite license for United States theatrical performance rights for a sum equal to the worldwide synchronization fee. Thus, where the co-ownership includes only the United States, the agreement between the owners should provide for the division of the performance license fee in proportion to the writer interest controlled by the respective owners, whereas the worldwide synchronization fee should be so shared only in respect of the 45 or 50 percent attributable to the United States.

Foreign Rights

Agreements for the co-ownership of new songs should provide for one or the other of the owners to have sole control of foreign rights or should set forth the basic terms for acceptable foreign licensing contracts. This provision is essential because in a number of foreign countries, including England, either joint owner may arbitrarily veto a license negotiated by the other. This is in contrast to the freedom to license accorded to each co-owner under the United States law.

Where joint ownership pertains to pre-1978 songs for their United States renewal period, it may also involve foreign administration of the songs if the foreign rights were reacquired by the writers commencing with the renewal term of the United States copyright. Such reacquisition is provided for in The Songwriter Guild form of agreement between publishers and writers relating to pre-1978 songs. Most agreements with writers prior to the 1948 and 1969 AGAC forms did not limit the term of foreign rights.

Consent by Silence

Many joint-ownership agreements provide for consultation and reasonable consent before either owner licenses recording companies at rates less than the compulsory license maximum per composition. Under the 1976 Act the maximum since July 1, 1984 is $4\frac{1}{2}$ cents or 0.85 cent per minute or fraction thereof, whichever is greater. Where the co-owner is a busy recording star or for other reasons perhaps unavailable for such consultation and consent, it is advisable to provide that, following a reasonable period after the receipt of registered or certified mail requesting consent, consent shall be assumed in the absence of written objection.

Restrictions on Assignment

As in any partnership or joint venture, there may be strong elements of personal reliance in selecting the co-owner. If the joint owner is a top recording star or a respected enterprising publisher, it may be appropriate to have a different set of provisions for mutual relations than if ownership is shared merely with a speculator. Where the joint-administration agreement is based on special personal factors, it may be desirable to provide that neither co-owner may assign his interest without the approval of, or rights of first refusal in, the other owner.

Registration and Notice

Joint ownership of copyright is recognized as an appropriate matter of registration by the Copyright Office. When there is a joint ownership of copyright, the notice of copyright on printed copies should contain both names, and such names should coincide with the names of the copyright owners on the copyright registration form.

Writer Aspects

Especially with regard to renewal copyrights of pre-1978 compositions, writers are often cautioned against allowing joint ownership of copyrights. In actuality, there is little practical effect upon the writer's royalty computations, although there may be a more significant effect upon the exploitation of the song. Critics of the practice of "splitting copyrights" point out that the incentive to promote a song may be diminished when the share of a publisher is decreased.

If there are two writers on a musical work fixed before or after January 1, 1978 and each gives publishing rights to a different publisher, then unless both publishers agree that one of them will assume full writer royalty obligations with respect to the entire composition, the individual writer will normally look solely to his own publisher for his share of royalties. Thus, where two publishers share equally in the mechanical-license fees payable for a song, each publisher pays its own contributing writer as if there were no collaborator on the song. Each publisher would pay its writer one-half of its mechanical-license receipts (which is the usual aggregate writers' rate), and, since each publisher receives 50 percent of the total mechanical-license fees, each writer will in effect receive 25 percent of the combined publishers' receipts. This is the same rate and amount that would be payable to each writer if there were only one publisher and two writers.

For sheet music and other printed uses, there is no difference to the writers if the two publishers agree to account to each other and to the writers for their separate publications or if they use a third-party common printer and distributor, such as Warner Bros. Music, and require appropriate accountings to the separate publishers. In the absence of such arrangements, a writer obtains sheet music royalties only from his publisher and receives nothing from the other publisher. This may prove inequitable if the other publisher is more energetic and capable and achieves greater sales of printed editions; this situation may occur rarely, and in view of the limited sales of printed editions the harm to a writer is not likely to be serious.

It has been observed that joint-ownership publishers with only a half-interest in a song have used the "split copyright" as a loss leader in the form of reduced mechanical-license fees in order to induce a record company to take other songs from the publisher's catalog at a higher rate. Obviously, in such cases, the writer and the other publisher lose thereby. Flagrant abuses of this sort may lead to a claim by the writer of a breach of the obligation of the publisher to exploit the composition equitably and fairly and may result in an enforced accounting by the publisher for additional royalties. Similarly, the other co-owner may contend that any discount must apply to all the licensed compositions rather than to the one composition alone.

On the other hand, the participation of another publisher in the song proceeds may add an extra measure of exploitation, to the ultimate benefit of the song.

The "Cut-in"

As an alternative to joint ownership of copyrights, some songwriters and publishers recommend that wherever feasible the record artist or the record company should receive a "cut-in" on the proceeds of the publisher, instead of an interest in the copyright itself. Thus, the financial reward need not include management rights in the copyright. This would leave in the hands of the publisher the control of license rates, foreign deals, collection vigilance, and exploitation, subject only to money payments out of receipts to the person or firm that helps to launch or "break" the song. In some instances the "cut-in" will be limited to a share of the publisher's earnings derived from the particular recording.

When, in the expectation of obtaining a record, a "cut-in" is proposed to be granted to a record company or recording artist, care should be exercised to nullify the "cut-in" if the record is not released. The mere making of a recording is no guarantee that it will be released as a single. Accordingly, many publishers insist that the actual general release of a single record on a specified label, by a designated artist, must occur before the "cut-in" takes effect. Others permit the agreement to become effective but provide for a right of recapture in the event that the specified recording is not released within a given period of time.

The "cut-in" is a practice that is often condemned, and when it is given to record company personnel without the knowledge of the employer it may constitute the crime of commercial bribery under state laws. It can be argued that when properly and openly made a "cut-in" is acceptable as a reputable business device which preserves the integrity of management of a copyright and is an appropriate recognition that copyright laws give no benefit to the artist who establishes the popularity of the song or to the record company whose arrangers are responsible for its successful commercial presentation. The practice is not the same as demanding to be named as a writer of the composition so as to be able to obtain a share of the writer credits and payments from ASCAP or BMI; the practice of a "cut-in" on the writer's share through being falsely named as a writer may comprise a fraudulent registration in the Copyright Office.

23

Uses and New Versions of Public Domain Music

When the famed Hollywood composer Dmitri Tiomkin was called to the stage to receive an Oscar for an outstanding motion picture score, he gave frank and witty credit to his "collaborators," Bach, Beethoven, and Brahms. A number of years later, composer Marvin Hamlisch in accepting the Oscar for his contribution to *The Sting* acknowledged his debt to the original composer, Scott Joplin. Reliance upon public domain music may also be noted on the sheet music of such popular songs as "Our Love," "Til the End of Time," and "Suddenly." Experts can point out many thousands of additional songs based on undisclosed public domain sources. Unsophisticated members of the music industry may think there is something unethical or shameful about reliance upon the public domain, but certainly a great composer such as Tiomkin was no less creative for his recognition of a cultural debt to the ages. Goethe correctly stated: "The most original modern authors are not so because they advance what is new, but simply because they know how to put what they have to say, as if it had never been said before."

On the other hand, the frequent claim of full originality when a work in actuality is based partly on public domain sources has been a source of confusion and even unfair business practices. In this connection, the British Performing Right Society *Bulletin* noted that in the 1960s a growing problem in the distribution of performance fees was the false claim of full originality for works that deserve only partial credit, and went on to say that a majority of these false claims came from overseas.

It is the aim of this chapter to review the purposes, sources, and proper uses of public domain music in the industry, especially by publishers, writers, record companies, artists, and television background music scorers. Outstanding examples of such uses in the current music scene follow:

(1) Music publishers use public domain songs in many folios and instruction series for the dual purpose of budget economy and free adaptability.
(2) Record companies include varying numbers of public domain songs in LPs, especially in budget LPs, to avoid mechanical royalty payments.
(3) Artists who are composers obtain copyrights on arrangements of public domain songs presented in their repertoire.

249

(4) Television film scores and advertising jingles and announcements frequently use public domain music in order to avoid high synchronization fees and to have full freedom to adapt in any form.

What Is Public Domain?

Public domain is the other side of the coin to copyright. It is best defined in negative terms. It lacks the element of private property granted to copyright in that there is no restriction on others from making full and complete use of the public domain material. It is, literally, "free as the air."

A copyright is granted for a limited time only, and once published a work does not stay protected permanently. Find any sheet music published in the United States over 75 years ago, and you can be certain that the song thus published is in the public domain in the United States. The majority of works in the public domain are so categorized by reason of the expiration of the limited time of copyright protection. Included within this group are not only works whose renewal copyright period has expired but also the hundreds of thousands of songs which reached their 28th year of copyright protection and then were not registered for United States renewal copyright.

Other works fall into the public domain much earlier, or may join the public domain from the time of their creation. Generally anything written and published for the United States government is in the public domain from the outset. With limited exceptions, prior to January 1, 1978, the generally effective date of the 1976 Copyright Act, anything published without a copyright notice fell into the public domain regardless of later attempts to correct this situation. As famous a song as "The Caissons Go Rolling Along" became public domain material because of a defective copyright notice. The omission of copyright notices may invalidate a copyright under the 1976 Act but there is greater flexibility in respect of forgiveness of the omission. See Chapter 15, "The Nature of Copyright in the United States."

Inspection of the educational catalogs of American publishers shows apparent enthusiasm for the works of the Russian composer Kabalevsky. This is undoubtedly warranted on merit. But it is also convenient to American publishers to use these and other Soviet works without having to obtain a copyright license. This is due to the absence of copyright protection in the United States for Soviet works originally published in the Soviet Union before it became a party to the Universal Copyright Convention on May 27, 1973. Works published before that date are still deemed to be in the public domain but works published subsequently are subject to copyright protection.

The difficulty of ascertaining public domain or copyright status in the international field is increased by the fact that most foreign countries respect copyright in a work for 50 years after the death of the author, whereas under United States copyright law as to works first fixed before January 1, 1978, protection is measured in terms of specific years. This results in a lack of uniformity as to when a specific work enters public domain status throughout the world. Accordingly, if reliance is placed on public domain status in compiling a printed folio of songs or in making a budget LP or in synchronizing the score of a film, the United States user must investigate the foreign copyright status thoroughly before allowing the work to be exported.

Purposes of Public Domain

The United States Constitution authorizes copyright only for "limited times." Thus, the policy against perpetual private rights in writings is set forth in the highest law of the land. In a study issued by the Copyright Office, the following reasons for this policy are stated:

> It is generally believed to be to the benefit of the public that once the work has been created, and the author protected for a sufficient time to have produced the original incentive, the work should become available to be freely used by all. There is believed to be a greater probability of more varied editions of works of lasting value, and a wider opportunity to distribute existing works competitively, and use them as a basis for new creation, if they are freely available. It is basic to our economic system that profits in this area should be gained by more efficient manufacture, better distribution and the like, rather than by perpetual protection, once the purpose of the protection for a limited time has been achieved.

Judge Learned Hand stated the policy as follows: ". . . Congress has created the monopoly in exchange for a dedication, and when the monopoly expires the dedication must be complete."

The composer or music publisher, naturally enough, may object to not being able to pass on his property to his grandchildren as easily as a neighbor who creates a shoe factory. However, consideration should be given to policy favoring limited restraints on uses of what is deemed to be the national cultural heritage. Imagine the block on cultural development if each of the heirs of Beethoven, Bach, or Brahms would have to be located to grant a license either for a Moog Synthesizer or a New York Philharmonic performance of the classics. A renowned German music industry leader, Dr. Erich Schulze, has stated: "If the term were unlimited, arrangements would have to be made to ensure that the rights can be exercised even though a great number of heirs might be involved. If, at some later date, all of the heirs should have died, the copyright would have to pass to the state."

Prior to the enactment of the 1976 Copyright Act, arguments were advanced for a longer term of copyright and a more delayed entry into public domain. Dr. Schulze pointed out that United States life expectancy had changed since the 1909 Copyright Act gave a maximum 56 years of copyright protection. He stated: "At the turn of the century, (the life expectancy was) 48.23 years for new-born males and 51.01 for new-born females; in 1960, 67.4 for new-born males and 74.1 for new-born females." Later statistics indicated that life expectancy in the U.S.A. in 1982 was 70.6 for new-born males and 78.1 for new-born females.

Dr. Schulze contended that since medical science had achieved the extension of life expectancy, the term of copyright should be enlarged to fully cover the lifetime of the author and his immediate family. The 1976 Copyright Act makes provision for a longer term of copyright protection, namely, the life of the author plus 50 years. This is discussed more fully in Chapter 16, "Duration of Copyright and Limitation of Grants." This standard had been adopted previously by a very large majority of the world's countries.

In some countries, there is a unique "public domain payant." This is a form of state fund for collecting royalties on public domain material for distribution, not to heirs of the creator but to new and deserving artists and writers. This practice tends to reduce the incentive to users to favor public domain at the expense of copyrighted works. It encourages deserving new writers whose works may some day themselves be a part of a national cultural heritage.

Guide to Public Domain

The public domain is like a vast national park without a guard to stop wanton looting, without a guide for the lost traveler, and, in fact, without clearly defined roads or even borders to stop the helpless visitor from being sued for trespass by private abutting owners. Much of the music material in the public domain is tainted by vague and indefinite claims of copyright in minimal or obscure "new versions." Even more of the musical public domain is lost to the public by oblivion resulting from the failure to maintain complete public archives.

United States Copyright Office

The United States Copyright Office is exclusively concerned with works protected by copyright and has no jurisdiction over public domain. The Copyright Office states that it keeps no separate record of public domain works. It does *not* list works in the *Catalog of Copyright Entries* which have not been registered for the renewal period of copyright. Therefore, it is the potential user of public domain material who must ascertain whether or not the renewal copyright has been forfeited.

Moreover, if a faulty claim to copyright is presented to the Copyright Office, for example, there is a failure to place a notice of copyright on a published copy, there is no public notice of rejection by the Copyright Office.

Of course, the Copyright Office does perform some very valuable positive services in an investigation of copyright status. It will render a full written report on copyright registrations and claims in respect of any work for a fee of $10 an hour, upon receipt of a letter of request for a search report. It should be noted that time can be saved by sending an initial payment of the first hour's fee which is the minimum payment, and authority to bill the balance. Such a report will not certify the public domain status but will give essential information as to whether there is another claimant to the copyright, whether the copyright has been renewed, and whether the initial claim for copyright is of such a date that public domain status, by reason of expiration of the period of protection or failure to renew, has occurred. Other search services are available through the office of Brylawski & Cleary, of Washington, D.C. Some major users, rather than risk a judgment involving substantial investment on the basis of only one such report, rely upon two or more reports requested simultaneously.

It is the basic policy under the 1976 Copyright Act that copyright deposits should be kept as long as possible. However, the Register of Copyrights and the Librarian of Congress jointly have the power to dispose of them at their discretion when they no longer deem it practical or desirable to retain them. As to unpublished works, there is to be no destruction or other disposition during the term of copyright unless a facsimile copy is made for Copyright Office records.[1] Provision is made for the depositor of copies or the copyright owner of record to request retention under Copyright Office control of deposited material for a period of 75 years from the date of publication of a work, pursuant to regulations, including fees, to be prescribed by the Register of Copyrights. A fee of $135 per copyright deposit has been fixed pursuant to a 1983 Interim Regulation.

The Copyright Office does *not* keep previously deposited manuscripts of unpublished or published music once a copyright expires. Consequently it is up to the potential user to locate a copy of the public domain manuscript unless, perchance, the Library of Congress chose in its discretion to keep a copy. Accordingly, search for and inspection of copies of published or unpublished works registered for copyright should be made *in advance* of the expiration of copyright. The nature of copyright is such that the Copyright Office itself will not ordinarily make a copy of a published or unpublished work on deposit with it. Therefore, unless written permission of the owner is obtained to make a copy, in the absence of a certified need for litigation purposes, an on-the-spot inspection of a manuscript is required.

---

[1] The 1909 Act of forbade the destruction of the manuscript of an unpublished work during its term of copyright without notice to the copyright owner of record, permitting him to claim and remove it.

Library of Congress

Not all copyrighted works are destroyed or lost when they are no longer within the copyright term of protection. The purpose of requiring a *deposit* of two copies with the registration of claim to copyright is to afford the Library of Congress an opportunity, in its discretion, to keep a reference copy. Of course, even the 532 miles of bookshelves in the Library of Congress, holding more than 200 million volumes, do not make it a universal archive of all previous publications. The Library has the right to obtain the transfer to its permanent and reserve collections of one or both copies of the "two complete copies of the best edition" of domestic editions registered for copyright and the one copy deposited for foreign works. In practice, the Librarian of Congress determines which published deposits of the Copyright Office are to be transferred to the Library of Congress or other government libraries or used for exchanges or transfer to any other library. As to unpublished works, the Library of Congress may select any deposits for its collection or for transfer to the National Archives of the United States or to a federal records center.

Editions of Old Songs

If a copy of sheet music or other printed version bears a date earlier than 75 years ago, the music and lyrics may be assumed to be in the public domain in the United States. Thus a composition dated 1909 clearly falls into that category.

Sheet music and other published copies of old songs are often obtained from private collections or dealers. However, an extensive collection of old-time popular songs is maintained by the Lincoln Center Library of the Performing Arts, in New York City, and inspection of this collection is desirable for ascertaining information on actual early editions.

It is also of importance to have access to early editions so as to avoid copying a new version or new arrangement of a work that is otherwise in the public domain.

Some public domain users use a system of "most common denominator" as a means of ascertaining true public domain. This is a method of gathering together many versions of a known public domain work and copying only those portions of words or music which appear in several different sources. The services of an expert musicologist are sometimes desirable in this respect, especially in instances such as motion picture uses, as great financial inconvenience would occur were a valid claim to be presented after initial use.

In many cases where the underlying melodic source for a popular composition is in the public domain, the musical contributions made to the original source by a copyright claimant may be of a minor and limited nature. For example, a songwriter may write a song entitled "Darling, I Love You," based on a Bach sonata. Another songwriter would be entitled to found a new instrumental work on the same sonata or put new lyrics to it. In either case, the later songwriter will have a valid claim to copyright on his version, provided that he has not copied any of the earlier writer's musical or lyric additions to the underlying sonata. The later writer would be well advised, however, to use a new title for his version to avoid confusion in the collection of mechanical and performance fees.

ASCAP and BMI Catalogs

The ASCAP and BMI catalogs of songs in their repertoires afford convenient lists of copyright claimants and, by a special notation such as an asterisk in the ASCAP book, indicate the public domain status of the basic underlying work. Upon inquiry, ASCAP and BMI will indicate the public domain status of works. SESAC also has an extensive catalog of its works, which frequently shows underlying public domain status by reference to "arranger" instead of "composer." In certain instances the SESAC catalog has many listings of the same musical work under different SESAC publishers, making it evident that the underlying work is one in the public domain.

The failure of ASCAP, BMI, or SESAC to list a work as public domain does not necessarily determine the issue. Some works filed as completely original may be based on a public domain composition, and the societies may not look behind the filing.

The Harry Fox Agency

The Harry Fox Agency, Inc. maintains voluminous files which contain significant information regarding the public domain status of compositions. This is required for the licensing functions of the agency. Inquiry may be made of the agency regarding whether a composition is in the public domain.

Copyright Registration of New Versions and Arrangements

While a copyright claimant, in filing for registration of a new version of copyright material, must designate the new matter on which the claim is based, such designation rarely appears on printed copies of the music. For instance, a new arrangement of "The Star Spangled Banner" may show a copyright notice for the year 1971, in the same manner and form as would appear on a new and original composition. Accordingly, reference may have to be made to the application for registration in the Copyright Office to determine the new matter for which protection is claimed.

Standard procedures for registration of copyright are described in Chapter 15, "The Nature of Copyright in the United States." Further discussion of arrangements and new versions of public domain works is found in Chapter 21, "Arrangements and Abridgements of Music." The 1976 Copyright Act prescribes that applications for copyright registration shall include "in the case of a compilation or derivative work, an identification of any pre-existing work or works that it is based on or incorporates, and a brief general statement of the additional material covered by the copyright claim being registered." It has been stated by the Committee on the Judiciary of the House of Representatives that Congress intended that the "application covering a collection such as a songbook or hymnal would clearly reveal any works in the collection that are in the public domain, and the copyright status of all other previously published compositions. This information will be readily available in the Copyright Office."

Reference is made in Chapter 15, "The Nature of Copyright in the United States," to Form PA, which is promulgated by the Register of Copyrights under the 1976 Act for use as an application for copyright registration of works of the performing arts. This form encompasses musical compositions. Item 5 of the form contains questions designed to ascertain whether an earlier registration has been made for the work and, if so, whether there is any basis for a new registration. Item 6 of the form calls for information on compilation or derivative works. It requests the identification of any pre-existing work that the current works is based on or incorporate, for example, "Compilation of 19th Century Military Songs." It also asks that the applicant give a brief, general statement of the additional new material covered by the copyright claim for which registration is sought.

The Copyright Office has stated previously that "new matter may consist of musical arrangement, compilation, editorial revision, and the like, as well as additional words and music." Thus, if a new folio of public domain works is published, a claim of copyright may be based on a "new compilation" if nothing else has been added to the public domain works. Another possible description of added material might be "new compilation, fingering, stress marks, and introductory material." Claims premised on new lyrics should show where the new lyrics occur, such as "new first and third verses." Most claims based on a new music arrangement merely designate in what lines the changed arrangement occurs if limited to specified lines; or, if there is a new musical version arranged for soprano, alto, bass, etc., a statement to that effect may be made.

It is unfortunate for users that the designation of new material occurs only on official applications and is not available for inspection except in the files of the Copyright Office in Washington. However, copies of applications can be ordered, regardless of whether or not consent from the claimant is obtained. It is only the deposited copy itself which is not to be copied. A copy of the application itself can be obtained, after supplying the details of the registration number from a search report, upon request and payment of fees in accordance with the form supplied by the Copyright Office.

Applications for copyright registration by a composer who has based his work on a public domain source may contain no entry on Item 6. The composer, in failing to complete the item, may in effect be claiming that his work is completely original, although his claim is incorrect. Therefore, inspection of applications will not always reveal the extent of public domain material, if any, embodied in a particular composition.

Mechanical Reproduction of Pre-1909 Songs

The right of a copyright owner to license mechanical reproduction of phonograph records and tapes was first granted by the Copyright Act of 1909. That Act protected only musical works "published and copyrighted after July 1, 1909." No copyright mechanical license has ever been required for pre-1909 works. The pre-1909 exclusion does not necessarily apply to foreign countries, so that a mechanical copyright license for foreign sales of records and tapes may be needed.

As to pre-1909 songs in the United States, there has always been a limited aspect of public domain in the free right to make mechanical reproductions of phonograph records and tapes. This public domain characteristic is reinforced by the fact that *all* rights in songs published or registered for copyright more than 75 years ago are now in the public domain in the United States.

Mechanical Reproduction of Pre-1952 Literary and Poetic Works

Although the copyright owner's exclusive right of mechanical reproduction has encompassed musical material since 1909, such right did not then apply to literary or poetic works. It was only in 1952 that Congress saw fit to extend the exclusive right of mechanical reproduction to literary and poetic works. The July 17, 1952 legislation is not retroactive, and, if the literary or poetry recording is exactly as originally written before 1952, a recording would not constitute an infringement of the work, despite the fact that the work may not be *printed* without the copyright owner's consent.

Reference Materials

A list of reference materials is contained in Appendix Q. In addition to those materials, a relatively new listing of public domain titles is contained in the *Jass Guide to P.D. Music*. This reference work gives many titles that warrant further search for the original versions now in the public domain.

Status of Sound Recordings

Statutory federal copyright was initially extended to sound recordings first fixed and published in the United States on or after February 15, 1972. This does not mean that all prior recordings, no matter how widely distributed to the public, are in the public domain. Their protection in a number of states under common law copyright and in others under special antipiracy statutes is discussed in Chapter 12, "Counterfeiting, Piracy, and Bootlegging," and Chapter 3, "Copyright in Sound Recordings."

The 1976 Copyright Act contains a limitation on the duration of protection under state law of sound recordings fixed before February 15, 1972. It is provided that state law protection will no longer apply on and after February 15, 2047 and that federal protection will not ever apply thereto. Therefore on February 15, 2047, which is 75 years from the February 15, 1972 effective date of the statute which initially extended federal protection to recordings, sound recordings fixed before February 15, 1972 will be in the public domain.

24

The Writer as His Own Publisher

Thousands of publishers participate in the American popular music industry. Some, such as the Warner Bros. and the CBS group of publishers and Chappell & Co., Inc., have extensive administrative and promotional offices. Others share little rooms in the Brill Building at 1619 Broadway or at 1650 Broadway, in New York City, and some rarely have cash reserves equal to the next month's rent.

No license is required to become a music publisher. The Constitution of the United States provides for freedom of the press, which is not limited to newspaper or book publications. Anyone can publish in the printed sense. However, in the music industry a "publisher" is more likely to be interested in other and more profitable aspects of music publishing such as collecting broadcast and other performance fees through ASCAP or BMI and foreign performing-right societies and granting mechanical-right licenses for phonograph records. Both ASCAP and BMI are under consent decrees which tend to encourage qualifying as publishers. ASCAP is required to advertise in music trade journals that anyone can become a publisher member upon proof that he is actively engaged in the music publishing business and that his musical compositions have been used or distributed for at least one year. The BMI consent decree requires acceptance of any publisher engaged in the music publishing business whose musical publications have been commercially published or recorded and publicly promoted or distributed for at least one year. In fact, ASCAP and BMI move promptly to grant publisher membership to persons active as publishers, without insisting on any set prerequisite time period of operations. Writer membership in ASCAP or BMI is available to any composer or lyricist who has had at least one work published or recorded.

Publisher membership in ASCAP involves a $50 annual fee. BMI publisher status does not call for a fee except a $25 application charge; affiliation is generally available to all applicants, no matter how modest their publishing activities.

Writer-Publisher Joint Firms

Some successful writers such as Henry Mancini, Richard Rodgers, and the Gershwins founded publishing firms for their compositions in conjunction with and administered by established publishers. This type of writer-founded firm frequently involves common stock participation by the writer and the administering publisher in proportions commensurate with the bargaining power of the writer. An administration fee is usually requested by the supervising publisher, which is a fixed percentage fee ranging from 7½ to 25 percent of gross receipts in lieu of charges for rent, local telephone services, management salaries, and other general overhead. In some instances, again dependent upon the bargaining power of the composer or lyricist, the administration fee will be waived. In effect, the firm jointly owned by a writer and a publisher is a device for increasing the earnings of the writer and his control over his copyrights.

The songwriter who is his own publisher rarely prints his songs; if he desires to have printed copies he can deal with independent sheet music printer-distributors. He may arrange for The Harry Fox Agency to license and collect mechanical-license fees for recordings of his compositions. The Fox Agency will act in his behalf in the same manner as it represents larger publishers.

For some publisher services, writers may resort to the assistance of organizations such as the American Mechanical Rights Organization and the Copyright Service Bureau in New York City, and Mietus Copyright Management in Union, New Jersey. For a further discussion, see Chapter 20, "Mechanical Rights." The Songwriters Guild in New York City has recognized the increasing ownership of publishing rights by its songwriter members, through either initial retention of rights or their recapture of rights in renewal periods. The Guild offers a limited catalog administration plan for the worldwide administration of retained publishing rights for a fee of 7½ percent of the gross receipts, except for a lesser fee of 2 percent of worldwide publisher performance income, with certain minimum service charges and a minimum term of two years; negotiation of contracts for printed publications or foreign sub-publishing is not included in services offered.

In connection with the 19 years of added life to existing copyrights under the 1976 Copyright Act, a writer who has terminated a grant of rights may desire assistance in evaluating the monetary value of the additional period. This evaluation will help him to determine whether to keep the ownership of the publishing rights or to reassign the composition to a publisher. The Songwriters Guild, through its catalog evaluation plan, offers to provide the valuation for an hourly fee, which is lower for members than for nonmembers.

Writer Firms

Other successful writers such as Carly Simon and Bob Dylan may act as their own publishers, with limited administrative assistance supplemented by the services of regular accountants and attorneys.

For less successful writers, acting as a publisher sometimes becomes necessary because of the lack of interest in their compositions by publishing companies. They have to undertake the making of demonstration records and attempting to place their compositions with record companies and artists. Some composers are by nature very active in promoting the recording of their compositions and their performance on the air, and they can easily claim that they are performing as a publisher; until such time as they find an alert publisher who will match or exceed their efforts they see no reason to share publishing income with a publisher. They keep 100 percent of the publishing income by forming one of the thousands of music companies in existence and by qualifying the firm for membership in ASCAP or affiliation with BMI, depending on their own writer status. They also have to assume all the advertising, promotion, accounting, and other expenses, which may sometimes prove to be high.

In certain instances, a writer will make a joint copyright ownership arrangement with a publisher and retain a portion of the publisher's share of income. If the writer is able to retain a part interest in the copyright of a composition, he can organize a publishing firm and register as an ASCAP or BMI publisher-member. This procedure is often chosen by recording artists who write their own material. In fact, many record companies will negotiate with recording artists for a joint copyright ownership by the company and the artist of all original songs written or controlled by the artist and recorded during the term of the recording contract. Negotiations will determine who will administer the copyrights and the extent of any administration fee.

Under a BMI payment schedule, effective January 1, 1984, writers, in the absence of a publisher, are entitled to receive the performance fees ordinarily payable in the aggregate to both the publisher and the writer. Also, the publisher and a writer can agree that the writer may receive more than 50 percent of the combined writer and publisher performance fees, although the publisher's share cannot amount to more than one-half. This new practice eliminates the need for a writer to form a publishing firm for the purpose of collecting more than the usual BMI writer's share of performance fees. For a further discussion, see Chapter 18, "Performing-Right Organizations."

25

Demonstration Records

The key means of displaying a new song or artist is the demonstration record, familiarly known as the "demo." A songwriter will play a demo for a record company or a publisher to interest it in recording or publishing the tune; a publisher will use a demo to convince artist and repertoire men of record companies to record the song. Demos are also presented directly to recording artists who are seeking new material.

It pays to take pains to make a good demo. The advantage of the demo is that it eliminates the need for the publisher, artist and repertoire man, or artist to be a trained musician in order to be able to review sheet music or a music lead sheet and evaluate its commercial possibilities. Many persons in the music business are unable to read music. A demo can be listened to, thus bypassing this problem, and it may contain an attractive arrangement, thus emphasizing its commercial appeal.

Frequently a songwriter will invest in recording a demo at a studio, using several musicians and a professional singer. Sometimes he may record the tune himself on a tape recorder, accompanying his own voice with piano, guitar or other instrument; the resultant demo is likely to be less attractive than one produced in a studio. A publisher will most often favor the production of a more elaborate demo recorded under the supervision of the publisher's professional manager or, occasionally, supervised for the publisher by the writer. The better demos involve professional arrangements, rather than impromptu "head" arrangements, and a considered choice of the musicians and musical instruments to be used.

When a demo is submitted for review by publishers, artists, or others, it is commonly in cassette form. A recording made originally on tape will have to be transferred to a cassette for easy listening.

At times the aim of a demo producer is to achieve such quality that the demo may be acquired by a record company as a master recording for the production of phonograph records and tapes. For a further discussion, see Chapter 4, "Independent Record Producers."

Costs of a Demo

Certain smaller studios that specialize in the production of demos charge from $20 to $35 per hour for their facilities, which include a skilled studio engineer. The original recording is usually made on tape, from which cassette or disc demos are produced. There is likely to be a basic tape charge of about $30 that allows recording for about 30 minutes. For the duplication of a cassette copy, the charge by a studio is around $6 for a single song, $7 for a cassette containing two songs and $10 for a cassette with four songs. A demo disc copy costs about $10 for a single song on one side and $14 for a single song on each side. An LP demo disc copy that includes four songs on one side would incur a charge of approximately $14 for about 12 minutes of music.

Studios used for demo-making have singers and musicians on call for such work at rates averaging $25 to $50 per song for each individual. The making of demos is in the nature of "bread and butter" work, and there are fine singers and musicians who are available for demo sessions when they are not otherwise employed. Some of the vocalists and musicians are under exclusive recording contracts with record companies, but their contracts are not usually construed as prohibiting performance on demos.

As noted earlier, a demo may have sufficient quality to be released by a record company as a finished record, and many publishers who invest in better demos are hopeful that they will achieve such a quality. In that instance, the exclusive recording commitments of performers on the demo may bar its use as a master recording for a released record.

The costs of a final demo vary considerably, depending upon whether one or more musicians, impromptu or prepared arrangements, home or studio recordings, and other factors are involved. For the better demo made at a studio, the average cost of one song is close to $250–$300 for four or five musicians and a professional singer. Payment to musicians and vocalists for demos is customarily at a lower rate than the union scale for commercial recordings, although the AF of M agreements fail to differentiate between demo and master recordings. While under-scale payments to AF of M members are technically not permissible, such practices usually go unnoticed. However, if a demo is employed as a final master for release by a record company, the musician and vocalist must be paid the difference between union scale for commercial recordings and what they received for the demo session.

Publisher Demo Expenses

If a music publisher makes or authorizes the making of a demo, the publisher usually assumes the entire costs. Sometimes the demo costs are paid by writers prior to placing a song with a publisher, and, as a condition of an assignment of the copyright by the writers to the publisher, the latter is required to repay the demo costs to the writers. In either instance, the moneys paid by the publisher for demos are treated as publisher expenses, as in the case of advertising or promotion expenses. Some publishers require songwriters to agree that half or even all of the demo costs shall be an advance against writer royalties, although only partial recoupment by the publisher is common. If acceded to by the writer, it is in his interest to limit the recoupment of the demo costs to royalties on the song in the demo, rather than allowing the demo costs to be charged generally against the writer's royalties from all songs placed with the publisher. Writers will contend that the demo costs are in the nature of promotion expenses, since the making of a demo is an essential first step in promoting a song, and that no promotion expenses should be charged to the writer. On the other hand, publishers may point out that the writer's performance fees are untouched and they may argue that the recoupment of only one-half or more of the demo costs from mechanical royalties is fair and equitable.

26

Infringement of Copyrights

There are two basic types of infringers of copyrights: unauthorized *users* of previously copyrighted works and duplicating *suppliers* of such copyrighted works. The first type, whether broadcasters, record companies, or film producers, can avoid infringement by obtaining permission, in the form of a *license,* to use a copyrighted work. The second type is composed of a writer and his publisher who market copies of an original work which the writer has consciously or subconsciously copied after having had *access* to the original work. Not all competitive infringements are dastardly acts willfully carried out. For example, even the great composer Jerome Kern was found to have infringed an earlier work which had somehow crept into his subconscious and which erupted as a recognizable copy in an allegedly original work. His was nonetheless a copyright infringement. George Harrison, the former Beatle, was found guilty in a copyright infringement action for "subconsciously" plagiarizing a 1962 tune in a 1970 hit record composition credited to him.

Proof of Access

Whether conscious or subconscious infringement is involved, an indispensable prerequisite to a finding of infringement is the *access* of the second writer to the work of the first. No infringement occurs merely because the identical melody or lyric is reproduced in the second writer's song. The copyright owned by the first writer protects him from copying, but does not give a basis for a claim against a second person who independently creates the same result. An obvious example would be a copyrighted photograph of the George Washington Bridge at sunset taken from a position which permitted the inclusion of the little red lighthouse in the same picture. A second photographer might independently take the same picture at the same time of day and at the same place, without access to the first photograph and thus without infringement of copyright. Similarly, the simple melodic lines of popular songs can be the subject of duplication by sheer coincidence without copying.

Consequently, it is important for an infringement claimant to establish access by showing public dissemination of his song through sheet music or record releases and public performances or by proving actual personal contact of the defendant with the song. Clearly, the active wrongdoer will deny hearing or other contacts with the song, whether over the transom in a Brill Building office or otherwise, and this makes difficult the proof of access. However, the courts will recognize circumstantial evidence as establishing proof of access. Similar complexities in the original work and the copies are deemed to demonstrate the presence of access. A telephone directory containing the same fictional or erroneous listings as in an earlier copyrighted directory would constitute proof of access. In music, extended duplication in more than isolated instances can also prove copying, which, as one Court held, was "a striking similarity which passes the bounds of mere accident."

Another Court held that common errors in the plaintiff's version of public domain music and in the defendant's use of the same music, such as misspelling of an author's name and failure to carry over a musical "slur" mark at the same exact place in the composition, although technically and musically required, "are unmistakable signs of copying."

Public Domain Origin

A common defense of a person who is charged with having infringed a copyrighted song is that the musical work is in the public domain. This can arise from abandonment of the copyright by the plaintiff by failure to use proper notices of copyright, failure to renew the copyright, or other action or inaction on the part of the plaintiff. Or the defendant may prove that the duplicated melody line or lyric originated from sources other than the plaintiff. In an infringement action against the producers of the children's TV show "Sesame Street," the Court found the original source to be an old Russian folk tale and that "the most that could be said is that [the defendant] read the plaintiff's work and retold the story in [his] own words. Such a finding will not, given the derivative nature of plaintiff's work, support a course of action for copyright infringement."

Copyright is not jeopardized by acknowledgment that a public domain composition is the basis of the writer's song. However, in such a case, the copyright obtained is not on the public domain work but on the arrangement, revision, or other new material added. Thus, a user could, without infringement of "Til the End of Time," record the original Chopin "Polonaise" public domain version of the melody, but not the arrangement or adaptation contained in the song, "Til the End of Time."

Innocence as a Defense

The determination of wrongful infringement by the supplier of music or records is not usually a shield behind which the innocent retail store or other intermediary between a customer and the first infringer can hide. The H. L. Green chain store was held liable for infringement in connection with the sale of bootleg records by a concessionaire which operated its phonograph record department. Similarly, the advertising agency Batten, Barton, Durstine & Osborn, Inc., was held liable for a commercial jingle supplied by an infringer. Liability is "joint and several" among the various infringers and for this reason suits may be aimed at the more financially responsible member or members of the infringing group, be it a pressing plant, distributor, record or music store, or, at the originating end, the composer of the infringing work.

Generally, innocent intent does not safeguard an infringer from liability, although it may affect the remedies against the infringer. The 1976 Copyright Act, in liberalizing the effect of omissions or defects in copyright notices, may tend to mislead persons who assume that omission of notices or notice defects such as the omission of names or dates, mean that a composition is in the public domain. To alleviate this result the Act provides that where an infringer was misled by the omission of a copyright notice or by the fact that no name or date could reasonably be regarded as part of a notice, he is not liable for actual or statutory damages for acts prior to his receiving notice of a copyright registration. In that situation, the Court in its discretion may allow claims for the infringer's profits, may enjoin future infringement, or may require that to continue his venture the infringer pay the copyright owner a reasonable license fee fixed by the Court.

The 1976 Act grants a complete defense to an innocent infringer in cases of an incorrect name in a copyright notice. This is on condition that the infringer acted in good faith under authority of the person in the notice and that Copyright Office records did not show the real owner in a copyright registration or in a document executed by the person named in the notice.

In allowing or disallowing injunctive relief, the discretion of a Court is involved. The innocent intent of an infringer will be a factor in the exercise of a Court's discretion.

Who May Sue for Infringement

Prior to the 1976 Copyright Act, generally only the copyright proprietor of a work was deemed to be entitled to bring an action for infringement. Exclusive licensees might sue for infringement on condition that the copyright proprietor was joined as a party to the suit. This policy was aimed at avoiding multiplicity of suits. A copyright was usually regarded as an indivisible "bundle of rights" insofar as infringement actions were concerned.

The 1976 Act effected a major change. All rights under copyright, such as performance rights, printing rights, and mechanical reproduction rights, are clearly divisible. The owner of an exclusive right can bring an action in his own name for infringement of his right. For example, if a firm such as Columbia Pictures Publications is the exclusive licensee of the right to print a particular song, it can sue as such against infringers of that right, without the participation or joinder of the licensor.

The beneficial owner of an exclusive right, as distinct from the legal owner, is also entitled to sue for infringement. An example of a beneficial owner would be an author who had assigned his legal title to a copyright in consideration of the right to receive percentage royalties computed on the basis of sales fees or license fees.

In recognition of the fact that an action for infringement can affect the rights of others who have an interest in the copyright, a court may require that the plaintiff serve a written notice of the action on any interested parties. The court may further require or permit any persons whose rights may be affected to join in the action.

Remedies for Infringement

There are various remedies available to a plaintiff who complains of infringement. He may seek an injunction. He may request that the infringing copies, as well as plates, molds, matrices, tapes, and other means of reproduction, be impounded or destroyed. More commonly, he will claim his actual damages and any additional profits of the infringer from the infringement that are not taken into account in computing the actual damages.

In suits for an infringer's profits, the burden of proof tends to be on the defendant. The 1976 statute states that the copyright proprietor need prove only "the infringer's gross revenue, and the infringer is required to prove his or her deductible expenses and the elements of profits attributable to factors other than the copyrighted work."

In lieu of actual damages and the additional profits of the infringer, at any time before final judgment during a legal action, a plaintiff under the 1976 Act can elect to recover statutory damages. For such damages the Court, generally, must award between $250 and $10,000, in the Court's discretion, for all infringements with respect to a single work.[1] For that purpose the components "of a compilation or derivative work constitute one work." However, where there is a willful infringement, as in the case of a defendant who infringes after written notice, the Court in its discretion may award up to $50,000 for statutory damages. A reduction to a minimum of $100 can apply if the court finds that the defendant "was not aware and had no reason to believe" that his act was an infringement. The court may omit any award against instructors, librarians, and archivists in nonprofit institutions who honestly but mistakenly relied on fair use where there were reasonable grounds for the belief that fair use was applicable to their reproductions.

An example of the computation of statutory damages under the 1909 Act is given in a Court decision in an action for copyright infringement of songs from the musical play "Jesus Christ, Superstar." A series of 48 live performances in the United States resulted in a judgment for $48,000. The computation was based upon a statutory

---

[1] Under the 1909 Act an award might be made for each separate infringement of each separate copyright.

minimum amount of $250 per copyright for each of four infringed copyrights, multiplied by the number of performances. As previously noted, under the 1976 Act a Court would generally make a single statutory damage award for all infringements as to an individual work.

In addition to infringements by performances, statutory damages would also be applicable to other infringements, such as by printed copies, film synchronization, mechanical reproduction other than under a compulsory license, or transcriptions.

The reason for statutory minimum damages is that frequently proof of actual damages or profits is difficult or impossible to achieve although other elements of infringement, such as access to the plaintiff's original work and similarity thereto, are shown. The availability of minimum damages to a successful plaintiff is an important deterrent against infringements. In fact, such a remedy is considered valuable, if not essential, to performing rights societies such as ASCAP, BMI, and SESAC, especially in dealing with smaller broadcasting stations which might otherwise be tempted to risk infringement on the chance of nondiscovery or the inability of a plaintiff to prove damages or the defendant's profits.

Court Costs and Attorney Fees

Many copyright actions entail long, expensive, and burdensome trials with verdicts of fairly small awards based on actual or statutory damages. In such instances, the plaintiff would be faced with empty justice if he had to foot the bills for court costs and legal expenses. However, the prevailing party in a copyright proceeding in the Court's discretion may be awarded reasonable attorney's fees and Court costs. This is a double-edged sword since the prevailing defendant can also obtain such relief. Some copyright cases have proven to be so complex that attorney's fees, based on the amount of work, the skill shown, the results obtained, and the responsibility involved, have been awarded by the courts in the amounts of $7,500 to $10,000 in cases where the awards for infringement were less.

Criminal Remedies

The 1976 Copyright Act provides that a willful infringement for commercial advantage or private financial gain can result in a fine of not more than $25,000 or imprisonment for not more than one year, or both.

A special penalty now applies to such infringements, of a certain magnitude, of sound recordings or motion pictures or other audiovisual works. A fine of not more than $250,000 or imprisonment for not more than two years, or both, may be imposed if in any 180 day period there was an unauthorized reproduction or distribution of over 100 but less than 1,000 phonorecords or more than 7 but less than 65 copies of one or more motion pictures or other audiovisual works. The same maximum fine of $250,000, or imprisonment of up to five years, or both, may be the sentence if the offense involves (a) the production or distribution of at least 1,000 copies of phonorecords, or at least 65 copies of motion pictures or other audiovisual works, or (b) a subsequent offense in case the fine for any prior offense could have been up to $250,000.

Mechanical Right Infringement

The 1976 Copyright Act provides a special limitation on the exclusive right to record musical compositions. If the copyright owner has authorized a recording which has been distributed to the public in the United States, the compulsory mechanical-license provisions of the 1976 Act are applicable. In the absence of service of a proper notice of intention to rely on those compulsory license provisions, such provisions do not pertain and the making and distribution of records become actionable acts of infringement for which full civil and criminal remedies are available.

Under the compulsory license provisions the copyright owner is entitled to receive monthly payments and statements of mechanical royalties under oath, as well as cumulative annual statements certified by a certified public accountant.[2] In case the monthly payments and the monthly and annual statements are not received when due and the default is not remedied within 30 days after written notice by the copyright owner, the compulsory license is automatically terminated.[3] Thereupon the making or distribution of all records for which royalties had not been paid become acts of infringement for which civil and criminal remedies apply.

Infringing Importation

One of the rights of a copyright owner is to prevent the importation of copies or phonorecords of a work. This stems from the importation being an infringement of the owner's exclusive right to distribute copies or records; civil and criminal remedies for an infringement apply.

There are minor exceptions provided by the 1976 Copyright Act. A person may import not more than one copy or record at a time for his private use. An individual arriving from abroad can include copies or records as a part of his personal baggage. A nonprofit organization which operates for scholarly, educational, or religious purposes may import not more than one copy of an audiovisual work, such as a motion picture, for its archives, and not exceeding five copies or records of any other work for its archives or for library lending.

The 1976 Copyright Act bars the importation of piratical copies or phonorecords, namely, those whose manufacture would be a copyright infringement if the Act had been applicable. Hence, while the manufac-

---

[2]The 1909 Copyright Act also called for monthly payments and monthly statements under oath; however, cumulative annual statements were not required.

[3]Under the 1909 Copyright Act there was no comparable provision for automatic termination of the compulsory license.

ture may be lawful in the country where made because, perhaps, that country has no copyright relations with the United States, nevertheless importation is prohibited if the making would be illegal under the United States Copyright Act. The United States Customs Service is authorized to prevent the importation of such unlawful copies or records.

Whether the making is lawful or unlawful, the Secretary of the Treasury may promulgate procedures whereby an individual claiming an interest in a copyrighted work will for a fee become entitled to notice from the United States Customs Service of the importation of copies or phonorecords.

Copyright Registration

The 1976 Copyright Act encourages copyright registration by making it a prerequisite to the commencement of an infringement action. Failure to register is a complete defense, but after registration the suit can proceed as to both past and future infringements.

There is a penalty imposed by the Act for failure to register. Despite registration the remedies of statutory damages and attorney's fees are not available as to prior acts of infringements with respect to an unpublished work. The same remedies are foreclosed as to published works with respect to infringements between first publication and copyright registration unless the registration was made within three months after initial publication.

Recordation of Copyright Transfer

The owner of an allegedly infringed copyright or exclusive right, who obtained his rights by a transfer of copyright, must record the instrument of transfer in the Copyright Office before instituting an infringement action. After recordation he can sue on past infringements.

Time to Bring Action

The 1909 and 1976 Copyright Acts provide for a three-year statute of limitations for the commencement of a court action or criminal proceedings. This means that a court suit must be begun within three years after the claim arose, and a criminal proceeding must be instituted within three years after the cause of action accrued.

Infringements such as are committed by phonograph records or printed editions may continue for longer than three years. Only those infringements which occurred before the latest three-year period would be barred by the statute of limitations.

For injunctive relief, as distinguished from claims for monetary damages or profits, a suit should be brought within a reasonably prompt period after the discovery of the infringement. Failure to institute the action within such period, which is likely to be less than three years, may cause a court to deny the injunction on the ground of the plaintiff's "laches."

27

Show Music

It is a rare popular songwriter who doesn't aspire to write show music. Yet, it is a rare show music writer who writes popular music outside of the framework of a show. Ira Gershwin's "Fascinatin' Rhythm," "Embraceable You," and "It Ain't Necessarily So" are all strong contenders in any popular music category, and yet each of these was written for specific Broadway shows, as were Schwartz and Dietz's "Dancing in the Dark" and "I Love Louisa." At the same time, ask such show writers for a popular song written independently of a show and it is a scarce song that they can mention. Even the veteran show writer Stephen Sondheim, who wrote such shows as "A Little Night Music" and "Sweeney Todd," would have difficulty in pointing to a popular song written by him outside a show.

On the other hand, Carolyn Leigh, with "Young at Heart" to her credit, caught the attention of Mary Martin and got the assignment for *Peter Pan.* And the musical *Promises, Promises* was written by Burt Bacharach and Hal David after their successes in the popular field with "This Girl's in Love with You" and "What the World Needs Now Is Love." Cy Coleman, with "Witchcraft" and "The Best Is Yet To Come" as popular successes, later came to Broadway with the shows "I Love My Wife" and "Barnum."

Sometimes there is a successful crossover from film composing to show music. "A Chorus Line" represented the first Broadway credits for composer Marvin Hamlisch and lyricist Edward Kleban. The composer had won an Oscar for his earlier adaptation of Joplin's music for "The Sting" and awards for the score and song of the film "The Way We Were." Kleban previously had written only for television and was known as a composer rather than a lyricist.

A popular song can be launched with a few hundred dollars, a demonstration record or master, and a lot of effort. A Broadway musical show seldom comes in for under $2 million and the costs may exceed $5 million. Such extensive financing is obtained from individual and corporate "angels," who usually tend to rely on stars and an acceptable book even more than on the composer and the lyric writer. Nevertheless, the composer and the lyric writer may end up with the most attractive financial interest of all those involved in the show, including the producer.

Rights of Producers and Writers

The Dramatists Guild is not a union. It is a voluntary association that is responsible in large part for the contractual strength of composers and lyric writers. Both composers and lyric writers are accepted as full members of the Guild along with playwrights. The Dramatists Guild contract sets forth minimum terms acceptable with respect to the rights of composers and lyricists in show music. The basic concept expressed throughout the contract is that legal title to the music is at all times reserved by the writers, subject only to limited rights licensed to the producer and to a limited financial participation accorded to the producer in certain "subsidiary" rights. The latter include motion picture and television (or radio) rights to the play, touring-company rights (other than a first-class company), stock rights, amateur rights, concert-tour rights, and grand-opera versions. The producer is granted no interest in music publishing rights, which would include payments of mechanical-license fees by record companies for cast albums sold, all ASCAP or BMI performance payments for the songs, and all other royalties or income from printed editions or from licensing to record companies, Muzak, commercial jingles, or other music uses.

The producer's important rights are confined to uses on the stage in the United States and Canada, and even these rights are dependent upon the show reaching the stage in a specified reasonable time. These rights can be extended to the British Isles within six months from the closing of the play in New York City, upon payment of a specified advance to the writers, or without an advance if the New York run exceeded 208 performances. Even as to the exercise of the stage rights, the writers reserve the right to protect the integrity of their work. No interpolations of additional songs can be made without their approval, nor can deletions occur without their consent. Any deleted material belongs to the writers completely, and any corrections, additions, or changes made with or without their consent are nevertheless the property of the writer subject only to the limited rights licensed to the producer; consents are determined by the majority vote of the composer, lyricist, and author of the play. The writers have the right to approve the cast, director, conductor, and choreographer.

All writers receive fixed payments during the pre-production period of the show, and thereafter they are normally paid a minimum royalty of 6 percent of the gross weekly box office receipts, shared among the book writer, lyricist, and composer; and the payment is due whether or not the play is operating at a profit. In a typical case the book writer receives one-third of this payment, and the composer and lyricist share equally the remaining two-thirds.

In certain cases the writers may negotiate a royalty higher than 6 percent, such as 6 percent until recoupment of production costs and 7 percent thereafter. It is noteworthy that some writers are even successful in adding an optional clause in the Dramatists Guild contract whereby they participate in the producer's share of the net profits after the repayment to investors of their investment in the show.

Original Cast Albums

Original cast albums by their very nature require performances by the members of the cast as well as the use of the musical and literary material. Because of the cast participation and by custom the producer preserves a strong role in bargaining for the cast album placement. Frequently the producer and representatives of the writers collaborate in the bargaining. In all instances the approval of the writers is required. With respect to the cast album, the royalty for which is customarily 12–15 percent or even more, the writers ordinarily receive 60 percent of such royalty and the producer is paid the balance of 40 percent. Royalties are commonly subject to the recoupment therefrom of the cost of production of the cast album. The royalties payable to the writers will be divided two-thirds between the composer and lyricist and one-third to the book writer. The writers' music publisher, who is selected by the composer and lyricist without any voice, other than advisory, by the producer, will also be paid mechanical-license fees which recently have totaled about 40 cents for each cast album sold.

Subsidiary Rights

As noted above, the writers, including the composer, lyricist, and book author, are normally paid a minimum of 6 percent of the box office receipts during the Broadway and first class runs. It has also been previously indicated that the producer, on behalf of himself and the investors, receives from the writers the right to share in certain "subsidiary rights." As to such rights disposed of during the first ten years following the Broadway closing, the writers' share is 60 percent of net receipts (regardless of when paid), rising to 65 percent on disposals made in the next two years and up to 80 percent on disposals made after 16 years and through the eighteenth year. The balance in each case is paid to the producer. Receipts from disposals made after 18 years are not shared with the producer. In all of these instances the writers have the sole bargaining power as to subsidiary rights, except with respect to original cast albums and the sale or lease of motion picture rights. Film rights are within the purview of the Negotiator of the Dramatists Guild under special provision.

The growing use of musicals in stock and amateur productions is an important revenue source after the show has closed its Broadway run. Amateur groups may pay on the average between $75 and $125 a performance for the rights to an entire musical, while professional groups pay minimum weekly guarantees against up to 10 percent of box office receipts. Both types of groups must also pay rental fees for the conductor's score and choral parts. Licensing agents in the field include

Tams-Witmark Music Library, Inc., Music Theatre International, Rodgers & Hammerstein Repertory, and Samuel French, Inc.

British Isles and Other Foreign Areas

If a producer, whose domestic production qualifies him under the Dramatists Guild Contract, produces or with the consent of the writers arranges for the production of a show in the British Isles, royalties are payable to the writers based on gross weekly box office receipts. The minimum royalties are 6 percent of such receipts. If the producer fails to produce or so arrange for the production of the show, he and the investors participate to the extent of 25 percent of the net proceeds received by the writers on contracts for such production executed within five years from the New York opening.

In foreign areas other than the British Isles, the writers control the production of the show and they pay to the producer, on behalf of himself and the investors, 40 percent of the writers' net proceeds received by virtue of contracts made within seven years from the New York opening.

Writing a Show

On the practical side, how is the writing of a show score initiated? Sometimes the job is assigned by a producer who owns rights granted by the author of the book; usually the author will assign rights on options only, for a limited time. In recent years shows such as *Evita, Cats, Dream Girls,* and *Grease* originated in an active collaboration among the book writer, the composer, and the lyricist from the very start. Such collaboration may ensue prior to the solicitation of a producer. If underlying rights in a film or a book are involved they may negotiate for an option period which may expire unless a producer is obtained within a stated term, such as a year. The producer in turn will acquire a secondary option from the author for a given period, which under the Dramatists Guild Agreement is one year from the contract date or one year from delivery of the unfinished play, whichever is later, in which to produce a show. There are hundreds of abortive show ventures, with the composer and lyricist investing the time, talent and energy all for nothing. *Li'l Abner* went through three sets of writers before being produced. Even the great Alan Jay Lerner was in the also-ran category on this show. Similarly, Richard Rodgers was announced as working on many musical versions which failed of fruition. Dorothy Fields started work as lyricist on *Annie Get Your Gun* and then switched roles to writing the book for Irving Berlin's score and lyrics.

Music in Dramatic Shows

Some shows use music only as background to dramatic action. In such instances, the composer usually is not covered by the Dramatists Guild contract, and his compensation and rights will be different from those of the author of the play. A common arrangement is for the composer to receive a single stipulated payment plus specified amounts for each week of the run of the show, as distinguished from a royalty based on box office receipts. There is no fixed rule as to the amount or nature of payment, and a top-rated composer may be able to obtain an initial fixed payment plus a percentage of gross weekly box office receipts, such as one-half of 1 percent. The agreement with the composer will ordinarily cover the use of the music for stock and amateur rights or for a television production, with appropriate payment to the composer for such use.

Then, too, incidental music is often used in a straight drama, A script may, for example, call for putting on a record in a drama, for which the producer frequently pays a fee of $25 per week to the music publisher. Sometimes, an authorized title song is written for a Broadway hit, although this is more common with regard to motion pictures. Such a tie-in helps promote the play or film by disc jocky use and provides a promotional head start for the song based on public interest in the play.

Investment in Musical Plays

As a condition to becoming the publisher of a score or the original cast album manufacturer, music publishers and record companies may find it necessary to invest in musical plays. While relatively few musicals enter the "profitable" category, such an investment can be highly desirable if the play is a hit. The film rights alone of *Annie* were bought by Columbia Pictures Industries for $9.5 million. This followed the earlier purchase of film rights to *A Chorus Line* by Universal Pictures for $5.5 million, the same price paid for motion picture rights to *My Fair Lady*. By 1976 *My Fair Lady*, whose sole investor was CBS, had earned $30 million in pre-tax profits. On the other hand, the Coca-Cola Company, the sole backer of *1600 Pennsylvania Avenue*, the Leonard Bernstein/Alan Jay Lerner show, lost about $1 million on the musical, which ran for less than a week on Broadway. Columbia Pictures Industries invested money in *Georgy* in 1970 and it closed after four performances.

In recent years, record companies have generally had little interest in or incentive to finance musical plays in order to obtain cast album rights. The present tendency is for a record company to await the opening of a play in out-of-town tryouts or on Broadway before determining whether to invest in the play or in the large recording costs, often several hundred thousand dollars, of a cast album. Sales of more recent cast albums have greatly diminished as compared to the sales of such older popular musicals as *My Fair Lady*, *South Pacific*, and *Sound of Music*. Even successful recent Broadway shows have had cast albums with sales of well under 100,000 copies and frequently as few as 35,000.

As a matter of historical interest, it may be noted that past financial rewards from exploiting cast album rights are indicated in a report by the Columbia Broadcasting System to its stockholders in 1956. Referring to *My Fair Lady*, the report stated that "with sales exceeding 850,000 in less than a year on the market, the Columbia album outgrossed the box office receipts of Broadway's reigning show." Later sales of the album have caused the aggregate to exceed 5 million. Retail sales of the cast albums of *South Pacific* and *Sound of Music* were also very sizable.

The form of normal theatrical investment is a "limited partnership." There are one or more general partners who are the producers and who are the only persons with unlimited financial responsibility. The limited partners, who include all investors, are the financiers of the show: they put up the total required costs but have no voice whatsoever in the management or staging of the show. For their investment of 100 percent of the costs of the play, the limited partners as a group usually receive 50 percent of the net profits after they have recouped their total investment. The general partner ordinarily is paid the balance of the net profits after such recoupment.

Running expenses must be paid before investment is recouped or there are any profits to be shared. These expenses occur from the opening until the closing of the play and include royalties to authors, directors, and designers; salaries and other payments to cast, musicians, company, business managers, production secretaries and assistants, theater party representatives, and stagehands; and the expenses of advertising and publicity. Theater rentals are also included in running expenses.

Contained in the running expenses of a typical show will be payments of 6 to 8 percent of the box office gross for authors' royalties, star salaries of thousands of dollars per week plus a percentage of the box office gross receipts, fixed office expense allowances to the general partner plus 2 to 3 percent of the box office gross as a management fee, and the payment to the director of his salary plus a percentage of the box office gross.

There can be no question that music is an essential part of the Broadway scene and can prove highly rewarding to the writers, publishers, record companies, and others who participate in the benefits. The ever-present question, however, is how to get enough theaters, producers, stars, and audiences to justify the immense speculative effort of trying to reach the Broadway stage and how, having arrived, to survive the first week.

28

Music and the Movies

Today, music is big business and big business is into music. RCA Records is a division of the RCA Corporation and CBS Records is a division of CBS, Inc. Some of the major motion picture companies have music business affiliations. Universal Pictures (a division of MCA, Inc.) and Warner Bros., Inc. (a subsidiary of Warner Communications, Inc.) have their own record companies and music publishing firms. Paramount Pictures Corp., a subsidiary of the Gulf & Western Corporation, has a substantial music publishing interest. Columbia Pictures Publications is a significant factor in the printed music field and is itself a subsidiary of Coca-Cola.

Music is very important to the motion picture industry and, reciprocally, motion pictures are of prime importance to the music industry. A considerable amount of music appears in the average film. The exposure of a film to the public is usually broad, and there is commensurate exposure of the music in the picture. It is indisputable that motion pictures are a prime source of music evergreens, which, in turn, help the box office appeal of motion pictures. The songs "Days of Wine and Roses" and "Never on Sunday" and the composition "The Pink Panther Theme," for example, have contributed significantly to the success of the films named in the titles of the music, and the public distribution of the films has aided materially in popularizing the music. Similarly, the soundtracks of films can turn into best-selling record LPs, which tend to promote the films at the box office, as in the case of "Saturday Night Fever" and "Flashdance."

Performances in Europe

Composers are interested in motion picture music because of its financial rewards. Contractual compensation is relatively high and, in addition, the exploitation of the music may result in further significant emoluments. As noted previously, evergreens may evolve from film scores, with coincident mechanical, performance, and sheet music earnings, which accrue in favor of the composer. A great incentive arises from earnings in Europe based on the performance of the music in conjunction with the film. Under the system prevalent in Europe, performing-right societies license theatres on condition that the theaters pay to the societies a percentage of the box office receipts. Such payments, which are based on music cue sheets, a sample of which appears in Part 4 as Form 16, are then divided between the publishers and writers of the film scores. Payments are related to the success of a film, and it is not unusual for such money for a successful film to aggregate thousands of dollars. The percentages collected generally range between 1 and slightly over 2 percent of the net box office receipts after taxes, with England, France, and Italy constituting the countries which generate the greatest film performance earnings. Composers can also expect performance compensation when the films are shown on television in the United States and elsewhere.

Rights Required for Films

For a motion picture, the producer must acquire several fundamental rights in music: (a) the synchronization right, which is the right to record the music in synchronized or timed relation to the pictures in a film; (b) the right to perform publicly the music that is recorded under the synchronization right; and (c) the right to make copies of the film and to distribute them to the public by sales or rental. Ordinarily the right to make copies and distribute them, for the purpose of negotiations, is subsumed under the synchronization and performance rights. It may be assumed, in the discussion below, that when a producer applies for a synchronization and performance license for his film, he is seeking the fundamental rights required to make and exploit the film.

Employee-for-Hire Contracts

If the producer wishes to use original music created for the motion picture, the producer customarily makes an "employee-for-hire" contract with a composer, pursuant to which fundamental rights are acquired from the composer. Under the contract the composer will create the music and in addition will usually arrange the music and select and conduct the orchestra. All rights under copyright in the music will vest in the producer as the so-called author under copyright law, including all rights of recording, performance, and music publishing. As for motion pictures and in respect of certain other situations, the 1976 Copyright Act defines a "work made for hire" to include not only that prepared by an employee in the scope of his employment but also a work specially ordered or commissioned, if the parties expressly agree in writing that the work shall be considered one made for hire. Under the Copyright Act of 1909, as amended, the great body of motion picture music has been written on an employee-for-hire basis and the copyright renewal rights for the 28-year renewal period are therefore controlled by the copyright proprietor irrespective of whether the composer survives to the renewal copyright period. For a discussion of rights beyond the renewal period, in the 19-year extended period provided under the 1976 Copyright Act, see Chapter 16, "Duration of Copyright and Limitation of Grants."

Synchronization and Performance License

A more complicated situation may ensue if a producer wishes to use music not specifically composed for the picture. In that event, the producer will seek a synchronization and performance license from the copyright proprietor, who is likely to be a music publisher. A copy of such a license is included in Part 4 as Form 9. Many publishers license synchronization and performance rights for motion pictures through The Harry Fox Agency, Inc., as their agent in New York City. That office will supply information regarding who controls music rights and will, after consultations with the publishers it represents, quote prices to be paid for synchronization and performance rights. If music is not administered for licensing purposes through The Harry Fox Agency, the producer will have to deal directly with the music publisher. Among the larger publishers who license directly are Foster Music Publishers, Inc., Criterion Music Corp., Maclen Music, Inc., Acuff-Rose Publications, Inc., and Chappell & Co., Inc.

While the Harry Fox Agency is reliable in its information as to who controls music rights, the cautious motion picture producer will have his own search made in that respect. This is especially prudent because in issuing licenses publishers will commonly insist on limiting any liability, for breach of their warranties as to ownership or control of the music, to the consideration paid for the license.

Indeed, it is quite common for a producer to refer such a matter to the law firm of Brylawski & Cleary, of Washington, D.C., which specializes in rendering complete copyright reports that may include an interpretation of law if the facts warrant it. Frequently, the particular matter has been researched previously and a quick reply can be forwarded to the producer.

Assuming that the producer, after investigating the facts, desires the issuance of a synchronization and performance license, questions may arise as to the nature of the license that the publisher may be willing to grant. A producer will seek a broad license which will permit the exploitation of the film in all conceivable media throughout the world. The publisher, on the other hand, may wish to limit the license to theatrical exhibition in theatres, thus reserving the right to further fees for exhibition over free television or "pay TV," or in respect of exploitation via video cassettes, which may be sold or rented to the public. Prolonged negotiations may be necessary before a mutually agreeable license is arrived at.

It is imperative for a producer to obtain a broad, comprehensive synchronization license. It is also customary to acquire a performance license for the theatrical exhibition of the picture in the United States, since the courts have held in *Alden-Rochelle v. ASCAP*, decided by the Federal District Court of the Southern District of New York in 1948, that under antimonopoly laws performance licenses for ASCAP music in films cannot be required of theatres. However, in the more important countries outside the United States, theatres are granted blanket licenses by the local performing-right society for the performance of music in conjunction with films; as previously indicated, theatres usually pay a small percentage of their net box office receipts after taxes as consideration for the license. The local performing-right societies outside the United States operate under agreements with ASCAP and BMI pursuant to which the foreign societies are authorized to grant licenses for the performance of music controlled by ASCAP or BMI; most music in which the producer is interested is so controlled.

Thus, the producer may rely on performance licenses granted to theatres outside the United States. Similarly, the producer may depend upon the blanket licenses issued by the performing-right organizations to television stations throughout most of the world outside the United States.

In the past, producers of films could also depend on blanket performance licenses granted by performing-right organizations to television stations in the United States. This still applies to network television broadcasters. But a lower Federal court has held, in an antitrust suit brought by Buffalo Broadcasting Company and other local nonnetwork broadcasters, that performing-right organizations are restricted from entering into blanket licenses for syndicated programs with local television broadcasters. An appellate Federal Court has reversed the lower Court and has held that ASCAP and BMI can require blanket licenses from nonnetwork local television broadcasters. The broadcasters have announced their intention to seek an appeal to the United States Supreme Court and the final outcome is presently unknown.

If the Buffalo Broadcasting case is ultimately lost by ASCAP and BMI, it would appear that the program producer or packager would have to obtain the performance right to music to cover performance of a syndicated television program on local television. This would be done when a synchronization right is acquired in existing music or a composer is hired to write original music. There is a precedent in that film producers already seek licenses for United States theatrical performance when they obtain synchronization rights.

Prices charged by publishers for synchronization and performance licenses will vary with the proposed use of the music in the film For a background instrumental use, the price will be less than for a background vocal use, and visual performances command higher fees than background performances.

For a copy of a television synchronization license, see Part 4, Form 9A.

Videos

For the purpose of the discussion below, video cassettes and video discs may be referred to as software.

Motion pictures loom large in the software field, as to both sales and rentals. In a *Billboard* video cassette Top 40 chart of sales in a week chosen at random in 1984, of the top ten best-selling software, eight were motion picture feature films; and there were many other films in the balance of the list. The influence of motion pictures was even more striking in a comparable *Billboard* Top 40 video cassette rental chart for the same week. In that chart, the top ten were all motion pictures, and motion picture software competely dominated the remainder of that list.

Producers of feature films generally insist upon music licenses from publishers that will permit the use of their product in the form of software. Publishers, and through them the songwriters they represent, seek to share in the substantial revenues to be generated by software. Negotiations between producers and publishers will be initiated by a producer application for a synchronization license.

A publisher, where the use of music is limited, may agree to a customary type of synchronization fee, with an extra payment for software rights. Or the producer may be granted an option to secure software rights, for a fixed sum within a given period.

As an alternative to a stipulated sum, the license may require the payment of software royalties, for which standard forms are in an evolving stage in the United States. The parties may agree to defer to future negotiations the fixing of a fee for software usage, with possible resort to arbitration under then-prevailing standards in the event of disagreement.

Where recordings are licensed for inclusion in a film, producers will have to clear the right to incorporate the recordings into software. The bargaining with record companies will be analogous to negotiations with music publishers. A special obstacle may be the need to obtain the approval of the recording artists. For a further discussion see Chapter 10, "Licensing of Recordings for Motion Pictures."

For a further consideration of the problems in acquiring software rights, also see Chapter 7, "Music Videos."

Music Publishing Rights

Contracts with composers constitute publishing agreements insofar as they set forth rights granted and royalties payable. If commercial records may be made from the soundtrack, the agreement may set forth the elements of a recording agreement.

Music publishing rights are ordinarily covered by employee-for-hire language, by which all rights of every nature and description vest in the producer. The royalties to be paid a composer fall into several categories, similar to those in agreements with composers who are submitting "pop" tunes to a publisher. For printed editions, it may be provided that the composer will be paid a specified amount, perhaps 6 to 8 cents, for piano copies sold in the United States and Canada and 10 percent of the wholesale price (after trade discounts, if any) of other printed editions sold and paid for in those countries. For foreign printed editions, the standard royalty is 50 percent of the royalties received by the original publisher. The composer will usually be paid 50 percent of the mechanical-license receipts of the original publisher. Composer royalties will be split evenly with the lyricists, if any.

Recording Artist Royalty

Motion picture producers will be reluctant to provide contractually for a royalty to be paid to the composer-conductor in respect of sales of soundtrack recordings. The reason for this is that such a royalty, which is in the nature of a recording artist royalty, is ordinarily deducted from royalties otherwise payable to the producer. However, in the case of more prominent motion picture composers, some of whom are recording artists in their own right, the agreement will provide for a special royalty to be paid on the sale of commercial phonograph records manufactured from any part of the soundtrack recorded by the orchestra conducted by the composer. This royalty may tend to approximate 5 percent of the retail list price (less taxes and price of the album cover) of 90 percent of records sold in the United States, frequently with provision for lower royalties for foreign and record club sales. The royalties are generally subject to reduction to the extent that royalties are payable to other artists and are likely to be payable only after recoupment therefrom of all or a portion of union re-use fees which must be paid if records are manufactured from a soundtrack.

Union Re-Use Fees

For an understanding of re-use fees, it should be pointed out that producers enter into union agreements with the American Federation of Musicians covering the studio orchestra, arrangers, and copyists used to make the picture score. Under these agreements the union must consent to the use of a soundtrack for the manufacture of records. Consent is usually given on condition that the musicians, arrangers, and copyists involved in the original recording are paid full scale under phonograph company–AF of M agreements for the music which appears in the phonograph record. It is not unusual for union re-use fees to reach $10,000 and more for a soundtrack LP.

Soundtrack LP Contracts with Record Companies

From time to time, the larger record companies have complained that soundtrack LPSs are preempted by the record companies affiliated with the motion picture companies. This was more true of the past than the present when film companies such as MGM-UA, Columbia Pictures, Paramount Pictures and Twentieth-Century Fox no longer have active record company firms. Even when a motion picture company has its affiliated operative record firm, the soundtrack LP rights may go to an unaffiliated record label. For example, RCA has obtained rights to a number of soundtrack LPs because of an exclusive recording contract with Henry Mancini, the very popular motion picture composer. CBS

Records issued the soundtrack LP of *West Side Story,* since it had reserved the right to the soundtrack LP when it contracted for show album rights to the Broadway show. There are also instances of soundtrack LP rights being acquired by an unaffiliated record company for foreign motion pictures which are uncommitted to the record company subsidiaries of the film companies that are distributing the films.

In cases where soundtrack LP rights are acquired by unaffiliated record companies, the agreement between the record company and the producer may represent the result of intensive bargaining on such matters as the royalty percentage, advances against royalties, promises of singles records by outstanding artists, and the use, exclusive or otherwise, of the art, logo, and stills from the picture. If the soundtrack was recorded by members of the American Federation of Musicians, the problem of re-use fees would have to be covered, and it is usually provided that the record company will pay such fees as an advance against royalties.

There has been a noticeable trend toward re-recording soundtrack scores for the purpose of a soundtrack LP, rather than using the original soundtrack. Several advantages are achieved thereby. In the first place, it is possible to use a smaller orchestra and thus avoid excessive union re-use fees. Second, a new recording with an LP in mind, with arrangements and orchestrations appropriately modified, may result in a more listenable and commercial phonograph record.

Composers and Lyricists Guild of America

In the field of motion picture music, the most important union, other than the American Federation of Musicians, has been the Composers and Lyricists Guild of America. The union has not had an agreement with motion picture producers since November 30, 1971. In 1972, seventy-one composer and lyricist members of the union brought a class action suit against motion picture companies alleging a conspiracy in restraint of trade. The complaint charged that the defendants had agreed to insist on including certain standard terms in every individual contract as a precondition to contracting with composers and lyricists. These standard provisions relate essentially to (1) the defendants' retention of copyright ownership in music written by the plaintiffs and (2) the defendants' right to assign the music to publishers chosen by the defendants (usually their subsidiaries, it was alleged) with the express provision that neither the defendants nor the publishers are obliged to exploit the music. After many years, the litigation was settled on a basis which left the copyright ownership in essence undisturbed but gave the plaintiffs a limited right to exploit if the publisher failed to meet certain exploitation standards.

Under the Guild agreements, now expired, which had been negotiated with producers, a composer who was hired by a producer had, with rare exceptions, to be a member of the Guild or would have to join the

Guild within a stipulated period. The agreements stated that music would be deemed composed under an employee-for-hire status; this operated to protect the producer if he engaged a composer who commenced to write the score before the contract between them was executed. Provision was made in the Guild agreements for credit to be given on a film to composers. The Guild agreements covered minimum compensation to be paid to composers, although it is relatively rare that an established composer will receive minimum compensation. The Guild agreements also set forth minimum printed edition and mechanical rights royalties to be paid to composers. It recognized that composers are affiliated with ASCAP or BMI and that they reserved the right to collect the composer's share of performance fees through those organizations.

Component Parts of Films

Music publishers associated with film companies desire to be named as the copyright owners in notices of copyright for the new music in films. This is traditional and prestigious and facilitates administration and exploitation of the music.

For some years the Copyright Office, for purposes of deposit and registration, considered a copyrightable component part of a motion picture, such as the new music, an integral part of the film. If the film had been released prior to the publication or registration of a copyrightable component part, the Copyright Office would refuse separate registration for the component part unless a separate copyright notice for that part had been placed on the film, for example, an individual notice naming the music publisher as the copyright owner of the music.

The position of the Copyright Office has recently changed, based on the Copyright Act of 1976, which requires a copyright notice only on publicly distributed copies of works that can be "visually perceived." Music in films is not visually perceptible and the conclusion therefore is that a separate copyright notice for music in films is unnecessary.

The Copyright Office now accepts the simultaneous registration of separate copyright claims for a film and for the new music in the motion picture. The multiple registrations can be made by different copyright claimants with the deposits of only one "copy" of the film, which can be a video cassette. There is no need to make separate deposits of "lead sheets" or other copies of the music.

While a soundtrack recording is an integral part of a motion picture, record companies have not had the same problem with the Copyright Office as the music publishers. By reason of editing, mixing, assembling, and alteration of the soundtrack for the purpose of soundtrack albums, a record company becomes entitled to treat an album as a derivative work for which the notice of copyright can be in the name of the record company. For a further discussion, see Chapter 3, "Copyright in Sound Recordings."

Foreign Production

The foregoing has been mostly concerned with motion picture music composed in the United States and music licensed by United States publishers. Motion pictures are also made and scored abroad and there are special problems which may arise as a consequence. In particular, it should be noted that in the case of British and French composers their performing-right societies claim the exclusive right to license the performance of the music in United States theatrical exhibitions. This is in contrast to the practice in the United States, where composers hired to create motion picture scores offer to producers the exhibition rights to the music; pursuant to a Court consent decree entered into by ASCAP and the Antitrust Division of the Department of Justice, members of ASCAP are prohibited from granting a synchronization right to any film producer unless the member, or ASCAP, grants corresponding motion picture performance rights.

Assuming that the scoring will be done by a British or a French composer, the producer may initiate negotiations to obtain a United States theatrical performance license from the Performing Right Society Ltd. of London (P.R.S.) for the British composer, or from Société des Auteurs Compositeurs et Editeurs de Musique (SACEM) in Paris, for the French composer. At this writing P.R.S. applies fixed standards of compensation for licenses, namely, a flat rate of £400 plus an amount calculated on the duration of the P.R.S. music in the film. The first 30 minutes of P.R.S. music are charged at the rate of £100 per minute, and any subsequent minutes at the rate of £60 per minute. This applies to both music commissioned for the film and other P.R.S. music interpolated in the motion picture.

For non-French pictures there are several approaches to obtain from SACEM, in respect of its composer members, the rights to perform a film theatrically in the United States and in other territories where performance fees are not collected from cinemas. In certain instances, usually in respect of a well-known composer, the contract with the composer may provide that he is responsible for acquiring the SACEM license for no additional fee and SACEM will comply. An alternative is for the producer to agree to pay SACEM a fee of 3 percent of the net producer's share from the film. Another approach is for the producer to pay SACEM a flat fee based on the budget of the picture. Thus, if the budget is less than 2,500,000 francs, the fee is 50,000 francs, with the fee increasing on a sliding scale until for a budget of 24,999,999 francs. French producers who are parties to an agreement between SACEM and the French Producers Association pay a fee of 2.5 percent of the net producer's share from the film, while for other French producers the rate is 3 percent.

29

Buying and Selling Copyrights

Rumors are rife in the music publishing industry as to which publishing firms and which copyrights are for sale. In recent years, the pace of acquisition of larger catalogs has quickened. United Artists (Transamerica Corp.), which acquired The Big Three (Robbins, Feist, and Miller catalogs) from MGM, was itself bought later by MGM, which soon thereafter sold the Big Three and other United Artists music catalogs to CBS. EMI purchased Screen Gems and Colgems Music from Columbia Pictures Corp.; Chappell bought administration rights and ownership interests in Anne-Rachel and its affiliated firms; and Paul and Linda McCartney (of Beatles and currently Wings fame) have purchased Edwin H. Morris Music Co. Most recently, the Chappell/ Intersong worldwide publishing interests were sold to a consortium consisting of publishing firms headed by Fred Bienstock, and Williamson publishing interests, and the investment banking firm Wertheim & Co. for a price of about $100 million. The deal is said to be the largest music publishing sale in history.

In earlier transactions, MCA obtained the catalog of Leeds Music; the Bregman, Vocco, and Conn catalog was purchased by Twentieth Century Fox, which later sold it to Warner Communications; G. Schirmer, Inc. became a part of Macmillan, Inc.; and the worldwide Chappell & Co. publishing firms were acquired by Philips–Deutsche Grammaphon.

Certain publishers and individuals have engaged in a deliberate course of buying copyrights and interests in copyrights. They are convinced that copyrights represent excellent investments. Of course, their principal interest lies in established musical compositions, rather than in the untried, unproven ones. Some publishers have bought half and even quarter interests in musical copyrights and seem to have prospered thereby.

Larger Catalogs

There are varied incentives to be observed on the part of sellers of larger music publishing catalogs. Among the factors noted are death of the principal owner and the possible need to raise cash to pay estate taxes, retirement of a principal owner, disagreement among the owners, desire to make a stock-for-stock trade with tax-free consequences, the achievement of capital gain benefits, and fear of decreasing value as the catalogs grow older.

On the part of public corporations, the acquisition of a broad-based, well-managed music publishing catalog may be regarded as a sound entry or expansion into the rapidly growing leisure time field. It may also be seen as a means to enhance the earnings on their common stock.

Sources of Individual Copyrights

The sources of individual copyrights are largely smaller publishers and the composers who have obtained control of their copyrights during the renewal term of copyrights, that is, after the initial 28-year period. Under The Songwriters Guild form of contract promulgated in 1948 and utilized before the 1976 Copyright Act, worldwide ownership of copyrights in the renewal period vests in the writer. The better copyrights in the 1930s and early 1940s, written by writers who insisted on such Guild terms under a pre-1948 contract, have come under the control of the writers for the United States and Canada. Knowledgeable publishers who are interested in such copyrights will have studies made of the publications of the Register of Copyright for the purpose of ferreting out the better copyrights which will shortly be up for renewal, and they will initiate negotiations with the writers or their estates for the right to publish the copyrighted material in the renewal period. There are instances of publishing rights for the renewal period having been acquired five or even ten years before the expiration of the original copyright period.

The prospective buyer must make a full and thorough examination of the contracts entered into by the writers and the prior publishers so as to ascertain what rights and territories are available to a purchaser. When a composition becomes popular, there is a flurry of interest by overseas publishers who may write or telex offers to subpublish the composition in a particular territory. One may find that a single composition has been subpublished with ten different subpublishers throughout the world and that each arrangement entails a separate agreement with special terms. In certain areas the composition subpublishing rights may have been assigned for ten years, in others for the original period of the United States copyright, and in the balance for the entire period of copyright in the particular territory. In the important music subpublishing territories, that period is usually the life of the writer plus 50 years. The buyer will determine on the basis of the subpublishing agreements whether he can purchase the full publishing rights for each territory or only the right to receive royalties from a subpublisher already designated.

Renewal and Reversion Rights

As to any purchases made of compositions first "fixed" before 1978 and which are in the original 28-year period of the United States copyright, the status of the right to renew the United States copyright is important.

The buyer who purchases from a publisher who does not control the renewal right knows that the acquired rights for the United States will cease at the end of the 28th year from the inception of the copyright. If the selling publisher is also vending the renewal right, the buyer must recognize that the seller can convey only a contingent interest in the renewal period and that the contingent interest will become a vested one only if the writer who granted renewal rights to the seller is alive in the 28th year; the same contingency is present if the seller is the writer himself. Should the writer not live to the 28th year, under the Copyright Acts the renewal right belongs to his wife and children; if there is no wife or children and the writer left a will, the right goes to the executor of the writer's estate; if there is no will, the renewal right vests in the writer's next of kin. It should be remembered that as to compositions written on an employee-for-hire basis there is no reversion in the event of the writer's death before the 28th year.

A buyer will take steps to protect his rights to the renewal period in the event that period has been relied on in the fixing of the purchase price. In the case of a writer still in his forties or fifties, with the renewal period but a few years away, it may be regarded as a good business risk to assume that the writer will live to the 28th year of the copyright. A more practical approach is to require that the writer's wife and children join in the sale agreement and convey to the buyer their contingent interest in the renewal period. Locating the wife and children may be a protracted and expensive task, sometimes further complicated by the status of illegitimate children. The problem of illegitimacy was the subject of the case of *DeSylva v. Ballentine,* which involved a claim·by the illegitimate son of the deceased George G. DeSylva that the son was entitled to share in renewal rights under Section 24 of the Copyright Act of 1909. The Supreme Court of the United States in 1956 held in favor of the son, declaring that if an illegitimate child is considered to be an heir of a writer under the laws of the applicable state (here California), he is also in the class of "children" entitled to the benefits of copyright renewal rights.

Even the joinder of the wife and children as parties to the purchase agreement does not constitute full protection because if the children are minors they may disaffirm the agreement and grant their proportionate share of the renewal copyright to another publisher. But it is possible to dissuade such disaffirmance by a provision in the sale agreement that the adults in the family guarantee performance by the children; the adults would be personally liable if the children disaffirm, and the buyer would also be secured by the rights of the adults to receive writer royalties from the buyer-publisher during the renewal period.

For further protection against the loss of renewal rights, the buyer may take out insurance on the life of the writer since the buyer has acquired an insurable interest. Should the buyer have in mind such insurance, he should be careful to include in the sale agreement a provision that the writer will cooperate in the obtaining of such insurance, including appearing for medical examinations.

With respect to the possibility that renewal rights may vest in the executor of the writer's estate, if the writer dies and leaves no wife or children, the contract may require the writer to agree to execute a new will or a codicil to an old will wherein it is provided that the executor is instructed to convey renewal rights to the buyer.

As to compositions already in the renewal term, consideration must be given to the author's right under the 1976 Copyright Act, to terminate after the 56th year. For compositions first "fixed" after 1977, the author's right, under the same statute, to terminate after the 35th year should be weighed. For a further discussion, see Chapter 16, "Duration of Copyright and Limitation of Grants."

With regard to the purchase of copyright interests for countries such as the United Kingdom, Canada, Australia, and other members of the British Commonwealth, a special problem may exist as to works originating before 1956. Under the applicable law, in certain situations the assignments of copyright or grants by a writer cease to have effect 25 years after his death and the rights revert to his estate for the final 25-year period of the life of the copyright. This right of "reversion" of copyright must be reckoned with by any prospective buyer of older copyrights.

Past Earnings

In arriving at a price to be paid for a copyright, the buyer will require information as to the past earnings of the copyright. These earnings will fall into the categories of performance fees, mechanical and synchronization fees, and earnings from printed editions. The buyer will request that the owner of a copyright submit financial data for a period of years, including copies of statements rendered by ASCAP or BMI and by The Harry Fox Agency, Inc., if it represented the owner in the collection of mechanical and synchronization fees. If the printed editions were handled by independent organizations, the buyer would want access to the statements rendered by these organizations.

Purchase of Copyrights or Stock

Where all of the catalog of a publisher is for sale, the buyer will usually prefer to acquire the copyrights rather than the corporate stock of the publisher, so as to obtain the right to depreciate the cost of the acquisition for tax purposes. It is possible that the corporate entity of the publisher may offer some tax loss benefits, or that purchasing the corporate entity may have some advantage such as the avoidance of restrictions against the assignment of copyrights or writer contracts.

In some instances the seller will insist on the sale of the corporate stock. Acquiring the corporate entity may create complicated legal and accounting problems, since the buyer then inherits the corporate liabilities, including possible claims for back taxes, writer suits for royalties, etc.; in the average case, it would be simpler for the buyer to purchase the assets of the publisher rather than its stock. If the individuals who are the principals in the publishing firm are very responsible persons, it is possible for the buyer to achieve sufficient protection in buying the corporate stock by providing in the sale agreement for strong warranties and indemnities by the individual principals guaranteeing against any adverse claims. Satisfactory protection may also be provided if the consideration for the sale is payable over a period of years, so that any adverse claims will likely appear while a significant portion of the consideration is still unpaid; it may be specifically provided that a portion of the price will be held in escrow, for a certain period, for the satisfaction of tax and other claims. To ensure that tax claims are made promptly, the buyer may request a government tax audit of the returns for past years.

Whether purchase is made of the underlying copyrights or the corporate stock, the buyer will be wise to insist upon warranties and indemnities relating to the absence of litigation or threats of litigation and to the fact that the copyrights are original, do not infringe the rights of any third party, and are not subject to any liens or other encumbrances.

Price

In the past, a common rule of thumb in the music publishing industry was that the buyer would pay the seller a price equal to from five to eight times the average yearly performance earnings paid by ASCAP or BMI for a musical composition over a representative period such as five years. This figure was without reference to mechanical and synchronization fees or foreign earnings of any kind. There is a recent tendency to give more weight to mechanical earnings; one reason is the greater emphasis being accorded by ASCAP to current earnings rather than to historical earnings of a copyright. For a detailed discussion, see Chapter 18, "Performing-Right Organizations." A further reason was the possibility, realized in the 1976 Copyright Act, that there would be a raise in the compulsory mechanical-license rate set forth in the Copyright Act of 1909, with a resultant increase in mechanical earnings. Another factor is the potentiality of new mechanical uses of music. Also, the glamor of the music industry as a leisure time industry with stock market appeal has broadened its allure to prospective buyers, with resultant price benefits to sellers of copyrights.

As a consequence, the old rule of thumb of five to eight times average yearly performance earnings is now on the conservative side. A more likely figure is the same multiple applied to the aggregate of (1) such average performance earnings, (2) the average over the same period of the publisher's share of mechanical earnings, that is, the gross mechanical earnings less the writer's mechanical royalties, and (3) the average of the publisher's share of foreign performance income and foreign mechanical earnings remitted to the U.S.A.

Under the Internal Revenue Law a seller who receives all or part of the sale price after the year of sale can treat the transaction as an installment sale provided the sale is at a gain. Thereunder the seller will be entitled to file his return for each year showing only the payments received in that year. A portion of each payment will represent a part of the gain, with the profit percentage or ratio applied to each payment being computed by dividing the gross profit by the gross selling price. If, on a sale for more than $3,000, the contract fails to charge interest or charges interest of less than 9 percent on payments due more than one year from the date of sale, part of the installments will be deemed by the Internal Revenue Service as interest payable at a discount rate of 10 percent compounded semiannually.

Assuming in the case of a copyright purchase and sale for $10,000 that there is a 29 percent down payment and the balance is payable in installment payments of 18 percent per year for three years and 17 percent for one year, together with certain further assumptions discussed below, the investment and recoupment can be summarized roughly as in Table 29.1.

The table assumes that there is a depreciation of the purchase price of the copyright for tax purposes over a period of ten years. Ordinarily depreciation has been over the initial 28-year term of copyright established in the Copyright Act of 1909, but in practice shorter periods have been permitted. Under the assumption of a ten-year period of depreciation, a 50 percent income tax rate, and yearly earnings of 20 percent of the purchase price, 75 percent of the earnings from the composition would be available for recoupment of the purchase price. Thus, if the purchase price were $10,000, the yearly earnings before taxes $2,000, and the yearly depreciation $1,000 (i.e., one-tenth of $10,000), the net income before taxes would be $1,000 and the after tax net income $500. The aggregate of the depreciation ($1,000) plus the net income after taxes ($500) would be $1,500 or 75 percent of the yearly earnings of $2,000.

The table also assumes that the costs of administering the copyright would be absorbed as a part of the present overhead of the purchaser, which may not be entirely true but is in the main accurate for larger publisher-purchasers. There is a further assumption that interest on the investment is disregarded.

On the basis of the given assumptions, Table 29.1 indicates that for an investment averaging less than 20 percent of the purchase price for seven years one may acquire an interest in a copyright for up to the full period of copyright protection in the United States and elsewhere. (See Chapter 16, "Duration of Copyright and Limitation of Grants.") The table further shows that the pretax return on the average investment, after the sixth year, would tend to be 100 percent or more per year,

Table 29.1 Investment and Recoupment in a Copyright Purchase.* (Percentages Are of the Purchase Price.)

Year	*(1)* *Total Payment***	*(2)* *Average cumulative recoupment at 20% before taxes†*	*(3)* *Yearly cumulative taxes on assumption of 10-year duration & 50% tax rate††*	*(4)* *After tax cumulative recoupment (col. 2 minus col. 3)*	*(5)* *Net investment per year (col. 1 minus col. 4)*
1st	$2,900(29%)	$2,000(20%)	$500(5%)	$1,500(15%)	$1,400(14%)
2nd	$4,700(47%)	$4,000(40%)	$1,000(10%)	$3,000(30%)	$1,700(17%)
3rd	$6,500(65%)	$6,000(60%)	$1,500(15%)	$4,500(45%)	$2,000(20%)
4th	$8,300(83%)	$8,000(80%)	$2,000(20%)	$6,000(60%)	$2,300(23%)
5th	$10,000(100%)	$10,000(100%)	$2,500(25%)	$7,500(75%)	$2,500(25%)
6th	$10,000(100%)	$12,000(120%)	$3,000(30%)	$9,000(90%)	$1,000(10%)
7th	$10,000(100%)	$14,000(140%)	$3,000(30%)	$10,000(100%)	0(0%)

*Assumes a $10,000 purchase price. Percentages shown would apply to that and other purchase prices.

**Assumes 29% downpayment and installment payments of 18% per year for 3 years and 17% for the last year.

†Assumes annual earnings of $2,000 per year before taxes.

††Ten-year depreciation assumes annual depreciation of $1,000 per year as a deduction from $2,000 annual earnings, leaving a taxable balance of $1,000 per year which, after taxes at a 50% rate, amounts to a residual balance of $500 per year.

although the principal of the investment would have been recouped in full. Obviously, if depreciation were to extend over a period longer than ten years (e.g., 28 years) and costs of administration and interest on investment were to accrue, the average investment would be greater and the period of recoupment longer than demonstrated by the table, which is intended merely to illustrate the type of computations which may be made by a prospective buyer.

Users of Copyrights

Some purchasers of copyrights are in a special position in that they are users of copyrights, in addition to being music publishers. Such a company as MCA, Inc., for example, is a user through its MCA, Coral and other record company labels, and in its Universal television and motion picture productions. It is therefore capable of enhancing the value of a composition by planned exploitation which would result in increased earnings from mechanical fees, performance fees, and synchronization fees. The mechanical fees would result from recordings by the record company, and the performance fees would arise from performances of the records and of the television and motion pictures in which the composition appears. Synchronization fees would be payable for use in television and motion pictures. It is obvious that the user-purchaser is frequently able to justify a higher purchase price for a composition than a buyer who is not a user. With judicious, planned use of a composition, a user-buyer may recoup his investment more quickly than other buyers.

Capital Gain

A problem that confronts a seller of copyrights is whether he may report the sum received as the proceeds from the sale of "capital assets," which are taxable at capital gain rates, or whether he must consider the income as royalties. Under the Internal Revenue Code, if the seller is the writer or his donee, the term "capital asset" does not include musical copyrights held by the writer or his donee, and therefore such persons must report the amount received, or the value of property acquired in exchange, as royalty income, not as capital gain. Other sellers, including the heirs of a writer, do have the benefit of capital gains treatment. For a further discussion of capital gain, See Chapter 38, "Taxation in the Music Business."

For additional consideration of factors relevant to the buying and selling of copyrights, see Chapter 30, "Loans to Music Publishers."

30

Loans to Music Publishers

It is difficult to conceive of anything more foreign to a conservative banker than the thousands of music publishers in New York's Tin Pan Alley, in Nashville, and in Hollywood. Assets literally "worth no more than a song" and administered in a highly personalized manner that emphasizes promotion, contacts, and ever-changing market conditions would seem hardly reassuring to the potential lender.

Yet, recent years have marked the establishment of satisfactory banking relationships in the music industry. Knowledgeable bankers have noted the regularity in payments to music publishers of millions of dollars a year from ASCAP, BMI, and SESAC, the performing-right organizations. Many loans are made in reliance upon certified ASCAP and BMI reports of past performance fee earnings. Low-cost collection-agent services, such as that of The Harry Fox Agency, Inc., which collects mechanical license fees from record companies for a fee of $4\frac{1}{2}$ percent of gross receipts, help materially to bolster the credit rating of the music business.

Interest by the banking business in the music industry has been specially emphasized by some bankers. One Los Angeles bank, with clients including Helen Reddy, The Beach Boys, and Quincy Jones, announced, in 1976, the appointment of a vice-president for a new entertainment industries division, with special interest in music. He stated, "We are going into lending new acts money against their recording contracts and BMI. This is as good a collateral as anything else." He said he would refer acts to other people for help when, although meritorious, a loan request is not "bankable."

As the banking world acquires a basic understanding of the peculiar needs and resources of the music industry, increased loans to industry members may result.

Purposes of Loans

There are numerous constructive purposes of business loans to music publishers. These may include:

(1) New copyright catalog acquisitions from other domestic publishers or from foreign sources.
(2) New writer royalty advances in connection with exclusive writer contracts.
(3) New physical studio or equipment costs.
(4) Costs of preparing new demonstration records.

(5) Costs of preparing, or financing others to make, master tapes.

(6) Selective advertising and promotion of new songs or recordings.

Evaluation of Loans

Annually, over 100,000 new copyrighted songs compete fiercely for the few spots on the top hit charts. The actual fact is that most new songs make no impact whatsoever in the music marketplace. In evaluating proposed loans, attention from an income point of view should ordinarily be narrowed to the provable financial history of songs already in the publisher's catalog.

In considering the business expenses of a music publisher, a major cost represents the royalties payable to songwriters with respect to mechanical-license receipts from record companies; the royalty is usually 50 percent of the receipts. Rent, salaries to promotion men and bookkeepers, and travel and telephone costs are other principal items of expense.

Special Risks

However, the lender in the field of musical copyrights must also be aware of unusual risks involved in such loans. As noted above, writer royalties are a major expense; if unpaid, under certain circumstances the writer may become entitled to recapture the copyright.

An unscrupulous borrower may apply for a bank loan after having exhausted other methods of obtaining money advances against future earnings. Such advances may have been obtained from print licensees or from foreign subpublishers. The lender may have relied on earnings from such sources, only to find that the advances must first be recouped before the earnings are available to repay the loan.

Another special risk is the duration of the borrower's rights in a musical copyright. With respect to copyrights originating before 1978, the borrower may not possess rights beyond the original 28-year term of copyright, due to failure to obtain renewal rights from the author or a deceased author's statutory successors. As to all copyrights, consideration should be given to statutory rights of termination, granted under the 1976 Copyright Act. If the copyright is of foreign origin, the borrower may have acquired United States publishing rights for only a limited term, for example, ten years, from the foreign original publisher. It should be remembered that all copyrights go into the public domain after the expiration of the applicable statutory periods of copyright. For a discussion of such periods of copyright and rights of termination, reference should be made to Chapter 16, "Duration of Copyright and Limitation of Grants."

Other special risks are posed by the possible negligent administration of copyrights after a loan has been obtained. Under the Copyright Act of 1909, in general, a careless publisher could invalidate the copyright by printing or authorizing the printing of a song without an appropriate copyright notice. "The Caissons Go Rolling Along" was forfeited by permitting such a publication. Forfeiture is less likely under the 1976 Act with its more liberal treatment of omissions or imperfections in notices; see Chapter 15, "The Nature of Copyright in the United States." Nevertheless there are still circumstances in which failure to comply with notice requirements will cause the loss of copyright protection.

The 1909 Act provided for the jeopardization of the right to collect mechanical royalties for failure to file a "Notice of Use" with the Copyright Office upon authorization of the making of phonograph records by a mechanical license; while this might forfeit collections until filing, a late filing would protect the right of subsequent collections. The filing of a Notice of Use is not required by the 1976 Act. But that Act provides that a copyright owner cannot collect mechanical royalties under a compulsory license for records made and distributed before the owner is identified as such in the records of the Copyright Office, although recovery can be made for records made and distributed after such identification. A lender might therefore wish to check the status of current registrations of copyrights.

A more basic threat to music copyrights can be the failure to defend adequately against litigation that attacks the validity of the copyright. This may result from the frequent defense of nonoriginality in lawsuits brought by the borrower. In fact, one prominent music industry lawyer has ventured the guess that a majority of important songs could not withstand the scrutiny of experts involved in extended litigation. Many a sound action for copyright infringement is settled or never brought because of fear that a valuable copyright will be declared invalid upon attack by the defendant.

Limitation on Amount of Loan

A simple protection available to lenders in the music field is to limit the amount of a loan to the anticipated receipts of the borrower from sources akin to "accounts receivable" in other fields. This mitigates the necessity for a full investigation of copyright ownership and duration. It does, however, require access to information concerning (1) recent uses of compositions in the borrower's catalog, and (2) advances against earnings previously obtained by the borrower.

A typical anticipated payment is the quarterly accounting by AS-CAP or BMI based on public performances logged from six to nine months prior to the accounting. Similar in regularity are The Harry Fox Agency quarterly distributions of mechanical royalties collected on a quarterly or semiannual basis from record companies. More delayed payments, often as much as one or two years behind domestic payments, on a hit song may be forthcoming from foreign agents or licensees who ordinarily remit 50 percent or more of their territorial earnings from all sources, except from printed uses which are usually accounted for at a minimum rate of 10 to 12½ percent of the retail selling price.

These anticipated receipts, subject to outstanding advances, may be considered an appropriate basis for short-term loans to a publisher. There may be the added protection of a possible notification to the appropriate society or collecting agency to make payment directly to the lender. The Harry Fox Agency, Inc. will accept an irrevocable direction, signed by the publisher and the bank, for payment to the bank of moneys otherwise due to the publisher in respect of mechanical license and synchronization fees.

ASCAP permits a member to instruct ASCAP to pay to a bank all of the member's earnings for a certain period or indefinitely. ASCAP allows such instructions for a general assignment to be irrevocable, and the member can therefore not revoke the instructions.

BMI likewise sanctions a general irrevocable assignment to a bank of future earnings of a publisher.

Both ASCAP and BMI will promptly respond to written requests from an affiliated publisher for a statement of outstanding advances and of the amounts of the most recent distributions to the publisher.

An uncomplicated determination of uncollected mechanical royalties can sometimes be made on the basis of public announcements of verified sales of hit records. The song of a proposed borrower may be contained in an LP certified by the Recording Industry Association of America (R.I.A.A.) as a "gold record" or "platinum record" LP. The former relates to a certified sale by the manufacturer of 500,000 LP and tape units, and the latter to one million thereof. As to "singles," a commensurate R.I.A.A. certification is a million-unit sale for a "gold record" single and a two-million-unit sale for a "platinum record" single. Caution, however, must be exercised before anticipating royalty receipts computed on exactly the amount of such sales. Royalties are generally less than the simple arithmetic would indicate, due to possible returns, reserves, and non-royalty sales. Subject to such caution, however, a true sale of one million singles, if licensed by the publisher at 4½ cents per selection, would result in the publisher's collecting $45,000 per selection of which $22,500 would remain for the publisher after the usual 50 percent writer royalties. This computation makes no deduction for The Harry Fox Agency commissions which would reduce the amount collected by 4½ percent. Information as to R.I.A.A. million sellers may be obtained from the trade press hit record charts.

Copyright Registration Report

An advantage of the federal copyright system is the maintenance of a public registration procedure which makes available essential title information, including the history of recorded assignments. The original copyright registrations of published and unpublished musical works are listed in the Catalog of Copyright Entries issued by the Copyright Office and available at many libraries throughout the country. However, the prospective lender should not rely on this listing alone since no reference is made therein to assignments or other recorded documents relating to the work. Complete reports are obtainable only by actual inspection of the copyright records maintained by the Copyright Office in Washington, D.C.

The law firm of Brylawski & Cleary of Washington, D.C., makes private reports based upon actual inspection of Copyright Office records. The Copyright Office itself also offers search reports. Some lenders may prefer to use two or more of these services to cross-check for accuracy before making a substantial loan.

All search reports should be examined closely as to the effective date of the information contained and as to whether the report includes the inspection of pending files. Due to the tremendous volume of recordations and the intricacies of Copyright Office filings, there is some delay between the date of receipt of assignments or related documents and their actual recordation.

Also to be noted is the hiatus permitted under the 1976 Copyright Law whereby a prior assignee or mortgagee can delay recordation of a document for up to one month from execution in the United States and up to two months from execution abroad without losing his right to priority over a subsequent purchaser or mortgagee for value without notice who records.[1]

Mortgage Recordation in Copyright Office

In music copyright matters the preferred form of security for a loan is that referred to in the 1909 Federal Copyright statute as the mortgage of copyright, although the 1976 Act lumps mortgages with other assignments of copyright interests under the phrase "transfer of copyright ownership." Under the federal law a major advantage is available to the lender by recordation of his mortgages. Thereby, for a single fee and by a single act of filing with the Copyright Office in Washington, D.C., the lender can obtain a nationwide maximum protection against conflicting mortgages or assignments. The procedure for recordation of a mortgage is the same as the recordation of a regular assignment of copyright.

No specific form of mortgage is prescribed in the 1909 or 1976 Copyright Acts. Section 204 of the 1976 Act[2] provides that there may be a transfer of copyright ownership (which includes a mortgage) by an instrument in writing signed by the owner of the rights conveyed or his authorized agent.

[1]The corresponding greater periods under the 1909 Act were three months from execution in the United States and six months from execution abroad.
[2]The corresponding section of the 1909 Act is Section 28.

Recordation of a transfer of copyright ownership is provided for in Section 205 of the 1976 Copyright Act.[3]

As indicated above, the period within which a mortgage must be recorded for protection against subsequent assignees or mortgagees who obtained their interest for value without notice is set by the 1976 statute as one month from execution in the United States and two months from execution abroad. This permissible delay represents a convenience to a mortgagee. However, it creates a period of hiatus during which a lender cannot be certain that it is not a subsequent mortgagee being defrauded by the borrower. The only assurance possible is to make the mortgage commitment for payment effective two months after execution, provided there is a clear title report; of course, it may be a rare borrower who will wait that long. The study made by the Copyright Office, in preparation for copyright act revision, is somewhat reassuring to the prospective bona-fide lender in indicating that a significant majority of recordations of assignments or mortgages is made within one month of execution.

The procedure for recordation is to send the original mortgage document to the Copyright Office, preferably by registered or certified mail, together with a registration fee. The fee is $10.00 if the document is six pages or less, and there is an additional fee of 50 cents for each page over six pages; for each title over one, there is a 50 cent additional fee.

The document should be submitted with a letter requesting recordation and noting the enclosure of the required fee. There is no specific form for the letter. The document, once recorded, will be returned to the sender with a certificate of recordation. A copy of the original document can be submitted instead of the original if accompanied by a sworn or official certification that the copy is a true copy of the original.

Certificates of acknowledgment are not required under the 1976 Act to sustain the validity of a mortgage of copyright or other transfer of copyright ownership, whether executed in the United States or in a foreign country. This is in contrast to the 1909 Act insofar as it called for all such documents executed in a foreign country to be acknowledged before a consular officer or secretary of legation of the United States authorized to administer oaths or perform notarial acts. Under the 1976 Act certificates of acknowledgment of transfers of copyright ownership (which includes mortgages) executed in the United States or elsewhere are deemed to be prima facie evidence of the execution of the transfer.

Recording in Local Jurisdiction

It is generally considered that compliance by the mortgagee with state recordation law, in addition to federal recordation, is desirable for

---

[3]The corresponding section of the 1909 Act is Section 30.

maximum security. It is unclear to what extent the federal Copyright Act preempts the field so as to make state recordation unnecessary, but it is generally believed that there is no such preemption. One reason for compliance with state law is that the foreclosure of a copyright mortgage under Court decisions is currently recognized as a matter for state law. When foreclosure of a copyright mortgage is sought and an independent ground of federal jurisdiction is available, such as diversity of citizenship of the parties, a federal Court may accept jurisdiction over the controversy and apply state law to the foreclosure of a federally recorded mortgage.

State filing procedures are simplified in the music center states of New York, California, and Tennessee. Each state applies the Uniform Commercial Code which recognizes mortgages on intangible property, such as copyrights.

In addition to recordation of the security claim with the Secretary of State, recordation of a mortgage in applicable county offices is also recommended.

Sale of Property upon Default

In rare instances it may become necessary to sell the security in order to repay a loan. In such case, consideration must be given to whether there should be a public or a private sale. In some security agreements, it is expressly provided that in the event of a breach or default by the mortgagor, at the mortgagee's option the copyrights can be sold at either a private or a public sale after a specified reasonable notice to the mortgagor. The usual practice is to advertise the sale in trade papers such as *Billboard, Variety* or *Cash Box,* with the mortgagee reserving the right to bid at the sale. In bidding, the mortgagee may take credit for all or part of the indebtedness against the purchase price.

One notable foreclosure of a mortgage on music copyrights was that by the Union Planters Bank of Memphis, Tennessee against the East Memphis music catalog formerly owned by Stax Records. Preliminary to the auction a number of potential buyers made inquiries, but none made the requisite minimum bid to match the upset price of the bank. Accordingly, the bank became the owner and administrator, pending exploration of other sale possibilities. The upset price reported was about $2 million, representing at least that amount loaned upon such security.

Some modern mortgage agreements, instead of specifying the various remedies of the mortgagee in the event of a default, merely adopt by reference the "remedies of a secured party under the Uniform Commercial Code." The Code sets forth in detail rights of sale, etc.

Exclusive State Recordation for Certain Rights

As a part of the general assets of a music publisher given as security for a loan, there may be certain assets that relate to copyright and yet are not statutory copyrights. One such asset may be incomplete compositions not in "fixed" demo or other recording or appropriate manuscript form, for which no copyright registration has been obtained. Another asset may be compositions to be written in the future under exclusive songwriter agreements. These common law copyrights and rights to future works are not protected under federal law; the only recordation procedure available for such rights is under state law.

Identification of these assets is obviously difficult. They do not bear the simple, official Copyright Office assigned registration numbers which are convenient for identification as against other recordations. Identification for state recordation can be by composer and author names and, in the case of partially written compositions, by title or tentative title. However, a careful lender will insist that wherever possible actual registration of an unpublished work under federal registration procedures occur before granting a loan which relies in any part upon such work.

It should be noted that under the 1976 Copyright Act, even unpublished works are subject to automatic federal protection once "fixed" (as more fully discussed in Chapter 15, "The Nature of Copyright in the United States").

Exclusive Writer Contracts

On evaluating an exclusive writer contract as an asset, inspection of the contract should be made to ascertain whether there is any restriction on assignment in the event of foreclosure. Since the relationship between an exclusive writer and his publisher may be deemed highly personal, the contract should be expressly assignable if a lender is to be protected. In some instances, if the exclusive writer is friendly to his publisher, he may consent to a limited assignability in order to qualify the publisher for a loan which may also accrue to the writer's benefit. In connection with a writer's contract the lender should inquire as to whether, as may frequently happen, there are unrecouped advances by the publisher to the writer. Such unrecouped advances constitute a valuable and well-defined asset if the writer's royalty statements show a consistent earnings history since it is then clear the advances can be charged against future earnings of the writer. On the other hand, absent such earnings history, the advances should be largely disregarded because advances to writers are not ordinarily deemed to be personal loans and are recoupable commonly only out of royalties otherwise due from the publisher to the writer.

Conditions on Administration

It would be a foolish business practice for a lender to forbid, from a sense of extreme caution, any use, during the term of a loan, of copyrights which are security for the loan. Of course, through negligent administration a valuable copyright can be completely forfeited. Thus, a copyright may fall into the public domain for failure of an adequate copyright notice. Other risks can arise in numerous ways mentioned previously. However, there may be a greater risk to a lender through the deterioration of a valuable catalog by an extended period of nonexploitation.

Just as in regard to most business loans the trade reputation and skill of the borrower must be considered along with an analysis of his assets, so also the business skill of a music business borrower must be duly weighed. Even if the borrower is regarded as reputable and skillful, the lender is likely to condition the loan upon compliance with certain conditions in the conduct of the music business while the loan is unpaid. Some conditions which may be imposed follow:

(1) There shall be no publication (including but not limited to sheet music, folios, and orchestrations) of any of the mortgaged copyrights, by or with the consent of the mortgagor, unless an appropriate copyright notice is imprinted on each such copy in the appropriate location.

(2) During the term of the Security Agreement, no license shall be granted which extends beyond the mortgage term unless the specific written consent of the mortgagee is first obtained, except with respect to continued clearance of public performance rights through ASCAP or BMI and except as to phonograph record mechanical reproduction licenses.

(3) Any phonograph record mechanical reproduction license which is to extend beyond the term of the mortgage shall be issued at not less than the statutory rate for compulsory licenses, subject only to customary record club and budget record discounts.

(4) During the term of the Security Agreement, no license granted or agency relationship created should involve the payment of money advances recoupable from earnings which may accrue subsequent to the term of the mortgage.

(5) No new version or abridgement may be made during the term of the mortgage unless copyright thereon is obtained by the mortgagor at its expense and the copyright is expressly made subject to the terms and provisions of the mortgage.

(6) No new lyric writer, composer, or arranger may be given any participation or claim of participation in rights or earnings of any of said mortgaged property, except on customary terms in the ordinary course of business, without the specific written consent of the mortgagee.

(7) All songwriter and composer royalties that may become

due during the term of the security agreement shall be promptly segregated in a special bank account when collected, and shall be promptly remitted, together with required royalty statements, when contractually due. In the event the borrower receives a claim of nonpayment or other breach in respect of such obligations or payment, written notice thereof shall be promptly served upon the mortgagee.

(8) The provisions of Paragraph (7) above shall apply also to royalties due under other agreements such as with a foreign original publisher whose composition is sub-published by the mortgagor.

(9) The mortgagee shall be promptly notified in writing of any claim by a third party that any of the mortgaged property infringes another work or lacks the requisite originality for a valid copyright.

(10) No infringement action shall be brought by or with the consent of the mortgagor without the written consent of the mortgagee.

(11) The services of a particular individual as General Manager of the mortgagor shall continue during the term of the security agreement unless his replacement shall be approved by the mortgagee in writing.

If any of these conditions is breached, the mortgagee could declare the loan to be in default, and thereby become entitled to remedies to safeguard the security and limit the risk of bad management. It must be remembered that the violation of certain conditions may result in the forfeiture of the copyright and the irretrievable loss of the security.

Outstanding Advances at Time of Loan

The prospective lender should bear in mind that it is a well established custom in the music industry for a music publisher to seek advances against future royalties. Advances serve not only to finance the business but also act to assure proper exploitation by the firm which makes the advances. They also serve to ease the problem of collections from licensees, especially in fields such as foreign subpublishing and domestic printing.

Present normal sources of advances to music publishers are foreign subpublishers and printed music licensees. In the past, as regards advances, they were less important than the performing-right organizations, ASCAP and BMI. However, both organizations discontinued advances in 1983 after a lower Federal court decision in the Buffalo Broadcasting case which limited the right of performing-right societies to require blanket licenses from non-network local television broadcasters. The case was reversed by a Federal appellate court in 1984; the broadcasters have stated that they will seek an appeal to the United

States Supreme Court. The Harry Fox Agency, which functions as a collection agent for mechanical royalties payable by record companies, does not make advances to music publishers. Nor does the usual record company make advances in return for mechanical licenses.

There are two types of advances, specific and general. A specific advance is recoupable only from the earnings of specified musical works or a single work. A general advance is usually recoupable from the earnings of the entire catalog of the publisher. Even a general advance is not a general obligation of the publisher, and it bears no interest; it is a debit against a specific earnings account and does not ordinarily continue in effect beyond the term of the applicable agreement.

If advances exist at the time a loan is applied for, prudent business practice of the lender would dictate that the advance be given due weight in determining the size of the loan and whether the borrower should be required to repay the advances out of the loan proceeds.

On the other hand, some credit rating value should be given to a publisher in respect of his right to recover advances, made by him, from future writer or publisher royalty earnings.

Appraiser's Report and Representations of Borrower

It can be readily recognized that expert analysis from a business and legal standpoint is required for most music business loans. This is frequently the province of accountants and attorneys who specialize in the field. However, even the experts must be given an accurate description of the property to be reviewed. A prime source of this information is the borrower himself. This information is subject to verification through various sources such as the performing-right organizations, the Harry Fox Agency, and Copyright Office search reports.

The following is a basic list of items or representations which a music publisher may be required to supply before a loan is granted:

(1) Identification of the copyrights by title, author, composer, copyright registration number, and date of registration. Footnote details should be given if the balance of the current copyright term is not owned by the publisher, or if less than full ownership exists.

(2) A representative songwriter royalty agreement and a footnote designation of any songwriter agreement with terms less favorable to publisher.

(3) A representation that all songwriter royalty accounts are current except those otherwise stated.

(4) As to songs deriving from a foreign or other prime publisher, a representative subpublishing agreement, and a specification of less favorable agreements and noncurrent royalty accounts.

(5) With respect to any song owned less than 100 percent as to United States rights, a designation of who has administrative rights and the responsibility to pay songwriter royalties, etc.

(6) Copies of the last five years' ASCAP, BMI, Harry Fox, etc., distribution reports.

(7) A summary of all advances currently outstanding against the publisher's account.

(8) A summary of all unrecouped advances given by the publisher against songwriter, other publisher or other third party accounts and a designation of whether the advance is general or specific.

(9) A summary of miscellaneous income (i.e., from commercial jingles, printed music users, foreign licensees) for the past five years.

(10) The designation of music deriving from or used in motion picture scores or musical plays.

(11) A list of exclusive writer contracts, showing the names of writers, the duration of exclusivity, and obligations for future salary payments or advances.

(12) As to copyrights originating before 1978, a list of renewal copyright rights obtained from authors or their statutory successors (i.e., widows and children) as to both copyrights presently in the renewal term and copyrights in their original term, showing the grantor, the title of the song, the effective date of the renewal copyright period, whether any obligations were incurred over and above standard writer royalties, and whether life insurance has been obtained or is obtainable on the grantor's life; also whether a notice of termination has been received in respect of the 19-year extended period after the 56 years of copyright.

(13) The cost of acquisition of any portion of the catalog acquired from other publishers.

(14) A schedule of major physical assets such as recording equipment, studio, and real estate, and the date and cost of acquisition.

(15) A schedule of master recordings currently leased by the publisher and the royalty arrangements in connection therewith.

(16) An inventory of printed goods on hand.

(17) A salary schedule of the publisher's personnel.

(18) The publisher's rent and the duration of his lease.

(19) A schedule of the publisher's stockholders and outstanding stock as well as any pension or profit sharing plans.

From the above information, an expert appraiser can advise the prospective mortgagee regarding the potential future earnings and the resale value of the catalog involved. The appraiser should be selected by the lender, but his fee should be paid by the loan applicant, whether the loan is granted or denied. An appraisal may involve substantial work, and the fee therefore would be a bar to many small loans.

Bankruptcy of Borrower

Music is traditionally a business of optimism. The low-salaried promotion man, expecting early wealth from a sure-fire series of hits, may be spurred to quit his job and open a publishing firm. Many of the applicants for the over 100,000 copyright registrations each year expect that their composition will be among the few hundred that appear on trade paper hit charts annually. This enthusiasm and optimism are evidence of the music industry's individuality and free enterprise. However, business failures and possible bankruptcy must be considered.

The voluntary or involuntary bankruptcy of a publisher has far-reaching consequences which must be considered by potential creditors. Under The Songwriters Guild form of contract, and under many other writer or subpublication agreements as well, it is provided that the contract will terminate and the copyright will be subject to recapture in the event of bankruptcy. Thus the songs could become worthless to the potential creditor of a bankrupt.

It has been held judicially that the sale of copyrights by a trustee in bankruptcy does not destroy a contractual obligation to pay future royalties to writers. This continuing obligation to pay royalties means that the purchaser at a bankruptcy sale, including the lender, cannot acquire copyrights free of future royalty obligations.

31

Commercial Jingles

The early success of "Pepsi-Cola Hits the Spot" heralded an ever-growing reliance by the advertising industry upon commercial jingles. The production of commercial jingles has developed into a specialized segment of the music industry, employing not only composers and arrangers but also many successful recording stars, such as The Jacksons and Duran Duran. Some standards of the jingle world are Coca-Cola's "I Want to Teach the World to Sing" and McDonald's "You Deserve a Break Today."

Types of Use

There are several ways of using music for commercial messages. One type of use is that of original music or music and lyrics written to fit an advertising jingle. This is illustrated by the Pepsi-Cola jingle. Another type employs a familiar tune, with the lyric altered to present the advertising message. Examples of minor lyrical changes can be heard in such jingles as "Thank Heaven for Little Cars" for Renault automobiles and "Up, Up and Away, TWA." Or a popular instrumental can be adopted without substantial change for commercial use, as was the "Colonel Bogey March (from *Bridge On the River Kwai*) for Getty Oil Commercials.

Such works receive 3 percent of an ASCAP performance credit for all uses within any one-hour period, and 3/1000th of a credit for all uses in the second hour.

Two types of use mentioned above are defined more exactly by ASCAP, in connection with the sharply reduced performance credit accorded by ASCAP to jingles. A commercial jingle is "an advertising, promotional or public service announcement containing musical material (with or without lyrics)" in which:

(a) the musical material was originally written for advertising, promotional or public service announcement purposes, or (b) the performance is of a musical work, originally written for other purposes, with the lyrics changed for advertising, promotional or public service announcement purposes with the permission of the ASCAP member or members in interest, or (c) the performance is of a musical work, originally written for other purposes, which does not have at least five feature playings recorded in the Society's survey during the five preceding fiscal survey years.

308

A third type of advertising use of music is as background for a spoken message, such as a strain from "Night and Day" during a television presentation of automobiles. This category is defined by ASCAP as: "A musical work (other than a jingle) used in conjunction with an advertising, promotional, or public service announcement . . ." For such a use, ASCAP generally accords the same credit as for a theme—namely, one-half a performance credit for all uses in the first hour if the composition is a qualified work, and one-tenth of a credit if it is not a qualified work. But only one-tenth of otherwise applicable credit is granted by ASCAP in the event the announcement is itself sponsored by the station or network, as in the case of music behind a presentation of station call letters.

BMI Payments

Since July of 1981 BMI has been making payments for jingle usage of music. But no payments are forthcoming for (a) music used as "promos," in other words, commercial announcements relating to a local station or network or its program, or (b) commercials containing only background music behind a spoken commercial message.

To qualify for payment, the music must be the sole sound that is the focus of audience attention for at least 15 seconds during the commercial. With the notice to BMI of the commercial, BMI requires the submission of an audio tape of the commercial as broadcast; in the case of a television commercial, the sender can supply a video home size tape, if he desires to. Another item that must be submitted is a list of the initial broadcast time bought on behalf of the sponsor. The music will not qualify if written for the advertiser as a "work made for hire" or written pursuant to any agreement whereby BMI is unable to license the performing rights.

Recent rates paid by BMI, *each* for the writer and the publisher are: 1 cent for a local radio performance, $1.50 for a radio network performance, 30 cents for a local television performance, and $36 for a television network performance. The rates are subject to change by BMI.

Negotiations as to Jingles

Major sources of money in connection with jingles derive from licensing well-known songs for jingles or from the commissioning of the creation of original jingle music and lyrics. Over $100,000 is reported to have been paid for an exclusive jingle right to a well-known standard. This is impressive when compared to annual earnings of the same song from conventional music sources, but the amount is small by comparison to the many hundreds of thousands of dollars, or even millions, spent in the advertising campaign built upon the jingle. An agency may not wish to jeopardize a costly campaign by a nonexclusive license which might permit another advertiser to use the same tune. Usually an advertiser will save money by settling for category exclusivity, permitting the same song to be used to advertise a noncompeting product. Simultaneous use of one song for advertising different products is infrequent but is sometimes observed, as with the use of "The Pink Panther Theme" for commercials advertising an insurer and a supplier of building products. Negotiations for the appropriate license are often initiated by the advertiser through The Harry Fox Agency but are ordinarily concluded by the agency in consultation with the publisher and often with the composer involved.

Items of negotiation in the licensing of songs for jingles are exclusivity, the extent of the licensed territory, and the duration of the license. A very important bargaining factor is whether the song is widely known. If it is a current or recent hit, the advertiser will desire the release of the jingle while the tune is fresh in the listener's memory. The publisher and writer will usually prefer to wait until the song is retrogressing on hit charts, so as not to detract from record sales and regular air play. Some composers will object to any jingle use of their song, as an affront to artistic integrity and reputation or as detracting from normal use of the song. This was the case under an AGAC (now The Songwriter Guild) form of agreement in regard to "Muskrat Ramble," where a California court allowed a judgment of $10,000 to a writer whose consent was not obtained. Carole King, through her publishing firm, refused a substantial license fee for a proposed jingle usage of "You've Got A Friend," although permitting a license for a political campaign use by a Democratic presidential contender. It is clearly advisable for a publisher to check carefully the contractual need to obtain writer consent before issuing jingle licenses.

SAMPAC

Producers and composers of jingles have formed a guild for their association and protection, known as SAMPAC. Upon analysis of various forms of jingle contracts in use, SAMPAC has suggested contractual negotiation clauses favoring the creators. In the event of disputes with advertisers that require a compromise, SAMPAC also suggests the language of compromise. The clauses deal with such matters as the reservation of rights by creators, and indemnification. A suggestion to members is that they obtain the protection of an errors and omission insurance policy if they are required to give indemnification.

Performance and Synchronization Licenses

Uses of music "in conjunction with" advertising messages, such as in background instrumental form, fall within the general ASCAP license and do not usually require a special performance license for the arrangement or adaptation. However, advertising campaigns are not founded upon a live use of background music, and, accordingly, a license is necessary for synchronizing the music with the taped television film or for mechanical reproduction on a transcribed announcement. Some publishers, in view of the possibility of substantial ASCAP or BMI performance payments, issue such licenses for a modest charge. Others request significant fees. They regard $50,000 to $100,000 or more of fees as reasonable in relation to large budget, perhaps multimillion dollar, advertising campaigns. However, often an advertising agency will seek quotations from publishers in respect of a number of acceptable songs and thus reserve the right to choose another song if the quotation on one tune is deemed to be too high.

Jingle Packaging

Writers commissioned for tailor-made jingles will sometimes prepare the entire package of the musical composition, lyric, performance, and recording. They thereby reap a financial benefit in addition to the flat fee for composing and writing the jingle. While the advertiser receives rights free of writer royalty obligations, the writer may nevertheless attempt to retain the right to collect performance fees that may be payable by a performing-right organization; however, it is common for writers to reserve no rights whatsoever.

Today many commercial jingles are purchased in package deals from jingle producers. They specialize in music for commercials and frequently have their own staffs of writers and composers who receive guaranteed earnings either as salary or as advances. Participation in the creation and production of a jingle may carry with it the advantage of becoming one of, or selecting, the singers and musicians in the production sessions. These performers receive union residual payments that often rival the fixed fees paid to the creator or producer. Creators and producers sometimes successfully bargain that, if not engaged for a follow-up to the initial campaign, they will receive the union rate payable to a singer on future versions of their original jingle.

Singers and Instrumentalists

Minimum payment rates to singers who perform in commercial jingles are governed by the applicable AFTRA or SAG (Screen Actors Guild) rate schedules to which reference should be made for detailed information and jurisdictional aspects. In general, jingles for radio are subject to AFTRA jurisdiction, and those for television are subject to SAG jurisdiction. AF of M rate schedules cover minimum rates of payment to instrumentalists, orchestrators, arrangers, and copyists. Payments under union agreements are usually geared to particular periods or cycles of use, and additional payments are commonly required for continued use beyond the original period.

Simulation of Artist Style

It is obviously more economical for an advertiser to use studio musicians and singers for commercials than to hire famous stars. When a synchronization license for a commercial jingle is obtained from a music publisher of a song made famous by a top star, it is nevertheless quite tempting for the advertiser to simulate the star's arrangement and style in the jingle. Nancy Sinatra's rendition of "These Boots Were Made for Walking" was thus imitated for a Goodyear Tire and Rubber Company commercial, and The Fifth Dimension's style was used for TWA's "Up, Up and Away." In individual suits brought with respect to each usage, the Courts held that the artists had no property right in their style of rendition or arrangement and that there was no unfair competition.

32

International Copyright Protection

Until ratification by the United States of the Universal Copyright Convention (UCC) in 1955, American publishers desiring to protect their copyrights in foreign countries had to rely upon the International Copyright Union, to which most of the leading countries of the world, except the United States, Russia, China, and many of the Latin American countries, belonged. The Union is based upon adherence to the Berne Convention. Berne member countries are listed in Appendix E2.

Berne Convention

Under the Berne Convention, works first published or simultaneously published in a Union country are granted copyright protection in all countries which are members of the Union. The duration of copyright in a Union country normally is the author's lifetime plus 50 years, as a minimum. Publication requires that works be "issued and made available in sufficient quantities to the public"; exhibitions, performances, recitations, and broadcasting do not constitute publication.

To obtain simultaneous publication in a Union country, American publishers usually arrange for publication in England or Canada. Although the British statute calls for the deposit of one copy of the best edition in the British Museum within one month after publication, failure to do so does not invalidate the copyright and involves only a possible fine of up to £5 plus the value of a copy. In Canada, unlike Great Britain, a claim to copyright may be officially registered, but registration is not essential to Berne Convention protection. Such registration in Canada has the virtue of being prima facie evidence of copyright.

The enactment of the 1976 Copyright Act may make the United States eligible for full membership in the International Copyright Union, based on adherence to the Berne Convention. A requirement for Berne adherence has been that copyright protection continue for an author's life and for 50 years after his death. Whether other requirements are met and whether the United States will apply for membership remains to be seen.

Universal Copyright Convention

In 1955, the United States became one of the first signers of the Universal Copyright Convention, a copy of which is included in Appendix D. Under the UCC, to which many of the leading countries of the world belong, with the notable exception of China, works of a national of a signatory country or works first published in a signatory country must be given the same treatment in other signatory nations that such nations give their own nationals for works originally published there. For protection under UCC it is immaterial where the works are first published in the case of a national of a signatory nation; similarly, one need not be a national of a signatory nation to achieve protection if first publication takes place in the signatory nation.

While under the Berne Convention no formalities such as deposit, notice, registration, or fee are required to obtain copyright protection, for UCC, the symbol © and the name of the copyright proprietor and the year of first publication must be shown in all copies in such a manner and location as to provide reasonable notice of a claim of copyright. Other formalities are waived except that each UCC country can continue to require formalities for works of its own nationals and for works first published in its territory. Consequently, an American national must abide by the provisions of the United States Copyright Act with respect to registration and deposit of copies.

In contrast to the most recent version of the Berne Convention, which sets forth a minimum period of protection based on the life of the writer plus 50 years, under UCC the minimum term of protection of music is the life of the author plus 25 years, or 25 years from publication if the life of the author is not used to measure the period of copyright in the particular country.

Some publishers, despite UCC, will continue to seek protection in Berne Convention countries through simultaneous publication. This appears a prudent course as long as there are a number of countries, such as the Union of South Africa, which are Union countries but not members of UCC.

Buenos Aires Convention

The United States is a signatory to the Buenos Aires Convention of 1910, along with Argentina, Brazil, Chile, Colombia, Costa Rica, Dominican Republic, Ecuador, Guatemala, Haiti, Honduras, Nicaragua, Panama, Paraguay, Peru, and Uruguay. By this convention, compliance with the copyright law of the country of first publication qualifies the work for protection in the other signatories to the convention; however, to secure copyright in all such countries, each work must carry a notice to the effect that property rights in the copyright are reserved. While the United States copyright notice would appear to satisfy this requirement, it would seem advisable to add to the notice "All Rights Reserved."

Geneva Phonogram Convention

An international treaty to protect sound recordings against piracy was drafted in 1971. It is known as the "Geneva Convention of October 29,

1971 for the Protection of Producers of Phonograms against Unauthorized Duplication."

Under the treaty the contracting states agree to protect the nationals of other states against the production or importation of unauthorized duplicate recordings if the purpose is to distribute them to the public. The method to accomplish this result is to be determined by the domestic law of each contracting state and shall include one or more of the following: protection by means of the grant of copyright or other specific right; protection by means of the law relating to unfair competition; or protection by means of penal sanctions.

The United States became a member on March 10, 1974. It implements the treaty through the federal copyright in sound recordings. For a list of other members of the convention and for a description of other international copyright relations of the United States, see Appendix E1.

Part 3

GENERAL MUSIC INDUSTRY ASPECTS

33

Sources of Information

It is important for people in the music business to keep informed of news and developments in the business. A prime source of information of this kind is the trade press. Other suppliers of data are the various organizations in the field and the United States Copyright Office; diverse other reference materials are also available.

Trade Press

The leading trade publications in the music business are *Billboard, Cash Box,* and the weekly newspaper *Variety. Billboard* and *Cash Box* concentrate on music matters, whereas *Variety* ranges over the entire field of entertainment with only one section devoted to music news.

To keep abreast of developments in the music business, songwriters, performers, publishers, and record company personnel read at least one of the two weekly magazines. The range of possible information in the trade press is indicated by the many charts in a typical issue of *Billboard.* For example, in one week in 1984 there were separate charts as follows:

Hot 100 (singles)
Hot 100 Sales & Airplay
Top 200 Albums
Hot Black Singles
Hot Black Singles Sales
  & Airplay
Top Black Albums
Hot Country Singles
Hot Country Singles Sales
  & Airplay
Top Country Albums
Top Rock Tracks

Hot Adult Contemporary
Top Midline Albums
Top Classical Albums
Top Jazz Albums
Hot Dance/Disco
Hits Of The World
Top Computer Software
Top Videocassettes—Sales
Top Videocassettes—Rentals
Top Videodiscs

The *Cash Box* weekly charts are roughly comparable to those in *Billboard.*

Billboard's best-selling pop singles chart called the "Hot 100" lists records by title, name of the artist, name of the producer, and the record label number. Also indicated are the number of weeks a record has been on the chart, its standing in each of the two previous weeks, the availability of video clips, the names of its writer(s), publisher and sheet music supplier, and the publisher's affiliation with ASCAP or BMI.

Songs registering the greatest airplay and sales gains for the past week are marked by a bullet encircling the number of their standing on the chart. Each song certified as a "million seller" by the Record Industry Association of America is accompanied by a black circle, and for sales of 2 million there is a black triangle.

Cash Box has a comparable best-selling pop singles chart called "CASH BOX TOP 100 SINGLES" which contains information similar to that on the Billboard chart except that the name of the record producer and certification by the Record Industry Association of America are omitted. Songs with "exceptionally heavy radio activity" in the prior week are shown with a black circle containing a lightning flash design, and those with "exceptionally heavy sales activity" by a black circle enclosing a dollar sign.

The weekly Variety includes a top ten best-selling singles list headed "U. S. Singles Sellers."

Table 33.1 is a comparison of the Billboard and Cash Box top singles listings (song, artist, label), for a week in 1984.

Table 33.1: Billboard and Cash Box Singles Listings for the week of July 14, 1984

Billboard	Cash Box
1. When Doves Cry Prince Warner Bros.	1. When Doves Cry Prince Warner Bros.
2. Dancing in the Dark Bruce Springsteen Columbia	2. Dancing in the Dark Bruce Springsteen Columbia
3. Jump (For My Love) Pointer Sisters Planet/RCA	3. The Reflex Duran Duran Capitol
4. Eyes Without A Face Billy Idol Chrysalis	4. Eyes Without A Face Billy Idol Chrysalis
5. The Reflex Duran Duran Capitol	5. Self Control Laura Branigan Atlantic
6. Self Control Laura Branigan Atlantic	6. Jump (For My Love) Pointer Sisters Planet/RCA
7. Almost Paradise . . . Love Theme From Footloose Mike Reno and Ann Wilson Columbia	7. Almost Paradise . . . Love Theme From Footloose Mike Reno and Ann Wilson Columbia
8. Ghostbusters Ray Parker, Jr. Arista	8. Time After Time Cyndi Lauper Portrait/CBS

It is apparent that record listing is not an exact science and that differences may arise from, among other things, variations in samplings of markets and merchandisers.

Billboard ranks albums in a separate chart entitled "TOP 200 ALBUMS" which sets forth the 200 best-selling albums in the United States. LPs that register the greatest sales gains in the latest week are noted by a bullet encircling the number of their status on the chart. Those albums certified by the Recording Industry Association of America for sales of 500,000 units are marked by a black circular dot and for sales of 1 million units by a small black triangle. The comparable *Cash Box* chart lists 200 albums and uses gray circles to show the albums which have demonstrated a strong upward move. The weekly *Variety* album chart list merely indicates the 10 top-selling LPs.

Table 33.2 is a comparison of the *Billboard* and *Cash Box* top eight albums for a week in 1984.

Table 33.2: *Billboard* and *Cash Box* Album Charts for the Week of July 14, 1984

Billboard	*Cash Box*
1. Born in the U.S.A. Bruce Springsteen Columbia	1. Born in the U.S.A. Bruce Springsteen Columbia
2. Sports Huey Lewis & The News Chrysalis	2. Footloose Soundtrack Columbia
3. Heartbeat City The Cars Elektra	3. Sports Huey Lewis & The News Chrysalis
4. Footloose Soundtrack Columbia	4. Can't Slow Down Lionel Richie Motown
5. Can't Slow Down Lionel Richie Motown	5. Heartbeat City The Cars Elektra
6. Rebel Yell Billy Idol Chrysalis	6. Breakin' Soundtrack Polydor
7. 1984 Van Halen Warner Bros.	7. She's So Unusual Cyndi Lauper Portrait/CBS
8. Seven And The Ragged Tiger Duran Duran Capitol	8. Rebel Yell Billy Idol Chrysalis

The two trade magazines include weekly reviews of new singles and albums. Singles are subdivided by *Billboard* into "Pop," "Black,"

"Country," "AC" (Adult Contemporary), and "Disco/Dance." Each subclassification is further divided into "picks" and "recommended." The "picks" are new releases which, in the opinion of *Billboard* reviewers, have the greatest chart potential in the particular format. The "recommended" have the "potential for significant chart action." There is a separate category of "new and noteworthy" which highlights new and developing acts worthy of attention.

Cash Box's singles reviews indicate records which achieve the category of "Feature Picks" and also highlight an "Out of the Box" and a "New and Developing" single.

Billboard in its album reviews allocates the better albums to the subclassifications of "Pop," "Black," "Country," "Jazz-Fusion," "Gospel," "Classical," "Latin," and "Soundtrack/Theatre." Those albums classified as "picks" in one of these formats are predicted to hit the top half of the chart for that format. The most outstanding of the week's releases is given the *Billboard* "Spotlight" attribution and is thereby forecasted to reach the top 10 on *Billboard*'s TOP 200 Albums chart or to earn a platinum (that is a 1 million) sales certification from the Record Industry Association of America. There are also "recommended" LPs, which include other releases expected to reach the chart in the respective format, as well as other albums of superior quality.

Cash Box contains album reviews of the more meritorious albums. As in the case of singles reviews, the albums are categorized as "Feature Picks" and the reviews also highlight an "Out of the Box" and a "New and Developing" album.

Variety has reviews biweekly of a limited number of singles and albums.

The two trade weeklies contain sections on international news and list the best international sellers in certain international record markets.

A typical issue of *Billboard* or *Cash Box* reports changes in artist affiliations with record companies, visitors from foreign music circles to the United States, shifts in record company personnel, special sales promotions, news of governmental laws and investigations, meetings of distributors, discussions of publishing and record company business developments, and acquisitions and mergers of publishing and record companies.

Billboard and *Cash Box* issue annual directories which include valuable information about record manufacturers, music publishers, record wholesalers, and firms engaged in services and supplies for the music industry. The directories are international in scope, and reference to them can be of great aid in familiarizing American record people and publishers with their counterparts in foreign countries.

Subscription Services

The underlying data for the *Billboard* charts are available to special subscribers to the *Billboard* Information Network, which is operated as a division of *Billboard*. Subscribers can receive early reports on chart activity directly through their office data processing machines. The service also provides an analysis of individual station playlists, regional airplay, and individual and regional store activity. Professional promotion people employed by publishers and record companies find the service useful in pinpointing activity and in making prompt evaluations of results.

New On The Charts is a monthly information service sold on subscription only to professionals in the music industry. It supplies the names, addresses, and telephone numbers of producers, publishers, booking agents, record labels, and personal managers associated with the chart entries on the *Billboard* and *Cash Box* charts. Video producer information and other current material are also presented.

Other Publications

Radio & Records (R&R) is a weekly trade paper targeted to the radio industry. It furnishes playlists of major market stations, affording programmers an opportunity to compare current hit record rotations. As distinguished from *Billboard* and *Cash Box* charts, it does not utilize store activity information. Its multi-format charts are limited to reporting on radio stations, with weighting by Arbitron audience measurements. Record company and music publisher promotion personnel use R&R charts to assess the radio acceptance of new releases.

Spot Radio Rates and Data is a monthly publication directed toward supplying vital information concerning each of the over 8,000 U.S.A. radio stations. It sets forth essential data for advertisers, such as rates, audience, power, and time of broadcast hours. Each station identifies its current music format, that is, Gospel, Black, Adult Contemporary, Country, Concert, and so forth. Listings are by state, with each area identified by population and household income data from the most recent census.

Radio Facts is an annual report prepared by the Radio Advertising Bureau, Inc. to furnish the statistics of radio formats. The 1984 report indicates that of the 8,000-plus radio stations, 27.7 percent specialize in Country music, 23.9 percent in Adult Contemporary, 10 percent in Top 40/Rock, 8.5 percent in Nostalgia Middle of the Road, 6.5 percent in Beautiful Music/Easy Listening, 6.3 percent in Religious, and the balance in Black, R & B, Classical, Jazz, Golden Oldies and other formats.

Copyright Office

The physical destruction of buildings in the Second World War was accompanied by the loss of important copyright records. News came from Finland that its great composer Jan Sibelius had insuffecent data to furnish his advisors and was unable to keep abreast of the uses in the United States of his extensive catalog. The United States Copyright

Office, as a gesture of goodwill, made a complete analysis of his approximately 800 works registered at any time in the United States, setting forth the dates of original and renewal registrations, the history of any assignments, and the original recordings indicated by Notices of Use on file. This gift required 200 man-hours of work. A similar study was made of about 3,000 musical compositions of German origin, replacing catalog information that had been destroyed in wartime.

Facilities of the Copyright Office are available for such research services at a service charge of $10 per hour. When a search is requested, all known basic facts should be sent to the Copyright Office. In addition to its search services, the Copyright Office can be of value in furnishing copies of missing songs. Unpublished manuscripts and published songs which have been filed with a copyright registration will be photocopied, and the copy supplied, provided that the request for the photocopy is authorized in writing by the copyright owner or his agent, or the request is by an attorney for use in a court proceeding, or there is a court order requiring the making of the copy.

There is published through the Copyright Office a *Catalog of Copyright Entries* which is on file in larger public libraries and copies of which may be purchased by the public. Effective with the Fourth Series, Volume 2, 1979 catalogs the *Catalog of Copyright Entries* has been issued in microfiche form only. The catalog was previously published through 1978 in printed book form. It will continue to be published in eight parts. Among these are separate parts for Performing Arts (which includes musical works), Sound Recordings, and Renewals. Orders for subscriptions to one or more parts, or subscriptions for the entire catalog may be sent to the Superintendent of Documents, U. S. Government Printing Office, Washington, D.C. 20402. Unpublished as well as published materials are included in all parts except the part covering Renewals. The catalog is indexed by copyright registration number, title of the work, claimant's name, and in the case of sound recordings, the names of principal performers. The appropriate use of the catalog can satisfy simply and inexpensively many requests for information regarding copyrighted material.

In a study prepared under the supervision of the Copyright Office with a view to considering a general revision of the Copyright Law, it was stated:

> In summary, the "Catalog of Copyright Entries" makes an official registration record available for consultation outside of the Copyright Office. It can be used, chiefly through its . . . indexes, to ascertain the facts of original or renewal registration for any copyrighted work from 1897 to date, to determine whether a registered work is still within the term of copyright protection, and to identify the copyright owner at the time of registration. It cannot be used to trace subsequent transfers of

title, which must be searched in the Office. It also identifies the particular work registered. . . . This makes it time-consuming to search for a work if the approximate registration or publication date and the class in which it was registered are not known. The . . . indexes are especially useful to copyright owners in determining which works are entering the period in which renewal registration must be made.

The Copyright Office assembles important federal and state court decisions regarding copyrights and related subjects in the field of intellectual property; these are published in a series of bulletins entitled "Decisions of the United States Courts Involving Copyright." Orders for these bulletins should be sent to the Superintendent of Documents. The Copyright Office also issues gratis a series of individual circulars explaining various aspects of domestic and international copyright protection.

Archive of Folk Culture

In 1928 the Library of Congress established within its Music Division a national repository for documentary manuscripts and sound recordings of American folk music. In 1981 its official name was changed from the Archive of Folk Song to "The Archive of Folk Culture." The Archive also has acquired—through gift, exchange, and field-collecting projects—folk song material from Canada, Latin America, the British Isles, Europe, Africa, and certain areas of the Orient and the Pacific. Since its establishment, over 35,000 records and tapes containing more than 300,000 items of folk song, folk music, folk tale, oral history, and other types of folklore have been sent to the Library of Congress mainly from the United States but also from other parts of the world. From this extensive collection, the Library of Congress has over a period of years issued over 65 selected recordings for the use of universities, libraries, students, and other interested parties. These long-playing records include traditional sea chanteys, authentic songs of the cowboy, songs of the Mormons, ballads of the Civil War, Anglo-American songs and ballads, Negro work songs and spirituals, fiddle and banjo tunes, songs of many Indian tribes, and also folk songs and music of Brazil, Mexico, Puerto Rico, and Venezuela.

A catalog listing the entire series of LP records available from the Library of Congress may be obtained from the Recorded Sound Section, Music Division, Library of Congress, Washington, D.C. 20540. The Archive has available extensive field notes, many textual transcriptions, and some musical transcriptions, in folders and bound volumes, for supplementary information about the recordings. The Archive has compiled over 125 bibliographies and other reference lists covering over 100 areas and subjects in the field of folklore and folk music; an inventory of the bibliographies and lists is available upon request.

Organizations

ASCAP, BMI, and The Harry Fox Agency, Inc. are important sources of information regarding the history, ownership, and rights under copyright with respect to musical works. ASCAP and BMI maintain index departments which can and do supply information to the industry and the public concerning millions of old and more recent compositions. All new copyright registrations in the United States Copyright Office are entered into their indexes. The Harry Fox Agency also has a great volume of data on file which is made available to publisher participants and to record companies, motion picture producers, and other users of music.

The various unions and trade organizations in the music industry will furnish data on items of interest to them. A list of trade associations, unions, and guilds is given in Appendix P.

Professional Research Services

It is often necessary to locate the owners of musical copyrights in connection with prospective motion picture, television, stage, and record productions. As previously noted, ASCAP, BMI, The Harry Fox Agency and unions and trade organizations may be helpful. Reference has also been made to the services of the law firm of Brylawski and Cleary of Washington, D.C., which will research the files of the Copyright Office, and to the research services of the United States Copyright Office.

Where an initial request for information produces unsatisfactory results, or the inquirer does not have the staff, time, or expertise to make his own inquiries, professional services may be employed. The same services may be sought where expertise is needed for the negotiation of appropriate licenses.

Investigative and negotiating services are supplied by the Mary Williams Clearing Corporation of 6223 Selma Avenue, Hollywood, California 90028. Similar functions of investigation and negotiation are also performed by The Clearing House, Ltd. of 6605 Hollywood Blvd., Hollywood, California 90028.

The Business Affairs Corp., of 105 West 55th Street, Suite 9B, New York, N.Y. 10019, acts primarily as a negotiator, with more incidental services for locating prospective licensors.

Reference Materials

Diverse reference books and manuals are available to supplement other sources of information. The *Variety Cavalcade of Music* provides data on and indexes of songs in hit categories. *Phonolog,* a service designed for record stores, gives information on available recordings, with listings by artist or by the title of the song or album. The *Schwann-1* and *Schwann-2 Record and Tape Guides,* sold only in record stores, are useful for finding LPs by title. *Schwann-1* provides a monthly coverage of new releases. *Schwann-2* appears semiannually and lists spoken language, international pop and folk, and monaural LPs as well as stereo LPs that have been on the market at least two years. *Popular Recordaid* publishes a bimonthly listing similar to *Schwann-1*, and there are also quarterly issues having an alphabetical title section for single records. In the past, *Song Dex* supplied index cards listing writers, publisher, copyright data and the identifying lyric and melody line of songs. The *Burns Mantle Annual* for Broadway shows indicates composers and lyric writers as well as other information about a show and its stars. The *Film Daily Year Book* contains similar data for films.

Joel Whitburn's Record Research is a series of books prepared under license from *Billboard* showing the history of all *Billboard* chart action singles and LPs. Essentially organized alphabetically by artist name, but also utilizing song title lists, it furnishes research and programming material plus some incidental facts concerning the records and the artists.

Billboard itself is selling chart-action research packages. For example, the "Number One Pop Singles, 1941 through 1983," "Top Ten Singles, 1947 through 1983," and "Top Country Albums of the Year, 1965 through 1983."

An important reference source for serious music is the massive 20-volume 1980 edition of *The New Grove Dictionary of Music and Musicians*.

A list of reference materials on songs, records, shows, films, composers, and publishers is given in Appendix Q.

International Meetings

In every year since 1967, there has been an international meeting of music business participants such as publishers, record companies, managers, performance societies, and equipment manufacturers and suppliers. This meeting is called MIDEM—International Music and Publishing Market—and is held in Cannes, France at the end of January. Information brochures and fliers, as well as samples, are distributed at participants' booths. MIDEM organizes lectures and seminars of interest to the music industry.

Throughout the year, *Billboard* organizes and sponsors trade meetings in the United States and abroad. The subject matter ranges broadly, covering diverse topics such as music programming, music videos, and international music business trade.

34

Names and Trademarks

One cannot generalize as to the value of names in the music industry. The tremendous variety in names of artists, record companies, and publishers ranges from names which simply identify, such as Ferrante and Teicher, Columbia Records, and Famous Music Corporation, to such extremely fanciful names as Creedence Clearwater Revival, Buddah Records, and Tuna Fish Music.

Names of record companies and music publishers appear relatively insignificant in terms of their influence on consumer purchases in the popular music field. Rarely will an individual go to a music store and request a "Dwarf Music song" or a "Warner Brothers Music song." Rather, the identification of the song will probably be by the song title itself or by its composer. Dwarf Music publishes songs by Bob Dylan, who owns Dwarf Music, and the consumer seeking a Bob Dylan composition will refer to Bob Dylan and not to the name of the publisher. In the record market, the consumer may expect a certain level of technical and artistic quality when purchasing a record bearing the label of a well known firm such as RCA or CBS. However, the actual purchase of their records will probably be made on the basis of an artist name. The consumer will ask for The Cars (on Elektra) or The Pointer Sisters (on Planet/RCA).

The goodwill attendant upon names in the music business is more important in music trade circles. A dealer or jobber is more likely to stock and feature a new record released by a successful and established record label or artist than a record by a new firm or artist. An artist may favor a recording agreement with CBS Records over one with a lesser label. A writer may prefer to be contracted to Chappell Music than to a publisher not as well-known.

In the field of serious and educational music publishing, the names of established publishers tend to have greater value than the names of publishers in the popular music industry. Purchasers of serious music rely on and respect the editorial selection and quality standards of well-known serious music publishers, whereas, in the popular music field, printed sales usually depend upon prior popular music recordings to stimulate consumer interest.

The consumer seeking a classical music recording may be influenced by the reputation of the record company on whose label the recording is released; certain labels have achieved a reputation for both technical and artistic quality.

The selection, protection, and development of names and trademarks are complex matters. The names and trademarks should be distinctive enough so that property rights therein will accrue to the persons or firms involved. For product identification they should not impinge upon other persons' or firms' rights in names or trademarks previously used. Close similarity may lead to confusion as to product, credit problems, misdirection of mail and telephone service, and legal entanglements.

Copyrightability

There is no protection afforded to brand names, trademarks, slogans, and other short phrases or expressions under the United States copyright laws. Nor may familiar symbols or designs, of themselves, qualify for copyright registration. For legal protection of a name, slogan, phrase, or symbol, it is generally true that reliance must be placed on registration under the federal trademark law or on the rules of law relating to unfair competition.

However, the 1976 Copyright Act provides that copyright can be obtained in "pictorial, graphic and sculptural works."[1] In order to be copyrightable, a work must include an appreciable amount of original text or pictorial materials. Thus copyright may apply to qualifying prints and labels used in connection with the sale or advertisement of articles of merchanise. For example, a record label embodying the name "Mountainview" in conjunction with a photograph of Mt. Vesuvius might enjoy copyright protection, in addition to protection under trademark law. The copyright protection would not extend to the name apart from the pictorial matter.

Comparison between Copyright and Trademarks

There is a tendency among persons in the music business to refer to "copyright" when they mean exclusive rights that are available only through trademark protection or through rules of law relating to unfair competition. A simple distinction between copyright and trademarks is that copyright protects the *expression* of literary, artistic, and musical ideas, whereas trademarks serve as a *badge of identification* which protects goodwill attached to a particular product or service and safeguards the public from confusion as to the source or identity of the products involved. Other differences between copyright and trademarks are shown in Table 34.1.

Selection of a Name

Finding the right name may be a time-consuming and often fruitless task. All too frequently the selected name has been previously preempted by other persons. The means of avoiding conflicting names are

[1]There was similar protection under the 1909 Copyright Act.

Table 34.1 Differences between Copyright and Trademarks.

Copyright	_Trademark_
Duration ordinarily limited to life of author plus 50 years.*	Unlimited number of successive 20-year terms.
Certificate issued by government without prior search for conflicting claims or prior notice to public.	Certificate issued by government only after search for conflicting claims, notice to the public of the pending claim, and an opportunity for objections to be filed.
Notice of copyright required from the first publication.	Notice of trademark not permitted until after registration.
Statutory protection commences upon fixation in a copy.**	Common law protection begins upon use.
Registration of copyright permitted for unpublished music or published music at any time during subsistence of copyrights.	Registration of trademark not allowed until after proven use in interstate commerce or in commerce between a state and a foreign country.
Originality required for a valid copyright.	Originality or novelty not essential for a valid trademark. Identification with product or service is significant.
Copyright is fully assignable.	Trademark is assignable only with the product or service identified by the mark.
Licensee of copyright need not be supervised by owner of copyright.	Licensee of trademark must be under owner's supervision and control to ensure that the product's identity, quality, and character are preserved.

---

*Under the Copyright Act of 1909 duration was limited to the original 28-year term plus one 28-year renewal.

**Under the 1909 Act, the statutory protection of unpublished compositions was conditioned upon registration; prior to registration there was common law protection.

discussed later in this chapter. As to sources of inspiration for new names in the music field, the stories are numerous and legendary. The great historic record label, OKEH, which was revived by CBS Records, originated with the initials of the owner. Laura Nyro's firm, Tuna Fish Music, memorializes her favorite sandwich. Certain names represent an attempt to present a consolidated trade image. For example, United Artists Music and Unart Music evidence an identification with their original parent company, United Artists Corporation. MCA Music shows a relation to MCA, Inc. Warner Brothers Music is a change of name from the established Music Publishers Holding Company which published for decades the vast and numerous music catalogs purchased by Warner Brothers Pictures in 1929.

CBS, Inc. has two publishing firms, April Music and Blackwood Music, with the initial letters of their names providing an easy identification as to which is the ASCAP firm and which is the BMI affiliated firm.

Varying devices are employed to suggest names for corporations or trademarks. A choice may be made from different categories, just as the United States Weather Bureau utilizes boys' and girls' names in alphabetical order to denote successive hurricanes and the United States Navy uses fish names to differentiate individual submarines. For example, publishers may be named after fruits (Apple Music), birds (Thrush Music), geographic places (Broadway Music), and colleges (Harvard Music). Dictionaries, atlases, maps, and even telephone books are some sources of inspiration. A fairly common device is to spell names backwards (Patti Page's EGAP Music), use a child's name (Alice, Marie), combine the names of a husband and wife (Marydan), or join the syllables of partners' names (Franstan).

As noted above, many record companies are identified with parent firms such as Warners, RCA, CBS, and MCA, Others are unique to themselves, for example, Elektra, Epic, Reprise, and Polydor. Some common names, such as London, Capitol, and King, have their own special history and position. But, in general, a common name is less desirable for new companies for several reasons: First, a common name may be confused with the names of other companies in related or unrelated fields and thereby subject the new company to a possible lawsuit on the grounds of trademark infringement or unfair competition. Secondly, different rules of trademark registration apply to common names. Finally, previous use of the common name may present a bar to incorporation of a new firm.

The selection of an artist's name can be an art. There are many simple names. Johnny Cash, Frank Sinatra, Barbra Streisand, and Peter Frampton have not suffered from the use of their own names. However, the popular music field abounds in highly imaginative names. A review of a *Billboard* chart shows:

Culture Club	Alabama
The Pretenders	.38 Special
The Police	Quiet Riot
Yes	The Romantics
Eurythmics	U2
ZZ Top	Air Supply
Genesis	Utopia

Information about Prior and Conflicting Names and Marks

In the initial enthusiasm of starting a new business, a music publisher or record company will frequently be annoyed by the rejection of names by a Secretary of State who passes on proposed incorporation documents for a new company. Each of the 50 states has its own corporate registration procedures. Particularly in the music-oriented states of New York, California, and Tennessee, the Secretary of State will often refuse to accept a name regarded as unduly similar to other names. This should be appreciated as an early warning which aids in starting a new company on the right track.

In the music publishing field, all major performing-right organizations, ASCAP, BMI, and SESAC, should be consulted before a new publisher name is used. The many thousands of names already on the file should not be duplicated since important performance credits may be lost due to confusion of names. ASCAP and BMI issue alphabetical lists of current publisher affiliate names. These lists are available upon request from either organization. Moreover, in response to telephone or letter inquiry, both ASCAP and BMI give specific advice as to the availability of a name. In fact, it is the practice of BMI to reserve on request, for a limited period, a name determined to be available, so as to permit time to organize the new company.

Record company names and labels may be conveniently checked in the front pages of the publication known as *Phonolog,* where all current records are listed and where label abbreviations are identified. If not readily available in libraries or music business offices, this publication is often found in retail record outlets. The annual editions issued by music trade papers, such as the *Billboard International Buyer's Guide* and the *Cash Box Annual Worldwide Directory,* also list publishers and record company labels and names.

The Harry Fox Agency at 205 East 42nd Street, New York. N.Y. 10017, is another source of information as to possible conflicting names in the music industry. This office represents the majority of substantial music publishers in the United States and collects, on their behalf, mechanical royalties from nearly every existing record company. Accordingly, The Harry Fox Agency has on file information of vital importance in the selection of names. On its own behalf it desires to assist in the avoidance of duplicative and confusing names. In some instances, its information as to publisher and record company names may be more complete than *Phonolog* or the *Billboard* or *Cash Box* lists.

Search Organizations and Services

Listings in trade publications, telephone books, and the other information sources noted previously are not necessarily complete, and in some cases a new company may desire to avoid making its own search and will engage professional help. Of course, a trademark attorney has expertise in arranging for a search and interpreting the results and this expertise is significant in giving assurance to a proposed trademark user. There are trademark search organizations that are listed in the yellow pages of the telephone directories. For example, the Trademark Service Corp., located at 747 Third Avenue in New York City, will issue a prompt report to attorneys on trademarks registered with the United States Patent and Trademark Office in Washington, D.C. Upon request, it will also report on trademarks filed with the Secretary of State in one or more designated states. This organization's report may also be expanded to include similar names in telephone directories. Also the law firm of Brylawski & Cleary, of Washington, D.C., will conduct similar research in the trademark records, the Copyright Office records, music industry trade directories, and its own files and resource material. Sometimes such a report can be used in a defensive stage rather than in searching for a new name. Thus, if an investment has already been made in a name and a claim is asserted by a third party that the name is unduly similar to its prior name, a search may reveal many other usages of the name and that it should be regarded as public property available for further use.

Requests for a search should not be made to the United States Patent and Trademark Office since it does not offer a search service. On the other hand, its files are available for a personal search by interested parties or their representatives in the public search room of the Trademark Examining Operation of the Patent and Trademark Office, located at Crystal Plaza Building, No. 2, 2011 Jefferson Davis Highway, Arlington, Virginia 22202.

A primary source of information used by professional search organizations and available to the public is the *Index to the Trademark Register*. It is a convenient listing of registered names and marks. All registered music names and marks, whether on the principal or supplemental register and whether a trademark or service mark, are found in this listing. Thus, inspection of Class 41, Education and Entertainment, shows such diverse music registrations as The Beatles, Big Kahuna, The Champagne Music of Lawrence Welk, The Fugs, Glenn Miller Orchestra, Grand Ole Opry, Minnie Pearl, National Symphony Orchestra, and Tin Pan Alley Music Service.

Additional lists available to the music industry are in Class 15, Musical Instruments, and Class 16, publications.

A word of caution is appropriate with respect to research as to prior and conflicting names and marks. It is frequently difficult to decide whether names or marks are confusingly similar, under legal principles. It is prudent therefore to consult attorneys whenever problems arise which the layman cannot readily solve.

Information about Prior and Conflicting Names of Artists

Although, as previously noted, unique names for artists abound in the music field, some artists may be surprised to find that their flight of imagination in coining a name has been previously duplicated. Especially where the artist desires to use his or her natural name, which is not an unusual one, caution should be exercised. Undoubtedly, there are many girls named Judy Collins or Peggy Lee, and many males have been given the natural names of James Brown and Tom Jones. In many cases, it is advisable to change even a natural name so as to avoid confusing the public and the music trade.

It is prudent to check with the artist unions as to names before launching a public career. The American Federation of Television & Radio Artists (AFTRA) is the union for performers on radio, television, and records. Its principal office is at 1350 Avenue of Americas, New York, N.Y. 10036. The union will advise as to similar names of performers on its roster.

The American Guild of Variety Artists (AGVA) is the union for performers in night clubs and cabarets. Its office is at 184 Fifth Avenue, New York, N.Y. 10010. It, too, will search its roster and report on possible confusion of names.

Registration of Names

As noted previously, ASCAP, BMI, and SESAC should be consulted as to prior uses of a name by their affiliated music publishers; they may refuse to accept a new member or affiliate with a name that is confusingly similar to other names. In the area of records, the American Federation of Musicians enters into written union agreements with any record company covering the use of union musicians. It maintains extensive lists of and data concerning record companies and record labels for use in union negotiations and for contract enforcement as to pay and working conditions. Record producers or companies may file with the union a proposed record company or record label name; in response to inquiries, the union will advise subsequent inquirers of possible conflicting usage. Communications in that regard should be directed to the national office of the American Federation of Musicians, 1500 Broadway, New York, N.Y. 10036.

Record companies entering into labor agreements with the American Federation of Musicians are required to execute simultaneous agreements with the Recording Industries Music Performance Trust Fund to make pension and related payment to the Fund. This office is addressed c/o its Trustee, 1501 Broadway, New York, N.Y. 10036. Information comparable to that of the American Federation of Musicians may also be requested of the Trustee, whose files may supplement those of the union.

Governmental approval of a corporate name, as previously mentioned, is a necessity before incorporation under such name. This is the province of the particular state in which incorporation is requested. One state does not require a search of the lists of names approved by other states. Only local clearance of names is involved in state incorporation procedures. But each state will crosscheck proposed names not only in the music industry involved but in all other fields. Thus, a "Whiz Bang Music Corporation" may fail of clearance in a state which has previously granted such name clearance for a hat company or for a company in other unrelated activities. If interest in a name persists despite the rejection by the Secretary of State, in some instances clearance may be obtained through obtaining waivers from prior users in the state.

An example of corporate name clearance procedure is that followed by the New York Secretary of State. A simple letter, without filing fee or further information, may be sent to the Secretary of State at Albany, New York, to request information as to the availability of one or more corporate names. The reply will set forth the available names. In effect, this constitutes a free search service by the state as to its corporation division files and a free evaluation of possible conflict with corporate names already in existence. An available name can be reserved for 60 days upon payment of a $10 fee, and upon good cause the reservation will be extended for an additional 60 days; during these periods the registration of incorporation documents can be perfected. There are also reservation-of-name procedures in the states of Delaware and California, and such procedures may apply in other states.

Registration of Marks

Under the United States trademark law, provision is made for the registration of a trademark, which distinguishes a product and identifies its origins, as for example, the RCA Victor name and the logo of a dog with a phonograph. Provision is also made for the registration of a service mark, which is used in the sale or advertising of services to identify the services of one person and distinguish them from the services of others, as with the Glenn Miller Orchestra. There is no statutory basis for the registration of trade or commercial names utilized merely to identify a business entity, but, if also used as a trademark or service mark, then, as such, the name is protected by statute, in addition to possible common law protection discussed above.

No time limit exists within which an application for registration should be filed. It may be filed at any time after the mark has been used in interstate, foreign, or territorial commerce. This use in relation to goods or products means that the mark has been affixed to goods or their containers and the product has been sold or shipped in such commerce. With respect to a service mark, it denotes that the mark is utilized or displayed in the sale or advertising of services rendered in commerce in more than one state or in any one state of the United States and a foreign country.

Once a mark has been registered, a registrant should give public notice of the registration by using, in conjunction with the mark, the words "Registered in U. S. Patent and Trademark Office" or "Reg. U.S. and Tm Pat. Off.," or the letter R enclosed in a circle, thus: ®. In suits for infringement under Federal Trademark Law, known as the Lanham Act, failure to give such notice of registration will prevent the registrant from recovering profits or damages unless the defendant had actual notice of the registration. It is legally improper to utilize such notice before the issuance of a registration and certificate. The impropriety may be a cause for refusal of registration and may result in fraud sanctions under the Lanham Act.

Prior to the completion of registration of a mark, consideration should be given to using the letters TM to indicate a claim to trademark rights. When the registration has been issued the TM can be replaced by the symbol® or words denoting registration.

A complete application for the registration of a trademark or service mark consists of (1) a written notarized application, (2) a drawing of the mark, (3) five specimens of facsimiles of the mark as used in commerce, and (4) the filing fee of $175. In the case of service marks not employed in printed or written form, three single-face, unbreakable disc recordings will be accepted; the speed at which the recordings are to be played must be specified thereon. Upon request, forms for the registration of trademarks or service marks may be obtained from the Patent and Trademark Office in Washington, D.C. An applicant may file his own application but in most instances it is desirable to appoint an attorney for that purpose.

A registration issued by the Patent and Trademark Office remains in force for 20 years from the date of registration and may be renewed, by the filing of a renewal application, for additional 20-year periods provided the mark is in use in commerce when the renewal application is filed.

Trademark and service mark registrants must avoid official cancellation for abandonment of the mark. This requires the filing of an affidavit or declaration of continued use of the mark before the end of the sixth year following the date of registration.

Advantages of Registration

Under the Trademark Act of 1946, there is provision for the establishment of two registers, known as the *Principal Register* and the *Supplemental Register*.

To qualify for registration on the *Principal Register* a mark must be arbitrary, fanciful, or in any event "distinctive," as opposed to a descriptive or common name. Other marks which are capable of distinguishing the applicant's products and which have been used in commerce for at least one year can be registered on the *Supplemental Register.*

As noted previously, it is not necessary for the owner of a trademark to register the mark. The common law protects trademark rights. However, registration results in certain advantages.

Registration on the *Principal Register* places the public on constructive notice of the registrant's claim to ownership. Registration also engenders certain presumptions of ownership and validity and of the exclusive right to use the mark on the goods for which the mark is registered. Registrants are given the right to sue in the United States Federal Courts, the right to prevent importation of goods bearing an infringing mark, and the benefit of incontestability after five years of registration.

Registration on the *Supplemental Register* does not give constructive notice to the public or presumptive evidence of ownership, validity, or the exclusive right to the mark, nor the right to prevent importation of goods carrying an infringing mark. It does not afford the benefit of incontestability. However, it does give the right to sue in the United States Federal Courts and the right to use lawfully the notice of registration which may be helpful in preventing infringement.

State Trademark Registration

Registration of trademarks can be made under state laws, as well as under the federal law. Usually a federal registration is deemed to give sufficient protection to the trademark without the need for additional registrations under state laws.

Registration in Foreign Countries

The diverse nature of trademark laws in foreign countries makes it imperative that businessmen who wish to protect their marks in such countries seek the advice of experts and act on such advice. In virtually all foreign countries a trademark need not have been used in commerce before it may be registered, and a registration may be used to bar the importation into the country of products to which the mark is affixed. In certain instances, individuals have been known to register the names and marks of world renowned corporations and have blocked the efforts of those companies to register their marks until financial settlements are made.

Where a businessman, as in the case of the music industry, proposes to license his product, it is important that trademark registrations be made in the foreign countries where licenses will prevail. In the absence of registrations, the legal protection of licenses may be questionable. It is also prudent to consider the necessity for proper trademark license agreements which must be recorded in many countries for appropriate protection.

The life of certificates of registration in foreign countries differs in accordance with the laws of each country.

As previously noted, the advice of trademark experts should be obtained in the complicated and technical field of foreign trademarks and licenses. Certain law firms in the United States and England specialize in foreign trademark registrations. Their services are utilized by other attorneys but may also be availed of directly.

Who Owns Rights in an Artist's Name?

In the field of music, numerous parties may claim the right to use and participate in the benefits from the use of an artist's name. These may include record companies, managers, and, in the case of a group, its co-members.

A record company will usually have the exclusive right, by contract, to use and exploit an artist's name in connection with recordings made during the term of his exclusive recording contract; in addition, the company, after the expiration of the contract, will have the continued right under the original contract to use the artist's name to identify, advertise, and promote the product previously made. This is discussed at greater length below.

When popular group names such as The Ink Spots, Buffalo Springfield, and The 1910 Fruit Gum Company become the subject of disputes among former members of the group, concepts of partnership property law become applicable to resolve the dispute. This is considered further below.

Sometimes a performer changes his name along the way, and questions will arise as to whether the right to use the former name also encompasses the new name. For example, Tiny Tim was formerly known as Darry Dover. A record company was barred by a Court from attempting to use Tiny Tim's current name, and "unique style, appearance, and personality" to identify, advertise, and promote records made when he was identified as Darry Dover. However, some artist contracts specifically provide for the right to use names by which the artist may be known either now or in the future. Such a clause might have led to a different result in the Tiny Tim controversy.

The unwarranted use of a name may cause the intercession of the Federal Trade Commission or of local criminal authorities interested in protecting the consumer from the fraudulent or deceptive use of popular artist names. A record company may confuse the public or subject itself to a possible lawsuit by use of record titles such as "A Tribute to Dylan" or "The Best of Sinatra" when the record contains performances by artists other than those named in the title. The public may buy the record on the supposition that only performances by the artist whose name appears in the title will be contained in the record. To avoid confusion, the cover of the record should clarify whether only the artist's performances are included therein or whether the record contains performances by other artists, either in the style of the named artist or of repertoire made popular by the named artist.

Record Company Rights in Name

So that the record company can protect its investment in recordings and promotion, the typical artist's contract with a record company specifies that the record company has exclusive rights to use the artist's name in connection with the recordings made thereunder. Sometimes, the right to the artist's name is limited to use in connection with the recordings of the particular artist. More often, the record company will obtain the right to exploit the name for its own institutional advertising purposes, even without reference to specific recordings of the artist.

The typical clause forbids the artist from utilizing his name to advertise or promote records made by other persons or firms. This restriction seems natural and justified. However, if the artist is likely to *produce* records of other artists, he may seek to exclude such activities from the restriction. A typical clause submitted by a company to artists is as follows:

> We shall have the worldwide right in perpetuity to use and to permit others to use your name (both legal and professional) and likeness and biographical material concerning you for advertising and purposes of trade, and otherwise without restriction, in connection with our business and products. We shall have the further right to refer to you, by your legal or professional name, as our exclusive artist, and you shall, in your activities in the entertainment field, use your best efforts to be billed and advertised as our exclusive artist. During the term of this contract you shall not authorize your legal or professional name or your likeness to be used in connection with the advertising or sale of phonograph records other than those manufactured and sold by us.

Group Member Rights in Name

Most popular music groups have a highly informal arrangement among the individual members. The groups are often born in a spirit of great mutual enthusiasm and optimism, and rarely do the groups have the business acumen or exercise the caution to require the drafting and execution of a formal partnership agreement. Yet, the typical popular music group is a partnership, no matter how informal the arrangement. When the group splits up, dissolves, or looks for substitutions, it must cope with principles of partnership law with regard to the asset of the group name.

The situations that may arise are legion. In the case of the original

Mills Brothers, there was a profusion of groups resulting from the diverse paths of the original members.

When the Buffalo Springfield broke up, the drummer formed a new group under that name. The other original members objected to the new group, labeling it "phony" in a statement to the public. The drummer then obtained a temporary restraining order by a Court against such statements, asserting his right as a partner to use the group name. However, another Court later dissolved the temporary restraining order on the ground that the other partners, even though no longer active, had the right to protect the name as a partnership asset by insisting on its use as identification of only the original group.

In their early days as a band, The Beatles had a drummer other than Ringo Starr. Although The Beatles were reorganized with the approval of the various members, the original drummer was not barred from referring to his "original" Beatles membership in connection with his new recordings.

The Chad Mitchell Trio broke up when Chad Mitchell himself decided to become a solo performer. In that instance an amicable mutual agreement resulted in the surviving members having the right to use the name, The Mitchell Trio.

One of the better transitions from a group to a solo name is to be found in the divorce of Diana Ross, the soloist, from the group known as The Supremes. For a considerable period of time before she left the group, with the cooperation of their record company, in public exploitation her personal and individual name preceded the group name, so that the public would associate her as a solo artist. After the separation, Miss Ross and the remainder of the group continued to enjoy public success.

The 1910 Fruit Gum Company had an express agreement among the members acknowledging the exclusive right in surviving members to use the name and to substitute new members for a resigning member. When litigation developed, resigning members were barred from diluting the value of the name.

Doing Business under Assumed Names

It is not essential in all business dealings to form a corporation for doing business under an assumed name. In early stages, and continuing indefinitely in many cases, a person or a group of persons may choose to do business under a company name. Thus, the Ace Music Company, or The Jeff Tracy Music Associates, or Gladstone-Black Company may be a convenient name selected for a business entity made up of an individual or a partnership. When this is done, however, a practical problem arises in cashing checks or in opening bank accounts under the assumed name. The solution is compliance with state requirements for doing business under an assumed name. This requires, in New York, for example, the filing of a sworn statement of identification of the true persons behind the new name.

An advantage of registering under the state statutes relating to doing business under an assumed name is that it may help to establish priority of use in the event groups with conflicting names are formed later.

Protection of Names or Marks

The courts will protect trade names against use or imitation on the doctrine of unfair competition. This is a form of unlawful business injury which consists in the passing off or attempting to pass off, on the public, the goods or business of one person as the goods or business of another, or in the conduct of a trade or business in such manner that there is an express or implied representation to that effect. There may also be unfair competition by misappropriation as well as by misrepresentation, where there was no fraud on the public but where the defendant for his advantage has misappropriated the benefit or property right of another.

The law of trademarks is a branch of the broader law of unfair competition. The test of a claim of trademark infringement is one of confusion regarding the source of origin of a product, in other words, whether the public would be misled into believing the product of the infringer was manufactured or sold by the original trademark proprietor.

A remedy ordinarily available to redress or prevent infringement of trademarks or unfair competition is a suit for an injunction against the continuation of the wrong. If the wrongdoer did not act innocently, there may also be an action for an accounting and recovery of damages and profits based on the past infringement.

The Federal Lanham Act itself provides that the Federal District Courts shall have the power to grant injunctions to prevent the violation of the rights of the registrant of a mark, and that in any action which establishes the infringement of the rights of the registrant the court may order the destruction of the infringing labels, signs, prints, packages, plates, molds, matrices, and other reproductions or imitations of the mark or the means of making same.

Under the Lanham Act, when a breach of the rights of the registrant has been established, under certain circumstances the plaintiff is entitled to recover (1) defendant's profits, (2) any damages suffered by the plaintiff, and (3) the costs of the action. With respect to defendant's profits, the plaintiff need prove only sales by the defendant, which must prove all elements of cost or claimed deductions. As to damages, the court may enter judgment for up to three times the actual damages. Should the court find the amount of recovery based on profits to be either inadequate or excessive, the court in its discretion may enter judgment for such sum as it shall deem just.

In a number of states, it is a criminal offense to infringe, imitate, or counterfeit trademarks or to sell goods under such marks. Under the terms of some statutes, the offender is also subject to a penalty recoverable in a civil or quasi-criminal action. Offenders must be found guilty of a fraudulent or criminal intent in order for the offense to constitute a violation of the statutes.

35

Protection of Ideas and Titles

The originators of the Hustle and the Twist dance steps receive no royalties from other persons who have capitalized on the ideas. Chubby Checker, who became the foremost exponent of the Twist in the public eye, with resultant financial rewards, owed no financial obligations to the inventor of the Twist. A rival network with impunity could copy the idea of the superstrong "Six Million Dollar Man" in a counterpart program entitled "The Bionic Woman."

While ideas as such are not copyrightable and are ordinarily free for the taking, it being considered that society benefits from the free dissemination of ideas, the courts sometimes protect ideas. Thus, the concrete expression of an idea may be the subject of copyright. For example, a song lyric about men from Mars cannot be copied, although another writer may pen a new lyric concerning such men; to the extent the original lyric cannot be copied there is an indirect protection of the idea.

One copyright concept that affects ideas is the exclusive right to develop copyrighted material for further exploitation. A novel can be dramatized only by the copyright owner of the novel or with his permission. A song such as "Frosty the Snow Man" can be developed into a story-book form with the consent of the copyright owner. The reproduction of a doll or other three-dimensional form based on a character in story or song is also an exclusive right stemming from copyright. Comic-strip heroes such as Superman help to demonstrate the concept of continuing rights in characters from copyrighted stories, separate and apart from the dialogue of the characters in the story. An example from the world of popular music is "Alvin" and his brother chipmunks. The legal bases for the protection of the development of such characters would appear to be a mixture of copyright law (for artistic, written, or three-dimensional reproduction of a fictional character) and unfair competition. The latter principle has been applied to prevent the misappropriation by one person of the results of another's labors.

Compensation for Ideas

Ideas themselves will be safeguarded when disclosed privately under circumstances indicating a mutual understanding, express or implied, that the idea will be paid for if used. In one case, the plaintiff had submitted to the secretary of a movie producer orally and by a short outline in writing the idea for a motion picture on the life of Floyd Collins, who had been trapped and had died in a cave after extensive rescue efforts. The plaintiff alleged that he had made it clear he was to be paid if the idea were used and the secretary had assented. The defendant subsequently made a motion picture on the life of Collins. The Appellate Court in California held that on the basis of the plaintiff's allegations there was an implied contract to pay for the plaintiff's services and that there was an issue of fact to be heard by the trial court regarding the existence of the contract and whether the defendant used the plantiff's synopsis. This ruling was made despite the fact that the story was in the public domain, having been fully explored in the press.

In the absence of an express or implied contract to pay, the courts have sometimes held a defendant liable for the use of a plaintiff's idea on the theory that otherwise the defendant would be unjustly enriched. This may arise when the situation is akin to a contract relationship but essential elements of contractual agreement are lacking. For example, if an agent unauthorizedly promises to pay for an idea accepted on behalf of a defendant, the defendant may be held liable if he uses the idea.

Some courts will protect ideas on the ground of a breach of a confidential relationship. This will occur, for example, with regard to secret ideas disclosed in an employer-employee relationship.

Concreteness and Originality

While it is sometimes stated that a plaintiff must prove that his idea was novel and original and that it was reduced to concrete form, the facts necessary for such proof may vary widely. For example, the combination of three old ideas has been held to constitute a novel and original idea.

For an idea to be concrete, it is generally accepted that it need not be reduced to writing. To some courts, a concrete idea is one that has been developed to the point of availability for use. A concrete idea is sometimes discussed as one different from an abstract idea and as having a "property" status.

Manifestly, if an idea is reduced to writing it may be protectible by copyright. Thus where a musical idea is the subject of a written expression it can be submitted for registration as an unpublished work in the Copyright Office by the deposit of a manuscript copy. Similarly a recording of an idea may be registered as an unpublished work under the 1976 Copyright Act, whereas prior thereto only a "published" record could be registered. A further method employed by songwriters or record producers to establish creation and date of origin is to enclose their material in carefully sealed envelopes and to mail the material to themselves by registered mail, which when received remains unopened. As compared to registration, this approach may be more effective in maintaining the privacy of the idea, but is less reliable than an official registration.

In all cases, for their protection, the informed songwriter, music publisher, or record producer should keep businesslike reference material showing when and to whom proposals were submitted; index cards or files of letters accompanying enclosures may be maintained.

Unsolicited Ideas

Mindful of potential litigation which may arise from the disclosure of ideas, some companies, including music publishers and record companies, have adopted a policy of not considering unsolicited ideas. Thereby lawsuits and attorneys' fees can be clearly avoided. If possible the incoming material should be routed to persons such as the comptroller who have no responsibility for creative endeavors and should be handled by form replies with which the material is returned. It can be argued that valuable ideas may be lost through this practice. However, professionals in the field can be trusted to supply most market requirements of ideas.

Other companies insist that they will not review an idea unless the submitter signs a release. One form of release makes the company and its officers the sole arbiter of the novelty, usability, and value of the idea. Since the obligation on the part of the company may be considered illusory, there is some doubt as to the legal enforceability of this type of release.

Another form of release provides that the parties will mutually agree on the value of an idea which is used, but that if they disagree the maximum value of the idea is fixed at a certain sum, such as $500 or $1,000. Or, the release may provide initially that the value is a sum fixed at, say, $500. This type of release would seem to be more enforceable than the release under which the company and its officers have sole discretion.

As a word of caution, it should be recognized that even a release form may prove to be inadequate protection against a bad faith appropriation of an idea without adequate consideration.

Titles

Titles are not subject to copyright protection. For example, the title "Stardust" is not secured by the Copyright Act. Titles have long been protected by the doctrine of unfair competition, which will be applied to titles that have achieved a secondary meaning in the eyes of the public as being associated with particular works. Most titles do not have a secondary meaning. Any casual check of the ASCAP or BMI indexes or of the Copyright Office records will reveal numerous instances of title duplications. Indirectly, some copyright protection of titles can be accomplished by their insertion in the body of the song lyric.

To achieve a secondary meaning more readily, a title should ordinarily be fanciful and use arbitrarily selected word groupings, rather than generally descriptive or frequently used phrases. For example, "My Only Love" or "Yours Sincerely" are general phrases that probably could not be pre-empted. On the other hand, "Begin the Beguine" is a fanciful, unique title. It is possible that even a geographic description or other nonunique title such as "Oklahoma!" or "South Pacific" can, over the years or other period required to establish a solid public acceptance, establish a secondary meaning of commercial value that cannot be usurped.

A secondary meaning is not necessarily permanent. Since unfair competition is not a copyright concept, there is no fixed period of exclusive protection and no easily determined date when the protection ceases and the title is in the public domain. The determinant is the matter of abandonment by failure to use or exploit. "Information Please" was a very valuable title during its use on radio. If not for the almanac using the title *Information Please*, it might be considered abandoned today and therefore available for anyone. Public identification does not necessarily mean that the title is associated with public success. *Slightly Scandalous* had a short life and was a failure as a play, but it nevertheless had sufficient secondary meaning to serve as the basis for an injunction against a motion picture of the same name.

Music is an essential ingredient of, and sister field to, motion pictures. It is common for a major motion picture to popularize a theme song from the picture with the same title as the picture. Many a film trades upon the established goodwill of a well-known song title. Irving Berlin's "White Christmas" came from *Holiday Inn* and thereafter, after a great song success, was used for another film entitled *White Christmas*. The film originally identified with the biography *The Jane Froman Story* was released, finally, under the title *With a Song in My Heart*. The publisher of the relatively new success at the time, "Young at Heart," was paid $15,000 for a synchronization license and title use for a Warner Brothers picture of the same name. A popular song known as "Ode to Billy Joe" was featured in the music and story line of a film with that title.

Song titles are frequently used as the titles of record albums, as a natural identification of the type of music in the LP, although the title song is often only one-tenth of the contents of the record. "Love Story," a composition from the popular film of the same title, was the title of a number of albums issued by different record companies. Rarely is the publisher paid a premium for such title use, but in one case, where the song was omitted from the record, a special royalty was paid. It is arguable that, on the same theory that a motion picture producer pays for the use of a song title for a motion picture, a record company should make a special payment for the right to utilize a song title as the title of an album.

36

Privacy and Publicity Rights

The music and record industries thrive on publicity. Sales of records are stimulated by the use of a top artist's name or portrait on an album jacket. The use of an artist's name and likeness on printed music editions such as sheet music and song folios is a valuable marketing device. Television and radio commercials often utilize an artist's name in advertising products. Hotels, resorts, and amusement parks frequently announce by name and photograph a personal appearance of or other association with top artists. Album jackets of many mood and instrumental albums use pictures of attractive models who have no relation to the contents of the album, but have eye-catching appeal. Merchandise such as T-shirts, buttons, and posters featuring the recording artist's likeness are a valuable tie-in with his record sales. Although most of these uses are eagerly sought by the artist and the industry and may be permissible by virtue of the operative contractual provisions, careful consideration must be given in each instance to the individual's right to control and benefit from his so-called "right of publicity."

Right of Privacy

The right of privacy or the personal right "to be let alone" is a relatively new Anglo-American legal concept. Impetus to the development of this right is largely attributed to a *Harvard Law Review* article of 1890 by Samuel D. Warren and Louis D. Brandeis. They wrote:

> The press is overstepping in every direction the obvious bounds of propriety and of decency. Gossip is no longer the resource of the idle and of the vicious, but has become a trade, which is pursued with industry as well as effrontery. To satisfy a prurient taste the details of sexual relations are spread broadcast in the columns of the daily papers. To occupy the indolent, column upon column is filled with idle gossip, which can only be procured by intrusion upon the domestic circle. The intensity and complexity of life, attendant upon advancing civilization, have rendered necessary some retreat from the world, and man, under the refining influence of culture, has become more sensitive to publicity, so that solitude and privacy have become more essential to the individual; but modern enterprises and inventions have, through invasions upon his privacy, subjected him to mental pain and distress, far greater than could be inflicted by mere bodily injury.

Warren and Brandeis sought recognition of a separate right distinct from defamation, contract, or property rights.

At first there was some hesitation in legal circles to endorse this right of privacy. Indeed, the first state to directly confront the concept, New York, had its highest court reject the notion that there existed a separate legal right of privacy in the state. In reaction to this decision, the New York legislature enacted a statute which today is found in sections 50 and 51 of the Civil Rights Law. This statute makes it a misdemeanor for a person, firm, or corporation to use for "advertising purposes, or for the purpose of trade, the name, portrait or picture of any living person" without first obtaining written consent. The statute also permits suit for injunctive relief as well as damages, including, in some cases, punitive damages.

As time went by, other states, Oklahoma, Utah, Virginia, and California, also adopted acts similar to New York's. Today the right of privacy in some form is recognized either by statute or through judicial decision in all but a few jurisdictions in the United States. Furthermore, the Supreme Court of the United States has said that an independent right of privacy is guaranteed by the U.S. Constitution against certain governmental interference.

The Constitutional guarantees of the freedom of speech and of the press may be raised in opposition to a claim for invasion of privacy. Under the U.S. Supreme Court's holdings, the right of privacy cannot be asserted to prohibit the publication of matters which are "newsworthy," that is, matters in the public interest, even if the report is false, unless there is proof that the defendant published the report with knowledge of its falsity or in reckless disregard of its truth. This doctrine applies to an individual who has become a "public figure" or an individual who may have been thrust into an event of public interest. A performing artist may well be viewed as a "public figure" in connection with his public activities. Furthermore, news functions or informative presentations are not deemed to be limited to newspapers; magazines, newsreels, radio, television, and books have been deemed privileged. Generally, the defense of freedom of speech or press would not apply to certain types of commercial speech, for example, an advertisement using the endorsement of a public figure, such as a celebrity.

A defense of express waiver may be asserted, in other words, that the individual consented to the use. Under certain statutes this consent would have to have been in writing. Other defenses may be that the use was incidental or insignificant, such as the mere mention of a celebrity's name in a film or book, or that the use was not for purposes of "advertising" or "trade" in jurisdictions where this type of use is prohibited by statute.

To the music and record industries, of concern in their daily operations is how the exploitation of a personality is affected by the individual's right to privacy and publicity. This is discussed in the next section, "Right of Publicity."

Right of Publicity

The real concern of an artist in most cases is to obtain publicity and in having his name and likeness recognized by the public. He does not seek privacy so much as he seeks to control and benefit from the commercial use of his name, photograph, and likeness. Some jurisdictions have recognized the legitimacy of this right of publicity and have granted it recognition either by statute or by case law. This right protects the right of an individual to control and profit from the publicity values which he has achieved. It is similar in theory to the exclusive right of a commercial enterprise to the benefits that goodwill and secondary meaning of its name produce. In those cases in which pure privacy theory might be unsuccessfully invoked, as where the artist with a celebrity status may be deemed a public figure, the right of publicity may nevertheless be successfully asserted.

This concept is generally credited as having grown from a case dealing with baseball cards. In that case a chewing gum manufacturer had entered into agreements with ballplayers giving it the exclusive right for a limited time to use the ballplayers' likenesses on baseball cards. Subsequently another gum manufacturer obtained similar rights from the same ballplayers. The first gum manufacturer sued the second to protect its exclusive rights in the photographs. The defendant argued in defense that the action was in privacy, that privacy actions were personal and not assignable and that only the ballplayers had standing to sue. The late Judge Jerome Frank said:

> in addition to and independent of that right of privacy . . . a man has a right in the publicity value of his photograph, i.e., the right to grant the exclusive privilege of publishing his picture. . . . This right might be called a "right of publicity." For it is common knowledge that many prominent persons (especially actors and ballplayers) far from having their feelings bruised through public exposure of their likenesses would feel sorely deprived if they no longer received money for authorizing advertisements. . . .

Thus, the court recognized the right of publicity and distinguished the right from pure privacy theory. This was also significant because, absent a contrary statute, the right of privacy is a personal right which terminates on the death of the individual. As a right distinct from that of pure privacy, the right of publicity could be held to survive the death of the individual. In fact, the law regarding the transfer to heirs of the right of publicity is presently undergoing change. A majority of the cases has held that the right survives death; however, as a precondition in such cases the courts generally require that the right must have been exploited during the lifetime of the celebrity, for example, by the licensing of merchandising rights.[1]

In right of publicity cases, the unauthorized use of a celebrity's name or likeness in connection with the dissemination of news or information of public interest is usually held to be privileged under the constitutional guarantees of the freedom of speech and of the press. This treatment is similar to that accorded in right of privacy cases. The constitutional privilege would not ordinarily apply where the unauthorized use is solely for commercial exploitation.

Use for Trade or Advertising

In those jurisdictions which recognize that the individual has the right to control the use of his name or likeness, whether under a right of publicity or a right of privacy, the individual is protected against the unauthorized commercial use of his name or likeness, such as in an advertisement on T-shirts or in posters endorsing a commercial product.

As noted, under the New York statute, it is a criminal misdemeanor and the basis for an action for injunction and damages to use the name, portrait, or picture, for advertising or trade purposes, of any living person without his written consent, or, if a minor, the consent of his parent or guardian. At the same time, the New York statute sets forth that it shall not be construed to prevent the use of the "name, portrait or picture of any author, composer or artist in connection with his literary, musical or artistic productions which he has sold or disposed of with such name, portrait, or picture used in connection therewith." Thus the name of a composer can be used without his written consent in connection with an authorized record of his composition.

Although California courts have recognized a right of privacy under the common law, the California legislature has enacted a statute dealing with the use of a person's name, photograph, or likeness for purposes of advertising products or services or for purposes of solicitation of purchases of products or services. Under this statute, any person who knowingly makes such use without the injured person's prior consent or, if a minor, the prior consent of his parent or guardian, shall be liable for any damages sustained by the injured person. In addition, the person violating this law will be liable to the injured party for no less than three hundred dollars. The statute provides, however, that the "use of a name, photograph, or likeness in connection with any news, public affairs or sports broadcast or account, or political campaign shall not constitute a use for purposes of advertising or solicitation."

In contrast to New York practice, most states which recognize the individual's right to control the use of his name or likeness do not

[1]California and Tennessee recently passed special legislation affecting unauthorized posthumous exercise of rights of publicity, for commercial purposes, for periods of 50 years and 10 years, respectively, after death. Reference should be made to the legislation for details.

require written consent to the use of such name or picture. Such consent may be oral or may be established by the custom of the business involved.

Privacy Contract Clauses

Contracts in the fields of music and records, in many instances, obviate problems of the right of privacy or the right of publicity by specific provisions regarding the use of name, picture, or biographical material. Exclusive recording contracts between an artist and a record company usually state that the record company has the sole right to use and to authorize others to use the artist's name, signature, likeness, and biographical material in connection with the artist's services under the agreement. This not only grants the required consent to the record company, but may also serve as the basis for prohibiting another record company from similar use. Some record contracts provide for the record company to handle "merchandising rights" in an artist's name and likeness. This covers such situations as the licensing of posters, buttons, and similar items, frequently on a basis that the artist will receive 50 percent of the company's net receipts.

Under the form of agreement promulgated by the American Federation of Musicians between a musician and a booking agent, the agent is granted rights to use the musician's name and likeness, and the right to authorize others to make such use for advertising and publicity.

Careful draftsmanship is necessary to delineate properly the rights which are to be transferred from the artist to the contracting company. In cases involving merchandising rights to the character of Count Dracula as portrayed by Bela Lugosi, and the commercial rights to the names and likenesses of Laurel and Hardy, the courts were called upon to decide whether, under certain types of grant clauses, the performers had transferred their entire exclusive merchandising rights. In both instances, the Courts held that they had not and that the film companies had acquired only the right to use their name and likenesses in connection with specific films for which the performers rendered their services. Where the contract is silent with respect to the rights, the courts may find that the rights remain with the artist.

Similarly, a divergence between the use authorized by the artist and the actual use made of his name, likeness, or biographical material may lead to a privacy suit. A slight variation in use may be insufficient to be actionable.

Public Domain Works

Reliance on the right of privacy was unsuccessful in preventing the publication of uncopyrighted works of Mark Twain under his name. The same theory was also rejected in the use of uncopyrighted Russian music with accurate composer credits given to Khatchaturian, Prokofieff, and Shostakovich. When a work is unprotected by copyright, there is no obligation to drop author credit, and, in fact, failing to give credit would appear to be more objectionable.

False attribution of a writer as author of a work may itself be held an invasion of the right of privacy.

Remedies

There are three types of relief granted by courts in cases where the right of privacy has been found to have been invaded. Courts may grant damages, issue injunctions enjoining such conduct, or impose criminal penalties against the defendant.

Criminal penalties where available are rarely imposed. In New York, Virginia, Utah, and Oklahoma a violation of the "privacy" statute is a misdemeanor. Yet the vast majority of cases brought under a statute such as New York's are civil actions.

Generally, a plaintiff in a privacy action will be seeking redress in compensatory damages, and, for certain abuses where malice is shown, punitive damages. There may be a damage award for mental pain and suffering, without proof by the plaintiff of actual monetary losses. In "right of publicity" cases, the measure of damages may be what the misappropriated right is worth, rather than actual damages.

37

Contracts with Minors

Although in recent years there has been a statutory trend to lower the age of legal maturity from 21 to 18, for centuries the age of legal maturity was 21. Before that age a person was regarded as an "infant" or a "minor." While legally regarded as "infants" because less than 21 years old, such stars as Elvis Presley, Paul Anka, and Bob Dylan earned large amounts and had considerable moneys invested in their careers by record companies, managers, or other entities in the entertainment business. The success stories of many such celebrities tend to obscure the legal difficulties engendered in their being minors.

Inherent in contracts with minors are financial risks based on the danger that because of their minority they may legally disaffirm their agreements. This has acted to discourage considerable expenditures in training minors, in promotional activities on behalf of minors, and in the preparation for events and productions in which a minor is to perform.

The statutes of the more important music industry states, California, New York, Tennessee, and Illinois, now all provide that 18 years is the age of majority. In those states, a contract signed by a person 18 years of age or older cannot be disaffirmed on the ground of infancy. Naturally this has helped to ease the problems of the entertainment industry in dealing with young artists who are legally regarded as minors for contractual purposes.

Various states, in recognition of the difficulties, have established procedures for court approval of the agreements with minors, which approval has the effect of preventing disaffirmance.

Voidability under Common Law

For an understanding of the matter, it is necessary to refer to the common law treatment of minors. For centuries, the common law has regarded minors as not having the full maturity of mind or judgment prerequisite to being legally bound by their agreements. Unless a contract involves necessaries such as food, clothing, or housing required for the infant's welfare, the agreement is voidable at the sole option of the infant. This may occur at any time during infancy or within a reasonable time after reaching the age of majority. On the other hand, the other party to the agreement cannot avoid the obligations to the infant and will be bound by the contract if the infant desires to enforce it. In fact, disaffirmance is not ordinarily conditioned upon a return by the infant of the goods, services, or other consideration received, and such consideration can be recaptured only to the extent not dissipated by the infant. This is justified on the ground that an immature person cannot be expected to demonstrate prudence in preserving the consideration handled by him.

Age Misrepresentation

The minor's act of fraud in misrepresenting his age, a common occurrence in the search for employment and a career, is not sufficient legal ground to enforce a contract against him or to collect damages from the infant for failure to live up to his agreement. The risk in dealing with the infant is placed on the other party.

Ratification

Just as a contract entered into after the age of legal maturity is fully enforceable against the adult, so is a contract of a minor enforceable if ratified by him after he has reached his majority. Ratification need not be in the form of a written document. Silence for an unreasonable time after maturity will be deemed sufficient ratification of a completed transaction. Where the contract has not been fully performed, ratification will be found in certain acts by the artist after he has reached the age of majority: for example, appearing for a recording session, accepting compensation for future performances, and like acts denoting an intent to continue with the agreement.

Disaffirmance

Acts to disaffirm or to void a minor's agreement need not follow any particular pattern. A typical act of this kind would be a written notice of disaffirmance on the ground of infancy. Other such acts would be the making of contracts inconsistent with the agreement in question, or pleading infancy as a defense in an action brought under the contract.

Statutory Provisions

In various states, statutes deal with the enforceability of contracts with minors. Since New York and California are leading centers of the music industry, reference will be made in particular to the statutes in those states.

For contracts for the services of persons under 18, regarding their employment as performers in the field of entertainment or professional sports, New York has provided a statutory method of ensuring that the agreements cannot be disaffirmed on the grounds of infancy. A procedure has been established for court review and approval of the contracts. This procedure also covers agreements for managerial and agency services to infants in the entertainment business. It does not pertain to music publishing agreements such as an exclusive writer's contract, other songwriter agreements, or a child's approval of the transfer by his parents of their renewal rights in the copyrights of songs.

Certain standards are set forth in the New York statute as the basis for court approval. In general the terms must be reasonable, and there will usually be a court requirement that a portion of the net earnings be set aside under a guardianship for the benefit of the infant. A contract cannot be approved if its term of service, including any extensions by option or otherwise, extends for a period of more than three years from the date of approval of the agreement. However, it may contain any covenants or conditions binding upon the minor beyond such three years if the same are found by the court to be reasonable. For example, the New York Law Revision Commission has gone on record in favor of permitting an agent's commissions to continue beyond three years on royalty-producing property created during the original three years. It also recommended that a minor who is a recording artist should be allowed to agree not to re-record a song for a competitor for a period longer than three years; the normal clause in the record business restricts for at least five years from the date of recording of the record. The New York statute ensures fairness to the minor by providing that, following a hearing on a claim that the well-being of the minor is being impaired by performance of the contract, the court which approved the agreement may either revoke the approval or declare that the approval is revoked unless an appropriate modification of the contract is made.

Under California statutes, court approval can be sought as to specified types of agreements with minors under 18; the California laws impose fewer restrictions on the courts than the New York statutes. These agreements include ones for the employment of a minor in the entertainment field as an actor, recording artist, or writer, or in other capacities. Also covered are agreements with minors for the purchase, sale, or licensing of literary, musical, or dramatic properties for entertainment purposes. Contracts for managerial and agency services by duly licensed managers or agencies to minors in the entertainment business may also be submitted for court approval. The employment or other contracts cannot be disaffirmed by a minor after court approval.

The California law does not contain the three-year limit found in the New York statute, and there may be approval of a term of employment of up to seven years. As in New York, the California Court may require the setting aside of earnings for the benefit of the infant.

Since the procedure for seeking approval usually entails attorney's fees and expenses and court appearances of the infant, guardians, and other parties to the agreement, it is reasonable to assume that applications for approval will be filed with respect to only a small minority of contracts with infants. This assumption is founded also on the practical knowledge that most new artists disappear from the public eye after one or two recordings are released. In fact, making application for court approval regarding the contract of an infant amounts to a recognition of his or her expected growth and continued stature in the entertainment business.

Parent's Guarantee of Performance

Cautious draftsmen who prepare contracts with minors have sometimes insisted on having parents or guardians of the minor become a party to or a guarantor of the contract for the minor's performance. This may have strong psychological value in enforcing performance by the child, although it does not prevent the child from disaffirming the agreement. Many parents or guardians who have signed such contracts become potentially liable for large sums representing damages for nonperformance by the minor.

New York has specifically provided by statute that, unless the contract is approved by the court, a parent or guardian is not liable as a party to or guarantor of a contract for the services of a minor under 18 as a performer in the field of entertainment. There is no similar provision in California.

38

Taxation in the Music Business

The Internal Revenue Laws of the United States make few specific references to copyrights, musical compositions, and other artistic creations. However, in those instances, preferential treatment as well as discrimination may be observed. For example, by a special statute passed in 1950, no author or composer or donee of an author or composer can qualify for the reduced capital gain tax rates available to inventors, investors, and even music publishers. On the other hand, in 1964, Congress showed appreciation of the feast-or-famine problems of artistic creators and others by permitting an averaging of income over five years; this period was reduced to four years, effective with the 1984 tax year.

Many a motion picture star or executive with unusually high current income is envious of a built-in factor of the music industry, namely, the spreading of royalty payments over many years. Many accountants and attorneys in the entertainment field try to achieve for their clients the spread-forward of earnings which is provided naturally by performance payments through ASCAP and BMI, record royalties, foreign royalties, and other revenue from slow and steady sources. Even with popular hits that do not become long-range standards, it takes years before all earnings from the initial success have been received. This natural spread-forward of earnings can sometimes be arranged for artists through contractual provisions which limit the annual earnings to be paid to them and provide for the excess to be paid in later years.

Accountants and attorneys in the tax field often advise clients of the truism that "tax avoidance is not tax evasion." The United States Supreme Court has expressed approval of avoidance as the act of an informed taxpayer who takes advantage by legal means of his legal right to decrease the amount he would otherwise have to pay for taxes. A familiar example is the taxpayer in a high bracket who reduces taxes by capital gain transactions which, with certain exceptions, in 1984 were subject to an overall maximum tax rate of 20 percent. Tax savings at this writing may also be achieved through depreciation allowances, certain charitable contributions, and the use of corporate entities. In addition to these factors, the discussion that follows also considers the transfer of rights in copyrights to a child or other person in a lower bracket of taxes, and the deduction of permissible business and professional expenses.

Capital Gains

In 1949, General Eisenhower, as the author of *Crusade in Europe,* obtained a reported half-million-dollar tax benefit by qualifying for capital gain treatment of the receipts from the sale of the copyright of the book. This was followed by an amendment to the tax laws, in 1950, sometimes referred to as the "Eisenhower Amendment," which barred any author, whether amateur (as General Eisenhower was considered) or professional, from a similar favored tax position. This does not mean that all copyrighted works are excluded from capital gain treatment. The "Eisenhower Amendment" applies only to authors and composers and to persons who receive rights in copyrighted works as donees by virtue of gifts or trusts.

The amendment does not include purchasers, or heirs, and they are still entitled to the benefit of capital gain tax rates on sales by them, to the extent that there is a gain after depreciation recapture. By an amendment to the Internal Revenue Code, Congress provided that if there was a sale of property for a consideration in excess of its depreciated value, there must first be recognized, as ordinary income, the amount of depreciation taken after 1961. In the event there is still a recognizable gain (and if the transaction is one that qualifies for capital gain treatment), then the excess gain is to be accorded capital gain treatment. For example, if a spouse inherited a copyright at a value of $20,000, depreciated it by $4,000 to a base of $16,000, and then sold it for $25,000, the first $4,000 of gain would be considered ordinary income (to "offset" the ordinary deduction for depreciation taken in prior years) and the remaining gain of $5,000 would be treated as capital gain.

The advantage of capital gain treatment is that profits received after holding a capital asset for more than 12 months plus a day are taxed at the applicable ordinary tax rate on only 40 percent of the capital gain, effective with the 1984 tax year and through 1987. The period for assets acquired after June 22, 1984 has been reduced to six months plus a day, with reversion to the one year plus a day period to apply after 1987. Therefore, for even the maximum rate (50 percent) taxpayer the maximum capital gain tax is 20 percent (i.e., 50 percent of 40 percent). However, the computed tax is subject to being superseded if an alternate minimum tax exceeds the computed tax. In determining the alternate minimum tax, an individual taxpayer with net long-term capital gains will ascertain the sum of his taxable income plus his "tax preference items" (including the excluded 60 percent of his capital gains and certain tax shelter deductions), less itemized deductions in his tax return for home mortgage interest, charitable deductions, and certain other items. From the total there will be deducted an additional $40,000 if the taxpayer is married and filing jointly, or $30,000 if single. The alternate minimum tax is 20 percent of the remainder and the taxpayer will then pay the higher of the alternative minimum tax or his "regular" income tax.

For an example of capital gain treatment, in the case of a married taxpayer otherwise earning $22,000 of taxable income, a capital gain of an additional $10,000 would result in adding only 40 percent of that amount ($4,000) to be taxed as ordinary taxable income, at an overall ordinary income tax rate in 1984 of 25 percent. In effect there would be a tax rate of 10 percent on the total capital gain since only 40 percent of the total capital gain, that is, $4,000, is subjected to the ordinary income tax. The tax savings of a taxpayer who has the benefit of capital gain rates will increase as his taxable income graduates upward.

Note the word "gain" in the phrase "capital gain." There is no tax whatsoever on the basic cost recouped by the sale. For example, disregarding the factor of allowable depreciation (which is discussed later), a music publisher who acquires a copyright at a cost of $15,000 and resells it a year later for $20,000 is not taxed on the first $15,000 and pays at capital gain rates on the $5,000 profit. In general, the cost basis allowed to be recovered, in the case of a sale by the author, is the sum of the costs he incurred in obtaining the copyright, less any depreciation he may have taken on such costs, with any excess over cost to be treated as ordinary income. For sales by purchasers of copyrights the basis is the consideration paid by the purchaser, less any depreciation taken, with any excess of the sale price to be treatable as ordinary income to the extent of the depreciation already taken and any additional gain to be treated as capital gain.

As to deceased authors, if a copyright is sold by the estate or a person deriving rights through the estate, a capital gain may be claimed generally by use of a higher cost basis. For inherited property the basis is usually the fair market value at date of death. If a federal tax return has to be filed, the basis will be the fair market value at date of death, or if elected on behalf of the estate, a date six months later. In the event a federal tax return need not be filed, the basis will be the appraised value at the date of death for state inheritance or transmission taxes. The basis referred to above is utilized for both capital gain and depreciation purposes.

For the situation involving inheritance from an heir of the author or the formula for increasing the cost basis for estate taxes paid on appreciation, it is suggested that there be a consultation with attorneys and accountants for appropriate advice as to tax consequences.

Generally, in the case of gifts of property, the donee retains the donor's basis. Accordingly, the donee ascertains his basis by determining what the donor's basis was. If the donee sells for an amount less than his basis, resulting in a loss, then, to reduce the loss, he is required to adopt the fair market value of the property at the date of the gift, if that is less than the donor's basis. If the donee sells for an amount in excess of his basis, the excess is subject to capital gain treatment if otherwise qualified; in case the donor was the author capital gain treatment would not apply.

Considerable difficulty was encountered in the past in determining the type of sale which qualifies for capital gain treatment. The difficulty existed because copyright was regarded as an indivisible entity for copyright purposes despite the various elements such as motion picture rights, performance rights, mechanical rights, and publication rights, all of which make up what has been called a "bundle of rights." It was questionable whether the sale of particular rights would qualify for capital gain treatment for tax purposes. However, in 1948, in a case involving the film rights to *Forever Amber,* it was judicially determined that for capital gain tax purposes there is nothing inherent in the nature of a copyright which renders impossible the separate sales of the several parts which comprise the whole. This position would seem to be reinforced by the 1976 Copyright Act which by its terms recognizes the divisibility of the various exclusive rights which comprise a copyright. Therein it is provided that any of such exclusive rights may be transferred and owned separately. Notwithstanding the recognition of the grant of the exclusive and perpetual right to exploit a copyright in a medium as a sale, possibly entitled to capital gain treatment, a patent case has held that the grant of such rights in a territory constituted a license, and not a sale. The similarity between patents and copyrights suggests that such result might also apply in the case of a copyright and one would be advised to move with caution in that regard.

Even the sale of rights by one music publisher to another under an agreement where the purchase price is a percentage (akin to a royalty) of future earnings is sufficient for capital gain treatment if the sale is full and final and the purchase price is not merely an anticipation of future income such as an advance against future royalties. There may be installment recognition of the gain so that the seller reports gains only as it actually receives payments.

No capital gain advantages are available to persons or firms which hold properties "primarily for sale to customers in the ordinary course of . . . business." Music publishers are normally licensors of copyrights and are thus excluded from that category of merchants who are required to apportion their sales receipts on an ordinary income tax basis.

In the current music industry market, it is a rare instance when the heirs of authors seek capital gain treatment. This situation may be in large part the result of a tradition against outright sale by the authors' widows and children; they honor the authors' decision to keep a continuing royalty interest and forego the attraction of an outright sale that may prove to be improvident. This attitude is easily understood in terms of an earlier era when a leading publisher paid $500 for Fats Waller's interest in "Ain't Misbehavin' " and certain other songs, but it is reasonable to inquire whether it should continue in a more recent era when $100,000 was paid for half of the publishing rights in a popular hit and another $100,000 changed hands for a portion of the rights to the Buddy DeSylva catalog. An author's heirs must bear in mind that the right to receive a substantial sum yearly in royalties over the remaining life of a copyright carries with it the obligation to pay income tax at ordinary rates, except as the copyright may be depreciated. The effect of depreciation is discussed below. Furthermore, the heirs should be aware of the possibility of capital gain treatment for an outright sale of their interest where the purchase price is a percentage (akin to a royalty) of future earnings.

Depreciation

A Treasury Department publication specifies copyrights as subject to depreciation and states, "The purpose of depreciation is to let you recover your investment over the useful life of the property." A copyright is recognized as an intangible capital asset of diminishing value. Accordingly, a proper portion of receipts from licenses or other uses of the copyright may be deemed to be not ordinary income but a payment in lieu of diminishing capital value. Unlike capital gain, the depreciation allowance is available to authors and composers as well as to music publishers. However, in practical effect, the depreciation allowance in the case of writers and the original publisher is small in that normally there can be depreciated only the copyright registration and the attorney fees involved in establishing the copyright, there being no taxable value attributable to the services of the author or composer in creating the property values unless the author or composer was an employee-for-hire, in which case his compensation could become an element of cost. The right to depreciate is applicable not only to purchasers or copyrights but also to estates, heirs, and trusts of deceased writers. This right is substantial in respect of purchases. It can also be substantial for heirs of writers since the depreciable value generally is the fair market value of the copyright at the date of death of the last owner, or six months later, if the estate was subject to Federal Estate Tax and there was a valid election by the executor or administrator to value the estate at the later date. When one "takes over" a predecessor's basis, as in the case of a donee, the new owner assumes both the full basis and the accumulated depreciation of the former owner. Thus, in determining the amount of depreciation to be recaptured as ordinary income, in the event of a sale, depreciation taken by both the seller and the prior owners (whose basis was assumed) must be considered.

For an example of the application of a depreciation allowance, the purchase by a music publisher of a copyright for the sum of $10,000 can be assumed. The music publisher would determine, after consultation with his accountant and attorney, the period over which the cost would be depreciated for tax purposes. If the period is ten years, the $10,000 cost would be depreciated in ten equal installments of $1,000 each and the publisher would have a nontaxable allowance of $1,000 a year deductible from the earnings in the full ten-year period. In effect, at the end of ten years, the publisher would have recaptured the basic investment and would be in a position to replenish his catalog by the purchase of another song.

A record company, in respect of the costs of its master recordings, is in a similar position with relation to the right to take allowances for depreciation.

Until recently the tax laws as interpreted by the Treasury Department singled out copyrights and other intangibles in the matter of depreciation and required that a depreciation computation must be made on a "straight-line" basis without the alternative methods available to other property owners. This meant that each year would be treated uniformly and that the tax basis, less salvage value at the end of the depreciation period, would be depreciated in equal installments over the period. In the event that a copyright became valueless in any year before the end of the depreciation term, the unrecovered cost or other basis for depreciation might be deducted in that year.

It is probable that a flow of income method is now required with respect to amounts paid after December 31, 1975 for certain property whose principal production began after that date. The Tax Reform Act of 1976 provides in effect that, for noncorporate producers (but including S corporations and personal holding companies), amounts attributable to the production of a film, sound recording, book, or similar property and which are otherwise eligible shall be deductible pro rata over the years in which the income is received on a flow of income basis. The provision defines the terms "film" and "sound recording" but does not define either "book" or "similar property." Nevertheless the Senate Committee Report on the proposed act appears to mandate the use of the flow of income method, for noncorporate producers, with respect to a musical copyright on the theory that it is "similar property." Thus the flow of income method is definitely required for the depreciation by noncorporate producers of record master costs and would appear to be required as to musical copyrights. For corporate producers, there would seem to be an option to depreciate on either a straight-line basis or a flow of income basis.

Under the flow of income method, an estimate is made of the total amount of income that is to be received over the economic life of the asset, and the depreciable basis of the assets is written down each year by the proportion that the receipts of the year bear to the total anticipated receipts. In this manner, the years with the greatest proportion of receipts will bear the greatest proportion of depreciation and there is a closer matching of expenses with income. Where investments are made in new items of depreciable tangible personal property with a minimum life of three years, such as equipment, for instance a typewriter or a demonstration record studio for a music publisher, consideration should be given to the possible availability of investment tax credits whereby credits are allowed directly against tax bills otherwise due. Consultation with accountants and attorneys is advised in this regard.

Tax Treatment of Record Masters

It is well recognized in the record industry that the overwhelming majority of all currently produced record masters have a useful commercial life of less than a year from the date of release. This is primarily due to the fact that most popular music masters do not reach the break-even point of return of cost and are discontinued for lack of popularity. However, there are evergreens in the record field just as there are standards in the music publishing field. Vintage recordings of Duke Ellington, Hank Williams, Fats Waller, and even Caruso still have regular sales long after their original cost has been recouped. The tax problem of whether to treat recording costs as totally current expenses to be deducted from current income before computing taxable income, or whether to establish a capital base subject to regular depreciation deductions no longer exists, except in the case of corporations, it being mandated in the Tax Reform Act of 1976 that, except for corporations, the flow of income basis is to be observed.

Nearly all record artist contracts state that the costs of the recording sessions, be they studio costs, arranger fees, or artist and accompanying musician union minimum payments, should be treated as "advances" chargeable against artist royalties. As such, on the face of the contract, there is justification for the common practice in the record industry of charging all recording costs as current expenses fully deductible in the year incurred, just as artist royalties themselves are fully deductible. However, courts have stated that, in tax matters, the government is not bound by the strict terms of the agreement and can examine the circumstances to determine the actualities. It is the official position of the Internal Revenue Service that the costs incurred in preparing master recordings, used for substantially more than one year to produce records for sale, are required to be depreciated over the period that the master recordings are utilized for that purpose. While no tax claim against a record company for taking improperly full current deductions for record productions appears to have been fully tested in the courts to date, questions have been raised by the government on audits.

In some instances it may actually suit the tax planning needs of a record company to establish a depreciation basis for the gradual recoupment of costs, rather than treat recording costs as a current expense. Thereby, increased current profits can be shown since there are fewer expenses to be deducted. Even a depreciation basis does not prejudice the right of the company to take a write-off of the undepreciated costs in the year when the record itself is discontinued from the company catalog and its inventory of such discontinued records is sold as scrap. However, most smaller companies seek maximum current deductions in order to decrease their taxes immediately and conserve their cash.

A corporate producer of phonograph records might want to consider utilization of a flow of income method for depreciating the recording costs, which method is now required of noncorporate producers. This method might prove advantageous, for example, if a master is to be used over 24 months, but 75 percent of the total revenue is to be earned during the first 12 months. The even write-off method would reduce income by 50 percent of the recording costs during the first 12 months, whereas the flow of income method would permit a 75 percent deduction for depreciation.

It should be remembered that the treatment of recording costs will affect the tax results applicable to gains on the sales of masters. When depreciation has been taken, the gains equal to the depreciation will be considered as ordinary income and the remaining balance as capital gain if the master is a capital asset in the hands of the seller. The tax benefit rule is equally applicable where an expense other than depreciation is deducted. If, for example, the cost of producing a master recording is written off in the year of production, and the master is later sold, the gain, to the extent of the original write-off, is considered ordinary income, and the remaining balance as capital gain provided the master is a capital asset of the seller.

Research and Experimental Expenses

Demonstration records often involve substantial outlays for studio costs and artist fees. This outlay would seem to be a capital expenditure to develop a new copyright just as much as copyright and attorney's fees, which are deemed a basis for depreciation. However, such expenses are not allowed for depreciation purposes. Instead, the taxpayer can choose between an immediate full deduction in the year of outlay, or a special allowance permitted for "research and experimental expenses" so similar to depreciation that it is difficult to see the reason for a distinction. Under the special allowance, which applies only to costs of assets that have no determinable useful life, the expense is spread over a period of 60 or more months. For example, if a music publisher with limited activity and earnings for any one year were to make a substantial outlay for research and experimental purposes, he might understandably prefer to use the special allowance procedure instead of the full deduction in the year of outlay.

Musical arrangements for various possible uses of a song might also be regarded as being in the area of research and development expenses. If the composer himself makes the arrangement while owner of the copyright, he cannot charge for his own services as an expense; but if he engages outside arrangers, orchestrators, or copyists, he has the privilege of charging the expense against current income, or resorting to the special allowance by which the expense is spread over 60 or more months.

Some writers or estates of writers assemble folios of songs or publish descriptive promotional material for distribution to disc jockeys or record companies. These do not constitute experimental or research expenditures and are to be deemed either current promotional expense or allocable as an item of cost against gross receipts from the sales of printed copies.

Charitable Contributions

Charitable gifts of appreciated property can sometimes provide tax benefits to the donor. A recorded tape library of unreleased masters or a valuable copyright are examples of such appreciated property within the music industry. In certain cases, a donor can deduct the fair market value of his gift, as determined by an expert appraiser, from his taxable income. In contrast to a sale, a donor need not trouble to find a purchaser willing and able to pay the appraised value of the property.

The tax laws impose several limitations on the tax benefits of gifts of appreciated property. The benefits are largely unavailable to the taxpayer such as a composer or lyricist who created the subject of the gift or to the donee of a composer or lyricist; he can only deduct the original cost of creation, which is usually negligible. This limitation, however, would not ordinarily be applicable to publishers or heirs. There is also a limitation if the donee's use of the gift is unrelated to the donee's charitable function.

Income tax deductions for charitable contributions of individuals are restricted to 50 percent of adjusted gross income, subject, however, to a ceiling of 30 percent with certain carryover rights on the excess if a sale of a property would have resulted in a long-term capital gain; but, deduction under the 50 percent limitation is permitted if the appreciated contribution is reduced by 40 percent of the potential long-term capital gain. For corporations, the percentage restriction is 10 percent of taxable income, computed subject to certain adjustments.

At one time, for certain taxpayers in high income tax brackets, the tax savings of charitable contributions of appreciated property could have been greater than the after-tax proceeds of a sale of the property. However, recent tax legislation has largely eliminated this situation although possibilities of tax advantages still exist.

Deduction For Home Use as Office or Studio

Many free-lance vocalists and musicians require extensive rehearsals, coaching and practice to maintain their income producing skills. They carry on these activities in their home, in a portion used on an exclusive and regular basis.

The Internal Revenue Service allows the deduction of operating and depreciation expenses allocable to the portion of a home used for business purposes where the use is on an exclusive and regular basis as a principal place of business, or as a place for seeing business clients, or as a separate business structure. If the taxpayer is an employee, he must also show that the home office is being used for the "convenience" of his employer.

Items such as heat, electricity, insurance and rent, or in the case of home ownership, taxes, mortgage interest, and depreciation may be deducted on an allocated basis. If all rooms at home are approximately the same size, the taxpayer may compute the business portion of office or studio-in-home expenses by the ratio of the number of rooms used for business purposes to the total number of rooms. Thus one room divided by ten rooms equals 10 percent. In other instances, the ratio will be the number of square feet in the business space to the total square feet. For example, 330 square feet divided by 3,300 square feet, or 10 percent.

The deduction cannot be more than the total gross income from the business use of the home, after deduction therefrom of business expenses other than home expenses. Only household expenses and repairs which benefit the business use space are deductible. The cost of painting another room would thus not be deductible although the cost of painting the outside of the house may be deductible. Lawn care and landscaping costs are not deductible.

Shifting Taxable Income to Persons in Lower Tax Brackets

Many a successful parent would like to avoid additional income at his current high tax rate by shifting the income to a child or other dependent in a lower tax bracket. This cannot be done with ordinary personal service income but is perfectly legal in the case of music royalties. The mere reallocation of actual or anticipated income within a family group is not permissible, and the government looks with a jaundiced eye upon such transactions. However, it is deemed proper to make a bona fide gift or transfer of copyright since the conveyance is then not of income but of property capable of producing income. Where there is a direct transfer to a beneficiary, there can be no strings attached such as a right of recapture after college graduation. The assignment cannot be hazy; it is best to document it fully by written notice to the publisher, by registration of copyright assignment, if any, and perhaps even by appointment of a bank or other institution to collect and distribute the moneys. Properly accomplished, it is clear that the income tax is chargeable to the new owner of the income-producing property and not to the assignor, although the assignor may be liable for gift taxes if the gift does not come within the statutory exemptions to which the donor may be entitled.

There may also be a conveyance of property in trust for the family member. In such case there may be a reversionary interest in the grantor provided it may not be reasonably expected to take effect within ten years. Thus there can be the creation of a ten-year trust, at the end of which the property reverts to the grantor. In general, the grantor cannot retain the power to administer the property or to control the beneficial enjoyment of the property. He will be taxed on income applied for his benefit, including income used to maintain a person whom he is obligated to support. This has the effect of limiting the use of trusts to shift income to dependents if the intent is to employ trust income for support. In determining the virtues of a trust, consideration should be given to the effects of the "throw back" rule on distributions of accumulated income.

Some successful songwriters have established trust funds for their children without including ASCAP or BMI performance moneys. While it may be contended that this attempt to divide copyrights technically constitutes a failure to make a full and complete assignment, the divisibility of copyright is accepted for tax purposes. No capital gain on resale can eventually be claimed by the child or trustee who received the gift from the songwriter because, under tax law, a donee of an author or composer is treated the same as the donor and is therefore barred from the benefit of capital gains.

When an aged person, such as a parent, is dependent upon a successful songwriter for support, consideration may be given to shifting income by a transfer of copyright or of the property right to a royalty contract. The transfer may be in the form of a trust to last for at least ten years or until the happening of an event not likely to occur within ten years; if the trust is to run for the lifetime of a person—such as the grantor—he must have a life expectancy of at least ten years, except that the trust may be arranged to last for the beneficiary's lifetime, regardless of how short his life expectancy is. Or there can be a direct conveyance to the parent, provided there is no obligation to return the property in the future; it is reasonable to expect that the parent will express appreciation by a bequest back to the assignor. By virtue of the trust or conveyance, the assignor will be relieved of taxes on the income. Taxes paid by the dependent are likely to be lower than those that would be payable by the assignor if the income were attributable to him; in 1984, the first $1,000 is tax free for a person under 65, and an additional $1,000, or a total of $2,000, is tax free after the age of 65. There is the further benefit of the possible use of the standard deduction by the dependent, and any remaining income would probably be taxed at a lesser rate than would be applicable if the income belonged to the assignor for tax purposes.

In determining whether to shift income to the dependent, the grantor must consider the possible loss of a dependency deduction on his own tax return if the dependent's income would increase beyond certain limits. This should not prove detrimental. For example, assigning property that is productive of $3,100 of income to a widowed parent over 65 reduces the income of the donor by $3,100. It causes him to lose the deduction for the dependent, equal to $1,000, but nevertheless results in a tax saving at the donor's top tax bracket on $2,100. There is no tax to the donee assuming he has no other income and uses the tax tables in effect for 1984.

Shifting Income from One Year to Other Years

The taxpayer on either a fiscal or calendar year may benefit by deferring the receipt and reporting of income to a future date, despite the loss of use of the money until its receipt. One reason for this is the continued availability to the taxpayer of moneys which would otherwise have to be paid as taxes. Another reason may be the expectation that there will be lower earnings in future years, and therefore the deferred income will be reported at a lower tax rate. Some writers, publishers, and record artists contract for and obtain delays in payments of royalties until a subsequent year.

In each case of income deferral, the question of "constructive receipt" arises. This problem is present if the taxpayer waives receipt of moneys to which he is entitled in the tax year, or delays cashing a check which is in his hands before the end of the current tax year. The petty subterfuge involved can be avoided by a forthright provision in a royalty agreement, designed to accomplish the same benefit.

A typical acceptable provision, in the instance of a recording artist, provides that the royalties payable in any one year may not exceed a stated maximum, and that any excess is accumulated for disbursement in future years when the current earnings do not reach the earnings ceiling. Other contracts, such as that between a show music writer and a music publisher, or an exclusive service contract between a songwriter and publisher for the services of the writer, may call for an annual minimum guaranteed payment to the writer on the understanding that the publisher can withhold earnings in excess of a ceiling figure fixed in the agreement. At the end of the term of the agreement, the accumulated amount withheld, if any, is disbursed over a stated number of years at an annual figure set forth in the contract.

When this method of income deferral is utilized, it is a requisite that the funds being held by the publisher or the recording company remain in the business and be subject to the risk of the business. A contractual provision whereby the person liable for the payment of the deferred amount places the funds in escrow or in trust, or in some other manner earmarks the funds and removes them from the possible claims of creditors, destroys the advantage sought, and results in a constructive receipt of the funds by the person entitled to them.

Keogh Plan

The Internal Revenue Code, in a different form, permits the deferral of a limited amount of such income, without undertaking the afore-described risk. A self-employed individual is permitted to set up a self-employed pension plan (often called a "Keogh" Plan).

There are two general types of Keogh Plans: defined-benefit plans and defined-contribution plans. Most persons have a defined-contribution plan, the two main types of which are money-purchase plans and profit-sharing plans. In the case of money-purchase plans the participant agrees to put a certain minimum percentage of self-employed income into the account each year. Most Keogh Plan holders who receive income from freelancing, such as self-employed songwriters, and who do not have employees have money-purchase plans. Where the holder has employees, it is likely that a profit-sharing plan is utilized.

Under either type of defined-contribution plan there can be contributed up to the lower of 25 percent of earned income or $30,000. For this purpose earned income consists of net earnings from self-employment less the Keogh contribution; this in effect limits the contribution to 20 percent of the net earnings from self-employment before the Keogh contribution. As to a money-purchase plan, the full amount of the contribution is deductible for tax purposes from gross income in the computation of adjusted gross income. Where there is a profit-sharing plan the deduction from gross income for tax purposes is limited to 15 percent of the net earnings from self-employment, and it is not clear at this writing whether the Keogh contribution is deductible from the net earnings in computing the 15 percent.

The effect of the use of the Keogh Plan is virtually the same as if the writer had arranged for the deferment of the payment of the amount contributed to the plan. However, by utilizing the plan he currently obtains the funds, thereby removing them from the risk of the publisher's or recording company's business. He effectively pays no current tax on the contribution, and he earns interest on his contribution (no interest is earned when funds are left with the publisher) and he need not pay tax on the interest until it is withdrawn.

In the situation of an ordinary deferment of income, the contract would have to provide how much is to be paid (or deferred) each year. Under the Keogh Plan, annual determinations may be made as to how much to "defer" by making the contribution, so long as the limitations are observed. Contracts providing for deferments set forth the time and amount of pay-out. Pay-outs under the Keogh Plan are generally not permitted to commence before age 59½ without penalty (except in case of total disability) and in any event must commence no later than the year when the participant reaches age 70½. If not fully withdrawn by such year, the plan must provide for ultimate pay-out over a period that does not extend beyond the life expectancy of the participant, or the joint lives of the participant and his beneficiary, as computed in accordance with Internal Revenue Service regulations.

Since, by virtue of having taken the deduction at the time of contribution, the self-employed individual has not paid tax in the earlier year, the entire amount drawn later, including the interest earned, is subject to tax.

A word of caution is required with respect to employees. In all probability, a self-employed composer or recording artist does not have employees, but if he does, and if he adopts a Keogh Plan, the plan must usually provide benefits for all full time employees whose period of service extends to three years or more.

Individual Retirement Accounts (IRAs)

Employed workers as well as self-employed workers may establish Individual Retirement Accounts (IRAs), which as in the case of Keogh Plans permit the deferral, for income tax purposes, of a certain amount of income and of future earnings on such deferred income, for example, interest.

Under an IRA plan, in 1984 a worker might make deductible contributions of up to $2,000 of earned income annually, which amount might rise to $2,250 if the worker had an unemployed spouse. If earnings were less than $2,000, the contribution might be for up to the full amount earned. A self-employed person may contribute to both an IRA and a Keogh Plan, except that after age 70½ he may no longer contribute to his IRA plan. An individual may be both employed, such as a member of a band, and self-employed, for instance, a songwriter who receives royalties from ASCAP and a music publisher. He may also establish and contribute to both an IRA and a Keogh Plan. If both the participant and his spouse work, each may establish an IRA and contribute, in 1984, up to $2,000 annually; the couple's total IRA annual contribution might thus aggregate $4,000.

Under an IRA, as in the case of a Keogh Plan, distributions to the participant may commence at age 59½ without penalty but need not begin before age 70½. If the amount in the plan is not fully withdrawn in that year, the withdrawal must not extend over a period longer than the life expectancy of the participant, or the joint lives of the participant and his beneficiary, as computed in accordance with Internal Revenue Service regulations.

All amounts withdrawn are subject to income tax at the time of withdrawal. All IRA withdrawals are fully taxable, although regular income averaging may be resorted to.

Keogh Plan distributions are treated in the same manner as IRA distributions for income tax purposes, except that certain favorable tax provisions apply to lump-sum Keogh distributions. In effect, the recipient may use a special ten-year averaging method to compute the tax due.

Income Averaging

Congress has recognized that artistic creators, actors, and others often have a boom or bust economic life. Under a so-called spread-back income averaging provision originally enacted in 1964 and later amended, the taxpayer in 1984 could in effect average income over a four-year period when income in the current year exceeded the average of the three prior years by more than 40 percent and this excess was more than $3,000. The "averageable income," which is the income in excess of 40 percent of the three-year average, is taxed as if it had been received over a four-year period. The result achieved is substantially similar to including 46⅔ percent of the income eligible for averaging in the taxable income base of each of the three prior years and of the current year. An advantage of the computation is that it is not necessary to recompute the tax for each of the three prior years in order to obtain the result.

The following indicates a computation to arrive at averageable income: It may be assumed that for 1984 the taxpayer had adjusted taxable income of $65,000 and that for the base period (the prior 3 years) his total adjusted income was $120,000.

Adjusted taxable income for 1984	$65,000
Minus 46⅔% of the adjusted total base period income of $120,000	56,000
Averageable income	$9,000

The taxpayer may use the income averaging method since the averageable income exceeds $3,000.

Income averaging is not available to corporations and partnerships.

S Corporations

An "S" corporation is one whose income and losses are allocable to its stockholders as if they were the stockholder's direct income or loss. For tax purposes, it is as if the corporation were a partnership or a sole proprietorship.

Through use of an S corporation a stockholder can achieve the limited liability afforded by a corporation and also avoid the double taxation of corporate profits and stockholder dividends.

The tax treatment is particularly beneficial in the case of new businesses expected to lose money at their beginning. A shareholder will be entitled to take tax losses which may be offset against income from other sources.

An S corporation must have one class of stock and all of its shareholders must agree to the S status. Shareholders who work for the corporation are treated as employees for Social Security tax payments. They do not pay self-employment tax on their salary income or other receipts from the corporation. An attorney should be consulted as to requirements and aspects of S corporations.

Contractual Formats

Despite the right of the tax authorities to review documentation for the purpose of distinguishing substance from form, it is clear that a taxpayer's right to qualify for certain tax treatment may depend on the contractual format which has been chosen for a particular transaction.

For example, if services are rendered to produce a master recording, the proceeds from the services might qualify as earned income; if there is a "lease" of the master recording, the proceeds might be regarded as ordinary income, whereas the proceeds from its "sale" might qualify for capital gains treatment. In each case, qualified attorneys and accountants should be consulted to consider alternative contractual formats.

The corporation approach to lower taxes can prove to be treacherous. Even if the corporation is not classified as a personal holding company, the accumulated income, to the extent it exceeds $250,000 ($150,000 if a service corporation in the field of performing arts) and is not required for the reasonable needs of the business, may be subjected to certain surtaxes.

The income of a personal holding company is subject to regular corporate tax rates, and its undistributed income is taxed at 50 percent. A personal holding company is defined as a corporation a majority of whose stock is held, directly or indirectly, by not more than five persons and at least 60 percent of whose gross income is within the definition of personal holding company income. The latter income includes, among other types of receipts, the income from copyright and other royalties.

The extent of the various activities needed to exclude personal holding company surtaxes and other techniques for using corporations to reduce taxes should be explored carefully with attorneys and accountants before action is taken.

Royalties as "Earned Income"

The Internal Revenue Code contains special provisions, whereby "earned income" is never taxed at a rate in excess of 50 percent. Before an author or composer undertakes any of the other tax saving devices discussed, he should bear this fact in mind, inasmuch as the royalties that he receives are considered to be earned income. Comparative calculations are advisable to ascertain whether there is sufficient tax advantage to warrant the utilization of one of the other methods, as compared with the payment of the ordinary income tax on royalties, with a maximum rate of 50 percent. However, if the royalties are received by one who is not the author, as for example his donee or heir, the maximum rate limitation is not applicable, since that owner did not produce the property that is earning the royalty.

Foreign Royalties Subject Only to United States Tax

By reciprocal treaties with many countries, American taxpayers are exempt from foreign income tax on royalties earned abroad. For example, the treaty between the United States and the United Kingdom provides for a tax exemption in the country of source of income, and taxation in the country of residence, with respect to royalties from copyrights and like property. This exemption does not apply if the taxpayer has a permanent establishment in the country that is the source of income and the royalties are directly associated with the business operations carried on by the permanent establishment.

Most publishers and record companies are aware of the necessity for filing nonresident alien tax exemption certificates with foreign governments either directly or through foreign subpublishers or agents. Authors and composers encounter this necessity only when they deal directly with foreign music or record companies, instead of in the customary manner through an American firm. Reciprocal treaties are designed to avoid double taxation and the inconvenience of having to file for refunds of moneys withheld at the source. Treaties are not uniform and specific reference should be made to the particular treaty when a question arises. Specific treaties will be supplied by the Superintendent of Documents, United States Government Printing Office, Washington, D.C. 20005.

With respect to royalties earned in a foreign country in which the recipient maintains a permanent establishment (so that the tax treaty would not be applicable), or earned in a country with which the United States does not have a tax treaty, there is a probability that the source country will impose a tax on the income there derived, and that the United States will also tax that income. However, some or all of the adverse effects of that double taxation might be ameliorated by appropriate use of the foreign tax credit in the United States return.

Part 4

APPENDIXES AND MUSIC INDUSTRY FORMS

Appendix A

Selected Extracts from the 1976 Copyright Act of the United States of America (United States Code, Title 17—Copyrights)*

Chapter 1.—Subject Matter and Scope of Copyright

---

*Pub. Law 94-553. The Act was enacted on October 19, 1976. Its effective date was January 1, 1978 except for Sections 118, 304 (b), and 801 through 810, which became effective on enactment of the Act. The Act has been amended as follows:

Section	Statute
101	Act of December 12, 1980 (Pub. Law 96-517)
109	Act of October 4, 1984 (Pub. Law 98-450)
110	Act of November 24, 1982 (Pub. Law 97-366)
115 (c)	Act of October 4, 1984 (Pub. Law 98-450)
117	Act of December 12, 1980 (Pub. Law 96-517)
201 (e)	Act of November 6, 1978 (Pub. Law 95-598)
506 (a)	Act of May 24, 1982 (Pub. Law 97-180)
601 (a)	Act of July 13, 1982 (Pub. Law 97-215)
798 (c)	Act of August 5, 1977 (Pub. Law 95-94), and further amended by Act of October 25, 1982 (Pub. Law 97-366)

17 USC 101.   **§ 101. Definitions**

As used in this title, the following terms and their variant forms mean the following:

An "anonymous work" is a work on the copies or phonorecords of which no natural person is identified as author.

"Audiovisual works" are works that consist of a series of related images which are intrinsically intended to be shown by the use of machines or devices such as projectors, viewers, or electronic equipment, together with accompanying sounds, if any, regardless of the nature of the material objects, such as films or tapes, in which the works are embodied.

The "best edition" of a work is the edition, published in the United States at any time before the date of deposit, that the Library of Congress determines to be most suitable for its purposes.

A person's "children" are that person's immediate offspring, whether legitimate or not, and any children legally adopted by that person.

A "collective work" is a work, such as a periodical issue, anthology, or encyclopedia, in which a number of contributions, constituting separate and independent works in themselves, are assembled into a collective whole.

A "compilation" is a work formed by the collection and assembling of preexisting materials or of data that are selected, coordinated, or arranged in such a way that the resulting work as a whole constitutes an original work of authorship. The term "compilation" includes collective works.

"Copies" are material objects, other than phonorecords, in which a work is fixed by any method now known or later developed, and from which the work can be perceived, reproduced, or otherwise communicated, either directly or with the aid of a machine or device. The term "copies" includes the material object, other than a phonorecord, in which the work is first fixed.

"Copyright owner", with respect to any one of the exclusive rights comprised in a copyright, refers to the owner of that particular right.

A work is "created" when it is fixed in a copy or phonorecord for the first time; where a work is prepared over a period of time, the portion of it that has been fixed at any particular time constitutes the work as of that time, and where the work has been prepared in different versions, each version constitutes a separate work.

A "derivative work" is a work based upon one or more preexisting works, such as a translation, musical arrangement, dramatization, fictionalization, motion picture version, sound recording, art reproduction, abridgment, condensation, or any other form in which a work may be recast, transformed, or adapted. A work consisting of editorial revisions, annotations, elaborations, or other modifications which, as a whole, represent an original work of authorship, is a "derivative work".

A "device", "machine", or "process" is one now known or later developed.

To "display" a work means to show a copy of it, either directly or by means of a film, slide, television image, or any other device or process or, in the case of a motion picture or other audiovisual work, to show individual images nonsequentially.

A work is "fixed" in a tangible medium of expression when its embodiment in a copy or phonorecord, by or under the authority of the author, is sufficiently permanent or stable to permit it to be perceived, reproduced, or otherwise communicated for a period of more than transitory duration. A work consisting of sounds, images, or both, that are being transmitted, is "fixed" for purposes of this title if a fixation of the work is being made simultaneously with its transmission.

The terms "including" and "such as" are illustrative and not limitative.

A "joint work" is a work prepared by two or more authors with the intention that their contributions be merged into inseparable or interdependent parts of a unitary whole.

"Literary works" are works, other than audiovisual works, expressed in words, numbers, or other verbal or numerical symbols or indicia, regardless of the nature of the material objects, such as books, periodicals, manuscripts, phonorecords, film, tapes, disks, or cards, in which they are embodied.

"Motion pictures" are audiovisual works consisting of a series of related images which, when shown in succession, impart an impression of motion, together with accompanying sounds, if any.

To "perform" a work means to recite, render, play, dance, or act it, either directly or by means of any device or process or, in the case of a motion picture or other audiovisual work, to show its images in any sequence or to make the sounds accompanying it audible.

"Phonorecords" are material objects in which sounds, other than those accompanying a motion picture or other audiovisual work, are fixed by any method now known or later developed, and from which the sounds can be perceived, reproduced, or otherwise communicated, either directly or with the aid of a machine or device. The term "phonorecords" includes the material object in which the sounds are first fixed.

"Pictorial, graphic, and sculptural works" include two-dimensional and three-dimensional works of fine, graphic, and applied art, photographs, prints and art reproductions, maps, globes, charts, technical drawings, diagrams, and models. Such works shall include works of artistic craftsmanship insofar as their form but not their mechanical or utilitarian aspects are concerned; the design of a useful article, as defined in this section, shall be considered a pictorial, graphic, or sculptural work only if, and only to the extent that, such design incorporates pictorial, graphic, or sculptural features that can be identified separately from, and are capable of existing independently of, the utilitarian aspects of the article.

A "pseudonymous work" is a work on the copies or phonorecords of which the author is identified under a fictitious name.

"Publication" is the distribution of copies or phonorecords of a work to the public by sale or other transfer of ownership, or by rental, lease, or lending. The offering to distribute copies or phonorecords to a group of persons for purposes of further distribution, public performance, or public display, constitutes publication. A public performance or display of a work does not of itself constitute publication.

To perform or display a work "publicly" means—

(1) to perform or display it at a place open to the public or at any place where a substantial number of persons outside of a normal circle of a family and its social acquaintances is gathered; or

(2) to transmit or otherwise communicate a performance or display of the work to a place specified by clause (1) or to the public, by means of any device or process, whether the members of the public capable of receiving the performance or display receive it in the same place or in separate places and at the same time or at different times.

"Sound recordings" are works that result from the fixation of a series of musical, spoken, or other sounds, but not including the sounds accompanying a motion picture or other audiovisual work, regardless of the nature of the material objects, such as disks, tapes, or other phonorecords, in which they are embodied.

"State" includes the District of Columbia and the Commonwealth of Puerto Rico, and any territories to which this title is made applicable by an Act of Congress.

A "transfer of copyright ownership" is an assignment, mortgage, exclusive license, or any other conveyance, alienation, or hypothecation of a copyright or of any of the exclusive rights comprised in a copyright, whether or not it is limited in time or place of effect, but not including a nonexclusive license.

A "transmission program" is a body of material that, as an aggregate, has been produced for the sole purpose of transmission to the public in sequence and as a unit.

To "transmit" a performance or display is to communicate it by any device or process whereby images or sounds are received beyond the place from which they are sent.

The "United States", when used in a geographical sense, comprises the several States, the District of Columbia and the Commonwealth of Puerto Rico, and the organized territories under the jurisdiction of the United States Government.

A "useful article" is an article having an intrinsic utilitarian function that is not merely to portray the appearance of the article or to convey information. An article that is normally a part of a useful article is considered a "useful article".

The author's "widow" or "widower" is the author's surviving spouse under the law of the author's domicile at the time of his or her death, whether or not the spouse has later remarried.

A "work of the United States Government" is a work prepared by an officer or employee of the United States Government as part of that person's official duties.

A "work made for hire" is—

(1) a work prepared by an employee within the scope of his or her employment; or

(2) a work specially ordered or commissioned for use as a contribution to a collective work, as a part of a motion picture or other audiovisual work, as a translation, as a supplementary work, as a compilation, as an instructional text, as a test, as answer material for a test, or as an atlas, if the parties expressly agree in a written instrument signed by them that the work shall be considered a work made for hire. For the purpose of the foregoing sentence, a "supplementary work" is a work prepared for publication as a secondary adjunct to a work by another author for the purpose of introducing, concluding, illustrating, explaining, revising, commenting upon, or assisting in the use of the other work, such as forewords, afterwords, pictorial illustrations, maps, charts, tables, editorial notes, musical arrangements, answer material for tests, bibliographies, appendixes, and indexes, and an "instructional text" is a literary, pictorial, or graphic work prepared for publication and with the purpose of use in systematic instructional activities.

A "computer program" is a set of statements or instructions to be used directly or indirectly in a computer in order to bring about a certain result.

17 USC 102.	**§ 102. Subject matter of copyright: In general**
	(a) Copyright protection subsists, in accordance with this title, in original works of authorship fixed in any tangible medium of expression, now known or later developed, from which they can be perceived, reproduced,
Works of authorship.	or otherwise communicated, either directly or with the aid of a machine or device. Works of authorship include the following categories:

(1) literary works;
(2) musical works, including any accompanying words;
(3) dramatic works, including any accompanying music;
(4) pantomimes and choreographic works;
(5) pictorial, graphic, and sculptural works;
(6) motion pictures and other audiovisual works; and
(7) sound recordings.

(b) In no case does copyright protection for an original work of authorship extend to any idea, procedure, process, system, method of operation, concept, principle, or discovery, regardless of the form in which it is described, explained, illustrated, or embodied in such work.

17 USC 103.

§ 103. Subject matter of copyright: Compilations and derivative works

(a) The subject matter of copyright as specified by section 102 includes compilations and derivative works, but protection for a work employing preexisting material in which copyright subsists does not extend to any part of the work in which such material has been used unlawfully.

(b) The copyright in a compilation or derivative work extends only to the material contributed by the author of such work, as distinguished from the preexisting material employed in the work, and does not imply any exclusive right in the preexisting material. The copyright in such work is independent of, and does not affect or enlarge the scope, duration, ownership, or subsistence of, any copyright protection in the preexisting material.

17 USC 104.

§ 104. Subject matter of copyright: National origin

(a) UNPUBLISHED WORKS.—The works specified by sections 102 and 103, while unpublished, are subject to protection under this title without regard to the nationality or domicile of the author.

(b) PUBLISHED WORKS.—The works specified by sections 102 and 103, when published, are subject to protection under this title if—

(1) on the date of first publication, one or more of the authors is a national or domiciliary of the United States, or is a national, domiciliary, or sovereign authority of a foreign nation that is a party to a copyright treaty to which the United States is also a party, or is a stateless person, wherever that person may be domiciled; or

(2) the work is first published in the United States or in a foreign nation that, on the date of first publication, is a party to the Universal Copyright Convention; or

(3) the work is first published by the United Nations or any of its specialized agencies, or by the Organization of American States; or

(4) the work comes within the scope of a Presidential proclamation. Whenever the President finds that a particular foreign nation extends, to works by authors who are nationals or domiciliaries of the United States or to works that are first published in the United States, copyright protection on substantially the same basis as that on which the foreign nation extends protection to works of its own nationals and domiciliaries and works first published in that nation, the President may by proclamation extend protection under this title to works of which one or more of the authors is, on the date of first publication, a national, domiciliary, or sovereign authority of that nation, or which was first published in that nation. The President may revise, suspend, or revoke any such proclamation or impose any conditions or limitations on protection under a proclamation.

17 USC 105.

§ 105. Subject matter of copyright: United States Government works

Copyright protection under this title is not available for any work of the United States Government, but the United States Government is not precluded from receiving and holding copyrights transferred to it by assignment, bequest, or otherwise.

17 USC 106.

§ 106. Exclusive rights in copyrighted works

Subject to sections 107 through 118, the owner of copyright under this title has the exclusive rights to do and to authorize any of the following:

(1) to reproduce the copyrighted work in copies or phonorecords;

(2) to prepare derivative works based upon the copyrighted work;

(3) to distribute copies or phonorecords of the copyrighted work to the public by sale or other transfer of ownership, or by rental, lease, or lending;

(4) in the case of literary, musical, dramatic, and choreographic works, pantomimes, and motion pictures and other audiovisual works, to perform the copyrighted work publicly; and

(5) in the case of literary, musical, dramatic, and choreographic works, pan-

tomimes, and pictorial, graphic, or sculptural works, including the individual images of a motion picture or other audiovisual work, to display the copyrighted work publicly.

17 USC 107.   **§ 107. Limitations on exclusive rights: Fair use**

Notwithstanding the provisions of section 106, the fair use of a copyrighted work, including such use by reproduction in copies or phonorecords or by any other means specified by that section, for purposes such as criticism, comment, news reporting, teaching (including multiple copies for classroom use), scholarship, or research, is not an infringement of copyright. In determining whether the use made of a work in any particular case is a fair use the factors to be considered shall include—

(1) the purpose and character of the use, including whether such use is of a commercial nature or is for nonprofit educational purposes;

(2) the nature of the copyrighted work;

(3) the amount and substantiality of the portion used in relation to the copyrighted work as a whole; and

(4) the effect of the use upon the potential market for or value of the copyrighted work.

17 USC 108.   **§ 108. Limitations on exclusive rights: Reproduction by libraries and archives**

(a) Notwithstanding the provisions of section 106, it is not an infringement of copyright for a library or archives, or any of its employees acting within the scope of their employment, to reproduce no more than one copy or phonorecord of a work, or to distribute such copy or phonorecord, under the conditions specified by this section, if

(1) the reproduction or distribution is made without any purpose of direct or indirect commercial advantage;

(2) the collections of the library or archives are (i) open to the public, or (ii) available not only to researchers affiliated with the library or archives or with the institution of which it is a part, but also to other persons doing research in a specialized field; and

(3) the reproduction or distribution of the work includes a notice of copyright.

(b) The rights of reproduction and distribution under this section apply to a copy or phonorecord of an unpublished work duplicated in facsimile form solely for purposes of preservation and security or for deposit for research use in another library or archives of the type described by clause (2) of subsection (a), if the copy or phonorecord reproduced is currently in the collections of the library or archives.

(c) The right of reproduction under this section applies to a copy or phonorecord of a published work duplicated in facsimile form solely for the purpose of replacement of a copy or phonorecord that is damaged, deteriorating, lost, or stolen, if the library or archives has, after a reasonable effort, determined that an unused replacement cannot be obtained at a fair price.

(d) The rights of reproduction and distribution under this section apply to a copy, made from the collection of a library or archives where the user makes his or her request or from that of another library or archives, of no more than one article or other contribution to a copyrighted collection or periodical issue, or to a copy or phonorecord of a small part of any other copyrighted work, if—

(1) the copy or phonorecord becomes the property of the user, and the library or archives has had no notice that the copy or phonorecord would be used for any purpose other than private study, scholarship, or research; and

(2) the library or archives displays prominently, at the place where orders are accepted, and includes on its order form, a warning of copyright in accordance with requirements that the Register of Copyrights shall prescribe by regulation.

(e) The rights of reproduction and distribution under this section apply to the entire work, or to a substantial part of it, made from the collection of a library or archives where the user makes his or her request or from that of another library or archives, if the library or archives has first determined, on the basis of a reasonable investigation, that a copy or phonorecord of the copyrighted work cannot be obtained at a fair price, if—

(1) the copy or phonorecord becomes the property of the user, and the library or archives has had no notice that the copy or phonorecord would be used for any purpose other than private study, scholarship, or research; and

(2) the library or archives displays prominently, at the place where orders are accepted, and includes on its order form, a warning of copyright in accordance with requirements that the Register of Copyrights shall prescribe by regulation.

(f) Nothing in this section—

(1) shall be construed to impose liability for copyright infringement upon a library or archives or its employees for the unsupervised use of reproducing equipment located on its premises: *Provided,* That such equipment displays a notice that the making of a copy may be subject to the copyright law;

(2) excuses a person who uses such reproducing equipment or who requests a copy or phonorecord under subsection (d) from liability for copyright infringement for any such act, or for any later use of such copy or phonorecord, if it exceeds fair use as provided by section 107;

(3) shall be construed to limit the reproduction and distribution by lending of a limited number of copies and excerpts by a library or archives of an audiovisual news program, subject to clauses (1), (2), and (3) of subsection (a); or

(4) in any way affects the right of fair use as provided by section 107, or any contractual obligations assumed at any time by the library or archives when it obtained a copy or phonorecord of a work in its collections.

(g) The rights of reproduction and distribution under this section extend to the isolated and unrelated reproduction or distribution of a single copy or phonorecord of the same material on separate occasions, but do not extend to cases where the library or archives, or its employee—

(1) is aware or has substantial reason to believe that it is engaging in the related or concerted reproduction or distribution of multiple copies or phonorecords of the same material, whether made on one occasion or over a period of time, and whether intended for aggregate use by one or more individuals or for separate use by the individual members of a group; or

(2) engages in the systematic reproduction or distribution of single or multiple copies or phonorecords of material described in subsection (d): *Provided,* That nothing in this clause prevents a library or archives from participating in interlibrary arrangements that do not have, as their purpose or effect, that the library or archives receiving such copies or phonorecords for distribution does so in such aggregate quantities as to substitute for a subscription to or purchase of such work.

(h) The rights of reproduction and distribution under this section do not apply to a musical work, a pictorial, graphic or sculptural work, or a motion picture or other audiovisual work other than an audiovisual work dealing with news, except that no such limitation shall apply with respect to rights granted by subsections (b) and (c), or with respect to pictorial or graphic works published as illustrations, diagrams, or similar adjuncts to works of which copies are reproduced or distributed in accordance with subsections (d) and (e).

Report to Congress.

(i) Five years from the effective date of this Act, and at five-year intervals thereafter, the Register of Copyrights, after consulting with representatives of authors, book and periodical publishers, and other owners of copyrighted materials, and with representatives of library users and librarians, shall submit to the Congress a report setting forth the extent to which this section has achieved the intended statutory balancing of the rights of creators, and the needs of users. The report should also describe any problems that may have arisen, and present legislative or other recommendations, if warranted.

17 USC 109.

§ 109. **Limitations on exclusive rights: Effect of transfer of particular copy or phonorecord**

Disposal.

(a) Notwithstanding the provisions of section 106(3), the owner of a particular copy or phonorecord lawfully made under this title, or any person authorized by such owner, is entitled, without the authority of the copyright owner, to sell or otherwise dispose of the possession of that copy or phonorecord.

(b) (1) Notwithstanding the provisions of subsection (a), unless authorized by the owners of copyright in the sound recording and in the musical works embodied therein, the owner of a particular phonorecord may not, for purposes of direct or indirect commercial advantage, dispose of, or authorize the disposal of, the possession of that phonorecord by rental, lease, or lending, or by any other act or practice in the nature of rental, lease, or lending. Nothing in the preceding sentence shall apply to the rental, lease, or lending of a phonorecord for nonprofit purposes by a nonprofit library or nonprofit educational institution.

(2) Nothing in this subsection shall affect any provision of the antitrust laws. For purposes of the preceding sentence, 'antitrust laws' has the meaning given that term in the first section of the Clayton Act and includes section 5 of the Federal Trade Commission Act to the extent that section relates to unfair methods of competition.

(3) Any person who distributes a phonorecord in violation of clause (1) is an infringer of copyright under section 501 of this title and is subject to the remedies set forth in sections 502, 503, 504, 505, and 509. Such violation shall not be a criminal offense under section 506 or cause such person to be subject to the criminal penalties set forth in section 2319 of title 18.[1]

Public display.

(c) Notwithstanding the provisions of section 106(5), the owner of a particular copy lawfully made under this title, or any person authorized by such owner, is entitled, without the authority of the copyright owner, to display that copy publicly, either directly or by the projection of no more than one image at a time, to viewers present at the place where the copy is located.

(d) The privileges prescribed by subsections (a) and (b) do not, unless authorized by the copyright owner, extend to any person who has acquired possession of the copy or phonorecord from the copyright owner, by rental, lease, loan, or otherwise, without acquiring ownership of it.

17 USC 110.

§ 110. **Limitations on exclusive rights: Exemption of certain performances and displays**

Notwithstanding the provisions of section 106, the following are not infringements of copyright:

(1) performance or display of a work by instructors or pupils in the course of face-to-face teaching activities of a nonprofit educational institution, in a

---

[1]The Act of October 4, 1984 (Pub. Law 98-450) which enacted Section 109 (b) provides that its provisions ''shall not affect the right of an owner of a particular phonorecord of a sound recording, who acquired such ownership before the date of the enactment of this Act, to dispose of the possession of that particular phonorecord on or after such date of enactment in any manner permitted by section 109 of title 17, United States Code, as in effect on the day before the date of the enactment of this Act.'' The Act also provides that its provisions will become ineffective after five years from October 4, 1984.

classroom or similar place devoted to instruction, unless, in the case of a motion picture or other audiovisual work, the performance, or the display of individual images, is given by means of a copy that was not lawfully made under this title, and that the person responsible for the performance knew or had reason to believe was not lawfully made;

(2) performance of a nondramatic literary or musical work or display of a work, by or in the course of a transmission, if—

    (A) the performance or display is a regular part of the systematic instructional activities of a governmental body or a nonprofit educational institution; and

    (B) the performance or display is directly related and of material assistance to the teaching content of the transmission; and

    (C) the transmission is made primarily for—

        (i) reception in classrooms or similar places normally devoted to instruction, or

        (ii) reception by persons to whom the transmission is directed because their disabilities or other special circumstances prevent their attendance in classrooms or similar places normally devoted to instruction, or

        (iii) reception by officers or employees of governmental bodies as a part of their official duties or employment;

(3) performance of a nondramatic literary or musical work or of a dramatico-musical work of a religious nature, or display of a work, in the course of services at a place of worship or other religious assembly;

(4) performance of a nondramatic literary or musical work otherwise than in a transmission to the public, without any purpose of direct or indirect commercial advantage and without payment of any fee or other compensation for the performance to any of its performers, promoters, or organizers, if—

    (A) there is no direct or indirect admission charge; or

Notice of objection to performance.

    (B) the proceeds, after deducting the reasonable costs of producing the performance, are used exclusively for educational, religious, or charitable purposes and not for private financial gain, except where the copyright owner has served notice of objection to the performance under the following conditions:

        (i) the notice shall be in writing and signed by the copyright owner or such owner's duly authorized agent; and

        (ii) the notice shall be served on the person responsible for the performance at least seven days before the date of the performance, and shall state the reasons for the objection; and

        (iii) the notice shall comply, in form, content, and manner of service, with requirements that the Register of Copyrights shall prescribe by regulation;

(5) communication of a transmission embodying a performance or display of a work by the public reception of the transmission on a single receiving apparatus of a kind commonly used in private homes, unless—

    (A) a direct charge is made to see or hear the transmission; or

    (B) the transmission thus received is further transmitted to the public;

(6) performance of a nondramatic musical work by a governmental body or a nonprofit agricultural or horticultural organization, in the course of an annual agricultural or horticultural fair or exhibition conducted by such body or organization; the exemption provided by this clause shall extend to any liability for copyright infringement that would otherwise be imposed on such body or organization, under doctrines of vicarious liability or related infringement, for a performance by a concessionnaire, business establishment, or other person at such fair or exhibition, but shall not excuse any such person from liability for the performance;

(7) performance of a nondramatic musical work by a vending establishment open to the public at large without any direct or indirect admission charge, where the sole purpose of the performance is to promote the retail sale of copies or phonorecords of the work, and the performance is not transmit-

ted beyond the place where the establishment is located and is within the immediate area where the sale is occurring;

(8) performance of a nondramatic literary work, by or in the course of a transmission specifically designed for and primarily directed to blind or other handicapped persons who are unable to read normal printed material as a result of their handicap, or deaf or other handicapped persons who are unable to hear the aural signals accompanying a transmission of visual signals, if the performance is made without any purpose of direct or indirect commercial advantage and its transmission is made through the facilities of: (i) a governmental body; or (ii) a noncommercial educational broadcast station (as defined in section 397 of title 47); or (iii) a radio subcarrier authorization (as defined in 47 CFR 73.293–73.295 and 73.593–73.595); or (iv) a cable system (as defined in section 111(f)).

(9) performance on a single occasion of a dramatic literary work published at least ten years before the date of the performance, by or in the course of a transmission specifically designed for and primarily directed to blind or other handicapped persons who are unable to read normal printed material as a result of their handicap, if the performance is made without any purpose of direct or indirect commercial advantage and its transmission is made through the facilities of a radio subcarrier authorization referred to in clause (8) (iii), *Provided,* That the provisions of this clause shall not be applicable to more than one performance of the same work by the same performers or under the auspices of the same organization.

(10) notwithstanding paragraph 4 above, the following is not an infringement of copyright: performance of a nondramatic literary or musical work in the course of a social function which is organized and promoted by a nonprofit veterans' organization or a nonprofit fraternal organization to which the general public is not invited, but not including the invitees of the organizations, if the proceeds from the performance, after deducting the reasonable costs of producing the performance, are used exclusively for charitable purposes and not for financial gain. For purposes of this section the social functions of any college or university fraternity or sorority shall not be included unless the social function is held solely to raise funds for a specific charitable purpose.

17 USC 111.   **§ 111. Limitations on exclusive rights: Secondary transmissions**

(a) CERTAIN SECONDARY TRANSMISSIONS EXEMPTED.—The secondary transmission of a primary transmission embodying a performance or display of a work is not an infringement of copyright if—

(1) the secondary transmission is not made by a cable system, and consists entirely of the relaying, by the management of a hotel, apartment house, or similar establishment, of signals transmitted by a broadcast station licensed by the Federal Communications Commission, within the local service area of such station, to the private lodgings of guests or residents of such establishment, and no direct charge is made to see or hear the secondary transmission; or

(2) the secondary transmission is made solely for the purpose and under the conditions specified by clause (2) of section 110; or

(3) the secondary transmission is made by any carrier who has no direct or indirect control over the content or selection of the primary transmission or over the particular recipients of the secondary transmission, and whose activities with respect to the secondary transmission consist solely of providing wires, cables, or other communications channels for the use of others: *Provided,* That the provisions of this clause extend only to the activities of said carrier with respect to secondary transmissions and do not exempt from liability the activities of others with respect to their own primary or secondary transmissions; or

(4) the secondary transmission is not made by a cable system but is made by a governmental body, or other nonprofit organization, with-

out any purpose of direct or indirect commercial advantage, and without charge to the recipients of the secondary transmission other than assessments necessary to defray the actual and reasonable costs of maintaining and operating the secondary transmission service.

(b) SECONDARY TRANSMISSION OF PRIMARY TRANSMISSION TO CONTROLLED GROUP.—Notwithstanding the provisions of subsections (a) and (c), the secondary transmission to the public of a primary transmission embodying a performance or display of a work is actionable as an act of infringement under section 501, and is fully subject to the remedies provided by sections 502 through 506 and 509, if the primary transmission is not made for reception by the public at large but is controlled and limited to reception by particular members of the public: *Provided,* however, That such secondary transmission is not actionable as an act of infringement if—

    (1)   the primary transmission is made by a broadcast station licensed by the Federal Communications Commission; and

    (2)   the carriage of the signals comprising the secondary transmission is required under the rules, regulations, or authorizations of the Federal Communications Commission; and

    (3)   the signal of the primary transmitter is not altered or changed in any way by the secondary transmitter.

(c) SECONDARY TRANSMISSIONS BY CABLE SYSTEMS.—

    (1)   Subject to the provisions of clauses (2), (3), and (4) of this subsection, secondary transmissions to the public by a cable system of a primary transmission made by a broadcast station licensed by the Federal Communications Commission or by an appropriate governmental authority of Canada or Mexico and embodying a performance or display of a work shall be subject to compulsory licensing upon compliance with the requirements of subsection (d) where the carriage of the signals comprising the secondary transmission is permissible under the rules, regulations, or authorizations of the Federal Communications Commission.

    (2)   Notwithstanding the provisions of clause (1) of this subsection, the willful or repeated secondary transmission to the public by a cable system of a primary transmission made by a broadcast station licensed by the Federal Communications Commission or by an appropriate governmental authority of Canada or Mexico and embodying a performance or display of a work is actionable as an act of infringement under section 501, and is fully subject to the remedies provided by sections 502 through 506 and 509, in the following cases:

        (A)   where the carriage of the signals comprising the secondary transmission is not permissible under the rules, regulations, or authorizations of the Federal Communications Commission; or

        (B)   where the cable system has not recorded the notice specified by subsection (d) and deposited the statement of account and royalty fee required by subsection (d).

Alteration, deletion, or substitution.

Prior consent of advertiser.

    (3)   Notwithstanding the provisions of clause (1) of this subsection and subject to the provisions of subsection (e) of this section, the secondary transmission to the public by a cable system of a primary transmission made by a broadcast station licensed by the Federal Communications Commission or by an appropriate governmental authority of Canada or Mexico and embodying a performance or display of a work is actionable as an act of infringement under section 501, and is fully subject to the remedies provided by sections 502 through 506 and sections 509 and 510, if the content of the particular program in which the performance or display is embodied, or any commercial advertising or station announcements transmitted by the primary transmitter during, or immediately before or after, the transmission of such program, is in any way willfully altered by the cable system through changes, deletions, or additions, except for the alteration, deletion, or substitution of commercial advertisements performed by those engaged in television commercial advertising market

research: *Provided,* That the research company has obtained the prior consent of the advertiser who has purchased the original commercial advertisement, the television station broadcasting that commercial advertisement, and the cable system performing the secondary transmission: *And provided further,* That such commercial alteration, deletion, or substitution is not performed for the purpose of deriving income from the sale of that commercial time.

(4)   Notwithstanding the provisions of clause (1) of this subsection, the secondary transmission to the public by a cable system of a primary transmission made by a broadcast station licensed by an appropriate governmental authority of Canada or Mexico and embodying a performance or display of a work is actionable as an act of infringement under section 501, and is fully subject to the remedies provided by sections 502 through 506 and section 509, if (A) with respect to Canadian signals, the community of the cable system is located more than 150 miles from the United States-Canadian border and is also located south of the forty-second parallel of latitude, or (B) with respect to Mexican signals, the secondary transmission is made by a cable system which received the primary transmission by means other than direct interception of a free space radio wave emitted by such broadcast television station, unless prior to April 15, 1976, such cable system was actually carrying, or was specifically authorized to carry, the signal of such foreign station on the system pursuant to the rules, regulations, or authorizations of the Federal Communications Commission.

(d) Compulsory License for Secondary Transmissions by Cable Systems.—

Notice.

(1)   For any secondary transmission to be subject to compulsory licensing under subsection (c), the cable system shall, at least one month before the date of the commencement of operations of the cable system or within one hundred and eighty days after the enactment of this Act, whichever is later, and thereafter within thirty days after each occasion on which the ownership or control or the signal carriage complement of the cable system changes, record in the Copyright Office a notice including a statement of the identity and address of the person who owns or operates the secondary transmission service or has power to exercise primary control over it, together with the name and location of the primary transmitter or primary transmitters whose signals are regularly carried by the cable system, and thereafter, from time to time, such further information as the Register of Copyrights, after consultation with the Copyright Royalty Tribunal (if and when the Tribunal has been constituted), shall prescribe by regulation to carry out the purpose of this clause.

(2)   A cable system whose secondary transmissions have been subject to compulsory licensing under subsection (c) shall, on a semiannual basis, deposit with the Register of Copyrights, in accordance with requirements that the Register shall, after consultation with the Copyright Royalty Tribunal (if and when the Tribunal has been constituted), prescribe by regulation—

Statement of account.

(A)   a statement of account, covering the six months next preceding, specifying the number of channels on which the cable system made secondary transmissions to its subscribers, the names and locations of all primary transmitters whose transmissions were further transmitted by the cable system, the total number of subscribers, the gross amounts paid to the cable system for the basic service of providing secondary transmissions of primary broadcast transmitters, and such other data as the Register of Copyrights may, after consultation with the Copyright Royalty Tribunal (if and when the Tribunal has been constituted), from time to time prescribe by regulation. Such statement shall also

Nonnetwork television programming.

include a special statement of account covering any nonnetwork television programming that was carried by the cable system in whole or in part beyond the local service area of the primary transmitter, under rules, regulations, or authorizations of the Federal Communications Commission permitting the substitution or addition of signals under certain circumstances, together with logs showing the times, dates, stations, and programs involved in such substituted or added carriage; and

Total royalty fee.

(B) except in the case of a cable system whose royalty is specified in subclause (C) or (D), a total royalty fee for the period covered by the statement, computed on the basis of specified percentages of the gross receipts from subscribers to the cable service during said period for the basic service of providing secondary transmissions of primary broadcast transmitters, as follows:

(i) 0.675 of 1 per centum of such gross receipts for the privilege of further transmitting any nonnetwork programing of a primary transmitter in whole or in part beyond the local service area of such primary transmitter, such amount to be applied against the fee, if any, payable pursuant to paragraphs (ii) through (iv);

(ii) 0.675 of 1 per centum of such gross receipts for the first distant signal equivalent;

(iii) 0.425 of 1 per centum of such gross receipts for each of the second, third, and fourth distant signal equivalents;

(iv) 0.2 of 1 per centum of such gross receipts for the fifth distant signal equivalent and each additional distant signal equivalent thereafter; and

in computing the amounts payable under paragraph (ii) through (iv), above, any fraction of a distant signal equivalent shall be computed at its fractional value and, in the case of any cable system located partly within and partly without the local service area of a primary transmitter, gross receipts shall be limited to those gross receipts derived from subscribers located without the local service area of such primary transmitter; and

(C) if the actual gross receipts paid by subscribers to a cable system for the period covered by the statement for the basic service of providing secondary transmissions of primary broadcast transmitters total $80,000 or less, gross receipts of the cable system for the purpose of this subclause shall be computed by subtracting from such actual gross receipts the amount by which $80,000 exceeds such actual gross receipts, except that in no case shall a cable system's gross receipts be reduced to less than $3,000. The royalty fee payable under this subclause shall be 0.5 of 1 per centum, regardless of the number of distant signal equivalents, if any; and

(D) if the actual gross receipts paid by subscribers to a cable system for the period covered by the statement, for the basic service of providing secondary transmissions of primary broadcast transmitters, are more than $80,000 but less than $160,000, the royalty fee payable under this subclause shall be (i) 0.5 of 1 per centum of any gross receipts up to $80,000; and (ii) 1 per centum of any gross receipts in excess of $80,000 but less than $160,000, regardless of the number of distant signal equivalents, if any.

Statements of account, submittal to Copyright Royalty Tribunal.

(3) The Register of Copyrights shall receive all fees deposited under this section and, after deducting the reasonable costs incurred by the Copyright Office under this section, shall deposit the balance in the Treasury of the United States, in such manner as the Secretary of the Treasury directs. All funds held by the Secretary of the Treasury shall be invested in interest-bearing United States securities for later distribution with interest by the Copyright Royalty Tribunal as provided by this title. The Register shall submit to the Copyright Roy-

alty Tribunal, on a semiannual basis, a compilation of all statements of account covering the relevant six-month period provided by clause (2) of this subsection.

Royalty fees, distribution.

(4) The royalty fees thus deposited shall, in accordance with the procedures provided by clause (5), be distributed to those among the following copyright owners who claim that their works were the subject of secondary transmissions by cable systems during the relevant semiannual period:

(A) any such owner whose work was included in a secondary transmission made by a cable system of a nonnetwork television program in whole or in part beyond the local service area of the primary transmitter; and

(B) any such owner whose work was included in a secondary transmission identified in a special statement of account deposited under clause (2)(A); and

(C) any such owner whose work was included in nonnetwork programing consisting exclusively of aural signals carried by a cable system in whole or in part beyond the local service area of the primary transmitter of such programs.

Distribution procedures.

(5) The royalty fees thus deposited shall be distributed in accordance with the following procedures:

(A) During the month of July in each year, every person claiming to be entitled to compulsory license fees for secondary transmissions shall file a claim with the Copyright Royalty Tribunal, in accordance with requirements that the Tribunal shall prescribe by regulation. Notwithstanding any provisions of the antitrust laws, for purposes of this clause any claimants may agree among themselves as to the proportionate division of compulsory licensing fees among them, may lump their claims together and file them jointly or as a single claim, or may designate a common agent to receive payment on their behalf.

(B) After the first day of August of each year, the Copyright Royalty Tribunal shall determine whether there exists a controversy concerning the distribution of royalty fees. If the Tribunal determines that no such controversy exists, it shall, after deducting its reasonable administrative costs under this section, distribute such fees to the copyright owners entitled, or to their designated agents. If the Tribunal finds the existence of a controversy, it shall, pursuant to chapter 8 of this title, conduct a proceeding to determine the distribution of royalty fees.

(C) During the pendency of any proceeding under this subsection, the Copyright Royalty Tribunal shall withhold from distribution an amount sufficient to satisfy all claims with respect to which a controversy exists, but shall have discretion to proceed to distribute any amounts that are not in controversy.

(e) Nonsimultaneous Secondary Transmissions by Cable Systems.—

(1) Notwithstanding those provisions of the second paragraph of subsection (f) relating to nonsimultaneous secondary transmissions by a cable system, any such transmissions are actionable as an act of infringement under section 501, and are fully subject to the remedies provided by sections 502 through 506 and sections 509 and 510, unless—

(A) the program on the videotape is transmitted no more than one time to the cable system's subscribers; and

(B) the copyrighted program, episode, or motion picture videotape, including the commercials contained within such program, episode, or picture, is transmitted without deletion or editing; and

(C) an owner or officer of the cable system (i) prevents the duplication of the videotape while in the possession of the system, (ii) prevents unauthorized duplication while in the possession of the facility making the videotape for the system if the system owns or controls the facility, or takes reasonable precautions to prevent such duplication if it does not own or control the facility, (iii) takes adequate precautions to prevent duplication while the tape is being transported, and (iv) subject to clause (2), erases or destroys, or causes the erasure or destruction of, the videotape; and

(D) within forty-five days after the end of each calendar quarter, an owner or officer of the cable system executes an affidavit attesting (i) to the steps and precautions taken to prevent duplication of the videotape, and (ii) subject to clause (2), to the erasure or destruction of all videotapes made or used during such quarter; and

(E) such owner or officer places or causes each such affidavit, and affidavits received pursuant to clause (2)(C), to be placed in a file, open to public inspection, at such system's main office in the community where the transmission is made or in the nearest community where such system maintains an office; and

(F) the nonsimultaneous transmission is one that the cable system would be authorized to transmit under the rules, regulations, and authorizations of the Federal Communications Commission in effect at the time of the nonsimultaneous transmission if the transmission had been made simultaneously, except that this subclause shall not apply to inadvertent or accidental transmissions.

(2) If a cable system transfers to any person a videotape of a program nonsimultaneously transmitted by it, such transfer is actionable as an act of infringement under section 501, and is fully subject to the remedies provided by sections 502 through 506 and 509, except that, pursuant to a written, nonprofit contract providing for the equitable sharing of the costs of such videotape and its transfer, a videotape nonsimultaneously transmitted by it, in accordance with clause (1), may be transferred by one cable system in Alaska to another system in Alaska, by one cable system in Hawaii permitted to make such nonsimultaneous transmissions to another such cable system in Hawaii, or by one cable system in Guam, the Northern Mariana Islands, or the Trust Territory of the Pacific Islands, to another cable system in any of those three territories, if—

(A) each such contract is available for public inspection in the offices of the cable systems involved, and a copy of such contract is filed, within thirty days after such contract is entered into, with the Copyright Office (which Office shall make each such contract available for public inspection); and

(B) the cable system to which the videotape is transferred complies with clause (1)(A), (B), (C)(i), (iii), and (iv), and (D) through (F); and

(C) such system provides a copy of the affidavit required to be made in accordance with clause (1)(D) to each cable system making a previous nonsimultaneous transmission of the same videotape.

(3) This subsection shall not be construed to supersede the exclusivity protection provisions of any existing agreement, or any such agreement hereafter entered into, between a cable system and a television broadcast station in the area in which the cable system is located, or a network with which such station is affiliated.

"Videotape." (4) As used in this subsection, the term "videotape", and each of its variant forms, means the reproduction of the images and sounds of a program or programs broadcast by a television broadcast station licensed by the Federal Communications Commission, regardless of the nature of the material objects, such as tapes or films, in which the reproduction is embodied.

(f) DEFINITIONS.—As used in this section, the following terms and their variant forms mean the following:

A "primary transmission" is a transmission made to the public by the transmitting facility whose signals are being received and further transmitted by the secondary transmission service, regardless of where or when the performance or display was first transmitted.

A "secondary transmission" is the further transmitting of a primary transmission simultaneously with the primary transmission, or nonsimultaneously with the primary transmission if by a "cable system" not located in whole or in part within the boundary of the forty-eight contiguous States, Hawaii, or Puerto Rico: *Provided, however,* That a nonsimultaneous further transmission by a cable system located in Hawaii of a primary transmission shall be deemed to be a secondary transmission if the carriage of the television broadcast signal comprising such further transmission is permissible under the rules, regulations, or authorizations of the Federal Communications Commission.

A "cable system" is a facility, located in any State, Territory, Trust Territory, or Possession, that in whole or in part receives signals transmitted or programs broadcast by one or more television broadcast stations licensed by the Federal Communications Commission, and makes secondary transmissions of such signals or programs by wires, cables, or other communications channels to subscribing members of the public who pay for such service. For purposes of determining the royalty fee under subsection (d)(2), two or more cable systems in contiguous communities under common ownership or control or operating from one head-end shall be considered as one system.

The "local service area of a primary transmitter", in the case of a television broadcast station, comprises the area in which such station is entitled to insist upon its signal being retransmitted by a cable system pursuant to the rules, regulations, and authorizations of the Federal Communications Commission in effect on April 15, 1976, or in the case of a television broadcast station licensed by an appropriate governmental authority of Canada or Mexico, the area in which it would be entitled to insist upon its signal being retransmitted if it were a television broadcast station subject to such rules, regulations, and authorizations. The "local service area of a primary transmitter", in the case of a radio broadcast station, comprises the primary service area of such station, pursuant to the rules and regulations of the Federal Communications Commission.

A "distant signal equivalent" is the value assigned to the secondary transmission of any nonnetwork television programing carried by a cable system in whole or in part beyond the local service area of the primary transmitter of such programing. It is computed by assigning a value of one to each independent station and a value of one-quarter to each network station and noncommercial educational station for the nonnetwork programing so carried pursuant to the rules, regulations, and authorizations of the Federal Communications Commission. The foregoing values for independent, network, and noncommercial educational stations are subject, however, to the following exceptions and limitations. Where the rules and regulations of the Federal Communications Commission require a cable system to omit the further transmission of a particular program and such rules and regulations also permit the substitution of another program embodying a performance or display of a work in place of the omitted transmission, or where such rules and regulations in effect on the date of enactment of this Act permit a cable system, at its election, to effect such deletion and substitution of a nonlive program or to carry additional programs not transmitted by primary transmitters within whose local service area the cable system is located, no value shall be assigned for the substituted or additional program; where the rules, regulations, or authorizations of the Federal Communications Commission in effect on the date of enactment of this Act permit a cable system, at its election, to omit the further transmission of a particular program and such rules, regulations, or authorizations also permit the substitution of another program embodying a performance or display of a work in place of the omitted transmission, the value assigned for the substituted or additional program shall be, in the case of a live program, the value of one full distant signal equivalent multiplied by a fraction that has as its numerator the number of days in the year in which such substitution occurs and as its denominator the number of days in the year. In the case of a station carried pursuant to the late-night or specialty programing rules of the Federal Communications Commission, or a station carried on a part-time basis where full-time carriage is not possible because the cable system lacks the activated channel capacity to retransmit on a full-time basis all signals which it is authorized to carry, the values for independent, network, and noncommercial educational stations set forth above, as the case may be, shall be multiplied by a fraction which is equal to the ratio of the broadcast hours of such station carried by the cable system to the total broadcast hours of the station.

A "network station" is a television broadcast station that is owned or operated by, or affiliated with, one or more of the television networks in the United States providing nationwide transmissions, and that transmits a substantial part of the programing supplied by such networks for a substantial part of that station's typical broadcast day.

An "independent station" is a commercial television broadcast other than a network station.

A "noncommercial educational station" is a television station that is a noncommercial educational broadcast station as defined in section 397 of title 47.

47 USC 397.

17 USC 112.

§ 112. Limitations on exclusive rights: Ephemeral recordings

(a) Notwithstanding the provisions of section 106, and except in the case of a motion picture or other audiovisual work, it is not an infringement of copyright for a transmitting organization entitled to transmit to the public a performance or display of a work, under a license or transfer of the copyright or under the limitations on exclusive rights in sound recordings specified by section 114(a), to make no more than one copy or phonorecord of a particular transmission program embodying the performance or display, if—

    (1) the copy or phonorecord is retained and used solely by the transmitting organization that made it, and no further copies or phonorecords are reproduced from it; and

    (2) the copy or phonorecord is used solely for the transmitting organization's own transmissions within its local service area, or for purposes of archival preservation or security; and

    (3) unless preserved exclusively for archival purposes, the copy or phonorecord is destroyed within six months from the date the transmission program was first transmitted to the public.

(b) Notwithstanding the provisions of section 106, it is not an infringement of copyright for a governmental body or other nonprofit organization entitled to transmit a performance or display of a work, under section 110(2) or under the limitations on exclusive rights in sound recordings specified by section 114(a), to make no more than thirty copies or phonorecords of a particular transmission program embodying the performance or display, if—

    (1) no further copies or phonorecords are reproduced from the copies or phonorecords made under this clause; and

    (2) except for one copy or phonorecord that may be preserved exclusively for archival purposes, the copies or phonorecords are destroyed within seven years from the date the transmission program was first transmitted to the public.

(c) Notwithstanding the provisions of section 106, it is not an infringement of copyright for a governmental body or other nonprofit organization to make for distribution no more than one copy or phonorecord, for each transmitting organization specified in clause (2) of this subsection, of a particular transmission program embodying a performance of a nondramatic musical work of a religious nature, or of a sound recording of such a musical work, if—

    (1)   there is no direct or indirect charge for making or distributing any such copies or phonorecords; and

    (2)   none of such copies or phonorecords is used for any performance other than a single transmission to the public by a transmitting organization entitled to transmit to the public a performance of the work under a license or transfer of the copyright; and

    (3)   except for one copy or phonorecord that may be preserved exclusively for archival purposes, the copies or phonorecords are all destroyed within one year from the date the transmission program was first transmitted to the public.

  (d) Notwithstanding the provisions of section 106, it is not an infringement of copyright for a governmental body or other nonprofit organization entitled to transmit a performance of a work under section 110(8) to make no more than ten copies or phonorecords embodying the performance, or to permit the use of any such copy or phonorecord by any governmental body or nonprofit organization entitled to transmit a performance of a work under section 110(8), if—

    (1)   any such copy or phonorecord is retained and used solely by the organization that made it, or by a governmental body or nonprofit organization entitled to transmit a performance of a work under section 110(8), and no further copies or phonorecords are reproduced from it; and

    (2)   any such copy or phonorecord is used solely for transmissions authorized under section 110(8), or for purposes of archival preservation or security; and

    (3)   the governmental body or nonprofit organization permitting any use of any such copy or phonorecord by any governmental body or nonprofit organization under this subsection does not make any charge for such use.

  (e) The transmission program embodied in a copy or phonorecord made under this section is not subject to protection as a derivative work under this title except with the express consent of the owners of copyright in the preexisting works employed in the program.

17 USC 113.

§ 113. Scope of exclusive rights in pictorial, graphic, and sculptural works

  (a) Subject to the provisions of subsections (b) and (c) of this section, the exclusive right to reproduce a copyrighted pictorial, graphic, or sculptural work in copies under section 106 includes the right to reproduce the work in or on any kind of article, whether useful or otherwise.

17 USC 1 *et seq.*

  (b) This title does not afford, to the owner of copyright in a work that portrays a useful article as such, any greater or lesser rights with respect to the making, distribution, or display of the useful article so portrayed than those afforded to such works under the law, whether title 17 or the common law or statutes of a State, in effect on December 31, 1977, as held applicable and construed by a court in an action brought under this title.

  (c) In the case of a work lawfully reproduced in useful articles that have been offered for sale or other distribution to the public, copyright does not include any right to prevent the making, distribution, or display of pictures or photographs of such articles in connection with advertisements or commentaries related to the distribution or display of such articles, or in connection with news reports.

17 USC 114.

§ 114. Scope of exclusive rights in sound recordings

  (a) The exclusive rights of the owner of copyright in a sound recording are limited to the rights specified by clauses (1), (2), and (3) of section 106, and do not include any right of performance under section 106(4).

  (b) The exclusive right of the owner of copyright in a sound recording under clause (1) of section 106 is limited to the right to duplicate the sound recording in the form of phonorecords, or of copies of motion pictures and other audiovisual works, that directly or indirectly recapture the actual sounds fixed in the recording. The exclusive right of the owner of copyright in a sound recording under clause (2) of section 106 is limited to the right to prepare a derivative work in which the actual sounds fixed in the sound recording are rearranged, remixed, or otherwise altered in sequence or quality. The exclusive rights of the owner of copyright in a sound recording under clauses (1) and (2) of section 106 do not extend to the making or duplication of another sound recording that consists entirely of an independent fixation of other sounds, even though such sounds imitate or simulate those in the copyrighted sound recording. The exclusive rights of the owner of copyright in a sound recording under clauses (1), (2), and (3) of section 106 do not apply to sound recordings included in educational television and radio programs (as defined in section 397 of title 47) distributed or transmitted by or through public broadcasting entities (as defined by section 118(g)): *Provided,* That copies or phonorecords of said programs are not commercially distributed by or through public broadcasting entities to the general public.

47 USC 397.

(c) This section does not limit or impair the exclusive right to perform publicly, by means of a phonorecord, any of the works specified by section 106(4).

Report to Congress.

(d) On January 3, 1978, the Register of Copyrights, after consulting with representatives of owners of copyrighted materials, representatives of the broadcasting, recording, motion picture, entertainment industries, and arts organizations, representatives of organized labor and performers of copyrighted materials, shall submit to the Congress a report setting forth recommendations as to whether this section should be amended to provide for performers and copyright owners of copyrighted material any performance rights in such material. The report should describe the status of such rights in foreign countries, the views of major interested parties, and specific legislative or other recommendations, if any.

17 USC 115.

§ 115. Scope of exclusive rights in nondramatic musical works: Compulsory license for making and distributing phonorecords

In the case of nondramatic musical works, the exclusive rights provided by clauses (1) and (3) of section 106, to make and to distribute phonorecords of such works, are subject to compulsory licensing under the conditions specified by this section.

(a) AVAILABILITY AND SCOPE OF COMPULSORY LICENSE.—

(1) When phonorecords of a nondramatic musical work have been distributed to the public in the United States under the authority of the copyright owner, any other person may, by complying with the provisions of this section, obtain a compulsory license to make and distribute phonorecords of the work. A person may obtain a compulsory license only if his or her primary purpose in making phonorecords is to distribute them to the public for private use. A person may not obtain a compulsory license for use of the work in the making of phonorecords duplicating a sound recording fixed by another, unless: (i) such sound recording was fixed lawfully; and (ii) the making of the phonorecords was authorized by the owner of copyright in the sound recording or, if the sound recording was fixed before February 15, 1972, by any person who fixed the sound recording pursuant to an express license from the owner of the copyright in the musical work or pursuant to a valid compulsory license for use of such work in a sound recording.

(2) A compulsory license includes the privilege of making a musical arrangement of the work to the extent necessary to conform it to the style or manner of interpretation of the performance involved, but the arrangement shall not change the basic melody or fundamental character of the work, and shall not be subject to protection as a

derivative work under this title, except with the express consent of the copyright owner.

(b) NOTICE OF INTENTION TO OBTAIN COMPULSORY LICENSE.—

(1) Any person who wishes to obtain a compulsory license under this section shall, before or within thirty days after making, and before distributing any phonorecords of the work, serve notice of intention to do so on the copyright owner. If the registration or other public records of the Copyright Office do not identify the copyright owner and include an address at which notice can be served, it shall be sufficient to file the notice of intention in the Copyright Office. The notice shall comply, in form, content, and manner of service, with requirements that the Register of Copyrights shall prescribe by regulation.

Failure to serve or file notice, penalty.

(2) Failure to serve or file the notice required by clause (1) forecloses the possibility of a compulsory license and, in the absence of a negotiated license, renders the making and distribution of phonorecords actionable as acts of infringement under section 501 and fully subject to the remedies provided by sections 502 through 506 and 509.

(c) ROYALTY PAYABLE UNDER COMPULSORY LICENSE.—

(1) To be entitled to receive royalties under a compulsory license, the copyright owner must be identified in the registration or other public records of the Copyright Office. The owner is entitled to royalties for phonorecords made and distributed after being so identified, but is not entitled to recover for any phonorecords previously made and distributed.

(2) Except as provided by clause (1), the royalty under a compulsory license shall be payable for every phonorecord made and distributed in accordance with the license. For this purpose, a phonorecord is considered "distributed" if the person exercising the compulsory license has voluntarily and permanently parted with its possession. With respect to each work embodied in the phonorecord, the royalty shall be either two and three-fourths cents, or one-half of one cent per minute of playing time or fraction thereof, whichever amount is larger.

(3) A compulsory license under this section includes the right of the maker of a phonorecord of a nondramatic musical work under subsection (a)(1) to distribute or authorize distribution of such phonorecord by rental, lease, or lending (or by acts or practices in the nature of rental, lease, or lending). In addition to any royalty payable under clause (2) and chapter 8 of this title, a royalty shall be payable by the compulsory licensee for every act of distribution of a phonorecord by or in the nature of rental, lease, or lending, by or under the authority of the compulsory licensee. With respect to each nondramatic musical work embodied in the phonorecord, the royalty shall be a proportion of the revenue received by the compulsory licensee from every such act of distribution of the phonorecord under this clause equal to the proportion of the revenue received by the compulsory licensee from distribution of the phonorecord under clause (2) that is payable by a compulsory licensee under that clause and under chapter 8. The Register of Copyrights shall issue regulations to carry out the purpose of this clause.[1]

Royalty payments. Regulations.

(4) Royalty payments shall be made on or before the twentieth day of each month and shall include all royalties for the month next preceding. Each monthly payment shall be made under oath and shall comply with requirements that the Register of Copyrights shall prescribe by regulation. The Register shall also prescribe regulations under which detailed cumulative annual statements of account, cer-

---

[1]The Act of October 4, 1984 (Pub. Law 98-450) which enacted Section 115 (c)(3) provides that its provisions will become ineffective after five years from that date.

tified by a certified public accountant, shall be filed for every compulsory license under this section. The regulations covering both the monthly and the annual statements of account shall prescribe the form, content, and manner of certification with respect to the number of records made and the number of records distributed.

(5) If the copyright owner does not receive the monthly payment and the monthly and annual statements of account when due, the owner may give written notice to the licensee that, unless the default is remedied within thirty days from the date of the notice, the compulsory license will be automatically terminated. Such termination renders either the making or the distribution, or both, of all phonorecords for which the royalty has not been paid, actionable as acts of infringement under section 501 and fully subject to the remedies provided by sections 502 through 506 and 509.

17 USC 116. **§ 116. Scope of exclusive rights in nondramatic musical works: Public performances by means of coin-operated phonorecord players**

(a) LIMITATION ON EXCLUSIVE RIGHT.—In the case of a nondramatic musical work embodied in a phonorecord, the exclusive right under clause (4) of section 106 to perform the work publicly by means of a coin-operated phonorecord player is limited as follows:

(1) The proprietor of the establishment in which the public performance takes place is not liable for infringement with respect to such public performance unless—

(A) such proprietor is the operator of the phonorecord player; or

(B) such proprietor refuses or fails, within one month after receipt by registered or certified mail of a request, at a time during which the certificate required by clause (1)(C) of subsection (b) is not affixed to the phonorecord player, by the copyright owner, to make full disclosure, by registered or certified mail, of the identity of the operator of the phonorecord player.

(2) The operator of the coin-operated phonorecord player may obtain a compulsory license to perform the work publicly on that phonorecord player by filing the application, affixing the certificate, and paying the royalties provided by subsection (b).

(b) RECORDATION OF COIN-OPERATED PHONORECORD PLAYER, AFFIXATION OF CERTIFICATE, AND ROYALTY PAYABLE UNDER COMPULSORY LICENSE.

(1) Any operator who wishes to obtain a compulsory license for the public performance of works on a coin-operated phonorecord player shall fulfill the following requirements:

(A) Before or within one month after such performances are made available on a particular phonorecord player, and during the month of January in each succeeding year that such performances are made available on that particular phonorecord player, the operator shall file in the Copyright Office, in accordance with requirements that the Register of Copyrights, after consultation with the Copyright Royalty Tribunal (if and when the Tribunal has been constituted), shall prescribe by regulation, an application containing the name and address of the operator of the phonorecord player and the manufacturer and serial number or other explicit identification of the phonorecord player, and deposit with the Register of Copyrights a royalty fee for the current calendar year of $8 for that particular phonorecord player. If such performances are made available on a particular phonorecord player for the first time after July 1 of any year, the royalty fee to be deposited for the remainder of that year shall be $4.

(B) Within twenty days of receipt of an application and a royalty fee pursuant to subclause (A), the Register of Copyrights shall issue to the applicant a certificate for the phonorecord player.

(C) On or before March 1 of the year in which the certificate prescribed by subclause (B) of this clause is issued, or within ten days after the date of issue of the certificate, the operator shall affix to the particular phonorecord player, in a position where it can be readily examined by the public, the certificate, issued by the Register of Copyrights under subclause (B), of the latest application made by such operator under subclause (A) of this clause with respect to that phonorecord player.

(2) Failure to file the application, to affix the certificate, or to pay the royalty required by clause (1) of this subsection renders the public performance actionable as an act of infringement under section 501 and fully subject to the remedies provided by sections 502 through 506 and 509.

(c) DISTRIBUTION OF ROYALTIES.—

Statements of account, submittal to Copyright Royalty Tribunal. Claims.

(1) The Register of Copyrights shall receive all fees deposited under this section and, after deducting the reasonable costs incurred by the Copyright Office under this section, shall deposit the balance in the Treasury of the United States, in such manner as the Secretary of the Treasury directs. All funds held by the Secretary of the Treasury shall be invested in interest-bearing United States securities for later distribution with interest by the Copyright Royalty Tribunal as provided by this title. The Register shall submit to the Copyright Royalty Tribunal, on an annual basis, a detailed statement of account covering all fees received for the relevant period provided by subsection (b).

(2) During the month of January in each year, every person claiming to be entitled to compulsory license fees under this section for performances during the preceding twelve-month period shall file a claim with the Copyright Royalty Tribunal, in accordance with requirements that the Tribunal shall prescribe by regulation. Such claim shall include an agreement to accept as final, except as provided in section 810 of this title, the determination of the Copyright Royalty Tribunal in any controversy concerning the distribution of royalty fees deposited under subclause (A) of subsection (b)(1) of this section to which the claimant is a party. Notwithstanding any provisions of the antitrust laws, for purposes of this subsection any claimants may agree among themselves as to the proportionate division of compulsory licensing fees among them, may lump their claims together and file them jointly or as a single claim, or may designate a common agent to receive payment on their behalf.

(3) After the first day of October of each year, the Copyright Royalty Tribunal shall determine whether there exists a controversy concerning the distribution of royalty fees deposited under subclause (A) of subsection (b)(1). If the Tribunal determines that no such controversy exists, it shall, after deducting its reasonable administrative costs under this section, distribute such fees to the copyright owners entitled, or to their designated agents. If it finds that such a controversy exists, it shall, pursuant to chapter 8 of this title, conduct a proceeding to determine the distribution of royalty fees.

Distribution procedures.

(4) The fees to be distributed shall be divided as follows:

(A) to every copyright owner not affiliated with a performing rights society, the pro rata share of the fees to be distributed to which such copyright owner proves entitlement.

(B) to the performing rights societies, the remainder of the fees to be distributed in such pro rata shares as they shall by agreement stipulate among themselves, or, if they fail to agree, the pro rata share to which such performing rights societies prove entitlement.

(C) during the pendency of any proceeding under this section, the Copyright Royalty Tribunal shall withhold from distribution an amount sufficient to satisfy all claims with respect to which a controversy exists, but shall have discretion to proceed to distribute any amounts that are not in controversy.

Regulations.

(5) The Copyright Royalty Tribunal shall promulgate regulations under which persons who can reasonably be expected to have claims may, during the year in which performances take place, without expense to or harassment of operators or proprietors of establishments in which phonorecord players are located, have such access to such establishments and to the phonorecord players located therein and such opportunity to obtain information with respect thereto as may

Civil action.

be reasonably necessary to determine, by sampling procedures or otherwise, the proportion of contribution of the musical works of each such person to the earnings of the phonorecord players for which fees shall have been deposited. Any person who alleges that he or she has been denied the access permitted under the regulations prescribed by the Copyright Royalty Tribunal may bring an action in the United States District Court for the District of Columbia for the cancellation of the compulsory license of the phonorecord player to which such access has been denied, and the court shall have the power to declare the compulsory license thereof invalid from the date of issue thereof.

(d) CRIMINAL PENALTIES.—Any person who knowingly makes a false representation of a material fact in an application filed under clause (1)(A) of subsection (b), or who knowingly alters a certificate issued under clause (1)(B) of subsection (b) or knowingly affixes such a certificate to a phonorecord player other than the one it covers, shall be fined not more than $2,500.

(e) DEFINITIONS.—As used in this section, the following terms and their variant forms mean the following:

(1) A "coin-operated phonorecord player" is a machine or device that—

(A) is employed solely for the performance of nondramatic musical works by means of phonorecords upon being activated by insertion of coins, currency, tokens, or other monetary units or their equivalent;

(B) is located in an establishment making no direct or indirect charge for admission;

(C) is accompanied by a list of the titles of all the musical works available for performance on it, which list is affixed to the phonorecord player or posted in the establishment in a prominent position where it can be readily examined by the public; and

(D) affords a choice of works available for performance and permits the choice to be made by the patrons of the establishment in which it is located.

(2) An "operator" is any person who, alone or jointly with others:

(A) owns a coin-operated phonorecord player; or

(B) has the power to make a coin-operated phonorecord player available for placement in an establishment for purposes of public performance; or

(C) has the power to exercise primary control over the selection of the musical works made available for public performance on a coin-operated phonorecord player.

(3) A "performing rights society" is an association or corporation that licenses the public performance of nondramatic musical works on behalf of the copyright owners, such as the American Society of Composers, Authors and Publishers, Broadcast Music, Inc., and SESAC, Inc.

17 USC 117.

§117. Limitations on exclusive rights: Computer programs

Notwithstanding the provisions of §106, it is not an infringement for the owner of a copy of a computer program to make or authorize the making of another copy or adaptation of that computer program provided:

(1) that such a new copy or adaptation is created as an essential step in the

utilization of the computer program in conjunction with a machine and that it is used in no other manner; or

(2) that such new copy or adaptation is for archival purposes only and that all archival copies are destroyed in the event that continued possession of the computer program should cease to be rightful.

Any exact copies prepared in accordance with the provisions of this section may be leased, sold or otherwise transferred, along with the copy from which such copies were prepared, only as part of the lease, sale or other transfer of all rights in the program. Adaptations so prepared may be transferred only with the authorization of the copyright owner.

17 USC 118.

§118. Scope of exclusive rights: Use of certain works in connection with noncommercial broadcasting

(a) The exclusive rights provided by section 106 shall, with respect to the works specified by subsection (b) and the activities specified by subsection (d), be subject to the conditions and limitations prescribed by this section.

Notice, publication in Federal Register.

(b) Not later than thirty days after the Copyright Royalty Tribunal has been constituted in accordance with section 802, the Chairman of the Tribunal shall cause notice to be published in the Federal Register of the initiation of proceedings for the purpose of determining reasonable terms and rates of royalty payments for the activities specified by subsection (d) with respect to published nondramatic musical works and published pictorial, graphic, and sculptural works during a period beginning as provided in clause (3) of this subsection and ending on December 31, 1982. Copyright owners and public broadcasting entities shall negotiate in good faith and cooperate fully with the Tribunal in an effort to reach reasonable and expeditious results. Notwithstanding any provision of the antitrust laws, any owners of copyright in works specified by this subsection and any public broadcasting entities, respectively, may negotiate and agree upon the terms and rates of royalty payments and the proportionate division of fees paid among various copyright owners, and may designate common agents to negotiate, agree to, pay, or receive payments.

(1) Any owner of copyright in a work specified in this subsection or any public broadcasting entity may, within one hundred and twenty days after publication of the notice specified in this subsection, submit to the Copyright Royalty Tribunal proposed licenses covering such activities with respect to such works. The Copyright Royalty Tribunal shall proceed on the basis of the proposals submitted to it as well as any other relevant information. The Copyright Royalty Tribunal shall permit any interested party to submit information relevant to such proceedings.

(2) License agreements voluntarily negotiated at any time between one or more copyright owners and one or more public broadcasting entities shall be given effect in lieu of any determination by the Tribunal: *Provided,* That copies of such agreements are filed in the Copyright Office within thirty days of execution in accordance with regulations that the Register of Copyrights shall prescribe.

Rates and terms, publication in Federal Register.

(3) Within six months, but not earlier than one hundred and twenty days, from the date of publication of the notice specified in this subsection the Copyright Royalty Tribunal shall make a determination and publish in the Federal Register a schedule of rates and terms which, subject to clause (2) of this subsection, shall be binding on all owners of copyright in works specified by this subsection and public broadcasting entities, regardless of whether or not such copyright owners and public broadcasting entities have submitted proposals to the Tribunal. In establishing such rates and terms the Copyright Royalty Tribunal may consider the rates for comparable circumstances under voluntary license agreements negotiated as provided in clause (2) of this subsection. The Copyright Royalty Tribunal shall also establish requirements by which copyright owners may receive reasonable notice of the use of their works under this section, and under which

records of such use shall be kept by public broadcasting entities.

(4) With respect to the period beginning on the effective date of this title and ending on the date of publication of such rates and terms, this title shall not afford to owners of copyright or public broadcasting entities any greater or lesser rights with respect to the activities specified in subsection (d) as applied to works specified in this subsection than those afforded under the law in effect on December, 31, 1977, as held applicable and construed by a court in an action brought under this title.

(c) The initial procedure specified in subsection (b) shall be repeated and concluded between June 30 and December 31, 1982, and at five-year intervals thereafter, in accordance with regulations that the Copyright Royalty Tribunal shall prescribe.

(d) Subject to the transitional provisions of subsection (b)(4), and to the terms of any voluntary license agreements that have been negotiated as provided by subsection (b)(2), a public broadcasting entity may, upon compliance with the provisions of this section, including the rates and terms established by the Copyright Royalty Tribunal under subsection (b)(3), engage in the following activities with respect to published nondramatic musical works and published pictorial, graphic, and sculptural works:

(1) performance or display of a work by or in the course of a transmission made by a noncommercial educational broadcast station referred to in subsection (g); and

(2) production of a transmission program, reproduction of copies or phonorecords of such a transmission program, and distribution of such copies or phonorecords, where such production, reproduction, or distribution is made by a nonprofit institution or organization solely for the purpose of transmissions specified in clause (1); and

(3) the making of reproductions by a governmental body or a nonprofit institution of a transmission program simultaneously with its transmission as specified in clause (1), and the performance or display of the contents of such program under the conditions specified by clause (1) of section 110, but only if the reproductions are used for performances or displays for a period of no more than seven days from the date of the transmission specified in clause (1), and are destroyed before or at the end of such period. No person supplying, in accordance with clause (2), a reproduction of a transmission program to governmental bodies or nonprofit institutions under this clause shall have any liability as a result of failure of such body or institution to destroy such reproduction: *Provided,* That it shall have notified such body or institution of the requirement for such destruction pursuant to this clause: *And provided further,* That if such body or institution itself fails to destroy such reproduction it shall be deemed to have infringed.

(e) Except as expressly provided in this subsection, this section shall have no applicability to works other than those specified in subsection (b).

(1) Owners of copyright in nondramatic literary works and public broadcasting entities may, during the course of voluntary negotiations, agree among themselves, respectively, as to the terms and rates of royalty payments without liability under the antitrust laws. Any such terms and rates of royalty payments shall be effective upon filing in the Copyright Office, in accordance with regulations that the Register of Copyrights shall prescribe.

Report to Congress.

(2) On January 3, 1980, the Register of Copyrights, after consulting with authors and other owners of copyright in nondramatic literary works and their representatives, and with public broadcasting entities and their representatives, shall submit to the Congress a report setting forth the extent to which voluntary licensing arrangements have been reached with respect to the use of nondramatic literary works by such broadcast stations. The report should also describe any problems that may have arisen, and present legislative or other recom-

mendations, if warranted.

(f)   Nothing in this section shall be construed to permit, beyond the limits of fair use as provided by section 107, the unauthorized dramatization of a nondramatic musical work, the production of a transmission program drawn to any substantial extent from a published compilation of pictorial, graphic, or sculptural works, or the unauthorized use of any portion of an audiovisual work.

(g)   As used in this section, the term "public broadcasting entity" means a noncommercial educational broadcast station as defined in section 397 of title 47 and any nonprofit institution or organization engaged in the activities described in clause (2) of subsection (d).

Chapter 2.—Copyright ownership and Transfer

Sec.
201. Ownership of copyright.
202. Ownership of copyright as distinct from ownership of material object.
203. Termination of transfers and licenses granted by the author.
204. Execution of transfers of copyright ownership.
205. Recordation of transfers and other documents.

17 USC 201.

§201. Ownership of copyright

(a)   INITIAL OWNERSHIP.—Copyright in a work protected under this title vests initially in the author or authors of the work. The authors of a joint work are coowners of copyright in the work.

(b)   WORKS MADE FOR HIRE.—In the case of a work made for hire, the employer or other person for whom the work was prepared is considered the author for purposes of this title, and, unless the parties have expressly agreed otherwise in a written instrument signed by them, owns all of the rights comprised in the copyright.

(c)   CONTRIBUTIONS TO COLLECTIVE WORKS.—Copyright in each separate contribution to a collective work is distinct from copyright in the collective work as a whole, and vests initially in the author of the contribution. In the absence of an express transfer of the copyright or of any rights under it, the owner of copyright in the collective work is presumed to have acquired only the privilege of reproducing and distributing the contribution as part of that particular collective work, any revision of that collective work, and any later collective work in the same series.

(d)   TRANSFER OF OWNERSHIP.—

(1)   The ownership of a copyright may be transferred in whole or in part by any means of conveyance or by operation of law, and may be bequeathed by will or pass as personal property by the applicable laws of intestate succession.

(2)   Any of the exclusive rights comprised in a copyright, including any subdivision of any of the rights specified by section 106, may be transferred as provided by clause (1) and owned separately. The owner of any particular exclusive right is entitled, to the extent of that right, to all of the protection and remedies accorded to the copyright owner by this title.

(e)   INVOLUNTARY TRANSFER.—When an individual author's ownership of a copyright, or of any of the exclusive rights under a copyright, has not previously been transferred voluntarily by that individual author, no action by any governmental body or other official or organization purporting to seize, expropriate, transfer, or exercise rights of ownership with respect to the copyright, or any of the exclusive rights under a copyright, shall be given effect under this title, except as provided in title 11.

17 USC 202.

§202. Ownership of copyright as distinct from ownership of material object

Ownership of a copyright, or of any of the exclusive rights under a copyright, is distinct from ownership of any material object in which the work is embodied. Transfer of ownership of any material object, including the copy or phonorecord in which the work is first fixed, does not of itself convey any rights in the copyrighted work embodied in the object; nor, in the absence of an agreement, does transfer of ownership of a copyright or of any exclusive rights under a copyright convey property rights in any material object.

17 USC 203.

§203. Termination of transfers and licenses granted by the author

(a) CONDITIONS FOR TERMINATIONS.—In the case of any work other than a work made for hire, the exclusive or nonexclusive grant of a transfer or license of copyright or of any right under a copyright, executed by the author on or after January 1, 1978, otherwise than by will, is subject to termination under the following conditions:

(1) In the case of a grant executed by one author, termination of the grant may be effected by that author or, if the author is dead, by the person or persons who, under clause (2) of this subsection, own and are entitled to exercise a total of more than one-half of that author's termination interest. In the case of a grant executed by two or more authors of a joint work, termination of the grant may be effected by a majority of the authors who executed it; if any of such authors is dead, the termination interest of any such author may be exercised as a unit by the person or persons who, under clause (2) of this subsection, own and are entitled to exercise a total of more than one-half of that author's interest.

(2) Where an author is dead, his or her termination interest is owned, and may be exercised, by his widow or her widower and his or her children or grandchildren as follows:

(A) the widow or widower owns the author's entire termination interest unless there are any surviving children or grandchildren of the author, in which case the widow or widower owns one-half of the author's interest;

(B) the author's surviving children, and the surviving children of any dead child of the author, own the author's entire termination interest unless there is a widow or widower, in which case the ownership of one-half of the author's interest is divided among them;

(C) the rights of the author's children and grandchildren are in all cases divided among them and exercised on a per stirpes basis according to the number of such author's children represented; the share of the children of a dead child in a termination interest can be exercised only by the action of a majority of them.

(3) Termination of the grant may be effected at any time during a period of five years beginning at the end of thirty-five years from the date of execution of the grant; or, if the grant covers the right of publication of the work, the period begins at the end of thirty-five years from the date of publication of the work under the grant or at the end of forty years from the date of execution of the grant, whichever term ends earlier.

Notice.

(4) The termination shall be effected by serving an advance notice in writing, signed by the number and proportion of owners of termination interests required under clauses (1) and (2) of this subsection, or by their duly authorized agents, upon the grantee or the grantee's successor in title.

(A) The notice shall state the effective date of the termination, which shall fall within the five-year period specified by clause (3) of this subsection, and the notice shall be served not less than two or more than ten years before that date. A copy of the notice shall be recorded in the Copyright Office before the effective date of termination, as a condition to its taking effect.

(B) The notice shall comply, in form, content, and manner of service, with requirements that the Register of Copyrights shall prescribe by regulation.

(5) Termination of the grant may be effected notwithstanding any agree-

ment to the contrary, including an agreement to make a will or to make any future grant.

(b) EFFECT OF TERMINATION.—Upon the effective date of termination, all rights under this title that were covered by the terminated grants revert to the author, authors, and other persons owning termination interests under clauses (1) and (2) of subsection (a), including those owners who did not join in signing the notice of termination under clause (4) of subsection (a), but with the following limitations:

Limitations.

(1)   A derivative work prepared under authority of the grant before its termination may continue to be utilized under the terms of the grant after its termination, but this privilege does not extend to the preparation after the termination of other derivative works based upon the copyrighted work covered by the terminated grant.

(2)   The future rights that will revert upon termination of the grant become vested on the date the notice of termination has been served as provided by clause (4) of subsection (a). The rights vest in the author, authors, and other persons named in, and in the proportionate shares provided by, clauses (1) and (2) of subsection (a).

(3)   Subject to the provisions of clause (4) of this subsection, a further grant, or agreement to make a further grant, of any right covered by a terminated grant is valid only if it is signed by the same number and proportion of the owners, in whom the right has vested under clause (2) of this subsection, as are required to terminate the grant under clauses (1) and (2) of subsection (a). Such further grant or agreement is effective with respect to all of the persons in whom the right it covers has vested under clause (2) of this subsection, including those who did not join in signing it. If any person dies after rights under a terminated grant have vested in him or her, that person's legal representatives, legatees, or heirs at law represent him or her for purposes of this clause.

(4)   A further grant, or agreement to make a further grant, of any right covered by a terminated grant is valid only if it is made after the effective date of the termination. As an exception, however, an agreement for such further grant may be made between the persons provided by clause (3) of this subsection and the original grantee or such grantee's successor in title, after the notice of termination has been served as provided by clause (4) of subsection (a).

(5)   Termination of a grant under this section affects only those rights covered by the grants that arise under this title, and in no way affects rights arising under any other Federal, State, or foreign laws.

(6)   Unless and until termination is effected under this section, the grant, if it does not provide otherwise, continues in effect for the term of copyright provided by this title.

17 USC 204.   **§204. Execution of transfers of copyright ownership**

(a)   A transfer of copyright ownership, other than by operation of law, is not valid unless an instrument of conveyance, or a note or memorandum of the transfer, is in writing and signed by the owner of the rights conveyed or such owner's duly authorized agent.

(b)   A certificate of acknowledgement is not required for the validity of a transfer, but is prima facie evidence of the execution of the transfer if—

(1)   in the case of a transfer executed in the United States, the certificate is issued by a person authorized to administer oaths within the United States; or

(2)   in the case of a transfer executed in a foreign country, the certificate is issued by a diplomatic or consular officer of the United States, or by a person authorized to administer oaths whose authority is proved by a certificate of such an officer.

17 USC 205.   **§205. Recordation of transfers and other documents**

(a)   CONDITIONS FOR RECORDATION.—Any transfer of copyright ownership or other document pertaining to a copyright may be recorded in the Copyright Office if the document filed for recordation bears the actual signature of the person who executed it, or if it is accompanied by a sworn or official certification that it is a true copy of the original, signed document.

(b) CERTIFICATE OF RECORDATION.—The Register of Copyrights shall, upon receipt of a document as provided by subsection (a) and of the fee provided by section 708, record the document and return it with a certificate of recordation.

(c) RECORDATION AS CONSTRUCTIVE NOTICE.—Recordation of a document in the Copyright Office gives all persons constructive notice of the facts stated in the recorded document, but only if—

    (1) the document, or material attached to it, specifically identifies the work to which it pertains so that, after the document is indexed by the Register of Copyrights, it would be revealed by a reasonable search under the title or registration number of the work; and

    (2) registration has been made for the work.

(d) RECORDATION AS PREREQUISITE TO INFRINGEMENT SUIT.—No person claiming by virtue of a transfer to be the owner of copyright or of any exclusive right under a copyright is entitled to institute an infringement action under this title until the instrument of transfer under which such person claims has been recorded in the Copyright Office, but suit may be instituted after such recordation on a cause of action that arose before recordation.

(e) PRIORITY BETWEEN CONFLICTING TRANSFERS.—As between two conflicting transfers, the one executed first prevails if it is recorded, in the manner required to give constructive notice under subsection (c), within one month after its execution in the United States or within two months after its execution outside the United States, or at any time before recordation in such manner of the later transfer. Otherwise the later transfer prevails if recorded first in such manner, and if taken in good faith, for valuable consideration or on the basis of a binding promise to pay royalties, and without notice of the earlier transfer.

(f) PRIORITY BETWEEN CONFLICTING TRANSFER OF OWNERSHIP AND NON-EXCLUSIVE LICENSE.—A nonexclusive license, whether recorded or not, prevails over a conflicting transfer of copyright ownership if the license is evidenced by a written instrument signed by the owner of the rights licensed or such owner's duly authorized agent, and if—

    (1) the license was taken before execution of the transfer; or

    (2) the license was taken in good faith before recordation of the transfer and without notice of it.

Chapter 3.—Duration of Copyright

Sec.

17 USC 301.

§301. Preemption with respect to other laws

(a) On and after January 1, 1978, all legal or equitable rights that are equivalent to any of the exclusive rights within the general scope of copyright as specified by section 106 in works of authorship that are fixed in a tangible medium of expression and come within the subject matter of copyright as specified by sections 102 and 103, whether created before or after that date and whether published or unpublished, are governed exclusively by this title. Thereafter, no person is entitled to any such right or equivalent right in any such work under the common law or statutes of any State.

(b) Nothing in this title annuls or limits any rights or remedies under the common law or statutes of any State with respect to—

(1) subject matter that does not come within the subject matter of copyright as specified by sections 102 and 103, including works of authorship not fixed in any tangible medium of expression; or

(2) any cause of action arising from undertakings commenced before January 1, 1978; or

(3) activities violating legal or equitable rights that are not equivalent to any of the exclusive rights within the general scope of copyright as specified by section 106.

(c) With respect to sound recordings fixed before February 15, 1972, any rights or remedies under the common law or statutes of any State shall not be annulled or limited by this title until February 15, 2047. The preemptive provisions of subsection (a) shall apply to any such rights and remedies pertaining to any cause of action arising from undertakings commenced on and after February 15, 2047. Notwithstanding the provisions of section 303, no sound recording fixed before February 15, 1972, shall be subject to copyright under this title before, on, or after February 15, 2047.

(d) Nothing in this title annuls or limits any rights or remedies under any other Federal statute.

17 USC 302.   **§302. Duration of copyright: Works created on or after January 1, 1978**

(a) IN GENERAL.—Copyright in a work created on or after January 1, 1978, subsists from its creation and, except as provided by the following subsections, endures for a term consisting of the life of the author and fifty years after the author's death.

(b) JOINT WORKS.—In the case of a joint work prepared by two or more authors who did not work for hire, the copyright endures for a term consisting of the life of the last surviving author and fifty years after such last surviving author's death.

(c) ANONYMOUS WORKS, PSEUDONYMOUS WORKS, AND WORKS MADE FOR HIRE.—In the case of an anonymous work, a pseudonymous work, or a work made for hire, the copyright endures for a term of seventy-five years from the year of its first publication, or a term of one hundred years from the year of its creation, whichever expires first. If, before the end of such term, the identity of one or more of the authors of an anonymous or pseudonymous work is revealed in the records of a registration made for that work under subsections (a) or (d) of section 408, or in the records provided by this subsection, the copyright in the work endures for the term specified by subsection (a) or (b), based on the life of the author or authors whose identity has been revealed. Any person having an interest in the copyright in an anonymous or pseudonymous work may at any time record, in records to be maintained by the Copyright Office for that purpose, a statement identifying one or more authors of the work; the statement shall also identify the person filing it, the nature of that person's interest, the source of the information recorded, and the particular work affected, and shall comply in form and content with requirements that the Register of Copyrights shall prescribe by regulation.

(d) RECORDS RELATING TO DEATH OF AUTHORS.—Any person having an interest in a copyright may at any time record in the Copyright Office a statement of the date of death of the author of the copyrighted work, or a statement that the author is still living on a particular date. The statement shall identify the person filing it, the nature of that person's interest, and the source of the information recorded, and shall comply in form and content with requirements that the Register of Copyrights shall prescribe by regulation. The Register shall maintain current records of information relating to the death of authors of copyrighted works, based on such recorded statements and, to the extent the Register considers practicable, on data contained in any of the records of the Copyright Office or in other reference sources.

Record-
keeping.

(e) PRESUMPTION AS TO AUTHOR'S DEATH.—After a period of seventy-five years from the year of first publication of a work, or a period of one hundred years from the year of its creation, whichever expires first, any person who obtains from the Copyright Office a certified report that the records provided by subsection (d) disclose nothing to indicate that the author of the work is living, or died less than fifty years before, is entitled to the benefit of a presumption that the author has been dead for at least fifty years. Reliance in good faith upon this presumption shall be a complete defense to any action for infringement under this title.

17 USC 303.

§303. Duration of copyright: Works created but not published or copyrighted before January 1, 1978

Copyright in a work created before January 1, 1978, but not theretofore in the public domain or copyrighted, subsists from January 1, 1978, and endures for the term provided by section 302. In no case, however, shall the term of copyright in such a work expire before December 31, 2002; and, if the work is published on or before December 31, 2002, the term of copyright shall not expire before December 31, 2027.

17 USC 304.

§304. Duration of copyright: Subsisting copyrights

(a) COPYRIGHTS IN THEIR FIRST TERM ON JANUARY 1, 1978.—Any copyright, the first term of which is subsisting on January 1, 1978, shall endure for twenty-eight years from the date it was originally secured: *Provided,* That in the case of any posthumous work or of any periodical, cyclopedic, or other composite work upon which the copyright was originally secured by the proprietor thereof, or of any work copyrighted by a corporate body (otherwise than as assignee or licensee of the individual author) or by an employer for whom such work is made for hire, the proprietor of such copyright shall be entitled to a renewal and extension of the copyright in such work for the further term of forty-seven years when application for such renewal and extension shall have been made to the Copyright Office and duly registered therein within one year prior to the expiration of the original term of copyright: *And provided further,* That in the case of any other copyrighted work, including a contribution by an individual author to a periodical or to a cyclopedic or other composite work, the author of such work, if still living, or the widow, widower, or children of the author, if the author be not living, or if such author, widow, widower, or children be not living, then the author's executors, or in the absence of a will, his or her next of kin shall be entitled to a renewal and extension of the copyright in such work for a further term of forty-seven years when application for such renewal and extension shall have been made to the Copyright Office and duly registered therein within one year prior to the expiration of the original term of copyright: *And provided further,* That in default of the registration of such application for renewal and extension, the copyright in any work shall terminate at the expiration of twenty-eight years from the date copyright was originally secured.

(b) COPYRIGHTS IN THEIR RENEWAL TERM OR REGISTERED FOR RENEWAL BEFORE JANUARY 1, 1978.—The duration of any copyright, the renewal term of which is subsisting at any time between December 31, 1976, and December 31, 1977, inclusive, or for which renewal registration is made between December 31, 1976, and December 31, 1977, inclusive, is extended to endure for a term of seventy-five years from the date copyright was originally secured.

(c) TERMINATION OF TRANSFERS AND LICENSES COVERING EXTENDED RENEWAL TERM.—In the case of any copyright subsisting in either its first or renewal term on January 1, 1978, other than a copyright in a work made for hire, the exclusive or nonexclusive grant of a transfer or license of the renewal copyright or any right under it, executed before January 1, 1978, by any of the persons designated by the second proviso of subsection (a) of this section, otherwise than by will, is subject to termination under the following conditions:

(1) In the case of a grant executed by a person or persons other than the author, termination of the grant may be effected by the surviving person or persons who executed it. In the case of a grant executed

by one or more of the authors of the work, termination of the grant may be effected, to the extent of a particular author's share in the ownership of the renewal copyright, by the author who executed it or, if such author is dead, by the person or persons who, under clause (2) of this subsection, own and are entitled to exercise a total of more than one-half of that author's termination interest.

(2) Where an author is dead, his or her termination interest is owned, and may be exercised, by his widow or her widower and his or her children or grandchildren as follows:

    (A) the widow or widower owns the author's entire termination interest unless there are any surviving children or grandchildren of the author, in which case the widow or widower owns one-half of the author's interest;

    (B) the author's surviving children, and the surviving children of any dead child of the author, own the author's entire termination interest unless there is a widow or widower, in which case the ownership of one-half of the author's interest is divided among them;

    (C) the rights of the author's children and grandchildren are in all cases divided among them and exercised on a per stirpes basis according to the number of such author's children represented; the share of the children of a dead child in a termination interest can be exercised only by the action of a majority of them.

(3) Termination of the grant may be effected at any time during a period of five years beginning at the end of fifty-six years from the date copyright was originally secured, or beginning on January 1, 1978, whichever is later.

Advance notice.

(4) The termination shall be effected by serving an advance notice in writing upon the grantee or the grantee's successor in title. In the case of a grant executed by a person or persons other than the author, the notice shall be signed by all of those entitled to terminate the grant under clause (1) of this subsection, or by their duly authorized agents. In the case of a grant executed by one or more of the authors of the work, the notice as to any one author's share shall be signed by that author or his or her duly authorized agent or, if that author is dead, by the number and proportion of the owners of his or her termination interest required under clauses (1) and (2) of this subsection, or by their duly authorized agents.

    (A) The notice shall state the effective date of the termination, which shall fall within the five-year period specified by clause (3) of this subsection, and the notice shall be served not less than two or more than ten years before that date. A copy of the notice shall be recorded in the Copyright Office before the effective date of termination, as a condition to its taking effect.

    (B) The notice shall comply, in form, content, and manner of service, with requirements that the Register of Copyrights shall prescribe by regulation.

(5) Termination of the grant may be effected notwithstanding any agreement to the contrary, including an agreement to make a will or to make any future grant.

Reversion.

(6) In the case of a grant executed by a person or persons other than the author, all rights under this title that were covered by the terminated grant revert, upon the effective date of termination, to all of those entitled to terminate the grant under clause (1) of this subsection. In the case of a grant executed by one or more of the authors of the work, all of a particular author's rights under this title that were covered by the terminated grant revert, upon the effective date of termination, to that author or, if that author is dead, to the persons owning his or her termination interest under clause (2) of this subsection, including those owners who did not join in signing the notice of termination under clause (4) of this subsection. In all cases the

Limitations.

reversion of rights is subject to the following limitations:

(A) A derivative work prepared under authority of the grant before its termination may continue to be utilized under the terms of the grant after its termination, but this privilege does not extend to the preparation after the termination of other derivative works based upon the copyrighted work covered by the terminated grant.

(B) The future rights that will revert upon termination of the grant become vested on the date the notice of termination has been served as provided by clause (4) of this subsection.

(C) Where the author's rights revert to two or more persons under clause (2) of this subsection, they shall vest in those persons in the proportionate shares provided by that clause. In such a case, and subject to the provisions of subclause (D) of this clause, a further grant, or agreement to make a further grant, of a particular author's share with respect to any right covered by a terminated grant is valid only if it is signed by the same number and proportion of the owners, in whom the right has vested under this clause, as are required to terminate the grant under clause (2) of this subsection. Such further grant or agreement is effective with respect to all of the persons in whom the right it covers has vested under this subclause, including those who did not join in signing it. If any person dies after rights under a terminated grant have vested in him or her, that person's legal representatives, legatees, or heirs at law represent him or her for purposes of this subclause.

(D) A further grant, or agreement to make a further grant, of any right covered by a terminated grant is valid only if it is made after the effective date of the termination. As an exception, however, an agreement for such a further grant may be made between the author or any of the persons provided by the first sentence of clause (6) of this subsection, or between the persons provided by subclause (C) of this clause, and the original grantee or such grantee's successor in title, after the notice of termination has been served as provided by clause (4) of this subsection.

(E) Termination of a grant under this subsection affects only those rights covered by the grant that arise under this title, and in no way affects rights arising under any other Federal, State, or foreign laws.

(F) Unless and until termination is effected under this subsection, the grant, if it does not provide otherwise, continues in effect for the remainder of the extended renewal term.

17 USC 305.

§305. Duration of copyright: Terminal date

All terms of copyright provided by sections 302 through 304 run to the end of the calendar year in which they would otherwise expire.

Chapter 4.—Copyright Notice, Deposit, and Registration

Sec.

410. Registration of claim and issuance of certificate.
411. Registration as prerequisite to infringement suit.
412. Registration as prerequisite to certain remedies for infringement.

17 USC 401.

§401. Notice of copyright: Visually perceptible copies

(a) GENERAL REQUIREMENT.—Whenever a work protected under this title is published in the United States or elsewhere by authority of the copyright owner, a notice of copyright as provided by this section shall be placed on all publicly distributed copies from which the work can be visually perceived, either directly or with the aid of a machine or device.

(b) FORM OF NOTICE.—The notice appearing on the copies shall consist of the following three elements:
   (1) the symbol © (the letter C in a circle), or the word "Copyright", or the abbreviation "Copr."; and
   (2) the year of first publication of the work; in the case of compilations or derivative works incorporating previously published material, the year date of first publication of the compilation or derivative work is sufficient. The year date may be omitted where a pictorial, graphic, or sculptural work, with accompanying text matter, if any, is reproduced in or on greeting cards, postcards, stationery, jewelry, dolls, toys, or any useful articles; and
   (3) the name of the owner of copyright in the work, or an abbreviation by which the name can be recognized, or a generally known alternative designation of the owner.

(c) POSITION OF NOTICE.—The notice shall be affixed to the copies in such manner and location as to give reasonable notice of the claim of copyright. The Register of Copyrights shall prescribe by regulation, as examples, specific methods of affixation and positions of the notice on various types of works that will satisfy this requirement, but these specifications shall not be considered exhaustive.

17 USC 402.

§402. Notice of copyright: Phonorecords of sound recordings

(a) GENERAL REQUIREMENT.—Whenever a sound recording protected under this title is published in the United States or elsewhere by authority of the copyright owner, a notice of copyright as provided by this section shall be placed on all publicly distributed phonorecords of the sound recording.

(b) FORM OF NOTICE.—The notice appearing on the phonorecords shall consist of the following three elements:
   (1) the symbol ℗ (the letter P in a circle); and
   (2) the year of first publication of the sound recording; and
   (3) the name of the owner of copyright in the sound recording, or an abbreviation by which the name can be recognized, or a generally known alternative designation of the owner; if the producer of the sound recording is named on the phonorecord labels or containers, and if no other name appears in conjunction with the notice, the producer's name shall be considered a part of the notice.

(c) POSITION OF NOTICE.—The notice shall be placed on the surface of the phonorecord, or on the phonorecord label or container, in such manner and location as to give reasonable notice of the claim of copyright.

17 USC 403.

§403. Notice of copyright: Publications incorporating United States Government works

Whenever a work is published in copies or phonorecords consisting preponderantly of one or more works of the United States Government, the notice of copyright provided by sections 401 or 402 shall also include a statement identifying, either affirmatively or negatively, those portions of the copies or phonorecords embodying any work or works protected under this title.

17 USC 404.

§404. Notice of copyright: Contributions to collective works

(a) A separate contribution to a collective work may bear its own notice of copyright, as provided by sections 401 through 403. However, a single notice applicable to the collective work as a whole is sufficient to satisfy the requirements of sections 401 through 403 with respect to the separate contributions it contains (not including advertisements inserted on behalf of persons other than the owner of copyright in the collective work), regardless of the ownership of copyright in the contributions and whether or not they have been previously published.

(b) Where the person named in a single notice applicable to a collective work as a whole is not the owner of copyright in a separate contribution that does not bear its own notice, the case is governed by the provisions of section 406(a).

17 USC 405.   §405. Notice of copyright: Omission of notice

(a) EFFECT OF OMISSION ON COPYRIGHT.—The omission of the copyright notice prescribed by sections 401 through 403 from copies or phonorecords publicly distributed by authority of the copyright owner does not invalidate the copyright in a work if—

　(1)　the notice has been omitted from no more than a relatively small number of copies or phonorecords distributed to the public; or

　(2)　registration for the work has been made before or is made within five years after the publication without notice, and a reasonable effort is made to add notice to all copies or phonorecords that are distributed to the public in the United States after the omission has been discovered; or

　(3)　the notice has been omitted in violation of an express requirement in writing that, as a condition of the copyright owner's authorization of the public distribution of copies or phonoecords, they bear the prescribed notice.

(b) EFFECT OF OMISSION ON INNOCENT INFRINGERS.—Any person who innocently infringes a copyright, in reliance upon an authorized copy or phonorecord from which the copyright notice has been omitted, incurs no liability for actual or statutory damages under section 504 for any infringing acts committed before receiving actual notice that registration for the work has been made under section 408, if such person proves that he or she was misled by the omission of notice. In a suit for infringement in such a case the court may allow or disallow recovery of any of the infringer's profits attributable to the infringement, and may enjoin the continuation of the infringing undertaking or may require, as a condition or permitting the continuation of the infringing undertaking, that the infringer pay the copyright owner a reasonable license fee in an amount and on terms fixed by the court.

(c) REMOVAL OF NOTICE.—Protection under this title is not affected by the removal, destruction, or obliteration of the notice, without the authorization of the copyright owner, from any publicly distributed copies or phonorecords.

17 USC 406.   §406. Notice of copyright: Error in name or date

(a) ERROR IN NAME.—Where the person named in the copyright notice on copies or phonorecords publicly distributed by authority of the copyright owner is not the owner of copyright, the validity and ownership of the copyright are not affected. In such a case, however, any person who innocently begins an undertaking that infringes the copyright has a complete defense to any action for such infringement if such person proves that he or she was misled by the notice and began the undertaking in good faith under a purported transfer or license from the person named therein, unless before the undertaking was begun—

　(1)　registration for the work had been made in the name of the owner of copyright; or

　(2)　a document executed by the person named in the notice and showing the ownership of the copyright had been recorded.

The person named in the notice is liable to account to the copyright owner for all receipts from transfers or licenses purportedly made under the copyright by the person named in the notice.

(b) ERROR IN DATE.—When the year date in the notice on copies or phonorecords distributed by authority of the copyright owner is earlier than the year in which publication first occurred, any period computed from the year of first publication under section 302 is to be computed from the year in the notice. Where the year date is more than one year later than the year in which publication first occurred, the work is considered to have been published without any notice and is governed by the provisions of section 405.

(c) OMISSION OF NAME OR DATE.—Where copies or phonorecords publicly distributed by authority of the copyright owner contain no name or no date that could reasonably be considered a part of the notice, the work is considered to have been published without any notice and is governed by the provisions of section 405.

17 USC 407. §407. **Deposit of copies or phonorecords for Library of Congress**

(a) Except as provided by subsection (c), and subject to the provisions of subsection (e), the owner of copyright or of the exclusive right of publication in a work published with notice of copyright in the United States shall deposit, within three months after the date of such publication—

(1) two complete copies of the best edition; or

(2) if the work is a sound recording, two complete phonorecords of the best edition, together with any printed or other visually perceptible material published with such phonorecords.

Neither the deposit requirements of this subsection nor the acquisition provisions of subsection (e) are conditions of copyright protection.

(b) The required copies or phonorecords shall be deposited in the Copyright Office for the use or disposition of the Library of Congress. The Register of Copyrights shall, when requested by the depositor and upon payment of the fee prescribed by section 708, issue a receipt for the deposit.

Exemption.

(c) The Register of Copyrights may by regulation exempt any categories of material from the deposit requirements of this section, or require deposit of only one copy or phonorecord with respect to any categories. Such regulations shall provide either for complete exemption from the deposit requirements of this section, or for alternative forms of deposit aimed at providing a satisfactory archival record of a work without imposing practical or financial hardships on the depositor, where the individual author is the owner of copyright in a pictorial, graphic, or sculptural work and (i) less than five copies of the work have been published, or (ii) the work has been published in a limited edition consisting of numbered copies, the monetary value of which would make the mandatory deposit of two copies of the best edition of the work burdensome, unfair, or unreasonable.

(d) At any time after publication of a work as provided by subsection (a), the Register of Copyrights may make written demand for the required deposit on any of the persons obligated to make the deposit under subsection (a).

Penalties.

Unless deposit is made within three months after the demand is received, the person or persons on whom the demand was made are liable—

(1) to a fine of not more than $250 for each work; and

(2) to pay into a specially designated fund in the Library of Congress the total retail price of the copies or phonorecords demanded, or, if no retail price has been fixed, the reasonable cost of the Library of Congress of acquiring them; and

(3) to pay a fine of $2,500, in addition to any fine or liability imposed under clauses (1) and (2), if such person willfully or repeatedly fails or refuses to comply with such a demand.

Regulations.

(e) With respect to transmission programs that have been fixed and transmitted to the public in the United States but have not been published, the Register of Copyrights shall, after consulting with the Librarian of Congress and other interested organizations and officials, establish regulations governing the acquisition, through deposit or otherwise, of copies or pho-

norecords of such programs for the collections of the Library of Congress.
(1) The Librarian of Congress shall be permitted, under the standards and conditions set forth in such regulations, to make a fixation of a transmission program directly from a transmission to the public, and to reproduce one copy or phonorecord from such fixation for archival purposes.
(2) Such regulations shall also provide standards and procedures by which the Register of Copyrights may make written demand, upon the owner of the right of transmission in the United States, for the deposit of a copy or phonorecord of a specific transmission program. Such deposit may, at the option of the owner of the right of transmission in the United States, be accomplished by gift, by loan for purposes of reproduction, or by sale at a price not to exceed the cost of reproducing and supplying the copy or phonorecord. The regulations established under this clause shall provide reasonable periods of not less than three months for compliance with a demand, and shall allow for extensions of such periods and adjustments in the scope of the demand or the methods for fulfilling it, as reasonably warranted by the circumtances. Willful failure or refusal to comply with the conditions prescribed by such regulations shall subject the owner of the right of transmission in the United States to liability for an amount, not to exceed the cost of reproducing and supplying the copy or phonorecord in question, to be paid into a specially designated fund in the Library of Congress.
(3) Nothing in this subsection shall be construed to require the making or retention, for purposes of deposit, of any copy or phonorecord of an unpublished transmission program, the transmission of which occurs before the receipt of a specific written demand as provided by clause (2).
(4) No activity undertaken in compliance with regulations prescribed under clauses (1) or (2) of this subsection shall result in liability if intended solely to assist in the acquisition of copies or phonorecords under this subsection.

17 USC 408. **§408. Copyright registration in general**

(a) REGISTRATION PERMISSIVE.—At any time during the subsistence of copyright in any published or unpublished work, the owner of copyright or of any exclusive right in the work may obtain registration of the copyright claim by delivering to the Copyright Office the deposit specified by this section, together with the application and fee specified by sections 409 and 708. Subject to the provisions of section 405(a), such registration is not a condition of copyright protection.

(b) DEPOSIT FOR COPYRIGHT REGISTRATION.—Except as provided by subsection (c), the material deposited for registration shall include—
(1) in the case of an unpublished work, one complete copy or phonorecord;
(2) in the case of a published work, two complete copies or phonorecords of the best edition;
(3) in the case of a work first published outside the United States, one complete copy or phonorecord as so published;
(4) in the case of a contribution to a collective work, one complete copy or phonorecord of the best edition of the collective work.

Regulations. Copies or phonorecords deposited for the Library of Congress under section 407 may be used to satisfy the deposit provisions of this section, if they are accompanied by the prescribed application and fee, and by any additional identifying material that the Register may, by regulation, require. The Register shall also prescribe regulations establishing requirements under which copies or phonorecords acquired for the Library of Congress under subsection (e) of section 407, otherwise than by deposit, may be used to satisfy the deposit provisions of this section.

(c) ADMINISTRATIVE CLASSIFICATION AND OPTIONAL DEPOSIT.—

    (1) The Register of Copyrights is authorized to specify by regulation the administrative classes into which works are to be placed for purposes of deposit and registration, and the nature of the copies or phonorecords to be deposited in the various classes specified. The regulations may require or permit, for particular classes, the deposit of identifying material instead of copies or phonorecords, the deposit of only one copy or phonorecord where two would normally be required, or a single registration for a group of related works. This administrative classification of works has no significance with respect to the subject matter of copyright or the exclusive rights provided by this title.

Regulations.

    (2) Without prejudice to the general authority provided under clause (1), the Register of Copyrights shall establish regulations specifically permitting a single registration for a group of works by the same individual author, all first published as contributions to periodicals, including newspapers, within a twelve-month period, on the basis of a single deposit, application, and registration fee, under all of the following conditions—

        (A) if each of the works as first published bore a separate copyright notice, and the name of the owner of copyright in the work, or an abbreviation by which the name can be recognized, or a generally known alternative designation of the owner was the same in each notice; and

        (B) if the deposit consists of one copy of the entire issue of the periodical, or of the entire section in the case of a newspaper, in which each contribution was first published; and

        (C) if the application identifies each work separately, including the periodical containing it and its date of first publication.

    (3) As an alternative to separate renewal registrations under subsection (a) of section 304, a single renewal registration may be made for a group of works by the same individual author, all first published as contributions to periodicals, including newspapers, upon the filing of a single application and fee, under all of the following conditions:

        (A) the renewal claimant or claimants, and the basis of claim or claims under section 304(a), is the same for each of the works; and

        (B) the works were all copyrighted upon their first publication, either through separate copyright notice and registration or by virtue of a general copyright notice in the periodical issue as a whole; and

        (C) the renewal application and fee are received not more than twenty-eight or less than twenty-seven years after the thirty-first day of December of the calendar year in which all of the works were first published; and

        (D) the renewal application identifies each work separately, including the periodical containing it and its date of first publication.

(d) CORRECTIONS AND AMPLIFICATIONS.—The Register may also establish, by regulation, formal procedures for the filing of an application for supplementary registration, to correct an error in a copyright registration or to amplify the information given in a registration. Such application shall be accompanied by the fee provided by section 708, and shall clearly identify the registration to be corrected or amplified. The information contained in a supplementary registration augments but does not supersede that contained in the earlier registration.

(e) PUBLISHED EDITION OF PREVIOUSLY REGISTERED WORK.—Registration for the first published edition of a work previously registered in unpublished form may be made even though the work as published is substantially the same as the unpublished version.

17 USC 409.   **§409. Application for copyright registration**

The application for copyright registration shall be made on a form prescribed by the Register of Copyrights and shall include—

 (1) the name and address of the copyright claimant;

 (2) in the case of a work other than an anonymous or pseudonymous work, the name and nationality or domicile of the author or authors, and, if one or more of the authors is dead, the dates of their deaths;

 (3) if the work is anonymous or pseudonymous, the nationality or domicile of the author or authors;

 (4) in the case of a work made for hire, a statement to this effect;

 (5) if the copyright claimant is not the author, a brief statement of how the claimant obtained ownership of the copyright;

 (6) the title of the work, together with any previous or alternative titles under which the work can be identified;

 (7) the year in which creation of the work was completed;

 (8) if the work has been published, the date and nation of its first publication;

 (9) in the case of a compilation or derivative work, an identification of any preexisting work or works that it is based on or incorporates, and a brief, general statement of the additional material covered by the copyright claim being registered;

 (10) in the case of a published work containing material of which copies are required by section 601 to be manufactured in the United States, the names of the persons or organizations who performed the processes specified by subsection (c) of section 601 with respect to that material, and the places where those processes were performed; and

 (11) any other information regarded by the Register of Copyrights as bearing upon the preparation or identification of the work or the existence, ownership, or duration of the copyright.

17 USC 410.   **§410. Registration of claim and issuance of certificate**

 (a) When, after examination, the Register of Copyrights determines that, in accordance with the provisions of this title, the material deposited constitutes copyrightable subject matter and that the other legal and formal requirements of this title have been met, the Register shall register the claim and issue to the applicant a certificate of registration under the seal of the Copyright Office. The certificate shall contain the information given in the application, together with the number and effective date of the registration.

 (b) In any case in which the Register of Copyrights determines that, in accordance with the provisions of this title, the material deposited does not constitute copyrightable subject matter or that the claim is invalid for any other reason, the Register shall refuse registration and shall notify the applicant in writing of the reasons for such refusal.

Prima facie evidence.

 (c) In any judicial proceedings the certificate of a registration made before or within five years after first publication of the work shall constitute prima facie evidence of the validity of the copyright and of the facts stated in the certificate. The evidentiary weight to be accorded the certificate of a registration made thereafter shall be within the discretion of the court.

Effective date.

 (d) The effective date of a copyright registration is the day on which an application, deposit, and fee, which are later determined by the Register of Copyrights or by a court of competent jurisdiction to be acceptable for registration, have all been received in the Copyright Office.

17 USC 411.   **§411. Registration as prerequisite to infringement suit**

 (a) Subject to the provisions of subsection (b), no action for infringement of the copyright in any work shall be instituted until registration of the copyright claim has been made in accordance with this title. In any case, however, where the deposit, application, and fee required for registration have been delivered to the Copyright Office in proper form and registration has been refused, the applicant is entitled to institute an action for infringement if notice thereof, with a copy of the complaint, is served on the Register of Copyrights. The Register may, at his or her option, become a party to the action with respect to the issue of registrability of the copyright claim by entering an appearance within sixty days after such service, but the Register's failure to become a party shall not deprive the court of jurisdiction to determine that issue.

(b) In the case of a work consisting of sounds, images, or both, the first fixation of which is made simultaneously with its transmission, the copyright owner may, either before or after such fixation takes place, institute an action for infringement under section 501, fully subject to the remedies provided by sections 502 through 506 and sections 509 and 510, if, in accordance with requirements that the Register of Copyrights shall prescribe by regulation, the copyright owner—

    (1) serves notice upon the infringer, not less than ten or more than thirty days before such fixation, identifying the work and the specific time and source of its first transmission, and declaring an intention to secure copyright in the work; and

    (2) makes registration for the work within three months after its first transmission.

17 USC 412.

§412. Registration as prerequisite to certain remedies for infringement

In any action under this title, other than an action instituted under section 411(b), no award of statutory damages or of attorney's fees, as provided by sections 504 and 505, shall be made for—

    (1) any infringement of copyright in an unpublished work commenced before the effective date of its registration; or

    (2) any infringement of copyright commenced after first publication of the work and before the effective date of its registration, unless such registration is made within three months after the first publication of the work.

Chapter 5.—Copyright Infringement and Remedies

Sec.
501. Infringement of copyright.
502. Remedies for infringement: Injunctions.
503. Remedies for infringement: Impounding and disposition of infringing articles.
504. Remedies for infringement: Damage and profits.
505. Remedies for infringement: Costs and attorney's fees.
506. Criminal offenses.
507. Limitations on actions.
508. Notification of filing and determination of actions.
509. Seizure and forfeiture.
510. Remedies for alteration of programing by cable systems.

17 USC 501.

§501. Infringement of copyright

(a) Anyone who violates any of the exclusive rights of the copyright owner as provided by sections 106 through 118, or who imports copies or phonorecords into the United States in violation of section 602, is an infringer of the copyright.

(b) The legal or beneficial owner of an exclusive right under a copyright is entitled, subject to the requirements of sections 205(d) and 411, to institute an action for any infringement of that particular right committed while he or she is the owner of it. The court may require such owner to serve written notice of the action with a copy of the complaint upon any person shown, by the records of the Copyright Office or otherwise, to have or claim an interest in the copyright, and shall require that such notice be served upon any person whose interest is likely to be affected by a decision in the case. The court may require the joinder, and shall permit the intervention, of any person having or claiming an interest in the copyright.

(c) For any secondary transmission by a cable system that embodies a performance or a display of a work which is actionable as an act of infringement under subsection (c) of section 111, a television broadcast station holding a copyright or other license to transmit or perform the same version of that work shall, for purposes of subsection (b) of this section, be treated as a legal or beneficial owner if such secondary transmission occurs within the local service area of that television station.

(d) For any secondary transmission by a cable system that is actionable as an act of infringement pursuant to section 111(c)(3), the following shall also have standing to sue: (i) the primary transmitter whose transmission has been altered by the cable system; and (ii) any broadcast station within whose local service area the secondary transmission occurs.

17 USC 502.

§502. Remedies for infringement: Injunctions

(a) Any court having jurisdiction of a civil action arising under this title may, subject to the provisions of section 1498 of title 28, grant temporary and final injunctions on such terms as it may deem reasonable to prevent or restrain infringement of a copyright.

(b) Any such injunction may be served anywhere in the United States on the person enjoined; it shall be operative throughout the United States and shall be enforceable, by proceedings in contempt or otherwise, by any United States court having jurisdiction of that person. The clerk of the court granting the injunction shall, when requested by any other court in which enforcement of the injunction is sought, transmit promptly to the other court a certified copy of all the papers in the case on file in such clerk's office.

17 USC 503.

§503. Remedies for infringement: Impounding and disposition of infringing articles

(a) At any time while an action under this title is pending, the court may order the impounding, on such terms as it may deem reasonable, of all copies or phonorecords claimed to have been made or used in violation of the copyright owner's exclusive rights, and of all plates, molds, matrices, masters, tapes, film negatives, or other articles by means of which such copies or phonorecords may be reproduced.

(b) As part of a final judgment or decree, the court may order the destruction or other reasonable disposition of all copies or phonorecords found to have been made or used in violation of the copyright owner's exclusive rights, and of all plates, molds, matrices, masters, tapes, film negatives, or other articles by means of which such copies or phonorecords may be reproduced.

17 USC 504.

§504. Remedies for infringement: Damages and profits

(a) IN GENERAL.—Except as otherwise provided by this title, an infringer of copyright is liable for either—

(1) the copyright owner's actual damages and any additional profits of the infringer, as provided by subsection (b); or

(2) statutory damages, as provided by subsection (c).

(b) ACTUAL DAMAGES AND PROFITS.—The copyright owner is entitled to recover the actual damages suffered by him or her as a result of the infringement, and any profits of the infringer that are attributable to the infringement and are not taken into account in computing the actual damages. In establishing the infringer's profits, the copyright owner is required to present proof only of the infringer's gross revenue, and the infringer is required to prove his or her deductible expenses and the elements of profit attributable to factors other than the copyrighted work.

(c) STATUTORY DAMAGES.—

(1) Except as provided by clause (2) of this subsection, the copyright owner may elect, at any time before final judgment is rendered, to recover, instead of actual damages and profits, an award of statutory damages for all infringements involved in the action, with respect to any one work, for which any one infringer is liable individually, or

for which any two or more infringers are liable jointly and severally, in a sum of not less than $250 or more than $10,000 as the court considers just. For the purposes of this subsection, all the parts of a compilation or derivative work constitute one work.

(2) In a case where the copyright owner sustains the burden of proving, and the court finds, that infringement was committed willfully, the court in its discretion may increase the award of statutory damages to a sum of not more than $50,000. In a case where the infringer sustains the burden of proving, and the court finds, that such infringer was not aware and had no reason to believe that his or her acts constituted an infringement of copyright, the court in its discretion may reduce the award of statutory damages to a sum of not less than $100. The court shall remit statutory damages in any case where an infringer believed and had reasonable grounds for believing that his or her use of the copyrighted work was a fair use under section 107, if the infringer was: (i) an employee or agent of a nonprofit educational institution, library, or archives acting within the scope of his or her employment who, or such institution, library, or archives itself, which infringed by reproducing the work in copies or phonorecords; or (ii) a public broadcasting entity which or a person who, as a regular part of the nonprofit activities of a public broadcasting entity (as defined in subsection (g) of section 118) infringed by performing a published nondramatic literary work or by reproducing a transmission program embodying a performance of such a work.

17 USC 505. **§505. Remedies for infringement: Costs and attorney's fees**

In any civil action under this title, the court in its discretion may allow the recovery of full costs by or against any party other than the United States or an officer thereof. Except as otherwise provided by this title, the court may also award a reasonable attorney's fee to the prevailing party as part of the costs.

17 USC 506. **§506. Criminal offenses**

(a) CRIMINAL INFRINGEMENT.—Any person who infringes a copyright willfully and for purposes of commercial advantage or private financial gain shall be punished as provided in section 2319 of title 18.[1]

---

[1]Section 2319 of title 18 of the U.S. Code (Act of May 24, 1982-Pub. Law 97-180) reads as follows:

18 USC 2319. **"§2319. Criminal infringement of a copyright**

"(a) Whoever violates section 506(a) (relating to criminal offenses) of title 17 shall be punished as provided in subsection (b) of this section and such penalties shall be in addition to any other provisions of title 17 or any other law.

"(b) Any person who commits an offense under subsection (a) of this section—

"(1) shall be fined not more than $250,000 or imprisoned for not more than five years, or both, if the offense—

"(A) involves the reproduction or distribution, during any one-hundred-and-eighty-day period, of at least one thousand phonorecords or copies infringing the copyright in one or more sound recordings;

"(B) involves the reproduction or distribution, during any one-hundred-and-eighty-day period, of at least sixty-five copies infringing the copyright in one or more motion pictures or other audiovisual works; or

"(C) is a second or subsequent offense under either of subsection (b)(1) or (b)(2) of this section, where a prior offense involved a sound recording, or a motion picture or other audiovisual work;

(b) FORFEITURE AND DESTRUCTION.—When any person is convicted of any violation of subsection (a), the court in its judgment of conviction shall, in addition to the penalty therein prescribed, order the forfeiture and destruction or other disposition of all infringing copies or phonorecords and all implements, devices, or equipment used in the manufacture of such infringing copies or phonorecords.

(c) FRAUDULENT COPYRIGHT NOTICE.—Any person who, with fraudulent intent, places on any article a notice of copyright or words of the same purport that such person knows to be false, or who, with fraudulent intent, publicly distributes or imports for public distribution any article bearing such notice or words that such person knows to be false, shall be fined not more than $2,500.

(d) FRAUDULENT REMOVAL OF COPYRIGHT NOTICE.—Any person who, with fraudulent intent, removes or alters any notice of copyright appearing on a copy of a copyrighted work shall be fined not more than $2,500.

(e) FALSE REPRESENTATION.   Any person who knowingly makes a false representation of a material fact in the application for copyright registration provided for by section 409, or in any written statement filed in connection with the application, shall be fined not more than $2,500.

17 USC 507.

§507. Limitations on actions

(a) CRIMINAL PROCEEDINGS.—No criminal proceeding shall be maintained under the provisions of this title unless it is commenced within three years after the cause of action arose.

(b) CIVIL ACTIONS.—No civil action shall be maintained under the provisions of this title unless it is commenced within three years after the claim accrued.

§508. Omitted

17 USC 509.

§509. Seizure and forfeiture

(a) All copies or phonorecords manufactured, reproduced, distributed, sold, or otherwise used, intended for use, or possessed with intent to use in violation of section 506(a), and all plates, molds, matrices, masters, tapes, film negatives, or other articles by means of which such copies or phono-

---

"(2) shall be fined not more than $250,000 or imprisoned for not more than two years, or both, if the offense—

"(A) involves the reproduction or distribution, during any one-hundred-and-eighty-day period, of more than one hundred but less than one thousand phonorecords or copies infringing the copyright in one or more sound recordings; or

"(B) involves the reproduction or distribution, during any one-hundred-and-eighty-day period, of more than seven but less than sixty-five copies infringing the copyright in one or more motion pictures or other audiovisual works; and

"(3) shall be fined not more than $25,000 or imprisoned for not more than one year, or both, in any other case.

Definitions.

"(c) As used in this section—

"(1) the terms 'sound recording,' 'motion picture,' 'audiovisual work,' 'phonorecord,' and 'copies' have, respectively, the meanings set forth in section 101 (relating to definitions) of title 17; and

"(2) the terms 'reproduction' and 'distribution' refer to the exclusive rights of a copyright owner under clauses (1) and (3) respectively of section 106 (relating to exclusive rights in copyrighted works), as limited by sections 107 through 118, of title 17.''

records may be reproduced, and all electronic, mechanical, or other devices for manufacturing, reproducing, or assembling such copies or phonorecords may be seized and forfeited to the United States.

19 USC 1
et seq.

(b) The applicable procedures relating to (i) the seizure, summary and judicial
forfeiture, and condemnation of vessels, vehicles, merchandise, and baggage for violations of the customs laws contained in title 19, (ii) the disposition of such vessels, vehicles, merchandise, and baggage or the proceeds from the sale thereof, (iii) the remission or mitigation of such
forfeiture, (iv) the compromise of claims, and (v) the award of compensation to informers in respect of such forfeitures, shall apply to seizures
and forfeitures incurred, or alleged to have been incurred, under the provisions of this section, insofar as applicable and not inconsistent with the
provisions of this section; except that such duties as are imposed upon any
officer or employee of the Treasury Department or any other person with
respect to the seizure and forfeiture of vessels, vehicles, merchandise; and
baggage under the provisions of the customs laws contained in title 19 shall
be performed with respect to seizure and forfeiture of all articles described
in subsection (a) by such officers, agents, or other persons as may be
authorized or designated for that purpose by the Attorney General.

§510. Omitted

Chapter 6.—Manufacturing Requirements and Importation

Sec.
601. Manufacture, importation, and public distribution of certain copies.
602. Infringing importation of copies or phonorecords.
603. Importation prohibitions: Enforcement and disposition of excluded articles.

17 USC 601.

§ 601. Manufacture, importation, and public distribution of certain copies

(a) Prior to July 1, 1986 and except as provided by subsection (b), the
importation into or public distribution in the United States of copies of
a work consisting preponderantly of nondramatic literary material that
is in the English language and is protected under this title is prohibited
unless the portions consisting of such material have been manufactured
in the United States or Canada.

(b) The provisions of subsection (a) do not apply—

(1) where, on the date when importation is sought or public distribution
in the United States is made, the author of any substantial part of
such material is neither a national nor a domiciliary of the United
States or, if such author is a national of the United States, he or
she has been domiciled outside the United States for a continuous
period of at least one year immediately preceding that date; in the
case of a work made for hire, the exemption provided by this clause
does not apply unless a substantial part of the work was prepared
for an employer or other person who is not a national or domiciliary
of the United States or a domestic corporation or enterprise;

(2) where the United States Customs Service is presented with an import statement issued under the seal of the Copyright Office, in
which case a total of no more than two thousand copies of any one
such work shall be allowed entry; the import statement shall be
issued upon request to the copyright owner or to a person designated by such owner at the time of registration for the work under
section 408 or at any time thereafter;

(3) where importation is sought under the authority or for the use, other
than in schools, of the Government of the United States or of any
State or political subdivision of a State;

(4) where importation, for use and not for sale, is sought—

(A) by any person with respect to no more than one copy of any
work at any one time;

       (B) by any person arriving from outside the United States, with respect to copies forming part of such person's personal baggage; or

       (C) by an organization operated for scholarly, educational, or religious purposes and not for private gain, with respect to copies intended to form a part of its library;

  (5) where the copies are reproduced in raised characters for the use of the blind; or

  (6) where, in addition to copies imported under clauses (3) and (4) of this subsection, no more than two thousand copies of any one such work, which have not been manufactured in the United States or Canada, are publicly distributed in the United States; or

  (7) where, on the date when importation is sought or public distribution in the United States is made—

       (A) the author of any substantial part of such material is an individual and receives compensation for the transfer or license of the right to distribute the work in the United States; and

       (B) the first publication of the work has previously taken place outside the United States under a transfer or license granted by such author to a transferee or licensee who was not a national or domiciliary of the United States or a domestic corporation or enterprise; and

       (C) there has been no publication of an authorized edition of the work of which the copies were manufactured in the United States; and

       (D) the copies were reproduced under a transfer or license granted by such author or by the transferee or licensee of the right of first publication as mentioned in subclause (B), and the transferee or the licensee of the right of reproduction was not a national or domiciliary of the United States or a domestic corporation or enterprise.

(c) The requirement of this section that copies be manufactured in the United States or Canada is satisfied if—

  (1) in the case where the copies are printed directly from type that has been set, or directly from plates made from such type, the setting of the type and the making of the plates have been performed in the United States or Canada; or

  (2) in the case where the making of plates by a lithographic or photoengraving process is a final or intermediate step preceding the printing of the copies, the making of the plates has been performed in the United States or Canada; and

  (3) in any case, the printing or other final process of producing multiple copies and any binding of the copies have been performed in the United States or Canada.

(d) Importation or public distribution of copies in violation of this section does not invalidate protection for a work under this title. However, in any civil action or criminal proceeding for infringement of the exclusive rights to reproduce and distribute copies of the work, the infringer has a complete defense with respect to all of the nondramatic literary material comprised in the work and any other parts of the work in which the exclusive rights to reproduce and distribute copies are owned by the same person who owns such exclusive rights in the nondramatic literary material, if the infringer proves—

  (1) that copies of the work have been imported into or publicly distributed in the United States in violation of this section by or with the authority of the owner of such exclusive rights; and

  (2) that the infringing copies were manufactured in the United States or Canada in accordance with the provisions of subsection (c); and

  (3) that the infringement was commenced before the effective date of registration for an authorized edition of the work, the copies of which have been manufactured in the United States or Canada in

accordance with the provisions of subsection (c).

(e) In any action for infringement of the exclusive rights to reproduce and distribute copies of a work containing material required by this section to be manufactured in the United States or Canada, the copyright owner shall set forth in the complaint the names of the persons or organizations who performed the processes specified by subsection (c) with respect to that material, and the places where those processes were performed.

17 USC 602.

§602. Infringing importation of copies or phonorecords

(a) Importation into the United States, without the authority of the owner of copyright under this title, of copies or phonorecords of a work that have been acquired outside the United States is an infringement of the exclusive right to distribute copies or phonorecords under section 106, actionable under section 501. This subsection does not apply to—

(1) importation of copies or phonorecords under the authority or for the use of the Government of the United States or of any State or political subdivision of a State, but not including copies or phonorecords for use in schools, or copies of any audiovisual work imported for purposes other than archival use;

(2) importation, for the private use of the importer and not for distribution, by any person with respect to no more than one copy or phonorecord of any one work at any one time, or by any person arriving from outside the United States with respect to copies or phonorecords forming part of such person's personal baggage; or

(3) importation by or for an organization operated for scholarly, educational, or religious purposes and not for private gain, with respect to no more than one copy of an audiovisual work solely for its archival purposes, and no more than five copies or phonorecords of any other work for its library lending or archival purposes, unless the importation of such copies or phonorecords is part of an activity consisting of systematic reproduction or distribution, engaged in by such organization in violation of the provisions of section 108(g)(2).

(b) In a case where the making of the copies or phonorecords would have constituted an infringement of copyright if this title had been applicable, their importation is prohibited. In a case where the copies or phonorecords were lawfully made, the United States Customs Service has no authority to prevent their importation unless the provisions of section 601 are applicable. In either case, the Secretary of the Treasury is authorized to prescribe, by regulation, a procedure under which any person claiming an interest in the copyright in a particular work may, upon payment of a specified fee, be entitled to notification by the Customs Service of the importation of articles that appear to be copies or phonorecords of the work.

Regulations.

17 USC 603.

§603. Importation prohibitions: Enforcement and disposition of excluded articles

Regulations.

(a) The Secretary of the Treasury and the United States Postal Service shall separately or jointly make regulations for the enforcement of the provisions of this title prohibiting importation.

(b) These regulations may require, as a condition for the exclusion or articles under section 602—

(1) that the person seeking exclusion obtain a court order enjoining importation of the articles; or

Surety bond.

(2) that the person seeking exclusion furnish proof, of a specified nature and in accordance with prescribed procedures, that the copyright in which such person claims an interest is valid and that the importation would violate the prohibition in section 602; the person seeking exclusion may also be required to post a surety bond for any injury that may result if the detention or exclusion of the articles proves to be unjustified.

(c) Articles imported in violation of the importation prohibitions of this title are subject to seizure and forfeiture in the same manner as property imported in violation of the customs revenue laws. Forfeited articles shall be destroyed as directed by the Secretary of the Treasury or the court, as the case may be; however, the articles may be returned to the country of export whenever it is shown to the satisfaction of the Secretary of the Treasury that the importer had no reasonable grounds for believing that his or her acts constituted a violation of law.

Chapter 7.—Copyright Office

Sec.
701. The Copyright Office: General responsibilities and organization.
702. Copyright Office regulations.
703. Effective date of actions in Copyright Office.
704. Retention and disposition of articles deposited in Copyright Office.
705. Copyright Office records: Preparation, maintenance, public inspection, and searching.
706. Copies of Copyright Office records.
707. Copyright Office forms and publications.
708. Copyright Office fees.
709. Delay in delivery caused by disruption of postal or other services.
710. Reproductions for use of the blind and physically handicapped: Voluntary licensing forms and procedures.

17 USC 701.

§701. The Copyright Office: General responsibilities and organization

(a) All administrative functions and duties under this title, except as otherwise specified, are the responsibility of the Register of Copyrights as director of the Copyright Office of the Library of Congress. The Register of Copyrights, together with the subordinate officers and employees of the Copyright Office, shall be appointed by the Librarian of Congress, and shall act under the Librarian's general direction and supervision.

Seal.

(b) The Register of Copyrights shall adopt a seal to be used on and after January 1, 1978, to authenticate all certified documents issued by the Copyright Office.

Report to Librarian of Congress.

(c) The Register of Copyrights shall make an annual report to the Librarian of Congress of the work and accomplishments of the Copyright Office during the previous fiscal year. The annual report of the Register of Copyrights shall be published separately and as a part of the annual report of the Librarian of Congress.

(d) Except as provided by section 706(b) and the regulations issued thereunder, all actions taken by the Register of Copyrights under this title are subject to the provisions of the Administrative Procedure Act of June 11, 1946, as amended (c. 324, 60 Stat. 237, title 5, United States Code, Chapter 5, Subchapter II and Chapter 7).

5 USC 551, 701.

17 USC 702.

§702. Copyright Office regulations

The Register of Copyrights is authorized to establish regulations not inconsistent with law for the administration of the functions and duties made the responsibility of the Register under this title. All regulations established by the Register under this title are subject to the approval of the Librarian of Congress.

17 USC 703.

§703. Effective date of actions in Copyright Office

In any case in which time limits are prescribed under this title for the performance of an action in the Copyright Office, and in which the last day of the prescribed period falls on a Saturday, Sunday, holiday, or other nonbusiness day within the District of Columbia or the Federal Government, the action may be taken on the next succeeding business day, and is effective as of the date when the period expired.

17 USC 704.

§704. Retention and disposition of articles deposited in Copyright Office

(a) Upon their deposit in the Copyright Office under sections 407 and 408, all copies, phonorecords, and identifying material, including those deposited in connection with claims that have been refused registration, are the property of the United States Government.

Regulations.

(b) In the case of published works, all copies, phonorecords, and identifying material deposited are available to the Library of Congress for its collections, or for exchange or transfer to any other library. In the case of unpublished works, the Library is entitled, under regulations that the Register of Copyrights shall prescribe, to select any deposits for its collections or for transfer to the National Archives of the United States or to a Federal records center, as defined in section 2901 of title 44.

(c) The Register of Copyrights is authorized, for specific or general categories of works, to make a facsimile reproduction of all or any part of the material deposited under section 408, and to make such reproduction a part of the Copyright Office records of the registration, before transferring such material to the Library of Congress as provided by subsection (b), or before destroying or otherwise disposing of such material as provided by subsection (d).

(d) Deposits not selected by the Library under subsection (b), or identifying portions or reproductions of them, shall be retained under the control of the Copyright Office, including retention in Government storage facilities, for the longest period considered practicable and desirable by the Register of Copyrights and the Librarian of Congress. After that period it is within the joint discretion of the Register and the Librarian to order their destruction or other disposition; but, in the case of unpublished works, no deposit shall be knowingly or intentionally destroyed or otherwise disposed of during its term of copyright unless a facsimile reproduction of the entire deposit has been made a part of the Copyright Office records as provided by subsection (c).

(e) The depositor of copies, phonorecords, or identifying material under section 408, or the copyright owner of record, may request retention, under the control of the Copyright Office, of one or more of such articles for the full term of copyright in the work. The Register of Copyrights shall prescribe, by regulation, the conditions under which such requests are to be made and granted, and shall fix the fee to be charged under section 708(a)(11) if the request is granted.

17 USC 705.

§705. Copyright Office records: Preparation, maintenance, public inspection, and searching

(a) The Register of Copyrights shall provide and keep in the Copyright Office records of all deposits, registrations, recordations, and other actions taken under this title, and shall prepare indexes of all such records.

(b) Such records and indexes, as well as the articles deposited in connection with completed copyright registrations and retained under the control of the Copyright Office, shall be open to public inspection.

Report.

(c) Upon request and payment of the fee specified by section 708, the Copyright Office shall make a search of its public records, indexes, and deposits, and shall furnish a report of the information they disclose with respect to any particular deposits, registrations, or recorded documents.

17 USC 706.

§706. Copies of Copyright Office records

(a) Copies may be made of any public records or indexes of the Copyright Office; additional certificates of copyright registration and copies of any public records or indexes may be furnished upon request and payment of the fees specified by section 708.

(b) Copies or reproductions of deposited articles retained under the control of the Copyright Office shall be authorized or furnished only under the conditions specified by the Copyright Office regulations.

§707. Omitted

17 USC 708.

§708. Copyright Office fees

(a) The following fees shall be paid to the Register of Copyrights:

(1) On filing each application for registration of a copyright claim or a supplementary registration under section 408, including the issuance of a certificate of registration, $10;

(2) On filing each application for registration of a claim to renewal of a subsisting copyright in its first term under section 304(a), including the issuance of a certificate of registration, $6;

(3) for the issuance of a receipt for a deposit under section 407, $2;

(4) for the recordation, as provided by section 205, of a transfer of copyright ownership or other document of six pages or less, covering no more than one title, $10; for each page over six and each title over one, 50 cents additional;

(5) for the filing, under section 115(b), of a notice of intention to make phonorecords, $6;

(6) for the recordation, under section 302(c), of a statement revealing the identity of an author of an anonymous or pseudonymous work, or for the recordation, under section 302(d), of a statement relating to the death of an author, $10 for a document of six pages or less, covering no more than one title; for each page over six and for each title over one, $1 additional;

(7) for the issuance, under section 601, of an import statement, $3;

(8) for the issuance, under section 706, of an additional certificate of registration, $4;

(9) for the issuance of any other certification, $4; the Register of Copyrights has discretion, on the basis of their cost, to fix the fees for preparing copies of Copyright Office records, whether they are to be certified or not;

(10) for the making and reporting of a search as provided by section 705, and for any related services, $10 for each hour or fraction of an hour consumed;

(11) for any other special services requiring a substantial amount of time or expense, such fees as the Register of Copyrights may fix on the basis of the cost of providing the service.

Waiver.

(b) The fees prescribed by or under this section are applicable to the United States Government and any of its agencies, employees, or officers, but the Register of Copyrights has discretion to waive the requirement of this subsection in occasional or isolated cases involving relatively small amounts.

Regulations.

(c) The Register of Copyrights shall deposit all fees in the Treasury of the United States in such manner as the Secretary of the Treasury directs. The Register may, in accordance with regulations that he or she shall prescribe, refund any sum paid by mistake or in excess of the fee required by this section,

17 USC 709.

§709. Delay in delivery caused by disruption of postal or other services

In any case in which the Register of Copyrights determines, on the basis of such evidence as the Register may by regulation require, that a deposit, application, fee, or any other material to be delivered to the Copyright Office by a particular date, would have been received in the Copyright Office in due time except for a general disruption or suspension of postal or other transportation or communications services, the actual receipt of such material in the Copyright Office within one month after the date on which the Register determines that the disruption or suspension of such services has terminated, shall be considered timely.

§710. Omitted

Chapter 8.—Copyright Royalty Tribunal

Sec.
801. Copyright Royalty Tribunal: Establishment and purpose.

17 USC 801. **§801. Copyright Royalty Tribunal: Establishment and purpose**

(a) There is hereby created an independent Copyright Royalty Tribunal in the legislative branch.

(b) Subject to the provisions of this chapter, the purposes of the Tribunal shall be—

   (1) to make determinations concerning the adjustment of reasonable copyright royalty rates as provided in sections 115 and 116, and to make determinations as to reasonable terms and rates of royalty payments as provided in section 118. The rates applicable under sections 115 and 116 shall be calculated to achieve the following objectives:

     (A) To maximize the availability of creative works to the public;

     (B) To afford the copyright owner a fair return for his creative work and the copyright user a fair income under existing economic conditions;

     (C) To reflect the relative roles of the copyright owner and the copyright user in the product made available to the public with respect to relative creative contribution, technological contribution, capital investment, cost, risk, and contribution to the opening of new markets for creative expression and media for their communication;

     (D) To minimize any disruptive impact on the structure of the industries involved and on generally prevailing industry practices.

   (2) to make determinations concerning the adjustment of the copyright royalty rates in section 111 solely in accordance with the following provisions:

     (A) The rates established by section 111(d)(2)(B) may be adjusted to reflect (i) national monetary inflation or deflation or (ii) changes in the average rates charged cable subscribers for the basic service of providing secondary transmissions to maintain the real constant dollar level of the royalty fee per subscriber which existed as of the date of enactment of this Act: *Provided,* That if the average rates charged cable system subscribers for the basic service of providing secondary transmissions are changed so that the average rates exceed national monetary inflation, no change in the rates established by section 111(d)(2)(B) shall be permitted: *And provided further,* That no increase in the royalty fee shall be permitted based on any reduction in the average number of distant signal equivalents per subscriber. The Commission may consider all factors relating to the maintenance of such level of payments including, as an extenuating factor, whether the cable industry has been restrained by subscriber rate regulating authorities from increasing the rates for the basic service of providing secondary transmissions.

     (B) In the event that the rules and regulations of the Federal Communications Commission are amended at any time after April 15, 1976, to permit the carriage by cable systems of additional television broadcast signals beyond the local service area of the primary transmitters of such signals, the royalty rates established by section 111(d)(2)(B) may be adjusted to insure that the rates for the additional distant signal equivalents resulting from such carriage are reasonable in the light of the changes effected by the amendment to such rules and regulations. In determining the reasonableness of rates proposed following an amendment of Federal Communications Commission rules and regulations, the Copyright Royalty Tribunal shall consider, among other factors, the economic impact on copyright owners and users: *Provided,* That no adjustment in royalty rates shall be made under this subclause with respect to any distant signal equivalent or fraction thereof represented by (i) carriage of any signal permitted under the rules and regulations of the Federal Communications Commission in effect on April 15, 1976, or the carriage of a signal of the same type (that is, independent, network, or noncommercial educational) substituted for such permitted signal, or (ii) a television broadcast signal first carried after April 15, 1976, pursuant to an individual waiver of the rules and regulations of the Federal Communications Commission, as such rules and regulations were in effect on April 15, 1976.

(C) In the event of any change in the rules and regulations of the Federal Communications Commission with respect to syndicated and sports program exclusivity after April 15, 1976, the rates established by section 111(d)(2)(B) may be adjusted to assure that such rates are reasonable in light of the changes to such rules and regulations, but any such adjustment shall apply only to the affected television broadcast signals carried on those systems affected by the change.

(D) The gross receipts limitations established by section 111(d)(2)(C) and (D) shall be adjusted to reflect national monetary inflation or deflation or changes in the average rates charged cable system subscribers for the basic service of providing secondary transmissions to maintain the real constant dollar value of the exemption provided by such section; and the royalty rate specified therein shall not be subject to adjustment; and

(3) to distribute royalty fees deposited with the Register of Copyrights under sections 111 and 116, and to determine, in cases where controversy exists, the distribution of such fees.

Notice.

(c) As soon as possible after the date of enactment of this Act, and no later than six months following such date, the President shall publish a notice announcing the initial appointments provided in section 802, and shall designate an order of seniority among the initially-appointed commissioners for purposes of section 802(b).

17 USC 802.

§802. Membership of the Tribunal

(a) The Tribunal shall be composed of five commissioners appointed by the President with the advice and consent of the Senate for a term of seven years each; of the first five members appointed, three shall be designated to serve for seven years from the date of the notice specified in section 801(c), and two shall be designated to serve for five years from such date, respectively. Commissioners shall be compensated at the highest rate now or hereafter prescribed for grade 18 of the General Schedule pay rates (5 U.S.C. 5332).

(b) Upon convening the commissioners shall elect a chairman from among the commissioners appointed for a full seven-year term. Such chairman shall serve for a term of one year. Thereafter, the most senior commissioner who has not previously served as chairman shall serve as chairman for a period of one year, except that, if all commissioners have served a full term as chairman, the most senior commissioner who has served the least number of terms as chairman shall be designated as chairman.

(c) Any vacancy in the Tribunal shall not affect its powers and shall be filled, for the unexpired term of the appointment, in the same manner as the original appointment was made.

17 USC 803.   **§803. Procedures of the Tribunal**

(a) The Tribunal shall adopt regulations, not inconsistent with law, governing its procedure and methods of operation. Except as otherwise provided in this chapter, the Tribunal shall be subject to the provisions of the Admin-

5 USC 551, 701.

Publication in Federal Register.
istrative Procedure Act of June 11, 1946, as amended (c. 324, 60 Stat. 237, title 5, United States Code, chapter 5, subchapter II and chapter 7.).

(b) Every final determination of the Tribunal shall be published in the Federal Register. It shall state in detail the criteria that the Tribunal determined to be applicable to the particular proceeding, the various facts that it found relevant to its determination in that proceeding, and the specific reasons for its determination.

17 USC 804.   **§804. Institution and conclusion of proceedings**

(a) With respect to proceedings under section 801(b)(1) concerning the adjustment of royalty rates as provided in sections 115 and 116, and with respect to proceedings under section 801(b)(2)(A) and (D)—

(1) on January 1, 1980, the Chairman of the Tribunal shall cause to be published in the Federal Register notice of commencement of proceedings under this chapter; and

(2) during the calendar years specified in the following schedule, any owner or user of a copyrighted work whose royalty rates are specified by this title, or by a rate established by the Tribunal, may file a petition with the Tribunal declaring that the petitioner requests an adjustment of the rate. The Tribunal shall make a determination as to whether the applicant has a significant interest in the royalty rate in which an adjustment is requested. If the Tribunal determines that the petitioner has a significant interest, the Chairman shall cause notice of this determination, with the reasons therefor, to be published in the Federal Register, together with notice of commencement of proceedings under this chapter.

(A) In proceedings under section 801(b)(2)(A) and (D), such petition may be filed during 1985 and in each subsequent fifth calendar year.

(B) In proceedings under section 801(b)(1) concerning the adjustment of royalty rates as provided in section 115, such petition may be filed in 1987 and in each subsequent tenth calendar year.

(C) In proceedings under section 801(b)(1) concerning the adjustment of royalty rates under section 116, such petition may be filed in 1990 and in each subsequent tenth calendar year.

(b) With respect to proceedings under subclause (B) or (C) of section 801(b)(2), following an event described in either of those subsections, any owner or user of a copyrighted work whose royalty rates are specified by section 111, or by a rate established by the Tribunal, may, within twelve months, file a petition with the Tribunal declaring that the petitioner requests an adjustment of the rate. In this event the Tribunal shall proceed as in subsection (a)(2), above. Any change in royalty rates made by the Tribunal pursuant to this subsection may be reconsidered in 1980, 1985, and each fifth calendar year thereafter, in accordance with the provisions in section 801(b)(2)(B) or (C), as the case may be.

(c) With respect to proceedings under section 801(b)(1), concerning the determination of reasonable terms and rates of royalty payments as provided in section 118, the Tribunal shall proceed when and as provided by that section.

(d) With respect to proceedings under section 801(b)(3), concerning the distribution of royalty fees in certain circumstances under sections 111 or 116, the Chairman of the Tribunal shall, upon determination by the Tribunal that a controversy exists concerning such distribution, cause to be published in the Federal Register notice of commencement of proceedings under this chapter.

(e) All proceedings under this chapter shall be initiated without delay following publication of the notice specified in this section, and the Tribunal shall render its final decision in any such proceeding within one year from the date of such publication.

§805. Omitted
§806. Omitted

17 USC 807.

§807. Deduction of costs of proceedings

Before any funds are distributed pursuant to a final decision in a proceeding involving distribution of royalty fees, the Tribunal shall assess the reasonable costs of such proceeding.

§808. Omitted

17 USC 809.

§809. Effective date of final determinations

Any final determination by the Tribunal under this chapter shall become effective thirty days following its publication in the Federal Register as provided in section 803(b), unless prior to that time an appeal has been filed pursuant to section 810, to vacate, modify, or correct such determination, and notice of such appeal has been served on all parties who appeared before the Tribunal in the proceeding in question. Where the proceeding involves the distribution of royalty fees under sections 111 or 116, the Tribunal shall, upon the expiration of such thirty-day period, distribute any royalty fees not subject to an appeal filed pursuant to section 810.

17 USC 810.

§810. Judicial review

Any final decision of the Tribunal in a proceeding under section 801(b) may be appealed to the United States Court of Appeals, within thirty days after its pub-

5 USC 701.

lication in the Federal Register by an aggrieved party. The judicial review of the decision shall be had, in accordance with chapter 7 of title 5, on the basis of the record before the Tribunal. No court shall have jurisdiction to review a final decision of the Tribunal except as provided in this section.

Transitional and Supplementary Provisions

17 USC note prec. 101.

SEC. 102. This Act becomes effective on January 1, 1978, except as otherwise expressly provided by this Act, including provisions of the first section of this Act. The provisions of sections 118, 304(b), and chapter 8 of title 17, as amended by the first section of this Act, take effect upon enactment of this Act.

17 USC note prec. 101.

SEC. 103. This Act does not provide copyright protection for any work that goes into the public domain before January 1, 1978. The exclusive rights, as provided by section 106 of title 17 as amended by the first section of this Act, to reproduce a work in phonorecords and to distribute phonorecords of the work, do not extend to any nondramatic musical work copyrighted before July 1, 1909.

17 USC note prec. 101.

SEC. 104. All proclamations issued by the President under section 1(e) or 9(b) of title 17 as it existed on December 31, 1977, or under previous copyright statutes of the United States, shall continue in force until terminated, suspended, or revised by the President.

§105. Omitted

17 USC 115 note.

SEC. 106. In any case where, before January 1, 1978, a person has lawfully made parts of instruments serving to reproduce mechanically a copyrighted work under the compulsory license provisions of section 1(e) of title 17 as it existed on December 31, 1977, such person may continue to make and distribute such parts embodying the same mechanical reproduction without obtaining a new compulsory license under the terms of section 115 of title 17 as amended by the first section of this Act. However, such parts made on or after January 1, 1978, constitute phonorecords and are otherwise subject to the provisions of said section 115.

17 USC 304 note.

SEC. 107. In the case of any work in which an ad interim copyright is subsisting or is capable of being secured on December 31, 1977, under section 22 of title 17 as it existed on that date, copyright protection is hereby extended to endure for the term or terms provided by section 304 of title 17 as amended by the first section of this Act.

17 USC 401
note.

Sec. 108. The notice provisions of sections 401 through 403 of title 17 as amended by the first section of this Act apply to all copies or phonorecords publicly distributed on or after January 1, 1978. However, in the case of a work published before January 1, 1978, compliance with the notice provisions of title 17 either as it existed on December 31, 1977, or as amended by the first section of this Act, is adequate with respect to copies publicly distributed after December 31, 1977.

17 USC 410
note.

Sec. 109. The registration of claims to copyright for which the required deposit, application, and fee were received in the Copyright Office before January 1, 1978, and the recordation of assignments of copyright or other instruments received in the Copyright Office before January 1, 1978, shall be made in accordance with title 17 as it existed on December 31, 1977.

17 USC 407
note.

Sec. 110. The demand and penalty provisions of section 14 of title 17 as it existed on December 31, 1977, apply to any work in which copyright has been secured by publication with notice of copyright on or before that date, but any deposit and registration made after that date in response to a demand under that section shall be made in accordance with the provisions of title 17 as amended by the first section of this Act.

§111. Omitted

49 USC 1301.

Sec. III. Section 2318 of title 18 of the United States Code is amended to read as follows:

§2318 Trafficking in counterfeit labels for phonorecords, and copies of motion pictures and other audiovisual works

"(a) Whoever, in any of the circumstances described in subsection (c) of this section, knowingly traffics in a counterfeit label affixed or designed to be affixed to a phonorecord, or a copy of a motion picture or other audiovisual work, shall be fined not more than $250,000 or imprisoned for not more than five years, or both.

Definitions.

"(b) As used in this section—

"(1) the term 'counterfeit label' means an identifying label or container that appears to be genuine, but is not;

"(2) the term 'traffic' means to transport, transfer or otherwise dispose of, to another, as consideration for anything of value or to make or obtain control of with intent to so transport, transfer or dispose of; and

"(3) the terms 'copy', 'phonorecord', 'motion picture', and 'audiovisual work' have, respectively, the meanings given those terms in section 101 (relating to definitions) of title 17.

"(c) The circumstances referred to in subsection (a) of this section are—

"(1) the offense is committed within the special maritime and territorial jurisdiction of the United States; or within the special aircraft jurisdiction of the United States (as defined in section 101 of the Federal Aviation Act of 1958);

"(2) the mail or a facility of interstate or foreign commerce is used or intended to be used in the commission of the offense; or

"(3) the counterfeit label is affixed to or encloses, or is designed to be affixed to or enclose, a copyrighted motion picture or other audiovisual work, or a phonorecord of a copyrighted sound recording.

"(d) When any person is convicted of any violation of subsection (a), the court in its judgment of conviction shall in addition to the penalty therein prescribed, order the forfeiture and destruction or other disposition of all counterfeit labels and all articles to which counterfeit labels have been affixed or which were intended to have had such labels affixed.

17 USC 501
note.

Sec. 112. All causes of action that arose under title 17 before January 1, 1978, shall be governed by title 17 as it existed when the cause of action arose.

§113. Omitted
§114. Omitted
§115. Omitted

Fair Use Guidelines for Educational Uses of Music under Copyright Act of 1976*

In a joint letter dated April 30, 1976, representatives of the Music Publishers' Association of the United States, Inc., the National Music Publishers' Association, Inc., the Music Teachers National Association, the Music Educators National Conference, the National Association of Schools of Music, and the Ad Hoc Committee on Copyright Law Revision, wrote to Chairman Kastenmeier of the House of Representatives Committee on the Judiciary as follows:

> During the hearings on H.R. 2223 in June 1975, you and several of your subcommittee members suggested that concerned groups should work together in developing guidelines which would be helpful to clarify Section 107 of the bill.
>
> Representatives of music educators and music publishers delayed their meeting until guidelines had been developed relative to books and periodicals. Shortly after that work was completed and those guidelines were forwarded to your subcommittee, representatives of the undersigned music organizations met together with representatives of the Ad Hoc Committee on Copyright Law Revision to draft guidelines relative to music.
>
> We are very pleased to inform you that the discussions thus have been fruitful on the guidelines which have been developed. Since private music teachers are an important factor in music education, due consideration has been given to the concerns of that group.
>
> We trust that this will be helpful in the report on the bill to clarify Fair Use as it applies to music.

The text of the guidelines accompanying this letter is as follows:

Guidelines for Educational Uses of Music

The purpose of the following guidelines is to state the minimum and not the maximum standards of educational fair use under Section 107 of HR 2223. The parties agree that the conditions determining the extent of permissible copying for educational purposes may change in the future; that certain types of copying permitted under these guidelines may not be permissible in the future, and conversely that in the future other types of copying not permitted under these guidelines may be permissible under revised guidelines.

Moreover, the following statement of guidelines is not intended to limit the types of copying permitted under the standards of fair use under judicial decision and which are stated in Section 107 of the Copyright Revision Bill. There may be instances in which copying which does not fall within the guidelines stated below may nonetheless be permitted under the criteria of fair use.

---

* The above guidelines have been approved by the House of Representatives and the U.S. Senate conferees who recommended the final draft of the Copyright Act of 1976.

A. Permissible Uses.

1. Emergency copying to replace purchased copies which for any reason are not available for an imminent performance provided purchased replacement copies shall be substituted in due course.

2. For academic purposes other than performance, multiple copies of excerpts of works may be made, provided that the excerpts do not comprise a part of the whole which would constitute a performable unit such as a section, movement or aria, but in no case more than 10% of the whole work. The number of copies shall not exceed one copy per pupil.

3. Printed copies which have been purchased may be edited or simplified provided that the fundamental character of the work is not distorted or the lyrics, if any, altered or lyrics added if none exist.

4. A single copy of recordings of performances by students may be made for evaluation or rehearsal purposes and may be retained by the educational institution or individual teacher.

5. A single copy of a sound recording (such as a tape, disc or cassette) of copyrighted music may be made from sound recordings owned by an educational institution or an individual teacher for the purpose of constructing aural exercises or examinations and may be retained by the educational institution or individual teacher. (This pertains only to the copyright of the music itself and not to any copyright which may exist in the sound recording.)

B. Prohibitions

1. Copying to create or replace or substitute for anthologies, compilations or collective works.

2. Copying of or from works intended to be "consumable" in the course of study or of teaching such as workbooks, exercises, standardized tests and answer sheets and like material.

3. Copying for the purpose of performance, except as in A(1) above.

4. Copying for the purpose of substituting for the purchase of music, except as in A(1) and A(2) above.

5. Copying without inclusion of the copyright notice which appears on the printed copy.

Appendix B

List of Regulations of the Copyright Office Promulgated Under the Copyright Act of 1976

---

[1] Set forth in full in Appendix C1
[2] Set forth in full in Appendix C3

---

[3]Set forth in full in Appendix C2

Copyright Office Regulation Pursuant to Section 304(c) of the 1976 Copyright Act on Termination of Transfers and Licenses Covering Extended Renewal Term

Part 201 of 37 CFR Chapter II is amended by adding a new §201.10 to read as follows:

§201.10 Notice of termination of transfers and licenses covering extended renewal term

(a) *Form.* The Copyright Office does not provide printed forms for the use of persons serving notices of termination.

(b) *Contents.*

    (1) A notice of termination must include a clear identification of each of the following:

        (i) The name of each grantee whose rights are being terminated, or the grantee's successor in title, and each address at which service of the notice is being made;

        (ii) The title and the name of at least one author of, and the date copyright was originally secured in, each work to which the notice of termination applies; and, if possible and practicable, the original copyright registration number;

        (iii) A brief statement reasonably identifying the grant to which the notice of termination applies;

        (iv) The effective date of termination; and,

        (v) In the case of a termination of a grant executed by a person or persons other than the author, a listing of the surviving person or persons who executed the grant. In the case of a termination of a grant executed by one or more of the authors of the work where the termination is exercised by the successors of a deceased author, a listing of the names and relationships to that deceased author of all of the following, together with specific indication of the person or persons executing the notice who constitute more than one-half of that author's termination interest: That author's surviving widow or widower; and all of that author's surviving children; and, where any of that author's children are dead, all of the surviving children of any such deceased child of that author; however, instead of the information required by this subdivision (v), the notice may contain both of the following: (A) A statement of as much of such information as is currently available to the person or persons signing the notice, with a brief explanation of the reasons why full information is or may be lacking; together with (B) a statement that, to the best knowledge and belief of the person or persons signing the notice, the notice has been signed by all persons whose signature is necessary to terminate the grant under section 304(c) of title 17, U.S.C., or by their duly authorized agents.

    (2) Clear identification of the information specified by paragraph (b)(1) of this section requires a complete and unambiguous statement of facts in the notice itself, without incorporation by reference of information in other documents or records.

(c) *Signature*.
  (1) In the case of a termination of a grant executed by a person or persons other than the author, the notice shall be signed by all of the surviving person or persons who executed the grant, or by their duly authorized agents.
  (2) In the case of a termination of a grant executed by one or more of the authors of the work, the notice as to any one author's share shall be signed by that author or by his or her duly authorized agent. If that author is dead, the notice shall be signed by the number and proportion of the owners of that author's termination interest required under clauses (1) and (2) of section 204(c) of title 17, U.S.C., or by their duly authorized agents, and shall contain a brief statement of their relationship or relationships to that author.
  (3) Where a signature is by a duly authorized agent, it shall clearly identify the person or persons on whose behalf the agent is acting.
  (4) The handwritten signature of each person effecting the termination shall either be accompanied by a statement of the full name and address of that person, typewritten or printed legibly by hand, or shall clearly correspond to such a statement elsewhere in the notice.
(d) *Service*.
  (1) The notice of termination shall be served upon each grantee whose rights are being terminated, or the grantee's successor in title, by personal service, or by first-class mail sent to an address which, after a reasonable investigation, is found to be the last known address of the grantee or successor in title.
  (2) The service provision of section 304(c)(4) of title 17, U.S.C., will be satisfied if, before the notice of termination is served, a reasonable investigation is made by the person or persons executing the notice as to the current ownership of the rights being terminated, and based on such investigation: (i) If there is no reason to believe that such rights have been transferred by the grantee to a successor in title, the notice is served on the grantee; or (ii) if there is reason to believe that such rights have been transferred by the grantee to a particular successor in title, the notice is served on such successor in title.
  (3) For purposes of subparagraph (2) of this paragraph (d), a "reasonable investigation" includes, but is not limited to, a search of the records in the Copyright Office; in the case of a musical composition with respect to which performing rights are licensed by a performing rights society, as defined by section 116(e)(3) of title 17, U.S.C., a "reasonable investigation" also includes a report from that performing rights society identifying the person or persons claiming current ownership of the rights being terminated.
  (4) Compliance with the provisions of clauses (2) and (3) of this paragraph (d) will satisfy the service requirements of section 304(c)(4) of title 17, U.S.C. However, as long as the statutory requirements have been met, the failure to comply with the regulatory provisions of subparagraph (2) or (3) of this paragraph (d) will not affect the validity of the service.
(e) *Harmless errors*.
  (1) Harmless errors in a notice that do not materially affect the adequacy of the information required to serve the purposes of section 304(c) of title 17, U.S.C., shall not render the notice invalid.
  (2) Without prejudice to the general rule provided by subparagraph (1) of this paragraph (e), errors made in giving the date or registration number referred to in paragraph (b)(1)(ii) of this section, or in complying with the provisions of paragraph (b)(1)(v) of this section, or in describing the precise relationships under clause (2) of paragraph (c) of this section, shall not affect the validity of the notice if the errors were made in good faith and without any intention to deceive, mislead, or conceal relevant information.
(f) *Recordation*.
  (1) A copy of the notice of termination will be recorded in the Copyright Office upon payment of the fee prescribed by subparagraph (2) of this paragraph (f) and upon compliance with the following provisions:
      (i) The copy submitted for recordation shall be a complete and exact duplicate of the notice of termination as served and shall include the actual signature or signatures, or a reproduction of the actual signature or signatures, appearing on the notice; where separate copies of the same notice were served on more than

one grantee or successor in title, only one copy need be submitted for recordation; and

(ii) The copy submitted for recordation shall be accompanied by a statement setting forth the date on which the notice was served and the manner of service, unless such information is contained in the notice.

(2) For a document consisting of six pages or less, covering no more than one title, the basic recordation fee is $5 if recorded before January 1, 1978, and $10 if recorded after December 31, 1977; in either case an additional charge of 50 cents is made for each page over six and each title over one. The statement referred to in paragraph (f)(1)(ii) of this section will be considered a part of the document for this purpose.

(3) The date of recordation is the date when all of the elements required for recordation, including the prescribed fee and, if required, the statement referred to in paragraph (f)(1)(ii) of this section, have been received in the Copyright Office. After recordation the document, including any accompanying statement, is returned to the sender with a certificate of record.

(4) Recordation of a notice of termination by the Copyright Office is without prejudice to any party claiming that the legal and formal requirements for issuing a valid notice have not been met.

Copyright Office Regulation on Renewal of Copyright

Part 202 of 37 C.F.R. Chapter II is amended by revising §202.17 to read as follows:

§202.17. Renewals.

(a) *General.* This section prescribes rules pertaining to the application for renewal copyright under section 304(a) of title 17 of the United States Code, as amended by Pub. L. 94-553.

(b) *Definition.* For purposes of this section, the term "posthumous work" means a work that was unpublished on the date of the death of the author and with respect to which no copyright assignment or other contract for exploitation of the work occurred during the author's lifetime.

(c) *Renewal Time-Limits.*

    (1) For works originally copyrighted between January 1, 1950 and December 31, 1977, claims to renewal copyright must be registered within the last year of the original copyright term, which begins on December 31 of the 27th year of the copyright, and runs through December 31, of the 28th year of the copyright. The original copyright term for a published work is computed from the date of first publication; the term for a work originally registered in unpublished form is computed from the date of registration in the Copyright Office. Unless the required application and fee are received in the Copyright Office during the prescribed period before the first term of copyright expires, the copyright in the unrenewed work terminates at the expiration of twenty-eight years from the end of the calendar year in which copyright was originally secured. The Copyright Office has no discretion to extend the renewal time limits.

    (2) The provisions of paragraph (c)(1) of this section are subject to the following qualification: In any case where the year date in the notice on copies distributed by authority of the copyright owner is earlier than the year of first publication, claims to renewal copyright must be registered within the last year of the original copyright term, which begins on December 31 of the 27th year from the year contained in the notice, and runs through December 31 of the 28th year from the year contained in the notice.

    (3) Whenever a renewal applicant has cause to believe that a formal application for renewal (Form RE), and in the case of works under paragraph (d)(2) of this section, an accompanying affidavit and submission relating to the subsistence of first-term copyright, if sent to the Copyright Office by mail, might not be received in the Copyright Office before expiration of the time limits provided by 17 U.S.C., section 304(a), he or she may apply for renewal registration by telegraphic or similar unsigned written communication. An application made by this method only will be accepted if: (i) The message is received in the Copyright Office within the specified time limits; (ii) the applicant adequately identifies the work involved, the date of first publication or original registration, the name and address of the renewal claimant, and the statutory basis of the renewal claim; (iii) the fee for renewal registration, if not already on deposit, is received in the Copyright Office before the time for renewal registration has expired; and (iv) a formal application for renewal (Form RE), and in the case of works under paragraph (d)(2) of this section,

an accompanying affidavit and submission relating to subsistence of the first-term copyright are also received in the Copyright Office before February 1 of the following year.

(d) *Original Registration.*

    (1) Except as provided by paragraph (d)(2) of this section, copyright in a work will not be registered for a renewal term unless an original registration for the work has been made in the Copyright Office.

    (2) An original registration in the Copyright Office is not a condition precedent for renewal registration in the case of a work in which United States copyright subsists by virtue of section 9(c) of title 17 of the United States Code, in effect on December 31, 1977 (which implemented the Universal Copyright Convention) provided, however, that the application for renewal registration is accompanied by:

        (i) An affidavit identified as ''Renewal Affidavit for a U.C.C. Work'' and containing the following information:

            (A) The date of first publication of the work;

            (B) The place of first publication of the work;

            (C) The citizenship of the author on the date of first publication of the work;

            (D) The domicile of the author on the date of first publication of the work;

            (E) An averment that, at the time of first publication, all the copies of the work published under the authority of the author or other copyright proprietor bore the symbol © accompanied by the name of the copyright proprietor and the year of first publication, and the United States copyright subsists in the work;

            (F) The handwritten signature of the renewal claimant or the duly authorized agent of the renewal claimant. The signature shall (1) be accompanied by the printed or typewritten name of the person signing the affidavit and by the date of the signature; and (2) shall be immediately preceded by the following printed or typewritten statement in accordance with section 1746 of title 28 of the United States Code: I certify under penalty of perjury under the laws of the United States of America that the foregoing is true and correct.

        (ii) A submission relating to the notice of copyright and copyrightable content which shall be, in descending order of preference, comprised of:

            (A) One complete copy of the work as first published; or

            (B) (*1*) A photocopy of the title page of the work as first published, and

                (*2*) A photocopy of the page of the work as first published bearing the copyright notice, and

                (*3*) A specification as to the location, relative to each other, of the title and notice pages of the work as first published, if the pages are different, and

                (*4*) A brief description of the copyrightable content of the work, and

                (*5*) An explanation of the inability to submit one complete copy of the work as first published; or

            (C) A statement describing the position and contents of the copyright notice as it appeared on the work as first published, and a brief description of the copyrightable content. The statement shall be made and signed in accordance with paragraph (d)(2)(i)(F) of this section and shall also include an explanation of the inability to submit either one complete copy of the work as first published or photocopies of the title and notice pages of the work as first published.

(e) *Application for Renewal Registration.*

    (1) Each application for renewal registration submitted on or after January 1, 1978 shall be furnished on Form RE. Copies of Form RE are available free upon request to the Public Information Office, United States Copyright Office, Library of Congress, Washington, D.C. 20559.

    (2) (i) An application for renewal registration may be submitted by any eligible renewal claimant as specified in paragraph (f) of this section or by the duly authorized agent of any such claimant.

        (ii) An application for renewal registration shall be accompanied by a fee of $6. The application shall contain the information required by the form and its accompanying instructions, and shall include a certification. The certification shall consist of: (A) A designation of whether the applicant is the renewal claimant, or the duly authorized agent of such claimant (whose identity shall also be given); (B) the handwritten signature of such claimant or agent, accompanied by the typewritten or printed name of that person; (C) a declaration that the statements made in the application are correct to the best of that person's knowledge; and (D) the date of certification.

(iii) In the case of an application for renewal registration for a foreign work protected under the U.C.C. which has not been the subject of an original copyright registration, the application shall be accompanied by a "Renewal Affidavit for a U.C.C. Work" and a submission relating to the notice of copyright and the copyrightable content in accordance with paragraph (d)(2) of this section.

(3) Once a renewal registration has been made, the Copyright Office will not accept a duplicate application for renewal registration on behalf of the same renewal claimant.

(f) *Renewal Claimants.*

(1) Except as otherwise provided by paragraphs (f)(2) and (3) of this section, renewal claims may be registered only in the name(s) of the eligible person(s) falling within one of the following classes of renewal claimants specified in section 304(a) of the copyright law. If the work was a new version of a previous work, renewal may be claimed only in the new matter.

(i) In the case of any posthumous work or of any periodical, cyclopedic, or other composite work upon which the copyright was originally secured by the proprietor thereof, the renewal claim may be registered in the name of the proprietor;

(ii) In the case of any work copyrighted by a corporate body (otherwise than as assignees or licensees of the individual author) or by an employer for whom such work is made for hire, the renewal claim may be registered in the name of the proprietor; and

(iii) In the case of any other copyrighted work, including a contribution by an individual author to a periodical or to a cyclopedic or other composite work, the renewal claim may be registered in the name(s) of the following person(s) in descending order of eligibility:

(A) The author of the work, if still living;

(B) The widow, widower, or children of the author, if the author is not living;

(C) The author's executors, if there is a will and neither the author nor any widow, widower, or child of the author is living;

(D) The author's next of kin, in the absence of a will and if neither the author nor any widow, widower, or child of the author is living.

(2) The provisions of paragraph (f)(1) are subject to the following qualification: Notwithstanding the definition of "posthumous work" in paragraph (b) of this section, a renewal claim may be registered in the name of the proprietor of the work, as well as in the name of the appropriate claimant under paragraph (f)(1)(iii), in any case where a contract for exploitation of the work but no copyright assignment in the work has occurred during the author's lifetime. However, registration by the Copyright Office in this case should not be interpreted as evidencing the validity of the claim.

(3) The provisions of paragraph (f)(1)(iii)(C) and (D) of this section are subject to the following qualifications:

(i) In any case where: (A) The author has left a will which names no executor; (B) the author has left a will which names an executor who cannot or will not serve in that capacity; or (C) the author has left a will which names an executor who has been discharged upon settlement of the estate or removed before the estate has been completely administered, the renewal claim may be registered either in the name of an administrator cum testamento annexo (administrator c.t.a.) or an administrator de bonis non cum testamento annexo (administrator d.b.n.c.t.a.) so appointed by a court of competent jurisdiction;

(ii) In any case described in paragraph (f)(3)(i) of this section, except in the case where the author has left a will without naming an executor and a court appointed administrator c.t.a. or administrator d.b.n.c.t.a. is in existence at the time of renewal registration, the renewal claim also may be registered in the name of the author's next of kin. However, registration by the Copyright Office of the conflicting renewal claims in these cases should not be interpreted as evidencing the validity of either claim.

(17 U.S.C. 304, 205, 702, and 708)
[46 FR 58671, Dec. 3, 1981]

Copyright Office Regulation on Methods of Affixation and Positions of the Copyright Notice

Part 201 of 37 C.F.R. Chapter II is amended by adding a new §201.20 to read as follows:

§201.20. Methods of affixation and positions of the copyright notice on various types of works.

(a) *General*

    (1) This section specifies examples of methods of affixation and positions of the copyright notice on various types of works that will satisfy the notice requirement of section 401(c) of title 17 of the United States Code, as amended by Pub. L. 94-553. A notice considered ''acceptable'' under this regulation shall be considered to satisfy the requirement of that section that it be ''affixed to the copies in such manner and location as to give reasonable notice of the claim of copyright.'' As provided by that section, the examples specified in this regulation shall not be considered exhaustive of methods of affixation and positions giving reasonable notice of the claim of copyright.

    (2) The provisions of this section are applicable to copies publicly distributed on or after December 1, 1981. This section does not establish any rules concerning the form of the notice or the legal sufficiency of particular notices, except with respect to methods of affixation and positions of notice. The adequacy or legal sufficiency of a copyright notice is determined by the law in effect at the time of first publication of the work.

(b) *Definitions.* For the purposes of this section:

    (1) The terms ''audiovisual works,'' ''collective works,'' ''copies,'' ''device,'' ''fixed,'' ''machine,'' ''motion picture,'' ''pictorial, graphic, and sculptural works,'' and their variant forms, have the meanings given to them in section 101 of title 17.

    (2) ''Title 17'' means title 17 of the United States Code, as amended by Pub. L. 94-553.

    (3) In the case of a work consisting preponderantly of leaves on which the work is printed or otherwise reproduced on both sides, a ''page'' is one side of a leaf; where the preponderance of the leaves are printed on one side only, the terms ''page'' and ''leaf'' mean the same.

    (4) A work is published in ''book form'' if the copies embodying it consist of multiple leaves bound, fastened, or assembled in a predetermined order, as, for example, a volume, booklet, pamphlet, or multipage folder. For the purpose of this section, a work need not consist of textual matter in order to be considered published in ''book form.''

    (5) A ''title page'' is a page, or two consecutive pages facing each other, appearing at or near the front of the copies of a work published in book form, on which the complete title of the work is prominently stated and on which the names of the author or authors, the name of the publisher, the place of publication, or some combination of them, are given.

    (6) The meaning of the terms ''front,'' ''back,'' ''first,'' ''last,'' and ''following,'' when used in connection with works published in book form, will vary in relation

to the physical form of the copies, depending upon the particular language in which the work is written.

(7) In the case of a work published in book form with a hard or soft cover, the "front page" and "back page" of the copies are the outsides of the front and back covers; where there is no cover, the "front page," and "back page" are the pages visible at the front and back of the copies before they are opened.

(8) A "masthead" is a body of information appearing in approximately the same location in most issues of a newspaper, magazine, journal, review, or other periodical or serial, information about the staff, periodicity of issues, operation, and subscription and editorial policies, of the publication.

(9) A "single-leaf work" is a work published in copies consisting of a single leaf, including copies on which the work is printed or otherwise reproduced on either one side or on both sides of the leaf, and also folders which, without cutting or tearing the copies, can be opened out to form a single leaf. For the purpose of this section, a work need not consist of textual matter in order to be considered a "single-leaf work."

(c) *Manner of Affixation and Position Generally.*

(1) In all cases dealt with in this section, the acceptability of a notice depends upon its being permanently legible to an ordinary user of the work under normal conditions of use, and affixed to the copies in such manner and position that, when affixed, it is not concealed from view upon reasonable examination.

(2) Where, in a particular case, a notice does not appear in one of the precise locations prescribed in this section but a person looking in one of those locations would be reasonably certain to find a notice in another somewhat different location, that notice will be acceptable under this section.

(d) *Works Published in Book Form.* In the case of works published in book form, a notice reproduced on the copies in any of the following positions is acceptable:

(1) The title page, if any;

(2) The page immediately following the title page, if any;

(3) Either side of the front cover, if any; or, if there is no front cover, either side of the front leaf of the copies;

(4) Either side of the back cover, if any; or, if there is no back cover, either side of the back leaf of the copies;

(5) The first page of the main body of work;

(6) The last page of the main body of the work;

(7) Any page between the front page and the first page of the main body of the work, if: (i) There are no more than ten pages between the front page and the first page of the main body of the work; and (ii) the notice is reproduced prominently and is set apart from other matter on the page where it appears;

(8) Any page between the last page of the main body of the work and back page, if: (i) There are no more than ten pages between the last page of the main body of the work and the back page; and (ii) the notice is reproduced prominently and is set apart from the other matter on the page where it appears.

(9) In the case of a work published as an issue of a periodical or serial, in addition to any of the locations listed in paragraphs (d)(1) through (8) of this section, a notice is acceptable if it is located: (i) As a part of, or adjacent to, the masthead; (ii) on the page containing the masthead if the notice is reproduced prominently and is set apart from the other matter appearing on the page; or (iii) adjacent to a prominent heading, appearing at or near the front of the issue, containing the title of the periodical or serial and any combination of the volume and issue number and date of the issue.

(10) In the case of a musical work, in addition to any of the locations listed in paragraphs (d)(1) through (9) of this section, a notice is acceptable if it is located on the first page of music.

(e) *Single-Leaf Works.* In the case of single-leaf works, a notice reproduced on the copies anywhere on the front or back of the leaf is acceptable.

(f) *Contributions to Collective Works.* For a separate contribution to a collective work to be considered to "bear its own notice of copyright," as provided by 17 U.S.C. 404, a notice reproduced on the copies in any of the following positions is acceptable:

(1) Where the separate contribution is reproduced on a single page, a notice is acceptable if it appears: (i) Under the title of the contribution on that page; (ii)

adjacent to the contribution; or (iii) on the same page if, through format, wording, or both, the application of the notice to the particular contribution is made clear;

(2) Where the separate contribution is reproduced on more than one page of the collective work, a notice is acceptable if it appears: (i) Under a title appearing at or near the beginning of the contribution; (ii) on the first page of the main body of the contribution; (ii) immediately following the end of the contribution; or (iv) on any of the pages where the contribution appears, if: (A) The contribution is reproduced on no more than twenty pages of the collective work; (B) the notice is reproduced prominently and is set apart from other matter on the page where it appears; and (C) through format, wording, or both, the application of the notice to the particular contribution is made clear;

(3) Where the separate contribution is a musical work, in addition to any of the locations listed in paragraphs (f)(1) and (2) of this section, a notice is acceptable if it is located on the first page of music of the contribution;

(4) As an alternative to placing the notice on one of the pages where a separate contribution itself appears, the contribution is considered to "bear its own notice" if the notice appears clearly in juxtaposition with a separate listing of the contribution by title, or if the contribution is untitled, by a description reasonably identifying the contribution: (i) On the page bearing the copyright notice for the collective work as a whole, if any; or (ii) in a clearly identified and readily-accessible table of contents or listing of acknowledgements appearing near the front or back of the collective work as a whole.

(g) *Works Reproduced in Machine-Readable Copies.* For works reproduced in machine-readable copies (such as magnetic tapes or disks, punched cards, or the like, from which the work cannot ordinarily be visually perceived except with the aid of a machine or device,[1] each of the following constitute examples of acceptable methods of affixation and position of notice:

(1) A notice embodied in the copies in machine-readable form in such a manner that on visually perceptible printouts it appears either with or near the title, or at the end of the work;

(2) A notice that is displayed at the user's terminal at sign on;

(3) A notice that is continuously on terminal display; or

(4) A legible notice reproduced durably, so as to withstand normal use, on a gummed or other label securely affixed to the copies or to a box, reel, cartridge, cassette, or other container used as a permanent receptacle for the copies.

(h) *Motion Pictures and Other Audiovisual Works.*

(1) The following constitute examples of acceptable methods of affixation and positions of the copyright notice on motion pictures and other audiovisual works: A notice that is embodied in the copies by a photomechanical or electronic process, in such a position that it ordinarily would appear whenever the work is performed in its entirety, and that is located: (i) With or near the title; (ii) with the cast, credits, and similar information; (iii) at or immediately following the beginning of the work; or (iv) at or immediately preceding the end of the work.

(2) In the case of an untitled motion picture or other audiovisual work whose duration is sixty seconds or less, in addition to any of the locations listed in paragraph (h)(1) of this section, a notice that is embodied in the copies by a photomechanical or electronic process, in such a position that it ordinarily would appear to the projectionist or broadcaster when preparing the work for performance, is acceptable if it is located on the leader of the film or tape immediately preceding the beginning of the work.

(3) In the case of the motion picture or other audiovisual work that is distributed to the public for private use, the notice may be affixed, in addition to the locations specified in paragraph (h)(1) of this section, on the housing or container, if it is a permanent receptacle for the work.

---

[1] Works published in a form requiring the use of a machine or device for purposes of optical enlargement (such as film, filmstrips, slide films, and works published in any variety of microform) and works published in visually perceptible form but used in connection with optical scanning devices, are not within this category.

(i) *Pictorial, Graphic, and Sculptural Works.* The following constitute examples of acceptable methods of affixation and positions of the copyright notice on various forms of pictorial, graphic, and sculptural works:

(1) Where a work is reproduced in two-dimensional copies, a notice affixed directly or by means of a label cemented, sewn, or otherwise attached durably, so as to withstand normal use, of the front or back of the copies, or to any backing, mounting, matting, framing, or other material to which the copies are durably attached, so as to withstand normal use, or in which they are permanently housed, is acceptable.

(2) Where a work is reproduced in three-dimensional copies, a notice affixed directly or by means of a label cemented, sewn, or otherwise attached durably, so as to withstand normal use, to any visible portion of the work, or to any base, mounting, framing, or other material on which the copies are durably attached, so as to withstand normal use, or in which they are permanently housed, is acceptable.

(3) Where, because of the size or physical characteristics of the material in which the work is reproduced in copies, it is impossible or extremely impracticable to affix a notice to the copies directly or by means of a durable label, a notice is acceptable if it appears on a tag that is of durable material, so as to withstand normal use, and that is attached to the copy with sufficient durability that it will remain with the copy while it is passing through its normal channels of commerce.

(4) Where a work is reproduced in copies consisting of sheet-like or strip material bearing multiple or continuous reproductions of the work, the notice may be applied: (i) To the reproduction itself; (ii) to the margin, selvage, or reverse side of the material at frequent and regular intervals; or (iii) if the material contains neither a selvage nor a reverse side, to tags or labels, attached to the copies and to any spools, reels, or containers housing them in such a way that a notice is visible while the copies are passing through their normal channels of commerce.

(5) If the work is permanently housed in a container, such as a game or puzzle box, a notice reproduced on the permanent container is acceptable.

(17 U.S.C. 401, 702)

[46 FR 58312, Dec. 1, 1981]

Copyright Office Regulation on Deposits for Library of Congress and for Copyright Registration

§202.15. Revoked
§202.16. Revoked

1. By revoking §§202.15 and 202.16; and
2. By adding new §§202.19, 202.20, and 202.21, to read as follows:

§202.19. Deposit of published copies or phonorecords for the Library of Congress

(a) *General.* This section prescribes rules pertaining to the deposit of copies and phonorecords of published works for the Library of Congress under section 407 of title 17 of the United States Code, as amended by Pub. L. 94–553. The provisions of this section are not applicable to the deposit of copies and phonorecords for purposes of copyright registration under section 408 of title 17, except as expressly adopted in §202.20 of these regulations.

(b) *Definitions.* For the purposes of this section:

    (1) (i) The "best edition' of a work is the edition, published in the United States at any time before the date of deposit, that the Library of Congress determines to be most suitable for its purposes.

        (ii) Criteria for selection of the "best edition" from among two or more published editions of the same version of the same work are set forth in the statement entitled "Best Edition of Published Copyrighted Works for the Collections of the Library of Congress" (hereafter referred to as the "Best Edition Statement") in effect at the time of deposit. Copies of the Best Edition Statement are available upon request made to the Acquisitions and Processing Division of the Copyright Office.

        (iii) Where no specific criteria for the selection of the "best edition" are established in the Best Edition Statement, that edition which, in the judgment of the Library of Congress, represents the highest quality for its purposes shall be considered the "best edition". In such cases: (A) When the Copyright Office is aware that two or more editions of a work have been published it will consult with other appropriate officials of the Library of Congress to obtain instructions as to the "best edition" and (except in cases for which special relief is granted) will require deposit of that edition; and (B) when a potential depositor is uncertain which of two or more published editions comprises the "best edition", inquiry should be made to the Acquisitions and Processing Division of the Copyright Office.

        (iv) Where differences between two or more "editions" of a work represent variations in copyrightable content, each edition is considered a separate version, and hence a different work, for the purpose of this section, and criteria of "best edition" based on such differences do not apply.

    (2) A "complete" copy includes all elements comprising the unit of publication of the best edition of the work, including elements that, if considered separately, would not be copyrightable subject matter or would otherwise be exempt from mandatory deposit requirements under paragraph (c) of this section. In the case of sound recordings, a "complete" phonorecord includes the phonorecord, together with any printed or other visually perceptible material published with such phonorecord (such as textual or pictorial matter appearing on record sleeves or album covers, or embodied in leaflets or booklets included in a sleeve, album, or other container). In the case of a musical composition published in copies only, or in both copies and phonorecords; (i) if the only publication of copies in the United States took place by the rental, lease, or lending of a full score and parts, a full score is a "complete" copy; and (ii) if the only publication of copies in the United States took place by the rental, lease, or lending of a conductor's score and parts, a conductor's score is a "complete" copy. In the case of a motion picture, a copy is "complete" if the reproduction of all of the visual and aural elements comprising the copyrightable subject matter in the work is

clean, undamaged, undeteriorated, and free of splices, and if the copy itself and its physical housing are free of any defects that would interfere with the performance of the work or that would cause mechanical, visual, or audible defects or distortions.

(3) The terms "copies", "collective work", "device", "fixed", "literary work", "machine", "motion picture", "phonorecord", "publication", "sound recording", and "useful article", and their variant forms, have the meanings given to them in section 101 of title 17.

(4) "Title 17" means title 17 of the United States Code, as amended by Pub. L. 94–553.

(c) *Exemptions from deposit requirements.* The following categories of material are exempt from the deposit requirements of section 407(a) of title 17:

(1) Diagrams and models illustrating scientific or technical works or formulating scientific or technical information in linear or three-dimensional form, such as an architectural or engineering blueprint, plan, or design, a mechanical drawing, or an anatomical model.

(2) Greeting cards, picture postcards, and stationery.

(3) Lectures, sermons, speeches, and addresses when published individually and not as a collection of the works of one or more authors.

(4) Literary, dramatic, and musical works published only as embodied in phonorecords. This category does not exempt the owner of copyright, or of the exclusive right of publication, in a sound recording resulting from the fixation of such works in a phonorecord from the applicable deposit requirements for the sound recording.

(5) Literary works, including computer programs and automated data bases, published in the United States only in the form of machine-readable copies (such as magnetic tape or disks, punched cards, or the like) from which the work cannot ordinarily be visually perceived except with the aid of a machine or device. Works published in a form requiring the use of a machine or device for purposes of optical enlargement (such as film, filmstrips, slide films and works published in any variety of microform), and works published in visually perceivable form but used in connection with optical scanning devices, are not within this category and are subject to the applicable deposit requirements.

(6) Three-dimensional sculptural works, and any works published only as reproduced in or on jewelry, dolls, toys, games, plaques, floor coverings, wallpaper and similar commercial wall coverings, textile and other fabrics, packaging material, or any useful article. Globes, relief models, and similar cartographic representations of area are not within this category and are subject to the applicable deposit requirements.

(7) Prints, labels, and other advertising matter published in connection with the rental, lease, lending, licensing, or sale of articles of merchandise, works of authorship, or services.

(8) Tests, and answer material for tests, when published separately from other literary works.

(9) Works first published as individual contributions to collective works. This category does not exempt the owner of copyright, or of the exclusive right of publication, in the collective work as a whole from the applicable deposit requirements for the collective work.

(10) Works first published outside the United States and later published in the United States without change in copyrightable content, if

    (i) registration for the work was made under §17 U.S.C. 408 before the work was published in the United States; or

    (ii) registration for the work was made under 17 U.S.C 408 after the work was published in the United States but before a demand for deposit is made under 17 U.S.C 407(d).

(11) Works published only as embodied in a soundtrack that is an integral part of a motion picture. This category does not exempt the owner of copyright, or of the exclusive right of publication, in the motion picture from the applicable deposit requirements for the motion picture.

(12) Motion pictures that consist of television transmission programs and that have been published, if at all, only by reason of a license or other grant to a nonprofit institution of the right to make a fixation of such programs directly from a transmission to the public, with or without the right to make further uses of such fixations.

(d) *Nature of required deposit.*

(1) Subject to the provisions of paragraph (d)(2) of this section, the deposit required to satisfy the provisions of section 407(a) of title 17 shall consist of

(i)   in the case of published works other than sound recordings, two complete copies of the best edition; and

(ii) in the case of published sound recordings, two complete phonorecords of the best edition.

(2) In the case of certain published works not exempt from deposit requirements under paragraph (c) of this section, the following special provisions shall apply:

(i)   In the case of published three-dimensional cartographic representations of area, such as globes and relief models, the deposit of one complete copy of the best edition of the work will suffice in lieu of the two copies required by paragraph (d)(1) of this section.

(ii) In the case of published motion pictures, the deposit of one complete copy of the best edition of the work will suffice in lieu of the two copies required by paragraph (d)(1) of this section. Any deposit for a published motion picture must be accompanied by a separate description of its contents, such as a continuity, pressbook, or synopsis. The Library of Congress may, at its sole discretion, enter into an agreement permitting the return of copies of published motion pictures to the depositor under certain conditions and establishing certain rights and obligations of the Library with respect to such copies. In the event of termination of such an agreement by the Library it shall not be subject to reinstatement, nor shall the depositor or any successor in interest of the depositor be entitled to any similar or subsequent agreement with the Library, unless at the sole discretion of the Library it would be in the best interests of the Library to reinstate the agreement or enter into a new agreement.

(iii) In the case of any published work deposited in the form of a hologram, the deposit shall be accompanied by: (A) Two sets of precise instructions for displaying the image fixed in the hologram; and (B) two sets of identifying material in compliance with §202.21 of these regulations and clearly showing the displayed image.

(iv) In any case where an individual author is the owner of copyright in a published pictorial or graphic work and (A) less than five copies of the work have been published, or (B) the work has been published and sold or offered for sale in a limited edition consisting of no more than three hundred numbered copies, the deposit of one complete copy of the best edition of the work or, alternatively, the deposit of photographs or other identifying material in compliance with §202.21 of these regulations, will suffice in lieu of the two copies required by paragraph (d)(1) of this section.

(v)   In the case of a musical composition published in copies only, or in both copies and phonorecords, if the only publication of copies in the United States took place by rental, lease, or lending, the deposit of one complete copy of the best edition will suffice in lieu of the two copies required by paragraph (d)(1) of this section.

(vi) In the case of published multimedia kits that are prepared for use in systematic instructional activities and that include literary works, audiovisual works, sound recordings, or any combination of such works, the deposit of one complete copy of the best edition will suffice in lieu of the two copies required by paragraph (d)(1) of this section.

(e) *Special relief.*

(1) In the case of any published work not exempt from deposit under paragraph (c) of this section, the Register of Copyrights may, after consultation with other appropriate officials of the Library of Congress and upon such conditions as the Register may determine after such consultation:

(i)   Grant an exemption from the deposit requirements of section 407(a) of title 17 on an individual basis for single works or series or groups of works; or

(ii) permit the deposit of one copy or phonorecord, or alternative identifying material, in lieu of the two copies or phonorecords required by paragraph (d)(1) of this section; or

(iii) permit the deposit of incomplete copies or phonorecords, or copies or phonorecords other than those normally comprising the best edition.

(2) Any decision as to whether to grant such special relief, and the conditions under which special relief is to be granted, shall be made by the Register of Copyrights after consultation with other appropriate officials of the Library of Congress, and shall be based upon the acquisition policies of the Library of Congress then in force.

(3) Requests for special relief under this paragraph shall be made in writing to the Chief,

Acquisitions and Processing Division of the Copyright Office, shall be signed by or on behalf of the owner of copyright or of the exclusive right of publication in the work, and shall set forth specific reason why the request should be granted.

(4) The Register of Copyrights may, after consultation with other appropriate officals of the Library of Congress, terminate any ongoing or continuous grant of special relief. Notice of termination shall be given in writing and shall be sent to the individual person or organization to whom the grant of special relief has been given, at the last address shown in the records of the Copyright Office. A notice of termination may be given at any time, but it shall state a specific date of termination that is at least 30 days later than the date the notice is mailed. Termination shall not affect the validity of any deposit earlier made under the grant of special relief.

(f) *Submission and receipt of copies and phonorecords.*

(1) All copies and phonorecords deposited in the Copyright Office will be considered to be deposited only in compliance with section 407 of title 17 unless they are accompanied by:

(i) An application for registration of claim to copyright, or

(ii) a clear written request that they be held for connection with a separately forwarded application.

Copies or phonorecords deposited without such an accompanying application or written request will not be connected with or held for receipt of separate applications, and will not satisfy the deposit provisions of section 408 of title 17 of §202.20 of these regulations. Any written request that copies or phonorecords be held for connection with a separately forwarded application must appear in a letter or similar document accompanying the deposit; a request or instruction appearing on the packaging, wrapping or container for the deposit will not be effective for this purpose.

(2) All copies and phonorecords deposited in the Copyright Office under section 407 of title 17, unless accompanied by written instructions to the contrary, will be considered to be deposited by the person or persons named in the copyright notice on the work.

(3) Upon request by the depositor made at the time of the deposit, the Copyright Office will issue a Certificate of Receipt for the deposit of copies or phonorecords of a work under this section. Certificates of Receipt will be issued in response to requests made after the date of deposit only if the requesting party is identified in the records of the Copyright Office as having made the deposit. In either case, requests for a Certificate of Receipt must be in writing and accompanied by a fee of $2. A Certificate of Receipt will include identification of the depositor, the work deposited, and the nature and format of the copy or phonorecord deposited, together with the date of receipt.

§202.20. Deposit of copies and phonorecords for copyright registration

(a) *General.* This section prescribes rules pertaining to the deposit of copies and phonorecords of published and unpublished works for the purpose of copyright registration under section 408 of title 17 of the United States Code, as amended by Pub. L. 94–553. The provisions of this section are not applicable to the deposit of copies and phonorecords for the Library of Congress under section 407 of title 17, except as expressly adopted in §202.19 of these regulations.

(b) *Definitions.* For the purposes of this section:

(1) The "best edition" of a work has the meaning set forth in §202.19(b)(1) of these regulations.

(2) A "complete" copy or phonorecord means the following:

(i) *Unpublished works.* Subject to the requirements of paragraph (vi) of this §202.20(b)(2), a "complete" copy or phonorecord of an unpublished work is a copy or phonorecord representing the entire copyrightable content of the work for which registration is sought;

(ii) *Published works.* Subject to the requirements of paragraphs (iii) through (vi) of this §202.20(b)(2), a "complete" copy or phonorecord of a published work includes all elements comprising the applicable unit of publication of the work, including elements that, if considered separately, would not be copyrightable subject matter. However, even where certain physically separable elements included in the applicable unit of publication are missing from the deposit, a copy or phonorecord will be considered "complete" for purposes of registration where: (A) The copy or phonorecord deposited contains all parts of the work for which copyright registration is sought; and (B) the removal of the missing elements did not physically damage the copy or phonorecord or garble its contents; and (C) the work is exempt from the mandatory deposit requirements under section 407 of title 17 of the United States Code and §202.19(c) of these regulations, or the copy deposited consists entirely of a container, wrapper, or holder, such as an envelope, sleeve, jacket, slipcase, box, bag, folder, binder, or other receptacle acceptable for deposit under paragraph (c)(2) of this section:

   (iii) *Contributions to collective works*. In the case of a published contribution to a collective work, a "complete" copy or phonorecord is the entire collective work including the contribution or, in the case of a newspaper, the entire section including the contribution;

   (iv) *Sound recordings*. In the case of published sound recordings, a "complete" phonorecord has the meaning set forth in §202.19(b)(2) of these regulations;

   (v) *Musical scores*. In the case of a musical composition published in copies only, or in both copies and phonorecords; (i) If the only publication of copies took place by the rental, lease, or lending of a full score and parts, a full score is a "complete" copy; and (ii) if the only publication of copies took place by the rental, lease, or lending of a conductor's score and parts, a conductor's score is a "complete" copy;

   (vi) *Motion pictures*. In the case of a published or unpublished motion picture, a copy is "complete" if the reproduction of all of the visual and aural elements comprising the copyrightable subject matter in the work is clean, undamaged, undeteriorated, and free of splices, and if the copy itself and its physical housing are free of any defects that would interfere with the performance of the work or that would cause mechanical, visual, or audible defects or distortions.

  (3) The terms "copy", "collective work", "device", "fixed", "literary work", "machine", "motion picture", "phonorecord", "publication", "sound recording", "transmission program", and "useful article", and their variant forms, have the meanings given to them in section 101 of title 17.

  (4) A "secure test" is a non-marketed test administered under supervision at specified centers on specific dates, all copies of which are accounted for and either destroyed or returned to restricted locked storage following each administration. For these purposes a test is not marketed if copies are not sold but it is distributed and used in such a manner that ownership and control of copies remain with the test sponsor or publisher.

  (5) "Title 17" means title 17 of the United States Code, as amended by Pub. L. 94–553.

  (6) For the purposes of determining the applicable deposit requirements under this §202.20 only, the following shall be considered as unpublished motion pictures: motion pictures that consist of television transmission programs and that have been published, if at all, only by reason of a license or other grant to a nonprofit institution of the right to make a fixation of such programs directly from a transmission to the public, with or without the right to make further uses of such fixations.

(c) *Nature of required deposit*.

  (1) Subject to the provisions of paragraph (c)(2) of this section, the deposit required to accompany an application for registration of claim to copyright under section 408 of title 17 shall consist of:

   (i) In the case of unpublished works, one complete copy or phonorecord.

   (ii) In the case of works first published in the United States before January 1, 1978, two complete copies or phonorecords of the work as first published.

   (iii) In the case of works first published in the United States on or after January 1, 1978, two complete copies or phonorecords of the best edition.

   (iv) In the case of works first published outside of the United States, whenever published, one complete copy or phonorecord of the work as first published. For the purposes of this section, any works simultaneously first published within and outside of the United States shall be considered to be first published in the United States.

  (2) In the case of certain works, the special provisions set forth in this clause shall apply. In any case where this clause specifies that one copy or phonorecord may be submitted, that copy or phonorecord shall represent the best edition, or the work as first published, as set forth in paragraph (c)(1) of this section.

   (i) *General*. In the following cases the deposit of one complete copy or phonorecord will suffice in lieu of two copies or phonorecords: (A) Published three-dimensional cartographic representations of area, such as globes and relief models; (B) published diagrams illustrating scientific or technical works or formulating scientific or technical information in linear or other two-dimensional form, such as an architectural or engineering blueprint, or a mechanical drawing; (C) published greeting cards, picture postcards and stationery; (D) lectures, sermons, speeches, and addresses published individually and not as a collection of the works of one or more authors; (E) published contributions to a collective work; (F) musical compositions published only by the rental, lease, or lending of copies; and (G) published multimedia kits that are prepared for use in systematic instructional activities and that include literary works, audiovisual works, sound recordings, or any combination of such works; and (H) works exempted from the requirement of depositing identifying material under §202.20(c)(2)(ix)(B)(5) of these regulations.

(ii) *Motion pictures.* In the case of published motion pictures, the deposit of one complete copy will suffice in lieu of two copies. The deposit of a copy or copies for any published or unpublished motion picture must be accompanied by a separate description of its contents, such as a continuity, pressbook, or synopsis. The Library of Congress may, at its sole discretion, enter into an agreement permitting the return of copies of published motion pictures to the depositor under certain conditions and establishing certain rights and obligations of the Library of Congress with respect to such copies. In the event of termination of such an agreement by the Library, it shall not be subject to reinstatement, nor shall the depositor or any successor in interest of the depositor be entitled to any similar or subsequent agreement with the Library, unless at the sole discretion of the Library it would be in the best interests of the Library to reinstate the agreement or enter into a new agreement. In the case of unpublished motion pictures (including television transmission programs that have been fixed and transmitted to the public, but have not been published), the deposit of identifying material in compliance with §202.21 of these regulations may be made and will suffice in lieu of an actual copy.

(iii) *Holograms.* In the case of any work deposited in the form of a hologram, the copy or copies shall be accompanied by: (A) Precise instructions for displaying the image fixed in the hologram; and (B) photographs or other identifying material complying with §202.21 of these regulations and clearly showing the displayed image. The number of sets of instructions and identifying material shall be the same as the number of copies required.

(iv) *Certain pictorial and graphic works.* In the case of any unpublished pictorial or graphic work, deposit of identifying material in compliance with §202.21 of these regulations may be made and will suffice in lieu of deposit of an actual copy. In the case of a published pictorial or graphic work, deposit of one complete copy, or of identifying material in compliance with §202.21 of these regulations, may be made and will suffice in lieu of deposit of two actual copies where an individual author is the owner of copyright, and either: (A) Less than five copies of the work have been published; or (B) the work has been published and sold or offered for sale in a limited edition consisting of no more than 300 numbered copies.

(v) *Commercial prints and labels.* In the case of prints, labels, and other advertising matter published in connection with the rental, lease, lending, licensing, or sale of articles of merchandise, works of authorship, or services, the deposit of one complete copy will suffice in lieu of two copies. Where the print or label is published in a larger work, such as a newspaper or other periodical, one copy of the entire page or pages upon which it appears may be submitted in lieu of the entire larger work. In the case of prints or labels physically inseparable from a three-dimensional object, identifying material complying with §202.21 of these regulations must be submitted rather than an actual copy or copies except under the conditions of paragraph (c)(2)(ix)(B)(6) of this section.

(vi) *Tests.* In the case of tests, and answer material for tests, published separately from other literary works, the deposit of one complete copy will suffice in lieu of two copies. In the case of any secure test the Copyright Office will return the deposit to the applicant promptly after examination: *Provided,* That sufficient portions, description, or the like are retained so as to constitute a sufficient archival record of the deposit.

(vii) *Machine-readable works.* In cases where an unpublished literary work is fixed, or a published literary work is published in the United States, only in the form of machine-readable copies (such as magnetic tape or disks, punched cards, or the like) from which the work cannot ordinarily be perceived except with the aid of a machine or device.[1] the deposit shall consist of:

(A) For published or unpublished computer programs, one copy of identifying portions of the program, reproduced in a form visually perceptible without the aid of a machine or device, either on paper or in microform. For these purposes, "identifying portions" shall mean either the first and last twenty-five pages or equivalent units of the program if reproduced on paper, or at least the first and last twenty-five pages or equivalent units of the program if reproduced in microform, together with the page or equivalent unit containing the copyright notice, if any.

(B) For published and unpublished automated data bases, compilations, statistical compendia, and other literary works so fixed or published, one copy of identifying portions of the work, reproduced in a form visually perceptible without the aid of a machine or device, either on paper or in microform. For these purposes: (*1*) "identifying portions" shall mean either the first and last twenty-five pages or equivalent units of the work if reproduced on paper, or at least the first and last twenty-five pages or equivalent units of work if reproduced on microform, or, in the case of automated data bases comprising separate and distinct data files, representative portions of each separate data file consisting of either 50 complete data records from each file or the entire file, whichever is less; and (*2*) "data file" and "file" mean a group of data records pertaining to a common subject matter, regardless of the physical size of the records or the number of data items included in them. (In the case of revised versions of such data bases, the portions deposited must contain representative data records which have been added or modified.) In any case where the deposit comprises representative portions of each separate file of an automated data base as indicated above, it shall be accompanied by a typed or printed descriptive statement containing: The title of the data base; the name and address of the copyright claimant; the name and content of each separate file within the data base, including the subject matter involved, the origin(s) of the data, and the approximate number of individual records within the file; and a description of the exact contents of any machine-readable copyright notice employed in or with the work and the manner and frequency with which it is displayed (e.g., at user's terminal only at sign-on, or continuously on terminal display, or on printouts, etc.). If a visually-perceptible copyright notice is placed on any copies of the work (such as magnetic tape reels) or their container, a sample of such notice must also accompany the statement.

(viii) *Works reproduced in or on sheet-like materials.* In the case of any unpublished work that is fixed, or any published work that is published, only in the form of a two-dimensional reproduction on sheet-like materials such as textile and other fabrics, wallpaper and similar commercial wall coverings, carpeting, floor tile, and similar commercial floor coverings, and wrapping paper and similar packaging material, the deposit shall consist of one copy in the form of an actual swatch or piece of such material sufficient to show all elements of the work in which copyright is claimed and the copyright notice appearing on the work, if any. If the work consists of a repeated pictorial or graphic design, the complete design and at least one repetition must be shown. If the sheet-like material in or on which a published work has been reproduced has been embodied in or attached to a three-dimensional object, such as wearing apparel, furniture, or any other three-dimensional manufactured article, and the work has been published only in that form, the deposit must consist of identifying material complying with §202.21 of these regulations instead of a copy.

(ix) *Works reproduced in or on three-dimensional objects.*

(A) In the following cases the deposit must consist of identifying material complying with §201.21 of these regulations instead of a copy or copies: (*1*) Any three-dimensional sculptural work, including any illustration or formulation of artistic expression or information in three-dimensional form. Examples of such works include statues, carvings, ceramics, moldings, constructions, models, and maquettes; and (*2*) Any two-dimensional or three-dimensional work that, if unpublished, has been fixed, or, if published, has been published only in or on jewelry, dolls toys, games, or any three-dimensional useful article.

---

[1] Works published in a form requiring the use of a machine or device for purposes of optical enlargement (such as film, filmstrips, slide films, and works published in any variety of microform), and works published in visually perceptible form but used in connection with optical scanning devices, are not within this category.

(B) In the following cases, the requirements of paragraph (A) of this §202.20(c)(2)(ix) for the deposit of identifying material shall not apply; (*1*) Works that are reproduced by intaglio or relief printing methods on two-dimensional materials such as paper or fabrics; (*2*) Three-dimensional cartographic representations of area, such as globes and relief models; (*3*) Works that have been fixed or published in or on a useful article that comprises one of the elements of the unit of publication of an educational or instructional kit which also includes a literary or audiovisual work, a sound recording, or any combination of such works; and (*4*) Published works exempt from the deposit of copies under section 407 of title 17 and §202.19(c) of these regulations, where the "complete" copy of the work within the meaning of paragraph (b)(2) of this section consists of a reproduction of the work on a two-dimensional materials such as paper or fabrics; and (*5*) published works consisting of multiple parts that are packaged and published in a box or similar container with flat sides and with dimensions of no more than 12 × 24 × 6 inches, and that include among the copyrightable elements of the work, in addition to any copyrightable element on the box or other container, three or more three-dimensional, physically separable parts; and (*6*) works reproduced on three-dimensional containers or holders such as boxes, cases, and cartons, where the container or holder can be readily opened out, unfolded, slit at the corners, or in some other way made adaptable for flat storage, and the copy, when flattened, does not exceed 96 inches in any dimension.

(x) *Soundtracks.* For separate registration of an unpublished work that is fixed, or a published work that is published, only as embodied in a soundtrack that is an integral part of a motion picture, the deposit of identifying material in compliance with §202.21 of these regulations will suffice in lieu of an actual copy or copies of the motion picture.

(xi) *Oversize deposits.* In any case where the deposit otherwise required by this section exceeds ninety-six inches in any dimension, identifying material complying with §202.21 of these regulations must be submitted instead of an actual copy or copies.

(d) *Special relief.*

(1) In any case the Register of Copyrights may, after consultation with other appropriate officials of the Library of Congress and upon such conditions as the Register may determine after such consultation: (i) Permit the deposit of one copy or phonorecord, or alternative identifying material, in lieu of the one or two copies or phonorecords otherwise required by paragraph (c)(1) of this section; (ii) permit the deposit of incomplete copies or phonorecords, or copies or phonorecords other than those normally comprising the best edition; or (iii) permit the deposit of an actual copy or copies, in lieu of the identifying material otherwise required by this section.

(2) Any decision as to whether to grant such special relief, and the conditions under which special relief is to be granted, shall be made by the Register of Copyrights after consultation with other appropriate officials of the Library of Congress, and shall be based upon the acquisition policies of the Library of Congress then in force and the archival and examining requirements of the Copyright Office.

(3) Requests for special relief under this paragraph may be combined with requests for special relief under §202.19 (e) of these regulations. Whether so combined or made solely under this paragraph, such requests shall be made in writing to the Chief, Examining Division of the Copyright Office, shall be signed by or on behalf of the person signing the application for registration, and shall set forth specific reasons why the request should be granted.

(4) The Register of Copyrights may, after consultation with other appropriate officials of the Library of Congress, terminate any ongoing or continuous grant of special relief. Notice of termination shall be given in writing and shall be sent to the individual person or organization to whom the grant of special relief had been given, at the last address shown in the records of the Copyright Office. A notice of termination may be given at any time, but it shall state a specific date of termination that is at least 30 days later than the date the notice is mailed. Termination shall not affect the validity of any deposit or registration earlier made under the grant of special relief.

(e) *Use of copies and phonorecords deposited for the Library of Congress.* Copies and phonorecords deposited for the Library of Congress under section 407 of title 17 and §202.19 of these regulations may be used to satisfy the deposit provisions of this section if they are accompanied by an application for registration of claim to copyright in the work represented by the deposit, or connected with such an application under the conditions set forth in §202.19(f)(1) of these regulations.

§202.21. Deposit of identifying material instead of copies

(a) *General*. Subject to the specific provisions of paragraphs (f) and (g) of this section, in any case where the deposit of identifying material is permitted or required under §202.19 or §202.20 of these regulations for published or unpublished works, the material shall consist of photographic prints, transparencies, photostats, drawings, or similar two-dimensional reproductions or renderings of the work, in a form visually perceivable without the aid of a machine or device. In the case of pictorial or graphic works, such material shall reproduce the actual colors employed in the work. In all other cases, such material may be in black and white or may consist of a reproduction of the actual colors.

(b) *Completeness; number of sets*. As many pieces of identifying material as are necessary to show clearly the entire copyrightable content of the work for which deposit is being made, or for which registration is being sought, shall be submitted. Except in cases falling under the provisions of §202.19 (d)(2)(iii) or §202.20 (c)(2)(iii) with respect to holograms, only one set of such complete identifying material is required.

(c) *Size*. All pieces of identifying material (except drawings or the like of copyright notices under paragraph (e) of this section) must be of uniform size. Photographic transparencies must be at least 35 mm. in size, and, if such transparencies are 3 × 3 inches or less, must be fixed in cardboard, plastic, or similar mounts to facilitate identification, handling, and storage. The Copyright Office prefers that transparencies larger than 3 × 3 inches be mounted in a way that facilitates handling and preservation, and reserves the right to require such mounting in particular cases. All types of identifying material must be not less than 3 × 3 inches and not more than 9 × 12 inches, but preferably 8 × 10 inches. Except in the case of transparencies, the image of the work must be either lifesize or larger, or if less than lifesize must be large enough to show clearly the entire copyrightable content of the work.

(d) *Title and dimensions*. At least one piece of identifying material must, on its front, back, or mount, indicate the title of the work and an exact measurement of one or more dimensions of the work.

(e) *Copyright notice*. In the case of works published with notice of copyright, the notice and its position on the work must be clearly shown on at least one piece of identifying material. Where necessary because of the size or position of the notice, a separate drawing or the like, no larger than 9 × 12 inches, showing the exact appearance and content of the notice, its dimensions, and its specific position on the work shall be submitted.

(f) For separate registration of an unpublished work that is fixed, or a published work that is published, only as embodied in a soundtrack that is an integral part of a motion picture, identifying material deposited in lieu of an actual copy or copies of the motion picture shall consist of:

 (1) a transcription of the entire work, or a reproduction of the entire work on a phonorecord; and

 (2) photographs or other reproductions from the motion picture showing the title of the motion picture, the soundtrack credits, and the copyright notice for the soundtrack, if any.

The provisions of paragraphs (b), (c), (d), and (e) of this §202.21 do not apply to identifying material deposited under this paragraph (f).

(g) In the case of unpublished motion pictures (including transmission programs that have been fixed and transmitted to the public, but have not been published), identifying material deposited in lieu of an actual copy shall consist of either:

 (1) an audio cassette or other phonorecord reproducing the entire soundtrack or other sound portion of the motion picture, and a description of the motion picture; or

 (2) a set consisting of one frame enlargement or similar visual reproduction from each ten minute segment of the motion picture, and a description of the motion picture.

In either case the "description" may be a continuity, a pressbook, or a synopsis, but in all cases it must include: (i) the title or continuing title of the work, and the episode title, if any: (ii) the nature and general content of the program; (iii) the date when the work was first fixed and whether or not fixation was simultaneous with first transmission; (iv) the date of first transmission, if any; (v) the running time; and (vi) the credits appearing on the work, if any. The provisions of paragraphs (b), (c), (d), and (e) of this §202.21 do not apply to identifying material submitted under this paragraph (g).

(17 U.S.C. 407, 408, 702)

[FR Doc. 78–26108 Filed 9–18–78; 8:45 am]

Appendix C5

Best Edition of Published Works for the Collections of the Library of Congress and for Copyright Registration

The Library of Congress has set forth, for the guidance of the public in complying with deposit requirements of the Copyright Law, a Best Edition Statement which reads as follows:

Appendix—"Best Edition" of Published Copyrighted Works for the Collections of the Library of Congress

The Copyright Law (Title 17, United States Code) requires that copies or phonorecords deposited in the Copyright Office be of the "best edition" of the work. The law states that "The 'best edition' of a work is the edition, published in the United States at any time before the date of deposit, that the Library of Congress determines to be most suitable for its purposes."

When two or more editions of the same version of a work have been published, the one of the highest quality is generally considered to be the best edition. In judging quality, the Library of Congress will adhere to the criteria set forth below in all but exceptional circumstances.

Where differences between editions represent variations in copyrightable content, each edition is a separate version and "best edition" standards based on such differences do not apply. Each such version is a separate work for the purposes of the Copyright Law.

Appearing below are lists of criteria to be applied in determining the best edition of each of several types of material. The criteria are listed in descending order of importance. In deciding between two editions, a criterion-by-criterion comparison should be made. The edition which first fails to satisfy a criterion is to be considered of inferior quality and will not be an acceptable deposit. For example, if a comparison is made between two hardbound editions of a book, one a trade edition printed on acid-free paper and the other a specially bound edition printed on average paper, the former will be the best edition because the type of paper is a more important criterion than the binding.

Under regulations of the Copyright Office, potential depositors may request authorization to deposit copies or phonorecords of other than the best edition of a specific work (e.g., a microform rather than a printed edition of a serial).

I. Printed Textual Matter

  A. *Paper, Binding, and Packaging*:
    1. Archival-quality rather than less-permanent paper.
    2. Hard cover rather than soft cover.
    3. Library binding rather than commercial binding.
    4. Trade edition rather than book club edition.
    5. Sewn rather than glue-only binding.
    6. Sewn or glued rather than stapled or spiral-bound.
    7. Stapled rather than spiral-bound or plastic-bound.
    8. Bound rather than looseleaf, except when future looseleaf insertions are to be issued.
    9. Slipcased rather than nonslipcased.
    10. With protective folders rather than without (for broadsides).
    11. Rolled rather than folded (for broadsides).
    12. With protective coatings rather than without (except broadsides, which should not be coated).

B. *Rarity*:
    1.   Special limited edition having the greatest number of special features.
    2.   Other limited edition rather than trade edition.
    3.   Special binding rather than trade binding.

C. *Illustrations*:
    1.   Illustrated rather than unillustrated.
    2.   Illustrations in color rather than black and white.

D. *Special features*:
    1.   With thumb notches or index tabs rather than without.
    2.   With aids to use such as overlays and magnifiers rather than without.

E. *Size*:
    1.   Larger rather than smaller sizes. (Except that large-type editions for the partially-sighted are not required in place of editions employing type of more conventional size)

II. Photographs

A. Size and finish, in descending order of preference:
    1.   The most widely distributed edition.
    2. 8×10-inch glossy print.
    3.   Other size or finish.

B. Unmounted rather than mounted.

C. Archival-quality rather than less permanent paper stock or printing process.

III. Motion Pictures

A. Film rather than another medium. Film editions are listed below in descending order of preference.
    1.   Preprint material, by special arrangement.
    2.   Film gauge in which most widely distributed.
    3.   35 mm rather than 16 mm.
    4.   16 mm rather than 8 mm.
    5.   Special formats (e.g., 65 mm) only in exceptional cases.
    6.   Open reel rather than cartridge or cassette.

B. Videotape rather than videodisc. Videotape editions are listed below in descending order of preference.
    1.   Tape gauge in which most widely distributed.
    2.   Two-inch tape.
    3.   One-inch tape.
    4.   Three-quarter-inch tape cassette.
    5.   One-half-inch tape cassette.

IV. Other Graphic Matter

A. *Paper and Printing*:
    1.   Archival quality rather than less-permanent paper.
    2.   Color rather than black and white.

B. *Size and Content*:
    1.   Larger rather than smaller size.
    2.   In the case of cartographic works, editions with the greatest amount of information rather than those with less detail.

C. *Rarity*:
    1.   The most widely distributed edition rather than one of limited distribution.
    2.   In the case of a work published only in a limited, numbered edition, one copy outside the numbered series but otherwise identical.
    3.   A photographic reproduction of the original, by special arrangement only.

D. *Text and Other Materials*: 1. Works with annotations, accompanying tabular or textual matter, or other interpretative aids rather than those without them.

E. *Binding and Packaging*:
    1.   Bound rather than unbound.
    2.   If editions have different binding, apply the criteria in I.A.2—I.A.7, above.
    4.   Rolled rather than folded.
    5.   With protective coatings rather than without.

V. Phonorecords
  A. Disc rather than tape.
  B. With special enclosures rather than without.
  C. Open-reel rather than cartridge.
  D. Cartridge rather than cassette.
  E. Quadraphonic rather than stereophonic.
  F. True stereophonic rather than monaural.
  G. Monaural rather than electronically rechanneled stereo.

VI. Musical Compositions
  A. *Fullness of Score*:
    1. *Vocal music*
      a. With orchestral accompaniment—
        i. Full score and parts, if any, rather than conductor's score and parts, if any. (In cases of compositions published only by rental, lease, or lending, this requirement is reduced to full score only.)
        ii. Conductor's score and parts, if any, rather than condensed score and parts, if any. (In cases of compositions published only by rental, lease, or lending, this requirement is reduced to conductor's score only.)
      b. Unaccompanied. Open score (each part on separate staff) rather than closed score (all parts condensed to two staves).
    2. *Instrumental music*:
      a. Full score and parts, if any, rather than conductor's score and parts, if any. (In cases of compositions published only by rental, lease, or lending, this requirement is reduced to full score only.)
      b. Conductor's score and parts, if any, rather than condensed score and parts, if any. (In cases of compositions published only by rental, lease, or lending, this requirement is reduced to conductor's score only.)
  B. *Printing and Paper*:
    1. Archival-quality rather than less-permanent paper.
  C. *Binding and Packaging*:
    1. Special limited editions rather than trade editions.
    2. Bound rather than unbound.
    3. If editions have different binding, apply the criteria in I.A.2—I.A.12, above.
    4. With protective folders rather than without.

VII. Microforms
  A. *Related Materials*:
    1. With indexes, study guides, or other printed matter rather than without.
  B. *Permanence and Appearance*:
    1. Silver halide rather than any other emulsion.
    2. Positive rather than negative.
    3. Color rather than black and white.
  C. *Format (newspapers and newspaper-formatted serials)*:
    1. Reel microfilm rather than any other microform.
  D. *Format (all other materials)*:
    1. Microfiche rather than reel microfilm.
    2. Reel microfilm rather than microform cassettes.
    3. Microfilm cassettes rather than micro-opaque prints.
  E. *Size:*
    1. 35 mm rather than 16 mm.

VIII. Works Existing in More Than One Medium

  Editions are listed below in descending order of preference.
  A. Newspapers, dissertations and theses, newspaper-formatted serials:
    1. Microform.
    2. Printed matter.
  B. All other materials:
    1. Printed matter.
    2. Microform.
    3. Phonorecord.
(Effective: January 1, 1978.)

Appendix D

Universal Copyright Convention*

The Contracting States,

Moved by the desire to assure in all countries copyright protection of literary, scientific and artistic works,

Convinced that a system of copyright protection appropriate to all nations of the world and expressed in a universal convention, additional to, and without impairing international systems already in force, will ensure respect for the rights of the individual and encourage the development of literature, the sciences and the arts,

Persuaded that such a universal copyright system will facilitate a wider dissemination of works of the human mind and increase international understanding,

Have agreed as follows:

Article I

Each Contracting State undertakes to provide for the adequate and effective protection of the rights of authors and other copyright proprietors in literary, scientific and artistic works, including writings, musical, dramatic and cinematographic works, and paintings, engravings and sculpture.

Article II

1. Published works of nationals of any Contracting State and works first published in that State shall enjoy in each other Contracting State the same protection as that other State accords to works of its nationals first published in its own territory.

2. Unpublished works of nationals of each Contracting State shall enjoy in each other Contracting State the same protection as that other State accords to unpublished works of its own nationals.

3. For the purpose of this Convention any Contracting State may, by domestic legislation, assimilate to its own nationals any person domiciled in that State.

Article III

1. Any Contracting State which, under its domestic law, requires as a condition of copyright, compliance with formalities such as deposit, registration, notice, notarial certificates, payment of fees or manufacture or publication in that Contracting State, shall regard these requirements as satisfied with respect to all works protected in accordance wth this Convention and first published outside its territory and the author of which is not one of its nationals, if from the time of the first

---

* Effective Sept. 16, 1955. There was a subsequent revision at Paris in 1971, to which the U.S.A. adhered on August 14, 1972 and which became effective on July 10, 1974. The new 1971 text retains the basic provisions of the original Convention but enumerates certain fundamental rights of authors, including exclusive rights of reproduction by any means, public performance, and broadcasting. In addition exceptions were instituted for developing countries whereby they are given the power to institute procedures for the compulsory licensing of translations and re-productions of certain works for educational purposes, subject to certain limitations, if the works are not made available in the country concerned within stated time periods. Adherents to the original convention are not required to ratify the newer version. Some 70 nations are members of one or both versions.

publication all the copies of the work published with the authority of the author or other copyright proprietor bear the symbol © accompanied by the name of the copyright proprietor and the year of first publication placed in such manner and location as to give reasonable notice of claim of copyright.

2. The provisions of paragraph 1 of this Article shall not preclude any Contracting State from requiring formalities or other conditions for the acquisition and enjoyment of copyright in respect of works first published in its territory or works of its nationals wherever published.

3. The provisions of paragraph 1 of this Article shall not preclude any Contracting State from providing that a person seeking judicial relief must, in bringing the action, comply with procedural requirements, such as that the complainant must appear through domestic counsel or that the complainant must deposit with the court or an administrative office, or both, a copy of the work involved in the litigation; provided that failure to comply with such requirements shall not affect the validity of the copyright, nor shall any such requirement be imposed upon a national of another Contracting State if such requirement is not imposed on nationals of the State in which protection is claimed.

4. In each Contracting State there shall be legal means of protecting without formalities the unpublished works of nationals of other Contracting States.

5. If a Contracting State grants protection for more than one term of copyright and the first is for a period longer than one of the minimum periods prescribed in Article IV, such State shall not be required to comply with the provisions of paragraph 1 of this Article III in respect of the second or any subsequent term of copyright.

Article IV

1. The duration of protection of a work shall be governed, in accordance with the provisions of Article II and this Article, by the law of the Contracting State in which protection is claimed.

2. The term of protection for works protected under this Convention shall not be less than the life of the author and 25 years after his death.

However, any Contracting State which, on the effective date of this Convention in that State, has limited this term for certain classes of works to a period computed from the first publication of the work, shall be entitled to maintain these exceptions and to extend them to other classes of works. For all these classes the term of protection shall not be less than 25 years from the date of first publication.

Any Contracting State which, upon the effective date of this Convention in that State, does not compute the term of protection upon the basis of the life of the author, shall be entitled to compute the term of protection from the date of the first publication of the work or from its registration prior to publication, as the case may be, provided the term of protection shall not be less than 25 years from the date of first publication or from its registration prior to publication, as the case may be.

If the legislation of a Contracting State grants two or more successive terms of protection, the duration of the first term shall not be less than one of the minimum periods specified above.

3. The provisions of paragraph 2 of this Article shall not apply to photographic works or to works of applied art; provided, however, that the term of protection in those Contracting States which protect photographic works, or works of applied art in so far as they are protected as artistic works, shall not be less than 10 years of said classes of works.

4. No Contracting State shall be obliged to grant protection to a work for a period longer than that fixed for the class of works to which the work in question belongs, in the case of unpublished works by the law of the contracting state of which the author is a national, and in the case of published works by the law of the Contracting State in which the work has been first published.

For the purposes of the application of the preceding provision, if the law of any Contracting State grants two or more successive terms of protection, the period of protection of that State shall be considered to be the aggregate of those terms. However, if a specified work is not protected by such State during the second or any subsequent term for any reason, the other Contracting States shall not be obliged to protect it during the second or any subsequent term.

5. For the purposes of the application of paragraph 4 of this Article the work of a national of a Contracting State, first published in a non-Contracting State, shall be treated as though first published in the Contracting State of which the author is a national.

6. For the purposes of the application of paragraph 4 of this Article, in case of simultaneous publication in two or more Contracting States, the work shall be treated as though first published in the State which affords the shortest term; any work published in two or more Contracting States within 30 days of its first publication shall be considered as having been published simultaneously in said Contracting States.

Article V

1. Copyright shall include the exclusive right of the author to make, publish, and authorize the making and publication of translations of works protected under this Convention.

2. However, any Contracting State may, by its domestic legislation, restrict the right of translation of writings, but only subject to the following provisions:

If, after the expiration of a period of seven years from the date of the first publication of a writing, a translation of such writing has not been published in the national language or languages, as the case may be, of the Contracting State, by the owner of the right of translation or with his authorization, any national of such Contracting State may obtain a non-exclusive license from the competent authority thereof to translate the work and publish the work so translated in any of the national languages in which it has not been published; provided that such national, in acccordance with the procedure of the State concerned, establishes either that he has requested, and been denied, authorization by the proprietor of the right to make and publish the translation, or that, after due diligence on his part, he was unable to find the owner of the right. A license may also be granted on the same conditions if all previous editions of a translation in such language are out of print.

If the owner of the right of translation cannot be found, then the applicant for a license shall send copies of his application to the publisher whose name appears on the work and, if the nationality of the owner of the right of translation is known, to the diplomatic or consular representative of the State of which such owner is a national, or the organization which may have been designated by the government of that State. The license shall not be granted before the expiration of a period of two months from the date of the dispatch of the copies of the application.

Due provision shall be made by domestic legislation to assure to the owner of the right of translation a compensation which is just and conforms to international standards, to assure payment and transmittal of such compensation, and to assure a correct translation of the work.

The original title and the name of the author of the work shall be printed on all copies of the published translation. The license shall be valid only for publication of the translation in the territory of the Contracting State where it has been applied for. Copies so published may be imported and sold in another Contracting State if one of the national languages of such other State is the same language as that into which the work has been translated, and if the domestic law in such other State makes provision for such licenses and does not prohibit such importation and sale. Where the foregoing conditions do not exist, the importation and sale of such copies in a Contracting State shall be governed by its domestic law and its agreements. The license shall not be transferred by the licensee.

The license shall not be granted when the author has withdrawn from circulation all copies of the work.

Article VI

"Publication," as used in this Convention, means the reproduction in tangible form and the general distribution to the public of copies of a work from which it can be read or otherwise visually perceived.

Article VII

This Convention shall not apply to works or rights in works which, at the effective date of the Convention in a Contracting State where protection is claimed, are permanently in the public domain in the said Contracting State.

Article VIII

1. This Convention, which shall bear the date of 6 September 1952, shall be deposited with the Director-General of the United Nations Educational, Scientific and Cultural Organization and shall remain open for signature by all States for a period of 120 days after that date. It shall be subject to ratification or acceptance by the signatory States.

2. Any State which has not signed this Convention may accede thereto.

3. Ratification, acceptance or accession shall be effected by the deposit of an instrument to that effect with the Director-General of the United Nations Educational, Scientific and Cultural Organization.

Article IX

1. This Convention shall come into force three months after the deposit of twelve instruments of ratification, acceptance or accession, among which there shall be those of four States which are not members of the International Union for the Protection of Literary and Artistic Works.

2. Subsequently, this Convention shall come into force in respect of each State three months after that State has deposited its instrument of ratification, acceptance or accession.

Article X

1. Each State party to this Convention undertakes to adopt, in accordance with its Constitution, such measures as are necessary to ensure the application of this Convention.

2. It is understood, however, that at the time an instrument of ratification, acceptance or accession is deposited on behalf of any State, such State must be in a position under its domestic law to give effect to the terms of this Convention.

Article XI

1. An Inter-governmental Committee is hereby established with the following duties:
   (a) to study the problems concerning the application and operation of this Convention;
   (b) to make preparation for periodic revisions of this Convention;
   (c) to study any other problems concerning the international protection of copyright, in co-operation with the various interested international organizations, such as the United Nations Educational, Scientific and Cultural Organization, the International Union for the Protection of Literary and Artistic Works and the Organization of American States;
   (d) to inform the Contracting States as to its activities.

2. The Committee shall consist of the representatives of twelve Contracting States to be selected with due consideration to fair geographical representation and in conformity with the Resolution relating to this article, annexed to this Convention.

The Director-General of the United Nations Educational, Scientific and Cultural Organization, the Director of the Bureau of the International Union for the Protection of Literary and Artistic Works and the Secretary-General of the Organization of American States, or their representatives, may attend meetings of the Committee in an advisory capacity.

Article XII

The Inter-governmental Committee shall convene a conference for revision of this Convention whenever it deems necessary, or at the request of at least ten Contracting States, or of a majority of the Contracting States if there are less than twenty Contracting States.

Article XIII

Any Contracting State may, at the time of deposit of its instrument of ratification, acceptance or accession, or at any time thereafter declare by notification addressed to the Director-General of the United Nations Educational, Scientific and Cultural Organization that this Convention shall apply to all or any of the countries or territories for the international relations of which it is responsible and this Convention shall thereupon apply to the countries or territories named in such notification after the expiration of the term of three months provided for in Article IX. In the absence of such notification, this Convention shall not apply to any such country or territory.

Article XIV

1. Any Contracting State may denounce this Convention in its own name or on behalf of all or any of the countries or territories as to which a notification has been given under Article XIII. The denunciation shall be made by notification addressed to the Director-General of the United Nations Educational, Scientific and Cultural Organization.

2. Such denunciation shall operate only in respect of the State or of the country or territory on whose behalf it was made and shall not take effect until twelve months after the date of receipt of the notification.

Article XV

A dispute between two or more Contracting States concerning the interpretation or application of this Convention, not settled by negotiation, shall, unless the States concerned agree on some other method of settlement, be brought before the International Court of Justice for determination by it.

Article XVI

1. This Convention shall be established in English, French and Spanish. The three texts shall be signed and shall be equally authoritative.
2. Official texts of this Convention shall be established in German, Italian and Portuguese.

Any Contracting State or group of Contracting States shall be entitled to have established by the Director-General of the United Nations Educational, Scientific and Cultural Organization other texts in the language of its choice by arrangement with the Director-General.

All such texts shall be annexed to the signed texts of this Convention.

Article XVII

1. This Convention shall not in any way affect the provisions of the Berne Convention for the Protection of Literary and Artistic Works or membership in the Union created by that Convention.
2. In application of the foregoing paragraph, a Declaration has been annexed to the present article. This Declaration is an integral part of this Convention for the States bound by the Berne Convention on January 1, 1951, or which have or may become bound to it at a later date. The signature of this Convention by such States shall also constitute signature of the said Declaration, and ratification, acceptance or accession by such States shall include the Declaration as well as the Convention.

Article XVIII

This Convention shall not abrogate multilateral or bilateral copyright conventions or arrangements that are or may be in effect exclusively between two or more American Republics. In the event of any difference either between the provisions of such existing conventions or arrangements and the provisions of this Convention, or between the provisions of this Convention and those of any new convention or arrangement which may be formulated between two or more American Republics after this Convention comes into force, the convention or arrangement most recently formulated shall prevail between the parties thereto. Rights in works acquired in any Contracting State under existing conventions or arrangements before the date this Convention comes into force in such State shall not be affected.

Article XIX

This Convention shall not abrogate multilateral or bilateral conventions or arrangements in effect between two or more Contracting States. In the event of any difference between the provisions of such existing conventions or arrangements and the provisions of this Convention, the provisions of this Convention shall prevail. Rights in works acquired in any Contracting State under existing conventions or arrangements before the date on which this Convention comes into force in such State shall not be affected. Nothing in this article shall affect the provisions of Articles XVII and XVIII of this Convention.

Article XX

Reservations to this Convention shall not be permitted.

Article XXI

The Director-General of the United Nations Educational, Scientific and Cultural Organization shall send duly certified copies of this Convention to the States interested, to the Swiss Federal Council and to the Secretary-General of the United Nations for registration by him.

He shall also inform all interested States of the ratifications, acceptances and accessions which have been deposited, the date on which this Convention comes into force, the notifications under Article XIII of this Convention, and denunciations under Article XIV.

Appendix Declaration Relating to Article XVII

The States which are members of the International Union for the Protection of Literary and Artistic Works, and which are signatories to the Universal Copyright Convention,

Desiring to reinforce their mutual relations on the basis of the said Union and to avoid any conflict which might result from the co-existence of the Convention of Berne and the Universal Convention,

Have, by common agreement, accepted the terms of the following declaration:

(a) Works which, according to the Berne Convention, have as their country of origin a country which has withdrawn from the International Union created by the said Convention, after January 1, 1951, shall not be protected by the Universal Copyright Convention in the countries of the Berne Union;

(b) The Universal Copyright Convention shall not be applicable to the relationships among countries of the Berne Union insofar as it relates to the protection of works having as their country of origin, within the meaning of the Berne Convention, a country of the International Union created by the said Convention.

International Copyright Relations of the United States of America*

General information

This sets forth U.S. copyright relations of current interest with the other independent nations of the world. Each entry gives country name (and alternate name) and a statement of copyright relations. The following code is used:

Bilateral	Bilateral copyright relations with the United States by virtue of a proclamation or treaty, as of the date given. Where there is more than one proclamation or treaty, only the date of the first one is given.
BAC	Party to the Buenos Aires Convention of 1910, as of the date given. U.S. ratification deposited with the Government of Argentina, May 1, 1911; proclaimed by the President of the United States, July 13, 1914.
None	No copyright relations with the United States.
Phonogram	Party to the Convention for the Protection of Producers of Phonograms Against Unauthorized Duplication of Their Phonograms, Geneva, 1971, as of the date given. The effective date for the United States was March 10, 1974.
UCC Geneva	Party to the Universal Copyright Convention, Geneva, 1952, as of the date given. The effective date for the United States was September 16, 1955.
UCC Paris	Party to the Universal Copyright convention as revised at Paris, 1971, as of the date given. The effective date for the United States was July 10, 1974.
Unclear	Became independent since 1943. Has not established copyright relations with the United States, but may be honoring obligations incurred under former political status.

Relations as of July 31, 1983

Afghanistan
None
Albania
None
Algeria
UCC Geneva Aug. 28, 1973
UCC Paris July 10, 1974
Andorra
UCC Geneva Sept. 16, 1955
Angola
Unclear
Antigua and Barbuda
Unclear
Argentina
Bilateral Aug. 23, 1934
BAC April 19, 1950
UCC Geneva Feb. 13, 1958
Phonogram June 30, 1973

Australia
Bilateral March 15, 1918
UCC Geneva May 1, 1969
Phonogram June 22, 1974
UCC Paris Feb. 28, 1978
Austria
Bilateral Sept. 20, 1907
UCC Geneva July 2, 1957
UCC Paris Aug. 14, 1982
Phonogram Aug. 21, 1982
Bahamas, The
UCC Geneva Dec. 27, 1976
UCC Paris Dec. 27, 1976
Bahrain
None
Bangladesh
UCC Geneva Aug. 5, 1975
UCC Paris Aug. 5, 1975

Barbados
Phonogram July 29, 1983
Belau
Unclear
Belgium
Bilateral July 1, 1891
UCC Geneva Aug. 31, 1960
Belize
Unclear
Benin (formerly Dahomey)
Unclear
Bhutan
None
Bolivia
BAC May 15, 1914
Botswana
Unclear

---

*Reprinted from Circular 38a of the Copyright Office, as of July 31, 1983.

Brazil
BAC Aug. 31, 1915
Bilateral April 2, 1957
UCC Geneva Jan. 13, 1960
Phonogram Nov. 28, 1975
UCC Paris Dec. 11, 1975
Bulgaria
UCC Geneva June 7, 1975
UCC Paris June 7, 1975
Burma
Unclear
Burundi
Unclear
Cambodia
(See entry under Kampuchea)
Cameroon
UCC Geneva May 1, 1973
UCC Paris July 10, 1974
Canada
Bilateral Jan. 1, 1924
UCC Geneva Aug. 10, 1962
Cape Verde
Unclear
Central African Empire
Unclear
Chad
Unclear
Chile
Bilateral May 25, 1896
BAC June 14, 1955
UCC Geneva Sept. 16, 1955
Phonogram March 24, 1977
China
Bilateral Jan. 13, 1904
Colombia
BAC Dec. 23, 1936
UCC Geneva June 18, 1976
UCC Paris June 18, 1976
Comoros
Unclear
Congo
Unclear
Costa Rica[1]
Bilateral Oct. 19, 1899
BAC Nov. 30, 1916
UCC Geneva Sept. 16, 1955
UCC Paris March 7, 1980
Phonogram June 17, 1982
Cuba
Bilateral Nov. 17, 1903
UCC Geneva June 18, 1957
Cyprus
Unclear
Czechoslovakia
Bilateral March 1, 1927
UCC Geneva Jan. 6, 1960
UCC Paris April 17, 1980
Denmark
Bilateral May 8, 1893
UCC Geneva Feb. 9, 1962

Phonogram March 24, 1977
UCC Paris July 11, 1979
Djibouti
Unclear
Dominica
Unclear
Dominican Republic[1]
BAC Oct. 31, 1912
Ecuador
BAC Aug. 31, 1914
UCC Geneva June 5, 1957
Phonogram Sept. 14, 1974
Egypt[2]
Phonogram April 23, 1978
El Salvador
Bilateral June 30, 1908
by virtue of Mexico City
Convention, 1902
Phonogram February 9,1979
UCC Geneva March 29,
1979
UCC Paris March 29, 1979
Equatorial Guinea
Unclear
Ethiopia
None
Fiji
UCC Geneva Oct. 10, 1970
Phonogram April 18, 1973
Finland
Bilateral Jan. 1, 1929
UCC Geneva April 16, 1963
Phonogram April 18, 1973
France
Bilateral July 1, 1891
UCC Geneva Jan. 14, 1956
Phonogram April 18, 1973
UCC Paris July 10, 1974
Gabon
Unclear
Gambia, The
Unclear
Germany
Bilateral April 15, 1892
UCC Geneva with Federal
Republic of Germany
Sept. 16, 1955
UCC Geneva with German
Democratic Republic Oct.
5, 1973
Phonogram with Federal
Republic of Germany May
18, 1974
UCC Paris with Federal Republic of Germany July
10, 1974
UCC Paris with German
Democratic Republic
Dec. 10, 1980
Ghana
UCC Geneva Aug. 22, 1962

Greece
Bilateral March 1, 1932
UCC Geneva Aug. 24, 1963
Grenada
Unclear
Guatemala[1]
BAC March 28, 1913
UCC Geneva Oct. 28, 1964
Phonogram Feb. 1, 1977
Guinea
UCC Geneva Nov. 13, 1981
UCC Paris Nov. 13, 1981
Guinea-Bissau
Unclear
Guyana
Unclear
Haiti
BAC Nov. 27, 1919
UCC Geneva Sept. 16, 1955
Holy See
(See entry under Vatican
City)
Honduras[1]
BAC April 27, 1914
Hungary
Bilateral Oct. 16, 1912
UCC Geneva Jan. 23, 1971
UCC Paris July 10, 1974
Phonogram May 28, 1975
Iceland
UCC Geneva Dec. 18, 1956
India
Bilateral Aug. 15, 1947
UCC Geneva Jan. 21, 1958
Phonogram Feb. 12, 1975
Indonesia
Unclear
Iran
None
Iraq
None
Ireland
Bilateral Oct. 1, 1929
UCC Geneva Jan. 20, 1959
Israel
Bilateral May 15, 1948
UCC Geneva Sept. 16, 1955
Phonogram May 1, 1978
Italy
Bilateral Oct. 31, 1892
UCC Geneva Jan. 24, 1957
Phonogram March 24, 1977
UCC Paris Jan. 25, 1980
Ivory Coast
Unclear
Jamaica
None
Japan[3]
UCC Geneva April 28, 1956
UCC Paris Oct. 21, 1977
Phonogram Oct. 14, 1978

Jordan
Unclear
Kampuchea
UCC Geneva Sept. 16, 1955
Kenya
UCC Geneva Sept. 7, 1966
UCC Paris July 10, 1974
Phonogram April 21, 1976
Kiribati
Unclear
Korea
Unclear
Kuwait
Unclear
Laos
UCC Geneva Sept. 16, 1955
Lebanon
UCC Geneva Oct. 17, 1959
Lesotho
Unclear
Liberia
UCC Geneva July 27, 1956
Libya
Unclear
Liechtenstein
UCC Geneva Jan. 22, 1959
Luxembourg
Bilateral June 29, 1910
UCC Geneva Oct. 15, 1955
Phonogram March 8, 1976
Madagascar (Malagasy Republic)
Unclear
Malawi
UCC Geneva Oct. 26, 1965
Malaysia
Unclear
Maldives
Unclear
Mali
Unclear
Malta
UCC Geneva Nov. 19, 1968
Mauritania
Unclear
Mauritius
UCC Geneva March 12, 1968
Mexico
Bilateral Feb. 27, 1896
UCC Geneva May 12, 1957
BAC April 24, 1964
Phonogram Dec. 21, 1973
UCC Paris Oct. 31, 1975
Monaco
Bilateral Oct. 15, 1952
UCC Geneva Sept. 16, 1955
Phonogram Dec. 2, 1974
UCC Paris Dec. 13, 1974
Mongolia
None

Morocco
UCC Geneva May 8, 1972
UCC Paris Jan. 28, 1976
Mozambique
Unclear
Nauru
Unclear
Nepal
None
Netherlands
Bilateral Nov. 20, 1899
UCC Geneva June 22, 1967
New Zealand
Bilateral Dec. 1, 1916
UCC Geneva Sept. 11, 1964
Phonogram Aug. 13, 1976
Nicaragua[1]
BAC Dec. 15, 1913
UCC Geneva Aug. 16, 1961
Niger
Unclear
Nigeria
UCC Geneva Feb. 14, 1962
Norway
Bilateral July 1, 1905
UCC Geneva Jan. 23, 1963
UCC Paris Aug. 7, 1974
Phonogram Aug. 1, 1978
Oman
None
Pakistan
UCC Geneva Sept. 16, 1955
Panama
BAC Nov. 25, 1913
UCC Geneva Oct. 17, 1962
Phonogram June 29, 1974
UCC Paris Sept. 3, 1980
Papua New Guinea
Unclear
Paraguay
BAC Sept. 20, 1917
UCC Geneva March 11, 1962
Phonogram Feb. 13, 1979
Peru
BAC April 30, 1920
UCC Geneva Oct. 16, 1963
Philippines
Bilateral Oct. 21, 1948
UCC status undetermined by UNESCO.
(Copyright Office considers that UCC relations do not exist.)
Poland
Bilateral Feb. 16, 1927
UCC Geneva March 9, 1977
UCC Paris March 9, 1977
Portugal
Bilateral July 20, 1893
UCC Geneva Dec. 25, 1956

UCC Paris July 30, 1981
Qatar
None
Romania
Bilateral May 14, 1928
Rwanda
Unclear
Saint Lucia
Unclear
Saint Vincent and the Grenadines
Unclear
San Marino
None
Sao Tome and Principe
Unclear
Saudi Arabia
None
Senegal
UCC Geneva July 9, 1974
UCC Paris July 10, 1974
Seychelles
Unclear
Sierra Leone
None
Singapore
Unclear
Solomon Islands
Unclear
Somalia
Unclear
South Africa
Bilateral July 1, 1924
Soviet Union
UCC Geneva May 27, 1973
Spain
Bilateral July 10, 1895
UCC Geneva Sept. 16, 1955
UCC Paris July 10, 1974
Phonogram Aug. 24, 1974
Sri Lanka (formerly Ceylon)
Unclear
Sudan
Unclear
Surinam
Unclear
Swaziland
Unclear
Sweden
Bilateral June 1, 1911
UCC Geneva July 1, 1961
Phonogram April 18, 1973
UCC Paris July 10, 1974
Switzerland
Bilateral July 1, 1891
UCC Geneva March 30, 1956
Syria
Unclear
Tanzania
Unclear

Thailand
Bilateral Sept. 1, 1921
Togo
Unclear
Tonga
None
Trinidad and Tobago
Unclear
Tunisia
UCC Geneva June 19, 1969
UCC Paris June 10, 1975
Turkey
None
Tuvalu
Unclear
Uganda
Unclear
United Arab Emirates
None

United Kingdom
Bilateral July 1, 1891
UCC Geneva Sept. 27, 1957
Phonogram April 18, 1973
UCC Paris July 10, 1974
Upper Volta
Unclear
Uruguay
BAC Dec. 17, 1919
Phonogram Jan. 18, 1983
Vanuatu
Unclear
Vatican City (Holy See)
UCC Geneva Oct. 5, 1955
Phonogram July 18, 1977
UCC Paris May 6, 1980
Venezuela
UCC Geneva Sept. 30, 1966
Phonogram Nov. 18, 1982

Vietnam
Unclear
Western Samoa
Unclear
Yemen (Aden)
Unclear
Yemen (San'a)
None
Yugoslavia
UCC Geneva May 11, 1966
UCC Paris July 10, 1974
Zaire[4]
Phonogram Nov. 29, 1977
Zambia
UCC Geneva June 1, 1965
Zimbabwe
Unclear

---

[1] This country became a party to the Mexico City Convention, 1902, effective June 30, 1908, to which the United States also became a party, effective on the same date. As regards copyright relations with the United States, this convention is considered to have been superseded by adherence of this country and the United States to the Buenos Aires Convention of 1910.

[2] For works other than sound recordings, none.

[3] Bilateral copyright relations between Japan and the United States, which were formulated effective May 10, 1906, are considered to have been abrogated and superseded by the adherence of Japan to the UCC Geneva, effective April 28, 1956.

[4] For works other than sound recordings, unclear.

Contracting Berne Union Countries*

Argentina	Libyan Arab Republic
Australia	Liechtenstein
Austria	Luxembourg
Bahamas	Madagascar
Barbados	Mali
Belgium	Malta
Benin	Mauritania
Brazil	Mexico
Bulgaria	Monaco
Camaroon	Morocco
Canada	Netherlands
Central African Empire	New Zealand
Chad	Niger
Chile	Norway
Congo (Brazzaville)	Pakistan
Costa Rica	Philippines
Cyprus	Poland
Czechoslovakia	Portugal
Denmark	Romania
Egypt	Rwanda
Fiji	Senegal
Finland	South Africa
France	Spain
Gabon	Sri Lanka
Germany (Democratic Republic)	Suriname
Germany (Federal Republic)	Sweden
Greece	Switzerland
Guinea	Thailand
Holy See	Togo
Hungary	Tunisia
Iceland	Turkey
India	United Kingdom
Ireland	Upper Volta
Israel	Uruguay
Italy	Venezuela
Ivory Coast	Yugoslavia
Japan	Zaire
Lebanon	Zimbabwe

*As of January 1, 1984

Copyright Registration Forms under the Copyright Act of 1976

On the following pages, instructions and application forms for copyright registration are reproduced. They include:

FORM PA: APPLICATION FOR COPYRIGHT REGISTRATION FOR A WORK OF THE PERFORMING ARTS

FORM SR: APPLICATION FOR COPYRIGHT REGISTRATION FOR A SOUND RECORDING

FORM TX: APPLICATION FOR COPYRIGHT REGISTRATION FOR A WORK OF THE VISUAL ARTS

FORM RE: APPLICATION FOR RENEWAL REGISTRATION

FORM CA: APPLICATION FOR SUPPLEMENARY COPYRIGHT REGISTRATION

Original forms, which must be used when applying for copyright, may be obtained by writing to:

UNITED STATES COPYRIGHT OFFICE
LIBRARY OF CONGRESS
WASHINGTON, D.C. 20559

Filling Out Application Form PA

*Detach and read these instructions before completing this form. Make sure all applicable spaces have been
filled in before you return this form.*

BASIC INFORMATION

When to Use This Form: Use Form PA for registration of published or unpublished works of the performing arts. This class includes works prepared for the purpose of being "performed" directly before an audience or indirectly "by means of any device or process." Works of the performing arts include: (1) musical works, including any accompanying words; (2) dramatic works, including any accompanying music; (3) pantomimes and choreographic works; and (4) motion pictures and other audiovisual works.

Deposit to Accompany Application: An application for copyright registration must be accompanied by a deposit consisting of copies or phonorecords representing the entire work for which registration is to be made. The following are the general deposit requirements as set forth in the statute:

Unpublished Work: Deposit one complete copy (or phonorecord).

Published Work: Deposit two complete copies (or phonorecords) of the best edition.

Work First Published Outside the United States: Deposit one complete copy (or phonorecord) of the first foreign edition.

Contribution to a Collective Work: Deposit one complete copy (or phonorecord) of the best edition of the collective work.

Motion Pictures: Deposit *both* of the following: (1) a separate written description of the contents of the motion picture; and (2) for a published work, one complete copy of the best edition of the motion picture; or, for an unpublished work, one complete copy of the motion picture or identifying material. Identifying material may be either an audiorecording of the entire soundtrack or one frame enlargement or similar visual print from each 10-minute segment.

The Copyright Notice: For published works, the law provides that a copyright notice in a specified form "shall be placed on all publicly distributed copies from which the work can be visually perceived." Use of the copyright notice is the responsibility of the copyright owner and does not require advance permission from the Copyright Office. The required form of the notice for copies generally consists of three elements: (1) the symbol "©", or the word "Copyright," or the abbreviation "Copr."; (2) the year of first publication; and (3) the name of the owner of copyright. For example: "© 1981 Constance Porter." The notice is to be affixed to the copies "in such manner and location as to give reasonable notice of the claim of copyright."

For further information about copyright registration, notice, or special questions relating to copyright problems, write:

Information and Publications Section, LM-455
Copyright Office
Library of Congress
Washington, D.C. 20559

LINE-BY-LINE INSTRUCTIONS

1 SPACE 1: Title

Title of This Work: Every work submitted for copyright registration must be given a title to identify that particular work. If the copies or phonorecords of the work bear a title (or an identifying phrase that could serve as a title), transcribe that wording *completely* and *exactly* on the application. Indexing of the registration and future identification of the work will depend on the information you give here. If the work you are registering is an entire "collective work" (such as a collection of plays or songs), give the overall title of the collection. If you are registering one or more individual contributions to a collective work, give the title of each contribution, followed by the title of the collection. Example: "'A Song for Elinda' in *Old and New Ballads for Old and New People*."

Previous or Alternative Titles: Complete this space if there are any additional titles for the work under which someone searching for the registration might be likely to look, or under which a document pertaining to the work might be recorded.

Nature of This Work: Briefly describe the general nature or character of the work being registered for copyright. Examples: "Music"; "Song Lyrics"; "Words and Music"; "Drama"; "Musical Play"; "Choreography"; "Pantomime"; "Motion Picture"; "Audiovisual Work."

2 SPACE 2: Author(s)

General Instructions: After reading these instructions, decide who are the "authors" of this work for copyright purposes. Then, unless the work is a "collective work," give the requested information about every "author" who contributed any appreciable amount of copyrightable matter to this version of the work. If you need further space, request additional Continuation Sheets. In the case of a collective work, such as a songbook or a collection of plays, give information about the author of the collective work as a whole.

Name of Author: The fullest form of the author's name should be given. Unless the work was "made for hire," the individual who actually created the work is its "author." In the case of a work made for hire, the statute provides

that "the employer or other person for whom the work was prepared is considered the author."

What is a "Work Made for Hire"? A "work made for hire" is defined as: (1) "a work prepared by an employee within the scope of his or her employment"; or (2) "a work specially ordered or commissioned for use as a contribution to a collective work, as a part of a motion picture or other audiovisual work, as a translation, as a supplementary work, as a compilation, as an instructional text, as a test, as answer material for a test, or as an atlas, if the parties expressly agree in a written instrument signed by them that the work shall be considered a work made for hire." If you have checked "Yes" to indicate that the work was "made for hire," you must give the full legal name of the employer (or other person for whom the work was prepared). You may also include the name of the employee along with the name of the employer (for example: "Elster Music Co., employer for hire of John Ferguson").

"Anonymous" or "Pseudonymous" Work: An author's contribution to a work is "anonymous" if that author is not identified on the copies or phonorecords of the work. An author's contribution to a work is "pseudonymous" if that author is identified on the copies or phonorecords under a fictitious name. If the work is "anonymous" you may: (1) leave the line blank; or (2) state "anonymous" on the line; or (3) reveal the author's identity. If the work is "pseudonymous" you may: (1) leave the line blank; or (2) give the pseudonym and identify it as such (for example: "Huntley Haverstock, pseudonym"); or (3) reveal the author's name, making clear which is the real name and which is the pseudonym (for example: "Judith Barton, whose pseudonym is Madeline Elster"). However, the citizenship or domicile of the author **must** be given in all cases.

Dates of Birth and Death: If the author is dead, the statute requires that the year of death be included in the application unless the work is anonymous or pseudonymous. The author's birth date is optional, but is useful as a form of identification. Leave this space blank if the author's contribution was a "work made for hire."

Author's Nationality or Domicile: Give the country of which the author is a citizen, or the country in which the author is domiciled. Nationality or domicile **must** be given in all cases.

Nature of Authorship: Give a brief general statement of the nature of this particular author's contribution to the work. Examples: "Words"; "Co-Author of Music"; "Words and Music"; "Arrangement"; "Co-Author of Book and Lyrics"; "Dramatization"; "Screen Play"; "Compilation and English Translation"; "Editorial Revisions."

3 SPACE 3: Creation and Publication

General Instructions: Do not confuse "creation" with "publication." Every application for copyright registration must state "the year in which creation of the work was completed." Give the date and nation of first publication only if the work has been published.

Creation: Under the statute, a work is "created" when it is fixed in a copy or phonorecord for the first time. Where a work has been prepared over a period of time, the part of the work existing in fixed form on a particular date constitutes the created work on that date. The date you give here should be the year in which the author completed the particular version for which registration is now being sought, even if other versions exist or if further changes or additions are planned.

Publication: The statute defines "publication" as "the distribution of copies or phonorecords of a work to the public by sale or other transfer of ownership, or by rental, lease, or lending"; a work is also "published" if there has been an "offering to distribute copies or phonorecords to a group of persons for purposes of further distribution, public performance, or public display." Give the full date (month, day, year) when, and the country where, publication first occurred. If first publication took place simultaneously in the United States and other countries, it is sufficient to state "U.S.A."

4 SPACE 4: Claimant(s)

Name(s) and Address(es) of Copyright Claimant(s): Give the name(s) and address(es) of the copyright claimant(s) in this work even if the claimant is the same as the author. Copyright in a work belongs initially to the author of the work (including, in the case of a work made for hire, the employer or other person for whom the work was prepared). The copyright claimant is either the author of the work or a person or organization to whom the copyright initially belonging to the author has been transferred.

Transfer: The statute provides that, if the copyright claimant is not the author, the application for registration must contain "a brief statement of how the claimant obtained ownership of the copyright." If any copyright claimant named in space 4 is not an author named in space 2, give a brief, general state-

---

earlier registration number and date. Otherwise, do not submit Form PA; instead, write the Copyright Office for information about supplementary registration or recordation of transfers of copyright ownership.

Changed Version: If the work has been changed, and you are now seeking registration to cover the additions or revisions, check the last box in space 5, give the earlier registration number and date, and complete both parts of space 6 in accordance with the instructions below.

Previous Registration Number and Date: If more than one previous registration has been made for the work, give the number and date of the latest registration.

6 SPACE 6: Derivative Work or Compilation

General Instructions: Complete space 6 if this work is a "changed version," "compilation," or "derivative work," and if it incorporates one or more earlier works that have already been published or registered for copyright, or that have fallen into the public domain. A "compilation" is defined as "a work formed by the collection and assembling of preexisting materials or of data that are selected, coordinated, or arranged in such a way that the resulting work as a whole constitutes an original work of authorship." A "derivative work" is "a work based on one or more preexisting works." Examples of derivative works include musical arrangements, dramatizations, translations, abridgments, condensations, motion picture versions, or "any other form in which a work may be recast, transformed, or adapted." Derivative works also include works "consisting of editorial revisions, annotations, or other modifications" if these changes, as a whole, represent an original work of authorship.

Preexisting Material (space 6a): Complete this space **and** space 6b for derivative works. In this space identify the preexisting work that has been recast, transformed, or adapted. For example, the preexisting material might be: "French version of Hugo's 'Le Roi s'amuse'." Do not complete this space for compilations.

Material Added to This Work (space 6b): Give a brief, general statement of the **additional** new material covered by the copyright claim for which registration is sought. In the case of a derivative work, identify this new material. Examples: "Arrangement for piano and orchestra"; "Dramatization for television"; "New film version"; "Revisions throughout; Act III completely new."

ment summarizing the means by which that claimant obtained ownership of the copyright. Examples: "By written contract"; "Transfer of all rights by author"; "Assignment"; "By will." Do not attach transfer documents or other attachments or riders.

5 SPACE 5: Previous Registration

General Instructions: The questions in space 5 are intended to find out whether an earlier registration has been made for this work and, if so, whether there is any basis for a new registration. As a general rule, only one basic copyright registration can be made for the same version of a particular work.

Same Version: If this version is substantially the same as the work covered by a previous registration, a second registration is not generally possible unless: (1) the work has been registered in unpublished form and a second registration is now being sought to cover this first published edition; or (2) someone other than the author is identified as copyright claimant in the earlier registration, and the author is now seeking registration in his or her own name. If either of these two exceptions apply, check the appropriate box and give the

If the work is a compilation, give a brief, general statement describing both the material that has been compiled **and the compilation itself.** Example: "Compilation of 19th Century Military Songs."

7,8,9 SPACE 7, 8, 9: Fee, Correspondence, Certification, Return Address

Deposit Account: If you maintain a Deposit Account in the Copyright Office, identify it in space 7. Otherwise leave the space blank and send the fee of $10 with your application and deposit.

Correspondence (space 7): This space should contain the name, address, area code, and telephone number of the person to be consulted if correspondence about this application becomes necessary.

Certification (space 8): The application cannot be accepted unless it bears the date and the **handwritten signature** of the author or other copyright claimant, or of the owner of exclusive right(s), or of the duly authorized agent of the author, claimant, or owner of exclusive right(s).

Address for Return of Certificate (space 9): The address box must be completed legibly since the certificate will be returned in a window envelope.

MORE INFORMATION

How To Register a Recorded Work: If the musical or dramatic work that you are registering has been recorded (as a tape, disk, or cassette), you may choose either copyright application Form PA or Form SR, Performing Arts or Sound Recordings, depending on the purpose of the registration.

Form PA should be used to register the underlying musical composition or dramatic work. Form SR has been developed specifically to register a "sound recording" as defined by the Copyright Act—a work resulting from the "fixation of a series of sounds," separate and distinct from the underlying musical or dramatic work. Form SR should be used when the copyright claim is limited to the sound recording itself. (In one instance, Form SR may also be used to file for a copyright registration for both kinds of works—see (4) below.) Therefore:

(1) File Form PA if you are seeking to register the musical or dramatic work, not the "sound recording," even though what you deposit for copyright purposes may be in the form of a phonorecord.

(2) File Form PA if you are seeking to register the audio portion of an audiovisual work, such as a motion picture soundtrack; these are considered integral parts of the audio-visual work.

(3) File Form SR if you are seeking to register the "sound recording" itself, that is, the work that results from the fixation of a series of musical, spoken, or other sounds, but not the underlying musical or dramatic work.

(4) File Form SR if you are the copyright claimant for both the underlying musical or dramatic work and the sound recording, *and* you prefer to register both on the same form.

(5) File both forms PA and SR if the copyright claimant for the underlying work and sound recording differ, or you prefer to have separate registration for them.

"Copies" and "Phonorecords": To register for copyright, you are required to deposit "copies" or "phonorecords." These are defined as follows:

Musical compositions may be embodied (fixed) in "copies," objects from which a work can be read or visually perceived, directly or with the aid of a machine or device, such as manuscripts, books, sheet music, film, and videotape. They may also be fixed in "phonorecords," objects embodying fixations of sounds, such as tapes and phonograph disks, commonly known as phonograph records. For example, a song (the work to be registered) can be reproduced in sheet music ("copies") or phonograph records ("phonorecords"), or both.

FORM PA

UNITED STATES COPYRIGHT OFFICE

REGISTRATION NUMBER

PA   PAU

EFFECTIVE DATE OF REGISTRATION

Month   Day   Year

DO NOT WRITE ABOVE THIS LINE. IF YOU NEED MORE SPACE, USE A SEPARATE CONTINUATION SHEET.

1   **TITLE OF THIS WORK ▼**

PREVIOUS OR ALTERNATIVE TITLES ▼

NATURE OF THIS WORK ▼   See instructions

2   **NAME OF AUTHOR ▼**

a

Was this contribution to the work a
"work made for hire"?

☐ Yes

☐ No

AUTHOR'S NATIONALITY OR DOMICILE
Name of Country

OR ⎰ Citizen of ▶

    ⎱ Domiciled in ▶

DATES OF BIRTH AND DEATH
Year Born ▼   Year Died ▼

**WAS THIS AUTHOR'S CONTRIBUTION TO
THE WORK**

Anonymous?   ☐ Yes   ☐ No

Pseudonymous? ☐ Yes   ☐ No

If the answer to either
of these questions is
"Yes," see detailed
instructions.

474

NOTE

Under the law, the "author" of a "work made for hire" is generally the employer, not the employee (see instructions). For any part of this work that was "made for hire" check "Yes" in the space provided, give the employer (or other person for whom the work was prepared) as "Author" of that part, and leave the space for dates of birth and death blank.

NATURE OF AUTHORSHIP Briefly describe nature of the material created by this author in which copyright is claimed. ▼

NAME OF AUTHOR ▼

DATES OF BIRTH AND DEATH
Year Born ▼   Year Died ▼

Was this contribution to the work a "work made for hire"?
☐ Yes
☐ No

AUTHOR'S NATIONALITY OR DOMICILE
Name of country
OR { Citizen of ▶ _____
Domiciled in ▶ _____

WAS THIS AUTHOR'S CONTRIBUTION TO THE WORK
Anonymous?   ☐ Yes ☐ No
Pseudonymous?   ☐ Yes ☐ No
If the answer to either of these questions is "Yes," see detailed instructions.

NATURE OF AUTHORSHIP Briefly describe nature of the material created by this author in which copyright is claimed. ▼

NAME OF AUTHOR ▼

DATES OF BIRTH AND DEATH
Year Born ▼   Year Died ▼

Was this contribution to the work a "work made for hire"?
☐ Yes
☐ No

AUTHOR'S NATIONALITY OR DOMICILE
Name of Country
OR { Citizen of ▶ _____
Domiciled in ▶ _____

WAS THIS AUTHOR'S CONTRIBUTION TO THE WORK
Anonymous?   ☐ Yes ☐ No
Pseudonymous?   ☐ Yes ☐ No
If the answer to either of these questions is "Yes," see detailed instructions.

NATURE OF AUTHORSHIP Briefly describe nature of the material created by this author in which copyright is claimed. ▼

3

YEAR IN WHICH CREATION OF THIS WORK WAS COMPLETED This information must be given in all cases.
▼ Year

DATE AND NATION OF FIRST PUBLICATION OF THIS PARTICULAR WORK
Complete this information Month ▶ _____ Day ▶ _____ Year ▶ _____
ONLY if this work has been published.   ◀ Nation

4

See instructions before completing this space.

COPYRIGHT CLAIMANT(S) Name and address must be given even if the claimant is the same as the author given in space 2.▼

TRANSFER If the claimant(s) named here in space 4 are different from the author(s) named in space 2, give a brief statement of how the claimant(s) obtained ownership of the copyright. ▶

OFFICE USE ONLY
DO NOT WRITE HERE

APPLICATION RECEIVED
ONE DEPOSIT RECEIVED
TWO DEPOSITS RECEIVED
REMITTANCE NUMBER AND DATE

MORE ON BACK ▶ • Complete all applicable spaces (numbers 5-9) on the reverse side of this page.
• See detailed instructions   • Sign the form at line 8

DO NOT WRITE HERE
Page 1 of _____ pages

475

EXAMINED BY

CHECKED BY

☐ CORRESPONDENCE
  Yes

☐ DEPOSIT ACCOUNT
  FUNDS USED

FOR
COPYRIGHT
OFFICE
USE
ONLY

DO NOT WRITE ABOVE THIS LINE. IF YOU NEED MORE SPACE, USE A SEPARATE CONTINUATION SHEET.

5

PREVIOUS REGISTRATION Has registration for this work, or for an earlier version of this work, already been made in the Copyright Office?

☐ **Yes** ☐ **No** If your answer is "Yes," why is another registration being sought? (Check appropriate box) ▶

☐ This is the first published edition of a work previously registered in unpublished form.

☐ This is the first application submitted by this author as copyright claimant.

☐ This is a changed version of the work, as shown by space 6 on this application.

If your answer is "Yes," give: **Previous Registration Number** ▼   **Year of Registration** ▼

6

DERIVATIVE WORK OR COMPILATION Complete both space 6a & 6b for a derivative work; complete only 6b for a compilation.

a. **Preexisting Material** Identify any preexisting work or works that this work is based on or incorporates. ▶

b. **Material Added to This Work** Give a brief, general statement of the material that has been added to this work and in which copyright is claimed. ▶

See instructions
before completing
this space.

7

DEPOSIT ACCOUNT If the registration fee is to be charged to a Deposit Account established in the Copyright Office, give name and number of Account.

Name ▼   **Account Number** ▼

CORRESPONDENCE Give name and address to which correspondence about this application should be sent. Name/Address/Apt/City/State/Zip ▶

Area Code & Telephone Number ▶

Be sure to give your daytime phone number.

8

CERTIFICATION* I, the undersigned, hereby certify that I am the

Check only one ▶

☐ author

☐ other copyright claimant

☐ owner of exclusive right(s)

☐ authorized agent of _____
　　　　Name of author or other copyright claimant, or owner of exclusive right(s) ▲

of the work identified in this application and that the statements made by me in this application are correct to the best of my knowledge.

Typed or printed name and date ▼ If this is a published work, this date must be the same as or later than the date of publication given in space 3.

_____ date ▶ _____

Handwritten signature (X) ▼

9

MAIL CERTIFI- CATE TO

Name ▼

Certificate will be mailed in window envelope

Number/Street/Apartment Number ▼

City/State ZIP ▼

Have you:
● Completed all necessary spaces?
● Signed your application in space 8?
● Enclosed check or money order for $10 payable to *Register of Copyrights*?
● Enclosed your deposit material with the application and fee?

MAIL TO: Register of Copyrights, Library of Congress, Washington, D.C. 20559.

☆ U.S. GOVERNMENT PRINTING OFFICE: 1982-361-278/64　　　　Sept. 1982—200,000

Filling Out Application Form SR

Detach and read these instructions before completing this form. Make sure all applicable spaces have been filled in before you return this form.

BASIC INFORMATION

When to Use This Form:
Use Form SR for copyright registration of published or unpublished sound recordings. It should be used where the copyright claim is limited to the sound recording itself, and it may also be used where the same copyright claimant is seeking simultaneous registration of the underlying musical, dramatic, or literary work embodied in the phonorecord.

With one exception, "sound recordings" are works that result from the fixation of a series of musical, spoken, or other sounds. The exception is for the audio portions of audiovisual works, such as a motion picture soundtrack or an audio cassette accompanying a filmstrip; these are considered a part of the audiovisual work as a whole.

Deposit to Accompany Application:
An application for copyright registration of a sound recording must be accompanied by a deposit consisting of phonorecords representing the entire work for which registration is to be made.

Unpublished Work: Deposit one complete phonorecord.

Published Work: Deposit two complete phonorecords of the best edition, together with "any printed or other visually perceptible material" published with the phonorecords.

Work First Published Outside the United States: Deposit one complete phonorecord of the first foreign edition.

Contribution to a Collective Work: Deposit one complete phonorecord of the best edition of the collective work.

The Copyright Notice:
For published sound recordings, the law provides that a copyright notice in a specified form "shall be placed on all publicly distributed phonorecords of the sound recording." Use of the copyright notice is the responsibility of the copyright owner and does not require advance permission from the Copyright Office. The required form of the notice for phonorecords of sound recordings consists of three elements: (1) the symbol "℗" (the letter "P" in a circle); (2) the year of first publication of the sound recording; and (3) the name of the owner of copyright. For example: "℗ 1981 Rittenhouse Record Co." The notice is to be "placed on the surface of the phonorecord, or on the label or container, in such manner and location as to give reasonable notice of the claim of copyright." For further information about copyright, write: Information and Publications Section, LM-455 Copyright Office, Library of Congress, Washington, D.C. 20559

LINE-BY-LINE INSTRUCTIONS

1 SPACE 1: Title

Title of This Work: Every work submitted for copyright registration must be given a title to identify that particular work. If the phonorecords or any accompanying printed material bear a title (or an identifying phrase that could serve as a title), transcribe that wording completely and exactly on the application. Indexing of the registration and future identification of the work may depend on the information you give here.

Nature of Material Recorded: Indicate the general type or character of the works or other material embodied in the recording. The box marked "Literary" should be checked for nondramatic spoken material of all sorts, including narration, interviews, panel discussions, and training material. If the material recorded is not musical, dramatic, or literary in nature, check "Other" and briefly describe the type of sounds fixed in the recording. For example: "Sound Effects"; "Bird Calls"; "Crowd Noises."

Previous or Alternative Titles: Complete this space if there are any additional titles for the work under which someone searching for the registration might be likely to look, or under which a document pertaining to the work might be recorded.

2 SPACE 2: Author(s)

General Instructions: After reading these instructions, decide who are the "authors" of this work for copyright purposes. Then, unless the work is a "collective work," give the requested information about every "author" who contributed any appreciable amount of copyrightable matter to this version of the work. If you need further space, request additional Continuation Sheets. In the case of a collective work, such as a collection of previously published or registered sound recordings, give information about the author of the collective work as a whole. If you are submitting this Form SR to cover the recorded musical, dramatic, or literary work as well as the sounds itself, it is important for space 2 to include full information about the various authors of all of the material covered by the copyright claim, making clear the nature of each author's contribution.

Name of Author: The fullest form of the author's name should be given. Unless the work was "made for hire," the individual who actually created the work is its "author." In the case of a work made for hire, the statute provides that "the employer or other person for whom the work was prepared is considered the author."

What is a "Work Made for Hire"? A "work made for hire" is defined as: (1) "a work prepared by an employee within the scope of his or her employment"; or (2) "a work specially ordered or commissioned for use as a contribution to a collective work, as a part of a motion picture or other audiovisual work, as a translation, as a supplementary work, as a compilation, as an instructional text, as a test, as answer material for a test, or as an atlas, if the parties expressly agree in a written instrument signed by them that the work shall be considered a work made for hire." If you have checked "Yes" to indicate that the work was "made for hire," you must give the full legal name of the employer (or other person for whom the work was prepared). You may also include the name of the employee along with the name of the employer (for example: "Elster Record Co., employer for hire of John Ferguson").

"Anonymous" or "Pseudonymous" Work: An author's contribution to a work is "anonymous" if that author is not identified on the copies or phonorecords of the work. An author's contribution to a work is "pseudonymous" if that author is identified on the copies or phonorecords under a fictitious name. If the work is "anonymous" you may: (1) leave the line blank; or (2) state "anonymous" on the line; or (3) reveal the author's identity. If the work is "pseudonymous" you may: (1) leave the line blank; or (2) give the pseudonym and identify it as such (for example: "Huntley Haverstock, pseudonym"); or (3) reveal the author's name, making clear which is the real name and which is the pseudonym (for example: "Judith Barton, whose pseudonym is Madeline Elster"). However, the citizenship or domicile of the author **must** be given in all cases.

Dates of Birth and Death: If the author is dead, the statute requires that the year of death be included in the application unless the work is anonymous or pseudonymous. The author's birth date is optional, but is useful as a form of identification. Leave this space blank if the author's contribution was a "work made for hire."

Author's Nationality or Domicile: Give the country of which the author is a citizen, or the country in which the author is domiciled. Nationality or domicile **must** be given in all cases.

Nature of Authorship: Give a brief general statement of the nature of this particular author's contribution to the work. If you are submitting this Form SR to cover both the sound recording and the underlying musical, dramatic, or literary work, make sure that the precise nature of each author's contribution is reflected here. Examples where the authorship pertains to the recording: "Sound Recording"; "Performance and Recording"; "Compilation and Remixing of Sounds." Examples where the authorship pertains to both the recording and the underlying work: "Words, Music, Performance, Record-ing"; "Arrangement of Music and Recording"; "Compilation of Poems and Reading."

3 SPACE 3: Creation and Publication

General Instructions: Do not confuse "creation" with "publication." Every application for copyright registration must state "the year in which creation of the work was completed." Give the date and nation of first publication only if the work has been published.

Creation: Under the statute, a work is "created" when it is fixed in a copy or phonorecord for the first time. Where a work has been prepared over a period of time, the part of the work existing in fixed form on a particular date constitutes the created work on that date. The date you give here should be the year in which the author completed the particular version for which registration is now being sought, even if other versions exist or if further changes or additions are planned.

Publication: The statute defines "publication" as "the distribution of copies or phonorecords of a work to the public by sale or other transfer of ownership, or by rental, lease, or lending"; a work is also "published" if there has been an "offering to distribute copies or phonorecords to a group of persons for purposes of further distribution, public performance, or public display." Give the full date (month, day, year) when, and the country where, publication first occurred. If first publication took place simultaneously in the United States and other countries, it is sufficient to state "U.S.A."

4 SPACE 4: Claimant(s)

Name(s) and Address(es) of Copyright Claimant(s): Give the name(s) and address(es) of the copyright claimant(s) in this work even if the claimant is the same as the author. Copyright in a work belongs initially to the author of the work (including, in the case of a work made for hire, the employer or other person for whom the work was prepared). The copyright claimant is either the author of the work or a person or organization to whom the copyright initially belonging to the author has been transferred.

Transfer: The statute provides that, if the copyright claimant is not the author, the application for registration must contain "a brief statement of how the claimant obtained ownership of the copyright." If any copyright claimant named in space 4 is not an author named in space 2, give a brief, general statement summarizing the means by which that claimant obtained ownership of the copyright. Examples: "By written contract"; "Transfer of all rights by

Changed Version: If the work has been changed, and you are now seeking registration to cover the additions or revisions, check the last box in space 5, give the earlier registration number and date, and complete both parts of space 6 in accordance with the instructions below.

Previous Registration Number and Date: If more than one previous registration has been made for the work, give the number and date of the latest registration.

6 SPACE 6: Derivative Work or Compilation

General Instructions: Complete space 6 if this work is a "changed version," "compilation," or "derivative work," and if it incorporates one or more earlier works that have already been published or registered for copyright, or that have fallen into the public domain, or sound recordings that were fixed before February 15, 1972. A "compilation" is defined as "a work formed by the collection and assembling of preexisting materials or of data that are selected, coordinated, or arranged in such a way that the resulting work as a whole constitutes an original work of authorship." A "derivative work" is "a work based on one or more preexisting works." Examples of derivative works include recordings reissued with substantial editorial revisions or abridgments of the recorded sounds, and recordings republished with new recorded material, or "any other form in which a work may be recast, transformed, or adapted." Derivative works also include works "consisting of editorial revisions, annotations, or other modifications" if these changes, as a whole, represent an original work of authorship.

Preexisting Material (space 6a): Complete this space and space 6b for derivative works. In this space identify the preexisting work that has been recast, transformed, or adapted. For example, the preexisting material might be: "1970 recording by Sperryville Symphony of Bach Double Concerto." Do not complete this space for compilations.

Material Added to This Work (space 6b): Give a brief, general statement of the additional new material covered by the copyright claim for which registration is sought. In the case of a derivative work, identify this new material. Examples: "Recorded performances on bands 1 and 3"; "Remixed sounds from original multitrack sound sources"; "New words, arrangement, and additional sounds." If the work is a compilation, give a brief, general statement "author"; "Assignment"; "By will." Do not attach transfer documents or other attachments or riders.

5 SPACE 5: Previous Registration

General Instructions: The questions in space 5 are intended to find out whether an earlier registration has been made for this work and, if so, whether there is any basis for a new registration. As a rule, only one basic copyright registration can be made for the same version of a particular work.

Same Version: If this version is substantially the same as the work covered by a previous registration, a second registration is not generally possible unless: (1) the work has been registered in unpublished form and a second registration is now being sought to cover this first published edition; or (2) someone other than the author is identified as copyright claimant in the earlier registration, and the author is now seeking registration in his or her own name. If either of these two exceptions apply, check the appropriate box and give the earlier registration number and date. Otherwise, do not submit Form SR; instead, write the Copyright Office for information about supplementary registration or recordation of transfers of copyright ownership.

describing both the material that has been compiled and the compilation itself. Example: "Compilation of 1938 Recordings by various swing bands."

7,8,9 SPACE 7, 8, 9: Fee, Correspondence, Certification, Return Address

Deposit Account: If you maintain a Deposit Account in the Copyright Office, identify it in space 7. Otherwise leave the space blank and send the fee of $10 with your application and deposit.

Correspondence (space 7): This space should contain the name, address, area code, and telephone number of the person to be consulted if correspondence about this application becomes necessary.

Certification (space 8): The application cannot be accepted unless it bears the date and the **handwritten signature** of the author or other copyright claimant, or of the owner of exclusive right(s), or of the duly authorized agent of the author, claimant, or owner of exclusive right(s).

Address for Return of Certificate (space 9): The address box must be completed legibly since the certificate will be returned in a window envelope.

MORE INFORMATION

"Works": "Works" are the basic subject matter of copyright; they are what authors create and copyright protects. The statute draws a sharp distinction between the "work" and "any material object in which the work is embodied."

"Copies" and "Phonorecords": These are the two types of material objects in which "works" are embodied. In general, "copies" are objects from which a work can be read or visually perceived, directly or with the aid of a machine or device, such as manuscripts, books, sheet music, film, and videotape. "Phonorecords" are objects embodying fixations of sounds, such as audio tapes and phonograph disks. For example, a song (the "work") can be reproduced in sheet music ("copies") or phonograph disks ("phonorecords"), or both.

"Sound Recordings": These are "works," not "copies" or "phonorecords." "Sound recordings" are "works that result from the fixation of a series of musical, spoken, or other sounds, but not including the sounds accompanying a motion picture or other audiovisual work." Example: When a record company issues a new release, the release will typically involve two distinct "works": the "musical work" that has been recorded, and the "sound recording" as a separate work in itself. The material objects that the record com-

pany sends out are "phonorecords": physical reproductions of both the "musical work" and the "sound recording."

Should You File More Than One Application?

If your work consists of a recorded musical, dramatic, or literary work, and both that "work," and the sound recording as a separate "work," are eligible for registration, the application form you should file depends on the following:

File Only Form SR if: The copyright claimant is the same for both the musical, dramatic, or literary work and for the sound recording, and you are seeking a single registration to cover both of these "works."

File Only Form PA (or Form TX) if: You are seeking to register only the musical, dramatic, or literary work, not the sound recording. Form PA is appropriate for works of the performing arts; Form TX is for nondramatic literary works.

Separate Applications Should Be Filed on Form PA (or Form TX) and on Form SR if: (1) The copyright claimant for the musical, dramatic, or literary work is different from the copyright claimant for the sound recording; or (2) You prefer to have separate registrations for the musical, dramatic, or literary work and for the sound recording.

FORM SR
UNITED STATES COPYRIGHT OFFICE

REGISTRATION NUMBER

SR   SRU

EFFECTIVE DATE OF REGISTRATION

Month   Day   Year

DO NOT WRITE ABOVE THIS LINE. IF YOU NEED MORE SPACE, USE A SEPARATE CONTINUATION SHEET.

1   **TITLE OF THIS WORK ▼**

PREVIOUS OR ALTERNATIVE TITLES ▼

NATURE OF MATERIAL RECORDED ▼ See instructions.
☐ Musical ☐ Musical-Dramatic
☐ Dramatic ☐ Literary
☐ Other

2   **NAME OF AUTHOR ▼**

a

Was this contribution to the work a
"work made for hire"?
☐ Yes
☐ No

AUTHOR'S NATIONALITY OR DOMICILE
Name of Country
OR { Citizen of ▶
{ Domiciled in ▶

DATES OF BIRTH AND DEATH
Year Born ▼   Year Died ▼

**WAS THIS AUTHOR'S CONTRIBUTION TO
THE WORK**
Anonymous?   ☐ Yes ☐ No
Pseudonymous? ☐ Yes ☐ No

If the answer to either
of these questions is
"Yes," see detailed
instructions.

482

NOTE

Under the law, the "author" of a "work made for hire" is generally the employer, not the employee (see instructions). For any part of this work that was "made for hire" check "Yes" in the space provided, give the employer (or other person for whom the work was prepared) as "Author" of that part, and leave the space for dates of birth and death blank.

See instructions before completing this space.

NATURE OF AUTHORSHIP Briefly describe nature of the material created by this author in which copyright is claimed. ▼

b

NAME OF AUTHOR ▼

DATES OF BIRTH AND DEATH
Year Born ▼   Year Died ▼

Was this contribution to the work a "work made for hire"?
☐ Yes
☐ No

AUTHOR'S NATIONALITY OR DOMICILE
Name of country
OR { Citizen of ▶ _____
Domiciled in ▶ _____

WAS THIS AUTHOR'S CONTRIBUTION TO THE WORK
Anonymous?   ☐ Yes ☐ No
Pseudonymous?   ☐ Yes ☐ No

If the answer to either of these questions is "Yes," see detailed instructions.

NATURE OF AUTHORSHIP Briefly describe nature of the material created by this author in which copyright is claimed. ▼

c

NAME OF AUTHOR ▼

DATES OF BIRTH AND DEATH
Year Born ▼   Year Died ▼

Was this contribution to the work a "work made for hire"?
☐ Yes
☐ No

AUTHOR'S NATIONALITY OR DOMICILE
Name of Country
OR { Citizen of ▶ _____
Domiciled in ▶ _____

WAS THIS AUTHOR'S CONTRIBUTION TO THE WORK
Anonymous?   ☐ Yes ☐ No
Pseudonymous?   ☐ Yes ☐ No

If the answer to either of these questions is "Yes," see detailed instructions.

NATURE OF AUTHORSHIP Briefly describe nature of the material created by this author in which copyright is claimed. ▼

3

YEAR IN WHICH CREATION OF THIS WORK WAS COMPLETED This information must be given in all cases.
▼ Year

DATE AND NATION OF FIRST PUBLICATION OF THIS PARTICULAR WORK
Complete this information ONLY if this work has been published.
Month ▶ _____ Day ▶ _____ Year ▶ _____
◀ Nation

4

COPYRIGHT CLAIMANT(S) Name and address must be given even if the claimant is the same as the author given in space 2. ▼

TRANSFER If the claimant(s) named here in space 4 are different from the author(s) named in space 2, give a brief statement of how the claimant(s) obtained ownership of the copyright. ▼

MORE ON BACK ▶ • Complete all applicable spaces (numbers 5-9) on the reverse side of this page.
• See detailed instructions.
• Sign the form at line 8.

DO NOT WRITE HERE
Page 1 of _____ pages

EXAMINED BY

CHECKED BY

DO NOT WRITE ABOVE THIS LINE. IF YOU NEED MORE SPACE, USE A SEPARATE CONTINUATION SHEET.

PREVIOUS REGISTRATION Has registration for this work, or for an earlier version of this work, already been made in the Copyright Office?

☐ **Yes** ☐ **No** If your answer is "Yes," why is another registration being sought? (Check appropriate box) ▼

☐ This is the first published edition of a work previously registered in unpublished form.

☐ This is the first application submitted by this author as copyright claimant.

☐ This is a changed version of the work, as shown by space 6 on this application.

If your answer is "Yes," give: **Previous Registration Number** ▼   **Year of Registration** ▼

5

DERIVATIVE WORK OR COMPILATION Complete both space 6a & 6b for a derivative work; complete only 6b for a compilation.

a. **Preexisting Material** Identify any preexisting work or works that this work is based on or incorporates. ▼

b. **Material Added to This Work** Give a brief, general statement of the material that has been added to this work and in which copyright is claimed. ▼

6

See instructions
before completing
this space.

DEPOSIT ACCOUNT If the registration fee is to be charged to a Deposit Account established in the Copyright Office, give name and number of Account.

Name ▼   **Account Number** ▼

7

CORRESPONDENCE Give name and address to which correspondence about this application should be sent. Name/Address/Apt/City/State/Zip ▶

_____

_____

Area Code & Telephone Number ▶

Be sure to
give your
daytime phone
▶ number.

8

CERTIFICATION* I, the undersigned, hereby certify that I am the

Check one ▶

☐ author

☐ other copyright claimant

☐ owner of exclusive right(s)

☐ authorized agent of _____
   Name of author or other copyright claimant, or owner of exclusive right(s) ◀

of the work identified in this application and that the statements made
by me in this application are correct to the best of my knowledge.

Typed or printed name and date ▼ If this is a published work, this date must be the same as or later than the date of publication given in space 3.

_____ date ▶ _____

Handwritten signature (X) ▼

_____

**MAIL
CERTIFI-
CATE TO**

**Certificate
will be
mailed in
window
envelope**

Name ▼
Number/Street/Apartment Number ▶
City/State/ZIP ▶

9

Have you:
- Completed all necessary spaces?
- Signed your application in space 8?
- Enclosed check or money order for $10 payable to _Register of Copyrights?_
- Enclosed your deposit material with the application and fee?

MAIL TO: Register of Copyrights, Library of Congress, Washington, D.C. 20559.

* 17 U.S.C. § 506(e): Any person who knowingly makes a false representation of a material fact in the application for copyright registration provided for by section 409 or in any written statement filed in connection with the application, shall be fined not more than $2,500.

☆ U.S. GOVERNMENT PRINTING OFFICE: 1982-361-278/63

Sept. 1982—210,000

Filling Out Application Form TX

Detach and read these instructions before completing this form. Make sure all applicable spaces have been filled in before you return this form.

BASIC INFORMATION

When to Use This Form: Use Form TX for registration of published or unpublished non-dramatic literary works, excluding periodicals or serial issues. This class includes a wide variety of works: fiction, non-fiction, poetry, textbooks, reference works, directories, catalogs, advertising copy, compilations of information, and computer programs. For periodicals and serials, use Form SE.

Deposit to Accompany Application: An application for copyright registration must be accompanied by a deposit consisting of copies or phonorecords representing the entire work for which registration is to be made. The following are the general deposit requirements as set forth in the statute:

Unpublished Work: Deposit one complete copy (or phonorecord).

Published Work: Deposit two complete copies (or phonorecords) of the best edition.

Work First Published Outside the United States: Deposit one complete copy (or phonorecord) of the first foreign edition.

Contribution to a Collective Work: Deposit one complete copy (or phonorecord) of the best edition of the collective work.

The Copyright Notice: For published works, the law provides that a copyright notice in a specified form "shall be placed on all publicly distributed copies from which the work can be visually perceived." Use of the copyright notice is the responsibility of the copyright owner and does not require advance permission from the Copyright Office. The required form of the notice for copies generally consists of three elements: (1) the symbol "©", or the word "Copyright," or the abbreviation "Copr."; (2) the year of first publication; and (3) the name of the owner of copyright. For example: "© 1981 Constance Porter." The notice is to be affixed to the copies "in such manner and location as to give reasonable notice of the claim of copyright."

For further information about copyright registration, notice, or special questions relating to copyright problems, write:

Information and Publications Section, LM-455
Copyright Office
Library of Congress
Washington, D.C. 20559

LINE-BY-LINE INSTRUCTIONS

1 SPACE 1: Title

Title of This Work: Every work submitted for copyright registration must be given a title to identify that particular work. If the copies or phonorecords of the work bear a title (or an identifying phrase that could serve as a title), transcribe that wording *completely* and *exactly* on the application. Indexing of the registration and future identification of the work will depend on the information you give here.

Previous or Alternative Titles: Complete this space if there are any additional titles for the work under which someone searching for the registration might be likely to look, or under which a document pertaining to the work might be recorded.

Publication as a Contribution: If the work being registered is a contribution to a periodical, serial, or collection, give the title of the contribution in the "Title of this Work" space. Then, in the line headed "Publication as a Contribution," give information about the collective work in which the contribution appeared.

2 SPACE 2: Author(s)

General Instructions: After reading these instructions, decide who are the "authors" of this work for copyright purposes. Then, unless the work is a "collective work," give the requested information about every "author" who contributed any appreciable amount of copyrightable matter to this version of the work. If you need further space, request additional Continuation sheets. In the case of a collective work, such as an anthology, collection of essays, or encyclopedia, give information about the author of the collective work as a whole.

Name of Author: The fullest form of the author's name should be given. Unless the work was "made for hire," the individual who actually created the work is its "author." In the case of a work made for hire, the statute provides that "the employer or other person for whom the work was prepared is considered the author."

What is a "Work Made for Hire"? A "work made for hire" is defined as: (1) "a work prepared by an employee within the scope of his or her employment"; or (2) "a work specially ordered or commissioned for use as a contribution to a collective work, as a part of a motion picture or other audiovisual work, as a translation, as a supplementary work, as a compilation, as an instructional text, as a test, as answer material for a test, or as an atlas, if the parties expressly agree in a written instrument signed by them that the work shall be considered a work made for hire." If you have checked "Yes" to indicate that the work was "made for hire," you must give the full legal name of the employer (or other person for whom the work was prepared). You may also include the name of the employee along with the name of the employer (for example: "Elster Publishing Co., employer for hire of John Ferguson").

"Anonymous" or "Pseudonymous" Work: An author's contribution to a work is "anonymous" if that author is not identified on the copies or phonorecords of the work. An author's contribution to a work is "pseudonymous" if that author is identified on the copies or phonorecords under a fictitious name. If the work is "anonymous" you may: (1) leave the line blank; or (2) state "anonymous" on the line; or (3) reveal the author's identity. If the work is "pseudonymous" you may: (1) leave the line blank; or (2) give the pseudonym and identify it as such (for example: "Huntley Haverstock, pseudonym"); or (3) reveal the author's name, making clear which is the real name and which is the pseudonym (for example: "Judith Barton, whose pseudonym is Madeline Elster"). However, the citizenship or domicile of the author **must** be given in all cases.

Dates of Birth and Death: If the author is dead, the statute requires that the year of death be included in the application unless the work is anonymous or pseudonymous. The author's birth date is optional, but is useful as a form of identification. Leave this space blank if the author's contribution was a "work made for hire."

Author's Nationality or Domicile: Give the country of which the author is a citizen, or the country in which the author is domiciled. Nationality or domicile **must** be given in all cases.

Nature of Authorship: After the words "Nature of Authorship" give a brief general statement of the nature of this particular author's contribution to the work. Examples: "Entire text"; "Coauthor of entire text"; "Chapters 11-14"; "Editorial revisions"; "Compilation and English translation"; "New text."

SPACE 3: Creation and Publication

General Instructions: Do not confuse "creation" with "publication." Every application for copyright registration must state "the year in which creation of the work was completed." Give the date and nation of first publication only if the work has been published.

Creation: Under the statute, a work is "created" when it is fixed in a copy or phonorecord for the first time. Where a work has been prepared over a period of time, the part of the work existing in fixed form on a particular date constitutes the created work on that date. The date you give here should be the year in which the author completed the particular version for which registration is now being sought, even if other versions exist or if further changes or additions are planned.

Publication: The statute defines "publication" as "the distribution of copies or phonorecords of a work to the public by sale or other transfer of ownership, or by rental, lease, or lending"; a work is also "published" if there has been an "offering to distribute copies or phonorecords to a group of persons for purposes of further distribution, public performance, or public display." Give the full date (month, day, year) when, and the country where, publication first occurred. If first publication took place simultaneously in the United States and other countries, it is sufficient to state "U.S.A."

4 SPACE 4: Claimant(s)

Name(s) and Address(es) of Copyright Claimant(s): Give the name(s) and address(es) of the copyright claimant(s) in this work even if the claimant is the same as the author. Copyright in a work belongs initially to the author of the work (including, in the case of a work made for hire, the employer or other person for whom the work was prepared). The copyright claimant is either the author of the work or a person or organization to whom the copyright initially belonging to the author has been transferred.

Transfer: The statute provides that, if the copyright claimant is not the author, the application for registration must contain "a brief statement of how the claimant obtained ownership of the copyright." If any copyright claimant named in space 4 is not an author named in space 2, give a brief, general statement summarizing the means by which that claimant obtained ownership of the copyright. Examples: "By written contract"; "Transfer of all rights by

a whole constitutes an original work of authorship." A "derivative work" is "a work based on one or more preexisting works." Examples of derivative works include translations, fictionalizations, abridgments, condensations, or "any other form in which a work may be recast, transformed, or adapted." Derivative works also include works "consisting of editorial revisions, annotations, or other modifications" if these changes, as a whole, represent an original work of authorship.

Preexisting Material (space 6a): For derivative works, complete this space and space 6b. In space 6a identify the preexisting work that has been recast, transformed, or adapted. An example of preexisting material might be: "Russian version of Goncharov's 'Oblomov.'" Do not complete space 6a for compilations.

Material Added to This Work (space 6b): Give a brief, general statement of the new material covered by the copyright claim for which registration is sought. **Derivative work** examples include: "Foreword, editing, critical annotations"; "Translation"; "Chapters 11-17." If the work is a **compilation**, describe both the compilation itself and the material that has been compiled. Example: "Compilation of certain 1917 Speeches by Woodrow Wilson." A work may be both a derivative work and compilation, in which case a sample statement might be: "Compilation and additional new material."

7 SPACE 7: Manufacturing Provisions

General Instructions: The copyright statute currently provides, as a general rule, that the copies of a published work "consisting preponderantly of nondramatic literary material in the English language" be manufactured in the United States or Canada in order to be lawfully imported and publicly distributed in the United States. If the work being registered is unpublished or not in English, leave this space blank. Complete this space if registration is sought for a published work "consisting preponderantly of nondramatic literary material that is in the English language." Identify those who manufactured the copies and where those manufacturing processes were performed. As an exception to the manufacturing provisions, the statute prescribes that, where manufacture has taken place outside the United States or Canada, a maximum of 2000 copies of the foreign edition may be imported into the United States without affecting the copyright owners' rights. For this purpose, the Copyright Office will issue an Import Statement upon request and payment of a fee of $3 at the time of registration or at any later time. For further information about import statements, write for Form IS.

"author"; "Assignment"; "By will." Do not attach transfer documents or other attachments or riders.

5 SPACE 5: Previous Registration

General Instructions: The questions in space 5 are intended to find out whether an earlier registration has been made for this work and, if so, whether there is any basis for a new registration. As a general rule, only one basic copyright registration can be made for the same version of a particular work.

Same Version: If this version is substantially the same as the work covered by a previous registration, a second registration is not generally possible unless: (1) the work has been registered in unpublished form and a second registration is now being sought to cover this first published edition; or (2) someone other than the author is identified as copyright claimant in the earlier registration, and the author is now seeking registration in his or her own name. If either of these two exceptions apply, check the appropriate box and give the earlier registration number and date. Otherwise, do not submit Form TX; instead, write the Copyright Office for information about supplementary registration or recordation of transfers of copyright ownership.

Changed Version: If the work has been changed, and you are now seeking registration to cover the additions or revisions, check the last box in space 5, give the earlier registration number and date, and complete both parts of space 6 in accordance with the instructions below.

Previous Registration Number and Date: If more than one previous registration has been made for the work, give the number and date of the latest registration.

6 SPACE 6: Derivative Work or Compilation

General Instructions: Complete space 6 if this work is a "changed version," "compilation," or "derivative work," and if it incorporates one or more earlier works that have already been published or registered for copyright, or that have fallen into the public domain. A "compilation" is defined as "a work formed by the collection and assembling of preexisting materials or of data that are selected, coordinated, or arranged in such a way that the resulting work as

8 SPACE 8: Reproduction for Use of Blind or Physically Handicapped Individuals

General Instructions: One of the major programs of the Library of Congress is to provide Braille editions and special recordings of works for the exclusive use of the blind and physically handicapped. In an effort to simplify and speed up the copyright licensing procedures that are a necessary part of this program, section 710 of the copyright statute provides for the establishment of a voluntary licensing system to be tied in with copyright registration. Copyright Office regulations provide that you may grant a license for such reproduction and distribution solely for the use of persons who are certified by competent authority as unable to read normal printed material as a result of physical limitations. The license is entirely voluntary, nonexclusive, and may be terminated upon 90 days notice.

How to Grant the License: If you wish to grant it, check one of the three boxes in space 8. Your check in one of these boxes, together with your signature in space 10, will mean that the Library of Congress can proceed to reproduce and distribute under the license without further paperwork. For further information, write for Circular R63.

9,10,11 SPACE 9, 10, 11: Fee, Correspondence, Certification, Return Address

Deposit Account: If you maintain a Deposit Account in the Copyright Office, identify it in space 9. Otherwise leave the space blank and send the fee of $10 with your application and deposit.

Correspondence (space 9): This space should contain the name, address, area code, and telephone number of the person to be consulted if correspondence about this application becomes necessary.

Certification (space 10): The application can not be accepted unless it bears the date and the **handwritten signature** of the author or other copyright claimant, or of the owner of exclusive right(s), or of the duly authorized agent of author, claimant, or owner of exclusive right(s).

Address for Return of Certificate (space 11): The address box must be completed legibly since the certificate will be returned in a window envelope.

FORM TX

UNITED STATES COPYRIGHT OFFICE

REGISTRATION NUMBER

TX   TXU

EFFECTIVE DATE OF REGISTRATION

Month	Day	Year

DO NOT WRITE ABOVE THIS LINE. IF YOU NEED MORE SPACE, USE A SEPARATE CONTINUATION SHEET.

1   **TITLE OF THIS WORK** ▼

PREVIOUS OR ALTERNATIVE TITLES ▼

PUBLICATION AS A CONTRIBUTION If this work was published as a contribution to a periodical, serial, or collection, give information about the collective work in which the contribution appeared. **Title of Collective Work** ▼

If published in a periodical or serial give: **Volume** ▼   **Number** ▼   **Issue Date** ▼   **On Pages** ▼

2   **NAME OF AUTHOR** ▼

a

Was this contribution to the work a "work made for hire"?

☐ Yes
☐ No

AUTHOR'S NATIONALITY OR DOMICILE
Name of Country

OR { Citizen of ▶ _____
    Domiciled in ▶ _____

DATES OF BIRTH AND DEATH
Year Born ▼   Year Died ▼

WAS THIS AUTHOR'S CONTRIBUTION TO THE WORK

Anonymous?   ☐ Yes ☐ No
Pseudonymous?   ☐ Yes ☐ No

If the answer to either of these questions is "Yes," see detailed instructions.

NOTE

Under the law, the "author" of a "work made for hire" is generally the employer, not the employee (see instructions). For any part of this work that was "made for hire" check "Yes" in the space provided, give the employer (or other person for whom the work was prepared) as "Author" of that part, and leave the space for dates of birth and death blank.

NATURE OF AUTHORSHIP Briefly describe nature of the material created by this author in which copyright is claimed. ▼

NAME OF AUTHOR ▼

DATES OF BIRTH AND DEATH
Year Born ▼   Year Died ▼

Was this contribution to the work a "work made for hire"?
☐ Yes
☐ No

AUTHOR'S NATIONALITY OR DOMICILE
Name of country
OR { Citizen of ▶
Domiciled in ▶

WAS THIS AUTHOR'S CONTRIBUTION TO THE WORK
Anonymous?   ☐ Yes ☐ No
Pseudonymous?   ☐ Yes ☐ No

If the answer to either of these questions is "Yes," see detailed instructions.

NATURE OF AUTHORSHIP Briefly describe nature of the material created by this author in which copyright is claimed. ▼

NAME OF AUTHOR ▼

DATES OF BIRTH AND DEATH
Year Born ▼   Year Died ▼

Was this contribution to the work a "work made for hire"?
☐ Yes
☐ No

AUTHOR'S NATIONALITY OR DOMICILE
Name of Country
OR { Citizen of ▶
Domiciled in ▶

WAS THIS AUTHOR'S CONTRIBUTION TO THE WORK
Anonymous?   ☐ Yes ☐ No
Pseudonymous?   ☐ Yes ☐ No

If the answer to either of these questions is "Yes," see detailed instructions.

NATURE OF AUTHORSHIP Briefly describe nature of the material created by this author in which copyright is claimed. ▼

YEAR IN WHICH CREATION OF THIS WORK WAS COMPLETED This information must be given in all cases.
◀ Year

DATE AND NATION OF FIRST PUBLICATION OF THIS PARTICULAR WORK
Complete this information Month ▶ _____ Day ▶ _____ Year ▶ _____
ONLY if this work has been published.
◀ Nation

COPYRIGHT CLAIMANT(S) Name and address must be given even if the claimant is the same as the author given in space 2. ▼

See instructions before completing this space.

TRANSFER If the claimant(s) named here in space 4 are different from the author(s) named in space 2, give a brief statement of how the claimant(s) obtained ownership of the copyright. ▶

OFFICE USE ONLY / **DO NOT WRITE HERE**

APPLICATION RECEIVED

ONE DEPOSIT RECEIVED

TWO DEPOSITS RECEIVED

REMITTANCE NUMBER AND DATE

DO NOT WRITE HERE

MORE ON BACK ▶ • Complete all applicable spaces (numbers 5-11) on the reverse side of this page.
• See detailed instructions.   • Sign the form at line 10.

DO NOT WRITE HERE

Page 1 of _____ pages

491

☐ CORRESPONDENCE
   Yes

☐ DEPOSIT ACCOUNT
   FUNDS USED

FOR
COPYRIGHT
OFFICE
USE
ONLY

DO NOT WRITE ABOVE THIS LINE. IF YOU NEED MORE SPACE, USE A SEPARATE CONTINUATION SHEET.

PREVIOUS REGISTRATION Has registration for this work, or for an earlier version of this work, already been made in the Copyright Office?

☐ **Yes** ☐ **No** If your answer is "Yes," why is another registration being sought? (Check appropriate box) ▼

☐ This is the first published edition of a work previously registered in unpublished form.

☐ This is the first application submitted by this author as copyright claimant.

☐ This is a changed version of the work, as shown by space 6 on this application.

If your answer is "Yes," give: **Previous Registration Number** ▼   **Year of Registration** ▼

5

DERIVATIVE WORK OR COMPILATION Complete both space 6a & 6b for a derivative work; complete only 6b for a compilation.

a. Preexisting Material Identify any preexisting work or works that this work is based on or incorporates. ▼

b. Material Added to This Work Give a brief, general statement of the material that has been added to this work and in which copyright is claimed. ▼

6

See instructions
before completing
this space.

MANUFACTURERS AND LOCATIONS If this is a published work consisting preponderantly of nondramatic literary material in English, the law may require that the copies be manufactured in the United States or Canada for full protection. If so, the names of the manufacturers who performed certain processes, and the places where these processes were performed **must** be given. See instructions for details.

Names of Manufacturers ▼   **Places of Manufacture** ▼

7

REPRODUCTION FOR USE OF BLIND OR PHYSICALLY HANDICAPPED INDIVIDUALS A signature on this form at space 10, and a check in one of the boxes here in space 8, constitutes a non-exclusive grant of permission to the Library of Congress to reproduce and distribute solely for the blind and physically handicapped and under the conditions and limitations prescribed by the regulations of the Copyright Office: (1) copies of the work identified in space 1 of this application in Braille (or similar tactile symbols); or (2) phonorecords embodying a fixation of a reading of that work; or (3) both.

a ☐ Copies and Phonorecords b ☐ Copies Only c ☐ Phonorecords Only See instructions

8

DEPOSIT ACCOUNT If the registration fee is to be charged to a Deposit Account established in the Copyright Office, give name and number of Account.

Name ▼ Account Number ▼

9

CORRESPONDENCE Give name and address to which correspondence about this application should be sent. Name/Address/Apt/City/State/Zip ▼

Area Code & Telephone Number ▶

Be sure to give your daytime phone number ▼

10

CERTIFICATION* I, the undersigned, hereby certify that I am the

Check one ▶
☐ author
☐ other copyright claimant
☐ owner of exclusive right(s)
☐ authorized agent of

_____
Name of author or other copyright claimant, or owner of exclusive right(s) ▲

of the work identified in this application and that the statements made by me in this application are correct to the best of my knowledge.

Typed or printed name and date ▼ If this is a published work, this date must be the same as or later than the date of publication given in space 3.

_____ date ▶ _____

☞ Handwritten signature (X) ▼

11

MAIL CERTIFI- CATE TO

Name ▼

Number/Street/Apartment Number ▼

City/State/ZIP ▼

Certificate will be mailed in window envelope

Have you:
• Completed all necessary spaces?
• Signed your application in space 10?
• Enclosed check or money order for $10 payable to Register of Copyrights?
• Enclosed your deposit material with the application and fee?

MAIL TO: Register of Copyrights, Library of Congress, Washington, D.C. 20559.

* 17 U.S.C. § 506(e): Any person who knowingly makes a false representation of a material fact in the application for copyright registration provided for by section 409, or in any written statement filed in connection with the application, shall be fined not more than $2,500.

☆ U.S. GOVERNMENT PRINTING OFFICE: 1982-361-278/58

Sept. 1982—600,000

493

Filling Out Application Form VA

Detach and read these instructions before completing this form. Make sure all applicable spaces have been filled in before you return this form.

BASIC INFORMATION

When to Use This Form: Use Form VA for copyright registration of published or unpublished works of the visual arts. This category consists of "pictorial, graphic, or sculptural works," including two-dimensional and three-dimensional works of fine, graphic, and applied art, photographs, prints and art reproductions, maps, globes, charts, technical drawings, diagrams, and models.

What Does Copyright Protect? Copyright in a work of the visual arts protects those pictorial, graphic, or sculptural elements that, either alone or in combination, represent an "original work of authorship." The statute declares: "In no case does copyright protection for an original work of authorship extend to any idea, procedure, process, system, method of operation, concept, principle, or discovery, regardless of the form in which it is described, explained, illustrated, or embodied in such work."

Works of Artistic Craftsmanship and Designs: "Works of artistic craftsmanship" are registrable on Form VA, but the statute makes clear that protection extends to "their form" and not to "their mechanical or utilitarian aspects." The "design of a useful article" is considered copyrightable "only if, and only to the extent that, such design incorporates pictorial, graphic, or sculptural features that can be identified separately from, and are capable of existing independently of, the utilitarian aspects of the article."

Labels and Advertisements: Works prepared for use in connection with the sale or advertisement of goods and services are registrable if they contain "original work of authorship." Use Form VA if the copyrightable material in the work you are registering is mainly pictorial or graphic; use Form TX if it consists mainly of text. NOTE: Words and short phrases such as names, titles, and slogans cannot be protected by copyright, and the same is true of standard symbols, emblems, and other commonly used graphic designs that are in the public domain. When used commercially, material of that sort can sometimes be protected under state laws of unfair competition or under the Federal trademark laws. For information about trademark registration, write to the Commissioner of Patents and Trademarks, Washington, D.C. 20231.

Deposit to Accompany Application: An application for copyright registration must be accompanied by a deposit consisting of copies representing the en-

tire work for which registration is to be made.

Unpublished Work: Deposit one complete copy.

Published Work: Deposit two complete copies of the best edition.

Work First Published Outside the United States: Deposit one complete copy of the first foreign edition.

Contribution to a Collective Work: Deposit one complete copy of the best edition of the collective work.

The Copyright Notice: For published works, the law provides that a copyright notice in a specified form "shall be placed on all publicly distributed copies from which the work can be visually perceived." Use of the copyright notice is the responsibility of the copyright owner and does not require advance permission from the Copyright Office. The required form of the notice for copies generally consists of three elements: (1) the symbol "©", or the word "Copyright," or the abbreviation "Copr."; (2) the year of first publication; and (3) the name of the owner of copyright. For example: "© 1981 Constance Porter." The notice is to be affixed to the copies "in such manner and location as to give reasonable notice of the claim of copyright."

For further information about copyright registration, notice, or special questions relating to copyright problems, write:

Information and Publications Section, LM-455
Copyright Office, Library of Congress, Washington, D.C. 20559

LINE-BY-LINE INSTRUCTIONS

1 SPACE 1: Title

Title of This Work: Every work submitted for copyright registration must be given a title to identify that particular work. If the copies of the work bear a title (or an identifying phrase that could serve as a title), transcribe that wording *completely* and *exactly* on the application. Indexing of the registration and future identification of the work will depend on the information you give here.

Previous or Alternative Titles: Complete this space if there are any additional titles for the work under which someone searching for the registration might be likely to look, or under which a document pertaining to the work might be recorded.

Publication as a Contribution: If the work being registered is a contribution to a periodical, serial, or collection, give the title of the contribution in the "Title of This Work" space. Then, in the line headed "Publication as a Contribution," give information about the collective work in which the contribution appeared.

Nature of This Work: Briefly describe the general nature or character of the pictorial, graphic, or sculptural work being registered for copyright. Examples: "Oil Painting"; "Charcoal Drawing"; "Etching"; "Sculpture"; "Map"; "Photograph"; "Scale Model"; "Lithographic Print"; "Jewelry Design"; "Fabric Design."

2 SPACE 2: Author(s)

General Instructions: After reading these instructions, decide who are the "authors" of this work for copyright purposes. Then, unless the work is a "collective work," give the requested information about every "author" who contributed any appreciable amount of copyrightable matter to this version of the work. If you need further space, request additional Continuation Sheets. In the case of a collective work, such as a catalog of paintings or collection of cartoons by various authors, give information about the author of the collec-

tive work as a whole.

Name of Author: The fullest form of the author's name should be given. Unless the work was "made for hire," the individual who actually created the work is its "author." In the case of a work made for hire, the statute provides that "the employer or other person for whom the work was prepared is considered the author."

What is a "Work Made for Hire"? A "work made for hire" is defined as: (1) "a work prepared by an employee within the scope of his or her employment"; or (2) "a work specially ordered or commissioned for use as a contribution to a collective work, as a part of a motion picture or other audiovisual work, as a translation, as a supplementary work, as a compilation, as an instructional text, as a test, as answer material for a test, or as an atlas, if the parties expressly agree in a written instrument signed by them that the work shall be considered a work made for hire." If you have checked "Yes" to indicate that the work was "made for hire," you must give the full legal name of the employer (or other person for whom the work was prepared). You may also include the name of the employee along with the name of the employer (for example: "Elster Publishing Co., employer for hire of John Ferguson").

"Anonymous" or "Pseudonymous" Work: An author's contribution to a work is "anonymous" if that author is not identified on the copies or phonorecords of the work. An author's contribution to a work is "pseudonymous" if that author is identified on the copies or phonorecords under a fictitious name. If the work is "anonymous" you may: (1) leave the line blank; or (2) state "anonymous" on the line; or (3) reveal the author's identity. If the work is "pseudonymous" you may: (1) leave the line blank; or (2) give the pseudonym and identify it as such (for example: "Huntley Haverstock, pseudonym"); or (3) reveal the author's name, making clear which is the real name and which is the pseudonym (for example: "Henry Leek, whose pseudonym is Priam Farrel"). However, the citizenship or domicile of the author **must be given in all cases.**

Dates of Birth and Death: If the author is dead, the statute requires that the year of death be included in the application unless the work is anonymous or pseudonymous. The author's birth date is optional, but is useful as a form of **identification.** Leave this space blank if the author's contribution was a "work **made for hire."**

Author's Nationality or Domicile: Give the country of which the author is a citizen, or the country in which the author is domiciled. Nationality or domicile **must** be given in all cases.

Nature of Authorship: Give a brief general statement of the nature of this particular author's contribution to the work. Examples: "Painting"; "Photograph"; "Silk Screen Reproduction"; "Co-author of Cartographic Material"; "Technical Drawing"; "Text and Artwork."

3 SPACE 3: Creation and Publication

General Instructions: Do not confuse "creation" with "publication." Every application for copyright registration must state "the year in which creation of the work was completed." Give the date and nation of first publication only if the work has been published.

Creation: Under the statute, a work is "created" when it is fixed in a copy or phonorecord for the first time. Where a work has been prepared over a period of time, the part of the work existing in fixed form on a particular date constitutes the created work on that date. The date you give here should be the year in which the author completed the particular version for which registration is now being sought, even if other versions exist or if further changes or additions are planned.

Publication: The statute defines "publication" as "the distribution of copies or phonorecords of a work to the public by sale or other transfer of ownership, or by rental, lease, or lending"; a work is also "published" if there has been an "offering to distribute copies or phonorecords to a group of persons for purposes of further distribution, public performance, or public display." Give the full date (month, day, year) when, and the country where, publication first occurred. If first publication took place simultaneously in the United States and other countries, it is sufficient to state "U.S.A."

4 SPACE 4: Claimant(s)

Name(s) and Address(es) of Copyright Claimant(s): Give the name(s) and address(es) of the copyright claimant(s) in this work even if the claimant is the same as the author. Copyright in a work belongs initially to the author of the work (including, in the case of a work made for hire, the employer or other person for whom the work was prepared). The copyright claimant is either the

---

one other than the author is identified as copyright claimant in the earlier registration, and the author is now seeking registration in his or her own name. If either of these two exceptions apply, check the appropriate box and give the earlier registration number and date. Otherwise, do not submit Form VA; instead, write the Copyright Office for information about supplementary registration or recordation of transfers of copyright ownership.

Changed Version: If the work has been changed, and you are now seeking registration to cover the additions or revisions, check the last box in space 5, give the earlier registration number and date, and complete both parts of space 6 in accordance with the instructions below.

Previous Registration Number and Date: If more than one previous registration has been made for the work, give the number and date of the latest registration.

6 SPACE 6: Derivative Work or Compilation

General Instructions: Complete space 6 if this work is a "changed version," "compilation," or "derivative work," and if it incorporates one or more earlier works that have already been published or registered for copyright, or that have fallen into the public domain. A "compilation" is defined as "a work formed by the collection and assembling of preexisting materials or of data that are selected, coordinated, or arranged in such a way that the resulting work as a whole constitutes an original work of authorship." A "derivative work" is "a work based on one or more preexisting works." Examples of derivative works include reproductions of works of art, sculptures based on drawings, lithographs based on paintings, maps based on previously published sources, or "any other form in which a work may be recast, transformed, or adapted." Derivative works also include works "consisting of editorial revisions, annotations, or other modifications" if these changes, as a whole, represent an original work of authorship.

Preexisting Material (space 6a): Complete this space and space 6b for derivative works. In this space identify the preexisting work that has been recast, transformed, or adapted. Examples of preexisting material might be "Grunewald Altarpiece"; or "19th century quilt design." Do not complete this space for compilations.

Material Added to This Work (space 6b): Give a brief, general statement of the additional new material covered by the copyright claim for which registration is sought. In the case of a derivative work, identify this new material.

author of the work or a person or organization to whom the copyright initially belonging to the author has been transferred.

Transfer: The statute provides that, if the copyright claimant is not the author, the application for registration must contain "a brief statement of how the claimant obtained ownership of the copyright." If any copyright claimant named in space 4 is not an author named in space 2, give a brief, general statement summarizing the means by which that claimant obtained ownership of the copyright. Examples: "By written contract"; "Transfer of all rights by author"; "Assignment"; "By will." Do not attach transfer documents or other attachments or riders.

5 SPACE 5: Previous Registration

General Instructions: The questions in space 5 are intended to find out whether an earlier registration has been made for this work and, if so, whether there is any basis for a new registration. As a rule, only one basic copyright registration can be made for the same version of a particular work.

Same Version: If this version is substantially the same as the work covered by a previous registration, a second registration is not generally possible unless: (1) the work has been registered in unpublished form and a second registration is now being sought to cover this first published edition; or (2) some-

Examples: "Adaptation of design and additional artistic work"; "Reproduction of painting by photolithography"; "Additional cartographic material"; "Compilation of photographs." If the work is a compilation, give a brief, general statement describing both the material that has been compiled and the compilation itself. Example: "Compilation of 19th Century Political Cartoons."

7,8,9 SPACE 7, 8, 9: Fee, Correspondence, Certification, Return Address

Deposit Account: If you maintain a Deposit Account in the Copyright Office, identify it in space 7. Otherwise leave the space blank and send the fee of $10 with your application and deposit.

Correspondence (space 7): This space should contain the name, address, area code, and telephone number of the person to be consulted if correspondence about this application becomes necessary.

Certification (space 8): The application cannot be accepted unless it bears the date and the **handwritten signature** of the author or other copyright claimant, or of the owner of exclusive right(s), or of the duly authorized agent of the author, claimant, or owner of exclusive right(s).

Address for Return of Certificate (space 9): The address box must be completed legibly since the certificate will be returned in a window envelope.

MORE INFORMATION

Form of Deposit for Works of the Visual Arts

Exceptions to General Deposit Requirements: As explained on the reverse side of this page, the statutory deposit requirements (generally one copy for unpublished works and two copies for published works) will vary for particular kinds of works of the visual arts. The copyright law authorizes the Register of Copyrights to issue regulations specifying "the administrative classes into which works are to be placed for purposes of deposit and registration, and the nature of the copies or phonorecords to be deposited in the various classes specified." For particular classes, the regulations may require or permit "the deposit of identifying material instead of copies of phonorecords," or "the deposit of only one copy or phonorecord where two would normally be required."

What Should You Deposit? The detailed requirements with respect to the kind of deposit to accompany an application on Form VA are contained in the Copyright Office Regulations. The following does not cover all of the deposit requirements, but is intended to give you some general guidance.

For an Unpublished Work, the material deposited should represent the entire copyrightable content of the work for which registration is being sought.

For a Published Work, the material deposited should generally consist of two complete copies of the best edition. Exceptions: (1) For certain types of works, one complete copy may be deposited instead of two. These include greeting cards, postcards, stationery, labels, advertisements, scientific drawings, and globes; (2) For most three-dimensional sculptural works, and for certain two-dimensional works, the Copyright Office Regulations require deposit of identifying material (photographs or drawings in a specified form) rather than copies; and (3) Under certain circumstances, for works published in five **copies or less or in limited, numbered editions, the deposit may consist of one copy or of identifying reproductions.**

FORM VA
UNITED STATES COPYRIGHT OFFICE

REGISTRATION NUMBER

VA   VAU

EFFECTIVE DATE OF REGISTRATION

Month   Day   Year

DO NOT WRITE ABOVE THIS LINE. IF YOU NEED MORE SPACE, USE A SEPARATE CONTINUATION SHEET.

1

TITLE OF THIS WORK ▼

NATURE OF THIS WORK ▼ See instructions

PREVIOUS OR ALTERNATIVE TITLES ▼

PUBLICATION AS A CONTRIBUTION If this work was published as a contribution to a periodical, serial, or collection, give information about the collective work in which the contribution appeared. **Title of Collective Work ▼**

If published in a periodical or serial give: **Volume ▼**   **Number ▼**   Issue Date ▼   On Pages ▼

2

NAME OF AUTHOR ▼

a

Was this contribution to the work a "work made for hire"?
☐ Yes
☐ No

AUTHOR'S NATIONALITY OR DOMICILE
Name of Country
OR { Citizen of ▶ _____
{ Domiciled in ▶ _____

DATES OF BIRTH AND DEATH
Year Born ▼   Year Died ▼

WAS THIS AUTHOR'S CONTRIBUTION TO THE WORK
Anonymous?   ☐ Yes ☐ No
Pseudonymous?   ☐ Yes ☐ No

If the answer to either of these questions is "Yes," see detailed instructions.

NOTE

Under the law, the "author" of a "work made for hire" is generally the employer, not the employee (see instructions). For any part of this work that was "made for hire" check "Yes" in the space provided, give the employer (or other person for whom the work was prepared) as "Author" of that part, and leave the space for dates of birth and death blank.

NATURE OF AUTHORSHIP Briefly describe nature of the material created by this author in which copyright is claimed. ▼

a

NAME OF AUTHOR ▼

DATES OF BIRTH AND DEATH
Year Born ▼   Year Died ▼

Was this contribution to the work a "work made for hire"?
☐ Yes
☐ No

AUTHOR'S NATIONALITY OR DOMICILE
Name of country
OR { Citizen of ▶ _____
     Domiciled in ▶ _____

WAS THIS AUTHOR'S CONTRIBUTION TO THE WORK
Anonymous?   ☐ Yes ☐ No
Pseudonymous?   ☐ Yes ☐ No

If the answer to either of these questions is "Yes," see detailed instructions.

NATURE OF AUTHORSHIP Briefly describe nature of the material created by this author in which copyright is claimed. ▼

b

NAME OF AUTHOR ▼

DATES OF BIRTH AND DEATH
Year Born ▼   Year Died ▼

Was this contribution to the work a "work made for hire"?
☐ Yes
☐ No

AUTHOR'S NATIONALITY OR DOMICILE
Name of Country
OR { Citizen of ▶ _____
     Domiciled in ▶ _____

WAS THIS AUTHOR'S CONTRIBUTION TO THE WORK
Anonymous?   ☐ Yes ☐ No
Pseudonymous?   ☐ Yes ☐ No

If the answer to either of these questions is "Yes," see detailed instructions.

NATURE OF AUTHORSHIP Briefly describe nature of the material created by this author in which copyright is claimed. ▼

3

YEAR IN WHICH CREATION OF THIS WORK WAS COMPLETED This information must be given in all cases.
◀ Year

DATE AND NATION OF FIRST PUBLICATION OF THIS PARTICULAR WORK
Complete this information Month ▶ _____ Day ▶ _____ Year ▶ _____
ONLY if this work has been published.   ◀ Nation

See instructions before completing this space.

4

COPYRIGHT CLAIMANT(S) Name and address must be given even if the claimant is the same as the author given in space 2. ▼

TRANSFER If the claimant(s) named here in space 4 are different from the author(s) named in space 2, give a brief statement of how the claimant(s) obtained ownership of the copyright. ▶

DO NOT WRITE HERE
OFFICE USE ONLY
DO NOT WRITE HERE

APPLICATION RECEIVED

ONE DEPOSIT RECEIVED

TWO DEPOSITS RECEIVED

REMITTANCE NUMBER AND DATE

MORE ON BACK ▶ • Complete all applicable spaces (numbers 5-9) on the reverse side of this page.   **DO NOT WRITE HERE**
                   • See detailed instructions.   • Sign the form at line 8.

499

EXAMINED BY

CHECKED BY

DO NOT WRITE ABOVE THIS LINE. IF YOU NEED MORE SPACE, USE A SEPARATE CONTINUATION SHEET.

5

PREVIOUS REGISTRATION Has registration for this work, or for an earlier version of this work, already been made in the Copyright Office?

☐ **Yes** ☐ **No** If your answer is "Yes," why is another registration being sought? (Check appropriate box) ▼

☐ This is the first published edition of a work previously registered in unpublished form.

☐ This is the first application submitted by this author as copyright claimant.

☐ This is a changed version of the work, as shown by space 6 on this application.

If your answer is "Yes," give: **Previous Registration Number** ▼   **Year of Registration** ▼

6

DERIVATIVE WORK OR COMPILATION Complete both space 6a & 6b for a derivative work; complete only 6b for a compilation.

a. Preexisting Material Identify any preexisting work or works that this work is based on or incorporates. ▼

See instructions
before completing
this space.

b. Material Added to This Work Give a brief, general statement of the material that has been added to this work and in which copyright is claimed. ▼

7

DEPOSIT ACCOUNT If the registration fee is to be charged to a Deposit Account established in the Copyright Office, give name and number of Account.

Name ▼   **Account Number** ▼

CORRESPONDENCE Give name and address to which correspondence about this application should be sent. Name/Address/Apt/City/State/Zip ▼

Be sure to
give your
daytime phone
▼ number.

8

_____

_____

Area Code & Telephone Number ▶

CERTIFICATION* I, the undersigned, hereby certify that I am the

Check only one ▼

☐ author

☐ other copyright claimant

☐ owner of exclusive right(s)

☐ authorized agent of _____
    Name of author or other copyright claimant, or owner of exclusive right(s) ▲

of the work identified in this application and that the statements made
by me in this application are correct to the best of my knowledge.

Typed or printed name and date ▼ If this is a published work, this date must be the same as or later than the date of publication given in space 3.

_____ **date** ▶ _____

👆 **Handwritten signature (X)** ▼

_____

9

**MAIL
CERTIFI-
CATE TO**

Name ▼

_____

Number/Street/Apartment Number ▼

_____

**Certificate
will be
mailed in
window
envelope**

City/State/ZIP ▼

_____

☆ U.S. GOVERNMENT PRINTING OFFICE: 1982-361-278/66

Sept. 1982—120,000

FORM RE

UNITED STATES COPYRIGHT OFFICE
LIBRARY OF CONGRESS
WASHINGTON, D.C. 20559

APPLICATION FOR
Renewal Registration

HOW TO REGISTER A RENEWAL CLAIM:

- **First:** Study the information on this page and make sure you know the answers to two questions:

  (1) What are the renewal time limits in your case?
  (2) Who can claim the renewal?

- **Second:** Turn this page over and read through the specific instructions for filling out Form RE. Make sure, before starting to complete the form, that the copyright is now eligible for renewal, that you are authorized to file a renewal claim, and that you have all of the information about the copyright you will need.

- **Third:** Complete all applicable spaces on Form RE, following the line-by-line instructions on the back of this page. Use typewriter, or print the information in dark ink.

- **Fourth:** Detach this sheet and send your completed Form RE to: Register of Copyrights, Library of Congress, Washington, D.C. 20559. Unless you have a Deposit Account in the Copyright Office, your application must be accompanied by a check or money order for $6, payable to: *Register of Copyrights*. Do not send copies, phonorecords, or supporting documents with your renewal application.

WHAT IS RENEWAL OF COPYRIGHT? For works originally copyrighted between January 1, 1950 and December 31, 1977, the statute now in effect provides for a first term of copyright protection lasting for 28 years, with the possibility of renewal for a second term of 47 years. If a valid renewal registration is made for a work, its total copyright term is 75 years (a first term of 28 years, plus a renewal term of 47 years). Example: For a work copyrighted in 1960, the first term will expire in 1988, but if renewed at the proper time the copyright will last through the end of 2035.

SOME BASIC POINTS ABOUT RENEWAL:

(1) There are strict time limits and deadlines for renewing a copyright.

(2) Only certain persons who fall into specific categories named in the law can claim renewal.

(3) The new copyright law does away with renewal requirements for works first copyrighted after 1977. However, copyrights that were already in their first copyright term on January 1, 1978 (that is, works originally copyrighted between January 1, 1950 and December 31, 1977) **still have to be renewed** in order to be protected for a second term.

TIME LIMITS FOR RENEWAL REGISTRATION: The new copyright statute provides that, in order to renew a copyright, the renewal application and fee must be received in the Copyright Office "within one year prior to the expiration of the copyright." It also provides that all terms of copyright will run through the end of the year in which they would otherwise expire. Since all copyright terms will expire on December 31st of their last year, all periods for renewal registration will run from December 31st of the 27th year of the copyright, and will end on December 31st of the following year.

To determine the time limits for renewal in your case:

(1) First, find out the date of original copyright for the work. (In the case of works originally registered in unpublished form, the date of copyright is the date of registration; for published works, copyright begins on the date of first publication.)

(2) Then add 28 years to the year the work was originally copyrighted.

Your answer will be the calendar year during which the copyright will be eligible for renewal, and December 31st of that year will be the renewal deadline. Example: a work originally copyrighted on April 19, 1957, will be eligible for renewal between December 31, 1984, and December 31, 1985.

WHO MAY CLAIM RENEWAL: Renewal copyright may be claimed only by those persons specified in the law. Except in the case of four specific types of works, the law gives the right to claim renewal to the individual author of the work, regardless of who owned the copyright during the original term. If the author is dead, the statute gives the right to claim renewal to certain of the author's beneficiaries (widow and children, executors, or next of kin, depending on the circumstances). The present owner (proprietor) of the copyright is entitled to claim renewal only in four specified cases, as explained in more detail on the reverse of this page.

CAUTION: Renewal registration is possible only if an acceptable application and fee are **received** in the Copyright Office during the renewal period and before the renewal deadline. If an acceptable application and fee are not received before the renewal deadline, the work falls into the public domain and the copyright cannot be renewed. The Copyright Office has no discretion to extend the renewal time limits.

INSTRUCTIONS FOR COMPLETING FORM RE

SPACE 1: RENEWAL CLAIM(S)

• **General Instructions:** In order for this application to result in a valid renewal, space 1 must identify one or more of the persons who are entitled to renew the copyright under the statute. Give the full name and address of each claimant, with a statement of the basis of each claim, using the wording given in these instructions.

• **Persons Entitled to Renew:**

A. The following persons may claim renewal in all types of works except those enumerated in Paragraph B, below:

1. The author, if living. State the claim as: *the author.*

2. The widow, widower, and/or children of the author, if the author is not living. State the claim as: *the widow (widower) of the author* . . . . *(Name of author)* . . . and/or the child (children) of the deceased author . . . . *(Name of author)*

3. The author's executor(s), if the author left a will and if there is no surviving widow, widower, or child. State the claim as: *the executor(s) of the author* . . . . *(Name of author)*

4. The next of kin of the author, if the author left no will and if there is no surviving widow, widower, or child. State the claim as: *the next of kin of the deceased author* . . . . *(Name of author)* . . . *there being no will.*

B. In the case of the following four types of works, the proprietor (owner of the copyright at the time of renewal registration) may claim renewal:

1. Posthumous work (a work as to which no copyright assignment or other contract for exploitation has occurred during the author's lifetime). State the claim as: *proprietor of copyright in a posthumous work.*

2. Periodic, cyclopedic, or other composite work. State the claim as: *proprietor of copyright in a composite work.*

3. "Work copyrighted by a corporate body otherwise than as assignee or licensee of the individual author." State the claim as: *proprietor of copyright in a work copyrighted by a corporate body otherwise than as assignee or licensee of the individual author.* (This type of claim is considered appropriate in relatively few cases.)

4. Work copyrighted by an employer for whom such work was made for hire. State the claim as: *proprietor of copyright in a work made for hire.*

SPACE 2: WORK RENEWED

• **General Instructions:** This space is to identify the particular work being renewed. The information given here should agree with that appearing in the certificate of original registration.

• **Title:** Give the full title of the work, together with any subtitles or descriptive wording included with the title in the original registration. In the case of a musical composition, give the specific instrumentation of the work.

• **Renewable Matter:** Copyright in a new version of a previous work (such as an arrangement, translation, dramatization, compilation, or work republished with new matter) covers only the additions, changes, or other new material appearing for the first time in that version. If this work was a new version, state in general the new matter upon which copyright was claimed.

• **Contribution to Periodical, Serial, or other Composite Work:** Separate renewal registration is possible for a work published as a contribution to a periodical, serial, or other composite work, whether the contribution was copyrighted independently or as part of the larger work in which it appeared. Each contribution published in a separate issue ordinarily requires a separate renewal registration. However, the new law provides an alternative, permitting groups of periodical contributions by the same individual author to be combined under a single renewal application and fee in certain cases.

If this renewal application covers a single contribution, give all of the requested information in space 2. If you are seeking to renew a group of contributions, include a reference such as "See space 5" in space 2 and give the requested information about all of the contributions in space 5.

504

SPACE 3: AUTHOR(S)

• **General Instructions:** The copyright secured in a new version of a work is independent of any copyright protection in material published earlier. The only "authors" of a new version are those who contributed copyrightable matter to it. Thus, for renewal purposes, the person who wrote the original version on which the new work is based cannot be regarded as an "author" of the new version, unless that person also contributed to the new matter.

• **Authors of Renewable Matter:** Give the full names of all authors who contributed copyrightable matter to this particular version of the work.

SPACE 4: FACTS OF ORIGINAL REGISTRATION

• **General Instructions:** Each item in space 4 should agree with the information appearing in the original registration for the work. If the work being renewed is a single contribution to a periodical or composite work that was not separately registered, give information about the particular issue in which the contribution appeared. You may leave this space blank if you are completing space 5.

• **Original Registration Number:** Give the full registration number, which is a series of numerical digits, preceded by one or more letters. The registration number appears in the upper right hand corner of the certificate of registration.

• **Original Copyright Claimant:** Give the name in which ownership of the copyright was claimed in the original registration.

• **Date of Publication or Registration:** Give only one date. If the original registration gave a publication date, it should be transcribed here; otherwise the registration was for an unpublished work, and the date of registration should be given.

SPACE 5: GROUP RENEWALS

• **General Instructions:** A single renewal registration can be made for a group of works if **all** of the following statutory conditions are met: (1) all of the works were written by the same author, who is named in space 3 and who is or was an individual (not an employer for hire); (2) all of the works were first published as contributions to periodicals (including newspapers) and were copyrighted on their first publication; (3) the renewal claimant or claimants, and the basis of claim or claims, as stated in space 1, is the same for all of the works; (4) the renewal application and fee are "received not more than 28 or less than 27 years after the 31st day of December of the calendar year in which all of the works were first published"; and (5) the renewal application identifies each work separately, including the periodical containing it and the date of first publication.

Time Limits for Group Renewals: To be renewed as a group, all of the contributions must have been first published during the same calendar year. For example, suppose six contributions by the same author were published on April 1, 1960, July 1, 1960, November 1, 1960, February 1, 1961, July 1, 1961, and March 1, 1962. The three 1960 copyrights can be combined and renewed at any time during 1988, and the two 1961 copyrights can be renewed as a group during 1989, but the 1962 copyright must be renewed by itself, in 1990.

Identification of Each Work: Give all of the requested information for each contribution. The registration number should be that for the contribution itself if it was separately registered, and the registration number for the periodical issue if it was not.

SPACES 6, 7 AND 8: FEE, MAILING INSTRUCTIONS, AND CERTIFICATION

• **Deposit Account and Mailing Instructions (Space 6):** If you maintain a Deposit Account in the Copyright Office, identify it in space 6. Otherwise, you will need to send the renewal registration fee of $6 with your form. The space headed "Correspondence" should contain the name and address of the person to be consulted if correspondence about the form becomes necessary.

• **Certification (Space 7):** The renewal application is not acceptable unless it bears the handwritten signature of the renewal claimant or the duly authorized agent of the renewal claimant.

• **Address for Return of Certificate (Space 8):** The address box must be completed legibly, since the certificate will be returned in a window envelope.

505

FORM RE

UNITED STATES COPYRIGHT OFFICE

REGISTRATION NUMBER

EFFECTIVE DATE OF RENEWAL REGISTRATION

....
(Month)   (Day)   (Year)

DO NOT WRITE ABOVE THIS LINE. **FOR COPYRIGHT OFFICE USE ONLY**

RENEWAL CLAIMANT(S), ADDRESS(ES), AND STATEMENT OF CLAIM: (See Instructions)

1

Renewal Claimant(s)

1

Name . . . .

Address . . . .

Claiming as . . . .

(Use appropriate statement from instructions)

2

Name . . . .

Address . . . .

Claiming as . . . .

(Use appropriate statement from instructions)

3

Name . . . .

Address . . . .

Claiming as . . . .

(Use appropriate statement from instructions)

②

Work Renewed

TITLE OF WORK IN WHICH RENEWAL IS CLAIMED:

RENEWABLE MATTER:

CONTRIBUTION TO PERIODICAL OR COMPOSITE WORK:

Title of periodical or composite work: . . . .

If a periodical or other serial, give: Vol. . . . . No. . . . . Issue Date . . . .

③

Author(s)

AUTHOR(S) OF RENEWABLE MATTER:

④

Facts of Original Registration

ORIGINAL REGISTRATION NUMBER:

. . . .

ORIGINAL COPYRIGHT CLAIMANT:

ORIGINAL DATE OF COPYRIGHT:

• If the original registration for this work was made in published form,

DATE OF PUBLICATION: . . . .
(Month)　　　　　(Day)　　　　　(Year)

OR

• If the original registration for this work was made in unpublished form, give:

DATE OF REGISTRATION: . . . .
(Month)　　　　　(Day)　　　　　(Year)

507

EXAMINED BY:	RENEWAL APPLICATION RECEIVED:
CHECKED BY:	
DEPOSIT ACCOUNT FUNDS USED: ☐	REMITTANCE NUMBER AND DATE:

FOR COPYRIGHT OFFICE USE ONLY

DO NOT WRITE ABOVE THIS LINE. FOR COPYRIGHT OFFICE USE ONLY

RENEWAL FOR GROUP OF WORKS BY SAME AUTHOR: To make a single registration for a group of works by the same individual author published as contributions to periodicals (see instructions), give full information about each contribution. If more space is needed, request continuation sheet (Form RE/CON).

5 Renewal for Group of Works

1	Title of Contribution: ....
	Title of Periodical: .... Vol. .... No. .... Issue Date ....
	Date of Publication: .... Registration Number: ....
	(Month) (Day) (Year)

2	Title of Contribution: ....
	Title of Periodical: .... Vol. .... No. .... Issue Date ....
	Date of Publication: .... Registration Number: ....
	(Month) (Day) (Year)

3	Title of Contribution: ....
	Title of Periodical: .... Vol. .... No. .... Issue Date ....
	Date of Publication: .... Registration Number: ....
	(Month) (Day) (Year)

4	Title of Contribution: ....
	Title of Periodical: .... Vol. .... No. .... Issue Date ....
	Date of Publication: .... Registration Number: ....
	(Month) (Day) (Year)

5	Title of Contribution: ....
	Title of Periodical: .... Vol. .... No. .... Issue Date ....
	Date of Publication: .... Registration Number: ....
	(Month) (Day) (Year)

6	Title of Contribution: .... Title of Periodical: .... Vol. ...... No. ...... Issue Date ...... Date of Publication: .... (Month) ...... (Day) ...... (Year) ...... Registration Number: ......
7	Title of Contribution: .... Title of Periodical: .... Vol. ...... No. ...... Issue Date ...... Date of Publication: .... (Month) ...... (Day) ...... (Year) ...... Registration Number: ......

⑥ Fee and Correspondence

DEPOSIT ACCOUNT: (If the registration fee is to be charged to a Deposit Account established in the Copyright Office, give name and number of Account.)

Name: ....

Account Number: ....

CORRESPONDENCE: (Give name and address to which correspondence about this application should be sent.)

Name: ....

Address: .... (Apt.)

.... (City) .... (State) .... (ZIP)

⑦ Certification (Application must be signed)

CERTIFICATION: I, the undersigned, hereby certify that I am the: (Check one)

□ renewal claimant   □ duly authorized agent of: .... (Name of renewal claimant)

of the work identified in this application, and that the statements made by me in this application are correct to the best of my knowledge.

Handwritten signature: (X) ....

Typed or printed name: .... Date: ....

⑧ Address for Return of Certificate

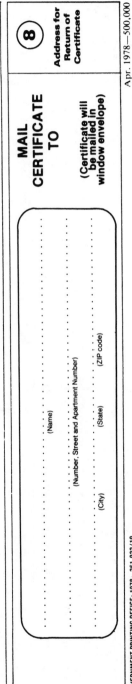

MAIL CERTIFICATE TO

(Certificate will be mailed in window envelope)

.... (Name)

.... (Number, Street and Apartment Number)

.... (City) .... (State) .... (ZIP code)

Apr. 1978—500,000

☆ U.S. GOVERNMENT PRINTING OFFICE: 1978—261-022/10

FORM CA

UNITED STATES COPYRIGHT OFFICE
LIBRARY OF CONGRESS
WASHINGTON, D.C. 20559

Application for Supplementary Copyright Registration

To Correct or Amplify Information Given in the
Copyright Office Record of an Earlier Registration

USE THIS FORM WHEN:

- An earlier registration has been made in the Copyright Office; and

- Some of the facts given in that registration are incorrect or incomplete; and

- You want to place the correct or complete facts on record.

How to Apply for Supplementary Registration:

First: Study the information on this page to make sure that filing an application on Form CA is the best procedure to follow in your case.

Second: Turn this page over and read through the specific instructions for filling out Form CA. Make sure, before starting to complete the form, that you have all of the detailed information about the basic registration you will need.

What is "Supplementary Copyright Registration"? Supplementary registration is a special type of copyright registration provided for in section 408(d) of the copyright law.

Purpose of Supplementary Registration. As a rule, only one basic copyright registration can be made for the same work. To take care of cases where information in the basic registration turns out to be incorrect or incomplete, the law provides for "the filing of an application for supplementary registration, to correct an error in a copyright registration or to amplify the information given in a registration."

Earlier Registration Necessary. Supplementary registration can be made only if a basic copyright registration for the same work has already been completed.

Who May File. Once basic registration has been made for a work, any author or other copyright claimant, or owner of any exclusive right in the work, who wishes to correct or amplify the information given in the basic registration, may submit Form CA.

Please Note:

• Do not use Form CA to correct errors in statements on the copies or phonorecords of the work in question, or to reflect changes in the content of the work. If the work has been changed substantially, you should consider making an entirely new registration for the revised version to cover the additions or revisions.

• Do not use Form CA as a substitute for renewal registration. For works originally copyrighted between January 1, 1950 and December 31, 1977, registration of a renewal claim within strict time limits is necessary to extend the first 28-year copyright term to the full term of 75 years. This cannot be done by filing Form CA.

• Do not use Form CA as a substitute for recording a transfer of copyright or other document pertaining to rights under a copyright. Recording a document under section 205 of the statute gives all persons constructive notice of the facts stated in the document and may have other important consequences in cases of infringement or conflicting transfers. Supplementary registration does not have that legal effect.

Third: Complete all applicable spaces on this form, following the line-by-line instructions on the back of this page. Use typewriter, or print the information in dark ink.

Fourth: Detach this sheet and send your completed Form CA to: Register of Copyrights, Library of Congress, Washington, D.C. 20559. Unless you have a Deposit Account in the Copyright Office, your application must be accompanied by a non-refundable filing fee in the form of a check or money order for $10 payable to: *Register of Copyrights*. Do not send copies, phonorecords, or supporting documents with your application, since they cannot be made part of the record of a supplementary registration.

What Happens When a Supplementary Registration is Made? When a supplementary registration is completed, the Copyright Office will assign it a new registration number in the appropriate registration category, and issue a certificate of supplementary registration under that number. The basic registration will not be expunged or cancelled, and the two registrations will both stand in the Copyright Office records. The supplementary registration will have the effect of calling the public's attention to a possible error or omission in the basic registration, and of placing the correct facts or the additional information on official record. Moreover, if the person on whose behalf Form CA is submitted is the same as the person identified as copyright claimant in the basic registration, the Copyright Office will place a note referring to the supplementary registration in its records of the basic registration.

PLEASE READ DETAILED INSTRUCTIONS ON REVERSE

Please read the following line-by-line instructions carefully and refer to them while completing Form CA.

INSTRUCTIONS

For Completing FORM CA (Supplementary Registration)

PART A: BASIC INSTRUCTIONS

• *General Instructions:* The information in this part identifies the basic registration to be corrected or amplified. Each item must agree exactly with the information as it already appears in the basic registration (even if the purpose of filing Form CA is to change one of these items).

• *Title of Work:* Give the title as it appears in the basic registration, including previous or alternative titles if they appear.

• *Registration Number:* This is a series of numerical digits, pre-ceded by one or more letters. The registration number appears in the upper right hand corner of the certificate of registration.

• *Registration Date:* Give the year when the basic registration was completed.

• *Name(s) of Author(s) and Name(s) of Copyright Claimant(s):* Give all of the names as they appear in the basic registration.

PART B: CORRECTION

• *General Instructions:* Complete this part **only** if information in the basic registration was incorrect at the time that basic registration was made. Leave this part blank and complete Part C, instead, if your purpose is to add, update, or clarify information rather than to rectify an actual error.

• *Location and Nature of Incorrect Information:* Give the line number and the heading or description of the the space in the basic registration where the error occurs (for example: "Line number 3 . . . Citizenship of author").

• *Incorrect Information as it Appears in Basic Registration:* Transcribe the erroneous statement exactly as it appears in the basic registration.

• *Corrected Information:* Give the statement as it should have appeared.

• *Explanation of Correction (Optional):* If you wish, you may add an explanation of the error or its correction.

PART C: AMPLIFICATION

• **General Instructions:** Complete this part if you want to provide any of the following: (1) additional information that could have been given but was omitted at the time of basic registration; (2) changes in facts, such as changes of title or address of claimant, that have occurred since the basic registration; or (3) explanations clarifying information in the basic registration.

• **Location and Nature of Information to be Amplified:** Give the line number and the heading or description of the space in the basic registration where the information to be amplified appears.

• **Amplified Information:** Give a statement of the added, updated, or explanatory information as clearly and succinctly as possible.

• **Explanation of Amplification (Optional):** If you wish, you may add an explanation of the amplification.

PARTS D, E, F, G: CONTINUATION, FEE, MAILING INSTRUCTIONS AND CERTIFICATION

• **Continuation (Part D):** Use this space if you do not have enough room in Parts B or C.

• **Deposit Account and Mailing Instructions (Part E):** If you maintain a Deposit Account in the Copyright Office, identify it in Part E. Otherwise, you will need to send the non-refundable filing fee of $10 with your form. The space headed "Correspondence" should contain the name and address of the person to be consulted if correspondence about the form becomes necessary.

• **Certification (Part F):** The application is not acceptable unless it bears the handwritten signature of the author, or other copyright claimant, or of the owner of exclusive right(s), or of the duly authorized agent of such author, claimant, or owner.

• **Address for Return of Certificate (Part G):** The address box must be completed legibly, since the certificate will be returned in a window envelope.

FORM CA

UNITED STATES COPYRIGHT OFFICE

REGISTRATION NUMBER

TX	TXU	PA	PAU	VA	VAU	SR	SRU	RE

Effective Date of Supplementary Registration

....
MONTH   DAY   YEAR

DO NOT WRITE ABOVE THIS LINE. FOR COPYRIGHT OFFICE USE ONLY

(A) Basic Instructions

TITLE OF WORK:

REGISTRATION NUMBER OF BASIC REGISTRATION:

YEAR OF BASIC REGISTRATION:

NAME(S) OF AUTHOR(S):

NAME(S) OF COPYRIGHT CLAIMANT(S):

(B) Correction

LOCATION AND NATURE OF INCORRECT INFORMATION IN BASIC REGISTRATION:

Line Number . . . . Line Heading or Description . . . .

INCORRECT INFORMATION AS IT APPEARS IN BASIC REGISTRATION:

CORRECTED INFORMATION:

EXPLANATION OF CORRECTION: (Optional)

LOCATION AND NATURE OF INFORMATION IN BASIC REGISTRATION TO BE AMPLIFIED:

Line Number . . . . Line Heading or Description . . . .

AMPLIFIED INFORMATION:

(C)

Amplification

EXPLANATION OF AMPLIFIED INFORMATION: (Optional)

FORM CA RECEIVED:

FOR
COPYRIGHT
OFFICE
USE
ONLY

EXAMINED BY: ....

CHECKED BY: ....

REMITTANCE NUMBER AND DATE:

CORRESPONDENCE:
☐ YES

REFERENCE TO THIS REGISTRATION
ADDED TO BASIC REGISTRATION:
☐ YES ☐ NO

DEPOSIT ACCOUNT FUNDS USED: ☐

DO NOT WRITE ABOVE THIS LINE. FOR COPYRIGHT OFFICE USE ONLY

CONTINUATION OF: (Check which) ☐ PART B OR ☐ PART C

(D) Continuation

DEPOSIT ACCOUNT: If the registration fee is to be charged to a Deposit Account established in the Copyright Office, give name and number of Account:

Name . . . . Account Number . . . .

(E) Deposit
Account and
Mailing
Instructions

CORRESPONDENCE: Give name and address to which correspondence should be sent:

Name . . . . Apt. No. . . . .

Address . . . .
. . . .
(Number and Street)   (City)   (State)   (ZIP Code)

(F)   **Certification (Application must be signed)**

CERTIFICATION ✱   I, the undersigned, hereby certify that I am the: (Check one)

☐ author   ☐ other copyright claimant   ☐ owner of exclusive right(s)   ☐ authorized agent of: . . . .
                                            (Name of author or other copyright claimant, or owner of exclusive right(s))
of the work identified in this application and that the statements made by me in this application are correct to the best of my knowledge.

Handwritten signature: (X) . . . .

Typed or printed name. . . . .

Date: . . . .

✱ 17 USC §506(e): FALSE REPRESENTATION—Any person who knowingly makes a false representation of a material fact in the application for copyright registration provided for by section 409, or in any written statement filed in connection with the application, shall be fined not more than $2,500.

(G)   **Address for Return of Certificate**

MAIL CERTIFICATE TO

(Certificate will be mailed in window envelope)

. . . .
. . . .
(Name)
. . . .
(Number, Street and Apartment Number)
. . . .
(City)   (State)   (ZIP code)

July 1983—30,000

U.S. GOVERNMENT PRINTING OFFICE 1983—381-278/502

517

Appendix G

ASCAP Writer Application

APPLICATION FOR WRITER-MEMBERSHIP
IN THE

AMERICAN SOCIETY of COMPOSERS, AUTHORS and PUBLISHERS
One Lincoln Plaza, New York, N.Y. 10023

W

I hereby apply for membership as a   FULL ☐   STANDARD ☐   AUTHOR ☐
ASSOCIATE ☐   POPULAR PRODUCTION ☐   COMPOSER ☐
in the American Society of Composers, Authors and Publishers. If elected, I agree to be bound by the Society's Articles of Association, as now in effect and as they may be amended, and I agree to execute agreements in such form and for such periods as the Board of Directors shall have approved or shall hereafter approve for all members.

The following information is submitted in support of this application:

1. Full Name: Mr.   Miss
   Mrs.   Ms. _____
   (First Name)   (Middle Name or Initial)   (Last Name)

2. Pseudonyms, if any (no more than four)

_____

_____

3. **Home Address:**

☐ _____
   (Street)   (City)   (State)   (Zip Code)   (Area Code & Tel #)
   Business Address (if same as above, write "same"):

☐ _____
   (Street)   (City)   (State)   (Zip Code)   (Area Code & Tel #)

Please check to which address your mail is to be sent.

4. **Date of Birth:** _____
   (month)   (day)   (year)

   Place of Birth: _____

5. **Citizen of:** _____

6. **Social Security #:** _____

7. I am ☐, or have been ☐, a member or affiliate of ASCAP, BMI or SESAC, or of a foreign performing rights licensing organization. (Check one if applicable)

   If you have checked one of the boxes above, please state the name of the organization with which you were affiliated and the period of your

   affiliation, and attach a copy of your release: _____

8. I have ☐, do not have ☐, a relative (including brother, sister, husband, wife, child or any other relation) who is affiliated with an organization referred to in item 7.   (Check the applicable box)

   If you answered affirmatively, please give the name of any such person, relationship to you and organization with which affiliated: _____

_____

9. I have ☐, have not ☐, paid to have the works submitted by me on behalf of this application published or recorded. (Check the applicable box)

   If you have answered affirmatively, please indicate which works submitted by you were the subject of such payment and to whom payment

   was made: _____

_____

518

10. **The musical works of which I am composer or author are listed on the opposite page. I represent that there are no existing assignments or licenses, direct or indirect, of non-dramatic performing rights in or to any of the works so listed, except with publishers of such works. If there are assignments or licenses other than with publishers, I have attached true copies. I have read the Society's Articles of Association and make this application with full knowledge of their contents.**

I warrant and represent that all of the information furnished in this application is true. I acknowledge that any contract between ASCAP and me will be entered into in reliance upon the representations contained in this application, and that the contract will be subject to cancellation if the information contained in this application is not complete and accurate.

Signature _____ Date _____

WRITER'S LIST OF WORKS

List of Domestic Copyrighted Musical Compositions Owned by the Applicant

TITLE	YEAR OF COPYRIGHT	COMPOSER	AUTHOR	PUBLISHER

Note:— For works based on compositions in the public domain, the title, author and composer of the public domain source must be indicated.

W

Appendix H

ASCAP Publisher Application

APPLICATION FOR PUBLISHER-MEMBERSHIP
IN THE
AMERICAN SOCIETY of COMPOSERS, AUTHORS and PUBLISHERS
One Lincoln Plaza, New York, N.Y. 10023

I(we) hereby apply for membership, as a ☐Standard/ ☐ Popular Production Music Publisher, in the American Society of Composers, Authors and Publishers. If elected I(we) agree to be bound by the Society's Articles of Association as now in effect, and as they may be amended, and I (we) agree to execute agreements in such form and for such periods as the Board of Directors shall have approved or shall hereafter approve for all members.

The following information is submitted in support of this application:

1. Firm Name _____

2. Business Address _____

_____

| City | State | Zip Code |

(_____)

3. Check and complete one of the following to indicate organization of company:

A. CORPORATION ☐   Corporate I.D. No._____

State of Incorporation _____Date of Charter _____

Name	Stockholders (list all stockholders)	Soc. Sec. No.	Home Address & Zip Code	Percentage of Ownership

Name	Officers (list all officers)	Soc. Sec. No.	Home Address & Zip Code	Office Held

B. PARTNERSHIP ☐ (list all partners)   Year Business Established _____

Name		Soc. Sec. No.	Home Address & Zip Code	Percentage of Ownership

C. INDIVIDUAL OWNERSHIP ☐ Year Business Established _____

Name_____ Soc. Sec. No. |___|___|___:___|___|___|___|___|

Home Address _____

| | Street Address | City | State | Zip Code |

Telephone Number:(_____)

4. Cities in Which Branch Offices Are Maintained

_____

_____

| City | State | Street Address | Area Code & Telephone # |

5. If any owner, stockholder, officer, or employee with any executive responsibilities, has been or is now connected with any publishing company, songwriter's agency, recording company, performance rights licensing organization (as an employee), or any other organization engaged in the solicitation, publication or exploitation of music, please fill in the information requested below:

Name of Individual	Telephone	Name of Company	If Publishing Company Indicate Performance Rights Affiliation	Position Held	Years of Association

6. If you have made, or intend to make, any charge to an author (lyricist), or composer in connection with the examination, publication, recording or exploitation of any composition published or to be published by you, please state the nature of the charge and the service to be performed.

7. I (we) have read ASCAP's Articles of Association and make this application with full knowledge of their contents. I (we) understand that any agreement entered into between ASCAP and me (us) will be in reliance upon the information contained in this application and attached schedules. I (we) understand that the agreement will be subject to cancellation if any information contained in this application is not fully and correctly provided or if the true name of each owner, stockholder, and officer is not provided as requested.

Firm Name

By

Date _____
 month   day   year

Title

DO NOT FILL IN BELOW

Received:	Presented:	Recommended by Membership Committee
		For _____ Date _____

10M-8/83

ASCAP Agreement with Writer or Publisher

AGREEMENT made between the Undersigned (for brevity called "*Owner*") and the American Society of Composers, Authors and Publishers (for brevity called "*Society*"), in consideration of the premises and of the mutual covenants hereinafter contained, as follows:

1. The *Owner* grants to the *Society* for the term hereof, the right to license non-dramatic public performances (as hereinafter defined), of each musical work:

Of which the *Owner* is a copyright proprietor; or

Which the *Owner,* alone, or jointly, or in collaboration with others, wrote, composed, published, acquired or owned; or

In which the *Owner* now has any right, title, interest or control whatsoever, in whole or in part; or

Which hereafter, during the term hereof, may be written, composed, acquired, owned, published or copyrighted by the *Owner,* alone, jointly or in collaboration with others; or

In which the *Owner* may hereafter, during the term hereof, have any right, title, interest or control, whatsoever, in whole or in part.

The right to license the public performance of every such musical work shall be deemed granted to the *Society* by this instrument for the term hereof, immediately upon the work being written, composed, acquired, owned, published or copyrighted.

The rights hereby granted shall include:

(a) All the rights and remedies for enforcing the copyright or copyrights of such musical works, whether such copyrights are in the name of the *Owner* and/or others, as well as the right to sue under such copyrights in the name of the *Society* and/or in the name of the *Owner* and/or others, to the end that the *Society* may effectively protect and be assured of all the rights hereby granted.

(b) The non-exclusive right of public performance of the separate numbers, songs, fragments or arrangements, melodies or selections forming part or parts of musical plays and dramatico-musical compositions, the *Owner* reserving and excepting from this grant the right of performance of musical plays and dramatico-musical compositions in their entirety, or any part of such plays or dramatico-musical compositions on the legitimate stage.

(c) The non-exclusive right of public performance by means of radio broadcasting, telephony, "wired wireless," all forms of synchronism with motion pictures, and/or any method of transmitting sound other than television broadcasting.

(d) The non-exclusive right of public performance by television broadcasting; provided, however, that:

(i) This grant does not extend to or include the right to license the public performance by television broadcasting or otherwise of any rendition or performance of (a) any opera, operetta, musical comedy, play or like production, as such, in whole or in part, or (b) any composition from any opera, operetta, musical comedy, play or like production (whether or not such opera, operetta, musical comedy, play or like production was presented on the stage or in motion picture form) in a manner which recreates the performance of such composition with substantially such distinctive scenery or costume as was used in the presentation of such opera, operetta, musical comedy, play or like production (whether or not such opera, operetta, musical comedy, play or like production was presented on the stage or in motion picture form): provided, however, that the rights hereby granted shall be deemed to include a grant of the right to license non-dramatic performances of compositions by television broadcasting of a motion picture containing such composition if the rights in such motion picture other than those granted hereby have been obtained from the parties in interest.

(ii) Nothing herein contained shall be deemed to grant the right to license the public performance by television broadcasting of dramatic performances. Any performance of a separate musical composition which is not a dramatic performance, as defined herein, shall be deemed to be a non-dramatic performance. For the purposes of this agreement, a dramatic performance shall mean a performance of a musical composition on a television program in which there is a definite plot depicted by action and where the performance of the musical composition is woven into and carries forward the plot and its accompanying action. The use of dialogue to establish a mere program format or the use of any non-dramatic device merely to introduce a performance of a composition shall not be deemed to make such performance dramatic.

(iii) The definition of the terms "dramatic" and "non-dramatic" performances contained herein are purely for the purposes of this agreement and for the term thereof and shall not be binding upon or prejudicial to any position taken by either of us subsequent to the term hereof or for any purpose other than this agreement.

(e) The *Owner* may at any time and from time to time, in good faith, restrict the radio or television broadcasting of compositions from musical comedies, operas, operettas and motion pictures, or any other composition being excessively broadcast, only for the purpose of preventing harmful effect upon such musical comedies, operas, operettas, motion pictures or compositions, in respect of other interests under the copyrights thereof; provided, however, that the right to grant limited licenses will be given, upon application, as to restricted compositions, if and when the *Owner* is unable to show reasonable hazards to his or its major interests likely to result from such radio or television broadcasting; and provided further that such right to restrict any such composition shall not be exercised for the purpose of permitting the fixing or regulating of fees for the recording or transcribing of such composition, and provided further that in no case shall any charges, "free plugs", or other consideration be required in respect of any permission granted to perform a restricted composition; and provided further that in no event shall any composition, after the initial radio or television broadcast thereof, be restricted for the purpose of confining further radio or television broadcasts thereof, to a particular artist, station, network or program. The *Owner* may also at any time and from time to time, in good faith, restrict the radio or television broadcasting of any composition, as to which any suit has been brought or threatened on a claim that such composition infringes a composition not contained in the repertory of *Society* or on a claim by a non-member of *Society* that *Society* does not have the right to license the public performance of such composition by radio or television broadcasting.

2. The term of this agreement shall be for a period commencing on the date hereof and expiring on the 31st day of December, 1985.

3. The *Society* agrees, during the term hereof, in good faith to use its best endeavors to promote and carry out the objects for which it was organized, and to hold and apply all royalties, profits, benefits and advantages arising from the exploitation of the rights assigned to it by its several members, including the *Owner*, to the uses and purposes as provided in its Articles of Association (which are hereby incorporated by reference), as now in force or as hereafter amended.

4. The *Owner* hereby irrevocably, during the term hereof, authorizes, empowers and vests in the *Society* the right to enforce and protect such rights of public performance under any and all copyrights, whether standing in the name of the *Owner* and/or others, in any and all works copyrighted by the *Owner*, and/or by others; to prevent the infringement thereof, to litigate, collect and receipt for damages arising from infringement, and in its sole judgment to join the *Owner* and/or others in whose names the copyright may stand, as parties plaintiff or defendants in suits or proceedings; to bring suit in the name of the *Owner* and/or in the name of the *Society*, or others in whose name the copyright may stand, or otherwise, and to release, compromise, or refer to arbitration any actions, in the same manner and to the same extent and to all intents and purposes as the *Owner* might or could do, had this instrument not been made.

5. The *Owner* hereby makes, constitutes and appoints the *Society*, or its successor, the *Owner's* true and lawful attorney, irrevocably during the term hereof, and in the name of the *Society* or its successor, or in the name of the *Owner*, or otherwise, to do all acts, take all proceedings, execute, acknowledge and deliver any and all instruments, papers, documents, process and pleadings that may be necessary, proper or expedient to restrain infringements and recover damages

in respect to or for the infringement or other violation of the rights of public performance in such works, and to discontinue, compromise or refer to arbitration any such proceedings or actions, or to make any other disposition of the differences in relation to the premises.

6. The *Owner* agrees from time to time, to execute, acknowledge and deliver to the *Society*, such assurances, powers of attorney or other authorizations or instruments as the *Society* may deem necessary or expedient to enable it to exercise, enjoy and enforce, in its own name or otherwise, all rights and remedies aforesaid.

7. It is mutually agreed that during the term hereof the Board of Directors of the *Society* shall be composed of an equal number of writers and publishers respectively, and that the royalties distributed by the Board of Directors shall be divided into two (2) equal sums, and one (1) each of such sums credited respectively to and for division amongst (a) the writer members, and (b) the publisher members, in accordance with the system of distribution and classification as determined by the Classification Committee of each group, in accordance with the Articles of Association as they may be amended from time to time, except that the classification of the *Owner* within his class may be changed.

8. The *Owner* agrees that his classification in the *Society* as determined from time to time by the Classification Committee of his group and/or The Board of Directors of the *Society*, in case of appeal by him, shall be final, conclusive and binding upon him.

The *Society* shall have the right to transfer the right of review of any classification from the Board of Directors to any other agency or instrumentality that in its discretion and good judgment it deems best adapted to assuring to the *Society's* membership a just, fair, equitable and accurate classification.

The *Society* shall have the right to adopt from time to time such systems, means, methods and formulae for the establishment of a member's status in respect of classification as will assure a fair, just and equitable distribution of royalties among the membership.

9. **"Public Performance" Defined.** The term *"public performance"* shall be construed to mean vocal, instrumental and/or mechanical renditions and representations in any manner or by any method whatsoever, including transmissions by radio and television broadcasting stations, transmission by telephony and/or "wired wireless"; and/or reproductions of performances and renditions by means of devices for reproducing sound recorded in synchronism or timed relation with the taking of motion pictures.

10. **"Musical Works" Defined.** The phrase *"musical works"* shall be construed to mean musical compositions and dramatico-musical compositions, the words and music thereof, and the respective arrangements thereof, and the selections therefrom.

11. The powers, rights, authorities and privileges by this instrument vested in the *Society*, are deemed to include the World, provided, however, that such grant of rights for foreign countries shall be subject to any agreements now in effect, a list of which are noted on the reverse side hereof.

12. The grant made herein by the owner is modified by and subject to the provisions of (a) the Amended Final Judgment (Civil Action No. 13–95) dated March 14, 1950 in U.S.A. v. ASCAP as further amended by Order dated January 7, 1960, (b) the Final Judgment (Civil Action No. 42–245) in U.S.A. v. ASCAP, dated March 14, 1950, and (c) the provisions of the Articles of Association and resolutions of the Board of Directors adopted pursuant to such judgments and order.

SIGNED, SEALED AND DELIVERED, on this . . . . day of . . . . , 19. . . .

Society $\left\{ \begin{array}{l} \text{AMERICAN SOCIETY OF COMPOSERS,} \\ \text{AUTHORS AND PUBLISHERS,} \\ \text{By. . . . .} \end{array} \right.$ Owner $\left\{ \begin{array}{l} \text{. . . . .} \\ \text{. . . . .} \end{array} \right.$

President

Summary of ASCAP Credit Weighting Formula

Type of Use	Applicable Credit	*References to ASCAP Weighting Formula of April, 1984*
Feature	Each feature performance gets 1 use credit for a single use regardless of whether the song is a qualifying work or not, but for network television performances, if a work has not had 5 local radio feature performances during the 5 preceding years, it shall receive 50% of otherwise applicable credit for performance between 15 and 44 seconds, and 25% of such credit for performance less than 15 seconds in duration. Subsequent uses on the same program get only 10% of a use credit with a maximum of 2 credits per work on any single program.	(B)(1)
	A performance is deemed "feature" and not "background" if a principal focus of audience attention and a broadcast musical subject matter, such as in synchronization with choreographic dancing, and is not a performance as a theme, jingle, background, cue or bridge. A visual instrumental or vocal rendition which is the principal focus of audience attention is not regarded as background music and is presumed to be "feature" unless a theme or jingle.	(A)(2), (A)(6)(a) and examples
	If more than 8 works are included in any 15 minutes as feature performances, there is a reduction of applicable credits pro rata to a maximum of 8 credits. Where radio performances of a single record side, or LP band which includes 3 or more works, there is a pro rata share of 8 use credits in ratio of duration of recording to 15 minutes.	(B)(2)

	Qualifying Work (See Comments and Definitions)	*Nonqualifying Work*	
Theme	½ credit for all uses of same work within first hour of any 2 hour period plus 5% of credit for all uses in second hour. (see footnotes A, B, C and E at page 485).	10% of a credit for all uses of same work as a theme within first hour of any 2-hour period plus 1% of a credit for all uses in second hour, but a	(C)(2) (C)(1)(h)

work used for more than 13 weeks as a theme of a prime time weekly network TV show receives 50% of a feature credit for uses thereafter (see footnotes A, B, C and E).

Background, Cue and Bridge	½ credit for first use of this type on a single program plus 5% of a credit for each subsequent such use on same program up to maximum of 1 credit. (see footnote C). *Special credit category:* Certain nonqualifying works with sheet music or a single record and which have had 5 logged feature local radio performances in last 5 years get, without being qualified works, 20% of a credit for first performance of this type plus 2% for each subsequent such use on same program, up to 40%.	36% of a credit for each 3 minutes aggregate duration on single program: if less duration 6% for each 16 to 36 seconds of aggregate duration and 1% for aggregate of less than 16 seconds attributable to same writer and publisher. See Special credit category under Qualifying Work.	(A)(2), (A)(4), (A)(5), (C)(3)
Jingle	There is no distinction as to qualifying or nonqualifying works used as a jingle. The credit is 3% of a credit for all uses in the first hour of a 2-hour period and .3% of a credit for all uses in second hour. But if a work has had 5 logged feature performances in the last 5 years it receives theme credit. (See "Theme" above.)		(A)(3) (C)(4)

Credits on Arrangements of Public Domain Works

Copyrighted arrangements get credits ranging from 2% up to 100% of otherwise applicable credit on the following basis: (G)

  A: 2% if the arrangement of work otherwise in the public domain is part of a copyrighted compilation and does not qualify for higher credit.

  B: 10% if the arrangement of a work otherwise in the public domain is separately published and separately copyrighted in the United States.

  C: 10% if the arrangement of a work otherwise in the public domain is included in a copyrighted collection of hymns or religious anthems which is offered for sale in a regular trade edition.

  D: Up to 35% if the arrangement contains new lyrics but uses the same title as the public domain version.

  E: Up to 50% if the arrangement uses new title and new lyrics.

  F: Additional 10 to 50% over C, D, and E above depending on extent of changes in music.

  G: 10 to 35% for primarily instrumental work being a transference from another medium.

  H: 35 to 100% for primarily instrumental work containing original musical characterization and exhibiting creative treatment as a set piece apart from its source. (Items "D" to "H" are subject to determination by the Special Classification Committee for Public Domain Arrangements.)

Comments and Definitions	

Theme—includes use "in conjunction" with advertising, promotional or public service announcements. — (A)(1)

Qualifying work—Any work having (a) an accumulation of 20,000 feature performance credits since January 1, 1943 of which (b) 2500 feature credits are attributable to the last five years but without including more than 750 such credits from any one of those five years. However, if the work was first performed before January 1, 1943, then regardless of having accumulated 20,000 credits, it is deemed to satisfy "(a)" above if it was among the top ten on the Lucky Strike Hit Parade or top ten weekly Variety or Billboard lists, or in 1952 Prentice-Hall Variety Music Cavalcade. Songs with less than five years of reports need satisfy only "(a)" of this paragraph plus maintaining at least 500 feature credits per year of available reports. — (C)

Note that for purposes of Theme credits, there is a partial type of qualification as follows: Where there is an accumulation of 2500 feature credits for the last five years, with no more than 750 credits from any one year, the themed use of this song gets 37.5% or 25% of a full use credit if it has accumulated, respectively, 15,000 or 10,000 feature performance credits since January 1, 1943. — (C)(1)(d) ... (B)(3)(b)

In computing these feature credits the rebuttable presumption is that any credits recorded before October 1, 1955 reflect feature performances if the work was first performed on or after January 1, 1943 and within the first two years of performances recorded, the song accumulated 20,000 credits, or if the title appears in the publications or lists referred to above. — (C)(1)(c)

Qualified work requirements as to feature performance credits are cut to 20% for works originally written for choral, symphonic or similar concert performance. — (C)(1)(g)

Recognized work—for ASCAP writer-members not on a 100% current performance basis there is a 20% writer's fund which is paid on performances of recognized works which are defined as works performed after one year from the earliest date of a performance of such work being logged by ASCAP. New works may qualify as recognized works immediately after receiving feature performance credits equal in number to the average number of feature credits received in each of the five latest available fiscal survey years by the fifty ASCAP works appearing for the first time in the survey and having the highest number of feature performance credits in such year: works performed after receiving feature performance credits in excess of one-half such averages and up to such average receive one-half of the recognized works credit for each performance credit in excess of one-half such average and up to such average. — (Does not appear in Weighting Formula —defined in ASCAP distribution formulas)

A: If in a 2-hour period the same work is performed both as a feature and as a theme or background, cue or bridge, such nonfeature additional credits cannot increase the aggregate to over 1 1/10 credits for the first 60 minutes or to more than 10% of a credit for the second hour. — (C)(2)(c)

B: On-camera performance of theme, at opening or closing of a television musical or variety program, which is principal focus of audience attention receives additional 25% of applicable credit, with limit of ½ additional credit for all such works on a particular program. — (C)(2)(d)

C: Reduce otherwise applicable credit to 10% of such applicable credit where the network or station using the work is the sponsor of the advertising or promotional announcement (other than jingle) involved. — (C)(5)(b)

D: For feature uses on a network program appearing four or more times per week of works written or published by persons regularly associated with the program and for nonfeature uses on a network program appearing four or — (C)(5)(a) more times per week the credit is 25% of the otherwise applicable credit.

E: Where any program results in more than ½ a credit per 15 minutes of   (C)(3)(c)
programming there is a pro rata reduction to a total of ½ a credit of all credits
given to works logged as themes and qualified works logged as background,
cue or bridge, or to nonqualified works getting special treatment due to fulfilling special criteria of 5 logged radio local performances, etc.

F: For network TV programs other than at prime time, credit is reduced   (D)
to 50% or 75% of other applicable credit, depending on time of day factor.

ASCAP Credit Weighting Formula

In awarding credit for a performance appearing in the Society's survey, no distinction shall be made on the basis of the identity or use of the work performed, except as provided in this Weighting Formula.

(A) *As used in this Weighting Formula:*

 (1) *"Theme"* shall mean a musical work used as the identifying signature of a radio or television personality or of all or part of a radio or television program or series of programs. A musical work (other than a jingle) used in conjunction with an advertising, promotional or public service announcement shall receive the same credit as a theme.

 (2) *"Background Music"* shall mean mood, atmosphere or thematic music performed as background to some non-musical subject matter being presented on a radio or television program. A vocal or a visual instrumental rendition which is a principal focus of audience attention shall not be regarded as background music regardless of the context in which performed.

 (3) *"Jingle"* shall mean an advertising, promotional or public service announcement containing musical material (with or without lyrics), where (a) the musical material was originally written for advertising, promotional or public service announcement purposes or (b) the performance is of a musical work, originally written for other purposes, with the lyrics changed for advertising, promotional or public service announcement purposes with the permission of the ASCAP member or members in interest or (c) the performance is of a musical work, originally written for other purposes, which does not have at least five feature playings recorded in the Society's survey during the five preceding fiscal survey years.

 (4) *"Cue Music"* shall mean music used on a radio or television program to introduce, but not to identify, a personality or event thereon. The term "cue music" includes, but is not limited to, introductions, "play-ons", and "play-offs".

 (5) *"Bridge Music"* shall mean music used on a radio or television program as a connective link between segments or portions thereof.

 (6) (a) *"Feature Performance"* shall mean any performance which is a principal focus of audience attention and which constitutes a musical subject matter on a radio or television program and is not a performance as a theme, jingle, background, cue or bridge music. A visual instrumental or vocal performance shall be presumed to be a feature performance unless such performance is as a theme or a jingle or is not a principal focus of audience attention.

 (b) *"Visual Instrumental Performance"* shall mean a performance by a musician or musicians who are seen by the television viewing audience.

 (c) *"Vocal Performance"* shall mean the performance of the lyrics of a composition or the on-camera humming or whistling of the music of a composition.

 (d) *"Musical Subject Matter"* shall mean the presentation in a program of an activity (i) which normally involves the performance of music—such as singing, playing a musical instrument, or dancing (including skating in a manner akin to dancing or ballet), and (ii) in which such music is the music written for or used in the original presentation as the work being sung, played, or danced to.

 (7) *"Qualifying Work"* shall mean a work meeting both of the criteria set forth in subpara-

graphs (a)(i) and (a)(ii) of paragraph (C) of this Weighting Formula. A work meeting the criteria set forth in subparagraph (d) of said paragraph (C) shall also be deemed a qualifying work to the extent that it shall receive the percentage set forth in said subparagraph (d) of the use credit provided in this Weighting Formula for qualifying works.

(8) *"Non-Qualifying Work"* shall mean a work not meeting the criteria set forth in paragraph (C) of this Weighting Formula.

(9) *"Single Program"* shall mean any substantially consecutive period of broadcasting which is presented by the same dominant personality, or is presented under substantially the same title, or is presented as a single show with separate segments. If any such period of broadcasting is more than two hours in duration, each two-hour segment thereof shall be treated as a single program, and any remaining fraction of less than two hours shall be treated as a single program.

(10) *"Use Credit"* shall mean a full credit for a single performance.

(11) *"Otherwise Applicable Credit"* shall mean the use credit or percentage of a use credit otherwise provided for in this Weighting Formula for a particular type of use of a qualifying or non-qualifying work.

(B) *Credit for Feature Performances*

(1) Each feature performance of a work (as distinguished from performance as a theme or jingle or as background, cue or bridge music) shall receive one use credit for the first performance and 10% of a use credit for each subsequent performance on a single program, provided that no work shall receive more than two use credits for a single program.

A feature performance on network television of a work which has had fewer than five feature playings recorded in the Society's local radio sample survey during the five preceding fiscal survey years shall receive 50% of the otherwise applicable credit for the first performance if it is between 15 and 44 seconds in duration and 25% of the otherwise applicable credit for the first performance if it is 14 seconds or less in duration. Each subsequent performance on a single program shall receive 10% of the otherwise applicable credit, provided that no work shall receive more than two use credits for a single program.

(2) In determining use credits for radio or television programs containing more than eight works per each quarter hour of programming (excluding themes, jingles, background, cue and bridge music), the use credit allotted to each work shall be reduced pro rata so that all works on the entire program shall receive in the aggregate the number of use credits which would have been allotted if the program had contained eight compositions per each quarter hour of programming (excluding themes, jingles, background, cue and bridge music).

In the case of radio performances, if a single side of a 45 rpm recording, or a single band on a long playing record, tape or other similar device includes three or more works, the use credit allocated to all works on the side or the band shall bear the same relationship to eight (8) use credits that the duration of the side or band bears to a quarter hour.

(3) If (i) analysis indicates that there are inaccuracies in listing the compositions performed or describing the manner of the performance on reports received for certain programs, and (ii) such information is prepared by a member or by a person associated with a member, and (iii) the Society does not have and the user or the member are unable to furnish the Society with a film, video tape, or other audio-visual recording of the program,—then it shall be presumed that the works of the member did not receive feature performances on the program.

(C) *Credit for Performances as a Theme, Background Music, or Cue or Bridge Music*

(1) *Qualifying Works:*

(a) A work complying with both of the following tests shall receive 50% of a use credit or other percentage thereof specified in this Weighting Formula for the performance of a qualifying work as a theme, background music, or cue or bridge music:

(i) an accumulation of 20,000 feature performance credits since January 1, 1943;

(ii) an accumulation of 2500 feature performance credits during the five latest available preceding fiscal survey years, toward which total not more than 750 credits shall be counted for any one of such survey years.

(b) Any work first performed before January 1, 1943 shall satisfy the requirements of subparagraph (a)(i) above, in the event such work has not accumulated 20,000 feature performance credits since such date, if the title of such work appears in the publication *Variety Music Cavalcade,* Prentice-Hall 1952, or among the top ten on the "Lucky Strike Hit Parade" or the top ten on the weekly list of the most popular songs published in *Variety* or *Billboard.*

(c)   If any work first performed on or after January 1, 1943 has earned the number of performance credits required pursuant to subparagraph (a)(i) above in the two consecutive fiscal survey years commencing with the year in which its first performance is recorded in the survey, or if the title of such work appears in the publication *Variety Music Cavalcade,* Prentice-Hall 1952, or among the top ten on the "Lucky Strike Hit Parade" or the top ten on the weekly list of the most popular songs published in *Variety* or *Billboard,* there shall be a rebuttable presumption that such performance credits recorded before October 1, 1955 reflect feature performances; otherwise, the burden shall be on the member or members in interest to establish that performance credits recorded before October 1, 1955 reflect feature performances.

(d)   A work performed as a theme and which complies with the requirements of subparagraph (a)(ii) above shall receive 37.5% or 25% of a full use credit if it has accumulated 15,000 or 10,000 feature performance credits, respectively, since January 1, 1943.

(e)   Until five years of records of feature performances are available the number of feature performance credits required pursuant to subparagraph (a)(ii) above shall be reduced proportionately to the number of years available. For a work whose first surveyed performance occurred within the five latest available preceding fiscal survey years, the requirement of said subparagraph (a)(ii) shall be satisfied when the work has met the requirements of subparagraph (a)(i) above and shall continue to be satisfied if in each subsequent year of such five years the work receives one-fifth the number of feature performance credits required by said subparagraph (a)(ii).

(f)   The number of performance credits needed to meet any requirement pursuant to subparagraph (a) above is premised on an annual total of approximately 25,000,000 performance credits recorded in the ASCAP survey; performance credits in years when the total number of performance credits recorded in the ASCAP survey was 20% greater or smaller than that number shall be adjusted proportionately.

(g)   For works which in their original form were composed for a choral, symphonic or similar concert performance (including chamber music), the numbers of feature performance credits required by subparagraphs (C)(1)(a), (b) and (d) shall be reduced to 20% of the numbers of feature performance credits prescribed therein.

(h)   When any work has been performed for more than 13 weeks as an opening or closing theme of a weekly network television program at least half of which is broadcast between the hours of 7 p.m. and 1:59 a.m. New York time, it shall receive 50% of a use credit when performed as such a theme for such program beginning with the fourteenth week. A work which qualifies both under this subparagraph and also any other subparagraphs of this paragraph (C)(1) shall receive the credit provided in this subparagraph (h).

(2) *Themes:*

(a)   When any qualifying work is performed as a theme, it shall receive only 50% of a use credit for all such performances within the first 60 minutes of any given two-hour period regardless of the number of actual such performances, and for all additional such performances during the second hour it shall receive only an additional 5% of a use credit regardless of the number of actual such performances.

(b)   When any non-qualifying work is performed as a theme, it shall receive only 10% of a use credit for all such performances within the first 60 minutes of any given two-hour period regardless of the number of actual such performances, and for all additional such performances during the second hour it shall receive only an additional 1% of a use credit regardless of the number of actual such performances.

(c)   When during any given two-hour period, any work is performed both
(i)   as a feature performance and
(ii) as a theme or background, cue or bridge music
it shall receive for its performances as a theme, background, cue or bridge music the percentage of a use credit herein provided therefor, except that in no event shall the addition of such percentage of use credit increase the aggregate use credit for such work to more than 1-1/10 use credits for the first 60 minutes of such two-hour period, or to more than 10% of a use credit for the second hour.

(d)   When any work is performed as a theme at the opening or closing of all or part of a television musical or variety program and the performance is rendered on-camera either vocally, instrumentally or by dancer(s) and constitutes a principal focus of audience attention, it shall receive an additional 25% of a use credit for the program (computed after the application of subparagraph (3)(c) of this paragraph (C)) provided, however, that the additional credit awarded hereunder for all works so performed on a particular program shall not aggregate more than 50% of a use credit, to be apportioned equally among all works so performed on the program.

(3) *Background, Cue and Bridge Music:*

   (a)   When any qualifying work is performed as background, cue or bridge music, it shall receive 50% of a use credit for the first such performance on a single program, and shall receive only 5% of a use credit for each subsequent such performance on such program, provided that no work shall receive more than one use credit for a single program.

   (b)   Non-qualifying works performed as background, cue or bridge music on each program shall receive, for each three minutes duration in the aggregate for that program, 30% of a use credit; fractions of three minutes shall be computed on the basis of 6% for each 36 seconds or major fraction thereof, and where the aggregated amount for any works written by the same writer or writers and published by the same publisher is in total a minor fraction of 36 seconds, 1% of a use credit. To determine use credits for performances in this classification where the time of actual performance cannot be established from the information available to the Society, 40% of the net program time will be considered as containing background, cue or bridge music and the computation of 30% will be based on such computed time. Where condensed versions of a program are presented and the actual music performed on this condensed version is unknown, the 40% computation will be made on the net program time and applied pro rata to all of the background, cue or bridge music in the original program. Where it is determined that the amount of music on particular types of programs deviates more than 20% from the 40% computation (*e.g.,* so that less than 32% of the net program time contains background, cue and bridge music) the percentage applicable to these types of programs will be determined through periodic samples of the amount of program time on these types of programs containing background, cue and bridge time determined as above will be divided among uses on a pro rata basis. Anything to the contrary notwithstanding, any non-qualifying work which five feature playings have been recorded in the Society's local radio sample survey during the five preceding fiscal survey years, shall receive not less than 20% of a use credit for the first performance as background, cue or bridge music on a single program and 2% of a use credit for each subsequent such performance on such program, provided that no work shall receive credit for background, cue or bridge use under this provision of more than 40% of a use credit for a single program.

   (c)   If the aggregate use credit allotted to works performed as themes and to qualifying works used as background, cue or bridge music and works described in the last sentence of subparagraph (3)(b) above performed as background, cue or bridge music per each quarter hour of programming would exceed 50% of a use credit, the use credit allotted to each such work shall be reduced pro rata so that all such works performed as theme, background, cue or bridge music on the entire program shall receive an aggregate of 50% of a use credit per each quarter hour of programming.

(4) *Jingles:* When any work is performed as a jingle it shall receive only 3% of a use credit for all such performances within the first 60 minutes of any given two-hour period regardless of the number of actual such performances, and for all additional such performances during the second hour it shall receive only an additional 10% of 3% of a use credit regardless of the number of actual such performances.

(5) *General Limitation:* Anything to the contrary notwithstanding:

   (a)   On any network program which is presented four or more times weekly, having the same dominant personality or under substantially the same title or format, the credit to be awarded for feature performances of works written or published by persons regularly associated with the program on which such performances are rendered and for performances of works as themes, background, cue or bridge music shall be 25% of the otherwise applicable credit. This limitation shall apply in the case of both individual credits and maximum aggregate credits on any such program.

   (b)   Any work (other than a jingle) used in conjunction with an advertising or promotional announcement sponsored by the network or station on which it appears shall receive 10% of the otherwise applicable credit.

(D) *Time-of-Day Factor for Network Television Programs*

Performances of works on television network programs other than those performances for which credits are limited under Paragraph (C)(5)(a) shall be credited as follows:

(1) *Monday through Friday*
   (a) If the program begins between 2:00 a.m. and 12:59 p.m., 50% of the otherwise applicable credit;
   (b) If the program begins between 1:00 p.m. and 6:59 p.m., 75% of the otherwise applicable credit;
   (c) If the program begins between 7:00 p.m. and 1:59 a.m., 100% of the applicable credit.
(2) *Saturday and Sunday*
   (a) If the program begins between 2:00 a.m. and 12:59 p.m., 50% of the otherwise applicable credit;
   (b) If the program begins between 1:00 p.m. and 1:59 a.m., 100% of the applicable credit.
(3) *New Year's Day, Memorial Day, Independence Day, Labor Day, Thanksgiving and Christmas:* If the program is broadcast on any of these holidays which falls on any weekday, performances shall be credited as if the program were broadcast on a Saturday or Sunday. For a program more than one hour in duration which begins in one time period, as defined above, and extends into another time period, the applicable credit for all performances on that program shall be determined as follows:

When more than half the program is in one time period, that time period shall govern; when the program is divided equally between time periods, the time period having the higher applicable credit shall govern.

For purposes of this rule, the time a program begins shall be New York broadcast time, except that if a network furnishes more than one program to its affiliates at the same time, such as different football games to different parts of the network, the times such program begin shall be the local times at the places the programs originate.

(E) *Serious Works Four Minutes or Longer in Duration*
   Works which require four minutes or more for a single, complete rendition thereof, and which in their original form were composed for a choral, symphonic, or similar concert performance (including chamber music), shall receive credit on the following basis when performed for the respective designated periods of time.

Minutes of Actual Performance	*The Otherwise Applicable Credit Is Multiplied by:*
4:00 to 5:30	2
5:31 to 10:30	6
10:31 to 15:30	12
15:31 to 20:30	20
20:31 to 25:30	30
25:31 to 30:30	40
30:31 to 35:30	50
35:31 to 40:30	60
40:31 to 45:30	70
45:31 to 50:30	80
50:31 to 55:30	90
55:31 to 60:30	100
Each additional 5 minutes or part thereof	10

(F) *Concert and Symphony Performances*
   The license fees which the Society receives from concert and symphony halls shall be multiplied by five in determining the credit to be awarded for performances of works in concert and symphony halls. For performances in concert and symphony halls, points shall be awarded as follows:

Point Award Minutes

	Up to 5	6 to 10	11 to 15	16 to 20	21 to 30	31 to 45	46 to 60
A) ENTERTAINMENT MUSIC—i.e. Light or Standard Instrumental and Choral Music ALL CATEGORIES	1	2	3	4	5	6	7
B) SERIOUS MUSIC IN THE ORIGINAL FORM							
a. Works for 1 or 2 instruments with or without voice	2	4	6	8	10	12	14
b. Works for 3 to 9 instruments with or without voice	3	6	9	12	15	20	25
c. Works for small orchestra with or without voice	4	9	18	24	30	40	50
d. Works for full orchestra with or without voice	8	18	36	48	60	80	100

For works in excess of 60 minutes, pro rata on the basis of the 60 minute points. The percentage of credit for arrangements of works in the public domain will be determined in accordance with Section (G).

(G) *Copyrighted Arrangements*
(1) Except as hereinafter specifically provided, any arrangement of a work otherwise in the public domain which
   (a)   is separately published and separately copyrighted in the United States; or
   (b)   is a work described in paragraph (6) below and is available on rental; or
   (c)   is included in a copyrighted collection of hymns or anthems which is offered for sale in a regular trade edition.
   shall receive 10% of the otherwise applicable credit.
(2) If an arrangement of a work otherwise in the public domain is included in a copyrighted collection and does not qualify for the 10% credit under the preceding paragraph it shall receive 2% of the otherwise applicable credit.
(3) If a copyrighted arrangement has the same title as the underlying original composition, but contains new lyrics it may receive up to 35% of the otherwise applicable credit depending upon the extent of new material.
(4) If a copyrighted arrangement has an entirely new title and contains new lyrics, it may receive up to 50% of the otherwise applicable credit depending upon the extent of new material.
(5) If a copyrighted arrangement has changes in the music, it may receive an additional 10% to 50% of the otherwise applicable credit depending upon the extent of new material.
(6) If a copyrighted arrangement is primarily an instrumental work, it may receive from 10% to 100% of the otherwise applicable credit, depending upon the extent to which it embodies changes in the music as follows:
   (a)   a transference from one medium to another, up to 35%;
   (b)   a development of a work which exhibits creative treatment and contains original musical characteristics and is identifiable as a set piece apart from the source material, 35% to 100%.
(7) All classifications pursuant to paragraphs 3, 4, 5 and 6 shall be made by the Special Classification Committee for Public Domain Arrangements.

(H) *Concert and Sympony Performances—Additional Credit*
In the case of any work which qualifies for credit under subdivision (B) of paragraph (F) above, and for which the Society holds the right to license such work from a writer member of the Society, or holds the right to license such work from the writer under Section I of the Order, such work shall receive for performances under paragraph (F) above, additional credit under this section. The additional credit shall be determined by multiplying the credit such work received

under paragraph (F) above by twice the ratio of (i) the license fees which the Society received from concert and symphony halls in the survey year October 1, 1963 through September 30, 1964 to (ii) the license fees which the Society received from concert and symphony halls in the year of the performance. Such additional credit shall in no event be more than twice the credit awarded under paragraph (F) above. Distribution based on the additional credits awarded under this paragraph shall be in addition to the distribution based upon credits awarded under paragraphs (F) above.

Procedure and specific situations in application of weighting formula provisions

The Board of Directors has considered in detail the procedure for implementing the Weighting Formula provisions and the way in which they will be applied to specific situations.

1. WEIGHTING FORMULA PROVISIONS—PROCEDURE:

The Society has for some time been reviewing on a regular basis information received concerning performances on network and local television programs. This review is being conducted by means of audio and visual examination of programs. The Society uses video-tape recording equipment in connection with this review.

Particular attention will be given to programs which, considering the nature of the program, generate an unusually large number of performance credits. Such programs will be checked by listening and viewing, or both, and comparing the results with the music information appearing on the program logs or cue sheets received by the Society.

2. WEIGHTING FORMULA PROVISIONS—SPECIFIC SITUATIONS AS GUIDES IN APPLICATION OF FORMULA:

The Survey and Distribution Committee has prepared, and the Board of Directors has approved, a series of illustrations of the way in which the formula provisions would be applied to specific situations.

The following are examples of performances other than as a theme, or a jingle, which *would* be credited as feature performances under the Weighting Formula:

1. A vocal or visual instrumental performance of a composition which is announced or to which the attention of the audience is otherwise specifically directed by a participant on the program.
2. A performance as part of a song or dance act which constitutes the principal activity on the program at the time it is rendered.
3. A performance on an audience participation program where the activity taking place is the identification by the participants on the program of the composition being performed.
4. Announced instrumentals at public spectacles such as football games.*

The following are examples of performances which would *not* be credited as feature performances under the Weighting Formula:

1. A performance where the orchestra or instrumentalist appears visually for a brief period while a participant on a program, such as a quiz game, panel, audience participation or similar program, is passing by or while the camera is panning.
2. A vocal or visual instrumental performance to introduce or accompany the following on quiz games, panel, audience participation or similar programs:
    (a) the description or presentation of prizes;
    (b) the appearance or departure of participants; or
    (c) the change of scene or subject.
3. Unannounced instrumental performances during public spectacles such as football games. (Performances at football games other than those indicated to have occurred during half-time periods will be presumed to be background music.)*
4. A vocal or visual instrumental performance used as a bridge to or from a commercial announcement or in a similar manner as a connective link.

*NOTE: A visual instrumental performance at a football game by a band which was actually viewed and heard by the television audience will be credited as a feature performance so long as the camera was focused on the band deliberately—that is, unless the band was visible for only a fleeting moment while, for example, the camera was focused on someone who just happened to be passing by the band or while the camera was panning.

5.   A vocal or visual instrumental performance used as a play-on or play-off.
6.   Non-visual instrumental performance as accompaniment to magicians or clowns, or acrobatic or animal acts.
7.   Humming or whistling off camera in a television program shall not be regarded as a feature performance.
8.   A performance with a film clip, newsreel, or documentary of dancers, skaters, instrumentalists or singers is not credited as a feature performance unless the music heard by the viewer is the music written for or used in the original presentation as the music being danced to, skated to, played, or sung by the performers being shown on the television screen.
9.   So-called "Mickey mousing" shall not receive feature credit. The term "Mickey mousing" refers to scoring on a film or similar program in which the music is very closely synchronized with movements, animation, or other activity on the program. The term does not include an activity which constitutes a musical subject matter.

The following is an example of a theme performance which would receive additional credit under Paragraph (C)(2)(d) of the Weighting Formula:

A performance at the opening or closing of a program or before or after a station break which serves as an identifying signature of all or part of the program is credited as a theme performance. However, where the performance is on a television musical or variety program, and is rendered on-camera, either vocally, instrumentally or by dancer(s) and constitutes a principal focus of audience attention, the performance will receive the additional credit for theme performances provided in Paragraph (C)(2)(d) of the Weighting Formula.

The following is an example of feature performances which would receive reduced credit under Paragraph (B)(2) of the Weighting Formula:

Three works with a running time of 5 minutes occupying one side of a 45 rpm or one cut of a 33⅓ rpm record will share 2.67 use credits, that is ⅓ of the eight (8) maximum use credits per quarter hour, because the duration of the record or cut is ⅓ of the quarter hour.

The foregoing illustrations are designed to serve as guides to the application of the Weighting Formula provisions. They are not, it must be emphasized, an all-inclusive listing of all possible situations, and they will be supplemented from time to time as additional illustrations are felt to be appropriate.

April 1, 1984

Appendix K

BMI Writer Application

1. NAME: MS. / MR. / MRS. / MISS ....
(First Name) (Middle Name or Initial) (Last Name)

2. ☐ HOME ADDRESS.

....
(Street) (City) (State) (Zip Code) (Phone Number)

☐ BUSINESS ADDRESS (If same as above, write "same")
(Include Company Room No. if necessary)

....
(Street) (City) (State) (Zip Code) (Phone Number)
(Check one address above to which all mail is to be sent)

3. DATE OF BIRTH: .... CITIZENSHIP: ....
Month Day Year Country

4. EDUCATIONAL BACKGROUND, ACADEMIC & MUSICAL: ....

....

5. DO YOU WRITE WORDS, MUSIC OR BOTH? ....

6. LIST ALL PEN NAMES AND PSEUDONYMS WHICH YOU HAVE USED OR WILL USE:

....

....

7. Are you now or have you ever been a writer member or writer-affliliate of BMI, ASCAP, SESAC, or of any foreign perform'ng rights licensing organization? If so, state name of organization and the period during which you were a member or affiliate. ....

....

8. Is your spouse, parent, brother, sister, child or any other relative or writer-member or writer-affilate of any organization specified in Paragraph 7? If so, give name, realtionship to you, and organization. ....

....

9. Have you ever written music or lyrics for a fee or in consideration of any payment from a composer or writer of the music or lyrics? Please state the circumstances under which you performed such services ....

....

....

10. Please list on the reverse side of this form at least one but not more than three compositions heretofore written by you, either alone or in collaboration with others, which are placed with a publisher, commercially recorded, being performed or likely to be performed.

STATE OF .... } ss.:
COUNTY OF ....

On the .... day of .... 19.....

before me came

to me known and known to me to be the individual described in and who executed the foregoing instrument, and (s)he duly acknowledged to me that (s)he executed the same.

....
Notary Public

My Notary Commission Expires ________

I warrant and represent that all of the information furnished on this application is true. I acknowledge that any contract consummated between me and BMI will be entered into in reliance upon the representations contained in this application, and that the contract will be subject to cancellation if any question herein contained is not answered fully or accurately.

Date ....

Social Security No. ....

Signature ....

APPLICATION WILL NOT BE ACCEPTED UNLESS IT IS NOTARIZED AND ALL QUESTIONS ARE FULLY ANSWERED

Return Completed Application to BMI, Attention of PERFORMING RIGHTS ADMINISTRATION

WR201-78

SCHEDULE OF WORKS

TITLE	FULL NAMES OF ALL CO-WRITERS, (INCLUDE AND ANY PSEUDONYM YOU MAY HAVE USED FOR EACH SPECIFIC TITLE).	Share of Writer Credit	FULL NAME OF PUBLISHER	Pub's Perf. Rights Organization BMI, ASCAP, SESAC, OTHER	IMPORTANT PLEASE GIVE INFORMATION ON RECORD RELEASES LABEL RELEASE DATE
1.					
2.					
3.					

BMI Publisher Application

NOTE:
ALL QUESTIONS MUST BE ANSWERED
APPLICATION MUST BE SIGNED ON LAST PAGE

1. NAME OF YOUR PROPOSED PUBLISHING COMPANY:

> (In order to eliminate confusion it is necessary to reject any name identical with, or similar to, that of an established publishing company. Also, any name using INITIALS as part of your company name cannot be accepted.)

1st   Choice: ....

2nd   Choice: ....

3rd   Choice: ....

2. BUSINESS ADDRESS:

.... Zip Code ....

Telephone No. ....

AREA CODE   TELEPHONE NO.

3. LIST 1 OR 2 TITLES of music owned by your publishing company which have been commercially recorded or are likely to be broadcast or performed in concerts or otherwise publicly performed.

TITLE	FULL NAME(S) OF WRITER(S)	WRITER(S) PER. RIGHTS AFFILIATION BMI, ASCAP, SESAC OR OTHER	COMMERCIAL RECORDING	
			NAME OF LABEL	RELEASE DATE
....	....	....	....	....
....	....	....	....	....
....	....	....	....	....
....	....	....	....	....

IF CUE SHEETS ARE NECESSARY, PLEASE SUBMIT.

4. COMPLETE A, B OR C TO INDICATE HOW YOUR COMPANY IS ORGANIZED:

A. INDIVIDUALLY OWNED:

Name of Individual .... Soc. Sec. No. ___ __ ____

Home Address ....

.... Zip Code ....

Are you now or have you ever been a writer member or writer-affiliate of BMI, ASCAP, SESAC. or of any foreign performing rights licensing organization? If so, state name of organization and the period during which you were a member or affiliate.

....

B. PARTNERSHIP: Fed. Tax Acct. No. __ _____

List all Partners

Name	Home Address & Zip Code	Soc. Sec. No.	Percentage of Ownership
		___ __ ____	
		___ __ ____	
		___ __ ____	

C. FORMALLY ORGANIZED CORPORATION:

PLEASE ATTACH A COPY OF YOUR **CERTIFICATE OF INCORPORATION.**

(Complete only if corporation is now in existence)

State in which incorporated ....Fed. Tax. Acct. No. __ _____

List all Stockholders

Name	Home Address & Zip Code	Percentage of Ownership

List all Officers

Name	Home Address & Zip Code	Office Held

5. LIST ALL OTHER EXECUTIVE EMPLOYEES, if any
   such as professional manager, contact man, etc.

NAME	HOME ADDRESS & ZIP CODE	POSITION HELD
....	....	....
	....	
....	....	....
	....	

6. If any owner, stockholder, officer or executive employee has been or is connected with any record company, publishing company, songwriters' agency, or any other organization engaged in the solicitation, publication or exploitation of music, please give the following information:

NAME OF INDIVIDUAL	NAME OF COMPANY	IF PUBLISHING Co., IS IT BMI?	POSITION HELD	YEARS OF ASSOCIATION FROM	To
....	....	....	....	....	....
....	....	....	....	....	....
....	....	....	....	....	....

7. Have you charged or do you intend to charge a fee to a songwriter for examining, publishing, recording or exploiting his songs? Please answer by checking the appropriate box below. If you answer yes, you must state the amount of the fee and what it is for.   NO ☐   YES ☐

....

....

N O T I C E

IT IS ACKNOWLEDGED THAT ANY CONTRACT CONSUMMATED BETWEEN APPLICANT AND BMI WILL BE ENTERED INTO IN RELIANCE UPON THE REPRESENTATIONS CONTAINED IN THIS APPLICATION AND THE REPRESENTATION THAT ALL OWNERS, INCLUDING PARTNERS, ARE OVER THE AGE OF EIGHTEEN. THE CONTRACT WILL BE SUBJECT TO CANCELLATION IF ANY QUESTION HEREIN CONTAINED IS NOT ANSWERED FULLY AND ACCURATELY OR IF THE TRUE NAME OF EACH OWNER, STOCKHOLDER, OFFICER AND/OR EXECUTIVE EMPLOYEE IS NOT REPORTED IN QUESTIONS 4 and 5 HEREOF.

Date ....   Signature ....

....
(Please print name of person signing)

1/82

BMI Agreement with Writer

Dear

The following shall constitute the agreement between us:

1. As used in this agreement:

(a) The word "period" shall mean the term from   to
               , and continuing thereafter for additional terms of two years each unless terminated by either party at the end of said initial term or any additional term, upon notice by registered or certified mail not more than six months or less than sixty (60) days prior to the end of any such term.

(b) The word "works" shall mean:

(i) All musical compositions (including the musical segments and individual compositions written for a dramatic or dramatico-musical work) composed by you alone or with one or more collaborators during the period; and

(ii) All musical compositions (including the musical segments and individual compositions written for a dramatic or dramatico-musical work) composed by you alone or with one or more collaborators prior to the period, except those in which there is an outstanding grant of the right of public performance to a person other than a publisher affiliated with BMI.

2. You agree that:

(a) Within ten (10) days after the execution of this agreement you will furnish to us two copies of a completed clearance sheet in the form supplied by us with respect to each work heretofore composed by you which has been published in printed copies or recorded commercially or which is being currently performed or which you consider as likely to be performed.

(b) In each instance that a work for which clearance sheets have not been submitted to us pursuant to sub-paragraph (a) hereof is published in printed copies or recorded commercially or in synchronization with film or tape or is considered by you as likely to be performed, whether such work is composed prior to the execution of this agreement or hereafter during the period, you will promptly furnish to us two copies of a completed clearance sheet in the form supplied by us with respect to each such work.

(c) If requested by us in writing, you will promptly furnish to us a legible lead sheet or other written or printed copy of a work.

3. The submission of clearance sheets pursuant to paragraph 2 hereof shall constitute a warranty by you that all of the information contained thereon is true and correct and that no performing rights in such work have been granted to or reserved by others except as specifically set forth therein in connection with works heretofore written or co-written by you.

4. Except as otherwise provided herein, you hereby grant to us for the period:

(a) All the rights that you own or acquire publicly to perform, and to license others to perform, anywhere in the world, any part or all of the works.

(b) The non-exclusive right to record, and to license others to record, any part or all of any of the works on electrical transcriptions, wire, tape, film or otherwise, but only for the purpose of performing such work publicly by means of radio and television or for archive or audition purposes and not for sale to the public or for synchronization (i) with motion pictures intended primarily for theatrical exhibition or (ii) with programs distributed by means of syndication to broadcasting stations.

(c) The non-exclusive right to adapt or arrange any part or all of any of the works for performance purposes, and to license others to do so.

542

5. (a) The rights granted to us by sub-paragraph (a) of paragraph 4 hereof shall not include the right to perform or license the performance of more than one song or aria from a dramatic or dramatico-musical work which is an opera, operetta, or musical show or more than five minutes from a dramatic or dramatico-musical work which is a ballet if such performance is accompanied by the dramatic action, costumes or scenery of that dramatic or dramatico-musical work.

(b) You, together with the publisher and your collaborators, if any, shall have the right jointly, by written notice to us, to exclude from the grant made by sub-paragraph (a) of paragraph 4 hereof performances of works comprising more than thirty minutes of a dramatic or dramatico-musical work, but this right shall not apply to such performances from (i) a score originally written for and performed as part of a theatrical or television film, (ii) a score originally written for and performed as part of a radio or television program, or (iii) the original cast, sound track or similar album of a dramatic or dramatico-musical work.

(c) You retain the right to issue non-exclusive licenses for performances of a work or works (other than to another performing rights licensing organization), provided that within ten (10) days of the issuance of such license we are given written notice of the titles of the works and the nature of the performances so licensed by you.

6. (a) As full consideration for all rights granted to us hereunder and as security therefor, we agree to pay to you, with respect to each of the works in which we obtain and retain performing rights during the period:

(i) For performances of a work on broadcasting stations in the United States, its territories and possessions, amounts calculated pursuant to our then current standard practices upon the basis of the then current performance rates generally paid by us to our affiliated writers for similar performances of similar compositions. The number of performances for which you shall be entitled to payment shall be estimated by us in accordance with our then current system of computing the number of such performances.

It is acknowledged that we license the works of our affiliates for performance by non-broadcasting means, but that unless and until such time as feasible methods can be devised for tabulation of and payment for such performances, payment will be based solely on broadcast performances. In the event that during the period we shall establish a system of separate payment for non-broadcasting performances, we shall pay you upon the basis of the then current performance rates generally paid by us to our other affiliated writers for similar performances of similar compositions.

(ii) In the case of a work composed by you with one or more collaborators, the sum payable to you hereunder shall be a pro rata share, determined on the basis of the number of collaborators, unless you shall have transmitted to us a copy of an agreement between you and your collaborators providing for a different division of payment.

(iii) All monies received by us from any performing rights licensing organization outside of the United States, its territories and possessions, which are designated by such performing rights licensing organization as the author's share of foreign performance royalties earned by your works after the deduction of our then current handling charge applicable to our affiliated writers.

(b) We shall have no obligation to make payment hereunder with respect to (i) any performance of a work which occurs prior to the date on which we have received from you all of the information and material with respect to such work which is referred to in paragraphs 2 and 3 hereof, or (ii) any performance as to which a direct license as described in sub-paragraph (c) of paragraph 5 hereof has been granted by you, your collaborator or publisher.

7. We will furnish statements to you at least twice during each year of the period showing the number of performances as computed pursuant to sub-paragraph (a) (i) of paragraph 6 hereof and at least once during each year of the period showing the monies due pursuant to sub-paragraph (a) (iii) of paragraph 6 hereof. Each statement shall be accompanied by payment to you, subject to all proper deductions for advances, if any, of the sum thereby shown to be due for such performances.

8. (a) Nothing in this agreement requires us to continue to license the works subsequent to the termination of this agreement. In the event that we continue to license any or all of the works, however, we shall continue to make payments to you for so long as you do not make or purport to make directly or indirectly any grant of performing rights in such works to any other licensing organization. The amounts of such payments shall be calculated pursuant to our then current standard practices upon the basis of the then current performance rates generally paid by us to our affiliated writers for similar performances of similar compositions. You agree to notify us by registered or certified mail of any grant or purported grant by you directly or indirectly of performing rights to any other performing rights organization within ten (10) days from the making of such grant or purported grant and if you fail so to inform us thereof and we make payments to you for any period after the making of any such grant or purported grant, you agree to repay to us all amounts so paid by us promptly on demand. In addition, if we inquire of you by registered or certified mail, addressed to your last known address, whether you have made any such grant or purported grant and you fail to confirm to us by registered or certified mail within thirty (30) days of the mailing of such inquiry that you have not made any such grant or purported grant, we may, from and after such date, discontinue making any payments to you.

(b) Our obligation to continue payment to you after the termination of this agreement for performances outside of the United States, its territories and possessions shall be dependent upon our receipt in the United States of payments designated by foreign performing rights organizations as the author's share of foreign performance royalties earned by your works. Payment of such foreign royalties shall be subject to deduction of our then current handling charge applicable to our affiliated writers.

(c) In the event that we have reason to believe that you will receive or are receiving payment from a performing rights licensing organization other than BMI for or based on United States performances of one or more of your works during a period when such works were licensed by us pursuant to this agreement, we shall have the right to withhold payment for such performances from you until receipt of evidence satisfactory to us of the amount so paid to you by such other organization or that you have not been so paid. In the event that you have been so paid, the monies payable by us to you for such performances during such period shall be reduced by the amount of the payment from such other organization. In the event that you do not supply such evidence within eighteen (18) months from the date of our request therefor, we shall be under no obligation to make any payment to you for performances of such works during such period.

9. In the event that this agreement shall terminate at a time when, after crediting all earnings reflected by statements rendered to you prior to the effective date of such termination, there remains an unearned balance of advances paid to you by us, such termination shall not be effective until the close of the calendar quarterly period during which (a) you shall repay such unearned balance of advances, or (b) you shall notify us by registered or certified mail that you have received a statement rendered by us at our normal accounting time showing that such unearned balance of advances has been fully recouped by us.

10. You warrant and represent that you have the right to enter into this agreement; that you are not bound by any prior commitments which conflict with your commitments hereunder; that each of the works, composed by you alone or with one or more collaborators, is original; and that exercise of the rights granted by you herein will not constitute an infringement of copyright or violation of any other right of, or unfair competition with, any person, firm or corporation. You agree to indemnify and hold harmless us and our licensees from and against any and all loss or damage resulting from any claim of whatever nature arising from or in connection with the exercise of any of the rights granted by you in this agreement. Upon notification to us or any of our licensees of a claim with respect to any of the works, we shall have the right to exclude such work from this agreement and/or to withhold payment of all sums which become due pursuant to this agreement or any modification thereof until receipt of satisfactory written evidence that such claim has been withdrawn, settled or adjudicated.

11. (a) We shall have the right, upon written notice to you, to exclude from this agreement, at any time, any work which in our opinion (i) is similar to a previously existing composition and might constitute a copyright infringement, or (ii) has a title or music or lyric similar to that of a previously existing composition and might lead to a claim of unfair competition, or (iii) is offensive, in bad taste or against public morals, or (iv) is not reasonably suitable for performance.

(b) In the case of works which in our opinion are based on compositions in the public domain, we shall have the right, upon written notice to you, either (i) to exclude any such work from this agreement, or (ii) to classify any such work as entitled to receive only a fraction of the full credit that would otherwise be given for performances thereof.

(c) In the event that any work is excluded from this agreement pursuant to paragraph 10 or sub-paragraph (a) or (b) of this paragraph 11, all rights in such work shall automatically revert to you ten (10) days after the date of our notice to you of such exclusion. In the event that a work is classified for less than full credit under sub-paragraph (b) (ii) of this paragraph 11, you shall have the right, by giving notice to us, within ten (10) days after the date of our letter advising you of the credit allocated to the work, to terminate our rights therein, and all rights in such work shall thereupon revert to you.

12. In each instance that you write, or are employed or commissioned by a motion picture producer to write, during the period, all or part of the score of a motion picture intended primarily for exhibition in theaters, or by the producer of a musical show or revue for the legitimate stage to write, during the period, all or part of the musical compositions contained therein, we agree to advise the producer of the film that such part of the score as is written by you may be performed as part of the exhibition of said film in theaters in the United States, its territories and possessions, without compensation to us, or to the producer of the musical show or revue that your compositions embodied therein may be performed on the stage with living artists as part of such musical show or revue, without compensation to us. In the event that we notify you that we have established a system for the collection of royalties for performance of the scores of motion picture films in theaters in the United States, its territories and possessions, we shall no longer be obligated to take such action with respect to motion picture scores.

13. You make, constitute and appoint us, or our nominee, your true and lawful attorney, irrevocably during the term hereof, in our name or that of our nominee, or in your name, or otherwise, to do all acts, take all proceedings, execute, acknowledge and deliver any and all instruments, papers, documents, process or pleadings that may be necessary, proper or expedient to restrain infringement of and/or to enforce and protect the rights granted by you hereunder, and to recover damages in respect to or for the infringement or other violation of the said rights, and in our sole judgment to join you and/or others in whose names the copyrights to any of the works may stand; to discontinue, compromise or refer to arbitration, any such actions or proceedings or to make any other disposition of the disputes in relation to the works, provided that any action or proceeding commenced by us pursuant to the provisions of this paragraph shall be at our sole expense and for our sole benefit.

14. You agree that you, your agents, employees or representatives will not, directly or indirectly, solicit or accept payment from writers for composing music for lyrics or writing lyrics to music or for reviewing, publishing, promoting, recording or rendering other services connected with the exploitation of any composition, or

permit use of your name or your affiliation with us in connection with any of the foregoing. In the event of a violation of any of the provisions of this paragraph 14, we shall have the right, in our sole discretion, by giving you at least thirty (30) days' notice by registered or certified mail, to terminate this agreement. In the event of such termination no payments shall be due to you pursuant to paragraph 8 hereof.

15. No monies due or to become due to you shall be assignable, whether by way of assignment, sale or power granted to an attorney-in-fact, without our prior written consent. If any assignment of such monies is made by you without such prior written consent, no rights of any kind against us will be acquired by the assignee, purchaser or attorney-in-fact.

16. In the event that during the period (a) mail addressed to you at the last address furnished by you pursuant to paragraph 19 hereof shall be returned by the post office, or (b) monies shall not have been earned by you pursuant to paragraph 6 hereof for a period of two consecutive years or more, or (c) you shall die, BMI shall have the right to terminate this agreement on at least thirty (30) days' notice by registered or certified mail addressed to the last address furnished by you pursuant to paragraph 19 hereof and, in the case of your death, to the representative of your estate, if known to BMI. In the event of such termination no payments shall be due to you pursuant to paragraph 8 hereof.

17. You acknowledge that the rights obtained by you pursuant to this agreement constitute rights to payment of money and that during the period we shall hold absolute title to the performing rights granted to us hereunder. In the event that during the period you shall file a petition in bankruptcy, such a petition shall be filed against you, you shall make an assignment for the benefit of creditors, you shall consent to the appointment of a receiver or trustee for all or part of your property, or you shall institute or shall have instituted against you any other insolvency proceeding under the United States bankruptcy laws or any other applicable law, we shall retain title to the performing rights in all works for which clearance sheets shall have theretofore been submitted to us and shall subrogate your trustee in bankruptcy or receiver and any subsequent purchasers from them to your right to payment of money for said works in accordance with the terms and conditions of this agreement.

18. Any controversy or claim arising out of, or relating to, this agreement or the breach thereof, shall be settled by arbitration in the City of New York, in accordance with the Rules of the American Arbitration Association, and judgment upon the award of the arbitrator may be entered in any Court having jurisdiction thereof. Such award shall include the fixing of the expenses of the arbitration, including reasonable attorney's fees, which shall be borne by the unsuccessful party.

19. You agree to notify our Department of Performing Rights Administration promptly in writing of any change in your address. Any notice sent to you pursuant to the terms of this agreement shall be valid if addressed to you at the last address so furnished by you.

20. This agreement cannot be changed orally and shall be governed and construed pursuant to the laws of the State of New York.

21. In the event that any part or parts of this agreement are found to be void by a court of competent jurisdiction, the remaining part or parts shall nevertheless be binding with the same force and effect as if the void part or parts were deleted from this agreement.

Very truly yours,

BROADCAST MUSIC, INC.

ACCEPTED AND AGREED TO:

By ....

....
Assistant Vice President

BMI Agreement with Publisher

AGREEMENT made on .... between BROADCAST MUSIC, INC. ("BMI"), a New York corporation, whose address is 320 West 57th Street, New York, N.Y. 10019 and

....,

a .... doing business as ....

....("Publisher"), whose address is ....

....

WITNESSETH:

FIRST: The term of this agreement shall be the period from .... to ...., and continuing thereafter for additional periods of five (5) years each unless terminated by either party at the end of such initial period, or any such additional five (5) year period, upon notice by registered or certified mail not more than six (6) months or less than three (3) months prior to the end of any such term.

SECOND: As used in this agreement, the word "works" shall mean:

A. All musical compositions (including the musical segments and individual compositions written for a dramatic or dramatico-musical work) whether published or unpublished, now owned or copyrighted by Publisher or in which Publisher owns or controls performing rights, and

B. All musical compositions (including the musical segments and individual compositions written for a dramatic or dramatico-musical work) whether published or unpublished, in which hereafter during the term Publisher acquires ownership or copyright or ownership or control of the performing rights, from and after the date of the acquisition by Publisher of such ownership or control.

THIRD: Except as otherwise provided herein, Publisher hereby sells, assigns and transfers to BMI, its successors or assigns, for the term of this agreement:

A. All the rights which Publisher owns or acquires publicly to perform, and to license others to perform, anywhere in the world, any part or all of the works.

B. The non-exclusive right to record, and to license others to record, any part or all of any of the works on electrical transcriptions, wire, tape, film or otherwise, but only for the purpose of performing such work publicly by means of radio and television or for archive or audition purposes and not for sale to the public or for synchronization (1) with motion pictures intended primarily for theatrical exhibition or (2) with programs distributed by means of syndication to broadcasting stations.

C. The non-exclusive right to adapt or arrange any part or all of any of the works for performance purposes, and to license others to do so.

FOURTH:

A. The rights granted to BMI by subparagraph A of paragraph THIRD hereof shall not include the right to perform or license the performance of more than one song or aria from a dramatic or dramatico-musical work which is an opera, operetta, or musical show or more than five (5) minutes from a dramatic or dramatico-musical work which is a ballet if such performance is accompanied by the dramatic action, costumes or scenery of that dramatic or dramatico-musical work.

B. Publisher, together with all the writers and co-publishers, if any, shall have the right jointly, by written notice to BMI, to exclude from the grant made by subparagraph A of paragraph THIRD hereof performances of works comprising more than thirty (30) minutes of a dramatic or dramatico-musical work, but this right shall not apply to such performances from (1) a score originally written for and performed as part of a theatrical or television film, (2) a score originally written for and performed as part of a radio or television program, or (3) the original cast, sound track or similar album of a dramatic or dramatico-musical work.

C. Publisher retains the right to issue non-exclusive licenses for performances of a work or works (other than to another performing rights licensing organization), provided that within ten (10) days of the issuance of such license BMI is given written notice of the titles of the works and the nature of the performances so licensed by Publisher.

FIFTH:

A. As full consideration for all rights granted to BMI hereunder and as security therefor, BMI agrees to make the following payments to Publisher with respect to each of the works in which BMI has performing rights:

(1) For performances of works on broadcasting stations in the United States, its territories and possessions BMI will pay amounts calculated pursuant to BMI's then standard practices upon the basis of the then current performance rates generally paid by BMI to its affiliated publishers for similar performances of similar compositions. The number of performances for which Publisher shall be entitled to payment shall be estimated by BMI in accordance with its then current system of computing the number of such performances.

It is acknowledged that BMI licenses the works of its affiliates for performance by non-broadcasting means, but that unless and until such time as feasible methods can be devised for tabulation of and payment for such performances, payment will be based solely on broadcast performances. In the event that during the term of this agreement BMI shall es ablish a system of separate payment for non-broadcasting performances, BMI shall pay Publisher upon the basis of the then current performance rates generally paid by BMI to its other affiliated publishers for similar performances of similar compositions.

(2) For performances of works outside of the United States, its territories and possessions BMI will pay to Publisher all monies received by BMI in the United States from any performing rights licensing organization which are designated by such organization as the publisher's share of foreign performance royalties earned by any of the works after the deduction of BMI's then current handling charge applicable to its affiliated publishers.

(3) In the case of works which, or rights in which, are owned by Publisher jointly with one or more other publishers who have granted performing rights therein to BMI, the sum payable to Publisher under this subparagraph A shall be a pro rata share determined on the basis of the number of publishers, unless BMI shall have received from Publisher a copy of an agreement or other document signed by all of the publishers providing for a different division of payment.

B. Notwithstanding the foregoing provisions of this paragraph FIFTH, BMI shall have no obligation to make payment hereunder with respect to (1) any performance of a work which occurs prior to the date on which BMI shall have received from Publisher all of the material with respect to such work referred to in subparagraph A of paragraph TENTH hereof, and in the case of foreign performances, the information referred to in subparagraph B of paragraph FOURTEENTH hereof, or (2) any performance as to which a direct license as described in subparagraph C of paragraph FOURTH hereof has been granted by Publisher, its co-publisher or the writer.

SIXTH:. BMI will furnish statements to Publisher at least twice during each year of the term showing the number of performances of the works as computed pursuant to subparagraph A(1) of paragraph FIFTH hereof, and at least once during each year of the term showing the monies received by BMI referred to in subparagraph A(2) of paragraph FIFTH hereof. Each such statement shall be accompanied by payment of the sum thereby shown to be due to Publisher, subject to all proper deductions, if any, for advances or amounts due to BMI from Publisher.

SEVENTH:

A. Nothing in this agreement requires BMI to continue to license the works subsequent to the termination of this agreement. In the event that BMI continues to license any or all of the works, however, BMI shall continue to make payments to Publisher for so long as Publisher does not make or purport to make directly or indirectly any grant of performing rights in such works to any other licensing organization. The amounts of such payments shall be calculated pursuant to BMI's then current standard practices upon the basis of the then current performance rates generally paid by BMI to its affiliated publishers for similar performances of similar compositions. Publisher agrees to notify BMI by registered or certified mail of any grant or purported grant by Publisher directly or indirectly of performing rights to any other performing rights organization within ten (10) days from the making of such grant or purported grant and if Publisher fails so to inform BMI thereof and BMI makes payments to Publisher for any period after the making of any such grant or purported grant, Publisher agrees to repay to BMI all amounts so paid by BMI promptly on demand. In addition, if BMI inquires of Publisher by registered or certified mail, addressed to Publisher's last known address, whether Publisher has made any such grant or purported grant and Publisher fails to confirm to BMI by registered or certified mail within thirty (30) days of the mailing of such inquiry that Publisher has not made any such grant or purported grant, BMI may, from and after such date, discontinue making any payments to Publisher.

B. BMI's obligation to continue payment to Publisher after the termination of this agreement for performances outside of the United States, its territories and possessions shall be dependent upon BMI's receipt in the United States of payments designated by foreign performing rights licensing organizations as the publisher's share of foreign performance royalties earned by any of the works. Payment of such foreign royalties shall be subject to deduction of BMI's then current handling charge applicable to its affiliated publishers.

C. In the event that BMI has reason to believe that Publisher will receive or is receiving payment from a performing rights licensing organization other than BMI for or based on United States performances of one or more of the works during a period when such works were licensed by BMI pursuant to this agreement, BMI shall have the right to withhold payment for such performances from Publisher until receipt of evidence satisfactory to BMI of the amount so paid to Publisher by such other organization or that Publisher has not been so paid. In the event that Publisher has been so paid, the monies payable by BMI to Publisher for such performances during such period shall be reduced by the amount of the payment from such other organization. In the event that Publisher does not supply such evidence within eighteen (18) months from the date of BMI's request therefor, BMI shall be under no obligation to make any payment to Publisher for performances of such works during such period.

EIGHTH: In the event that this agreement shall terminate at a time when, after crediting all earnings reflected by statements rendered to Publisher prior to the effective date of such termination, there remains an un-earned balance of advances paid to Publisher by BMI, such termination shall not be effective until the close of the calendar quarterly period during which (A) Publisher shall repay such unearned balance of advances, or (B) Publisher shall notify BMI by registered or certified mail that Publisher has received a statement rendered by BMI at its normal accounting time showing that such unearned balance of advances has been fully recouped by BMI.

NINTH:

A. BMI shall have the right, upon written notice to Publisher, to exclude from this agreement, at any time, any work which in BMI's opinion (1) is similar to a previously existing composition and might consti-tute a copyright infringement, or (2) has a title or music or lyric similar to that of a previously existing composi-tion and might lead to a claim of unfair competition, or (3) is offensive, in bad taste or against public morals, or (4) is not reasonably suitable for performance.

B. In the case of works which in the opinion of BMI are based on compositions in the public domain, BMI shall have the right, at any time, upon written notice to Publisher, either (1) to exclude any such work from this agreement, or (2) to classify any such work as entitled to receive only a stated fraction of the full credit that would otherwise be given for performances thereof.

C. In the event that any work is excluded from this agreement pursuant to subparagraph A or B of this paragraph NINTH, or pursuant to subparagraph C of paragraph TWELFTH hereof, all rights of BMI in such work shall automatically revert to Publisher ten (10) days after the date of the notice of such exclusion given by BMI to Publisher. In the event that a work is classified for less than full credit under subparagraph B(2) of this paragraph NINTH, Publisher shall have the right, by giving notice to BMI within ten (10) days after the date of BMI's notice to Publisher of the credit allocated to such work, to terminate all rights in such work granted to BMI herein and all such rights of BMI in such work shall revert to Publisher thirty (30) days after the date of such notice from Publisher to BMI.

TENTH:

A. With respect to each of the works which has been or shall be published or recorded com-mercially or synchronized with motion picture or television film or tape or which Publisher considers likely to be performed, Publisher agrees to furnish to BMI:

(1) Two copies of a completed clearance sheet in the form supplied by BMI, unless a cue sheet with respect to such work is furnished pursuant to subparagraph A(3) of this paragraph TENTH.

(2) If such work is based on a composition in the public domain, a legible lead sheet or other written or printed copy of such work setting forth the lyrics, if any, and music correctly metered; pro-vided that with respect to all other works, such copy need be furnished only if requested by BMI pursuant to sub-section (c) of subparagraph D(2) of this paragraph TENTH.

(3) If such work has been or shall be synchronized with or otherwise used in connec-tion with motion picture or television film or tape, a cue sheet showing the title, composers, publisher and nature and duration of the use of the work in such film or tape.

B. Publisher shall submit the material described in subparagraph A of this paragraph TENTH with respect to works heretofore published, recorded or synchronized within ten (10) days after the execution of this agreement and with respect to any of the works hereafter so published, recorded, synchronized or likely to be per-formed prior to the date of publication or release of the recording, film or tape or anticipated performance.

C. The submission of each clearance sheet or cue sheet shall constitute a warranty by Publisher that all of the information contained thereon is true and correct and that no performing rights in any of the works listed thereon has been granted to or reserved by others except as specifically set forth therein.

D. Publisher agrees:

(1) To secure and maintain copyright protection of the works pursuant to the Copy-right Law of the United States and pursuant to the laws of such other nations of the world where such protection is afforded; and to give BMI prompt written notice of the date and number of copyright registration and/or renewal of each work registered in the United States Copyright Office.

(2) At BMI's request:

(a) To register each unpublished and published work in the United States Copy-right Office pursuant to the Copyright Law of the United States.

(b) To record in the United States Copyright Office in accordance with the Copyright Law of the United States any agreements, assignments, instruments or documents of any kind by which Publisher obtained the right to publicly perform and/or the right to publish, co-publish or sub-publish any of the works.

(c) To obtain and deliver to BMI copies of: unpublished and published works; copyright registration and/or renewal certificates issued by the United States Copyright Office; any of the docu-ments referred to in sub-section (b) above.

E. Publisher agrees to give BMI prompt notice by registered or certified mail in each instance when, pursuant to the Copyright Law of the United States, (1) the rights granted to BMI by Publisher in any work shall revert to the writer or the writer's representative, or (2) copyright protection of any work shall terminate.

ELEVENTH: Publisher warrants and represents that:

A. Publisher has the right to enter into this agreement; Publisher is not bound by any prior commitments which conflict with its undertakings herein; the rights granted by Publisher to BMI herein are the sole and exclusive property of Publisher and are free from all encumbrances and claims; and exercise of such rights will not constitute infringement of copyright or violation of any right of, or unfair competition with, any person, firm, corporation or association.

B. Except with respect to works in which the possession of performing rights by another person, firm, corporation or association is specifically set forth on a clearance sheet or cue sheet submitted to BMI pursuant to subparagraph A of paragraph TENTH hereof, Publisher has exclusive performing rights in each of the works by virtue of written grants thereof to Publisher signed by all the authors and composers or other owners of such work.

TWELFTH:

A. Publisher agrees to defend, indemnify, save and hold BMI, its licensees, the advertisers of its licensees and their respective agents, servants and employees, free and harmless from and against any and all demands, loss, damage, suits, judgments, recoveries and costs, including counsel fees, resulting from any claim of whatever nature arising from or in connection with the exercise of any of the rights granted by Publisher in this agreement; provided, however, that the obligations of Publisher under this paragraph TWELFTH shall not apply to any matter added to, or changes made in, any work by BMI or its licensees.

B. Upon the receipt by any of the parties herein indemnified of any notice, demand, process, papers, writ or pleading, by which any such claim, demand, suit or proceeding is made or commenced against them, or any of them, which Publisher shall be obliged to defend hereunder, BMI shall, as soon as may be practicable, give Publisher notice thereof and deliver to Publisher such papers or true copies thereof, and BMI shall have the right to participate by counsel of its own choice, at its own expense. Publisher agrees to cooperate with BMI in all such matters.

C. In the event of such notification of claim or service of process on any of the parties herein indemnified, BMI shall have the right, from the date thereof, to exclude the work with respect to which a claim is made from this agreement and/or to withhold payment of all sums which may become due pursuant to this agreement or any modification thereof until receipt of satisfactory written evidence that such claim has been withdrawn, settled or adjudicated.

THIRTEENTH: Publisher makes, constitutes and appoints BMI, or its nominee, Publisher's true and lawful attorney, irrevocably during the term hereof, in the name of BMI or that of its nominee, or in Publisher's name, or otherwise, to do all acts, take all proceedings, and execute, acknowledge and deliver any and all instruments, papers, documents, process or pleadings that may be necessary, proper or expedient to restrain infringement of and/or to enforce and protect the rights granted by Publisher hereunder, and to recover damages in respect of or for the infringement or other violation of the said rights, and in BMI's sole judgment to join Publisher and/or others in whose names the copyrights to any of the works may stand, and to discontinue, compromise or refer to arbitration, any such actions or proceedings or to make any other disposition of the disputes in relation to the works; provided that any action or proceeding commenced by BMI pursuant to the provisions of this paragraph THIRTEENTH shall be at its sole expense and for its sole benefit.

FOURTEENTH:

A. It is acknowledged that BMI has heretofore entered into, and may during the term of this agreement enter into, contracts with performing rights licensing organizations for the licensing of public performing rights controlled by BMI in territories outside of the United States, its territories and possessions (hereinafter called "foreign territories"). Upon Publisher's written request, BMI agrees to permit Publisher to grant performing rights in any or all of the works for any foreign territory for which, at the time such request is received, BMI has not entered into any such contract with a performing rights licensing organization; provided, however, that any such grant of performing rights by Publisher shall terminate at such time when BMI shall have entered into such a contract with a performing rights licensing organization covering such foreign territory and shall have notified Publisher thereof. Nothing herein contained, however, shall be deemed to restrict Publisher from assigning to its foreign publisher or representative the right to collect a part or all of the publishers' performance royalties earned by any or all of the works in any foreign territory as part of an agreement for the publication, exploitation or representation of such works in such territory, whether or not BMI has entered into such a contract with a performing rights licensing organization covering such territory.

B. Publisher agrees to notify BMI promptly in writing in each instance when publication, exploitation or other rights in any or all of the works are granted for any foreign territory. Such notice shall set forth the title of the work, the country or countries involved, the period of such grant, the name of the person, firm, corporation or association entitled to collect performance royalties earned in the foreign territory and the amount of such share. Within ten (10) days after the execution of this agreement Publisher agrees to submit to BMI, in writing, a list of all works as to which Publisher has, prior to the effective date of this agreement, granted to any person, firm, corporation or association performing rights and/or the right to collect publisher performance royalties earned in any foreign territory.

C. In the event that BMI transmits to Publisher performance royalties designated as the writer's share of performance royalties earned by any of the works in any foreign territory, Publisher shall promptly pay such royalties to the writer or writers of the works involved. If Publisher is unable for any reason to locate and make payment to any of the writers involved within six (6) months from the date of receipt, the amounts due such writers shall be returned to BMI.

FIFTEENTH:

A. Publisher agrees that Publisher, its agents, employees, representatives or affiliated companies, will not directly or indirectly during the term of this agreement:

(1) Solicit or accept payment from or on behalf of authors for composing music for lyrics, or from or on behalf of composers for writing lyrics to music.

(2) Solicit or accept manuscripts from composers or authors in consideration of any payments to be made by or on behalf of such composers or authors for reviewing, arranging, promotion, publication, recording or any other services connected with the exploitation of any composition.

(3) Permit Publisher's name, or the fact of its affiliation with BMI, to be used by any other person, firm, corporation or association engaged in any of the practices described in subparagraphs A(1) and A(2) of this paragraph FIFTEENTH.

(4) Submit to BMI, as one of the works to come within this agreement, any musical composition with respect to which any payments described in subparagraphs A(1) and A(2) of this paragraph FIFTEENTH have been made by or on behalf of a composer or author to any person, firm, corporation or association.

B. Publisher agrees that Publisher, its agents, employees or representatives will not directly or indirectly during the term of this agreement make any effort to ascertain from, or offer any inducement or consideration to, anyone, including but not limited to any broadcasting licensee of BMI or to the agents, employees or representatives of BMI or of any such licensee, for information regarding the time or times when any such BMI licensee is to report its performances to BMI, or to attempt in any way to manipulate performances or affect the representative character or accuracy of BMI's system of sampling or logging performances.

C. Publisher agrees to notify BMI promptly in writing (1) of any change of firm name of Publisher, and (2) of any change of twenty percent (20%) or more in the ownership thereof.

D. In the event of the violation of any of the provisions of subparagraphs A, B or C of this paragraph FIFTEENTH, BMI shall have the right, in its sole discretion, to terminate this agreement by giving Publisher at least thirty (30) days' notice by registered or certified mail. In the event of such termination, no payments shall be due to Publisher pursuant to paragraph SEVENTH hereof.

SIXTEENTH: In the event that during the term of this agreement (1) mail addressed to Publisher at the last address furnished by it pursuant to paragraph TWENTIETH hereof shall be returned by the post office, or (2) monies shall not have been earned by Publisher pursuant to paragraph FIFTH hereof for a period of two consecutive years or more, or (3) the proprietor, if Publisher is a sole proprietorship, shall die, BMI shall have the right to terminate this agreement on at least thirty (30) days' notice by registered or certified mail addressed to the last address furnished by Publisher pursuant to paragraph TWENTIETH hereof and, in the case of the death of a sole proprietor, to the representative of said proprietor's estate, if known to BMI. In the event of such termination, no payments shall be due Publisher pursuant to paragraph SEVENTH hereof.

SEVENTEENTH: Publisher acknowledges that the rights obtained by it pursuant to this agreement constitute rights to payment of money and that during the term BMI shall hold absolute title to the performing rights granted to BMI hereunder. In the event that during the term Publisher shall file a petition in bankruptcy, such a petition shall be filed against Publisher, Publisher shall make an assignment for the benefit of creditors, Publisher shall consent to the appointment of a receiver or trustee for all or part of its property, Publisher shall file a petition for corporate reorganization or arrangement under the United States bankruptcy laws, Publisher shall institute or shall have instituted against it any other insolvency proceeding under the United States bankruptcy laws or any other applicable law, or, in the event Publisher is a partnership, all of the general partners of said partnership shall be adjudged bankrupts, BMI shall retain title to the performing rights in all works for which clearance sheets shall have theretofore been submitted to BMI and shall subrogate Publisher's trustee in bankruptcy or receiver and any subsequent purchasers from them to Publisher's right to payment of money for said works in accordance with the terms and conditions of this agreement.

EIGHTEENTH: Any controversy or claim arising out of, or relating to, this agreement or the breach thereof. shall be settled by arbitration in the City of New York, in accordance with the Rules of the American Arbitration Association, and judgment upon the award of the arbitrator may be entered in any court having jurisdiction thereof. Such award shall include the fixing of the expenses of the arbitration. including reasonable attorney's fees, which shall be borne by the unsuccessful party.

NINETEENTH: Publisher agrees that it shall not, without the written consent of BMI, assign any of its rights hereunder. No rights of any kind against BMI will be acquired by the assignee if any such purported assignment is made by Publisher without such written consent.

TWENTIETH: Publisher agrees to notify BMI's Department of Performing Rights Administration promptly in writing of any change in its address. Any notice sent to Publisher pursuant to the terms of this agreement shall be valid if addressed to Publisher at the last address so furnished by Publisher.

TWENTY-FIRST: This agreement cannot be changed orally and shall be governed and construed pursuant to the laws of the State of New York.

TWENTY-SECOND: In the event that any part or parts of this agreement are found to be void by a court of competent jurisdiction, the remaining part or parts shall nevertheless be binding with the same force and effect as if the void part or parts were deleted from this agreement.

IN WITNESS WHEREOF, the parties hereto have caused this agreement to be duly executed as of the day and year first above written.

BROADCAST MUSIC, INC.

By ....

Assistant Vice President

....

By ....

(Title of Signer)...

Appendix O

BMI Payment Schedule

Commencing with works cleared on and after January 1, 1984 BMI will adopt a system similar to that of other performing rights organizations throughout the world and consider the payments to writers and publishers as a single unit equal to 200%. Where there is the usual equal division of performance royalties between writer(s) and publisher(s), the total writer(s)' share will be 100%, (½ of the available 200%) and the total publisher(s)' share will be the remaining 100%.

Please note the following rules with respect to the division of the 200% royalty:

1. The publisher(s)' share may not exceed half of the total 200%.

2. If the agreement between the publisher(s) and writer(s) provides for the writer(s) to receive more than half of the 200%, the work should be cleared indicating the percentages allocable to all writers and all publishers so that the total is not more than 200%.

3. Where no rights have been assigned to a publisher, the writer(s) will receive the entire 200% in the same ratio as their respective writer shares.

If BMI is subsequently notified that rights have been assigned to a publisher, BMI will after receipt of such notice credit the publisher with the appropriate share for performances commencing with the quarter in which such notice is received. No retroactive adjustments will be made by BMI.

The following is the payment schedule in effect as of January 1, 1984. It does not constitute a modification or amendment of any agreement to which BMI is a party. The rates described are subject to change by BMI at any time.

PLEASE NOTE: THE RATES DESCRIBED ARE THE MINIMUM RATES WHICH BMI WILL PAY. BECAUSE WE OPERATE ON A NON-PROFIT BASIS, WE DISTRIBUTE ALL AVAILABLE INCOME AND MAY, FROM TIME TO TIME, VOLUNTARILY INCREASE SOME OR ALL OF THE RATES DESCRIBED HEREIN.

When computing royalties earned by a single performance, these minimum rates are multiplied in the case of a network performance by the number of interconnected stations carrying the broadcast. A performance on a local station is multiplied by a statistical multiplier based on the ratio of stations logged to stations licensed in each station classification.

BASE RATES

I. U.S. RADIO FEATURE PERFORMANCES

	LOCAL		NETWORK
	RADIO 1	RADIO 2	
Popular Song	12¢	6¢	12¢
Concert Work	32¢ per min.	14¢ per min.	32¢ per min.

II. U.S. RADIO THEMES

For performances of a work regularly used at the opening and closing of a regularly scheduled program of not less than 25 minutes duration, one-half feature credit is given. Where the theme is used only as opening or closing, payment is made only if the usage consists of a full chorus or a minimum of 45 seconds.

III. U.S. RADIO BACKGROUND MUSIC

No payment is made for performances by radio as background or cue music nor for any partial performance of a work except for thematic use or for the partial performance of a concert work.

IV. U.S. TELEVISION FEATURE PERFORMANCES

	LOCAL*	NETWORK	
		GROUP A	GROUP B
Popular Song	$1.50	$9.00 per station	$5.00 per station
Concert Work	$1.50 per min.	$9.00 per min. per station	$5.00 per min. per station

V. U.S. TELEVISION THEMES

LOCAL*	NETWORK	
	GROUP A	GROUP B
46¢ per ½ hr. show	72¢ per ½ hr. show per station	58¢ per ½ hr. show per station

Superthemes: Themes for shows which have been broadcast on U.S. network Group A for more than 13 weeks will be paid at $2.00 per network station, for a show of any duration of ½ hour or more. To qualify the theme must be the only theme used for the show (other than a theme incorporated in a motion picture or sports film) and must have a duration of not less than 40 seconds as opening and/or closing theme.

VI.   U.S. TELEVISION BACKGROUND MUSIC

LOCAL*	NETWORK	
	GROUP A	GROUP B
42¢ per min.	72¢ per min. per station	52¢ per min. per station

*Please note that all local television rates are subject to change by BMI without prior notice if BMI's income from local television stations is reduced as the direct or indirect result of pending litigation.

VII.   BONUS RATES

A work which has more than 25,000 logged U.S. feature broadcast performances as reflected by BMI's records will thereafter receive the bonus rates described below for U.S. feature broadcast performances other than television network or cable feature performances.

Plateau A: 25,000-49,999 performances: 1½ times the base payment rate
Plateau B: 50,000-299,000 performances: 2 times the base payment rate
Plateau C: 300,000-999,999 performances: 2½ times the base payment rate
Plateau D: 1,000,000 performances and over: 4 times the base payment rate

Please Note:

1. While United States television network, cable and public broadcasting station feature performances will be counted in computing the plateau of a work, such performances themselves are not subject to bonuses.

2. Performances are cumulative and need not have taken place in one specific period. All feature performances logged by BMI for a work from and after January 1, 1960 are counted in determining a song's plateau level.

3. "Special Credit Works": A Special Credit Work is one which meets the qualifications described in subdivisions (a) or (b) of this paragraph and is regarded as such for payment purposes only in connection with United States feature broadcast performances.

(a) "Show Music": a composition from an original score written for and performed for the run of the play in a musical comedy, revue or operetta in a professional production in the United States using Equity performers and for which an original cast album is released. If the musical comedy, revue or operetta is presented in a first-class legitimate Broadway theatre, the composition qualifies as a special credit work as of the opening date regardless of whether a cast album is released. The special credit is applicable to compositions from shows which are presented in theatres other than a first-class legitimate Broadway theatre only if the show opened after October 1, 1966. Such a composition is automatically entitled to Plateau D status.

(b) "Movie Work": a complete musical work originally written for and performed in full in a full-length motion picture released in the United States after October 1, 1966. The work, in order to qualify, must be performed for not less than 40 consecutive seconds as feature work or theme in the motion picture. The words "motion picture" as used herein include a film made for television release if the duration of the air time including commercial announcements and station breaks is not less than a 90 minute period. Such a work cleared prior to January 1, 1980 is entitled to start at Plateau B or, if cleared after January 1, 1980, at Plateau C.

VIII.   GENERAL RULES AND DEFINITIONS

A. A "concert work" is a symphony, concerto or other serious work originally written for concert or opera performance. The indicated credit per minute of performance will be allowed only for feature performances and will not be allowed for popular arrangements of concert works; such arrangements are credited at the applicable rate for a popular song. Such works are not eligible for plateau bonus credit as described in VII hereof.

B. Radio Networks at present are ABC, CBS, MUTUAL and NBC. Television Networks are ABC, CBS and NBC.

IX.   PAYMENT AND CREDITING RULES

A. No credit is given for any composition which has not been cleared through BMI in the manner required by BMI's contract with the affiliate claiming payment except that background credit will be given for television performance of music identified on cue sheets where authorship and/or proprietorship of the publishing rights can be established. A work identified as a feature work on cue sheets will only receive feature credit if it has been submitted via a separate clearance form.

B. BMI does not accept for clearance, license or make payment for material contained on spoken word records unless the music is original (not based on a public domain work) and a substantial part of the recording contains clearly audible music.

C. Payment is being made on an experimental basis for music used in commercials other than network or station promotional announcements. To qualify for payment for such performances, the music must be the sole focus of audience attention for not less than 15 seconds. Forms for submitting commercials should be requested of BMI's Commercial Jingle Department at 320 West 57th Street, New York, New York 10019. No submissions will be accepted hereafter relating to performances prior to July 1, 1983.

D. A work (other than a concert work) which exceeds 7 minutes as commercially recorded may be eligible for additional credit. The clearance form submitted to BMI for such work should be accompanied by a letter specifying that application is being made for consideration for additional credit. Jazz works of a concert nature of 4-6 minutes duration will receive double credit for a full broadcast performance and such works of 7 minutes duration or longer will receive treble credit for a full broadcast performance.

E. BMI cannot undertake to distinguish between lyric and instrumental performances of a work unless the two versions bear different titles.

If the lyric and instrumental versions are known by different titles, performances of the instrumental version will be credited solely to the composer and to the publisher of the instrumental version unless BMI is notified by all parties involved of an agreement between them that the author of the lyric and the publisher of the lyric version are entitled to share in performance royalties of the instrumental version.

Where the lyric and instrumental versions are known by the same title, the lyricist and the publisher of the lyric version will each be credited respectively with 100% of the applicable writer and publisher logging credit for all performances unless BMI is notified by all parties involved of an agreement between them that the lyricist and the publisher of the lyric version are to be credited only for a stated percentage of all logged performances.

F. If more than one musical work is recorded on one side of a 45 RPM record or other mechanical reproduction of equivalent duration: (1) if no more than 2 musical works are involved in such a recording each work receives full logging credit if the performances of each work consist of a full chorus or more or (2) if more than 2 works are used on such a recording, a single logging credit is divided among all the musical works so used in equal shares but BMI will accept a directive from all the publishers of the works involved to divide the single logging credit in percentages agreed upon by such publishers.

The above rule is also applicable to musical works used as a medley, unit or single band on a long playing record or tape except that, if such medley, unit or single band runs in excess of 5 minutes playing time, a full logging credit is awarded to each musical work of which a minute or more is performed and a single logging credit is divided equally among all other works comprising the medley, unit or single band.

G. A work assigned from one BMI publisher to another will be credited to the assignee commencing with the calendar quarter in which BMI receives notice of the assignment. The recognition of such assignment shall be subject to appropriate adjustment with respect to monies advanced by BMI to the assignor publishing company or any other outstanding financial obligation or liability to BMI of the assignor.

H. In the event that BMI has reason to believe that a publisher or writer will receive or is receiving payment from a performing rights licensing organization other than BMI for or based on United States performances of one or more of its works during a period when such works were licensed by BMI pursuant to the publisher's or writer's BMI contract, the monies payable by BMI to the publisher or writer for such performances during such a period shall be reduced by the amount of such payment from such other organization. BMI shall have the right to withhold payment for such performances from the publisher or writer until receipt of evidence satisfactory to BMI of the amount so paid to the publisher or writer by such other organization or that the publisher or writer has not been so paid. In the event that the publisher or writer does not supply such evidence within 18 months from the date of BMI's request therefor, BMI shall be under no obligation to make any payment to the publisher or writer for performances of such works for such period.

I. Performance royalties received by BMI from performing rights organizations outside the Untited States shall be distributed to the affiliate for whom they are, designated after deduction of 3% of the gross amount received for handling and administrative expense.

J. Payment for performances on public broadcasting stations, pay cable and usage of works as commercials will be made on an annual basis. Rates for public broadcasting performances are those applicable to local radio 2 or local television.

X. RADIO PERFORMANCE: RULES AND DEFINITIONS

A. A Radio 1 station is a station which, for the latest calendar year prior to the performance for which figures are available, has paid BMI $4,000 or more. A Radio 2 station is one which for the same period paid less than $4,000.

B. A feature performance is a performance of not less than 90 seconds duration which is the sole sound broadcast at the time of the performance and which therefore constitutes the sole focus of audience attention.

XI. TELEVISION PERFORMANCE: RULES AND DEFINITIONS

A. Group A and Group B Network Programs: A Group A program is any network television program broadcast between the hours of 7:00 P.M. and 1:00 A.M. All network television programs broadcast at other times are deemed Group B programs.

B. FEATURE PERFORMANCE

1. A feature performance is a performance that constitutes the main focus of audience attention at the time of the performance. The vocalists and/or instrumentalists, respectively, must be on camera except where the music is used as part of a choreographic routine which constitutes the main focus of attention.

2. Feature performances of less than 45 seconds will be credited on a pro rata basis. An untimed feature performance will be deemed to be a three second usage. At no time shall accumulation of partial credits for a work total more than one full credit per half-hour show.

C. THEME

A theme comprises both the opening and closing musical works performed on a program. Except for "superthemes", half payment is made where a work is used as an opening or closing but not both. Performances of the theme, other than opening and closing, are credited at background rates. For shows telecast more than three times weekly, theme payment will be at two-thirds of the usual rate.

D. BACKGROUND

1. Background music is music used other than as feature or theme. Music used as background to a promotional or commercial announcement receives no credit.

2. With respect to shows other than those specified in subdivisions 3 to 7 below:

(a) Payment for background music is based on the use of music up to one-half of the duration of the program. For uses in excess of one-half of the duration of the program, a proportional reduction will be made for the purpose of division among the publishers and writers entitled thereto, but payment will not exceed that which would have been made for a usage of one-half of the program duration.

(b) On Group B Network programs broadcast more than three times a week, the rate for background music is one-third the usual rate, unless the music is performed on a single instrument in which case it is computed at one-fourth the usual rate.

3. The rate of payment for background music in full-length motion pictures shown in motion picture theatres in the United States prior to television release or motion pictures made for television whose duration (including commercial and station break announcements) is not less than 90 minutes will be 72¢ per minute when performed as part of the broadcast of the motion picture if such broadcast is on Group A or Group B Network.

4. The rate of payment for background music used on quiz and audience participation shows of one-half hour duration is as follows: Music performed

(a) between one and one-half minutes and three minutes by less than four instruments: 12¢

(b) three minutes or more by less than four instruments, or between one and one-half minutes and three minutes, by four or more instruments: 34¢

(c) between three minutes and eight minutes by four or more instruments: 62¢

(d) more than eight minutes by four or more instruments: $1.24.

Proportional payment will be made for shows of duration other than one-half hour and for any show containing both music licensed by BMI and music not so licensed.

Two-thirds of the rates described in this subdivision shall be payable with respect to a quiz or audience participation show broadcast on Group B Network more than three times a week.

5. Where the log or cue sheet for a program, film or film series does not indicate the timing of the background music involved but indicates the music used and identifies its publishers and/or writers, BMI will assign the credits on the basis of four minutes per half-hour for all categories of shows other than those described in subdivision 6 of this paragraph.

6. Untimed background music used for debates, discussions, newscasts, lectures, commentaries and similar programs shall be deemed a four second usage for each work with a limit of 12 seconds per half-hour.

In the case of untimed music in motion pictures described in subdivision 3 of this paragraph, BMI shall assign the credits on the basis of eight minutes per half-hour.

7. Untimed background music used to mark entrances, exits, play-ons, play-offs and change of scene shall be deemed to be a five second usage for each untimed work.

January, 1984

Trade Associations, Unions, and Guilds

American Federation of Musicians (AF of M), 1500 Broadway, New York, New York 10036 Tel: 212-896-1330

American Federation of Television and Radio Artists (AFTRA) 1350 Avenue of the Americas, New York, New York 10036 Tel: 212-265-7700

American Guild of Musical Artists, 1841 Broadway, New York, New York 10036 Tel: 212-265-3687

American Guild of Variety Artists (AGVA), 184 Fifth Ave., New York, New York 10010 Tel: 212-675-1003

Amusement and Music Operators Assn. 2000 Spring Road, Oak Brook, Illinois 60521 Tel: 312-654-2662

Country Music Assn. (CMA), 7 Music Circle No., Nashville, Tennessee 37203 Tel: 615-244-2840

Dramatists Guild, 234 W. 44 Street, New York, N.Y. 10036 Tel: 212-391-3966

Electronic Industries Assn., Consumer Electronics Division, 2001 I Street, N.W., Wash., D.C. 20006 Tel: 202-457-4900

Gospel Music Assn., P. O. Box 23201 Nashville, Tenn. 37202 Tel: 615-242-0303

International Tape/Disc Association, 10 Columbus Circle, New York, New York 10019 Tel: 965-7110

Music Performance Trust Funds, 1501 Broadway, New York, New York 10036 Tel: 212-391-3950

National Academy of Recording Arts and Sciences (NARAS), Western Chapter, 4444 Riverside Dr., Suite 202, Burbank, Calif. 91505 Tel: 213-843-8233

National Association of Broadcasters, 1771 "N" St., N.W., Washington, D.C. Tel: 202-293-3500

National Assn. of Music Merchants, 500 N. Michigan Ave., Chicago, Illinois 60611 Tel: 312-527-3200

National Assn. of Record Merchandisers (NARM), 1008 F. Astoria Blvd, Suite 200, Cherry Hill, N.J. 08034 Tel: 609-427-1404

National Music Publishers Assn., 110 E. 59th St., New York, New York 10022 Tel: 212-PL 1-1930

Radio Advertising Bureau, 485 Lexington Avenue, New York, New York 10017 Tel: 212-599-6666

Recording Industry Assn. of America, Inc. (RIAA), 888 Seventh Ave., New York, New York 10106 Tel: 212-765-4330

The Songwriters Guild (formerly AGAC), 276 Fifth Ave. New York, New York 10001 Tel: 212-686-6820

Video Software Dealers Association, 1008 F Astoria Blvd, Cherry Hill, N.J. 08034 Tel: 609-424-7117

Reference Materials for Songs, Records, Shows, Films, Composers, and Publishers

All the Years of American Popular Music—A Comprehensive History, David Ewen. A history and survey of popular music with short biographies. Prentice Hall, 1977, 850 pp.

The American Dance Band Discography, Vols. 1 & 2, Brian Rust, discography of popular orchestras showing artists, songs, accompanists, record dates, catalog labels and numbers and brief biographical material, Arlington House, 1975, 2064 pp.

American Music Before 1865 in Print and on Records, a Biblio-Discography, Institute for Studies in American Music, Department of Music/School of Performing Arts, Brooklyn College, CUNY, Brooklyn, New York 11210, 130 pp.

American Music Center Library Catalog of Choral and Vocal Music, compiled by Judith Finnell, lists over 4,000 American works for voice and chorus: American Music Center, 250 W. 57th Street, New York, New York 10019.

American Music Recordings: A Discography of 20th Century U.S.A. Composers, edited by Carol J. Oja, Institute for Studies in American Music, Brooklyn College, CUNY, Brooklyn, New York, 11210, 1982, 10092 entries, 368 pages.

American Popular Songs—From Revolutionary War to the Present, David Ewen, Encyclopedia entries of over 4000 songs plus chronology of Hit Parade songs and best selling records through 1966. Random House, 1966, 505 pp.

An Inventory of the Bibliographies and Other Reference Aids, Prepared by the Archive of Folk Song, Library of Congress: Library of Congress, Music Division, Archive of Folk Song, Washington, D.C. 20540, 1975, 7 pp.

ASCAP 50th Anniversary Hit Tunes, chronological listing of ASCAP-licensed hit songs from 1892 to 1963, as well as ASCAP-licensed Motion Picture Academy Award songs from 1934 to 1963: ASCAP, 1964.

ASCAP Index of Performed Compositions, arranged by song title alphabetically, showing composer, author, and publisher: 3 Volumes, ASCAP, 1963; 2 Volumes, ASCAP, 1952; 1 Volume, ASCAP, 1942.

ASCAP Index of Program Listings, arranged by song title alphabetically, showing composer, author, and publisher, and respective shares and number of performance credits then recorded: 1 Volume, ASCAP, 1938.

ASCAP Biographical Dictionary of Composers, Authors and Publishers, 1966 Edition, compiled and edited by The Lynn Farnol Group, Inc.: brief authorized biographies of ASCAP writers showing date and place of birth and important songs, shows, and films, and names and addresses of ASCAP publishers: ASCAP, One Lincoln Plaza, New York, New York 10023, 845 pages.

Billboard Index, 1971, 1972–73, guide to articles, and features in *BILLBOARD* 1971, 1972, and 1973 issues, showing people, company or conceptual information: The Billboard Bookshelf, 2160 Patterson Street, Cincinnati, Ohio 45214.

Blue Book of Tin Pan Alley, Jack Burton. An anthology of American popular music containing lists of songs and short biographies of leading writers, without music and lyrics: Century House, Watkins Glen, N.Y., 1951, 520 pp.

Blue Book of Broadway Musicals, Jack Burton. Chronological list of musical plays from 1900 to 1950 indicating writers of play and of music and stars of show: Century House, Watkins Glen, N.Y., 1952, 320 pp. (New ed. available.)

Blue Book of Hollywood Musicals, Jack Burton. Songs from film soundtracks and the stars who sang them, listed chronologically from beginning of sound films to 1950, indicating names of writers, stars who sang them and some record album data: Century House, Watkins Glen, N.Y., 1953, 296 pp.

BMI Performindex No. 7, with alphabetical index and index by categories of Concert, Country, Film, Theatre, Television, Instrumental, Jazz, Latin-American, Popular, Religious, and Rhythm and Blues: 1 volume, BMI, 1964.

Check-List of Recorded Songs in the English Language in the Archive of American Folk Song to July, 1940, alphabetical list with geographical index: Arno Press, New York, 1971 reprint edition, 3 volumes.

Complete Encyclopedia of Pop Music & Jazz (4 volumes) 1900–1950 by Roger D. Kinkle— Arlington House.

Country Music Encyclopedia, Melvin Shestack, Over 200 artist biographies plus discography of artists showing title, label and record number and additional listing of radio stations specializing in country music showing call letters, place on dial and locale. Thomas Y. Crowell, 1974, 410 pp.

Dictionary of Musical Themes, Harold Barlow and Sam Morganstern, alphabetical listing by notation in common musical key of some 10,000 instrumental classical music themes and index of titles, useful for song sleuths, Crown 1948, 656 pp. (also companion volume of themes from operas etc. under title).

Dictionary of Opera and Song Themes, same authors and publishers, 1966, 547 pp.

Doctoral Dissertations in American Music: A Classified Bibliography, Rita H. Mead, surveys 1226 dissertations, Institute for Studies in American Music, Department of Music/School of Performing Arts, Brooklyn College, CUNY, Brooklyn, New York 11210, 1974.

Early American Sheet Music: Its Lure and Its Lore, Harry Dichter and Elliot Shapiro. Review of sheet music from 1768 to 1885 including a directory of early American Publishers: R. Bowker Co., N.Y., 1941, 287 pp.[1]

Encyclopedia of Folk, Country and Western Music, Irwin Stambler and Grelun Landon, artist and group brief biographies and some entries for instruments, festivals, etc. St. Martin's Press, 1969, 396 pp.

Encyclopedia of Pop, Rock and Soul, Irwin Stambler, artist and group biographies plus special similar section on British acts since the Beatles and appendices showing Record Industry Association of America Gold Records, Grammy Awards by category and Oscar Nominees and winners. Griffin Books, St. Martin's Press, 1974, 604 pp.

Encyclopedia of Popular Music, Irwin Stambler, Song histories and brief biographies of artists and composers—includes approximately 70 synopses of stage musicals from 1925 to 1965. St. Martin's Press, 1965, 359 pp.

Flashes of Merriment, Lester Levy, study of American sheet music: University of Oklahoma, Norman, Okla.

Folk Music Source Book, Larry Sandberg and Dick Weissman, a guide to North American folk music from blues to ragtime, string band, blue grass, Canadian and Chicano music. Annotated listings of artists, composers, music terms includes index to instruction books, record collections, etc. Alfred A. Knopf, 1976, 260 pp.

Folk Recordings, list of titles and contents of LP folk recordings selected from the Archive of Folk Song: Library of Congress, Music Division, Recorded Sound Section, Washington, D.C. 20540, rev. 8/76, 29 pp.

Give Me Yesterday, Lester Levy, third in a trilogy on American popular culture: University of Oklahoma, Norman, Oklahoma.

Grace Notes, Lester Levy, study of American sheet music: University of Oklahoma, Norman, Okla.

Great Songs of Madison Avenue, Edited by Peter and Craig Norback, musical arrangements and autography by Kenneth J. Costa. Words and music of 115 jingles, Quadrangle/The New York Times Book Company, 1976, 251 pages.

Index of American Popular Music, Jack Burton. Index of individual song titles for cross reference purposes to the Blue Book Series by same author for further information: Century House, Watkins Glen, N.Y., 1957, unpaged.[1]

---

[1] Out of print.

Music for Patriots, Politicians, and Presidents, Vera Brodsky Lawrence, American history through song, contains facsimiles, cartoons, engravings, broadsides, sheet music covers, the music itself and a fast-running text: Macmillan 866 Third Ave., New York, New York 10022, 1975.

New Grove Dictionary of Music and Musicians (20 volumes), 6th Edition, Stanley Sadie, a world encyclopedia of music covering every musical subject. Grove's Dictionary of Music, 1980.

Old English Popular Music, William Chappell (Revised Edition by Wooldridge). Melody and lyrics and musicology notes of songs, ballads and dance tunes from ancient days of 1251 through 1762: Jack Brussell, Publisher, 100 Fourth Ave., New York, New York 10003, 1961, 498 pp.

Popular Music, Volumes 1 through 6, Annotated index of songs from 1950 to 1959 (volume 1) and in successive chronology by other volumes, lists title, composer, publisher, record artists and label, Adrian Press, 1964–1973, 345 pp.

Record Research, Joel Whitburn. An index by artist and title of each singles and album recording which appeared in the following BILLBOARD charts: "Top Pop" 1940–1955, "Hot 100" 1955–1976, "Top LP's" 1945–1976, "Country & Western" 1949–1976, "Rhythm & Blues (Soul)" 1949–1976, and "Easy Listening" 1961–1974. Includes for each charted record: Date, top chart position, weeks on chart, and label and catalog number. Record Research Inc., P.O. Box 200, Menomonee Falls, Wis. 53051, 1976.

Rock Encyclopedia, Lillian Roxon, brief biographies of arts and groups and miscellaneous other entries, Grosset, 1969, 611 pp.

Schwann Record and Tape Guide, alphabetical and category listing of currently available discs and tapes, categories by "classical" "jazz", "musicals", "current popular" and "movies" showing artist, title, label, index number and price code issued with monthly supplements, W. Schwann, Inc., Boston, Mass.

Solid Gold, The Popular Record Industry, R. Serge Denisoff, the relationship of artist to record company, production, marketing and distribution of records, and special emphasis on demography of record buying public: Transaction Books, P.O. Box 978, Edison, N.J. 08903, 1975, 359 pp.

Song Index, Minnie Earl Sears. An index to more than 12,000 songs in 177 song collections (supplement contains 7,000 additional songs) indexed by song title, composer or author and first line with code reference to collections in which song is available. Does not include popular songs. Includes extensive bibliography: H.W. Wilson Co., 1926, 650 pp. supplement, 1934, 366 pp.; reprinted by Archen and Shoestring, 1966.

Songs of the American Theatre, Richard Lewine and Alfred Simon, a listing of more than 12,000 songs including selected titles from film and television productions through 1971, and all Broadway and off-Broadway productions since 1925 and selected works from earlier dates, indicates cast album and printed music issuance, Dodd, Mead & Co. 1971, 820 pp.

The Contemporary Music Performance Directory, compiled by Judith Finnell, everything you want to know about performing groups, facilities and concerts: American Music Center, 250 W. 57th Street, New York 10019.

United States Music, Sources of Bibliography and Collective Biography, Richard Jackson, Institute for Studies in American History, Department of Music/School of Performing Arts, Brooklyn College, New York 11210, 1973

Appendix R

Work Permit Map and Address List

Regional and District Office Locations

Regional Offices

Eastern Region (BUR)	Burlington, VT 05401 Federal Building Elmwood Ave.
Northern Region (TWC)	Federal Building Fort Snelling Twin Cities, MN 55111
Southern Region (DLS)	Dallas, TX 75270 Skyline Center Bldg. C 311 North Stemmons Freeway
Western Region (SPD)	San Pedro, CA 90731 Terminal Island

District Offices

District	
32 (ANC)	Anchorage, AK 99513 New Federal Building 701 C Street, Rm. D229
26 (ATL)	Atlanta, GA 30303 Richard B. Russell Federal Office Bldg. 75 Spring St. S.W., Rm. 1408
5 (BAL)	Baltimore, MD 21201 E. A. Garmatz Federal Building 100 South Hanover Street
2 (BOS)	Boston, MA 02203 John Fitzgerald Kennedy Federal Bldg., Government Center
7 (BUF)	Buffalo, NY 14202 68 Court Street
9 (CHI)	Chicago, IL 60604 Dirksen Federal Office Bldg. 219 South Dearborn St.
24 (CLE)	Cleveland, OH 44199 Rm. 1917, Anthony J. Celebreeze Federal Office Building 1240 East 9th Street
20 (DAL)	Dallas, TX 75242 Room 6A21, Federal Building 1100 Commerce Street

19 (DEN)	Denver, CO 80202 1787 Federal Building 1961 Stout Street
8 (DET)	Detroit, MI 48207 Federal Building 333 Mt. Elliott Street
15 (ELP)	El Paso, TX 79984 343 U.S. Courthouse P.O. Box 9398
40 (HLG)	Harlingen, TX 78550 2102 Teege Road
23 (HAR)	Hartford, CT 06105 900 Asylum Avenue
30 (HEL)	Helena, MT 59626 Federal Building, Room 512 301 South Park, Drawer 10036
17 (HHW)	Honolulu, HI 96809 P.O. Box 461 595 Ala Moana Boulevard
38 (HOU)	Houston, TX 77004 2627 Caroline Street
11 (KAN)	Kansas City, MO 64106 Suite 1100 324 E. Eleventh Street
16 (LOS)	Los Angeles, CA 90012 300 North Los Angeles Street
6 (MIA)	Miami, FL 33130 155 South Miami Ave.
21 (NEW)	Newark, NJ 07102 Federal Building 970 Broad Street
28 (NOL)	New Orleans, LA 70113 Postal Service Building 701 Loyola Avenue
3 (NYC)	New York, NY 10007 26 Federal Plaza
29 (OMA)	Omaha, NE 68102 Federal Office Building 106 South 15th Street, Room 1008
4 (PHI)	Philadelphia, PA 19106 Room 1321 U.S. Courthouse Independence Mall West 601 Market Street

District	District Offices
18 (PHO)	Phoenix, AZ 85025 Federal Building 230 North First Avenue
22 (POM)	Portland, ME 04112 76 Pearl Street
31 (POO)	Portland, OR 97209 Federal Office Bldg. 511 N.W. Broadway
1 (STA)	St. Albans, VT 05478 Federal Building P.O. Box 328
10 (SPM)	St. Paul, MN 55101 932 New Post Office Building 180 East Kellogg Blvd
14 (SNA)	San Antonio, TX 78206 U.S. Federal Building 727 East Durango Suite A301
39 (SND)	San Diego, CA 92188 880 Front Street
13 (SFR)	San Francisco, CA 94111 Appraisers Building 630 Sansome Street
27 (SAJ)	San Juan, PR 00936 GPO Box 5068 San Juan, P.R.
12 (SEA)	Seattle, WA 98134 815 Airport Way, South
25 (WAS)	Washington, DC 20538 25 E St. N.W.

District Offices in Foreign Countries

33 (HKC)	Hong Kong, B.C.C. District Director U.S. Immigration and Naturalization Service c/o American Consulate General Box 30 FPO San Francisco, CA 96659 Street Address (NOT FOR MAIL) St. John's Bldg., Room 39 Garden Road, Hong Kong, B.C.C.
35 (MEX)	Mexico City, Mexico District Director U.S. Immigration and Naturalization Service c/o American Embassy Aparato Postal 88 BIS Mexico 5, D.F., Mexico
37 (RIT)	Rome, Italy U.S. Immigration and Naturalization Service c/o American Embassy APO New York, N.Y. 09794 Street Address (NOT FOR MAIL) Via V. Veneto 119

Other Offices from which information concerning immigration and naturalization service matters may be obtained

17 (AGA)	Agana, GU 96910 U.S. Immigration and Naturalization Service 801 Pacific News Bldg. 238 O'Hara Street
7 (ALB)	Albany, NY 12207 Rm. 220, U.S. Post Office & Courthouse 445 Broadway
26 (CLT)	Charlotte, NC 28205 1111 Hawthorne Lane
24 (CIN)	Cincinnati, OH 45201 U.S. Post Office and Courthouse P.O. Box 537, 5th & Walnut Streets
9 (HMM)	Hammond, IN 46320 104 Federal Bldg., 507 State Street
13 (LVG)	Las Vegas, NV 89101 Federal Bldg., U.S. Courthouse 300 Las Vegas Blvd. South
28 (MEM)	Memphis, TN 38103 814 Federal Office Bldg. 167 North Main Street
9 (MIL)	Milwaukee, WI 53202 Room 186, Federal Building 517 East Wisconsin Avenue
25 (NOR)	Norfolk, VA 23510 Norfolk Federal Building 200 Granby Mall, Room 439
4 (PIT)	Pittsburgh, PA 15222 2130 Federal Building 1000 Liberty Avenue
2 (PRO)	Providence, RI 02903 Federal Building, U.S. Post Office Exchange Terrace
13 (REN)	Reno, NV 89502 Suite 150 350 South Center St.

11	St. Louis, MO 63101
(STL)	Room 423
	U.S. Courthouse and
	Customhouse
	1114 Market Street

19	Salt Lake City, UT 84138
(SLC)	Room 4103 Federal Building
	125 South State Street

| 12 | Spokane, WA 99201 |
| (SPO) | 691 U.S. Courthouse Building |

WORK PERMIT MAP

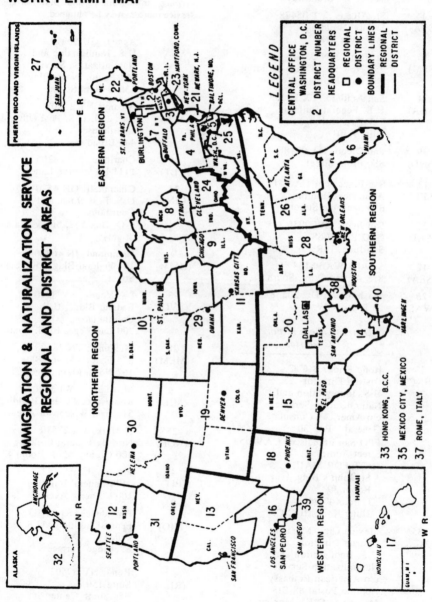

IMMIGRATION & NATURALIZATION SERVICE
REGIONAL AND DISTRICT AREAS

AFTRA Rates, April 1, 1985

1) PENSION AND WELFARE CONTRIBUTIONS—9%

2) ARTISTS RATES:

a) *Solos & Duos:*
   $110

b) *Groups:*

3–8	$50
9–16	$38
17–24	$33.25
25–35 (non-classical)	$28.25
36 or more (non-classical)	$24.00

   Min. Call—Twice the above figures

c) *Actors etc.:*

Actors & Comedians	$84.00
Narrators & Announcers	$95.00

   Min. Call—Twice the above figures

d) *Original Cast Albums:*

Broadway	Minimum $300
Off-Broadway	Minimum $220

e) *Sound Effects Artists:*

First hour	$79.50
Additional half-hour	$29.75

f) *Contractors:*

3–8	$25.00
9–16	$29.50
17–24	$35.25
25–35	$43.25
36 or more	$51.25

Selected Bibliographies on Copyright

This bibliography contains reference material relevant both to copyright issues under the Copyright Act of 1976 (the general revision of the copyright law which became effective January 1, 1978), and to the previous 1909 statute, which the revision supersedes. The copyright statute is found in title 17 of the United States Code.

The list of works is not intended to be exhaustive, nor does the Copyright Office necessarily endorse the works listed. Year dates of publications have not been given for works revised annually or at frequent intervals.

United States:

American Law Institute-American Bar Association. **The Copyright Act of 1976.** Philadelphia: American Law Institute-American Bar Association, 1977.

Bush, George P. **Technology and Copyright: Sources and Materials.** Mt. Airy, Md.: Lomond Books, 1979.

Chickering, Robert B., and Susan Hartman. **How to Register a Copyright and Protect Your Creative Work.** New York: Charles Scribner's Sons, 1980.

Commerce Clearing House. **Copyright Law Reporter.** Chicago: Commerce Clearing House, 1980. (2 v. looseleaf).

Copyright Law Symposium. Nathan Burkan Memorial Competition, sponsored by the American Society of Composers, Authors, and Publishers. New York: Columbia University Press, 1939—. (The essays contained in each volume are selected annually for inclusion.)

Copyright Society of the U.S.A. **Bulletin.** New York: New York University Law Center, 1953—. (Published bimonthly.)

Copyright Society of the U.S.A. **Studies on Copyright.** Compiled and edited under the supervision of the Copyright Society of the U.S.A. 2 v. Arthur Fisher Memorial Edition. South Hackensack, N.J.: F. B. Rothman, and Indianapolis: Bobbs-Merrill Co., 1963.

Crawford, Tad. **The Writer's Legal Guide.** New York: Hawthorn Books, Inc., 1977.

Gaston, Janice B. **The New Copyright Law: A Handbook for Noncommercial Broadcasters.** Washington, D.C.: National Public Radio, 1978 (loose-leaf).

Henn, Harry G. **Copyright Primer.** New York: Practicing Law Institute, 1979.

Hirsch, E. G. **Copyright It Yourself.** Wheeling, Ill.: Whitehall, Co., 1979.

Hurst, Walter E. **Copyright: How to Register Your Copyright & Introduction to New & Historical Copyright Law.** Hollywood, Cal.: Seven Arts Press, 1977.

Hurst, Walter E. **Copyright Registration Forms PA & SR: How to Prepare Applications to Register Songs, Movies, Performing Arts Works & Sound Recordings with the U.S. Copyright Office.** 1st ed. Hollywood, Cal.: Seven Arts Press, 1979.

Johnston, Donald F. **Copyright Handbook.** New York: R. R. Bowker Co., 1978.

Kaplan, Benjamin, and Ralph S. Brown, Jr. **Cases on Copyright, Unfair Competition, and Other Topics Bearing on the Protection of Literary, Musical, and Artistic Works.** 3d. ed. by Ralph S. Brown, Jr. Mineola, N.Y.: Foundation Press, 1978.

Latman, Alan. **The Copyright Law: Howell's Copyright Law Revised and the 1976 Act.** 5th ed. Washington, D.C.: Bureau of National Affairs, 1979.

Latman, Alan, and Ralph Gorman. **Copyright for the Eighties. Cases and Materials.** Charlottesville, Va.: Michie Bobbs-Merrill, 1981.

Lindey, Alexander. **Lindey on Entertainment, Publishing and Arts; Agreements and the Law.** New York: Clark Boardman, 1980— (loose-leaf).

Medical Library Association. **The Copyright Law and the Health Sciences Librarian.** Chicago: Medical Library Association, 1978.

Nimmer, Melville B. **Cases and Materials on Copyright and Other Aspects of Law Pertaining to Literary, Musical and Artistic Works.** 2d ed. (American Casebook Series). St. Paul: West Publishing Co., 1979.

Nimmer, Melville B. **Nimmer on Copyright.** Albany, N.Y.: M. Bender, 1982 (4 v. loose-leaf).

Patent, Trademark & Copyright Journal. Washington, D.C.: Bureau of National Affairs, 1970—. (Beginning with November 5, 1970, published every Thursday except the Thursday following July 4 and the last Thursday in December.)

Patterson, Lyman Ray. **Copyright in Historical Perspective.** Nashville: Vanderbilt University Press, 1968.

Ringer, Barbara. **The demonology of copyright.** New York: R.R. Bowker Co., 1974.

Rosenberg, Peter D. **Patent Law Fundamentals.** New York: Clark Boardman, 1980.

Shemel, Sidney, and M. William Krasilovsky. **This Business of Music.** Edited by Paul Ackerman. Rev. and enl. 4th ed. New York: Billboard Publications, Inc., 1979.

Sparkman, Joseph B. **Copyright Primer for Film and Video.** Portland, Ore.: Northwest Media Project, 1978.

Tucciarone, Angel. **Copyright and the Church Musician.** Pittsburgh: Diocese of Pittsburgh, 1977.

United States, National Commission on New Technological Uses of Copyrighted Works (CONTU). **Final Report of CONTU on New Technological Uses of Copyrighted Works.** Washington, D.C.: Library of Congress, 1979.

Wincor, Richard. **Copyright, Patents, and Trademarks: The Protection of Intellectual and Industrial Property.** Dobbs Ferry, N.Y.: Oceana Publications, 1980.

Wittenberg, Philip. **The Protection of Literary Property.** Boston: The Writer, Inc., 1978.

British and Canadian:

Copinger, Walter Arthur. **Copinger and Skone James on the Law of Copyright.** 12th ed., by E.P. Skone James. London: Sweet & Maxwell, 1980.

Fox, Harold G. **The Canadian Law of Copyright and Industrial Designs.** 2d ed. Toronto: Carswell Co., 1967.

Keyes, A.A. **Copyright in Canada: Proposals for a Revision of the Law.** Hull, Que.: Consumer and Corporate Affairs Canada, 1977.

International:

Bogsch, Arpad L. **The Law of Copyrights Under the Universal Convention.** 3d rev. ed. Leyden: A.W. Sijhoff; New York: R.R. Bowker, 1968.

Copyright; Monthly Review of the World Intellectual Property Organization (WIPO). Geneva: WIPO, 1965—.

Copyright Laws and Treaties of the World. Compiled by the United Nations Educational, Scientific, and Cultural Organization with the cooperation of the Copyright Office of the United States of America and the Industrial Property Department of the Board of Trade of the United Kingdom of Great Britain and Northern Ireland. Edited by Arpad L. Bogsch, Harold W. Clarke, Juan O. Diaz-Lewis, Abe A. Goldman, and Thomas Ilosvay. 3 v. Paris: UNESCO; Washington, D.C.: Bureau of National Affairs, 1956—(loose-leaf). Kept up-to-date by annual supplements, 1957—.

Newcity, Michael A. **Copyright Law in the Soviet Union.** New York: Praeger, 1978.

Russell-Clarke, Alan Daubeny. **Russell-Clarke on Copyright in Industrial Designs.** 5th ed. London: Sweet & Maxwell, 1974.

Thomas, Denis. **Copyright and the Creative Artist: The Protection of Intellectual Property with Special Reference to Music.** London: Institute of Economic Affairs, 1967.

United Nations Educational, Scientific and Cultural Organization. Copyright Division. **Copyright Bulletin.** Paris, 1967—. (Published quarterly.)

Universal Copyright Convention Analyzed. Edited by Theodore R. Kupferman and Mathew Foner. New York: Federal Legal Publications, 1955.

Selected Bibliography for Writers

Audiovisual Market Place. New York: R. R. Bowker Co.
Guide to Book-Publishing. New York: R. R. Bowker Co.
International Literary Market Place. New York: R. R. Bowker Co.
International Motion Picture Almanac. New York: Quigley Publishing Co., Inc.
International Television Almanac. New York: Quigley Publishing Co., Inc.
LMP (Literary Market Place). New York: R. R. Bowker Co.
Literary & Library Prizes. New York: R. R. Bowker Co.
The Writer. Boston: The Writer, Inc. (Published monthly.)
Writers' & Artists' Yearbook. Boston: The Writer, Inc.
Writer's Digest. Cincinnati: Writer's Digest, Inc. (Published monthly.)
Writer's Handbook. Boston: The Writer, Inc.
Writer's Market. Cincinnati: Writer's Digest, Inc.
Writer's Yearbook. Cincinnati: Writer's Digest, Inc.

Selected Bibliography for Artists

American Artist. New York: Billboard Publications, Inc. (Published monthly.)
Art in America. New York: Art in America. (Published bimonthly.)
Artist's Market. Cincinnati: Writer's Digest, Inc.
ARTnews. New York: ARTnews Associates. (Published ten times a year.)
Chamberlain, Betty. **The Artist's Guide to His Market.** New York: Watson-Guptill Publications.
Fine Arts Market Place. New York: R. R. Bowker Co.

Selected Bibliography for Musicians

Billboard. New York: Billboard Publications, Inc. (Published weekly.)
Dachs, David. **Anything Goes: The World of Popular Music.** Indianapolis: The Bobbs-Merrill Co., Inc.
Erickson, J. Gunnar; Hearn, Edward R., and Halloran, Mark E., **Musician's Guide to Copyright.** New York: Charles Scribner's Sons, 1983.
The Musician's Guide. New York: Music Information Service, Inc.
Pavlakis, Christopher. **The American Music Handbook.** New York: The Free Press.
Rachlin, Harvey. **The Encyclopedia of the Music Business.** New York: Harper and Row, 1981.
Shemel, Sidney, and M. William Krasilovsky, **More About This Business of Music.** New York: Billboard Publications, Inc., 1982.
Shemel, Sidney, and M. William Krasilovsky. **This Business of Music.** New York: Billboard Publications, Inc., 1979.
Variety. New York: Variety, Inc. (Published weekly.)

Form 1

Songwriter Contract Form of The Songwriters Guild (Formerly American Guild of Authors and Composers)

NOTE TO SONGWRITERS: (A) DO NOT SIGN THIS CONTRACT IF IT HAS ANY CHANGES UNLESS YOU HAVE FIRST DISCUSSED SUCH CHANGES WITH AGAC; (B) FOR YOUR PROTECTION PLEASE SEND A FULLY EXECUTED COPY OF THIS CONTRACT TO AGAC.

Popular Songwriters Contract   © Copyright 1978 AGAC

AGREEMENT made this ——————— day of ——————— , 19 ———— , between

———————————————————————————————————————

(hereinafter called "Publisher") and ———————————————————————

———————————————————————————————————————

(Jointly and/or severally hereinafter collectively called "Writer");

Witnesseth:

Composition
(Insert title of composition here) ⟶

1. The Writer hereby assigns, transfers and delivers to the Publisher a certain heretofore unpublished original musical composition, written and/or composed by the above-named Writer now entitled ———————————————

   (hereinafter referred to as "the composition"), including the title, words and music thereof, and the right to secure copyright therein throughout the entire world, and to have and to hold the said copyright and all rights of whatsoever nature

(Insert number of years here) ⟶ thereunder existing, for ———————————————

   not more than 40

   years from the date of this contract or 35 years from the date of the first release of a commercial sound recording of the composition, whichever term ends earlier, unless this contract is sooner terminated in accordance with the provisions hereof.

Performing
Rights Affiliation
(Delete Two) ⟶

2. In all respects this contract shall be subject to any existing agreements between the parties hereto and the following small performing rights licensing organization with which Writer and Publisher are affiliated:

   (ASCAP, BMI, SESAC). Nothing contained herein shall, or shall be deemed to, alter, vary or modify the rights of Writer and Publisher to share in, receive and retain the proceeds distributed to them by such small performing rights licensing organization pursuant to their respective agreement with it.

Warranty

3. The Writer hereby warrants that the composition is his sole, exclusive and original work, that he has full right and power to make this contract, and that there exists no adverse claim to or in the composition, except as aforesaid in Paragraph 2

571

hereof and except such rights as are specifically set forth in Paragraph 23 hereof.

Royalties 4. In consideration of this contract, the Publisher agrees to pay the Writer as follows:

(Insert amount of advance here) → (a) $ _____ as an advance against royalties, receipt of which is hereby acknowledged, which sum shall remain the property of the Writer and shall be deductible only from payments hereafter becoming due the Writer under this contract.

Piano Copies (b) In respect of regular piano copies sold and paid for in the United States and Canada, the following royalties per copy:

Sliding Scale → _____ % (in no case, however, less than 10%) of the wholesale selling price of the first 200,000 copies or less; plus

(Insert percentage here) → _____ % (in no case, however, less than 12%) of the wholesale selling price of copies in excess of 200,000 and not exceeding 500,000; plus

→ _____ % (in no case, however, less than 15%) of the wholesale selling price of copies in excess of 500,000.

Foreign Royalties *(Insert percentage here)* → (c) _____ % (in no case, however, less than 50%) of all net sums received by the Publisher in respect of regular piano copies, orchestrations, band arrangements, octavos, quartets, arrangements for combinations of voices and/or instruments, and/or other copies of the composition sold in any country other than the United States and Canada, provided, however, that if the Publisher should sell such copies through, or cause them to be sold by, a subsidiary or affiliate which is actually doing business in a foreign country, then in respect of such sales, the Publisher shall pay to the Writer not less than 5% of the marked retail selling price in respect of each such copy sold and paid for.

Orchestrations and Other Arrangements, etc. (d) In respect of each copy sold and paid for in the United States and Canada, or for export from the United States, of orchestrations, band arrangements, octavos, quartets, arrangements for combinations of voices and/or instruments, and/or other copies of the composition (other than regular piano copies) the following royalties on the wholesale selling price (after trade discounts, if any):

(Insert percentage here) → _____ % (in no case, however, less than 10%) on the first 200,000 copies or less; plus

→ _____ % (in no case, however, less than 12%) on all copies in excess of 200,000 and not exceeding 500,000; plus

→ _____ % (in no case, however, less than 15%) on all copies in excess of 500,000.

Publisher's Song Book, Folio, etc. (e) (i) If the composition, or any part thereof, is included in any song book, folio or similar publication issued by the Publisher containing at least four, but not more than twenty-five musical compositions, the royalty to be paid by the Publisher to the Writer shall be an amount determined by dividing 10% of the wholesale selling price (after trade discounts, if any) of the copies sold, among the total number of the Publisher's copyrighted musical compositions included in such publication. If such publication contains more than twenty-five musical compositions, the said 10% shall be increased by an additional ½% for each additional musical composition.

Licensee's
Song Book,
Folio, etc.

(ii) If, pursuant to a license granted by the Publisher to a licensee not controlled by or affiliated with it, the composition, or any part thereof, is included in any song book, folio or similar publication, containing at least four musical compositions, the royalty to be paid by the Publisher to the Writer shall be that proportion of 50% of the gross amount received by it from the licensee, as the number of uses of the composition under the license and during the license period, bears to the total number of uses of the Publisher's copyrighted musical compositions under the license and during the license period.

(iii) In computing the number of the Publisher's copyrighted musical compositions under subdivisions (i) and (ii) hereof, there shall be excluded musical compositions in the public domain and arrangements thereof and those with respect to which the Publisher does not currently publish and offer for sale regular piano copies.

(iv) Royalties on publications containing less than four musical compositions shall be payable at regular piano copy rates.

Professional Material
and Free Copies

(f) As to "professional material" not sold or resold, no royalty shall be payable. Free copies of the lyrics of the composition shall not be distributed except under the following conditions: (i) with the Writer's written consent; or (ii) when printed without music in limited numbers for charitable, religious or governmental purposes, or for similar public purposes, if no profit is derived, directly or indirectly; or (iii) when authorized for printing in a book, magazine or periodical, where such use is incidental to a novel or story (as distinguished from use in a book of lyrics or a lyric magazine or folio), provided that any such use shall bear the Writer's name and the proper copyright notice; or (iv) when distributed solely for the purpose of exploiting the composition, provided, that such exploitation is restricted to the distribution of limited numbers of such copies for the purpose of influencing the sale of the composition, that the distribution is independent of the sale of any other musical compositions, services, goods, wares or merchandise, and that no profit is made, directly or indirectly, in connection therewith.

(Insert percentage here) ⟶ (g)
Mechanicals, Electrical
Transcription,
Synchronization, All
Other Rights

_____ % (in no case, however, less than 50%) of: All gross receipts of the Publisher in respect of any licenses (including statutory royalties) authorizing the manufacture of parts of instruments serving to mechanically reproduce the composition, or to use the composition in synchronization with sound motion pictures, or to reproduce it upon electrical transcription for broadcasting purposes; and of any and all gross receipts of the Publisher from any other source or right now known or which may hereafter come into existence, except as provided in paragraph 2.

Licensing Agent's
Charges

(h) If the Publisher administers licenses authorizing the manufacture of parts of instruments serving to mechanically reproduce said composition, or the use of said composition in synchronization or in timed relation with sound motion pictures or its reproduction upon electrical transcriptions, or any of them, through an agent, trustee or other administrator acting for a substantial part of the industry and not under the exclusive control of the Publisher (hereinafter sometimes referred to as licensing agent), the Publisher, in determining his receipts, shall be entitled to deduct from gross license fees paid by the Licensees, a sum equal to the charges paid by the Publisher to said licensing agent, provided, however, that in respect to synchronization or timed relation with sound motion pictures, said deduction shall in no event exceed $150.00 or 10% of said gross license fee, whichever is less; in connection with the manufacture of parts of instruments serving to mechanically reproduce said composition, said deductions shall not exceed 5% of said gross license fee; and in connection with electrical transcriptions, said deduction shall not exceed 10% of said gross license fee.

Block Licenses (i) The Publisher agrees that the use of the composition will not be included in any bulk or block license heretofore or hereafter granted, and that it will not grant any bulk or block license to include the same, without the written consent of the Writer in each instance, except (i) that the Publisher may grant such licenses with respect to electrical transcription for broadcasting purposes, but in such event, the Publisher shall pay to the Writer that proportion of 50% of the gross amount received by it under each such license as the number of uses of the composition under each such license during each such license period bears to the total number of uses of the Publisher's copyrighted musical compositions under each such license during each such license period; in computing the number of the Publisher's copyrighted musical compositions for this purpose, there shall be excluded musical compositions in the public domain and arrangements thereof and those with respect to which the Publisher does not currently publish and offer for sale regular piano copies; (ii) that the Publisher may appoint agents or representatives in countries outside of the United States and Canada to use and to grant licenses for the use of the composition on the customary royalty fee basis under which the Publisher shall receive not less than 10% of the marked retail selling price in respect of regular piano copies, and 50% of all other revenue; if, in connection with any such bulk or block license, the Publisher shall have received any advance, the Writer shall not be entitled to share therein, but in part of said advance shall be deducted in computing the composition's earnings under said bulk or block license. A bulk or block license shall be deemed to mean any license or agreement, domestic or foreign, whereby rights are granted in respect of two or more musical compositions.

Television and New Uses (j) Except to the extent that the Publisher and Writer have heretofore or may hereafter assign to or vest in the small performing rights licensing organization with which Writer and Publisher are affiliated, the said rights or the right to grant licenses therefor, it is agreed that no licenses shall be granted without the written consent, in each instance, of the Writer for the use of the composition by means of television, or by any means, or for any purposes not commercially established, or for which licenses were not granted by the Publisher on musical compositions prior to June 1, 1937.

Writer's Consent to Licenses (k) The Publisher shall not, without the written consent of the Writer in each case, give or grant any right or license (i) to use the title of the composition, or (ii) for the exclusive use of the composition in any form or for any purpose, or for any period of time, or for any territory, other than its customary arrangements with foreign publishers, or (iii) to give a dramatic representation of the composition or to dramatize the plot or story thereof, or (iv) for a vocal rendition of the composition in synchronization with sound motion pictures, or (v) for any synchronization use thereof, or (vi) for the use of the composition or a quotation or excerpt therefrom in any article, book, periodical, advertisement or other similar publication. If, however, the Publisher shall give to the Writer written notice by certified mail, return receipt requested, or telegram, specifying the right or license to be given or granted, the name of the licensee and the terms and conditions thereof, including the price or other compensation to be received therefor, then, unless the Writer (or any one or more of them) shall, within five business days after the delivery of such notice to the address of the Writer hereinafter designated, object thereto, the Publisher may grant such right or license in accordance with the said notice without first obtaining the consent of the Writer. Such notice shall be deemed sufficient if sent to the Writer at the address or addresses hereinafter designated or at the address or addresses last furnished to the Publisher in writing by the Writer.

Trust for Writer (l) Any portion of the receipts which may become due to the Writer from license fees (in excess of offsets), whether received directly from the licensee or from any licensing agent of the Publisher, shall, if not paid immediately on the receipt thereof by the Publisher, belong to the Writer and shall be held in trust for the Writer until payment is made; the ownership of said trust fund by the Writer shall not be questioned whether the monies are physically segregated or not.

Writer Participation (m) The Publisher agrees that it will not issue any license as a result of which it will receive any financial benefit in which the Writer does not participate.

Writer Credit (n) On all regular piano copies, orchestrations, band or other arrangements, octavos, quartets, commercial sound recordings and other reproductions of the composition or parts thereof, in whatever form and however produced, Publisher shall include or cause to be included, in addition to the copyright notice, the name of the Writer, and Publisher shall include a similar requirement in every license or authorization issued by it with respect to the composition.

Writers' Respective Shares 5. Whenever the term "Writer" is used herein, it shall be deemed to mean all of the persons herein defined as "Writer" and any and all royalties herein provided to be paid to the Writer shall be paid equally to such persons if there be more than one, unless otherwise provided in Paragraph 23.

Release of Commercial Sound Recording *(Insert period not exceeding 12 months)* 6. (a) (i) The Publisher shall, within _____ months from the date of this contract (the "initial period"), cause a commercial sound recording of the composition to be made and released in the customary form and through the customary commercial channels. If at the end of such initial period a sound recording has not been made and released, as above provided, then, subject to the provisions of the next succeeding subdivision, this contract shall terminate.

Insert amount to be not less than $250)   (ii)   If, prior to the expiration of the initial period, Publisher pays the Writer the sum of $ _____
(Insert period not exceeding six months) (which shall not be charged against or recoupable out of any advances, royalties or other monies theretofor paid, then due, or which thereafter may become due the Writer from the Publisher pursuant to this contract or otherwise), Publisher shall have an additional _____ months (the "additional period") commencing with the end of the initial period, within which to cause such commercial sound recording to be made and released as provided in subdivision (i) above. If at the end of the additional period a commercial sound recording has not been made and released, as above provided, then this contract shall terminate.

(iii)   Upon termination pursuant to this Paragraph 6(a), all rights of any and every nature in and to the composition and in and to any and all copyrights secured thereon in the United States and throughout the world shall automatically re-vest in and become the property of the Writer and shall be reassigned to him by the Publisher. The Writer shall not be obligated to return or pay to the Publisher any advance or indebtedness as a condition of such re-assignment; the said re-assignment shall be in accordance with and subject to the provisions of Paragraph 8 hereof, and, in addition, the Publisher shall pay to the Writer all gross sums which it has theretofore or may thereafter receive in respect of the composition.

Writer's Copies   (b)   The Publisher shall furnish, or cause to be furnished, to the Writer six copies of the commercial sound recording referred to in Paragraph 6(a).

Piano Copies, Piano Arrangement or Lead Sheet *(Select (i) or (ii)*   (c)   The Publisher shall
☐ (i) within 30 days after the initial release of a commercial sound recording of the composition, make, publish and offer for sale regular piano copies of the composition in the form and through the channels customarily employed by it for that purpose;
☐ (ii) within 30 days after execution of this contract make a piano arrangement or lead sheet of the composition and furnish six copies thereof to the Writer.

In the event neither subdivision (i) nor (ii) of this subparagraph (c) is selected, the provisions of subdivision (ii) shall be automatically deemed to have been selected by the parties.

Foreign Copyright   7. (a)   Each copyright on the composition in countries other than the United States shall be secured only in the name of the Publisher, and the Publisher shall not at any time divest itself of said foreign copyright directly or indirectly.

Foreign Publication   (b)   No rights shall be granted by the Publisher in the composition to any foreign publisher or licensee inconsistent with the terms hereof, nor shall any foreign publication rights in the composition be given to a foreign publisher or licensee unless and until the Publisher shall have complied with the provisions of Paragraph 6 hereof.

Foreign Advance   (c)   If foreign rights in the composition are separately conveyed, otherwise than as a part of the Publisher's current and/or future catalog, not less than 50% of any advance received in respect thereof shall be credited to the account of and paid to the Writer.

Foreign Percentage	(d)	The percentage of the Writer on monies received from foreign sources shall be computed on the Publisher's net receipts, provided, however, that no deductions shall be made for offsets of monies due from the Publisher to said foreign sources; or for advances made by such foreign sources to the Publisher, unless the Writer shall have received at least 50% of said advances.
No Foreign Allocations	(e)	In computing the receipts of the Publisher from licenses granted in respect of synchronization with sound motion pictures, or in respect of any world-wide licenses, or in respect of licenses granted by the Publisher for use of the composition in countries other than the United States, no amount shall be deducted for payments or allocations to publishers or licensees in such countries.

Termination or Expiration of Contract
8. Upon the termination or expiration of this contract, all rights of any and every nature in and to the composition and in and to any and all copyrights secured thereon in the United States and throughout the world, shall re-vest in and become the property of the Writer, and shall be re-assigned to the Writer by the Publisher free of any and all encumbrances of any nature whatsoever, provided that:

(a) If the Publisher, prior to such termination or expiration, shall have granted a domestic license for the use of the composition, not inconsistent with the terms and provisions of this contract, the re-assignment may be subject to the terms of such license.

(b) Publisher shall assign to the Writer all rights which it may have under any such agreement or license referred to in subdivision (a) in respect of the composition, including, but not limited to, the right to receive all royalties or other monies earned by the composition thereunder after the date of termination or expiration of this contract. Should the Publisher thereafter receive or be credited with any royalties or other monies so earned, it shall pay the same to the Writer.

(c) The Writer shall not be obligated to return or pay to the Publisher any advance or indebtedness as a condition of the re-assignment provided for in this Paragraph 8, and shall be entitled to receive the plates and copies of the composition in the possession of the Publisher.

(d) Publisher shall pay any and all royalties which may have accrued to the Writer prior to such termination or expiration.

(e) The Publisher shall execute any and all documents and do any and all acts or things necessary to effect any and all re-assignments to the Writer herein provided for.

Negotiations for New or Unspecified Uses
9. If the Publisher desires to exercise a right in and to the composition now known or which may hereafter become known, but for which no specific provision has been made herein, the Publisher shall give written notice to the Writer thereof. Negotiations respecting all the terms and conditions of any such disposition shall thereupon be entered into between the Publisher and the Writer and no such right shall be exercised until specific agreement has been made.

Royalty Statements and Payments
10. The Publisher shall render to the Writer, hereafter, royalty statements accompanied by remittance of the amount due at the times such statements and remittances are customarily rendered by the Publisher, provided, however, that such statements and remittances shall be rendered either semi-annually or quarterly and not more than forty-five days after

the end of each such semi-annual or quarterly period, as the case may be. The Writer may at any time, or from time to time, make written request for a detailed royalty statement, and the Publisher shall, within sixty days, comply therewith. Such royalty statements shall set forth in detail the various items, foreign and domestic, for which royalties are payable thereunder and the amounts thereof, including, but not limited to, the number of copies sold and the number of uses made in each royalty category. If a use is made in a publication of the character provided in Paragraph 4, subdivision (e) hereof, there shall be included in said royalty statement the title of said publication, the publisher or issuer thereof, the date of and number of uses, the gross license fee received in connection with each publication, the share thereto of all the writers under contract with the Publisher, and the Writer's share thereof. There shall likewise be included in said statement a description of every other use of the composition, and if by a licensee or licensees their name or names, and if said use is upon a part of an instrument serving to reproduce the composition mechanically, the type of mechanical reproduction, the title of the label thereon, the name or names of the artists performing the same, together with the gross license fees received, and the Writer's share thereof.

Examination of Books 11. (a) The Publisher shall from time to time, upon written demand of the Writer or his representative, permit the Writer or his representative to inspect at the place of business of the Publisher, all books, records and documents relating to the composition and all licenses granted, uses had and payments made therefor, such right of inspection to include, but not by way of limitation, the right to examine all original accountings and records relating to uses and payments by manufacturers of commercial sound recordings and music rolls; and the Writer or his representative may appoint an accountant who shall at any time during usual business hours have access to all records of the Publisher relating to the composition for the purpose of verifying royalty statements rendered or which are delinquent under the terms hereof.

(b) The Publisher shall, upon written demand of the Writer or his representative, cause any licensing agent in the United States and Canada to furnish to the Writer or his representative, statements showing in detail all licenses granted, uses had and payments made in connection with the composition, which licenses or permits were granted, or payments were received, by or through said licensing agent, and to permit the Writer or his representative to inspect at the place of business of such licensing agent, all books, records and documents of such licensing agent, relating thereto. Any and all agreements made by the Publisher with any such licensing agent shall provide that any such licensing agent will comply with the terms and provisions hereof. In the event that the Publisher shall instruct such licensing agent to furnish to the Writer or his representative statements as provided for herein, and to permit the inspection of the books, records and documents as herein provided, then if such licensing agent should refuse to comply with the said instructions, or any of them, the Publisher agrees to institute and prosecute diligently and in good faith such action or proceedings as may be necessary to compel compliance with the said instructions.

(c) With respect to foreign licensing agents, the Publisher shall make available the books or records of said licensing agents in countries outside of the United States and Canada to the extent such books or records are available to the Publisher, except that the Publisher may in lieu thereof make available any accountants' reports and audits which the Publisher is able to obtain.

(d) If as a result of any examination of books, records or documents pursuant to Paragraphs 11(a), 11(b) or 11(c) hereof, it is determined that, with respect to any royalty statement rendered by or on behalf of the Publisher to the Writer, the Writer is owed a sum equal to or greater than five percent of the sum shown on that royalty statement as being due to the Writer, then the Publisher shall pay to the Writer the entire cost of such examination, not to exceed 50% of the amount shown to be due the Writer.

(e) (i) In the event the Publisher administers its own licenses for the manufacture of parts of instruments serving to mechanically reproduce the composition rather than employing a licensing agent for that purpose, the Publisher shall include in each license agreement a provision permitting the Publisher, the Writer or their respective representatives to inspect, at the place of business of such licensee, all books, records and documents of such licensee relating to such license. Within 30 days after written demand by the Writer, the Publisher shall commence to inspect such licensee's books, records and documents and shall furnish a written report of such inspection to the Writer within 90 days following such demand. If the Publisher fails, after written demand by the Writer, to so inspect the licensee's books, records and documents, or fails to furnish such report, the Writer or his representative may inspect such licensee's books, records and documents at his own expense.

(ii) In the further event that the Publisher and the licensee referred to in subdivision (i) above are subsidiaries or affiliates of the same entity or one is a subsidiary or affiliate of the other, then, unless the Publisher employs a licensing agent to administer the licenses referred to in subdivision (i) above, the Writer shall have the right to make the inspection referred to in subdivision (i) above without the necessity of making written demand on the Publisher as provided in subdivision (i) above.

(iii) If as a result of any inspection by the Writer pursuant to subdivisions (i) and (ii) of this subparagraph (e) the Writer recovers additional monies from the licensee, the Publisher and the Writer shall share equally in the cost of such inspection.

Default in Payment or Prevention of Examination

12. If the Publisher shall fail or refuse, within sixty days after written demand, to furnish or cause to be furnished, such statements, books, records or documents, or to permit inspection thereof, as provided for in Paragraphs 10 and 11 hereof, or within thirty days after written demand, to make the payment of any royalties due under this contract, then the Writer shall be entitled, upon ten days' written notice, to terminate this contract. However if the Publisher shall:

(a) Within the said ten-day period serve upon the Writer a written notice demanding arbitration; and

(b) Submit to arbitration its claim that it has complied with its obligation to furnish statements, books, records or documents, or permitted inspection thereof or to pay royalties, as the case may be, or both, and thereafter comply with any award of the arbitrator within ten days after such award or within such time as the arbitrator may specify;

then this contract shall continue in full force and effect as if the Writer had not sent such notice of termination. If the Publisher shall fail to comply with the foregoing provisions, then this contract shall be deemed to have been terminated as of the date of the Writer's written notice of termination.

Derivative Works
13. No derivative work prepared under authority of Publisher during the term of this contract may be utilized by Publisher or any other party after termination or expiration of this contract

Notices
14. All written demands and notices provided for herein shall be sent by certified mail, return receipt requested.

Suits for Infringement
15. Any legal action brought by the Publisher against any alleged infringer of the composition shall be initiated and prosecuted at its sole cost and expense, but if the Publisher should fail, within thirty days after written demand, to institute such action, the Writer shall be entitled to institute such suit at his cost and expense. All sums recovered as a result of any such action shall, after the deduction of the reasonable expense thereof, be divided equally between the Publisher and the Writer. No settlement of any such action may be made by either party without first notifying the other; in the event that either party should object to such settlement, then such settlement shall not be made if the party objecting assumes the prosecution of the action and all expenses thereof, except that any sums thereafter recovered shall be divided equally between the Publisher and the Writer after the deduction of the reasonable expenses thereof.

Infringement Claims
16. (a) If a claim is presented against the Publisher alleging that the composition is an infringement upon some other work or a violation of any other right of another, and because thereof the Publisher is jeopardized, it shall forthwith serve a written notice upon the Writer setting forth the full details of such claim. The pendency of said claim shall not relieve the Publisher of the obligation to make payment of the royalties to the Writer hereunder, unless the Publisher shall deposit said royalties as and when they would otherwise be payable, in an account in the joint names of the Publisher and the Writer in a bank or trust company in New York, New York, if the Writer on the date of execution of this contract resides East of the Mississippi River, or in Los Angeles, California, if the Writer on the date of execution of this contract resides West of the Mississippi River. If no suit be filed within nine months after said written notice from the Publisher to the Writer, all monies deposited in said joint account shall be paid over to the Writer plus any interest which may have been earned thereon.

(b) Should an action be instituted against the Publisher claiming that the composition is an infringement upon some other work or a violation of any other right of another, the Publisher shall forthwith serve written notice upon the Writer containing the full details of such claim. Notwithstanding the commencement of such action, the Publisher shall continue to pay the royalties hereunder to the Writer unless it shall, from and after the date the service of the summons, deposit said royalties as and when they would otherwise be payable, in an account in the joint names of the Publisher and the Writer in a bank or trust company in New York, New York, if the Writer on the date of execution of this contract resides East of the Mississippi River, or in Los Angeles, California, if the Writer on the date of execution of this contract resides West of the Mississippi River. If the said suit shall be finally adjudicated in favor of the Publisher or shall be settled, there shall be released and paid to the writer all of such sums held in escrow less any amount paid out of the Writer's share with the Writer's written consent in settlement of said action. Should the said suit finally result adversely to the Publisher, the said amount on deposit shall be released to the Publisher to the extent of any expense or damage it incurs and the balance shall be paid over to the Writer.

(c)   In any of the foregoing events, however, the Writer shall be entitled to payment of said royalties or the money so deposited at and after such time as he files with the Publisher a surety company bond, or a bond in other form acceptable to the Publisher, in the sum of such payments to secure the return thereof to the extent that the Publisher may be entitled to such return. The foregoing payments or deposits or the filing of a bond shall be without prejudice to the rights of the Publisher or Writer in the premises.

Arbitration   17. Any and all differences, disputes or controversies arising out of or in connection with this contract shall be submitted to arbitration before a sole arbitrator under the then prevailing rules of the American Arbitration Association. The location of the arbitration shall be New York, New York, if the Writer on the date of execution of this contract resides East of the Mississippi River, or Los Angeles, California, if the Writer on the date of execution of this contract resides West of the Mississippi River. The parties hereby individually and jointly agree to abide by and perform any award rendered in such arbitration. Judgment upon any such award rendered may be entered in any court having jurisdiction thereof.

Assignment   18. Except to the extent herein otherwise expressly provided, the Publisher shall not sell, transfer, assign, convey, encumber or otherwise dispose of the composition or the copyright or copyrights secured thereon without the prior written consent of the Writer. The Writer has been induced to enter into this contract in reliance upon the value to him of the personal service and ability of the Publisher in the exploitation of the composition, and by reason thereof it is the intention of the parties and the essence of the relationship between them that the rights herein granted to the Publisher shall remain with the Publisher and that the same shall not pass to any other person, including, without limitations, successors to or receivers or trustees of the property of the Publisher, either by act or deed of the Publisher or by operation of law, and in the event of the voluntary or involuntary bankruptcy of the Publisher, this contract shall terminate, provided, however, that the composition may be included by the Publisher in a bona fide voluntary sale of its music business or its entire catalog of musical compositions, or in a merger or consolidation of the Publisher with another corporation, in which event the Publisher shall immediately give written notice thereof to the Writer; and provided further that the composition and the copyright therein may be assigned by the Publisher to a subsidiary or affiliated company generally engaged in the music publishing business. If the Publisher is an individual, the composition may pass to a legatee or distributee as part of the inheritance of the Publisher's music business and entire catalog of musical compositions. Any such transfer or assignment shall, however, be conditioned upon the execution and delivery by the transferee or assignee to the Writer of an agreement to be bound by and to perform all of the terms and conditions of this contract to be performed on the part of the Publisher.

Subsidiary Defined   19. A subsidiary, affiliate, or any person, firm or corporation controlled by the Publisher or by such subsidiary or affiliate, as used in this contract, shall be deemed to include any person, firm or corporation, under common control with, or the majority of whose stock or capital contribution is owned or controlled by the Publisher or by any of its officers, directors, partners or associates, or whose policies and actions are subject to domination or control by the Publisher or any of its officers, directors, partners or associates.

Amounts   20. The amounts and percentages specified in this contract shall be deemed to be the amounts and percentages agreed upon by the parties hereto, unless other amounts or percentages are inserted in the blank spaces provided therefor.

Modifications   21. This contract is binding upon and shall enure to the benefit of the parties hereto and their respective successors in interest (as hereinbefore limited). If the Writer (or one or more of them) shall not be living, any notices may be given to, or consents given by, his or their successors in interest. No change or modification of this contract shall be effective unless reduced to writing and signed by the parties hereto.

The words in this contract shall be so construed that the singular shall include the plural and the plural shall include the singular where the context so requires and the masculine shall include the feminine and the feminine shall include the masculine where the context so requires.

Paragraph Headings   22. The paragraph headings are inserted only as a metter of convenience and for reference, and in no way define, limit or describe the scope or intent of this contract nor in any way affect this contract.

Special Provisions   23. _____

_____

_____

_____

_____

Witness:

_____

Witness:

_____

Witness:

_____

Witness:

_____

Publisher _____

By _____

Address _____

Writer _____ (L.S.)

Address _____

Soc. Sec. # _____

Writer _____ (L.S.)

Address _____

Soc. Sec. # _____

Writer _____ (L.S.)

Address _____

Soc. Sec. # _____

For Your Protection, Send a Copy of the Fully Signed Contract to The Songwriters Guild

Special Exceptions to apply only if filled in and initialed by the parties.
☐ The composition is part of an original score (not an interpolation) of
☐ Living Stage Production   ☐ Motion Picture   ☐ Night Club Revue
☐ Televised Musical Production
which is the subject of an agreement between the parties dated   , a copy of
which is hereto annexed. Unless said agreement requires compliance with Paragraph 6 in respect
of a greater number of musical compositions, the Publisher shall be deemed to have complied with
said Paragraph 6 with respect to the composition if it fully performs the terms of said Paragraph
6 in respect of any one musical composition included in said score.

Form 2

Publisher Popular Song Contract

AGREEMENT made this _____ day of _____ 19 _____ between
_____ (hereinafter called the "Publisher") and _____

jointly and/or severally (hereinafter called "Writer(s)"):

Witnesseth:

In consideration of the agreement herein contained and of the sum of One ($1.00) Dollar and other good and valuable consideration in hand paid by the Publisher to the Writer(s), receipt of which is hereby acknowledged, the parties agree as follows:

1. The Writer(s) hereby sells, assigns, transfers and delivers to the Publisher, its successors and assigns, a certain heretofore unpublished original musical composition, written and/or composed by the above named Writer(s), now entitled:

including the title, words and music, and all copyrights thereof, including but not limited to the copyright registration thereof No. _____ , and all rights, claims and demands in any way relating thereto, whether legal or equitable, including but not limited to the grand rights (which include among other rights the right to include the said composition in a dramatico-musical work or review), and the exclusive right to secure copyrights therein throughout the entire world, and to have and to hold the said copyrights and all rights of whatsoever nature now and hereafter thereunder existing and/or existing under any agreements or licenses relating thereto, for and during the full terms of all of said copyrights. In consideration of the agreement herein contained and the additional sum of One ($1.00) Dollar and other good and valuable consideration in hand paid by the Publisher to the Writer(s), receipt of which is hereby acknowledged, the Writer(s) hereby sells, assigns, transfers and delivers to the Publisher, its successors and assigns, the copyrights of said musical composition(s) whether now known or hereafter created throughout the world to which the Writer(s) may be entitled now or hereafter, and all registrations thereof, and all rights of any and every nature now and hereafter thereunder existing for the full terms of copyrights.

2. If any of the compositions referred to herein was, in whole or in part, subsisting in its original term of copyright as of January 1, 1978, Writer(s) shall so notify Publisher in writing and shall be entitled to demand as further consideration in connection therewith the additional sum of One Dollar ($1.00), and Publisher shall be entitled to all rights of renewal and extension of copyright therein and shall be empowered as attorney in fact for Writer(s), through any officer or employee of Publisher, to renew, pursuant to law, in the name of Writer(s), if living, the copyright in the said composition and to execute and deliver in the name of Writer(s), a formal assignment of each such renewal copyright to the Publisher, or to its assigns, under the terms and conditions hereof.

3. The Writer(s) hereby warrants that the said composition is his sole, exclusive and original work, and that he has full right and power to make the within agreement, and that there exists no adverse claims to or in the said composition.

4. The Writer(s) hereby warrants that the foregoing musical composition does not infringe any other copyrighted work and has been created by the joint collaboration of the Writers named herein and that said composition, including the title, words and music thereof, has been, unless herein otherwise specifically noted, the result of the joint efforts of all the undersigned Writers and not by way of any independent or separable activity by any of the Writers.

5. In consideration of this agreement, the Publisher agrees to pay the Writer(s) as follows:

a) _____ as a non-returnable advance against the royalties payable to Writer(s) hereunder, which sum, and all other advances which may be paid, shall be deductible from payments hereafter becoming due the Writer(s) hereunder or under any other agreement heretofore or hereafter made between the parties.

b) the royalties provided in Exhibit 1 annexed hereto on the dates and for the accounting periods therein specified.

6. It is understood and agreed by and between all the parties hereto that all sums hereunder payable jointly to the Writer(s) shall be paid to and divided amongst them respectively as follows:

NAME   SHARE

7. In the event that Publisher, within one (1) year from the date hereof, has not performed at least one of the following acts:

a) published and offered the musical composition for sale in regular piano copies or other customary form of trade publication; or

b) caused a commercial phonograph record embodying the musical composition to be made and distributed; or

c) licensed the use of the musical composition or any part thereof in or as part of a motion picture, or television picture, or live production, or dramatic or musical production; or

d) paid to the Writer(s) the sum of Fifty ($50.00) Dollars as an advance against all royalties hereunder.

Then, subject to the provisions of Paragraph 9 herein, the Writer(s) shall have the option to give Publisher, by certified mail, written notice to the effect Publisher shall have thirty (30) days after receipt of such notice from the Writer(s) in which to cure such failure by performing any one of the acts contained in subparagraphs a), b), c), or d) of this paragraph. In the event that Publisher shall not cure such failure within such thirty (30) day period, then all rights in and to the musical composition shall automatically revert to the Writer(s) without any further liability on the part of Publisher hereunder and subject to all licenses previously given by Publisher hereunder, provided that Publisher shall then advise such licensees to account directly to Writer(s) for any uses under their licenses, and if an advance is then outstanding in favor of any such licensee, Publisher shall remain liable to Writer(s) for the royalties herein stipulated if provision is not made for direct payment notwithstanding such advance.

8. The Writer(s) hereby consents to such changes, adaptations, dramatizations, transpositions, editing and arrangements of said composition, and the setting of words to the music and of music to the words, and the change of title as the Publisher deems desirable. In the event that the composition covered by this agreement is an instrumental composition, then and in such event the Writer(s) hereby irrevocably grants to the Publisher the sole and exclusive right and privilege to cause to have lyrics written for such composition by a writer or writers designated by the Publisher, which lyrics shall require only the approval of the Publisher, whereupon the Writer(s) shall be entitled to only one-half of the aforementioned royalties provided in this agreement. The Writer(s) hereby waive any and all claims which they have or may have against the Publisher and/or its associates, affiliated and subsidiary corporations by reason of the fact that the title of the said composition may be the same or similar to that of any musical composition or compositions heretofore or hereafter acquired by the Publisher and/or its associated, affiliated and subsidiary corporations. The Writer(s) consents to the use of his (their) name and likeness and the title to the said composition on and for the music, folios, recordings, performances, and player rolls of said composition and in connection with publicity and advertising concerning the Publisher, its successors, assigns and licensees, and said composition and agrees that the use of such name, likeness and title may commence prior to publication and may continue so long as the Publisher shall own and/or exercise any rights in said composition.

9. Writer(s) understands and agrees that in order to exploit effectively the said composition it is frequently necessary for the Publisher, or Writer(s), pursuant to instructions from the Publisher, to make recordings of the said composition for demonstration purposes. Said recordings are, in the trade, commonly referred to as "demo-records." Writer(s) agrees that effective from the date hereof, Publisher shall charge to Writer(s) and deduct from any royalty otherwise payable to Writer(s) (or in equal proportions from each Writer, if there be more than one) one-half ($\frac{1}{2}$) of the costs of production of demo-records embodying the said composition. If a demo-record has been paid for by Publisher, the provisions in Paragraph 7 shall not apply, unless costs of the demo-record have been reimbursed or recouped.

10. Written demands and notices other than royalty statements provided for herein shall be sent by certified mail.

11. Any legal action brought by the Publisher against any alleged infringer of said composition shall be initiated and prosecuted at the Publisher's sole expense, and of any recovery made by it as a result thereof, after deduction of the expense of the litigation, a sum equal to fifty per cent (50%) shall be paid to the Writer(s).

(a) If a claim is presented against the Publisher in respect of said composition, and because thereof the Publisher is jeopardized, it shall thereupon serve written notice upon the Writer(s), containing the full details of such claim known to the Publisher and thereafter until the claim has been adjudicated or settled shall hold any moneys coming due the Writer(s) in escrow pending the outcome of such claim or claims. The Publisher shall have the right to settle or otherwise dispose of such claims in any manner as it in its sole discretion may determine. In the event of any recovery against the Publisher, either by way of judgment or settlement, all of the costs, charges, disbursements, attorney fees and the amount of the judgment or settlement, may be deducted by the Publisher from any and all royalties or other payments theretofore or thereafter payable to the Writer(s) by the Publisher or by its associated, affiliated, or subsidiary corporations.

(b) From and after the service of summons in a suit for infringement filed against the Publisher with respect to said composition, any and all payments thereafter coming due the Writer(s) shall be held by the Publisher in trust until the suit has been adjudicated and then be disbursed accordingly, unless the Writer(s) shall elect to file an acceptable bond in the sum of payments, in which event the amounts due shall be paid to the Writer(s).

12. "Writer" as used herein shall be deemed to include all authors and composers signing this agreement.

13. The Writer(s), each for himself, hereby irrevocably constitutes and appoints the Publisher or any of its officers, directors, or general manager, his (their) attorney and representative, in the name(s) of the Writer(s), or any of them, or in the name of the Publisher, its successors and assigns, to make sign, execute, acknowledge and deliver any and all instruments which may be desirable or necessary in order to vest in the Publisher, its successors and assigns, any of the rights hereinabove referred to.

14. The Publisher shall have the right to assign this agreement and its obligations hereunder, or sell, assign, transfer, license or otherwise dispose of any of its rights and obligations in whole or in part under this agreement to any person, firm or corporation, but said disposition shall not affect the right of the Writer(s) to receive the royalties hereinabove set forth from the assignee.

15. This agreement shall be construed only under the laws of the State of New York. If any part of this agreement shall be invalid or unenforceable, it shall not affect the validity of the balance of this agreement.

16. This agreement shall be binding upon and shall inure to the benefit of the respective parties hereto, their respective successors in interest, legal representatives and assigns, and represents the entire understanding between the parties.

17. If the said composition has been recorded and released fill in:

    Date and place of first release: _____

    Record Company _____

    Record number _____

IN WITNESS WHEREOF, the parties hereto have hereunto set their hands and seals the day and year first above written.

_____   Writer _____

(Name of Publisher)   Address _____

By _____   Soc. Sec. # _____

    Year of Birth _____

_____   Writer _____

    Address _____

    Soc. Sec. # _____

    Year of Birth _____

_____   Writer _____

    Address _____

    Soc. Sec. # _____

    Year of Birth _____

Exhibit 1 (Songwriter Royalties)

(*a*) 8 cents per copy with respect to regular piano copies separately sold and paid for in the United States and Canada.

(*b*) 10% of the net wholesale selling price of each copy of all other printed editions, if any [except for the use thereof in folios or other composite works licensed and not issued by Publisher], sold and paid for in the United States and Canada.

(*c*) 50% of all net sums actually received by Publisher from the licensing of mechanical instrument, electrical transcription, motion picture and television synchronization rights and all other rights [including the use thereof in folios or other composite works licensed by Publisher] now known or hereafter to become known in the United States and Canada.

(*d*) No royalties shall be due for "professional copies" or other complimentary copies for advertising or promotional purposes not sold or resold.

(*e*) For use in folios or other composite works together with other compositions, the said royalty rate provided hereinbefore shall be prorated in the ratio of the musical composition to all works (including the musical composition) in such publication, except that with respect to royalties for such usage provided in paragraph (*c*) above, such pro rata computation shall be based on the relation between the musical composition and the total number of compositions so licensed by Publisher.

(*f*) 50% of all net sums actually received by Publisher from sales and uses in countries outside the United States and Canada. It is understood that in such outside countries publication may be made by an assignee, representative or licensee of Publisher.

(*g*) Writer(s) shall not be entitled to share in any sums distributed to Publisher by any performing-right organization which makes a direct or indirect distribution to writers. If, however, any small performance rights shall be administered directly by Publisher or its assignees, agents or licensees, Publisher shall pay hereunder 50% of all net sums received by Publisher therefrom.

(*h*) The Publisher agrees that it will render statements to the Writer(s) within forty-five (45) days after June 30th and December 31st of each year, and will accompany such statements with payments for any royalties earned by the Writer(s), in excess of advances previously paid, and due and owing at the end of each of such semiannual periods. Payments in amounts of less than ten ($10) dollars may be deferred to subsequent accounting periods until at least such sum on a cumulative basis is due. Said statements and payments, in the absence of written objection thereto by the Writer(s) within six (6) months from receipt, shall constitute an account stated as to all royalties due for the period encompassed by such statement and/or payment.

Form 3A

Exclusive Songwriter Term Contract

AGREEMENT made this day of _____ 19 _____ by and between _____(hereinafter referred to as the "Writer") and _____ _____ , a New York corporation (hereinafter referred to as the "Publisher").

Witnesseth:

WHEREAS, the Writer is a composer of music and/or an author of lyrics of musical compositions and/or an arranger of music in the public domain, and

WHEREAS, the Publisher is a corporation which is engaged in the business of publishing, selling and exploiting songs, music and other like literary, dramatic and artistic property,

NOW, THEREFORE, in consideration of the mutual covenants herein contained and other good and valuable consideration, it is agreed:

1. The Publisher agrees to pay to the Writer during the term hereof _____($____) dollars per week as a nonreturnable advance and to be deducted from any and all royalties accruing to the Writer hereinunder, the first such payment to be made _____ , 19_____

2. Writer hereby agrees, for the full term hereof and for any extensions thereof, to be exclusively employed by Publisher and to serve under Publisher's supervision and control, in the writing of compositions, alone or in collaboration with others, including the title, words and music thereof, and in connection therewith, Writer confirms that each of said compositions or parts thereof shall be considered works made for hire as contemplated and defined in Section 101 of the United States Copyright Act.

3. (a) As to compositions heretofore written or arranged in whole or in part by Writer, the Writer does hereby sell, assign and transfer to Publisher all rights whether legal or equitable, including but not limited to the grand rights (which include among other rights the right to include a musical composition in a dramatico-musical work or review), of whatsoever nature now known or which may hereafter come into existence. If any of such compositions was, in whole or in part, subsisting in its original term of copyright as of January 1, 1978, Writer shall so notify Publisher in writing and shall be entitled to demand as further consideration in connection therewith the additional sum of One Dollar ($1.00) and Publisher shall be entitled to all rights of renewal and extension of copyright therein and shall be empowered as attorney in fact for Writer, through any officer or employee of Publisher, to renew, pursuant to law, in the name of Writer, if living, the copyright in the said composition and to execute and deliver in the name of Writer a formal assignment of each such renewal copyright to the Publisher or its assigns, under the terms and conditions hereof.

   (b) With respect to any compositions heretofore written or arranged in whole or in part by Writer, it is understood by the parties that, notwithstanding the foregoing, the Writer does not herein assign any interest which may have been the subject of an assignment of copyright or other agreement with a music publisher which was duly recorded with the Copyright Office. Attached as Exhibit 2 is a list of such musical compositions and information regarding such recordation.

4. The Publisher agrees to pay to the Writer or, upon his death, to the person or persons legally entitled thereto, during the period of copyright protection of the compositions, the royalties provided in Exhibit I annexed hereto.

The royalties provided therein shall be paid in instances where the Writer was the sole author and composer of the musical composition and, with regard to compositions where the Writer has a collaborator, the Writer shall be paid only such portion of said royalties as if said total royalties were shared equally among all writers of such composition.

5. The Writer agrees that all of the lyrics and music delivered by the Writer to the Publisher hereunder shall be Writer's own original compositions or arrangements and that no part thereof shall be an imitation or copy of any other copyrighted work.

6. The term of this agreement shall commence as of the week of _____ 19_____ and shall continue for a period of fifty-two (52) weeks.

588

In addition thereto, Publisher is hereby granted an option, to be exercised by written notice sent to Writer within thirty (30) days prior to the termination of the initial term of this agreement, to extend this agreement for an additional term of fifty-two (52) weeks on the same terms, including the continuation of the same advance royalty payments during such extended term.

7. Writer understands and agrees that in order to exploit effectively the musical compositions it is frequently necessary for the Publisher, or Writer, pursuant to instructions from the Publisher, to make recordings of the musical compositions for demonstration purposes. Said recordings are, in the trade, commonly referred to as "demo-records." Writer agrees that effective from the date hereof, Publisher shall charge to Writer and deduct from any royalty otherwise payable to Writer (or in equal proportions from each writer, if there is more than one) one-half (½) of the costs of production of demo-records embodying a musical composition.

8. The Writer hereby consents that this contract and all copyrights and other rights hereunder may be assigned by the Publisher either expressly or by operation of law subject, however, to the payment of the royalties heretofore provided.

9. In the event that the Writer shall become mentally or physically incapacitated so that he is unable to, or in the event that he shall fail, refuse or neglect to carry out the provisions of this agreement upon his part to be performed, then in any such event the Publisher shall be relieved of any obligation to make further royalty advances pursuant to this agreement. The Publisher shall also be entitled to extend the term of this agreement during the period of such event.

10. The Writer hereby warrants and represents that he is under no legal restriction against entering into this agreement.

11. The Writer hereby agrees that during the term of this agreement, and any extension thereof, he shall obtain the Publisher's approval of any person with whom he shall collaborate.

12. All payments and notices hereunder shall be made to the Writer at the address of

---

unless otherwise directed in writing.

13. The term "Publisher" as used throughout this agreement shall be deemed to apply to the Publisher and its designees, successors and assigns.

14. This agreement shall be binding upon and shall enure to the benefit of the Publisher and its designees, successors and assigns, and the Writer and Writer's personal representatives and assigns.

IN WITNESS WHEREOF, the Writer and the Publisher have caused these presents to be executed as of the day and year first above written.

(Name of Publisher)

By ―――――――――――――――――――

(Writer)

(Address)

(Social Security Number)

(Date of Birth)

Exhibit 1

(*a*) 8 cents per copy with respect to regular piano copies separately sold and paid for in the United States and Canada.

(*b*) 10% of the net wholesale selling price of each copy of all other printed editions, if any [except for the use thereof in folios or other composite works licensed and not issued by Publisher], sold and paid for in the United States and Canada.

(*c*) 50% of all net sums actually received by Publisher from the licensing of mechanical instrument, electrical transcription, motion picture and television synchronization rights and all other rights [including the use thereof in folios or other composite works licensed by Publisher] now known or hereafter to become known in the United States and Canada.

(*d*) No royalties shall be due for "professional copies" or other complimentary copies for advertising or promotional purposes not sold or resold.

(e) For use in folios or other composite works together with other compositions, the said royalty rate provided hereinbefore shall be prorated in the ratio of the musical composition to all works (including the musical composition) in such publication, except that with respect to royalties for such usage provided in paragraph (c) above, such pro rata computation shall be based on the relation between the musical composition and the total number of compositions so licensed by Publisher.

(f) 50% of all net sums actually received by Publisher from sales and uses in countries outside the United States and Canada. It is understood that in such outside countries publication may be made by an assignee, representative or licensee of Publisher.

(g) Writer shall not be entitled to share in any sums distributed to Publisher by any performing-right organization which makes a direct or indirect distribution to writers. If, however, any small performance rights shall be administered directly by Publisher or its assignees, agents or licensees, Publisher shall pay hereunder 50% of all net sums received by Publisher therefrom.

(h) The Publisher agrees that it will render statements to the Writer(s) within forty-five (45) days after June 30th and December 31st of each year, and will accompany such statements with payments for any royalties earned by the Writer(s), in excess of advances previously paid, and due and owing at the end of each of such semiannual periods. Payments in amounts of less than ten ($10) dollars may be deferred to subsequent accounting periods until at least such sum on a cumulative basis is due. Said statements and payments, in the absence of written objection thereto by the Writer(s) within six (6) months from receipt, shall constitute an account stated as to all royalties due for the period encompassed by such statement and/or payment.

Form 3B

Letter Acknowledging Individual Song under Term Contract

(Publisher name
and address)

Date _____

Re: Exclusive Term Agreement
Dated _____

Dear Sirs:

This is to acknowledge that the following specific compositions were written by the undersigned and placed with your company pursuant to the above-referred-to exclusive term agreement on the basis provided therein:

Form 4

Acknowledgment by Arranger of Work-for-Hire Status*

WHEREAS, _____ (hereinafter referred to as "Arranger"), has at the request of _____ (Employer) and upon Employer's special order and commission made the following musical arrangements: _____

WHEREAS, Arranger and Employer agree that the said arrangements shall be considered as works made for hire as contemplated and defined in Section 101 of the United States Copyright Act;

NOW, THEREFORE, in consideration of the sum of _____ ($ _____) Dollars, and other good and valuable consideration, receipt of which is hereby acknowledged, Arranger does hereby acknowledge such employment, and that under the terms of such employment such arrangements and all rights appertaining thereto are entirely the property of Employer, its successors and assigns, absolutely and forever, for any and all copyright terms and all extension and renewal terms of copyright whether now known or hereafter created throughout the world, and for all uses and purposes whatsoever and free from the payment of any royalty or compensation whatsoever, and credit may be given for said arrangements to the Arranger in whole or in part, or not at all at the sole discretion of Employer.

IN WITNESS WHEREOF, the parties have hereunto set their hands and seals this _____ day of _____

Arranger _____
Employer _____
By _____

---

* The within form may be used for arrangements made on or after January 1, 1978 when the Copyright Act of 1976 became generally effective. For an employee-for-hire acknowledgement form, the two WHEREAS clauses in the above form may be replaced by the following single clause:

WHEREAS, _____ (hereinafter referred to as "Arranger"), an employee for hire of _____ (Employer), has at its request and under its direction, made the following musical arrangements:

Form 5

Agreement Cancelling Collaboration in an Unexploited Composition

This will confirm our mutual agreement concerning the following unexploited composition(s):

_____

_____

1. All agreements between us heretofore made concerning said composition(s) are cancelled and terminated.

2. The title, lyrics and melodies of said composition(s) are deemed separated and the rights in said component parts shall be vested and owned as follows:

Title to _____

Lyrics to _____

Melody to _____

3. Each of us agrees not to use or offer for publication or other purposes any of such component parts of said composition(s) which is herein transferred and released to the other writer(s).

Dated:

_____
(Signature)

_____
(Signature)

_____
(Signature)

Agreement as to Joint Ownership of Copyright

Date _____

Re: _____

Gentlemen:

The following is our understanding and agreement with respect to the above composition:

1. The undersigned warrants that it is the sole owner of the copyright and of any and all rights in and to the above composition throughout the world, subject only to the agreement with the writers of the above composition dated _____.

2. The undersigned will assign the copyright of the composition in or to the joint names of yourself and the undersigned, so that each party will own an undivided one-half interest in said copyright and in any claims or interests now or hereafter existing with respect thereto.

3. The undersigned shall have the sole and exclusive right to administer and protect said composition on behalf of both parties, and shall have the sole right to designate on behalf of both parties hereto all persons, firms or corporations to administer the said musical composition outside of the U.S. and Canada and, on behalf of or in the names of both parties, to enter into agreements with said persons, firms or corporations, which may be affiliated with the undersigned, to sub-publish or otherwise deal with said musical composition on subpublication royalty terms of not less than ten (10%) per cent of the retail price of printed editions and fifty (50%) per cent of all other income.

4. The undersigned will pay you fifty (50%) per cent of the net publisher's share actually received by it in the United States (and remaining after deduction of royalties payable to writers and of the costs of printing, engraving, copyrighting and trade advertising):

(a) By virtue of the sale or other distribution of printed editions, and;

(b) From mechanical license fees and all other sources including performance fees (except U.S.A. and Canadian performance fees), mechanical fees, transcription fees and synchronization fees which shall be paid in accordance with paragraph 6 hereof.

5. The undersigned shall be solely responsible for paying to the writers their share of royalties due in respect of its receipts and shall hold you harmless in that regard.

6. The undersigned will forward to Broadcast Music, Inc., if the composition is a BMI composition, or to the American Society of Composers, Authors, and Publishers in the case of an ASCAP composition, written instructions with respect to the distribution of U.S.A. and Canadian performance fees whereby you shall receive fifty (50%) per cent of the publisher's share with regard to the said composition; and the undersigned will forward to The Harry Fox Agency, Inc. or its successors in respect of the U.S.A., and to the Canadian Musical Reproduction Rights Agency Limited or its successors in respect of Canada, written instructions with respect to the distribution of U.S.A. and Canadian mechanical, transcription and synchronization fees whereby you shall receive twenty-five (25%) per cent of the gross receipts thereof [less fifty (50%) per cent of the publisher's share of the licensing agent charges with regard to the said composition] with the balance to be paid to the undersigned.

7. The undersigned agrees that within sixty (60) days after each June 30th and December 31st of each year it will prepare and furnish statements hereunder to you, and will make payment of all sums shown to be due thereby.

8. This agreement shall be for the full term of copyright throughout the world, including renewals and extensions to the extent owned or controlled by the parties.

9. This agreement shall be construed in accordance with the laws of the State of New York and shall be binding upon the parties hereto and their respective heirs and assigns, provided, however, that neither party may assign this agreement without notifying the other, in writing, of the terms of the said assignment, and further provided that the said assignment shall be made specifically subject to this agreement.

10. The parties hereto do hereby agree to submit to arbitration in New York City, under the rules of the American Arbitration Association and pursuant to the New York Arbitration Law, any differences arising under this agreement, and do hereby agree individually and jointly to abide by and perform any award rendered by the Arbitration and that a judgment of the Supreme Court of the State of New York may be entered upon such award.

11. Both parties shall share equally all costs and expenses, damages, losses and attorney's fees incurred in protecting said musical composition, with respect both to responding to claims of infringement brought as to said composition and as to bringing suit against any infringer of said composition.

12. This agreement shall not be deemed one of joint venture or partnership.

13. Notwithstanding any of the foregoing, Paragraphs 2, 3, 4, 5, 6, 7, 8 and 11 of this agreement shall not become effective unless and until you obtain a commercial recording of the above composition and the general release of copies of the said recording in the United States as a single recording by _____

_____ (artist) on the _____record label within _____ months from the date of this agreement. In the event the recording is not released within such period, this agreement shall be deemed null and void.

IN WITNESS WHEREOF, the parties have hereunto set their hands the day and year first above written.

By _____

AGREED TO AND ACCEPTED:

By _____

Publisher Instructions to Performing-Right Societies

Date _____

Index Department
Broadcast Music, Inc.
320 W. 57th Street
New York, N.Y. 10019

or

Index Department
ASCAP
1 Lincoln Plaza
New York, N.Y. 10023

Gentlemen:

This is to advise that performing rights in the following work, which is being or has heretofore been cleared with your society on behalf of the undersigned, are now jointly owned with another publisher(s). Accordingly, would you please adjust your records to reflect the following change in publisher credits:

1.   Title

_____

_____

_____

2.   Publishers   Shares

_____   _____

_____   _____

_____   _____

_____   _____

3. Effective
   date of
   split: _____
   (Must be as of the beginning of a calendar quarter, i.e., Jan. 1, Apr. 1, July 1 or Oct. 1)

4. Territory: _____

_____

   (World; U.S. and Canada; other)

Very truly yours,

_____

(Publisher for whom work cleared)

By _____

(Authorized signature)

Form 6C

Instructions to The Harry Fox Agency, Inc., by Joint Owners*

Date _____

The Harry Fox Agency, Inc.
205 E. 42nd Street
New York, New York 10017

Re: _____

Gentlemen:

The following is the correct publisher information with respect to the above composition, and licenses should be issued in the joint names of:

_____and,

_____

All royalties and fees for recordings or synchronization of this composition are to be paid irrevocably as follows, unless contrary instructions shall be jointly issued:

_____   _____ %

_____   _____ %

Please mark your records accordingly.

Sincerely,

By _____

By _____

---

* A similar form of instructions is appropriate for notification to the Canadian Musical Reproduction Rights Agency Limited (CMRRA) of 198 Davenport Road, Toronto, Ontario, Canada M5R152.

Form 7

Short Form Copyright Assignment

In consideration of the sum of one ($1.00) dollar and other good and valuable consideration, receipt of which is hereby acknowledged, the undersigned does (do) hereby sell, assign, transfer and set over unto _____ _____ ; its successors and assigns, the copyright(s) in and to the following musical composition(s) which was(were) written by the following indicated person(s):

Title	*Writer(s)*	*Copyright Office Identification No.*

and all of the right, title and interest of the undersigned, vested and contingent, therein and thereto, subject to the terms, conditions, restrictions and limitations of an agreement dated the _____ day of _____ between _____ and _____ ____ , and for the term or terms of copyright(s) provided in said agreement.[1]

IN WITNESS WHEREOF the undersigned has(have) hereunto set his(their) hand(s) and seal(s) this _____ day of _____

(IN WITNESS WHEREOF the undersigned has caused these presents to be executed by its duly authorized officer this _____ day of _____).

_____
(IF CORPORATE, NAME OF CORPORATION)

By _____

[1] For songs fixed on or after January 1, 1978, there is only a single term of copyright under the Copyright Act of 1976.

598

Form 8

U.S.A. Mechanical License

Date _____

Gentlemen:

Musical Work:

The undersigned (hereinafter designated as the "Publisher"), owns the copyright or controls the rights to reproduce in phonorecords and to distribute phonorecords of the below copyrighted musical work.

Music by _____

Words by _____

Phonorecord No. _____ Artist _____

You have advised the Publisher that you wish to use said copyrighted work under the compulsory license provision of Section 115 of the Copyright Act relating to the making and distribution of phonorecords of such work.

Upon your doing so, you shall have all the rights which are granted to, and all the obligations which are imposed upon, users of said copyrighted work under the compulsory license provisions of the Copyright Act, after distribution of phonorecords of the copyrighted work to the public in the United States by another person under authority of the copyright owner, except that with respect to phonorecords thereof made and distributed by you:

1. You shall pay royalties and account to the Publisher quarterly, within 45 days after the end of each calendar quarter, on the basis of phonorecords made and distributed; and

2. For such phonorecords made and distributed, the royalty shall be the statutory rate in effect at the time the phonorecord is made (and any royalty stated in terms of a percentage of the statutory rate shall apply to the statutory rate at such time); and

3. This compulsory license covers and is limited to one particular recording of said copyrighted work set forth above as performed by the artist and on the phonorecord number set forth above; and this compulsory license does not supersede nor in any way affect any prior agreements now in effect respecting phonorecords of said copyrighted work; and

4. If you fail to account to Publisher and pay royalties as herein provided, Publisher may give you written notice that, unless the default is remedied within 30 days from the date of the notice, this compulsory license will be automatically terminated. Such termination shall render either the making or the distribution, or both, of all phonorecords for which royalties have not been paid, actionable as acts of infringement under, and fully subject to the remedies provided by the Copyright Act.

5. You need not serve or file the notice of intention to obtain a compulsory license required by the Copyright Act.

We acknowledge receipt of a
copy hereof: Very truly yours,

_____   _____

      (Record Company)   (Publisher)

By _____   By _____

Synchronization and U.S.A. Theatrical Performing Right License for Motion Pictures

IN CONSIDERATION of and conditioned upon the payment of the sum of $_____ as a recording right license fee being paid to the undersigned upon the execution and delivery hereof, the undersigned (referred to as the "Licensor") hereby gives to: _____

(referred to as the "Licensee") the non-exclusive, irrevocable limited right, license, privilege and authority to record, in any manner, medium or form, in any country covered by this license, the musical composition hereinafter specified, and to make copies of such recordings and to import such copies into any country covered by this license, upon and subject to the terms, conditions, limitations, restrictions and reservations hereinafter contained.

1. The musical composition covered by this recording right license is: _____ by: _____

2. Said musical composition may only be recorded in the one motion picture entitled: _____

3. The type of use to be made of said musical composition for such recording is limited to: ___

4. The amount of such uses to be made for such recording is limited to: _____

5. The territory covered by this recording right license is: _____

6. In consideration of the additional sum of $ _____ as a performing license fee being paid to the undersigned upon the execution and delivery hereof, the Licensor, hereby gives to the Licensee the non-exclusive, irrevocable, limited right, license, privilege and authority to publicly perform and to authorize others to publicly perform, as hereinafter specifically provided, said musical composition as recorded in said motion picture, and in radio, screen and television trailers for the advertising and exploitation of the said motion picture, pursuant to the foregoing recording right license, in only the territory covered by this performing right license, upon and subject to the terms, conditions, limitations, restrictions and reservations hereinafter contained.

7. The right to publicly perform said recording of said musical composition pursuant to this performing right license shall be limited and confined to:

(a) The public performance thereof in the exhibition of said motion picture to audiences in motion picture theatres and other places of public entertainment where motion pictures are customarily exhibited, including by means of the televising of said motion picture direct to audiences in such motion picture theatres and other places of public entertainment where motion pictures are customarily exhibited.

(b) The public performance thereof in the exhibition of said motion picture by means of television (other than as provided in subdivision (a) hereof) upon the express condition, but not otherwise, that at the time of each such performance thereof, from, over or through each television station, such station, either directly or as an affiliated station of a television network, shall theretofore have obtained a valid license, separate and apart from this license, to so perform the same in the exhibition of said motion picture, from the Licensor or from ASCAP, BMI, or from any other society, association, agency or entity having the lawful right to issue such license for and on behalf of the Licensor and to collect the license fee for such performance thereof.

(c) The public performance by means of so-called "closed circuit television," "subscription television," "pay television," or CATV is subject to clearance of the performance right either from the Licensor or from ASCAP (BMI) or from any other society, association, agency or entity having the lawful right to issue such license for and on behalf of the Licensor and to collect the license fee for such performance thereof.

8. The territory covered by this performing right license is the *United States, its territories and possessions*.

9. The term of this performing right license is for the worldwide period of all copyrights in and to the musical composition, and any and all renewals or extensions thereof, that Licensor may now own or control or hereafter own or control.

10. The right to publicly perform said recording of said musical composition for every use and purpose and by every method and means whatsoever in the exhibition of said motion picture outside of the United States, its Territories and Possessions, shall be subject to the obtaining of separate licenses therefor from the performing right societies having the lawful right to issue such licenses, and to collect the license fees for such performance thereof.

11. This license in its entirety (both recording and performing right) shall terminate thirty (30) days after the date of the first public exhibition of said motion picture at which admission is charged (except so called "sneak" previews) unless prior to the expiration of said thirty day period the Licensee shall have furnished to the Licensor a cue sheet of said motion picture.

12. This license in its entirety (both recording and performing right) shall terminate, if prior to any public performance of said recording of said musical composition in the exhibition of said motion picture (a) the recording right license fee payable hereunder shall not have been paid to the Licensor and (b) the performing right license fee payable hereunder shall not have been paid to the Licensor.

13. Neither license hereunder authorizes or permits (a) any change to be made in the lyrics or in the fundamental character of the music of said musical composition, (b) the use of the title of said musical composition or any simulation thereof as the title of said motion picture, or (c) the use of the story of said musical composition as any part of the story of said motion picture.

14. The Licensor makes no warranty or representation, express or implied, except that the Licensor warrants that it has the right to grant such recording right and performing right licenses subject to the terms, conditions, limitations, restrictions and reservations therein contained, such licenses being granted without recourse for any other cause or in any other event whatsoever; the total liability of the Licensor under each such license being limited in any event to that part of the consideration paid hereunder by the Licensee to the Licensor for such license in respect to which such breach of warranty may relate.

15. The Licensor reserves to itself all rights and uses of every kind and nature whatsoever in and to said musical composition other than such limited right of recording and performance specifically licensed hereunder, whether now or hereafter known or in existence, including the sole right to exercise and to authorize others to exercise the same at any and all times and places and without limitation.

Dated:

New York, New York,

_____ (Licensor)

Form 9B

Television Film
Synchronization License

To: _____ TV Lic. # _____ Date _____
Composition: _____

1. In consideration of the sum of _____ payable upon the execution hereof, we grant you the non-exclusive right to record on film or video tape the above identified musical composition(s) in synchronization or timed relation with a single episode or individual program entitled _____
for television use only, subject to all of the terms and conditions herein provided.

2. (a) The type of use is to be _____
    (b) On or before the first telecast of the said film, you or your assigns agree to furnish to us a copy of the Cue Sheet prepared and distributed in connection therewith.

3. The territory covered by this license is the world.

4. (a) This license is for a period of _____ from the date hereof.
    (b) Upon the expiration of this license all rights herein granted shall cease and terminate and the right to make or authorize any further use or distribution of any recordings made hereunder shall also cease and terminate.

5. This is a license to record only and does not authorize any use of the aforesaid musical composition(s) not expressly set forth herein. By way of illustration but not limitation, this license does not include the right to change or adapt the words or to alter the fundamental character of the music of said musical composition(s) or to use the title(s) thereof as the title or sub-title of said film.

6. Performance of the said musical composition(s) in the exhibition of said film is subject to the condition that each television station over which the aforesaid musical composition(s) is (are) to be so performed shall have a performance license issued by us or from a person, firm, corporation, society, association or other entity having the legal right to issue such performance license.

7. No sound records produced pursuant to this license are to be manufactured, sold and/or used separately or independently of said film.

8. The film shall be for television use only and may not be televised into theatres or other places where admission is charged.

9. All rights not herein specifically granted are reserved by us.

10. We warrant only that we have the legal right to grant this license and this license is given and accepted without other warranty or recourse. If said warranty shall be breached in whole or in part with respect to (any of) said musical composition(s), our total liability shall be limited either to repaying to you the consideration theretofore paid under this license with respect to such musical composition to the extent of such breach or to holding you harmless to the extent of the consideration theretofore paid under this license with respect to such musical composition to the extent of said breach.

11. This license shall run to you, your successors and assigns, provided you shall remain liable for the performance of all of the terms and conditions of this license on your part to be performed and provided further that any disposition of said film or any prints thereof shall be subject to all the terms hereof, and you agree that all persons, firms or corporations acquiring from you any right, title, interest in or possession of said film or any prints thereof shall be notified of the terms and conditions of this license and shall agree to be bound thereby.

_____
(Licensor)

By _____

Video Synchronization and Distribution License

THIS AGREEMENT made and entered into this _____ day of _____by and be-tween _____("Publisher") and _____("Licensee")

WHEREAS Publisher owns or controls the musical composition ("Composition") entitled _____ , written by _____ ; and

WHEREAS Licensee desires to utilize the Composition in that certain production entitled _____("Production"), and to reproduce the Production and Composition in videocassettes and videodiscs (both devices being referred to herein as "Videograms");

NOW THEREFORE the parties hereto do hereby mutually agree as follows:

1. In consideration of the royalties to be paid hereunder by Licensee to Publisher and the other covenants herein on the part of the Licensee, the Publisher hereby grants to Licensee the nonexclusive right and license to reproduce and make copies of the Composition in Videogram copies of the Production and to distribute the Videograms to the public by sale or other transfer of ownership.

2. No right to rent Videograms is hereby granted. If Licensee wishes to utilize Videograms via rental Licensee shall advise Publisher in writing and the parties hereto shall negotiate in good faith the compensation or other participation to be paid to Publisher in respect of rental receipts.

3. This license and grant is for a term of _____years only, commencing on the date of this agreement. At the expiration or earlier termination of such period, all rights and licenses granted hereunder shall cease and terminate.

4. The rights granted hereunder are limited solely to the territory of _____ (the "licensed territory").

5. As compensation to the Publisher, Licensor agrees to pay to the Publisher the following royalties:

a) As to each copy of a videodisc sold in the licensed territory and paid for and not returned _____ , and

b) As to each copy of a videocassette sold in the licensed territory and paid for and not returned _____ .

6. Accountings shall be rendered by Licensee to Publisher within sixty (60) days after the close of each calendar quarter, showing in detail the royalties earned, and any deductions taken in computing royalties. Publisher shall be responsible for paying royalties to writers and any third party by reason of the grant and license hereunder. No statement shall be due for a period in which Videograms are not sold. All royalty statements shall be binding upon Publisher and not subject to any objection by Publisher for any reason unless specific objection in writing, stating the basis thereof, is given to Licensee within one (1) year from the date rendered.

7. Publisher shall have the right to inspect and make abstracts of the books and records of Licensee, insofar as said books and records pertain to the performance of Licensee's obligations hereunder; such inspection to be made on at least ten (10) days written notice, during normal business hours of normal business days but not more frequently than once annually in each year.

8. The rights and license granted hereunder may not be assigned or transferred, either affirmatively or by operation of law, without Publisher's written consent.

9. Publisher warrants and represents that it has full right, power and authority to enter into and to perform this agreement.

10. This agreement shall be deemed made in and shall be construed in accordance with the

laws of the State of New York. The agreement may not be modified orally and shall not be binding or effective unless and until it is signed by both parties hereto.

IN WITNESS WHEREOF the parties have entered into this agreement the day and year first above written.

Publisher

By ————————————————————

Licensee

By ————————————————————

Form 10

Agreement Licensing Recording for Film

THIS AGREEMENT, made and entered into this _____day of _____ by and between _____(hereinafter referred to as "LICENSOR") and _____ (hereinafter referred to as "LICENSEE").

A. LICENSOR is primarily engaged in producing, manufacturing, distributing and selling sound phonograph records, and has recorded and is the exclusive owner of certain master recordings, including any copyrights in the sound recordings therein, embodying the performances of the artists and musical compositions listed below (hereinafter referred to as "Said Master Recordings"):

B. LICENSEE is engaged in the business of producing and manufacturing a documentary motion picture film tentatively entitled, _____(hereinafter referred to as "Said Film").

C. It is the desire of LICENSEE to utilize Said Master Recordings in connection with Said Film.

NOW, THEREFORE, pursuant to the above facts and in consideration of the mutual covenants and conditions herein set forth, the parties do hereby agree as follows:

1) Subject to LICENSEE'S obtaining music publishing and union clearances referred to hereinafter, LICENSOR does hereby grant to LICENSEE the non-exclusive right to synchronize the Said Master Recording in time-relation on the soundtrack of Said Film, it being understood that the performances of the artist are not to be used or permitted to be used for release on phonograph records or tapes or other types of sound reproduction home use (including videocassettes or videodiscs for home use) other than through LICENSOR.

2) LICENSEE agrees to give LICENSOR and the artists credit on Said Film and on advertisements for the Said Film in substantially the following manner:

3) In consideration of the license and grant herein made, if the Said Master Recording is used, in whole or in part, in the Said Film, LICENSEE shall pay to LICENSOR, within _____ days after the first commercial release of Said Film, the sum of

4) LICENSEE is not required or obligated to use the Said Master Recording in the Said Film.

5) Except as provided in Paragraph 1) above, LICENSEE shall be entitled to exploit the Said Film in any and all media and modes of use throughout the world and in radio, television and screen trailers advertising Said Film. Said exploitation may include, but not be limited to, free television broadcasts, pay television, subscription television, CATV, cable television, and any transportation facility.

6) LICENSEE shall not be entitled to exercise any rights granted hereunder unless and until LICENSEE shall obtain AF of M and any governing union clearance, including payment of union reuse fees, and copyright synchronization licenses; and LICENSEE shall indemnify and hold LICENSOR free and harmless from any and all claims, liabilities, losses, damages or expenses, including attorneys' fees, arising out of or in any way connected with LICENSEE'S use of Said Master Recording hereunder, including but not limited to the claims of unions, union members, publishers and artists. LICENSOR shall give LICENSEE prompt notice of the amount of any applicable union reuse fees and LICENSEE shall not be obligated to pay same until such notice is given to it.

7) LICENSOR warrants and represents that, except for approvals of appropriate music publishers, it has the right and authority to make the license and grant of rights hereunder, including the approval of the artists and any producers of the Said Master Recording, and that except as set forth herein there shall be no further payments required of the LICENSEE.

8) The rights herein granted to LICENSEE may not be transferred or assigned by LICENSEE, in whole or in part, without the prior written consent of LICENSOR. In the event that LICENSEE should be adjudicated bankrupt or file a petition in bankruptcy or be in process of re-organization under the Bankruptcy Act of the United States, or take advantage of the insolvency laws of any state, territory or county, or if a permanent receiver, trustee, or similar court officer should be appointed by a court of competent jurisdiction to administer its affairs, or if it should voluntarily or involuntarily go out of business or attempt to assign, mortgage, or pledge all or substantially all of its assets for the benefit of its creditors, or attempt to assign this agreement, or sublicense or terminate any of its rights or duties hereunder, or attempt to sell, mortgage or pledge Said Master Recordings provided it hereunder without the prior written consent of LICENSOR, this agreement and the licenses granted hereunder shall automatically terminate immediately upon the occurrence of any such contingency without prejudice to any claim which LICENSOR may have for damages or otherwise in the premises.

9) This instrument constitutes the entire agreement between the parties and cannot be modified except by written instrument signed by the parties hereto. This agreement shall be governed by and interpreted in accordance with the laws of the State of New York. If either party shall institute any action or proceedings to enforce any of the terms and conditions of this agreement, the prevailing party in such action shall be entitled to receive, in addition to any other relief which might be granted by the court having jurisdiction over the action, reasonable attorneys' fees and costs.

10) LICENSOR agrees to supply LICENSEE with tape copies for use as specified herein for which LICENSEE agrees to reimburse LICENSOR the costs in connection with making and delivering such copies.

IN WITNESS WHEREOF, the parties hereto have executed this agreement on the day and year first above written.

LICENSOR

By _____

LICENSEE

By _____

Form 11

Foreign Subpublication Agreement

AGREEMENT made this _____ day of _____ by and between
_____ (hereinafter referred to as "Owner") and _____
_____ (hereinafter referred to as "Subpublisher").
IN CONSIDERATION of the sum of One Dollar by each to the other in hand paid and other good and valuable consideration, receipt whereof is hereby mutually acknowledged, and of the premises it is agreed:

1. Owner warrants and represents that it is the sole proprietor of all copyrights in, and is possessed of all copyrights in, and is possessed of all rights and interests in and to, the musical composition entitled " _____ " (hereinafter referred to as "Said Composition"), words by _____
   music by _____(who are respectively members
   of _____[performing right society])
   for the territory of _____
   _____ (which territory is hereinafter referred to as the "Licensed Territory"), free and clear of all claims and encumbrances for a term not less than the term of all rights granted herein.

2. Owner hereby transfers and assigns to Subpublisher the following rights in and to the Said Composition.
   a. The exclusive right to print, publish and vend copies of Said Composition in any and all parts of the Licensed Territory.
   b. The exclusive rights of public performance, including broadcasting and television rights, and of licensing such rights in any and all parts of the Licensed Territory, subject to the provisions of paragraph 3b hereof.
   c. The exclusive right, in any and all parts of the Licensed Territory, to grant non-exclusive licenses to manufacture parts serving to produce and reproduce, and make mechanical reproductions and electrical reproductions for piano rolls, phonograph records and transcriptions; to license such rights in and for the Licensed Territory; and to collect all royalties and fees payable by reason thereof. Such right shall not include the production and manufacture of copies of videocassettes or videodiscs of audiovisual productions produced outside the Licensed Territory unless Owner consents in writing.
   d. The non-exclusive right to grant non-exclusive world licenses for the synchronization, recording and use in and with motion pictures and television productions produced in the Licensed Territory, and to make copies of the recordings thereof, and to export such copies to all countries of the world.
   e. The right to make new adaptations and arrangements and to procure any new lyric or translation of lyric, to change the title and to make Said Composition suitable and proper for the authorized uses in the Licensed Territory. In no event shall any deduction be made from the gross sum of fees referred to in this agreement to pay or compensate the writer of new or revised lyrics or the composer of any arrangement. Such new matter shall be the sole property of Owner free from royalty obligations except as may be approved in writing by Owner.

3. Owner hereby reserves unto itself:
   a. The copyright in and to Said Composition in every country of the World including countries of the Licensed Territory.
   b. The exclusive right to grant licenses for the entire World or any part thereof including the Licensed Territory, for the synchronization, recording and use in and

with motion picture, television or other audiovisual productions produced outside of the Licensed Territory which right includes the right to export such productions to the Licensed Territory and the Subpublisher shall not be entitled to share in any worldwide or other fees received by the Owner or its assigns in respect of such licenses. Nothing contained in this paragraph 3b, however, shall bar participation of Subpublisher under paragraph 2b where public performance licenses are available and obtained from the performing right society of which Subpublisher is a member.

    c.   The exclusive right to dramatize and to license and use such dramatic versions throughout the World.

    d.   The exclusive right to make cartoon, literary, and other subsidiary uses of Said Composition and to license the use of the title apart from use in conjunction with Said Composition.

    e.   Any and all rights not herein specifically granted to Subpublisher.

4.   Owner shall provide to Subpublisher, without charge, six (6) printed copies of the pianoforte sale edition and dance orchestration and one (1) copy of each recording of Said Composition that Owner shall deem, in its sole discretion, useful in the Licensed Territory as soon as available.

5.   Subpublisher shall provide promptly to Owner, without charge, two (2) copies of each edition of Said Composition published in the Licensed Territory and one (1) copy of each recording released in the Licensed Territory.

6.   Subpublisher agrees that in each copy of Said Composition published by it or its licensees, there shall be printed the following notice of copyright on the title page or the first page of music:

        "Copyright © 19 _____ (name of Owner)
        All Rights Reserved
        Authorized for sale in _____(Licensed
        Territory) only."

Said Composition acquired by Subpubliser hereunder shall not be published in a folio, book, composite work or collection of works without Owner's express permission in writing. Subject to any applicable statute or treaty it is expressly understood that Subpublisher may publish, sell, and license the use of the Said Composition in the Licensed Territory only and may not export any copies or material therefrom.

7.   The rights acquired by the Subpublisher under this agreement shall be for a period of _____ years from the date of this agreement.

8.   In the event that the Subpublisher shall fail to publish Said Composition in a pianoforte sale edition or dance orchestration edition not later than one year from date hereof, or in the event that a commercial recording of Said Composition shall not be placed on sale in the Licensed Territory within one year from date hereof, then, in either of such events, all rights herein assigned to the Subpublisher shall automatically revert to the Owner without further notice by either party to the other and without releasing Subpublisher of any obligations to account to Owner for amounts previously earned or accrued.

9.   The grant of performing rights hereunder is subject to the rights of _____ _____ (name of performing right society with which Owner is affiliated). The entire publisher's share of performing fees for the Licensed Territory shall be collected by the Subpublisher subject to division with Owner as hereinafter provided and subject further to the right of the Owner to direct in writing that fifty (50%) per cent thereof shall be paid to the performing right society with which the Owner is affiliated, for payment to the Owner. In the event that the Owner directs that fifty (50%) per cent shall be paid to the performing right society with which the Owner is affiliated then the Subpublisher shall not be obliged to account to the Owner for any of said performing fee under Paragraph 10c.

10.   The Subpublisher shall pay to the Owner the following royalties with respect to the said Composition:

    a.   Ten (10%) per cent of the marked retail selling price of each copy of Said Composition in each and every printed edition (except for books and folios) sold, paid for and not returned to the Sub-Publisher in the Licensed Territory.

    b.   An amount equal to that proportion of ten (10%) per cent of the marked retail selling price of each copy of a book or folio issued by the Subpublisher and sold, paid for and not returned, as Said Composition bears to the total number of musical compositions in such book or folio on which the Subpublisher is obliged to make royalty payments.

c.   Fifty (50%) per cent of all moneys actually received by Subpublisher in respect of the rights acquired by it by virtue of Paragraph 2 subdivisions b, c, and d. In computing such amounts, no deductions shall be made except for collection fees customarily authorized by the majority of the music publishers in the Licensed Territory.

d.   Fifty (50%) per cent of any and all sums actually received by the Subpublisher from all other sources within the Licensed Territory.

e.   No royalties shall be paid by Subpublisher for professional copies distributed for professional exploitation or advertising purposes.

11. Subpublisher agrees to furnish to Owner semiannually statements of royalties for the periods ending June 30th and December 31st in each year within sixty (60) days after such dates, subject to deductions for income tax, if any, required to be paid for Owner's account. Within said sixty (60) days after such dates, Subpublisher shall apply to the proper government bureau for permission, if necessary, to make payment of the amount shown to be due on said statement. The rate of exchange prevailing on the day said permission is granted shall be used in determining the conversion to dollars and said payments shall be made in dollars by draft in New York promptly after permission is granted. Each such statement shall show for each individual composition by title the number of copies sold, the gross income for each type of income, i.e., mechanical royalties, performing fees, etc. and the rate of Owner's share of royalties from each source.

12. Subpublisher may assign any of its rights hereunder to any publishers affiliated with it for any countries of the Licensed Territory, provided that each assignee shall assume in writing all obligations of the subpublisher for the assigned territory, that each assignee shall account directly to the Owner, that the assignee shall compute royalties in accordance with Paragraph 10 hereof based on income at the source and that such assignment shall not result in any reduction of royalties that would be payable in the absence thereof. In the event of any assignment, written notice shall be served upon Owner by the Subpublisher within thirty (30) days of such assignment together with the written assumption of obligations by the assignee referred to hereinabove. Subpublisher, despite such assignment, shall remain liable for the payment of royalties hereunder.

13. Subject to the provisions of any applicable statute or treaty, including the regulations of the European Economic Community, Owner agrees that it will not ship or authorize anyone to ship into the Licensed Territory any copies of Said Composition except pursuant to the request of the Subpublisher.

14. Owner hereby authorizes and empowers Subpublisher to enforce and protect all rights in and to Said Composition and the copyright herein in the Licensed Territory in the name of the Owner or otherwise, and in its sole judgment to join the Owner and such others as it may deem advisable as parties plaintiff or defendant in suits or proceedings, and to proceed with and dispose of any such claim or action as Subpublisher may deem advisable (provided that such disposition shall not be prejudicial to Owner's rights in absence of Owner's written consent), at the sole expense of Subpublisher; its reasonable costs and expenses (including legal fees) may be recouped by Subpublisher from any recovery actually received, and the balance shall be evenly divided between the Owner and Subpublisher.

15. If Subpublisher fails to account and make payments hereunder and such failure is not cured within ten (10) days after written notice thereof sent by registered mail to Subpublisher, or if Subpublisher fails to perform any other obligations required of it hereunder and such failure is not cured within thirty (30) days after written notice by registered mail to Subpublisher, or in the event that Subpublisher shall go into compulsory liquidation, or shall go into bankruptcy or make an assignment for the benefit of creditors or make any compositions with creditors, or any insolvency or composition proceeding shall be commenced by or against Subpublisher, then and in any of such events Owner, in addition to such other rights or remedies which it may have at law or otherwise under this agreement, may elect to cancel or terminate this agreement without prejudice to any rights or claims it may have, and all rights hereunder shall forthwith revert to Owner and Subpublisher may not thereafter exercise any rights hereunder and shall destroy all printed copies in its possession. Owner's failure to terminate this agreement upon any default or defaults shall not be deemed to constitute a waiver of Owner's right to terminate the same upon any subsequent default.

16. All statements, notices and mailings of any kind or nature shall be addressed by each party to the other to their respective addresses as hereinabove set forth unless said party notifies the other in writing of a change of address, in which case all such mailings shall be addressed to the new address.

17. This agreement shall not be construed as one of partnership or joint venture.
18. This agreement shall be binding upon the respective parties, their successors and assigns, and shall be construed in accordance with the laws of the State of New York.

    IN WITNESS WHEREOF, the parties hereto have signed or caused these presents to be signed by an authorized officer, as of the day and year above written.

OWNER
By _____

SUBPUBLISHER
By _____

Agreement between Record Company and Recording Artist

Record Company ――――――――――
(Address) ――――――――――

――――――――――
――――――――――

(Date)

Dear Artist:

1. This contract for your personal services is made between Record Company as the employer and you. We hereby employ you to render personal services for us or in our behalf for the purpose of recording and making phonograph records.

2. Recordings will be made at times during the term hereof in studios as we may designate. A minimum of ―――――――――― 45 r.p.m. record sides, or their equivalent, per year shall be recorded during the initial period of this contract, and additional recordings shall be made at our election. The musical compositions to be recorded shall be designated by us, and each recording shall be subject to our approval as satisfactory for manufacture and sale. We reserve the right, at our election, to suspend the operation of this contract if, by reason of sickness, injury, accident or refusal to work, you fail to perform hereunder in accordance with the provisions hereof, or if, due to any labor controversy or adjustment thereof or to any other cause not entirely within our control or which we cannot by reasonable diligence have avoided, we are materially hampered in the recording, manufacture, distribution or sale of records, or our normal business operations become commercially impractical. Such suspension shall be upon written notice to you and shall last for the duration of any such contingency. At our election, a period of time equal to the duration of such suspension shall be added at the end of the then current period of the term hereof, and such period and the term hereof shall be accordingly extended.

3. For the rights herein granted and for the services to be rendered hereunder by you, we shall pay you as to records sold in the United States of America:

    a. a royalty of ―――――――――― (――――%) per cent in respect of master recordings made hereunder during the first term of this agreement.

    b. a royalty of ―――――――――― (――――%) per cent in respect of master recordings made hereunder during the second term of this agreement, if renewed.

    c. a royalty of ―――――――――― (――――%) per cent in respect of master recordings made hereunder during any subsequent term of this agreement, if renewed.

and as to records sold in other countries a royalty at the rate of one-half the aforesaid royalties, for the respective terms, of the retail list price (less governmental taxes and duties) of records in the country of manufacture of 90% of all double-faced records manufactured, sold, paid for and not subject to return on both faces of which are embodied only the selections recorded hereunder; and one-half the respective amounts of such royalty for 90% of all records manufactured, sold, paid for and not subject to return on only one face of which are embodied only selections hereunder; provided, however, that for records sold in foreign countries we may, from time to time, at our election base the percentages either upon the retail list prices in the country of manufacture, or the country of sale. If a manufacturer's suggested retail list price is not utilized or permitted, the generally accepted retail price shall be utilized.

In the event that any of the performances hereunder are released together with or in combination with other performances or recordings in a long playing or extended play record it is agreed that as to such record you shall receive that proportion of the royalties payable to you as provided hereinbefore as the number of selections included in such record which are performances recorded hereunder bears to the total number of selections embodied in such record. Royalties for records sold outside of the United States of America are to be computed in the national currency of the country where the retail list prices above mentioned apply, and are to be payable only with respect to records for which we receive payment in the United States of America, in dollar equivalent at the rate of exchange at the time we receive payment in the United States of America, and after proportionate deductions for income and remittance taxes withheld at the source.

As to records sold by direct mail operation or through record clubs or similar sales plans or devices, and as to sales of tape through licensees embodying performances hereunder, and as to sales by distribution through retail outlets in conjunction with special advertisements on radio or television, the royalty rate shall be one-half that provided hereinbefore but in the case of distribution through licensees the royalty shall not exceed one-half the net royalty received by us from any licensee. Royalties on sales of records on a mid-priced record line (i.e., bearing a suggested retail list price of more than sixty-six and two-thirds per cent (66 ⅔%) and less than eighty per cent (80%) of the suggested retail list price of top-line records on which recordings of the majority of our artists are initially released) shall be three-quarters (¾) of the otherwise applicable royalty rate provided hereinabove, and royalties on sales of records on a budget or low-price record line (i.e., bearing a suggested retail list price of sixty-six and two-thirds per cent (66 ⅔%) or less than the suggested retail list price of such top-line records) shall be one-half of such otherwise applicable royalty rate.

Royalties on records sold for use as premium or promotional merchandise shall be at one-half the rate provided hereinbefore and shall be based on the price (less governmental taxes and duties) received by us for such records. No royalty shall be payable as to records distributed to members of and/or subscribers to any "record club" operation, either as a result of joining or subscribing to such club, and/or as a result of the purchase of a required number of records, including but not limited to "bonus" and/or "free" records.

No royalties shall be payable in respect of records given away for promotional purposes or sold at below stated wholesale prices to disc jockeys, record reviewers, radio and television stations and networks, motion picture companies, music publishers, our employees, you or other customary recipients of promotional records or for use on transportation facilities, or records sold as scrap, salvage, overstock or "cut outs," or records sold below fifty per cent (50%) of our regular wholesale price to distributors or others. If records are shipped subject to a special discount or merchandise plan, the number of such records deemed to have been sold shall be determined by reducing the number of records shipped by the percentage of such discount granted and if a discount is granted in the form of "free" or "bonus" records, such "free" or "bonus" records shall not be deemed included in the number of records sold.

Our customary charges for albums, jackets, boxes, or other packaging and container will be excluded from the royalty base for the purposes of this Paragraph 3. At the present time there are deductions from the suggested retail list price (or other applicable price, if any, upon which royalties are computed) of phonograph records of a sum equal to ten per cent (10%) thereof in respect of single records which are packaged in color or other special printed sleeves; ten per cent (10%) thereof for standard long play "singlefold" disc album jackets without inserts or other special elements; fifteen per cent (15%) for other long play disc album jackets; twenty per cent (20%) thereof for reel-to-reel tapes, cartridges, cassettes and any other types of recordings other than discs; and twenty-five per cent (25%) for compact discs.

4. For your services rendered, and for the rights granted herein to us, we shall make a non-returnable advance payment to you, within fourteen (14) days after the services are rendered at each recording session, at the rate of union scale, and each such payment shall constitute an advance and be charged against your royalties, if and when earned, under this or any other agreement between you and us. Within fourteen (14) days after the services are rendered at each recording session we will pay for the services of the accompanying musicians, vocalists, arrangers and copyists at the rate of union scale, and such payments and other recording costs shall be charged against your royalties, if and when earned, under this or any other agreement between us.

5. In the event you accompany other royalty artists, it is agreed that the amount of your royalty shall be proportionately reduced by the total number of royalty artists and the costs under Paragraph 4 to be charged against your royalties shall be proportionately reduced.

6. Payment of accrued royalties shall be made semi-annually on the 1st day of May for the six months ending February 28th; and on the 1st day of November, for the six months ending August 31, in each year. However, we shall have the right to deduct from the amount of royalties due any advance royalties previously paid. All royalty statements, and all other accounts rendered by us to you, shall be binding upon you and not subject to any objection by you for any reason unless specific

objection in writing, stating the basis thereof, is given to us within one (1) year from the date rendered and unless an action, suit or proceeding is commenced against us in a court of competent jurisdiction within one (1) year from the date such specific objection is made in writing. In computing the royalties hereunder, we shall have the right to withhold reasonable reserves for record returns and for credits of any nature. Such reserves shall not be greater than fifty per cent (50%) of the monies otherwise due to you as royalties in connection with such records, and we agree to liquidate the reserves within two accounting periods subsequent to the accounting period in which the reserves were originally withheld.

7. During the term of this contract you will not perform for the purpose of making phonograph records for any person other than us; and after the expiration of the term of this contract you will not perform any selections recorded hereunder for any other person for the purpose of making phonograph records, within five (5) years after the completion of the recording, or two (2) years after the expiration of this contract, whichever is later. If during the term of this contract you perform any composition for the purpose of making any recording for any medium other than phonograph records you will do so only pursuant to a written contract containing an express provision that neither such performance nor any recording thereof will be used directly or indirectly for the purpose of making phonograph records or any other device for home use. You agree to supply us promptly with a signed copy or a photostat of a signed copy upon execution of such agreement. You acknowledge that your services are unique and extraordinary.

8. All recordings hereunder and all records and reproductions made therefrom, together with sound recording copyrights therein and the performances embodied therein, shall be entirely our property, free of any claims whatsoever by you or any person deriving any rights or interests from you. You acknowledge that your performances in the sound recordings hereunder were made for hire within the scope of your employment and that we are to be considered the author for the purpose of copyrights in sound recordings and that we own all of the rights comprised in such copyrights, including any rights to renew and extend the copyrights. Without limitation of the foregoing, we, and/or our subsidiaries, affiliates and licensees shall have the right to make records or other reproductions of the performances embodied in such recordings by any method now or hereafter known, and to sell and deal in the same under any trade-mark or trade-names or labels designated by us, or we may at our election refrain therefrom.

9. We shall have the right to use and to allow others to use your name, signature and likeness, and biographical material concerning you, for advertising and purposes of trade, and otherwise without restriction, in connection with the services performed. You agree that during the term of this agreement you will not permit or authorize anyone other than us to use your name, signature or likeness in connection with the making, advertising or marketing of phonograph records, except for phonograph records made by you prior to the term of this agreement under agreements with other recording companies.

10. Notwithstanding any provision in this contract to the contrary, it is specifically understood and agreed by all parties hereto:

a. They are bound by all the terms and provisions of the AFTRA CODE OF FAIR PRACTICE for Phonograph recordings:

b. That should there by any inconsistency between this contract and said CODE OF FAIR PRACTICE, the said CODE OF FAIR PRACTICE shall prevail, but nothing in this provision shall affect terms, compensation or conditions provided in this contract which are more favorable to members of AFTRA than the terms, compensation and conditions provided for in said CODE OF FAIR PRACTICE.

c. If the term of this contract is of longer duration than the term of said Code, then from and after the expiration date of the Code: (a) the provisions of this contract shall be deemed modified to conform to any agreement or modifications negotiated or agreed to in a renewal or extension of the Code; and (b) while no code is in effect the existence of this contract shall not prevent the artist from engaging in any strike or work stoppage without penalty by way of damage or otherwise to you or AFTRA. In the event you engage in such strike or stoppage we may suspend this contract for the duration of the strike or stoppage and may have the option of extending the term of this contract for a period of time equal to the length of such strike or stoppage which option must be exercised by written notice given to you within thirty (30) days after the end of the strike or stoppage.

d. The artist represents that (s) he is or will become a member of the American Federation of Television and Radio Artists in good standing.*

11. You represent and warrant that you are under no disability, restriction or prohibition, whether contractual or otherwise, with respect to your right to execute this contract and perform its terms and conditions, and with respect to your right to record any and all compositions here-

under. You agree to and do hereby indemnify, save and hold us harmless from any and all loss and damage (including attorneys' fees) arising out of or connected with any claim by a third party which is inconsistent with any of the warranties or representations made by you in this contract, and you agree to reimburse us, on demand, for any payment made by us at any time after the date hereof with respect to any liability or claim to which the foregoing indemnity applies.

12. (a) All compositions written or composed in whole or in part by you, or which are owned or controlled directly or indirectly in whole or in part by you ("Controlled Composition"), shall be licensed to us, at our election, at a rate per selection of _____ per cent (_____%) of the minimum statutory mechanical license fee rate per selection (or, with respect to compositions having a playing time of more than five (5) minutes, _____ per cent (_____%) of the amount set forth in the compulsory license provisions of the United States Copyright Act) in effect on the date of release of the particular record, on the basis of records sold and not returned. Arranged versions of musical compositions in the public domain, constituting a Controlled Composition, when recorded by you hereunder, shall be free from copyright royalties.

(b) The total mechanical license fees for all selections in an LP shall not exceed ten (10) times the current minimum statutory mechanical license fee rate for each LP sold and not returned.

(c) As to a Controlled Composition, if a record is excluded from royalty payments under the provisions of Paragraph 3 hereof, then no mechanical license royalty shall be payable in respect of that record.

(d) In the event that the mechanical rates payable by us are in excess of the amounts provided in subdivisions (a) and (b) above you agree to indemnify and save us harmless. If we should pay the excess, you owe the same to us; in addition to other remedies to which we may resort, we may recoup the excess from royalties otherwise due to you or from any other payments to be made hereunder to you.

(e) Any assignment made by you of the ownership or copyright in any such Controlled Composition shall be made by you subject to the provisions hereof.

13. For the purposes of this contract the terms "records" or "phonograph records" shall include all forms of recordings manufactured or sold primarily for use as home entertainment including, without limitation, discs of any speed or size, magnetic recording tape and any other medium for reproduction of artistic performances primarily for home entertainment now known or which may hereafter become known, whether embodying sound alone or sound synchronized with or accompanied by visual images, e.g. "sight and sound" devices. We agree not to make or exploit any audiovisual product embodying your performance without your prior written consent.[1]

14. This contract sets forth the entire agreement between us with respect to the subject matter hereof. No modification, amendment, waiver, termination or discharge of this contract or any provision hereof shall be binding upon us unless confirmed by a written instrument signed by an officer of our company. No waiver of any provision of this contract or of any default hereunder shall affect our rights thereafter to enforce such provision or to exercise any right or remedy in the event of any other default, whether or not similar.

15. This agreement shall be deemed to have been made in the State of New York, and its validity, construction and effect shall be governed by the laws of the State of New York.

16. The period of this contract shall be one (1) year commencing with the date hereof.

17. You grant us _____ (_____) successive options to extend the term of this agreement for periods of one (1) year each upon all the terms and conditions herein contained. Such extensions shall commence at the expiration of the term of this agreement, unless it shall have been extended, in which event it shall commence at the latest expiration date of any such extension. Any option to extend the term of this agreement may be exercised by us by giving you notice in writing at least thirty (30) days prior to the expiration of the term of this agreement or any extensions thereof. Such notice to you may be given by delivery to you personally or by mailing to you at your address last known to us. Such notice by mail shall be deemed to have been given on the date on which it is mailed by registered mail.

18. We may at our election assign this agreement or any of our rights hereunder.

Please date and sign all copies of this letter in the place provided and return same to the undersigned. One executed copy of this letter will be returned to you for your files.

---

[1]For a form of Rider covering video rights, see Form 12B hereinafter.

Very truly yours,
RECORD COMPANY

By _____

AGREED TO AND ACCEPTED:

_____

* In the event the artist is an instrumentalist and a member of the American Federation of Musicians, Paragraph 10 which refers to AFTRA will be omitted. Pursuant to the union agreement between the record company and the American Federation of Musicians, the recording contract will contain or be deemed to contain clauses substantially as follows:

a. the provision of Paragraphs 11 and 12 of the Phonograph Record Labor Agreement between the American Federation of Musicians and us shall be deemed incorporated herein to the same extent as if fully set forth herein, and the provisions of such paragraphs of such agreement shall govern in the case of any variance between them and the provisions of this agreement.

b. this agreement shall not become effective unless and until it shall be approved by the International Executive Board of the American Federation of Musicians or by a duly authorized agent thereof.

c. any assignment by us of this agreement or any of our rights hereunder shall not become effective unless and until it is approved in writing by the American Federation of Musicians.

Video Rights Rider

1. Definitions:
   As used in this Rider, the following definitions apply:
   a) "Video"—each and every original recording of sound, coupled with a visual image, by any method or on any substance or material, whether now or hereafter known, including by means of film, videotape or other audiovisual media, which is used or useful in the recording, production or manufacture of Videograms.
   b) "Videogram"—all forms of sound reproduction coupled with visual images, now or hereafter known, including but not limited to videocassettes, videodiscs, videotape or any other device now or hereafter devised and designed to be used in conjunction with a reproduction apparatus which causes a visual image to be seen on the screen of a television receiver or any comparable device now or hereafter devised.
   c) "Recording Costs"—as to Videos shall include costs connected with the preparation, pre-production, production, post-production, completion and delivery of the final master tape or film of videos, including payments to production companies (including without limitation, video producers, directors, writers and associate producers); technical, lighting and production crews; each and every individual (including Artist) who appears in or who rendered services or performances in or in connection with a Video; any union, guild, labor organization or trustee pursuant to the terms of any collective bargaining agreement or otherwise; studios, halls and facilities; set construction crews and materials; location and police permits and fees; transportation, living expenses and per diems incurred in connection with location scouting and the attendance of artists and all production personnel at pre-production, production and post-production sessions and the preparation therefor; equipment rental and cartage; insurance premiums paid in connection with the production of Videos; taxes and contingencies (including fees or mark-ups payable to any production company; tape, film or other stock; on-line and off-line editing, mixing, special effects, color correction, audio track transfer or dubbing, title cards and similar functions; creation of videocassette viewing copies from the final master tape or film; payments in connection with the production and utilization of the musical works embodied on Videos, including, without limitation, flat fee payments to the publishers of such musical works (or their agents for collection) but excluding any payments in the nature of a royalty or "per unit" fee arising out of or in connection with the distribution and sale of Videos; unreimbursed costs and expenses incurred in the duplication and delivery of copies of Videos for licensees; and all other costs and expenses (excluding Company's overhead costs and services of Company's employees) incurred with respect to Videos which are now or which may become generally recognized as production costs of audiovisual works.
   d) "Phonograph Records"—all forms of sound reproduction embodying sound alone, now or hereafter known, manufactured or distributed primarily for home use, school use, jukebox use or use in means of transportation.
   e) "Controlled Composition"—one wholly or partly written by Artist, or owned or controlled directly or indirectly in whole or in part by Artist.
   f) "Advance"—a prepayment of royalties.
2. You shall be available, from time to time, at our request and expense, to perform in order to record via film, videotape or other audiovisual media, performances by you of musical compositions on Videos delivered hereunder. Performances shall be scheduled so as not to unreasonably interfere with your other professional activities.
3. You and we shall mutually agree in writing on a) the compositions and other material to

be contained in Videos, b) the general concept or story, c) the producer and director, d) the production budget and e) the time and place of recording.

4. We shall be solely responsible for paying Recording Costs of the Videos up to the amount of the production budget mutually agreed in writing. If the Recording Costs exceed the production budget because of your acts or omissions, you shall be responsible for and shall pay such excess. Should we determine to pay such excess, although not obligated to do so, you shall reimburse us promptly on demand, without limitation of our other rights and remedies. We shall also have the right to recoup such excess from any monies payable to you hereunder.

5. Your fixed compensation in respect of performances to produce a Video shall be only the minimum amounts payable for such performances under applicable collective bargaining agreements. The foregoing is without prejudice to your right to receive the contingent compensation under Paragraph 8 hereof.

6. We or our designee, as employers for hire, shall own all right, title and interest in the said Videos in perpetuity throughout the world, from the inception of their origination, including the worldwide copyright therein. Each such audiovisual work shall be deemed a "work made for hire" that is specially ordered or commissioned within the meaning of Section 101 of the Copyright Act of 1976.

7. All Recording Costs shall be deemed Advances recoupable by us from (a) not to exceed fifty per cent (50%) of your royalties on the exploitation of Phonograph Records, b) your royalties as provided in Paragraph 8 a) in respect of the exploitation of Videograms, and c) from monies included in the computation of Net Receipts as provided in Paragraph 8 b).

8. Your royalties on our exploitation of Videograms shall be determined as follows:
   a) On Net Sales of units manufactured for distribution by us, the royalty will be computed at the following percentage rates:
      1) On units sold for distribution in the United States: twelve per cent (12%) of the Royalty Base Price.
      2) On units sold for distribution outside the United States: twelve per cent (12%) of the Royalty Base Price. The *Royalty Base Price* is our published wholesale price in effect at the commencement of the accounting period concerned less all taxes and less an applicable container charge of fifteen per cent (15%) of the said wholesale price. The wholesale price of Videograms sold expressly for rental will be computed so as to include any applicable renewal charges.
   b) On units manufactured for distribution by any Licensee of us, and on all other distribution or commercial exploitation (except exploitation as covered by Paragraph 8 a) (above), we shall pay you fifty per cent (50%) of the Net Receipts (as defined below). Monies earned and received by us from any Licensee (rather than monies earned and received by the Licensee) in respect of such exploitation shall be included in the computation of Net Receipts. We shall negotiate at arm's length with respect to such exploitation with any joint ventures, subsidiaries, wholly or partly owned, and other divisions of us. Net Receipts shall mean all monies earned and received by us from exploitation by means other than Videograms or Phonograph Records manufactured for distribution by us, less
      1) the distribution costs, including all direct out-of-pocket costs incurred in respect of the marketing, advertising or licensing, other than general overhead expenses.
      2) a twenty-five per cent (25%) distribution fee.
      3) payments to third parties, including but not limited to unions, guilds and publishers.
      4) any other item of direct expense attributable to exploitation, collection and receipt in the U.S.A. of such monies, and
      5) Recording Costs not previously recouped from Phonograph Record royalties.
   c) In respect of Paragraph 8a), as to Videograms sold by direct mail or through "clubs" or similar sales plans, and as to sales through retail outlets in conjunction with special advertisements on radio or television, the royalty rate shall be one-half that provided in Paragraph 8a).
   d) No royalties shall be payable in respect of Videograms furnished without charge for purposes of promotion, critique or review, or as a sales inducement to distributors, subdistributors and dealers. All such royalty-free units distributed for promotional purposes shall be stamped or marked with a legend to the effect that they are for promotional purposes only and are "not for sale." No royalties shall be payable on

units sold after deletion from our or our Licensees' or any sublicensees' catalogs at a price which is one-third (⅓) or less than the then current applicable subdistributor (or equivalent) price.

e) With respect to Joint Recordings of you with one or more other artists, the royalty rate to be used in determining the royalties payable to you shall be computed by multiplying the royalty rate otherwise applicable thereto by a fraction, the numerator of which shall be one and the denominator of which shall be the total number of royalty artists whose performances are embodied on a Joint Recording.

f) With respect to exploitation of a Video together with other audiovisual material not recorded hereunder, the following will apply in respect of the computation of royalties under Paragraph 8a): the royalty rate shall be multiplied by a fraction in which the denominator is the total playing time of the combined unit and the numerator is the playing time of the Video contained therein. As to the computation of Net Receipts under Paragraph 8b) the said Net Receipts attributable to the Video shall be at the same proportion indicated by the fraction referred to in the previous sentence.

9. During the term of this Rider, no third party other than us will be authorized to make, sell, broadcast or otherwise exploit audiovisual material consisting substantially of the musical performances of you, except as provided hereinafter. You may grant to a third party the right to create a program embodying a) your non-musical dramatic performance, or b) subject to our right of first refusal as described below, your musical performances for exploitation through theatrical exhibition and/or television broadcast or transmission. Such right of first refusal shall operate as follows: (1) You shall first notify us of all of the material terms and conditions of the proposed agreement, pursuant to which the audiovisual material is to be made, sold, broadcast or otherwise exploited, including but not limited to the titles of the Compositions covered by the proposed agreement, the format to be used, the manner of exploitation proposed and the identities of all proposed parties to the agreement. (2) You shall offer to enter into an agreement with us, containing the same terms and conditions with respect to advances, costs, royalties and other payments described in your notice and otherwise in the same form as in the agreement, but with payments to you that are ninety (90%) per cent of the payments to you in the proposed agreement. If we do not accept your offer within thirty (30) days after its receipt ("Offer Period"), you may then enter the proposed agreement with the same parties mentioned in your notice, subject to subparagraph a) below and provided that the agreement is concluded with those parties within thirty (30) days after the end of the Offer Period upon the same terms and conditions set forth in your notice to us. If the agreement with the third party or parties is not concluded within such thirty (30) day period, then the said first refusal procedure must be repeated.

a) If we do not accept an offer made to us pursuant to this paragraph, such non-acceptance shall not be considered a waiver of our other rights pursuant to this Rider and the main recording agreement. Thus, among other things, you and any third party or parties may not exploit audiovisual material featuring you in the form of Phonograph Records, and you may not authorize the use by any third party or parties of any non-visual or audiovisual recordings owned by or exclusively licensed to us. You agree not to act in contravention of our rights.

10. As to Controlled Compositions, we are hereby granted an irrevocable worldwide, nonexclusive license to reproduce such Compositions in Videos and Videograms and to distribute and perform such Videograms and to authorize others so to do. We will not be required to make any payment in connection with such reproduction, performance or distribution, and that license will apply whether or not we receive any payment in connection with such reproduction, performance or distribution.

Royalties in connection with licenses for the use of non-Controlled Compositions shall be borne equally by us and, to the extent of the royalties payable to you under subparagraph 8a), by you, i.e. either one-half of the said amounts shall be deducted from the royalties under that subparagraph or all of such amounts shall be deducted from Net Receipts under subparagraph 8b), whichever arises first.

Form 13

Artist/Producer
Development Agreement

AGREEMENT made this _____day of _____by and between _____ ("Producer") and _____("Artist")

Witnesseth:

In consideration of the mutual covenants herein contained, it is hereby agreed as follows:

1. Producer agrees to provide production services as an independent producer and the necessary studio facilities to Artist, for the immediate purpose of producing and exploiting a master demonstration record ("master demo") and for the further purpose of assisting in the development of the Artist's career.
2. Artist and Producer ("Parties") agree to seek an exclusive artist/producer recording contract with a nationally distributed record company ("Recording Contract"), providing for (a) a commitment of at least two (2) double-sided singles in the initial year and at least one (1) LP a year in not more than four (4) option years, and (b) a basic combined artist-producer royalty of not less than nine per cent (9%) of ninety per cent (90%) of the retail selling price, subject to customary adjustments for tape, foreign, record clubs, budget records, container charges, etc.
3. The Parties shall share equally in all advances and royalties received under the Recording Contract, and under any alternate or substitute agreement. The shares shall be payable only after recoupment of all recording costs and other disbursements under this agreement and the Recording Contract.
4. Artist agrees that Producer will continue as Artist's Producer for the full term, including any exercised options, of the Recording Contract, and of any alternate or substituted agreements with respect to the Recording Contract.
5. Artist agrees to execute, at Producer's request, a Recording Contract which contains terms and conditions no less favorable to the Artist than those set forth above.
6. In the event that Producer has not negotiated a Recording Contract within a period of one (1) year from the date hereof, Artist shall have the right to terminate this contract by written notice by registered or certified mail.
7. The Parties agree that the term of this agreement shall extend for the full term of the Recording Contract, as same may be extended through the exercise of options, and such term as extended of any alternate or substitute agreements. If an option is not exercised under any such agreement, the term of this agreement shall be deemed extended for an additional six (6) months for the purpose of obtaining an alternate or substitute agreement.
8. In the event that the Parties are unable to obtain a Recording Contract within nine (9) months from the date of this agreement, Producer may authorize the release, on a regional or national basis, of any master demo produced under this agreement upon the minimum royalty and the participation terms of Paragraphs 2 and 3 hereof.
9. As to any composition written or controlled directly or indirectly by Artist which is recorded and released pursuant to the provisions hereof, Artist agrees to assign to Producer a fifty per cent (50%) undivided interest in Artist's interest in the copyright of the composition, as well as the sole and exclusive right to administer and protect both Parties' interest in the composition throughout the world, for the full life of the copyright. Producer will account to Artist, and pay Artist, semiannually within sixty (60) days after July 1 and December 31 of each year, fifty per cent (50%) of the net publisher's share actually received by Producer or its representative in the U.S.A. and remaining after deduction of writer royalties and other direct costs. If Artist is a writer of such a composition, Artist and Producer shall enter into a songwriter-publisher contract on the terms of The Songwriters Guild (formerly known as AGAC) minimum basic form contract.

10. Producer agrees to be available for actual production services as an independent producer pursuant to this agreement. In the event of the Producer's disability or other unavailability for such services, any substitute for Producer must be mutually approved, which approval shall not be unreasonably withheld. The costs of any such substitute shall be charged against the participation of the Producer.

11. In the event of any unresolved controversy between the Parties relating to this agreement, the Parties shall submit the same to a single arbitrator for final determination under the then applicable rules of the American Arbitration Association in the City of New York, and judgment may be entered upon any such award in any court having jurisdiction.

12. No breach of this agreement by either Party shall be deemed material, unless the other Party gives written notice of the breach by registered or certified mail, and the recipient of the notice has failed to cure the breach within thirty (30) days after the receipt of such notice.

13. Producer shall account and pay royalties to Artist semiannually within sixty (60) days after receipt from a record company pursuant to a Recording Contract. Receipts contemplated under Paragraph 8 above shall also be so accounted for.

14. Artist shall have the right to audit the books and records of Producer, no more than once annually, upon reasonable written notice with respect to all matters hereunder. Audits shall be performed during business hours at Producer's offices by a certified public accountant.

15. Artist agrees that because his or her services are unique and extraordinary and cannot be adequately compensated for in damages, Producer shall be entitled to injunctive relief, in addition to damages, to enforce the provisions of this agreement.

16. Producer may assign its rights under this agreement, in whole or in part, to any subsidiary, affiliated or controlling corporation or to any other assignee, provided that such assignment shall not relieve Producer of its obligations under this agreement. Producer may also assign its rights under this agreement to any of its licensees, in the ordinary course of business, to the extent necessary or appropriate, in Producer's sole discretion, to implement the license granted.

17. This agreement shall be deemed made in and shall be construed in accordance with the laws of the State of New York.

18. This agreement may not be modified orally and shall not be binding until it is signed by both Parties hereto.

IN WITNESS WHEREOF, the parties hereto have entered into this agreement the day and year first above written.

ARTIST

_____

PRODUCER

_____

Form 14

Record Production Agreement

Date _____

Independent Producer
1420 Broadway
New York, New York

Dear Sir:

Reference is made to a recording agreement dated _____ between Record Company (herein referred to as "we" or "us" or "undersigned") and _____ (artist).

It is agreed between us as follows:

1. So long as you are available and are acceptable to the artist you shall supervise, direct and produce the recording sessions under the recording agreement up to the point of delivery to us of a finished tape in first-class condition and suitable for the purpose of manufacturing top quality phonograph records. For such services and your expenses you shall receive no consideration other than the royalties set forth below. All aspects of such production shall be subject to our approval.

2. As and when royalties become payable to the artist(s), after recoupment of advances against royalties, we shall pay you as to subsequent sales of records as follows.[1]

As to records sold in the United States of America a royalty of _____(_____%) per cent, and as to records sold in other countries a royalty of _____(_____%) per cent, of the retail list prices (less governmental taxes and duties) of records in the country of manufacture of 90% of all double-faced records manufactured and sold on both faces of which are embodied any of the selections recorded in the master recording(s) produced hereunder; and one-half the respective amounts of such royalty for 90% of all records manufactured and sold on only one face of which is embodied a selection recorded in the master recording(s) provided, however, that for records sold in foreign countries the undersigned may, from time to time, at its election, base the percentages upon the retail list prices in the country of manufacture or the country of sale. If a manufacturer's suggested retail list price is not utilized or permitted, the generally accepted retail price shall be utilized. In the event that any of the recordings in the master recording(s) produced hereunder are released together with or in combination with other performances or recordings in a long playing or extended play record, it is agreed that royalties will be paid for only those selections which are recordings in the master recording(s) produced hereunder and the royalties paid shall be prorated in the proportion that the number of selections included in such record which are recordings in the master recording(s) produced hereunder bears to the total number of selections embodied in such records. Royalties for records sold outside of the United States of America are to be computed in the national currency of the country where the retail list prices above mentioned apply, and are to be payable only with respect to records for which the undersigned receives payment in the United States of America, in dollar equivalent at the rate of exchange at the time the undersigned receives payment in the United States of America, and after proportionate deductions for taxes withheld at the source.

No royalties shall be payable in respect of records given away for promotional purposes or sold at below stated wholesale prices to disc jockeys, record reviewers, radio and television stations and networks, motion picture companies, music publishers, our employees, you or other customary recipients of promotional records or for use on transportation facilities, or records sold as scrap, salvage, overstock or "cut outs", or records sold below our cost of manufacturing. If records are shipped subject to a special discount or merchandise plan, the number of such records deemed to have been sold shall be determined by reducing the number of records shipped by the percentage of such discount granted and if a discount is granted in the form of "free" or "bonus" records, such "free" or "bonus" records shall not be deemed included in the number of records sold.

As to records sold by direct mail operation or through record clubs or similar sales plans or devices, and as to sales by distribution through retail outlets in conjunction with special advertisements on radio or television, and as to sales of tape through licensees embodying performances hereunder, the royalty shall be one-half that provided hereinbefore. Royalties on sales of records on a mid-priced record line (i.e. bearing a suggested retail list price of more than sixty-six and two-thirds per cent (66 ⅔%) and less than eighty per cent (80%) of the suggested retail list price of top-line records on which recordings of the majority of Company's artists are initially released) shall be three-quarters (¾) of the otherwise applicable royalty rate provided hereinabove, and royalties on sales of records on a budget or low-price record line (i.e. bearing a suggested retail list price of sixty-six and two-thirds per cent (66 ⅔%) or less than the suggested retail list price of such top-line records) shall be one-half of such otherwise applicable royalty rate.

No royalty shall be payable as to records distributed to members of and/or subscribers to any "record club" operation, either as a result of joining or subscribing to such club, and/or as a result of the purchase of a required number of records, including but not limited to "bonus" and/or "free" records or as to records sold or distributed as "premiums."

Our customary charges for albums, jackets, boxes or other packaging and container will be excluded from the royalty base for the purpose of this paragraph. At the present time there are deductions from the suggested retail list price (or other applicable price, if any, upon which royalties are computed) of phonograph records of a sum equal to ten per cent (10%) thereof in respect of single records which are packaged in color or other special printed sleeves; ten per cent (10%) thereof for standard long play "singlefold" disc album jackets without inserts or other special elements; fifteen per cent (15%) for other long play disc album jackets; twenty per cent (20%) thereof for reel-to-reel tapes, cartridges, cassettes and any other types of recordings other than discs; and twenty-five per cent (25%) for so-called compact discs.

3. Insofar as you are concerned, we alone shall own, without restrictions, the entire right, title and interest in and to any master recording produced and delivered to us hereunder and in and to the worldwide copyright in the sound recording thereof, and in and to any renewals and extensions of copyright, worldwide; we shall have the sole and exclusive right to manufacture, distribute, sell and in all ways exploit and deal in, throughout the world, or to refrain therefrom, all phonograph records and other musical devices which may be manufactured from the master recording, and the performances embodied thereon; and we shall have the sole and exclusive right to use and control any master recording as we see fit. in our absolute discretion.

4. Payment of all sums to be paid by us hereunder pursuant to paragraph 2 shall be made semi-iannually within sixty (60) days following the six months ending February 28th and August 31st and shall be accompanied by a statement setting forth in reasonable detail the computation of such sums. No statement shall be due for any period in which we do not sell records. All royalty statements, and all other accounts rendered by us to you, shall be binding upon you and not subject to any objection by you for any reason unless specific objection in writing, stating the basis thereof, is given to us within one (1) year from the date rendered, and unless an action, suit, or proceeding is commenced against us in a court of competent jurisdiction within one (1) year from the date such specific objection is made in writing. In computing the royalties hereunder, we shall have the right to withhold reasonable reserves for record returns and for credits of any nature. Such reserves shall not be greater than fifty per cent (50%) of the monies otherwise due to you as royalties in connection with such records, and we agree to liquidate the reserves within two accounting periods subsequent to the accounting period in which the reserves were originally withheld.

5. We shall have the right to use and to allow others to use your name, likeness and biography in connection with the advertising, publicizing or sale of phonograph records produced hereunder.

6. You and we shall agree on a written budget before any recording sessions. Any additional costs shall be borne by you unless we otherwise agree in writing.

---

[1]As an alternative it may be provided "we shall pay you retroactive to the first record sold hereunder as follows:"

7. We may assign this agreement or any interest therein.

8. This agreement shall be construed under the laws of the State of New York.

Please constitute the foregoing a binding agreement by signing at the place indicated below:

Very truly yours,

RECORD COMPANY

By _____
President

AGREED TO AND ACCEPTED

_____

Independent producer

Foreign Record Licensing Agreement

AGREEMENT made and entered into this _____ day of _____ 19 _____ by and between FOREIGN RECORD COMPANY, hereinafter referred to as a "Licensee", and U.S.A. RECORD COMPANY, hereinafter referred to as "Owner";

Witnesseth:

WHEREAS, Owner was organized for the purpose of and is engaged in the United States of America in the production of phonograph records (hereinafter referred to as "records"); and

WHEREAS, Licensee is in a position directly or indirectly to provide manufacturing and marketing facilities for records in the licensed territory referred to below;

NOW, THEREFORE, in consideration of the foregoing and of the mutual promises hereinafter set forth, it is agreed:

1. Owner hereby grants to Licensee, for a period of three years from the date of this agreement, the exclusive and non-assignable rights to manufacture, sell and distribute records, without limitation or restriction except as set forth herein, with respect to the recordings (herein sometimes called "master recordings") set forth in Exhibit A, attached hereto and made a part hereof, anywhere in and solely in the territory of _____ (herein called "licensed territory").

2. Except as provided for in this agreement all other rights of any nature whatsoever in the aforementioned recordings are reserved by Owner.

3. If Licensee fails to account and make payments hereunder and such failure is not cured within thirty (30) days after written notice thereof to Licensee, or if Licensee fails to perform any other obligations required of it hereunder and such failure is not cured within thirty (30) days after written notice thereof to Licensee, or in the event that Licensee shall go into compulsory liquidation, or shall go into bankruptcy or make an assignment for the benefit of creditors or make any compositions with creditors, or any insolvency or composition proceeding shall be commenced by or against Licensee, then and in any of such events Owner, in addition to such other rights or remedies which it may have at law or otherwise under this agreement, may elect to cancel or terminate this agreement without prejudice to any rights or claims it may have, and all rights hereunder shall forthwith revert to Owner and Licensee may not thereafter manufacture records from masters furnished under this agreement by Owner, or sell such records. Upon such cancellation or termination, Licensee shall destroy all such records in its possession and thereupon return all then existing tapes previously received from Owner, or any derivatives of same.

4. a. In consideration for the rights herein granted Licensee agrees to pay to Owner a sum equal to ten (10%) per cent of the suggested retail list price (less taxes and duties) in the licensed territory of ninety (90%) per cent of all records manufactured and sold hereunder. If there are no suggested retail list prices of records in a country in the licensed territory, then for the purpose of computing royalties hereunder the prices of records in such country generally regarded as the equivalent thereof shall be deemed the suggested retail list prices of such records. Licensee shall notify Owner of the suggested retail list price in the licensed territory within thirty (30) days from the date hereof, and will notify Owner of any changes thereof within fourteen (14) days of any such change. In the event payments due to Owner are delayed or denied by governmental regulations, Owner shall be entitled to designate a local depository in the licensed territory in which Licensee at the direction of Owner shall use its best efforts to deposit such moneys to the credit of Owner. There shall be no deductions for records returned by purchasers.

b. As additional royalty under the agreement, Licensee agrees to pay to Owner fifty (50%) per cent of all public performance and broadcasting fees, if any, received in respect of all records manufactured and sold under this agreement; provided, however, that whenever such fees are not computed and paid in direct relation to the public performances and broadcasts of such records, they shall be computed for the purpose of this agreement by determining the proportion of any such fee paid to Licensee as the number of records produced under this agreement and sold in the area from which the fee is derived bears to the total number of records sold in that area by Licensee.

5. Payments by Licensee to Owner of royalties due pursuant to Paragraphs 4a and 4b hereof shall be made semiannually in the United States and in United States dollars within forty-five (45) days following the end of June and December, of each year, and each such payment shall be accompanied by a statement setting forth in detail the computation of the amount thereof and include, without limitation of the generality of the foregoing, the number of records sold from each master during the accounting period, as well as all charges, royalties and claims hereunder. All payments made by Licensee hereunder shall be computed in local currency at official rates effective on the date provided for payment, subject to any governmental exchange regulations in effect from time to time in the territory.

6. The royalties to be paid by Licensee to Owner pursuant to Paragraph 4a hereof are intended to include provision for all recording artists' and other talent royalties which shall be entirely payable by Owner. Licensee shall be free of any obligations to pay the costs of recording sessions.

7. With respect to records manufactured or sold hereunder from master recordings which embody copyrighted musical or other material, Licensee agrees to pay or cause to be paid directly to the proprietors of the copyrights or their duly authorized agents all royalties which may be or become due to them.

8. With respect to records manufactured or sold hereunder from master recordings which were produced subject to the American Federation of Musicians Music Performance Trust Fund Agreement, Licensee agrees to pay to Owner all sums which may be or become due in accordance with such agreement and all sums which are payable to the Special Fund established under the 1964–1969 Phonograph Record Labor Agreement of the American Federation of Musicians.

9. Licensee agrees to commence the manufacture and sale of recordings hereunder within three (3) months from the date of this agreement, and in the event Licensee shall fail so to do all rights granted herein shall automatically cease and terminate.

10. Licensee agrees that all records manufactured by it under this agreement shall prominently bear the imprint, on the label and album cover and/or sleeve, of the words "Produced by U.S.A. Record Company." Licensee also agrees that each record manufactured or distributed by it under this agreement shall bear the following notice of copyright placed on the surface or reproduction or on the label or container in such manner and location as to give reasonable notice of the claim of copyright: ℗ 19   (name of Owner).

11. Licensee agrees to defend, indemnify and hold Owner harmless against any and all liability, loss, damage, cost or expense, including attorney's fees, paid or incurred, by reason of any breach or claim of breach of any of Licensee's covenants, warranties or representations hereunder or by reason of and in respect of the distribution, manufacture, sale or performance of records made by Licensee hereunder and not due to any violation or breach by Owner of its covenants, warranties or representations hereunder.

12. All recordings released hereunder shall be released in their entirety and without editing and in the manner and for the purpose originally recorded by or for Owner, unless Owner's prior written consent is secured. Adaptations by Licensee for different record speeds shall be deemed authorized. Licensee shall couple performances in a record only in the same manner as recordings manufactured by Owner and only the compositions contained in masters supplied by Owner, unless otherwise notified in writing by Owner.

Recordings shall not be supplied by Licensee to record clubs, nor for promotional giveaways or other devices for mass distribution involving the sale of records at reduced prices or their being given away without receipt of payment, without Owner's prior consent in writing. Advertising or disc jockey promotions shall be deemed exempted from the foregoing prohibitions.

13. Owner agrees to deliver master recordings hereunder by supplying to Licensee at Owner's cost price plus any actual expenses incurred for packing and shipping (including insurance), one or more duplicate tape recordings, acetate masters or metal mothers or stampers (as selected and ordered by Licensee) of each master recording subject to the provisions hereof. Owner may require that such payments shall be made by sight draft against bill of lading. Such tapes, acetates, stampers and mothers shall be delivered to Licensee as promptly as possible following the submission of written orders therefor to Owner. Licensee shall pay all customs, fees, duties and other expenses relating to the importation of the said items. At the time of the delivery to Licensee of the first such derivative from each master recording, Owner shall supply to Licensee, in writing, the correct title of the recorded work; the names of the author, composer and publisher thereof

together with any additional copyright information known to Owner; the names of the recording artists as Owner displays or intends to display them on the labels of the records marketed by Owner; and a statement of whether the recording was produced subject to the American Federation of Musicians Music Performance Trust Fund Agreement.

14. With respect to master recordings delivered hereunder, Owner agrees to supply to Licensee samples of its advertising and promotional material (exclusive of audiovisual material except as provided in Paragraph 22 hereinafter), including catalogues, supplements, release sheets, liners, photographs of artists, and the like, which shall be delivered to Licensee from time to time as prepared by Owner for use in the United States of America. All such samples will be free of charge, except that Licensee will pay all expenses for packing and shipping (including insurance) and customs and duty fees and expenses. Licensee shall have the right, insofar as Owner possesses the right, to use any part or all of such material, in its original form or with minor modifications, on or in connection with records produced hereunder. Owner agrees, upon request, to supply to Licensee any such material in quantity, or plates for reproducing the same, at Owner's cost price plus any actual expenses for packing and shipping (including insurance). Owner may require that such payments shall be made by sight draft against bill of lading. Licensee shall pay all customs fees, duties and other expenses relating to the importation of the material. Licensee shall have the right, at its option, to reproduce any or all such material for use as aforesaid, provided, that Owner itself has obtained the right to grant such right to Licensee and Licensee shall have made any payments necessary in such connection.

15. The rights hereby granted by Owner to Licensee are the following:

a. The right to manufacture, sell, publicly perform and advertise in the licensed territory only, records containing the performances embodied in the master recordings made available by Owner to Licensee as above provided;

b. The right to use in the licensed territory the name, likeness and biography of each artist whose performance is embodied in the said master recordings in connection with the advertising, publicizing or sale of phonograph records manufactured therefrom provided, however, that Licensee shall abide by any restrictions imposed upon Owner with respect thereto of which Owner has notified Licensee at the time of delivery under Paragraph 13.

c. The right to use in the licensed territory only the advertising and promotional material supplied to Licensee hereunder pursuant to the provisions of Paragraphs 14 and 22 hereof, subject to any restrictions imposed upon Owner in respect thereof of which Owner has notified Licensee at the time of delivery under such paragraphs.

16. Licensee shall supply Owner promptly with a minimum of three (3) sample copies of each release.

17. All masters, tapes, acetates, stampers, mothers or duplicates thereof of recordings hereunder, and all copyrights, ownerships and rights in and to such recordings, shall remain the sole and exclusive property of Owner, subject, however, to the rights of Licensee to make reproductions pursuant to the terms of this agreement.

18. Owner shall have the right to inspect and make extracts of the books and records of Licensee, its subsidiaries, affiliates, licensees and assigns wherever same may be, insofar as said books and records pertain to any monies payable to Owner under this agreement and any extension or modification thereof, or insofar as any said books or records pertain to the exercise by Licensee, of any rights granted to Licensee hereunder. Such inspection shall be made on ten (10) days written notice, during normal business hours of normal business days but not more frequently than once annually in each year.

19. Licensee shall refrain from releasing "cover" performances produced by Licensee of any musical composition embodied on a master recording subject to the terms thereof until a period of two (2) months have elapsed from the first day of the release in the licensed territory of records manufactured from such master recording.

20. Upon the expiration or other termination of this agreement, except as otherwise provided herein, all pressing by Licensee shall cease. With respect to all masters, including any made by Licensee, and any other material in Licensee's hands used in the manufacture of Owner's records, Licensee shall promptly at the option of Owner and upon its written instructions, either;

a. deliver same to Owner in the United States or licensed territory, as designated by Owner, at Owner's sole cost and expense of delivery, or

b. transfer same at Owner's sole cost and expense of delivery to any other company designated and approved by Owner, or

c. destroy same under Owner's supervision, or at Owner's request destroy same and supply Owner with an affidavit of such fact, sworn to by a principal officer of Licensee.

Notwithstanding the foregoing, upon the expiration or other termination of this agreement except for termination of this agreement by Owner by virtue of Licensee's breach or default under this agreement, Licensee shall have the right to sell, for a period of six months only, in normal course of business, any inventory of phonograph records previously manufactured hereunder, provided and on condition that within fifteen (15) days from such termination or other expiration Licensee furnishes to Owner a written list of such inventory which also shows the factory costs thereof. Such sales shall be subject to the payment of royalties by Licensee under the terms of this agreement.

However, at any time after the expiration or other termination of this agreement, Owner shall have the right to purchase from Licensee at Licensee's factory cost all or part of the inventory not theretofore sold by Licensee. Such sales shall not be subject to the payment of royalties under this agreement.

21. For the purposes of this agreement, the term "record" or "phonograph record" shall mean any disk record of any material and revolving at any speed, or any other device or contrivance of any type, character, or description, whether now or hereafter known, for the reproduction of sound, manufactured or sold primarily for home entertainment. Rights to sound synchronized with or accompanied by visual images, e.g. "sight and sound" devices are reserved to Owner and Licensee shall not be entitled to participate in any fees or other remuneration collected or to be collected therefor by Owner.

22. Notwithstanding any of the foregoing, to the extent of its rights only, Owner shall make available to Licensee, solely for promotional purposes in connection with records hereunder, videoclips of the artists' performances, not exceeding five minutes in length, owned by Owner and used or to be used for such purpose in Owner's original territory. Owner shall advise Licensee of the availability of such videoclips and Licensee may require that Owner supply a sample at Owner's cost price plus any actual expenses for packing and shipping (including insurance). Owner agrees, upon request, to supply to Licensee additional copies for promotional purposes at Owner's cost price plus any actual expenses for packing and shipping (including insurance). If Licensee proposes to duplicate the videoclips in the licensed territory, then Owner and Licensee shall agree mutually on the material to be supplied by Owner for such purpose, at Licensee's cost. Any right to reproduce shall be conditional upon the Owner itself having obtained the right to grant such right to Licensee and upon the Licensee having made any payments necessary in such connection. Licensee shall pay all customs fees, duties and other expenses relating to the importation of any material referred to in this paragraph. Licensee shall have no authority to license or exploit the said videoclips for commercial purposes, such right being reserved entirely to the Owner. Videoclips for a particular record may not be coupled with other audiovisual material without Owner's written consent.

23. Owner represents and warrants that it possesses full right, power and authority to enter into and to perform this agreement; and that it will not, so long as this agreement remains in effect, grant or attempt to grant to any other person, firm or corporation in the licensed territory, rights of any kind in any of the aforesaid master recordings, the exercise of which would derogate from or be inconsistent with the rights granted to Licensee hereunder. Owner also represents and warrants that there are no liens or encumbrances against any of the recordings which are the subject hereof, which would derogate from or be inconsistent with the rights granted to Licensee hereunder.

24. The covenants, representations and warranties hereunder are subject to applicable laws and treaties, including but not limited to those of the European Economic Community.

25. This agreement shall be deemed made in and shall be construed in accordance with the laws of the State of New York. If any part of this agreement shall be invalid or unenforceable, it shall not affect the validity of the balance of this agreement.

26. Owner may assign its rights hereunder.

27. This agreement may not be modified orally and shall not be binding or effective unless and until it is signed by the parties hereto.

IN WITNESS WHEREOF, the parties hereto have entered into this agreement the day and year first above written.

U.S.A. RECORD COMPANY

By _____

FOREIGN RECORD COMPANY

By _____

Form 16

Sample Motion Picture or Television Film Cue Sheet

LMN Production Company   *June 11, 1985*

JUNIOR LEAGUE

REELS 1 & 2

NO.	SELECTION	COMPOSER	PUBLISHER	EXTENT	HOW USED	TIME
1	Medley consisting of:					
	(a) SIGNATURE	JANE DOE	XYZ	ENTIRE	BKG. INST.	0.07
	(b) JUNIPER	JANE DOE	XYZ	ENTIRE	VIS. VOC.	5.37
2	COWBOYS	MIKE ROE	ABC	PARTIAL	BKG. INST.	0.34
3	Medley consisting of:					
	(a) JUNIPER	JANE DOE	XYZ	PARTIAL	BKG. INST.	0.09
	(b) COWBOYS	MIKE ROE	ABC	ENTIRE	BKG. INST.	0.45
	(c) JUNIPER	JANE DOE	FGH	PARTIAL	BKG. INST.	0.38
	(d) THE BOYS	IRV GROW	XYZ	PARTIAL	BKG. INST.	0.47
4	THE GIRLS	MAY JOE	ABC	ENTIRE	BKG. INST.	0.05
5	THE BIRDS	MAY JOE	ABC	ENTIRE	VIS. VOC.	2.45

REELS 3 & 4

NO.	SELECTION	COMPOSER	PUBLISHER	EXTENT	HOW USED	TIME
6	KERMIS	MAY LOE	ABC	ENTIRE	VIS. VOC.	2.09
7	KERMIS	MAY LOE	XYZ	PARTIAL	BKG. INST.	0.23
8	Medley consisting of:					
	(a) JUNIPER	JANE DOE	XYZ	PARTIAL	BKG. INST.	1.40
	(b) CLEO	BOB SMITH	ABC	ENTIRE	VIS. VOC.	1.50
	(c) KERMAC	MAY LOE	ABC	ENTIRE	BKG. INST.	1.30
9	KERMAC	MAY LOE	ABC	ENTIRE	VIS. VOC.	1.25
10	Medley consisting of:					
	(a) JUNIPER	JANE DOE	ABC	PARTIAL	BKG. INST.	0.24
	(b) COWBOYS	MIKE ROE	ABC	PARTIAL	BKG. INST.	0.24
	(c) JUNIPER	JANE DOE	XYZ	PARTIAL	BKG. INST.	0.12
	(d) COWBOYS	MIKE ROE	ABC	PARTIAL	BKG. INST.	0.14
	(e) JUNIPER	JANE DOE	XYZ	PARTIAL	BKG. INST.	0.30
	(f) COWBOYS	MIKE ROE	ABC	ENTIRE	BKG. INST.	0.45

Form 17A

Standard AFTRA Exclusive Agency Contract: Singer*

American Federation of Television and Radio Artists
Standard AFTRA Exclusive Agency Contract under Rule 12-B

THIS AGREEMENT, made and entered into at ————————————— , by and between
————————————————————————— , hereinafter called the "AGENT," and
————————————————————————— , hereinafter called the "ARTIST."

Witnesseth:

1. The Artist employs the Agent as his sole and exclusive Agent in the transcription, radio broadcasting and television industries (hereinafter referred to as the "broadcasting industries") within the scope of the regulations (Rule 12-B) of the American Federation of Television and Radio Artists (hereinafter called AFTRA), and agrees not to employ any other person or persons to act for him in like capacity during the term hereof, and the Agent accepts such employment. This contract is limited to the broadcasting industries and to contracts of the Artist as an artist in such fields and any reference hereinafter to contracts or employment whereby the Artist renders his services, refers to contracts or employment in the broadcasting industries, except as otherwise provided herein.

2. The Artist agrees that prior to any engagement or employment in the broadcasting industries, he will become a member of AFTRA in good standing and remain such a member for the duration of such engagement or employment. The Artist warrants that he has the right to make this contract and that he is not under any other agency contract in the broadcasting fields. The Agent warrants that he is and will remain a duly franchised agent of AFTRA for the duration of this contract. This paragraph is for the benefit of AFTRA and AFTRA members as well as for the benefit of the parties to this agreement.

3. The term of this contract shall be for a period of ————— , commencing the ————— day of ————————— 19————— (Note—The term may not be in excess of three years.)

4. (a) The Artist agrees to pay to the Agent a sum equal to ————————— per cent (not more than 10%) of all moneys or other consideration received by the Artist, directly or indirectly, under contracts of employment entered into during the term specified herein as provided in the Regulations. Commissions shall be payable when and as such moneys or other consideration are received by the Artist or by anyone else for or on the Artist's behalf.

(b) Any moneys or other consideration received by the Artist or by anyone for or on his behalf, in connection with any termination of any contract of the Artist on which the Agent would otherwise be entitled to receive commission, or in connection with the settlement of any such contract, or any litigation arising out of such contract, shall also be moneys in connection with which the Agent is entitled to the aforesaid commissions; provided, however, that in such event the Artist shall be entitled to deduct arbitration fees, attorney's fees, expenses and court costs before computing the amount upon which the Agent is entitled to his commissions.

(c) Such commissions shall be payable by the Artist to the Agent, as aforesaid, during the term of this contract and thereafter only where specifically provided herein.

---

* Reproduced with permission of the American Federation of Television and Radio Artists

(d) The agent shall be entitled to the aforesaid commissions after the expiration of the term specified herein, for so long a period thereafter as the Artist continues to receive moneys or other consideration under or upon employment contracts entered into by the Artist during the term specified herein, including moneys or other consideration received by the Artist under the extended term of such employment contracts, resulting from the exercise of an option or options given an employer under such employment contracts, extending the term of such employment contracts, whether such options be exercised prior to or after the expiration of the term specified herein.

(e) If after the expiration of the term of this agreement and during the period the Agent is entitled to commissions, a contract of employment of the Artist be terminated before the expiration thereof, as said contract may have been extended by the exercise of options therein contained, by joint action of the Artist and employer, or by the action of either of them, other than on account of an Act of God, illness or the like and the Artist enters into a new contract of employment with said employer within a period of sixty (60) days, such new contract shall be deemed to be in substitution of the contract terminated as aforesaid. In computing the said sixty (60) day period, each day between June 15th and September 15th shall be counted as three-fifths (3/5) of a day only. No contract entered into after said sixty (60) day period shall be deemed to be in substitution of the contract terminated as aforesaid. Contracts of substitution have the same effect as contracts for which they were substituted; provided, however, that any increase or additional salary, bonus or other compensation payable to the Artist (either under such contract of substitution or otherwise) over and above the amounts payable under the contract of employment entered into prior to the expiration of the term of this agreement shall be deemed an adjustment and unless the Agent shall have a valid Agency contract in effect at the time of such adjustment the Agent shall not be entitled to any commissions on any such adjustment. In no event may a contract of substitution with an employer entered into after the expiration of the term of this agreement, extend the period of time during which the Agent is entitled to commission beyond the period that the Agent would have been entitled to commission had no substitution taken place, except to the extent, if necessary, for the Agent to receive the same total amount of commission he would have received had no such substitution taken place; provided, however, that in no event shall the agent receive more than the above percentages as commissions on the Artist's adjusted compensation under the contract of substitution. A change in form of an employer for the purpose of evading this provision, or a change in the corporate form of an employer resulting from reorganization or like, shall not exclude the application of these provisions.

(f) So long as the Agent receives commissions from the Artist, the Agent shall be obligated to service the Artist and perform the obligations of this contract with respect to the services of the Artist on which such commissions are based, subject to AFTRA's Regulations Governing Agents.

(g) The Agent has no right to receive money unless the Artist receives the same, or unless the same is received for or on his behalf, and then only proportionate in the above percentages when and as received. Money paid pursuant to legal process to the Artist's creditors, or by virtue of assignment or direction of the Artist, and deductions from the Artist's compensation made pursuant to law in the nature of a collection or tax at the source, such as Social Security or Old Age Pension taxes, or income taxes withheld at the source, shall be treated as compensation received for or on the Artist's behalf.

5. Should the Agent, during the term or terms specified herein negotiate a contract of employment for the Artist and secure for the Artist a bona fide offer of employment, which offer is communicated by the Agent to the Artist in reasonable detail and in writing, which offer the Artist declines, and if, after the expiration of the term of this agreement and within ninety (90) days after the date upon which the Agent gives such written information to the Artist, the Artist accepts said offer of employment on substantially the same terms, then the Artist shall be required to pay commissions to the Agent upon such contract of employment. If an Agent previously employed under a prior agency contract is entitled to collect commissions under the foregoing circumstances, the Agent with whom the present contract is executed waives his commission to the extent that the prior agent is entitled to collect the same.

6. (a) If during any period of niney-one (91) days immediately preceding the giving of the notice of termination hereinafter mentioned in this paragraph, the Artist fails to be employed and receive, or be entitled to receive, compensation for fifteen (15) days' employment, whether such employment is from fields under AFTRA's jurisdiction or any other branch of the entertainment industry in which the Agent may be authorized by written contract to represent the Artist, then either the Artist or the Agent may terminate the employment of the Agent hereunder by written notice to the other party. (1) For purposes of computing the fifteen (15) days' employment required hereunder, each separate original radio broadcast, whether live or recorded, and each transcribed program, shall be considered a day's employment, but a rebroadcast, whether recorded or live,

or an off-the-line recording, or a prior recording or the time spent in rehearsal for any employment in the radio broadcasting or transcription industry, shall not be considered such employment. (2) During the months of June, July and August, each day's employment in the radio broadcasting industry, shall, for purposes of computing fifteen (15) days' employment under this sub-paragraph "(a)" and for no other purpose, be deemed one and one-half (1½) days' employment. (3) For the purposes of computing the fifteen (15) days' employment required hereunder, each separate television broadcast (including the rehearsal time) shall be considered two and one-half (2½) days' employment. However, any days spent in rehearsal over three days inclusive of the day of the telecast, and any days of exclusivity over three days inclusive of the day of telecast, will automatically extend the ninety-one (91) day period by such overage. (4) During the months of June, July and August, each day's employment in the television broadcasting field shall, for the purpose of computing fifteen (15) days' employment under this sub-paragraph "(a)" and for no other purpose, be deemed three and three-quarters (3¾) days' employment. (5) Each master phonograph record recorded by the Artist shall be one (1) day's employment.

(b) The ninety-one (91) day period which is the basis of termination shall be suspended during any period of time which the artist has declared himself to be unavailable or has so notified the agent in writing or has confirmed in writing a written communication from the agent to such effect. The said ninety-one (91) day period which is the basis of termination shall also be suspended (1) during the period of time in which the artist is unable to respond to a call for his services by reason of physical or mental incapacity or (2) for such days as the artist may be employed in a field in which the artist is not represented by the agent.

(c) In the event that the Agent has given the Artist notice in writing of a bona fide offer of employment as an Artist in the entertainment industry and at or near the Artist's usual places of employment at a salary and from an employer commensurate with the Artist's prestige (and there is in fact such an offer), which notice sets forth the terms of the proposed employment in detail and the Artist refuses or negligently fails to accept such proffered employment, then the period of guaranteed employment specified in said offer, and the compensation which would have been received thereunder shall be deemed as time worked or compensation received by the Artist in computing the money earned or time worked with reference to the right of the Artist to terminate under the provisions of this paragraph.

(d) No termination under paragraph 6 shall deprive the Agent of the right to receive commissions or compensation on moneys earned or received by the Artist prior to the date of termination, or earned or received by the Artist after the date of termination of the Agent's employment on contracts for the Artist's services entered into by the Artist prior to the effective date of any such termination and during the term or terms specified herein, or commission or compensation to which the Agent is entitled pursuant to paragraphs 4(e) and 5 hereof.

(e) The Artist may not exercise the right of termination if at the time he attempts to do so, either:

    (1)   the Artist is actually working under written contract or contracts which guarantee the Artist employment in the broadcasting industries for at least one program each week for a period of not less than thirteen (13) consecutive weeks. For the purposes of this sub-paragraph a "program" shall be either (i) a regional network program of one-half (½) hour length or more; (ii) a national network program of one-quarter (¼) hour length or more; or (iii) a program or programs the aggregate weekly compensation for which equals or exceeds the Artist's customary compensation for either (i) or (ii), or

    (2)   the Artist is under such written contract, as described in the preceding sub-paragraph (1) or in sub-paragraph (5) below, and such contract begins within forty-five (45) days after the time the Artist attempts to exercise the right of termination, or

    (3)   where the Artist attempts to exercise the right of termination during the months of August or September, and the Artist is under such written contract as described in the preceding sub-paragraph "(1)" or in sub-paragraph "(5)" below and such contract begins not later than the following October 15th, or

    (4)   If during any period of ninety-one (91) days immediately preceding the giving of notice of termination herein referred to, the Artist has received, or has been entitled to receive, compensation in an amount equal to not less than thirteen (13) times his past customary compensation for a national network program of one-half (½) hour's length, whether such employment or compensation is from the broadcasting industries or any other branch of the entertainment industry in which the agent may be authorized by written contract to represent the Artist.

    (5)   The Artist is actually working under written contract or contracts which guarantee the Artist either (a) employment in the television broadcasting field for at

least one (1) program every other week in a cycle of thirteen (13) consecutive weeks where the program is telecast on an alternate week basis, or (b) employment for at least eight (8) programs in a cycle of thirty-nine (39) consecutive weeks, where the program is telecast on a monthly basis or once every four (4) weeks.

In the cases referred to in sub-paragraphs (1), (2), (3) and (5) above, the ninety-one (91) day period begins upon the termination of the contract referred to in such sub-paragraphs; and for the purpose of such sub-paragraphs any local program which under any applicable AFTRA collective bargaining agreement is the equivalent of a regional or national network program, shall be considered a regional or national network program as the case may be.

(f) Where the Artist is under a contract or contracts for the rendition of his services in the entertainment industry in any field in which the agent is authorized to act for the Artist, during the succeeding period of One hundred and eighty-two (182) days after the expiration of the ninety-one (91) day period in question, at a guaranteed compensation for such services of Twenty-five Thousand ($25,000.00) Dollars or more, or where the Artist is under a contract or contracts for the rendition of his services during said 182 day period in the radio, phonograph recording and/or television fields at a guaranteed compensation for such services of Twenty thousand dollars ($20,000.00) or more, then the Artist may not exercise the right of termination.

(g) Periods of layoff or leave of absence under a term contract shall not be deemed to be periods of unemployment hereunder, unless under said contract the Artist has the right during such period to do other work in the radio or television field or in any other branch of the entertainment industry in which the Agent may be authorized by written contract to represent the Artist. A "term contract" as used herein means a contract under which the Artist is guaranteed employment in the broadcasting industries for at least one program each week for a period of not less than thirteen (13) consecutive weeks, and also includes any "term contract" as defined in the Regulations of the Screen Actors Guild, Inc. in respect to the motion picture industry, under which the Artist is working. Also, a "term contract" as used herein relating to the television field means a contract under which the Artist is guaranteed employment in the television field as set forth in sub-paragraph (e)(5) above.

(h) Where the Artist has a contract of employment in the broadcasting industries and either the said contract of employment, or any engagement or engagements thereunder, are cancelled by the employer pursuant to any provision of said contract which does not violate any rule or regulation of AFTRA, the Artist shall be deemed to have been employed and to have received compensation for the purposes of paragraph 6(a) for any such cancelled broadcasts, with the following limitation—where a contract providing for more than one program has been so cancelled, the Artist shall not be deemed to have been employed or to have received compensation under such contract, with respect to more than one such program on and after the effective date of cancellation of such contract.

(i) For the purposes of this paragraph 6, where the Artist does not perform a broadcast for which he has been employed but nevertheless is compensated therefor, the same shall be considered employment hereunder.

(j) If at any time during the original or extended term of this contract, broadcasting over a majority of both the radio stations as well as a majority of the television broadcasting stations shall be suspended, the ninety-one (91) days period mentioned in this paragraph 6 shall be extended for the period of such suspension.

7. The Agent may represent other persons. The Agent shall not be required to devote his entire time and attention to the business of the Artist. The Agent may make known the fact that he is the sole and exclusive representative of the Artist in the broadcasting industries. In the event of a termination of this contract, even by the fault of the Artist, the Agent has no rights or remedies under the preceding sentence.

8. The Agent agrees that the following persons, and the following persons only, namely
(HERE INSERT NOT MORE THAN FOUR NAMES)

shall personally supervise the Artist's business during the term of this contract. One of such persons shall be available at all reasonable times for consultation with the Artist at the city or cities named herein. The Agent, upon request of the Artist, shall assign any one of such persons who may be available (and at least one of them always shall be available upon reasonable notice from the Artist), to engage in efforts or handle any negotiations for the Artist at such city or its environs and such person shall do so. Employees of the Agent who had signed the AFTRA covenant and who are not named herein may handle agency matters for the Artist or may aid any of the named persons in handling agency matters for the Artist.

9. In order to provide continuity of management, the name or names of not more than four (4) persons connected with the Agent must be written in the following space, and this contract is not valid unless this is done:

(HERE INSERT NOT MORE THAN FOUR NAMES)

In the event three (3) or four (4) persons are so named, at least two (2) of such persons must remain active in the Agency throughout the term of this contract. In the event only one (1) or two (2) persons are so named, at least one (1) such person must remain active in the Agency throughout the term of this contract. If the required number of persons does not remain active with the Agency, the Artist may terminate this contract in accordance with Section XXIII of AFTRA's Regulations Governing Agents.

10. The Artist hereby grants to the Agent the right to use the name, portraits and pictures of the Artist to advertise and publicize the Artist in connection with Agent's representation of the Artist hereunder.

11. The Agent agrees:

(a) To make no deductions whatsoever from any applicable minimums established by the AFTRA under any collective bargaining agreement.

(b) At the request of the Artist, to counsel and advise him in matters which concern the professional interests of the Artist in the broadcasting industries.

(c) The Agent will be truthful in his statements to the Artist.

(d) The Agent will not make any binding engagement or other commitment on behalf of the Artist, without the approval of the Artist, and without first informing the Artist of the terms and conditions (including compensation) of such engagement.

(e) The Agent's relationship to the Artist shall be that of a fiduciary. The Agent, when instructed in writing by the Artist not to give out information with reference to the Artist's affairs, will not disclose such information.

(f) That the Agent is equipped, and will continue to be equipped, to represent the interests of the Artist ably and diligently in the broadcasting industry throughout the term of this contract, and that he will so represent the Artist.

(g) To use all reasonable efforts to assist the Artist in procuring employment for the services of the Artist in the broadcasting industries.

(h) The Agent agrees that the Agent will maintain an office and telephone open during all reasonable business hours (emergencies such as sudden illness or death excepted) within the city of _____ or its environs, throughout the term of this agreement, and that some representative of the Agent will be present at such office during such business hours. This contract is void unless the blank in this paragraph is filled in with the name of a city at which the Agent does maintain an office for the radio broadcasting and television agency business.

(i) At the written request of the Artist, given to the Agent not oftener than once every four (4) weeks, the Agent shall give the Artist information in writing, stating what efforts the Agent has rendered on behalf of the Artist within a reasonable time preceding the date of such request.

(j) The Agent will not charge or collect any commissions on compensation received by the Artist for services rendered by the Artist in a package show in which the Agent is interested, where prohibited by Section VIII of AFTRA's Regulations.

12. This contract is subject to AFTRA's Regulations Governing Agents (Rule 12-B). Any controversy under this contract, or under any contract executed in renewal or extension hereof or in substitution herefor or alleged to have been so executed, or as to the existence, execution or validity hereof or thereof, or the right of either party to avoid this or any such contract or alleged contract on any grounds, or the construction, performance, nonperformance, operation, breach, continuance or termination of this or any such contract, shall be submitted to arbitration in accordance with the arbitration provisions in the regulations regardless of whether either party has terminated or purported to terminate this or any such contract or alleged contract. Under this contract the Agent undertakes to endeavor to secure employment for the Artist.

For California only

This provision is inserted in this contract pursuant to a rule of AFTRA, a bona fide labor union, which Rule regulates the relations of its members to agencies or artists managers. Reasonable written notice shall be given to the Labor Commissioner of the State of California of the time and place of any arbitration hearing hereunder. The Labor Commissioner of the State of California, or his authorized representative, has the right to attend all arbitration hearings. The clauses relating to the Labor Commissioner of the State of California shall not be applicable to cases not falling under the provisions of Section 1647.5 of the Labor Code of the State of California.

Nothing in this contract nor in AFTRA's Regulations Governing Agents (Rule 12-B) shall be construed so as to abridge or limit any rights, powers or duties of the Labor Commissioner of the State of California.

WHETHER OR NOT THE AGENT IS THE ACTOR'S AGENT AT THE TIME THIS AGENCY CONTRACT IS EXECUTED, IT IS UNDERSTOOD THAT IN EXECUTING THIS CONTRACT EACH PARTY HAS INDEPENDENT ACCESS TO THE REGULATIONS AND HAS RELIED AND WILL RELY EXCLUSIVELY UPON HIS OWN KNOWLEDGE THEREOF.

IN WITNESS WHEREOF, the parties hereto have executed this agreement the _____ day of _____ , 19_____

_____

ARTIST

_____

AGENT

NOTE: This contract must be signed at least in triplicate. One copy must be promptly delivered by the Agent to AFTRA, one copy must be promptly delivered by the Agent to the Artist, and one copy must be retained by the Agent. If AFTRA has an office in the city where the contract is executed, AFTRA's copy of the contract must be delivered to that office within 15 days of execution; or at the Agent's option, to AFTRA's main office in New York City within 30 days of execution.

This agency or artists manager is licensed by the Labor Commissioner of the State of California.

This agency or artists manager is franchised by the American Federation of Television and Radio Artists.

This form of contract has been approved by the Labor Commissioner of the State of California on July 21, 1953 and by the American Federation of Television and Radio Artists.

(The foregoing references to California may be deleted or appropriate substitutions made in other states.)

Rider to be attached to AFTRA exclusive agency contract

Exhibit "C" Covering Phonograph Records

The following shall be deemed part of the standard AFTRA exclusive agency contract to which it is attached.

This contract also includes the Artist's services for phonograph records, and the term "broadcasting industry" shall also include the phonograph record field, provided the Artist has initialed this rider.

_____

Artist's Initials

Form 17B

Standard AF of M Exclusive Agent–Musician Agreement

(Three Years or Less)[1]
NOT FOR USE IN STATE OF CALIFORNIA

Name of Agent	Legal Name of Musician
Address of Agent	Professional Name of Musician
A.F.M. Booking Agent Number	Name of Musician's Orchestra or Group
	Musician's A.F.M. Locals

This Agreement Begins on _____ , 19_____ , and Ends on _____ , 19_____

1. Scope of agreement

Musician hereby employs Agent and Agent hereby accepts employment as Musician's exclusive booking agent, manager and representative throughout the world with respect to musician's services, appearances and endeavors as a musician. As used in this agreement "Musician" refers to the undersigned musician and to musicians performing with any orchestra or group which Musician leads or conducts and whom Musician shall make subject to the terms of this agreement; "A.F.M." refers to the American Federation of Musicians of the United States and Canada.

2. Duties of agent

(a) Agent agrees to use reasonable efforts in the performance of the following duties: assist Musician in obtaining, obtain offers of, and negotiate, engagements for Musician; advise, aid, counsel and guide Musician with respect to Musician's professional career; promote and publicize Musician's name and talents; carry on business correspondence in Musician's behalf relating to Musician's professional career; cooperate with duly constituted and authorized representatives of Musician in the performance of such duties.

(b) Agent will maintain office, staff and facilities reasonably adequate for the rendition of such services.

(c) Agent will not accept any engagements for Musician without Musician's prior approval which shall not be unreasonably withheld.

(d) Agent shall fully comply with all applicable laws, rules and regulations of governmental authorities and secure such licenses as may be required for the rendition of services hereunder.

3. Rights of agent

(a) Agent may render similar services to others and may engage in other businesses and ventures, subject, however, to the limitations imposed by 8 below.

---

[1] There is also a five-year form.

(b) Musician will promptly refer to Agent all communications, written or oral, received by or on behalf of Musician relating to the services and appearances by Musician.

(c) Without Agent's written consent, Musician will not engage any other person, firm or corporation to perform the services to be performed by Agent hereunder (except that Musician may employ a personal manager) nor will Musician perform or appear professionally or offer so to do except through Agent.

(d) Agent may publicize the fact that Agent is the exclusive booking agent and representative for Musician.

(e) Agent shall have the right to use or to permit others to use Musician's name and likeness in advertising or publicity relating to Musician's services and appearances but without cost or expense to Musician unless Musician shall otherwise specifically agree in writing.

(f) In the event of Musician's breach of this agreement, Agent's sole right and remedy for such breach shall be the receipt from Musician of the commissions specified in this agreement, but only if, as, and when, Musician receives moneys or other consideration on which such commissions are payable hereunder.

4. Compensation of agent

(a) In consideration of the services to be rendered by Agent hereunder, Musician agrees to pay to Agent commissions equal to the percentages, set forth below, of the gross moneys received by Musician, directly or indirectly, for each engagement on which commissions are payable hereunder:

    (i)   Fifteen per cent (15%) if the duration of the engagement is two (2) or more consecutive days per week.

    (ii)   Twenty per cent (20%) for Single Miscellaneous Engagements of one (1) day duration—each for a different employer in a different location.

    (iii)   In no event, however, shall the payment of any such commissions result in the retention by Musician for any engagement of net moneys or other consideration in an amount less than the applicable minimum scale of the A.F.M. or of any local thereof having jurisdiction over such engagement.

    (iv)   In no event shall the payment of any such commissions result in the receipt by Agent for any engagement of commissions, fees or other consideration, directly, or indirectly, from any person or persons, including the Musician, which in aggregate exceed the commissions provided for in this agreement. Any commission, fee, or other consideration received by Agent from any source other than Musician, directly or indirectly, on account of, as a result of, or in connection with supplying the services of Musician shall be reported to Musician and the amount thereof shall be deducted from the commissions payable by the Musician hereunder.

(b) Commissions shall become due and payable to Agent immediately following the receipt thereof by Musician or by anyone else in Musician's behalf.

(c) No commissions shall be payable on any engagement if Musician is not paid for such engagement irrespective of the reasons for such non-payment to Musician, including but not limited to non-payment by reason of the fault of Musician. This shall not preclude the awarding of damages by the International Executive Board to a booking agent to compensate him for actual expenses incurred as the direct result of the cancellation of an engagement when such cancellation was the fault of the member.

(d) Agent's commissions shall be payable on all moneys or other considerations received by Musician pursuant to contracts for engagements negotiated or entered into during the term of this agreement; *if specifically agreed to by Musician by initialing the margin hereof,* to contracts for engagements in existence at the commencement of the term hereof (excluding, however, any engagements as to which Musician is under prior obligation to pay commissions to another agent); and to any modifications, extensions and renewals thereof or substitutions therefor regardless of when Musician shall receive such moneys or other considerations.

(e) As used in this paragraph and elsewhere in this agreement the term "gross earnings" shall mean the gross amounts received by Musician for each engagement less costs and expenses incurred in collecting amounts due for any engagement, including costs of arbitration, litigation and attorney's fees.

(f) *If specifically agreed to by Musician by initialing the margin hereof, the following shall apply:*

    (i) Musician shall advance to Agent against Agent's final commissions an amount not exceeding the following percentages of the gross amounts received for each engagement: 15% on engagements of three (3) days or less; 10% on all other engagements.

(ii) If Musician shall so request and shall simultaneously furnish Agent with the data relating to deductions, the Agent within 45 days following the end of each 12 months period during the term of this agreement and within 45 days following the termination of this Agreement, shall account to and furnish Musician with a detailed statement itemizing the gross amounts received for all engagements during the period to which such accounting relates, the moneys or other considerations upon which Agent's commissions are based, and the amount of Agent's commissions resulting from such computations. Upon request, a copy of such statement shall be furnished promptly to the Office of the President of the A.F.M.

(iii) Any balances owed by or to the parties shall be paid as follows: by the Agent at the time of rendering such statement; by the Musician within 30 days after receipt of such statement.

5. Duration and termination of agreement

(a) The term of this agreement shall be as stated in the opening heading hereof, subject to termination as provided in 5(b), 6 and 10 below.

(b) In addition to termination pursuant to other provisions of this agreement, this agreement may be terminated by either party, by notice as provided below, if Musician

(i) is unemployed for four (4) consecutive weeks at any time during the term hereof; or

(ii) does not obtain employment for at least twenty (20) cumulative weeks of engagements to be performed during each of the first and second six (6) months periods during the term hereof; or

(iii) does not obtain employment for at least forty (40) cumulative weeks of engagements to be performed during each subsequent year of the term hereof.

(c) Notice of such termination shall be given by certified mail addressed to the addressee at his last known address and a copy thereof shall be sent to the A.F.M. Such termination shall be effective as of the date of mailing of such notice if and when approved by the A.F.M. Such notice shall be mailed no later than two (2) weeks following the occurrence of any event described in (i) above: two (2) weeks following a period in excess of thirteen (13) of the cumulative weeks of unemployment specified in (ii) above; and two (2) weeks following a period in excess of twenty-six (26) of the cumulative weeks of unemployment specified in (iii) above. Failure to give notice as aforesaid shall constitute a waiver of the right to terminate based upon the happening of such prior events.

(d) Musician's disability resulting in failure to perform engagements and Musician's unreasonable refusal to accept and perform engagements shall not by themselves either deprive Agent of its right to or give Musician the right to terminate (as provided in (b) above).

(e) As used in this agreement, a "week" shall commence on Sunday and terminate on Saturday. A "week of engagements" shall mean any one of the following:

(i) a week during which Musician is to perform on at least four (4) days; or

(ii) a week during which Musician's gross earnings equals or exceeds the lowest such gross earnings obtained by Musician for performances rendered during any one of the immediately preceding six (6) weeks; or

(iii) a week during which Musician is to perform engagements on commercial television or radio or in concert for compensation equal at least to three (3) times the minimum scales of the A.F.M. or of any local thereof having jurisdiction applicable to such engagements.

6. Agent's maintenance of A.F.M. booking agent agreement

Agent represents that Agent is presently a party to an A.F.M. Booking Agent Agreement which is in full force and effect. If such A.F.M. Booking Agent Agreement shall terminate, the rights of the parties hereunder shall be governed by the terms and conditions of said Booking Agent Agreement relating to the effect of termination of such agreements which are incorporated herein by reference.

7. No other agreements

This is the only and the complete agreement between the parties relating to all or any part of the subject matter covered by this agreement.[2] There is no other agreement, arrangement or participation between the parties, nor do the parties stand in any relationship to each other which is not created by this agreement,[2] whereby the terms and conditions of this agreement are avoided

---

[2] (A.F.M. Personal Management Agreement Excepted.)

or evaded, directly or indirectly, such as, by way of example but not limitation, contracts, arrangements, relationships or participations relating to publicity services, business management. personal management, music publishing, or instruction.

8. Incorporation of A.F.M. constitution, by-laws, etc.

There are incorporated into and made part of this agreement, as though fully set forth herein, the present and future provisions of the Constitution, By-laws, Rules, Regulations and Resolutions of the A.F.M. and those of its locals which do not conflict therewith. The parties acknowledge their responsibility to be fully acquainted, now and for the duration of this agreement, with the contents thereof.

9. Submission and determination of disputes

Every claim, dispute, controversy or difference arising out of, dealing with, relating to, or affecting the interpretation or application of this agreement, or the violation or breach, or the threatened violation or breach thereof shall be submitted, heard and determined by the International Executive Board of the A.F.M., in accordance with the rules of such Board (regardless of the termination or purported termination of this agreement or of the Agent's A.F.M. Booking Agent Agreement), and such determination shall be conclusive, final and binding on the parties.

10. No assignment of this agreement

This agreement shall be personal to the parties and shall not be transferable or assignable by operation of law or otherwise without the prior consent of the Musician and of the A.F.M. The obligations imposed by this agreement shall be binding upon the parties. The Musician may terminate this agreement at any time within ninety (90) days after the transfer of a controlling interest in the Agent.

11. Negotiation for renewal

Neither party shall enter into negotiations for or agree to the renewal or extension of this agreement prior to the beginning of the final year of the term hereof.

12. Approval by A.F.M.

This agreement shall not become effective unless, within thirty (30) days following its execution, an executed copy thereof is filed with and is thereafter approved in writing by the A.F.M.

IN WITNESS WHEREOF, the parties hereto have executed this agreement the _____ day of
_____ , 19_____.

_____	_____
Agent	Musician

By _____   _____
                  Title or Capacity   Residence Address

                                               _____
                                               City   State   Zip Code

Agent Representing No More Than Two Clients if specifically agreed to by the parties by signing below:

(a) Agent warrants and represents that Agent presently serves, and Agent agrees that during the term hereof Agent will restrict its activities to serving, as booking agent, or manager, or representative, no more than one other musical soloist, orchestra, band or performing group. If such warranty and representation is untrue, this agreement is null and void. If such agreement is broken, this agreement shall automatically terminate.

(b) In consideration thereof, the parties agree that the provisions of 4(a)(i) and (ii) and 4(f) above shall be inapplicable and that the compensation of Agent shall be as set forth in Schedule 1 attached. In no event, however, shall the payment of any commission result in the retention by Musician for any engagement of net moneys or other consideration in an amount less than the applicable minimum scale of the A.F.M. or of any local thereof.

_____	_____
Agent	Musician

By _____
                  Title or Capacity

INDEX